The Major Victorian Poets:
Tennyson, Browning, Arnold

The cover portraits, left to right, are
of Browning, Tennyson, Arnold.

Riverside Editions

The Major Victorian Poets:
Tennyson, Browning, Arnold

Edited with an Introduction and Notes by
William E. Buckler
New York University

Houghton Mifflin Company   Boston
Atlanta   Dallas   Geneva, Illinois   Hopewell, New Jersey   Palo Alto

To my once and future students

Printed in the U.S.A.

Library of Congress Catalog Card Number: 72–564.

ISBN: 0–395–14024–2

Contents

Preface

Students of Victorian poetry realize that general interest in the efforts of Tennyson and his contemporaries to express in poetry their acute consciousness of "modernism" has deepened so much in the last forty years that it is different now not by degree but by kind. Interest has become esteem. What we used to defend we now applaud. What we held suspect we now find not just credible but germane, cogent, and persuasively poetic. Indeed, we want more of the poems of more of the Victorian poets. It is no longer critically just to offer distinguished poets like Swinburne and Rossetti in bits and pieces that hardly allow them stature as poets at all.

Within the physical limits of a Riverside Edition it seemed best then to present a few of the Victorian poets in a critically valid quantity of their works, rather than to roughhew and in that way distort a larger number. Tennyson, Browning, and Arnold are considered the indispensable poets of their generation. Critical appreciation of their poetry has never been keener, and a worthy canon of criticism is persistently widening for each. These three are the foundation figures in the Victorian poetic tradition. Their works are major reference points in studies of the cultural ambiance from which they emerged; they themselves tended to see each other in a comparative light. Furthermore, each is, of and by himself, a poet of intrinsic interest and excellence.

W.E.B.

Introduction

In her sensitive, incisive review of the "Facsimile and Transcript of the Original Drafts" of T. S. Eliot's *The Waste Land,* Helen Vendler (*The New York Times Book Review,* November 7, 1971) wrote the following bold sentences:

> Matthew Arnold, in "The Study of Poetry," had isolated from the grandest poems he knew, their grandest lines, lines which he christened 'touchstones' by which all other poems could be tried. To read Arnold's 'touchstones' is to sense "The Waste Land" in embryo:
>
> > And what is else not to be overcome . . .
> >
> > De plusurs choses à remembrer li prist . . .
> >
> > Absent thee from felicity awhile . . .
> >
> > Καὶ σέ, γέρον, τὸ πρὶν μὲν ἀκούομεν ὅλβιον εἶναι.
> >
> > In la sua volontade è nostra pace.
>
> Just as Eliot's rhythms rise from the songs in "Empedocles on Etna," and just as his essays find their model in Arnold's, so "The Waste Land" is the anguished poem Arnold should have written, an antiphonal duet between his aridity and his touchstones.
>
> But there is a third, and un-Arnoldian component in "The Waste Land"—the modern talk. How did Eliot learn it? Where did he find the rhythms of the pub and the marital quarrel? Not even Browning, though he hovers behind these dialogues, ever quite conceived of anything so rapid and nervous. . . ."

The point need not be labored: one of the most accomplished critics of modern literature (of the later Yeats, of Wallace Stevens) sees Arnold and Browning as prominent progenitors of the rhythms, world view, and language of "the most famous of modern poems." This in itself is dramatically corrective to a provincial view of the Victorians' place in the continuity of English poetry.

Looking the other way along the continuum, one finds an even more patent relation of the Victorian poets to the work of their predecessors. The master of Tennyson's apprenticeship was Byron, especially the Byron of *Hebrew Melodies.* In his next phase of growth, Tennyson took as his models Shelley and Keats. Behind his maturest poetry stand the impressive blank verse of Wordsworth and Keats and the psychological penetration and moral seriousness of Wordsworth. Both Browning and Swinburne generously acknowledged the momentous importance of Shelley as an inspiriting force in their careers as poets. Through other poets of a certain temperament this influence persisted well into the twentieth century—through the major example of Yeats and the more modest examples of Hardy and Housman. Arnold was the most "Wordsworthian" of the major Victorian poets; and critics rightly see the aesthetic theories and practice of Keats as a useful norm for Arnold's evolution as a poet. So acute was Arnold's sensitivity to the worth of knowing the best of Wordsworth and of Byron to a generation who had almost forgotten them that, in the late seventies, he published works of each with critical introductions calculated to reconstitute their reputations among his younger contemporaries.

It is imprecise, except in the over-all context of post-Renaissance Europe, to speak of the Victorian poets as "modern"; and it gives inadequate definition to their peculiar struggle with both idiom and idea to emphasize their romanticism. Yet both points must be measured since Victorian poets were consciously and characteristically occupied with them.

The "over-all context of post-Renaissance Europe" is, therefore, an important consideration in any contemplation of the Victorians. They were acutely aware that they had inherited a psychologically and spiritually dismembered world, that they had inherited the "modern spirit" —which Arnold (in 1863) defined as "the sense of want of correspondence between the forms of modern Europe and its spirit, between the new wine of the eighteenth and nineteenth centuries, and the old bottles of the eleventh and twelfth centuries, or even of the sixteenth and seventeenth. . . ." They knew intensely, soulfully, that some force had been set in motion that had shattered into a million atoms the coherence of the Christian era. That force, in its multiple facets, was the Renaissance. And the Victorians knew (note Arnold's refinement "or even of the sixteenth and seventeenth") that their own age did not enjoy the compensatory excitement which had belonged to those in the sixteenth and seventeenth centuries who had adapted to their explosive age by assigning themselves the important new role of dealing with great and sudden issues in a new spirit of man's self-reliance. Except for a lonely prescient few who read the curve of the future quite differently (recall Donne's lines, "The new philosophy calls all in doubt,/ The element of fire is quite put out"), there seemed more than ample reason for most to rejoice in the new dispensation and no reason to say, with Empedocles or Julian, "I have lived long enough." But between this time and Arnold's age, there was not so much a shift in premises as a formulation of them (Hobbes, Locke, and Hume each left a hard deposit), a dogged determination to drive those premises to their conclusions, and a concurrent tendency to drop the opposing case or become hardened and eccentric in defending it. A young intellectual in the age of Elizabeth I could, with a good deal of conscientious ease, shift from Catholic to Protestant; a young intellectual in Victoria's age could rarely find sanctuary in religion at all. Arnold has again spoken (privately, in 1849) for his generation:

"these are damned times—everything is against one—the height to which knowledge has come, the spread of luxury, our physical enervation, the absence of great *natures*, the unavoidable contact with millions of small ones, newspapers, cities, light profligate friends, moral desperadoes like Carlyle, our own selves, and the sickening consciousness of our difficulties. . . ." The parallels which literary historians sometimes draw between the seventeenth and nineteenth centuries are ultimately superficial and obscure differences in degree that are of such magnitude as to be differences in kind.

The Victorian poets were aware, too, that with rare exceptions the models of their most celebrated predecessors in English poetry (before Wordsworth) were no longer available to them. The traditional epic, in a patently nonepical age, was anachronistic. The idiom of Elizabethan drama without the *esprit* of a living Elizabethan tradition, even if it led to a perfect imitation, was got-up and irrelevant. Their mammoth efforts to restore poetic drama on the Elizabethan model to the modern stage constituted one of their strangest exercises in futility. The coteries of Sidney and Spenser, Dryden and Pope, had no counterpart among the Victorians; the genre-tradition which they had learned from the Latins and through which they had achieved many of their most noteworthy effects had, in its remnants, been pulverized by the Romantic revolution in poetry; and the grandly hierarchical value-systems with which they had underpinned their world views had, above all else, ceased to satisfy. The shattered world of the Victorians could rescue only fragments from the tradition. Chaucer proved mildly useful to the "idle singer of an empty day," William Morris. Hopkins found valuable instruction in the metrics of *Piers Plowman* and in the choruses of *Samson Agonistes*, and Tennyson's conception of King Arthur apparently borrows something from *Piers*. Arnold failed to find in Chaucer the "high seriousness" (the determination to make basic moral choices) of the true classic, considered the Elizabethans the very worst models for the modern poet, judged Milton the perfect stylist in English but sought his models elsewhere, and, in the whole literature of the age of Dryden, Pope, and Johnson, discovered only "the scantiest and frailest of classics" in Thomas Gray. The heroic couplet was either transmuted out of recognition (as in Browning's *My Last Duchess*) or served for little more than the apprentice-imitations of Elizabeth Barrett Browning. The Spenserian revival, which had blossomed so lately and effectively for Keats and Byron and Shelley, died on the Victorian vine. Dante Gabriel Rossetti learned more about the sonnet from the Italians than from the Elizabethans; Arnold took his formula from Wordsworth; Tennyson and Browning wrote no sonnets of importance at all. Although exciting and apt parallels can be found between the "holy" sonnets of Donne and the "terrible" sonnets of Hopkins, it is fairly clear that, in terms of form, Hopkins was more affected by the experimental endeavors of Keats than by the example of the Anglican Divine. The Victorian period was a great period of scholarship and criticism in English literature, but the poets as poets could, like Hopkins, only "admire and do otherwise."

One likely explanation of this curious fact is the paradoxical nature of the Romantic revolution in poetry. While the Romantic poets redirected English poetic energy—gave it a new language, new themes, and a new national function—they also succeeded in updating, for the uses of the whole century, earlier English literature. In other words the viable strains of Spenser, Shakespeare, Milton, and Pope came to the Victorian "modernized" by Keats, Coleridge, Wordsworth, Byron, and Shelley.

As has already been indicated, the debt of the Victorian poets to the Romantics was enormous. Just how enormous can perhaps be dramatized by trying to imagine what Tennyson's poetry would have been like if he had been fourteen years old not when Byron died but when Pope died—or what Browning's poetry would have been like had he been a contemporary of Thomas Gray. In all likelihood they would have been "unsung Miltons," would never have spoken out in the sense that Arnold contended Gray *"never spoke out."* It was not simply a matter of a particular Romantic poet providing an aesthetic pressure to which a particular Victorian poet could fruitfully respond. Rather the Romantic movement as a whole broke the mold that had come to it from the past and remade it in a spirit of urgency and relevance. Romanticism changed the expectations of poetry for both the poet and the reader of poetry as fundamentally as the French Revolution changed the expectations of rulers and the ruled.

Yet the work of the major Victorian poets does not strike the reader as much *like* the work of the major Romantics. Browning and Tennyson, for example, are not Shelleyan and Keatsian, and *Wuthering Heights* is more "Byronic" than any Victorian poem is. A minor classic like Christina Rossetti's *Goblin Market* may call up parallels in the reader's mind with Coleridge's *Christabel*, and Tennyson's *Recollections of the Arabian Nights* can justly be said to have an analogue of sorts in Coleridge's *Kubla Khan*, but neither poet would be thought of as Coleridgean. There is not, among the Victorians, a satirist in any way comparable to Byron or a philosopher-poet in any way comparable to Wordsworth or Shelley. Even the Shelleyan "strain" which one can pinpoint in Tennyson, Browning, Swinburne, and Hardy is little more than a fragmentary linkage.

What, then, are the distinguishing characteristics of the poetry of Tennyson's generation?

The single, surest common denominator of Victorian poetry—the characteristic from which most of the others seem to flow—was its employment of the impersonative mode. By this device the Victorians converted their poetry, with its tremendous and precarious weight of thought, from a poetry of argument to a poetry of character. It enabled them to discipline Romanticism without destroying it. When Matthew Arnold sat down to write the preface to his *Poems* of 1853, he concerned himself with the need for a wholesome aesthetic for himself and for his contemporaries. The general principle which he attempted to counter, and the specific examples he cited, clearly show that Arnold was trying to lead English poetry away from the pageant of the naked heart which had been an important manifestation of Romanticism and to which he thought some members of his own generation were still too partial. "A true allegory of the state of one's own mind in a representative history is perhaps the highest thing that one can attempt in the way of poetry." (The formulation has been identified as David Masson's.) "No assuredly," said Arnold, "it is not, it never can be so: no great poetical work has ever been produced with such an aim." Arnold then proceeded, with an eye both to Aristotle's *Poetics* and to Wordsworth's *Preface* of 1800, to set forth an alternative to poetry as a "true allegory of the state of one's own mind."

It is important to see Wordsworth as one of the two significant points of reference in Arnold's preface in order to avoid several false starts when appraising its thrust and significance. One such false start would be to think Arnold, by returning exclusively to a Greek classic testament of a supremely integrated age, was being a bit precious siding with the Ancients in his generation's Ancients-Moderns debate. Another would be to place Arnold's arguments in a false, though provocative, context by seeing them as part of the "sensibility" dialogue through which the Longinian, psychological (as distinct from the Aristotelian, aesthetic) view of literature gained general credibility for a time. That dialogue had had creative vitality for the poets of the later eighteenth century (for Cowper, Burns, and Blake, for example); it was not the central problem of the early Victorian poets. A third (perhaps minor) false start would be to find Arnold less than a pure Aristotelian (as some critics do) and to think that the matter is settled. On the positive side, recognizing Wordsworth's place in Arnold's thoughts emphasizes their contemporaneity and helps us refine our understanding of their force.

Their two prefaces show Arnold and Wordsworth in essential agreement on basic issues. In the first place, they felt that their times were characterized by an unchaste and depraved taste. It demands "gross and violent stimulants" such as "frantic novels, sickly and stupid German Tragedies, and deluges of idle and extravagant stories in verse," said Wordsworth. Goethe and Niebuhr, said Arnold, have pointed up the moral grossness and spiritual torpor of this "modern" age. Secondly they insisted upon the great importance of selecting the subject for a poem. Wordsworth chose incidents and situations in which he could trace "truly though not ostentatiously, the primary laws of our nature. . . ." Arnold defined the true incidents and situations (he called them "great actions") of poetry as those which appeal to "the great primary human affections; to those elementary feelings which subsist permanently in the race, and which are independent of time." Thirdly they agreed that the action itself was the important thing, not the poet's personal reaction—more than a "wise passiveness"—to that action. In his poems, said Wordsworth, "the feeling . . . developed gives importance to the action and situation, and not the action and situation to the feeling." The poet, said Arnold, "needs . . . to be perpetually reminded to prefer his action to everything else; so to treat this, as to permit its inherent excellences to develop themselves, without interruption from the intrusion of his personal peculiarities: most fortunate, when he most entirely succeeds in effacing himself, and in enabling a noble action to subsist as it did in nature." In the fourth place, they both firmly rejected the notion of an artificial language of poetry and insisted that a plain and emphatic language was the appropriate language through which to develop situations touching the primary laws of our nature. Wordsworth opposed particularly the arid extravagance of neoclassical diction; Arnold opposed the ornateness of the Elizabethan-cum-Romantic tradition. (Going beyond Arnold's preface and its specific intent—to his poems and critical essays—one can easily document his concurrence with other points upon which Wordsworth touches: the poet's "more lively sensibility"; his "greater knowledge of human nature"; his "more comprehensive soul"; his contemplative joy in the spirit of life both in himself and in the "goings-on of the Universe"; his purposes—to please, to enlighten, to strengthen, and to purify man's critical and moral tastes.)

Wordsworth's preface was, of course, affixed to the second edition of *Lyrical Ballads*. Arnold used his preface, in part, as a justification for dropping *Empedocles on Etna* from currency and substituting *Sohrab and Rustum* as an example of how his theory worked *for him*. The nature of this example, an epic fragment in imitation of Homer, together with his frequent and favorable citation of classical models, led many of Arnold's contemporaries (and ours) to charge him with exclusive emphasis on antique subject matter and of having neglected lyric poetry. In a second preface (1854), Arnold commented briefly on these matters. He denied the charge of exclusive emphasis. He turned aside the question of lyric poetry in a peculiarly interesting way: "It [the preface of 1853] leaves . . . untouched the question, how far, and in what manner, the opinions there expressed respecting the choice of subjects apply to lyric poetry; that region of the poetical field which is chiefly cultivated at present." Arnold was an adept verbal strategist. He does not say here that the opinions expressed in the earlier preface do not apply to lyric poetry—in fact, he implies that they do. He says only that he is not at the moment inclined to say "how far, and in what manner" they apply. Having stated his belief that the former preface was "in the main, true," Arnold was not inclined to be drawn into the wholly distasteful role of publicly adjudicating the performances of his contemporaries—the new Laureate Tennyson, for example, or his friend Clough, or Elizabeth Barrett and Robert Browning. He had made his point on behalf of negative capability, against the "true allegory of the state of one's own mind." He had published what is now regarded as the most important poetic manifesto of his age. He stood on its validity.

The retrospect of one hundred and twenty years shows Arnold to have been in tune with the future. The impersonative mode, both lyrical and dramatic, became modern poetry's "one way of speaking truth." Indeed in the year of Arnold's second preface (1854), Tennyson published a most extraordinary lyrical drama entitled *Maud*, "a little *Hamlet*" as he described it, in which "different phases of passion in one person take the place of different characters." The seed-lyric of the poem had been written almost twenty years earlier ("O that 'twere possible"), and in 1842 Tennyson had published a soliloquy, *Locksley Hall*, that shows many points of contact with *Maud*. By restless experimentation he had found a unique dramatic formulation through which to project his "history of a morbid poetic soul, under the blighting influence of a recklessly speculative age." That the formula works (that *Maud* is a profoundly successful melding of form and content) modern criticism confirms. In 1855, Browning published his single most important collection of poems, *Men and Women*, in two volumes. After almost a decade of brilliant but inchoate verbal virtuosity (in the 1830's), Browning discovered how to rein in his genius and to make poetry instead of pyrotechnics. He did this through another decade of concentration on three related principles. He had verbalized them long before he could put them into sustained practice: to deal with "so many imaginary Characters," not his own; to concentrate on "Action in Character, rather than Character in Action"; to focus on incidents in the history of a soul. During the 1840's especially, Browning worked out the "technique of indirection" for which he is famous and which he stated most succinctly in the closing lines of *The Ring and the Book*:

> . . . Art may tell a truth
> Obliquely, do the thing shall breed the thought,
> Nor wrong the thought, missing the mediate word.

When Arnold was working out his defense of dramatic objectivity in 1853, he could not have known the degree to which Browning would confirm in 1855 the practical necessity of his principles, both in choice of subject and in the self-effaced handling of it. Before 1853 the body of Browning's lyrics dramatically conceived and executed, although significant, was obscured by the maelstrom of philosophical narrative and dramas in imitation of the Elizabethans he was too well known for. But with *Men and Women* one of the imperative models of modern poetry had been published, and the impersonative mode had been firmly established.

In order to accept "the impersonative mode" as indispensable to the way in which the Victorian poets moved the tradition forward toward the twentieth century (gave poetry a new psychological orientation and a new pace, variegated its language, and renovated for its use endless myths and prosodic models) one must amend quite dramatically the established tendency to impose upon Victorian works an autobiographical matrix. This tendency has been especially inimical to the creative efforts of Arnold, Swinburne, and Hardy. For each it has reduced the voices of his poetry to one voice (the author's), and all his subjects to one subject (the author). It has implicitly disqualified these poets from being what they tried to be—imaginative explorers of the human situation and creators of some artifice of humanity. Each protested vigorously against such an approach to his work and insisted that the lyricism used was dramatically conceived—in Hardy's phrase "even where not explicitly so," that is, even when a public myth or explicit dramatic frame has not been established. Criticism, in general, has not listened. Hardy's tentativeness has been packaged into a philosophy; Swinburne's examinations of the stranger fruit of human experience have been catalogued as personal perversions; and Arnold's most dramatically conceived poem (*Empedocles on Etna*) has been read as thinly disguised self-revelation. The cost to their poetry has been great because the author of such criticism, in Arnold's words, "has not really his eye upon the professed object of his criticism at all, but upon something else which he wants to prove by means of that object." As a result the work of these poets has been seen as involuted, as if they had capitulated to one of the demons of the age, the demon of self-consciousness. That the demon was real they all attest. But their search was for the not-self, and in pursuit of it they reached out to other ages (history) and other literatures (myth) for meaningful touchstones of human experience to achieve what Samuel Butler called "crossing"—getting yourself out of yourself and something else into you.

What about Tennyson before *Maud*, the Tennyson, say, of *In Memoriam* and of the poems on classical subject matter he spent so much time revising and perfecting before 1842? At first glance *In Memoriam* appears to be the kind of aberration Matthew Arnold warned against —a "true allegory of the state of one's own mind." In fact, it is not. *In Memoriam* is, in its way, just as dramatic a poem as *Maud*; and although it strikes quite a different groundtone (or succession of groundtones); it has its own independent *persona*, who is incrementally characterized as the poem progresses and who emerges from the dark night of the soul on the strength of personal qualities unmonitored from outside the poem. That he is a poet, the poem itself makes abundantly clear. The questions he asks, the inner allegories he projects, his modes of perception, the movement of his moods, the manner in which he re-assembles both his identity and his value-system (in addition, of course, to the explicit capsule-examinations of poetry's relationship to personality distributed throughout the poem) all confirm this indispensable symbolic fact. More than that, *In Memoriam*, in its carefully tentative, exploratory, experiential, but inevitable manner, posits the necessity of the imagination (not of fantasy or fable, not of unassisted reason or speculation) in any genuinely tenable modern faith.

This same impersonation is pervasive in Tennyson's early poems. In the sonnets among his *juvenilia*, he projected not his own voice but that of so many imaginary persons. For example "Nothing will die" finds its contrary in "All things will die." Later, in poems like *Supposed Confessions*, *The Two Voices*, and *The Palace of Art*, he created imaginary dialogues in order to project and cross-fertilize conflicting personalities and values (states of being). This is equally true of the cluster of "classical" poems (*The Hesperides*, *Œnone*, *The Lotos-Eaters*, *Ulysses*, *Tithonus*), in which there is no necessary deposit of belief, only a continuing, widening examination of interlocking themes, a projection not of conclusions but of awareness. It was this peculiar ability of Tennyson to enter into subtly differentiated states of being that enabled him to produce so early in the century such Symbolist poems as *Mariana* and *The Lady of Shalott* and to give a modern relevance to his exploration of myth and of historical personages.

Tennyson's fascination with states of being persisted throughout his life. It is one of the controlling concerns of the *Idylls of the King*, as it is of many later poems—*Rizpah*, for example, and *The Voyage of Maeldune*. Balin, in *Balin and Balan*, underscores the relationship between the sense of self (self-estimate) and the ability to believe in the not-self. Conversely Balin shows the disastrous consequences when a supportive assumption is abruptly withdrawn from someone who has inadequate knowledge of or faith in himself. Setting aside the Doppelganger strategy of the idyll, one can say that what Balin requires (a foreshadowing of the Grail quest) are signs, tokens, and symbols to uphold his wavering faith in himself and, therefore, in his mission. Both inner and outer supports are inadequate and give rise to extravagance and a psychological disorientation bordering on madness. The alternative which Vivien offers ("This old sun-worship . . . [which] will rise again,/ And beat the Cross to earth, and break the King/ And all his Table") is the only one available to Balin after his faith in himself crumbles: " 'Here I dwell/ Savage among the savage woods, here die—/ Die—let the wolves' black maws ensepulchre/ Their brother beast, whose anger was his lord!' " Merlin, in *Merlin and Vivien,* has lost hope and is visited by a deep, pervasive melancholy. Isolated by his prophetic insight into the dissolution not only of the Arthurian ideal but also of his own usefulness in the world, he with-draws to the wilderness, easy prey for the serpentine Vivien. There is a fitful dialogue between Merlin and Vivien rather than a debate, and this seems apt enough. For all her diabolical wiliness, it is unthinkable that Vivien could have outwitted the ancient seer. It is not, then, a battle of wits but a struggle between two states of being—malicious perseverance on her side and moral exhaustion on his. Merlin knows what a scourge his secret will be in her hands; but his global depres-sion, his longing for relief from painful visions, his world-weariness break him at last, and he re-enters the womb of nature. In *Lancelot and Elaine,* Elaine, like the variant lady of Shalott, is "cursed" with a willful nature which establishes a simple and simplistic dichotomy be-tween fulfillment of her love for Lancelot (as wife or as mistress) and death. This is the statement which her swan song makes:

> "Sweet is true love tho' given in vain, in vain;
> And sweet is death who puts an end to pain:
> I know not which is sweeter, no, not I."

Elaine, for all her beauty and purity, is a fairy-figure, and the world view by which she lives and dies is a simple, attractive, and fatal form of naturalism. She is *la belle dame* without mercy to herself. Lancelot is sharply contrasted with "the lily maid of Astolat." He is three times her age; the shield which he leaves in her care is storied over with the scars of his life-battles; he cannot love at the simple, unequivocal level of physical union; although he, too, is torn between the poles of a dichotomy, the warring elements are entirely within himself. The war between Sense and Soul, between infidelity and fidelity, is centered in Lancelot more than any other knight and he responds to it at various levels—in a longing for anonymity (as in the ninth tournament of the diamonds), in recurrent fits of madness, and in the agony of a death wish:

> "I needs must break
> These bonds that so defame me. Not without
> She wills it—would I, if she will'd it? nay,
> Who knows? but if I would not, then may God,
> I pray him, send a sudden angel down
> To seize me by the hair and bear me far,
> And fling me deep in that forgotten mere,
> Among the tumbled fragments of the hills."

Like Doctor Faustus Lancelot in his near-despair prays for release from his strange identity, for permission to merge once more with the ele-ments out of which he was mysteriously born.

Viewed from the vantage point suggested here, Tennyson's *Idylls*, and his poems generally, assume a substantially different character from the one usually assigned them. Allegory in the Spenserian sense and epic in the Miltonic sense, along with the value-systems they assume, simply do not apply. The modernization mentioned earlier takes on an Arnoldian coloration: that is most modern which is most relevant. The *Idylls* ceases to be either a "Victorian" or a "medieval" poem and becomes an eternally new, eternally old parabolic study of the role of the "abysmal deeps of personality" in human affairs. Tennyson's poetic concerns appear to have a great deal more in common with Browning's than has been traditionally asserted.

Browning ordered the experiences which his poems provide differently from Tennyson. He set clearer conditions for the reader's approach to them, moved language further and more abruptly from the standard poetic norm, and established a closer, less ambivalent relationship between himself and his reader by, as it were, joining the crowd. Despite these differences Browning, like Tennyson, was working in a new anti-epic frame of reference.

The length and the divisions of *The Ring and the Book* suggest clearly that Browning was working with epic models in mind. Linking this fact with Milton's intention (to "assert Eternal Providence,/ And justify the ways of God to men") draws one's thoughts toward *Paradise Lost*. Without questioning T. S. Eliot's estimate of Milton's epic, one can still accept Eliot's suggestion that for his generation of young poet-practitioners Milton could not serve as a model. Milton's conscious "elevation" and his effort to establish a marked distance between prose and poetry and between private and public myth disqualified him, at least *de facto*, as a model for the new poets of the twentieth century. The contrast of *Paradise Lost* and *The Ring and the Book* sharply demonstrates the anti-epic assumptions of Browning's poem and also its greater relevance for modern poetry.

In the first place, Browning does not take a traditional myth and modernize it. Instead he takes a long-forgotten "Roman murder-case" which, although true, can have only as much significance as the alloy of the poet's imagination gives it. Secondly there is no continuous story-line or odyssey; the poem does not depend on emblematic episodes or narratives. The speakers of the monologues *are* the narratives. The only thing of importance they tell us—truthfully or disingenuously and therefore truthfully still—is *who they are* and how they weigh in on this complex scale called man. Browning reduces the elaborate mythological machinery of a traditional epic to the realistic level of the actual machinery of justice. Therefore, thirdly, there is no preconceived poetic norm by which the verse must evolve. It uses, like *Paradise Lost*, "English heroic verse without rhyme" (blank verse), but each monologue takes the quality of its verse from the speaker—

his involvement, his sense of self, his ultimate purposes, whether and in what degree he is play-acting, and whether he is in fact searching after truth and at what level. What we have, then, are varying degrees of colloquialism with occasional variations into declamation and invocation. The metaphoric texture is cut from the same cloth; the manipulations of vowel, consonant, and rhythm by which the blank verse gets its variety and vitality reinforce the same ideal of effective plain-speaking.

It was said that Browning established a closer, less ambivalent relationship between himself and his reader than did Tennyson. One result is the greater immediacy one feels reading a Browning poem. In Books I and XII of *The Ring and the Book*, he carries this author-reader relationship to a new, more explicit level. These prologue-epilogue books accomplish many things, but two of them are worth special comment. Book I contains an extraordinarily dynamic rendering of the actual process of imaginative gestation. The speaker explains the ring-metaphor, certainly; but more importantly he involves the reader in the growth of the realization which became *The Ring and the Book* itself. From the day "a Hand," mid the busy life of San Lorenzo Square in Florence, pushed *his* hand toward the Old Yellow Book until the creative act is accomplished, there take place periods of excited familiarization with and corroboration of the "facts," of constant re-telling of the story, and of a gradual blending of imaginative perceptions with the raw record. People long dead live again, and the poet repeats "God's process in man's due degree . . ." (I, 717). The following verse-paragraph (I, 679–697) provides the central statement:

> This was it from, my fancy with those facts,
> I used to tell the tale, turned gay to grave,
> But lacked a listener seldom; such alloy,
> Such substance of me interfused the gold
> Which, wrought into a shapely ring therewith,
> Hammered and filed, fingered and favoured, last
> Lay ready for the renovating wash
> O' the water. "How much of the tale was true?"
> I disappeared; the book grew all in all;
> The lawyers' pleadings swelled back to their size,—
> Doubled in two, the crease upon them yet,
> For more commodity of carriage, see!—
> And these are letters, veritable sheets
> That brought posthaste the news to Florence, writ
> At Rome the day Count Guido died, we find,
> To stay the craving of a client there,
> Who bound the same and so produced my book.
> Lovers of dead truth, did ye fare the worse?
> Lovers of live truth, found ye false my tale?

The only troublesome element in the goldsmith-poet analogy is that of "the renovating wash." In this one respect the analogy (or metaphor) strains toward the metaphysical conceit. When the goldsmith has finished his "hammering and filing, fingering and favouring," he dips the ring in acid ("water"). This causes the surface alloy to burn away, and a film of pure gold covers the surface of the ring. To make this fit the poetic process Browning is describing, one has to assume that the extended period of learning, interpreting, and conceptualizing has been completed and that the appearance of the finished product is the issue. Hence "I disappeared; the book grew all in all" (l. 687) refers to the final stage of presentation—the writing—of Books II–XI. The imagination or fancy is not withdrawn from the art-work, but merely disappears below the surface.

In I, 838–1329, Browning characterizes each speaker of a monologue and pinpoints the dramatic situation in which each will function. He gives, in other words, a brief expository account (comparable, for example, to the method of Chaucer in the *General Prologue* to *The Canterbury Tales* and also to the *Arguments* which precede the several books of *Paradise Lost*) of what will be dramatized at length in the poem that follows. The example of Chaucer and Milton may in fact have been one of his reasons for doing so. But two other reasons, one traditional, and the other more idiosyncratic, seem, speculatively at least, more central. Browning was a life-long student and admirer of the Greek tragedians, especially of Aeschylus and Euripides. He knew the importance of public, well-known myths to the Greek tragedy-writers —that the "fiction" itself was a given, originality residing in the poet's handling of it (re-interpretation, characterization, group orchestration, language). Starting from the opposite point (a "Roman murder-case" *lost* from the annals of memory), the poet needed to compensate, to publicize the fiction so that it in itself would not magnetize the reader's interest. The more idiosyncratic reason is wholly consonant with this. Having judged the characters from the outset, so to speak, Browning wanted to enter into them, let them "swell back to their size," and to provide the reader with his turn to judge them from this inner vantage point. Thus the poet-speaker of Book I puts his own credibility on trial before the tribunal of the reader as well as those of the other monologuists.

Browning's buoyant efforts to involve the reader in the excitements of the creative process, to make him in his "due degree" a poet, is unique in the period. (There is, perhaps, a brief glimmer of it in Hopkins's *The Wreck of the Deutschland*, ll. 137–144, 217–222.) The poet (or artist) as subject was one of the dominant concerns of the whole century. It had always been a conventional subject but in the nineteenth century it became an obsession. Blake, Wordsworth, Keats, and Shelley had, each in a different way, launched versions of the question which successive poets turned round and round and round. Blake had given it an apocalyptic orientation, Wordsworth a psychological, Keats an aesthetic, and Shelley a vatic. Each of these, although modified, had a Victorian near-counterpart—Blake in Swinburne, Wordsworth in Arnold, Keats in Tennyson, and Shelley in Browning. The particular version of the question (the poet's nature, his function, his materials, his manner, his spiritual struggle, the discouragement of being misapprehended) that one can identify with this poem or that of this poet or that is not the primary matter. The shadings are infinite and necessarily inconclusive. What is important is this: that despite the multitudinous problems of their "deeply *unpoetical*" age and despite their penetrating sense of isolation, alienation, and the obscurity of their visions even to sympathetic readers, the Victorian poets managed to acclimate poetry to the new conditions of their fractured universe and to write their "sacred book."

A GENERAL BIBLIOGRAPHICAL NOTE

Hopefully some of the deficiencies of the above essay are supplied in the critical and explanatory notes at the end of this volume (pp. 632–688). The student must ultimately formulate his own sense of the peculiar pressures and counter-pressures which shape both the matter and the manner of the several Victorian poets. The following documents will provide genuine guidance in that formulation.

An annotated list of the year's work in Victorian studies is published annually in the periodical called *Victorian Studies*, and these have in turn been collected and indexed approximately once a decade: 1932–1944, 1945–1954, 1955–1964. Through these lists, the student can get a full view of the general concerns and the concentrations of scholars and critics of the last forty years. In addition there is an evaluative-descriptive volume devoted to the poets: *The Victorian Poets: A Guide to Research*, edited by Frederic E. Faverty, revised edition (Cambridge: Harvard University Press, 1964).

A general overview of the principal ideas and events identified with the period can be gleaned from any one of the following three books: D. C. Somervell, *English Thought in the Nineteenth Century* (London: Longmans, Green, 1929); J. H. Randall, Jr., *The Making of the Modern Mind*, revised edition (Boston: Houghton Mifflin, 1940); G. M. Young, *Victorian England: Portrait of an Age* (London: Oxford University Press, 1936).

Two more recent books reflect a considerable breakthrough in contemporary efforts to take a fresh look at the Victorians and their cultural crisis: Jerome H. Buckley, *The Victorian Temper: A Study in Literary Culture* (Cambridge: Harvard University Press, 1951) and Walter E. Houghton, *The Victorian Frame of Mind, 1830–1870* (New Haven: Yale University Press, 1957). Four other books have a "landmark" character because they had a seminal influence on the

Alfred Tennyson
August 6, 1809—October 6, 1892

A BIOGRAPHICAL SKETCH

Tennyson was born, the fourth of twelve children, to the rector of Somersby in Lincolnshire in 1809; in 1892 he died, peer of the realm, poet laureate for almost half a century, famous among the English-speaking peoples (and rewarded by them) to a degree unprecedented in a poet's lifetime. The crosscurrents of literary innovation were too turbulent during the sixty-five years in which he published poems for Tennyson's poetry to be, for long if ever, the dominant model of original practitioners. Browning and Arnold were attracted more to Tennyson's models than to Tennyson himself. The next generation labored at new subject matter and new poetic idioms; but, to the broadly literate man and to the versifier, Tennyson was throughout much of his career the great exemplar of modern poetry.

Tennyson's pre-university days were filled with compensated disquiet. His father was a highly cultivated, book-oriented man, but he was subject to terrifying bouts of the blackest melancholia that engendered in the young Alfred fundamental questions about the value of such a life. His mother was pious and long-suffering but inclined to simplify life-and-death questions along fundamentalist lines. His brothers and sisters were, for the most part, talented in a literary way and more than a little neurotic. Among these personal dynamics, Tennyson moved falteringly. He began to write verses almost as soon as he could write, and he often found solace and genuine satisfaction among the volumes of classical and English literature generously available in his father's library. When the atmosphere of his home became intolerably depressing, Tennyson escaped into the fields and forests and wrestled with his anxious spirit. He collaborated with his brothers, Frederick and Charles, in the production of a volume of poems imprecisely titled *Poems by Two Brothers* (1827).

When Tennyson entered Trinity College, an exciting and fruitful

1

phase of his life opened up. For the first time he was freed from the emotional buffetings at home, and he found in Cambridge a peer group among whom his gifts were prized and from whom he drew aesthetic nurture and intellectual stimulation different, in degree and kind, from anything he had ever known. As was the case with many of his contemporaries, the university regimen itself offered him little. But the group of undergraduates with whom he became identified (they called themselves flamboyantly "The Apostles") and by whom he was held in great account gave direction to his natural seriousness and moved him dramatically toward his majority as a poet. One of them, through his qualities of mind and character and by the happy fact that he and Tennyson were drawn together in what Browning would later call an "elective affinity" (or soul-mating), became an immeasurable source of stability and growth for the young poet. Arthur Henry Hallam exemplified to his entire group of Cambridge associates an important force for new values. To Tennyson Hallam was, besides, the only dependable referee of his new and strenuous efforts to become a poet of significance.

Tennyson published *Poems, Chiefly Lyrical* in 1830 and *Poems* in 1832 (dated 1833). Although their reception was generally favorable if innocuous, some of the big critical guns of the day riddled him mercilessly. Hallam, too, reviewed the earlier volume in an essay entitled "On Some of the Characteristics of Modern Poetry and on the Lyrical Poems of Alfred Tennyson" (*The Englishman's Magazine*, August 1831). Hallam's review is of first importance for several reasons. Tennyson himself said that he and Hallam thought as one about poetry at this time. Beyond much doubt the essay represents the substance of their conversations both while the poems were being written and while the lightning of some of the reviews was being grounded. In its theoretical parts it represents an effort of Tennyson and some of his contemporaries not only to write poetry but also to establish sound directions for it. Finally and somewhat incidentally, Hallam's review has been credited with an influence on the poetic principles of such later notables as William Butler Yeats ("Art and Ideas").

Classifying Tennyson generally but not imitatively with such "Poets of Sensation" as Shelley and Keats (who reflect a "powerful tendency of imagination to a life of immediate sympathy with the external universe"), Hallam catalogued "five distinctive excellencies" in Tennyson's manner:

> First, his luxuriance of imagination, and at the same time his control over it. Secondly his power of embodying himself in ideal characters, or rather moods of character, with such extreme accuracy of adjustment, that the circumstances of the narration seem to have a natural correspondence with the predominant feeling, and, as it were,

to be evolved from its assimilative force. Thirdly his vivid, picturesque delineation of objects, and the peculiar skill with which he holds all of them *fused*, to borrow a metaphor from science, in a medium of strong emotion. Fourthly, the variety of his lyrical measures, and exquisite modulation of harmonious words and cadences to the swell and fall of the feelings expressed. Fifthly, the elevated habits of thought, implied in these compositions, and imparting a mellow soberness of tone, more impressive, to our minds, than if the author had drawn up a set of opinions in verse, and sought to instruct the understanding rather than to communicate the love of beauty to the heart.

The essential justness of Hallam's views has not weakened with time.

In 1831 his father became seriously ill and Tennyson was forced to leave the supportive world of Cambridge and return to a family in financial straits. (A few weeks afterwards the elder Tennyson died.) The most shattering event of the young poet's life, however, was the sudden death of Hallam of a fever in Vienna in September 1833. The life of his perfect friend—"as near perfection as mortal man can be"—had been inexplicably wasted; and Tennyson had to search again the foundations of human experience to find fresh and non-dogmatic bases for believing "That men may rise on stepping-stones/ Of their dead selves to higher things." The results of that search turned into poetry, in part, with *In Memoriam* (1850). But his whole effort during the decade following Hallam's death to come to terms with his life and his art must be considered a single motion of mind and personality, which ended in quantum leaps in Tennyson's mastery of his craft, his confidence in a distinctive poetic role, and his perception of the "abysmal deeps of personality" that both plague and prompt modern man. Thus his two volumes of *Poems* (1842), *The Princess* (1847), and *Maud* (1855) are all parts of the same psychological and spiritual fabric from which *In Memoriam* was cut.

From 1842 onward Tennyson's life took a more tolerable, less chaotic turn. Readers of the 1842 *Poems* recognized him as the major poet of his generation. In 1845 he was awarded a Civil List pension of £200 a year. In 1850, the watershed year of his life, he published *In Memoriam*, married Emily Sellwood, and succeeded Wordsworth as poet laureate.

Tennyson took his vocation as a poet very seriously indeed. Between 1850 and 1892, he published the equivalent of fifteen volumes of poetry—from *Maud: A Monodrama* in 1855 to *The Death of Œnone, and Other Poems*, published posthumously in 1892. His later canon is deeply marked by three characteristics. One is craftsmanship. No English poet (not Spenser, not Keats) ever labored more meticulously than Tennyson did to make the thing that he was doing as artistically perfect as possible. Another is relevance. Whether his subject matter was classical or medieval or contemporaneous, he examined relentlessly the persistent human questions of identity and authority, usually in a heightened psychological and spiritual context. A third is experimentation. This point requires particular emphasis, perhaps, in the face of judgments like that of T. S. Eliot who claimed a degree of atrophy is apparent in Tennyson's work after *In Memoriam*. Against Eliot's thesis should be set numerous considerations, including the following. *Maud* (1855) is one of the boldest experiments in form and psychological disorientation since Marlowe's *The Tragical History of Doctor Faustus*. The work (as distinct from the subject matter) on which Tennyson labored recurrently for thirty years, *Idylls of the King*, is the most elaborate and successful modernization of Arthurian material in the language. It is a startling contradiction of the pressure from many of his contemporary readers and critics to force the poet to deal with current problems in current dress. Also it represents an unprecedented and precarious effort to examine basic problems of knowledge and faith in such a manner as to appeal simultaneously to readers-on-the-run and the "happy few." The poetic dramas—especially *Queen Mary* (1875), *Harold* (1876), and *Becket* (1884)—are not only far-reaching experiments in form but also a confirmation of Tennyson's impersonative tendency rarely credited in studies of his poetry. Several of his later volumes, e.g., *Locksley Hall Sixty Years After, and Other Poems* (1886) and *The Death of Œnone, Akbar's Dream, and Other Poems* (1892), show Tennyson's need to re-examine earlier subjects and themes with new perspective.

Tennyson was greatly honored by his countrymen. In 1855 he was awarded the degree of D.C.L. by Oxford; in 1884 he was made a peer by Queen Victoria; and in 1892 he was buried in Westminster Abbey.

A BIBLIOGRAPHICAL NOTE

The most frequently cited editions of Tennyson's complete works are the Eversley Edition, edited by his son Hallam Tennyson (6 volumes, London: Macmillan & Co., 1907–1908) and the Cambridge Edition, edited by W. J. Rolfe (Boston: Houghton Mifflin, 1898). His son also compiled the first biography, *Alfred Lord Tennyson: A Memoir* (2 volumes, London: Macmillan & Co., 1897). Tennyson's grandson, Sir Charles Tennyson, has published a modern biography, *Alfred Tennyson* (London and New York: Macmillan, 1949).

The best critical introductions to Tennyson's poems are found in *Critical Essays on the Poetry of Tennyson*, edited by John Killham (Boston: Houghton Mifflin, 1961) and in Jerome H. Buckley's *Tennyson: The Growth of a Poet* (Cambridge: Harvard University Press, 1960).

The selections in this text are based on the Cambridge Edition.

ODE TO MEMORY

I

Thou who stealest fire,
From the fountains of the past,
To glorify the present, O, haste,
        Visit my low desire!
Strengthen me, enlighten me!
I faint in this obscurity,
Thou dewy dawn of memory.

II

Come not as thou camest of late,
    Flinging the gloom of yesternight
On the white day, but robed in soften'd light   10
        Of orient state.
Whilome thou camest with the morning mist,
    Even as a maid, whose stately brow
The dew-impearled winds of dawn have kiss'd,
        When she, as thou,
Stays on her floating locks the lovely freight
Of overflowing blooms, and earliest shoots
Of orient green, giving safe pledge of fruits,
Which in wintertide shall star
The black earth with brilliance rare.   20

III

Whilome thou camest with the morning mist,
    And with the evening cloud,
Showering thy gleaned wealth into my open breast;
Those peerless flowers which in the rudest wind
        Never grow sere,
When rooted in the garden of the mind,
    Because they are the earliest of the year.
        Nor was the night thy shroud.
In sweet dreams softer than unbroken rest
Thou leddest by the hand thine infant Hope.   30
The eddying of her garments caught from thee
The light of thy great presence; and the cope
    Of the half-attain'd futurity,
        Tho' deep not fathomless,
Was cloven with the million stars which tremble
O'er the deep mind of dauntless infancy.
Small thought was there of life's distress;
For sure she deem'd no mist of earth could dull

Those spirit-thrilling eyes so keen and beautiful;
Sure she was nigher to heaven's spheres,   40
Listening the lordly music flowing from
      The illimitable years.
  O, strengthen me, enlighten me!
  I faint in this obscurity,
  Thou dewy dawn of memory.

IV

Come forth, I charge thee, arise,
Thou of the many tongues, the myriad eyes!
Thou comest not with shows of flaunting vines
    Unto mine inner eye,
    Divinest Memory!   50
  Thou wert not nursed by the waterfall
Which ever sounds and shines
  A pillar of white light upon the wall
Of purple cliffs, aloof descried:
Come from the woods that belt the gray hillside,
The seven elms, the poplars four
That stand beside my father's door,
And chiefly from the brook that loves
To purl o'er matted cress and ribbed sand,
Or dimple in the dark of rushy coves,   60
Drawing into his narrow earthen urn,
    In every elbow and turn,
The filter'd tribute of the rough woodland;
    O, hither lead thy feet!
Pour round mine ears the livelong bleat
Of the thick-fleeced sheep from wattled folds,
    Upon the ridged wolds,
When the first matin-song hath waken'd loud
Over the dark dewy earth forlorn,
What time the amber morn   70
Forth gushes from beneath a low-hung cloud.

V

Large dowries doth the raptured eye
  To the young spirit present
    When first she is wed,
      And like a bride of old
    In triumph led,
      With music and sweet showers
      Of festal flowers,
  Unto the dwelling she must sway.
Well hast thou done, great artist Memory

In setting round thy first experiment   80
    With royal framework of wrought gold;
Needs must thou dearly love thy first essay,
And foremost in thy various gallery
    Place it, where sweetest sunlight falls
    Upon the storied walls;
        For the discovery
And newness of thine art so pleased thee
That all which thou hast drawn of fairest
Or boldest since but lightly weighs   90
With thee unto the love thou bearest
The first-born of thy genius. Artist-like,
Ever retiring thou dost gaze
On the prime labor of thine early days,
No matter what the sketch might be:
Whether the high field on the bushless pike,
Or even a sand-built ridge
Of heaped hills that mound the sea,
Overblown with murmurs harsh,
Or even a lowly cottage whence we see   100
Stretch'd wide and wild the waste enormous marsh,
Where from the frequent bridge,
Like emblems of infinity,
The trenched waters run from sky to sky;
Or a garden bower'd close
With plaited alleys of the trailing rose,
Long alleys falling down to twilight grots,
Or opening upon level plots
Of crowned lilies, standing near
Purple-spiked lavender: 110
Whither in after life retired
From brawling storms,
From weary wind,
With youthful fancy re-inspired,
We may hold converse with all forms
Of the many-sided mind,
And those whom passion hath not blinded,
Subtle-thoughted, myriad-minded.

My friend, with you to live alone
Were how much better than to own   120
A crown, a sceptre, and a throne!
O, strengthen me, enlighten me!
I faint in this obscurity,
Thou dewy dawn of memory.
1826? (1830)

RECOLLECTIONS OF THE
ARABIAN NIGHTS

When the breeze of a joyful dawn blew free
In the silken sail of infancy,
The tide of time flow'd back with me,
  The forward-flowing tide of time;
And many a sheeny summer-morn,
Adown the Tigris I was borne,
By Bagdat's shrines of fretted gold,
High-walled gardens green and old;
True Mussulman was I and sworn,
  For it was in the golden prime   10
    Of good Haroun Alraschid.

Anight my shallop, rustling thro'
The low and bloomed foliage, drove
The fragrant, glistening deeps, and clove
The citron-shadows in the blue;
By garden porches on the brim,
The costly doors flung open wide,
Gold glittering thro' lamplight dim,
And broider'd sofas on each side.
  In sooth it was a goodly time,   20
  For it was in the golden prime
    Of good Haroun Alraschid.

Often, where clear-stemm'd platans guard
The outlet, did I turn away
The boat-head down a broad canal
From the main river sluiced, where all
The sloping of the moonlit sward
Was damask-work, and deep inlay
Of braided blooms unmown, which crept
Adown to where the water slept.   30
  A goodly place, a goodly time,
  For it was in the golden prime
    Of good Haroun Alraschid.

A motion from the river won
Ridged the smooth level, bearing on
My shallop thro' the star-strown calm,
Until another night in night
I enter'd, from the clearer light,
Imbower'd vaults of pillar'd palm,

Imprisoning sweets, which, as they clomb   40
Heavenward, were stay'd beneath the dome
   Of hollow boughs. A goodly time,
    For it was in the golden prime
     Of good Haroun Alraschid.

Still onward; and the clear canal
Is rounded to as clear a lake.
From the green rivage many a fall
Of diamond rillets musical,
Thro' little crystal arches low
Down from the central fountain's flow   50
Fallen silver-chiming, seemed to shake
The sparkling flints beneath the prow.
   A goodly place, a goodly time,
    For it was in the golden prime
     Of good Haroun Alraschid.

Above thro' many a bowery turn
A walk with vari-colored shells
Wander'd engrain'd. On either side
All round about the fragrant marge
From fluted vase, and brazen urn   60
In order, eastern flowers large,
Some dropping low their crimson bells
Half-closed, and others studded wide
   With disks and tiars, fed the time
   With odor in the golden prime
    Of good Haroun Alraschid.

Far off, and where the lemon grove
In closest coverture upsprung,
The living airs of middle night
Died round the bulbul as he sung;   70
Not he, but something which possess'd
The darkness of the world, delight,
Life, anguish, death, immortal love,
Ceasing not, mingled, unrepress'd,
   Apart from place, withholding time,
   But flattering the golden prime
    Of good Haroun Alraschid.

Black the garden-bowers and grots
Slumber'd; the solemn palms were ranged
Above, unwoo'd of summer wind;   80
A sudden splendor from behind
Flush'd all the leaves with rich gold-green,
And, flowing rapidly between
Their interspaces, counterchanged

The level lake with diamond-plots
   Of dark and bright. A lovely time,
   For it was in the golden prime
     Of good Haroun Alraschid.

Dark-blue the deep sphere overhead,
Distinct with vivid stars inlaid,   90
Grew darker from that under-flame;
So, leaping lightly from the boat,
With silver anchor left afloat,
In marvel whence that glory came
Upon me, as in sleep I sank
In cool soft turf upon the bank,
   Entranced with that place and time,
   So worthy of the golden prime
     Of good Haroun Alraschid.

Thence thro' the garden I was drawn—   100
A realm of pleasance, many a mound,
And many a shadow-chequer'd lawn
Full of the city's stilly sound,
And deep myrrh-thickets blowing round
The stately cedar, tamarisks,
Thick rosaries of scented thorn,
Tall orient shrubs, and obelisks
   Graven with emblems of the time,
   In honor of the golden prime
     Of good Haroun Alraschid.   110

With dazed vision unawares
From the long alley's latticed shade
Emerged, I came upon the great
Pavillion of the Caliphat.
Right to the carven cedarn doors,
Flung inward over spangled floors,
Broad-based flights of marble stairs
Ran up with golden balustrade,
   After the fashion of the time,
   And humor of the golden prime   120
     Of good Haroun Alraschid.

The fourscore windows all alight
As with the quintessence of flame,
A million tapers flaring bright
From twisted silvers look'd to shame
The hollow-vaulted dark, and stream'd
Upon the mooned domes aloof
In inmost Bagdat, till there seem'd
Hundreds of crescents on the roof

Of night new-risen, that marvellous time   130
To celebrate the golden prime
   Of good Haroun Alraschid.

Then stole I up, and trancedly
Gazed on the Persian girl alone,
Serene with argent-lidded eyes
Amorous, and lashes like to rays
Of darkness, and a brow of pearl
Tressed with redolent ebony,
In many a dark delicious curl,
Flowing beneath her rose-hued zone;   140
  The sweetest lady of the time,
  Well worthy of the golden prime
    Of good Haroun Alraschid.

Six columns, three on either side,
Pure silver, underpropt a rich
Throne of the massive ore, from which
Down-droop'd, in many a floating fold,
Engarlanded and diaper'd
With inwrought flowers, a cloth of gold.
Thereon, his deep eye laughter-stirr'd   150
With merriment of kingly pride,
  Sole star of all that place and time,
  I saw him—in his golden prime,
    The Good Haroun Alraschid.
1830

MARIANA

"Mariana in the moated grange."—*Measure for Measure.*

With blackest moss the flower-plots
  Were thickly crusted, one and all;
The rusted nails fell from the knots
  That held the pear to the gable-wall.
The broken sheds look'd sad and strange:
  Unlifted was the clinking latch;
  Weeded and worn the ancient thatch
Upon the lonely moated grange.
    She only said, "My life is dreary,
      He cometh not," she said;   10
    She said, "I am aweary, aweary,
      I would that I were dead!"

Her tears fell with the dews at even;
  Her tears fell ere the dews were dried;

She could not look on the sweet heaven,
　　Either at morn or eventide.
After the flitting of the bats,
　　When thickest dark did trance the sky,
　　She drew her casement-curtain by,
And glanced athwart the glooming flats.　　　　20
　　　　She only said, "The night is dreary,
　　　　　　He cometh not," she said;
　　　　She said, "I am aweary, aweary,
　　　　　　I would that I were dead!"

Upon the middle of the night,
　　Waking she heard the night-fowl crow;
The cock sung out an hour ere light;
　　From the dark fen the oxen's low
Came to her; without hope of change,
　　In sleep she seem'd to walk forlorn,　　　　30
　　Till cold winds woke the gray-eyed morn
About the lonely moated grange.
　　　　She only said, "The day is dreary,
　　　　　　He cometh not," she said;
　　　　She said, "I am aweary, aweary,
　　　　　　I would that I were dead!"

About a stone-cast from the wall
　　A sluice with blacken'd waters slept,
And o'er it many, round and small,
　　The cluster'd marish-mosses crept.　　　　40
Hard by a poplar shook alway,
　　All silver-green with gnarled bark:
　　For leagues no other tree did mark
The level waste, the rounding gray.
　　　　She only said, "My life is dreary,
　　　　　　He cometh not," she said;
　　　　She said, "I am aweary, aweary,
　　　　　　I would that I were dead!"

And ever when the moon was low,
　　And the shrill winds were up and away,　　　　50
In the white curtain, to and fro,
　　She saw the gusty shadow sway.
But when the moon was very low,
　　And wild winds bound within their cell,
　　The shadow of the poplar fell
Upon her bed, across her brow.
　　　　She only said, "The night is dreary,
　　　　　　He cometh not," she said;

She said, "I am aweary, aweary,
　　I would that I were dead!"　　　　　　　60

All day within the dreamy house,
　　The doors upon their hinges creak'd;
The blue fly sung in the pane; the mouse
　　Behind the mouldering wainscot shriek'd,
Or from the crevice peer'd about.
　　Old faces glimmer'd thro' the doors,
　　Old footsteps trod the upper floors,
Old voices called her from without.
　　　　She only said, "My life is dreary,
　　　　　　He cometh not," she said;　　　　70
　　　　She said, "I am aweary, aweary,
　　　　　　I would that I were dead!"

The sparrow's chirrup on the roof,
　　The slow clock ticking, and the sound
Which to the wooing wind aloof
　　The poplar made, did all confound
Her sense; but most she loathed the hour
　　When the thick-moted sunbeam lay
　　Athwart the chambers, and the day
Was sloping toward his western bower.　　　80
　　　　Then said she, "I am very dreary,
　　　　　　He will not come," she said;
　　　　She wept, "I am aweary, aweary,
　　　　　　O God, that I were dead!"
1830

THE LADY OF SHALOTT

PART I

On either side the river lie
Long fields of barley and of rye,
That clothe the wold and meet the sky;
And thro' the field the road runs by
　　　　To many-tower'd Camelot;
And up and down the people go,
Gazing where the lilies blow
Round an island there below,
　　　　The island of Shalott.

Willows whiten, aspens quiver,　　　　　　10
Little breezes dusk and shiver
Thro' the wave that runs for ever

By the island in the river
    Flowing down to Camelot.
Four gray walls, and four gray towers,
Overlook a space of flowers,
And the silent isle imbowers
    The Lady of Shalott.

By the margin, willow-veil'd,
Slide the heavy barges trail'd   20
By slow horses; and unhail'd
The shallop flitteth silken-sail'd
    Skimming down to Camelot:
But who hath seen her wave her hand?
Or at the casement seen her stand?
Or is she known in all the land,
    The Lady of Shalott?

Only reapers, reaping early
In among the bearded barley,
Hear a song that echoes cheerly   30
From the river winding clearly,
    Down to tower'd Camelot;
And by the moon the reaper weary,
Piling sheaves in uplands airy,
Listening, whispers " 'T is the fairy
    Lady of Shalott."

PART II

There she weaves by night and day
A magic web with colors gay.
She has heard a whisper say,
A curse is on her if she stay   40
    To look down to Camelot.
She knows not what the curse may be,
And so she weaveth steadily,
And little other care hath she,
    The Lady of Shalott.

And moving thro' a mirror clear
That hangs before her all the year,
Shadows of the world appear.
There she sees the highway near
    Winding down to Camelot;   50
There the river eddy whirls,
And there the surly village-churls,
And the red cloaks of market girls,
    Pass onward from Shalott.

Sometimes a troop of damsels glad,
An abbot on an ambling pad,
Sometimes a curly shepherd-lad,
Or long-hair'd page in crimson clad,
        Goes by to tower'd Camelot;
And sometimes thro' the mirror blue   60
The knights come riding two and two:
She hath no loyal knight and true,
        The Lady of Shalott.

But in her web she still delights
To weave the mirror's magic sights,
For often thro' the silent nights
A funeral, with plumes and lights
        And music, went to Camelot;
Or when the moon was overhead,
Came two young lovers lately wed: 70
"I am half sick of shadows," said
        The Lady of Shalott.

PART III

A bow-shot from her bower-eaves,
He rode between the barley-sheaves.
The sun came dazzling thro' the leaves,
And flamed upon the brazen greaves
        Of bold Sir Lancelot.
A red-cross knight for ever kneel'd
To a lady in his shield,
That sparkled on the yellow field,   80
        Beside remote Shalott.

The gemmy bridle glitter'd free,
Like to some branch of stars we see
Hung in the golden Galaxy.
The bridle bells rang merrily
        As he rode down to Camelot;
And from his blazon'd baldric slung
A mighty silver bugle hung,
And as he rode his armor rung,
        Beside remote Shalott.   90

All in the blue unclouded weather
Thick-jewell'd shone the saddle-leather,
The helmet and the helmet-feather
Burn'd like one burning flame together,
        As he rode down to Camelot;
As often thro' the purple night,

Below the starry clusters bright,
Some bearded meteor, trailing light,
    Moves over still Shalott.

His broad clear brow in sunlight glow'd;   100
On burnish'd hooves his war-horse trode;
From underneath his helmet flow'd
His coal-black curls as on he rode,
    As he rode down to Camelot.
From the bank and from the river
He flash'd into the crystal mirror,
"Tirra lirra," by the river
    Sang Sir Lancelot.

She left the web, she left the loom,
She made three paces thro' the room,   110
She saw the water-lily bloom,
She saw the helmet and the plume,
    She look'd down to Camelot.
Out flew the web and floated wide;
The mirror crack'd from side to side;
"The curse is come upon me," cried
    The Lady of Shalott.

PART IV

In the stormy east-wind straining,
The pale yellow woods were waning,
The broad stream in his banks complaining,   120
Heavily the low sky raining
    Over tower'd Camelot;
Down she came and found a boat
Beneath a willow left afloat,
And round about the prow she wrote
    The Lady of Shalott.

And down the river's dim expanse
Like some bold seër in a trance,
Seeing all his own mischance—
With a glassy countenance   130
    Did she look to Camelot.
And at the closing of the day
She loosed the chain, and down she lay;
The broad stream bore her far away,
    The Lady of Shalott.

Lying, robed in snowy white
That loosely flew to left and right—
The leaves upon her falling light—
Thro' the noises of the night

She floated down to Camelot;   140
And as the boat-head wound along
The willowy hills and fields among,
They heard her singing her last song,
    The Lady of Shalott.

Heard a carol, mournful, holy,
Chanted loudly, chanted lowly,
Till her blood was frozen slowly,
And her eyes were darken'd wholly,
    Turn'd to tower'd Camelot.
For ere she reach'd upon the tide   150
The first house by the water-side,
Singing in her song she died,
    The Lady of Shalott.

Under tower and balcony,
By garden-wall and gallery,
A gleaming shape she floated by,
Dead-pale between the houses high,
    Silent into Camelot.
Out upon the wharfs they came,
Knight and burgher, lord and dame,   160
And round the prow they read her name,
    The Lady of Shalott.

Who is this? and what is here?
And in the lighted palace near
Died the sound of royal cheer;
And they cross'd themselves for fear,
    All the knights at Camelot:
But Lancelot mused a little space;
He said, "She has a lovely face;
God in his mercy lend her grace,   170
    The Lady of Shalott."
1832, 1842

ŒNONE

There lies a vale in Ida, lovelier
Than all the valleys of Ionian hills.
The swimming vapor slopes athwart the glen,
Puts forth an arm, and creeps from pine to pine,
And loiters, slowly drawn. On either hand
The lawns and meadow-ledges midway down
Hang rich in flowers, and far below them roars

The long brook falling thro' the cloven ravine
In cataract after cataract to the sea.
Behind the valley topmost Gargarus   10
Stands up and takes the morning; but in front
The gorges, opening wide apart, reveal
Troas and Ilion's column'd citadel,
The crown of Troas.
              Hither came at noon
Mournful Œnone, wandering forlorn
Of Paris, once her playmate on the hills.
Her cheek had lost the rose, and round her neck
Floated her hair or seem'd to float in rest.
She, leaning on a fragment twined with vine,
Sang to the stillness, till the mountain shade   20
Sloped downward to her seat from the upper cliff.

  "O mother Ida, many-fountain'd Ida,
Dear mother Ida, harken ere I die.
For now the noonday quiet holds the hill;
The grasshopper is silent in the grass;
The lizard, with his shadow on the stone,
Rests like a shadow, and the winds are dead.
The purple flower droops, the golden bee
Is lily-cradled; I alone awake.
My eyes are full of tears, my heart of love,   30
My heart is breaking, and my eyes are dim,
And I am all aweary of my life.

  "O mother Ida, many-fountain'd Ida,
Dear mother Ida, harken ere I die.
Hear me, O earth, hear me, O hills, O caves
That house the cold crown'd snake! O mountain **brooks,**
I am the daughter of a River-God,
Hear me, for I will speak, and build up all
My sorrow with my song, as yonder walls
Rose slowly to a music slowly breathed,   40
A cloud that gather'd shape; for it may be
That, while I speak of it, a little while
My heart may wander from its deeper woe.

  "O mother Ida, many-fountain'd Ida,
Dear mother Ida, harken ere I die.
I waited underneath the dawning hills;
Aloft the mountain lawn was dewy-dark,
And dewy-dark aloft the mountain pine.
Beautiful Paris, evil-hearted Paris,
Leading a jet-black goat white-horn'd, white-hooved,   50
Came up from reedy Simois all alone.

"O mother Ida, harken ere I die.
Far-off the torrent call'd me from the cleft;
Far up the solitary morning smote
The streaks of virgin snow. With downdropt eyes
I sat alone; white-breasted like a star
Fronting the dawn he moved; a leopard skin
Droop'd from his shoulder, but his sunny hair
Cluster'd about his temples like a God's;
And his cheeks brighten'd as the foam-bow brightens   60
When the wind blows the foam, and all my heart
Went forth to embrace him coming ere he came.

"Dear mother Ida, harken ere I die.
He smiled, and opening out his milk-white palm
Disclosed a fruit of pure Hesperian gold,
That smelt ambrosially, and while I look'd
And listen'd, the full-flowing river of speech
Came down upon my heart:
                          " 'My own Œnone,
Beautiful-brow'd Œnone, my own soul,
Behold this fruit, whose gleaming rind ingraven   70
"For the most fair," would seem to award it thine,
As lovelier than whatever Oread haunt
The knolls of Ida, loveliest in all grace
Of movement, and the charm of married brows.'

"Dear mother Ida, harken ere I die.
He prest the blossom of his lips to mine,
And added, 'This was cast upon the board,
When all the full-faced presence of the Gods
Ranged in the halls of Peleus; whereupon
Rose feud, with question unto whom 't were due;   80
But light-foot Iris brought it yester-eve,
Delivering, that to me, by common voice
Elected umpire. Herè comes to-day,
Pallas and Aphrodite, claiming each
This meed of fairest. Thou, within the cave
Behind yon whispering tuft of oldest pine,
Mayst well behold them unbeheld, unheard
Hear all, and see thy Paris judge of Gods.'

"Dear mother Ida, harken ere I die.
It was the deep midnoon; one silvery cloud   90
Had lost his way between the piny sides
Of this long glen. Then to the bower they came,
Naked they came to that smooth-swarded bower,
And at their feet the crocus brake like fire,
Violet, amaracus, and asphodel,

Lotos and lilies; and a wind arose,
And overhead the wandering ivy and vine,
This way and that, in many a wild festoon
Ran riot, garlanding the gnarled boughs
With bunch and berry and flower thro' and thro'.   100

　　"O mother Ida, harken ere I die.
On the tree-tops a crested peacock lit,
And o'er him flow'd a golden cloud, and lean'd
Upon him, slowly dropping fragrant dew.
Then first I heard the voice of her to whom
Coming thro' heaven, like a light that grows
Larger and clearer, with one mind the Gods
Rise up for reverence. She to Paris made
Proffer of royal power, ample rule
Unquestion'd, overflowing revenue   110
Wherewith to embellish state, 'from many a vale
And river-sunder'd champaign clothed with corn,
Or labor'd mine undrainable of ore.
Honor,' she said, 'and homage, tax and toll,
From many an inland town and haven large,
Mast-throng'd beneath her shadowing citadel
In glassy bays among her tallest towers.'

　　"O mother Ida, harken ere I die.
Still she spake on and still she spake of power,
'Which in all action is the end of all;   120
Power fitted to the season; wisdom-bred
And throned of wisdom—from all neighbor crowns
Alliance and allegiance, till thy hand
Fail from the sceptre-staff. Such boon from me,
From me, heaven's queen, Paris, to thee king-born,
A shepherd all thy life, but yet king-born.
Should come most welcome, seeing men, in power
Only, are likest Gods, who have attain'd
Rest in a happy place and quiet seats
Above the thunder, with undying bliss   130
In knowledge of their own supremacy.'

　　"Dear mother Ida, harken ere I die.
She ceased, and Paris held the costly fruit
Out at arm's-length, so much the thought of power
Flatter'd his spirit; but Pallas where she stood
Somewhat apart, her clear and bared limbs
O'erthwarted with the brazen-headed spear
Upon her pearly shoulder leaning cold,
The while, above, her full and earnest eye
Over her snow-cold breast and angry cheek   140
Kept watch, waiting decision, made reply:

" 'Self-reverence, self-knowledge, self-control,
These three alone lead life to sovereign power.
Yet not for power (power of herself
Would come uncall'd for) but to live by law,
Acting the law we live by without fear;
And, because right is right, to follow right
Were wisdom in the scorn of consequence.'

"Dear mother Ida, harken ere I die.
Again she said: 'I woo thee not with gifts.   150
Sequel of guerdon could not alter me
To fairer. Judge thou me by what I am,
So shalt thou find me fairest.
                                        Yet, indeed,
If gazing on divinity disrobed
Thy mortal eyes are frail to judge of fair,
Unbias'd by self-profit, O, rest thee sure
That I shall love thee well and cleave to thee,
So that my vigor, wedded to thy blood,
Shall strike within thy pulses, like a God's,
To push thee forward thro' a life of shocks,   160
Dangers, and deeds, until endurance grow
Sinew'd with action, and the full-grown will,
Circled thro' all experiences, pure law,
Commeasure perfect freedom.'
                                        "Here she ceas'd,
And Paris ponder'd, and I cried, 'O Paris,
Give it to Pallas!' but he heard me not,
Or hearing would not hear me, woe is me!

"O mother Ida, many-fountain'd Ida,
Dear mother Ida, harken ere I die.
Idalian Aphrodite beautiful,   170
Fresh as the foam, new-bathed in Paphian wells,
With rosy slender fingers backward drew
From her warm brows and bosom her deep hair
Ambrosial, golden round her lucid throat
And shoulder; from the violets her light foot
Shone rosy-white, and o'er her rounded form
Between the shadows of the vine-bunches
Floated the glowing sunlights, as she moved.

"Dear mother Ida, harken ere I die.
She with a subtle smile in her mild eyes,   180
The herald of her triumph, drawing nigh
Half-whisper'd in his ear, 'I promise thee
The fairest and most loving wife in Greece.'
She spoke and laugh'd; I shut my sight for fear;
But when I look'd, Paris had raised his arm,

And I beheld great Here's angry eyes,
As she withdrew into the golden cloud,
And I was left alone within the bower;
And from that time to this I am alone,
And I shall be alone until I die.   190

    "Yet, mother Ida, harken ere I die.
Fairest—why fairest wife? am I not fair?
My love hath told me so a thousand times.
Methinks I must be fair, for yesterday,
When I past by, a wild and wanton pard,
Eyed like the evening star, with playful tail
Crouch'd fawning in the weed. Most loving is she?
Ah me, my mountain shepherd, that my arms
Were wound about thee, and my hot lips prest
Close, close to thine in that quick-falling dew   200
Of fruitful kisses, thick as autumn rains
Flash in the pools of whirling Simois!

    "O mother, hear me yet before I die.
They came, they cut away my tallest pines,
My tall dark pines, that plumed the craggy ledge
High over the blue gorge, and all between
The snowy peak and snow-white cataract
Foster'd the callow eaglet—from beneath
Whose thick mysterious boughs in the dark morn
The panther's roar came muffled, while I sat   210
Low in the valley. Never, never more
Shall lone Œnone see the morning mist
Sweep thro' them; never see them overlaid
With narrow moonlit slips of silver cloud,
Between the loud stream and the trembling stars.

    "O mother, hear me yet before I die.
I wish that somewhere in the ruin'd folds,
Among the fragments tumbled from the glens,
Or the dry thickets, I could meet with her
The Abominable, that uninvited came   220
Into the fair Peleïan banquet-hall,
And cast the golden fruit upon the board,
And bred this change; that I might speak my mind,
And tell her to her face how much I hate
Her presence, hated both of Gods and men.

    "O mother, hear me yet before I die.
Hath he not sworn his love a thousand times,
In this green valley, under this green hill,
Even on this hand, and sitting on this stone?
Seal'd it with kisses? water'd it with tears?   230

O happy tears, and how unlike to these!
O happy heaven, how canst thou see my face?
O happy earth, how canst thou bear my weight?
O death, death, death, thou ever-floating cloud,
There are enough unhappy on this earth,
Pass by the happy souls, that love to live;
I pray thee, pass before my light of life,
And shadow all my soul, that I may die.
Thou weighest heavy on the heart within,
Weigh heavy on my eyelids; let me die.   240

    "O mother, hear me yet before I die.
I will not die alone, for fiery thoughts
Do shape themselves within me, more and more,
Whereof I catch the issue, as I hear
Dead sounds at night come from the inmost hills,
Like footsteps upon wool. I dimly see
My far-off doubtful purpose, as a mother
Conjectures of the features of her child
Ere it is born. Her child!—a shudder comes
Across me: never child be born of me,   250
Unblest, to vex me with his father's eyes!

    "O mother, hear me yet before I die.
Hear me, O earth. I will not die alone,
Lest their shrill happy laughter come to me
Walking the cold and starless road of death
Uncomforted, leaving my ancient love
With the Greek woman. I will rise and go
Down into Troy, and ere the stars come forth
Talk with the wild Cassandra, for she says
A fire dances before her, and a sound   260
Rings ever in her ears of armed men.
What this may be I know not, but I know
That, wheresoe'er I am by night and day,
All earth and air seem only burning fire."
1832, 1842

TO ——

WITH THE FOLLOWING POEM

I send you here a sort of allegory—
For you will understand it—of a soul,
A sinful soul possess'd of many gifts,
A spacious garden full of flowering weeds,

A glorious devil, large in heart and brain,
That did love beauty only—beauty seen
In all varieties of mould and mind—
And knowledge for its beauty; or if good,
Good only for its beauty, seeing not
That Beauty, Good, and Knowledge are three sisters   10
That doat upon each other, friends to man,
Living together under the same roof,
And never can be sunder'd without tears.
And he that shuts Love out, in turn shall be
Shut out from Love, and on her threshold lie
Howling in outer darkness. Not for this
Was common clay ta'en from the common earth
Moulded by God, and temper'd with the tears
Of angels to the perfect shape of man.
1832

THE PALACE OF ART

I built my soul a lordly pleasure-house,
    Wherein at ease for aye to dwell.
I said, "O Soul, make merry and carouse,
    Dear soul, for all is well."

A huge crag-platform, smooth as burnish'd brass,
    I chose. The ranged ramparts bright
From level meadow-bases of deep grass
    Suddenly scaled the light.

Thereon I built it firm. Of ledge or shelf
    The rock rose clear, or winding stair.   10
My soul would live alone unto herself
    In her high palace there.

And "while the world runs round and round," I said,
    "Reign thou apart, a quiet king,
Still as, while Saturn whirls, his steadfast shade
    Sleeps on his luminous ring."

To which my soul made answer readily:
    "Trust me, in bliss I shall abide
In this great mansion, that is built for me,
    So royal-rich and wide."   20

. . . .
Four courts I made, East, West and South and North,
    In each a squared lawn, wherefrom
The golden gorge of dragons spouted forth
    A flood of fountain-foam.

And round the cool green courts there ran a row
    Of cloisters, branch'd like mighty woods,
Echoing all night to that sonorous flow
    Of spouted fountain-floods;

And round the roofs a gilded gallery
    That lent broad verge to distant lands,   30
Far as the wild swan wings, to where the sky
    Dipt down to sea and sands.

From those four jets four currents in one swell
    Across the mountain stream'd below
In misty folds, that floating as they fell
    Lit up a torrent-bow.

And high on every peak a statue seem'd
    To hang on tiptoe, tossing up
A cloud of incense of all odor steam'd
    From out a golden cup.   40

So that she thought, "And who shall gaze upon
    My palace with unblinded eyes,
While this great bow will waver in the sun,
    And that sweet incense rise?"

For that sweet incense rose and never fail'd,
    And, while day sank or mounted higher,
The light aerial gallery, golden-rail'd,
    Burnt like a fringe of fire.

Likewise the deep-set windows, stain'd and traced,
    Would seem slow-flaming crimson fires   50
From shadow'd grots of arches interlaced,
    And tipt with frost-like spires.

.   .   .   .
Full of long-sounding corridors it was,
    That over-vaulted grateful gloom,
Thro' which the livelong day my soul did pass,
    Well-pleased, from room to room.

Full of great rooms and small the palace stood,
    All various, each a perfect whole
From living Nature, fit for every mood
    And change of my still soul.   60

For some were hung with arras green and blue,
    Showing a gaudy summer-morn,
Where with puff'd cheek the belted hunter blew
    His wreathed bugle-horn.

One seem'd all dark and red—a tract of sand,
    And some one pacing there alone,

Who paced for ever in a glimmering land,
    Lit with a low large moon.

One show'd an iron coast and angry waves,
    You seem'd to hear them climb and fall   70
And roar rock-thwarted under bellowing caves,
    Beneath the windy wall.

And one, a full-fed river winding slow
    By herds upon an endless plain,
The ragged rims of thunder brooding low,
    With shadow-streaks of rain.

And one, the reapers at their sultry toil.
    In front they bound the sheaves. Behind
Were realms of upland, prodigal in oil,
    And hoary to the wind.   80

And one a foreground black with stones and slags;
    Beyond, a line of heights; and higher
All barr'd with long white cloud the scornful crags;
    And highest, snow and fire.

And one, an English home—gray twilight pour'd
    On dewy pastures, dewy trees,
Softer than sleep—all things in order stored,
    A haunt of ancient Peace.

Nor these alone, but every landscape fair,
    As fit for every mood of mind,   90
Or gay, or grave, or sweet, or stern, was there,
    Not less than truth design'd.

. . . .

Or the maid-mother by a crucifix,
    In tracts of pasture sunny-warm,
Beneath branch-work of costly sardonyx
    Sat smiling, babe in arm.

Or in a clear-wall'd city on the sea,
    Near gilded organ-pipes, her hair
Wound with white roses, slept Saint Cecily;
    An angel look'd at her.   100

Or thronging all one porch of Paradise
    A group of Houris bow'd to see
The dying Islamite, with hands and eyes
    That said, We wait for thee.

Or mythic Uther's deeply-wounded son
    In some fair space of sloping greens

Lay, dozing in the vale of Avalon,
    And watch'd by weeping queens.

Or hollowing one hand against his ear,
    To list a foot-fall, ere he saw   110
The wood-nymph, stay'd the Ausonian king to hear
    Of wisdom and of law.

Or over hills with peaky tops engrail'd,
    And many a tract of palm and rice,
The throne of Indian Cama slowly sail'd
    A summer fann'd with spice.

Or sweet Europa's mantle blew unclasp'd,
    From off her shoulder backward borne;
From one hand droop'd a crocus; one hand grasp'd
    The mild bull's golden horn.   120

Or else flush'd Ganymede, his rosy thigh
    Half-buried in the eagle's down,
Sole as a flying star shot thro' the sky
    Above the pillar'd town.

Nor these alone; but every legend fair
    Which the supreme Caucasian mind
Carved out of Nature for itself was there,
    Not less than life design'd.

.   .   .   .

Then in the towers I placed great bells that swung,
    Moved of themselves, with silver sound;   130
And with choice paintings of wise men I hung
    The royal dais round.

For there was Milton like a seraph strong,
    Beside him Shakespeare bland and mild;
And there the world-worn Dante grasp'd his song,
    And somewhat grimly smiled.

And there the Ionian father of the rest;
    A million wrinkles carved his skin;
A hundred winters snow'd upon his breast,
    From cheek and throat and chin.   140

Above, the fair hall-ceiling stately-set
    Many an arch high up did lift,
And angels rising and descending met
    With interchange of gift.

Below was all mosaic choicely plann'd
    With cycles of the human tale

Of this wide world, the times of every land
    So wrought they will not fail.

The people here, a beast of burden slow,
    Toil'd onward, prick'd with goads and stings;   **150**
Here play'd, a tiger, rolling to and fro
    The heads and crowns of kings;

Here rose, an athlete, strong to break or bind
    All force in bonds that might endure,
And here once more like some sick man declined,
    And trusted any cure.

But over these she trod; and those great bells
    Began to chime. She took her throne;
She sat betwixt the shining oriels,
    To sing her songs alone.   **160**

And thro' the topmost oriels' colored flame
    Two godlike faces gazed below;
Plato the wise, and large-brow'd Verulam,
    The first of those who know.

And all those names that in their motion were
    Full-welling fountain-heads of change,
Betwixt the slender shafts were blazon'd fair
    In diverse raiment strange;

Thro' which the lights, rose, amber, emerald, blue,
    Flush'd in her temples and her eyes,   **170**
And from her lips, as morn from Memnon, drew
    Rivers of melodies.

No nightingale delighteth to prolong
    Her low preamble all alone,
More than my soul to hear her echo'd song
    Throb thro' the ribbed stone;

Singing and murmuring in her feastful mirth,
    Joying to feel herself alive,
Lord over Nature, lord of the visible earth,
    Lord of the senses five;   **180**

Communing with herself: "All these are mine,
    And let the world have peace or wars,
'T is one to me." She—when young night divine
    Crown'd dying day with stars,

Making sweet close of his delicious toils—
    Lit light in wreaths and anadems,

And pure quintessences of precious oils
    In hollow'd moons of gems,

To mimic heaven; and clapt her hands and cried,
    "I marvel if my still delight   190
In this great house so royal-rich and wide
    Be flatter'd to the height.

"O all things fair to sate my various eyes!
    O shapes and hues that please me well!
O silent faces of the Great and Wise,
    My Gods, with whom I dwell!

"O Godlike isolation which art mine,
    I can but count thee perfect gain,
What time I watch the darkening droves of swine
    That range on yonder plain.   200

"In filthy sloughs they roll a prurient skin,
    They graze and wallow, breed and sleep;
And oft some brainless devil enters in,
    And drives them to the deep."

Then of the moral instinct would she prate
    And of the rising from the dead,
As hers by right of full-accomplish'd Fate;
    And at the last she said:

"I take possession of man's mind and deed.
    I care not what the sects may brawl.   210
I sit as God holding no form of creed,
    But contemplating all."

.   .   .   .
Full oft the riddle of the painful earth
    Flash'd thro' her as she sat alone,
Yet not the less held she her solemn mirth,
    And intellectual throne.

And so she throve and prosper'd; so three years
    She prosper'd; on the fourth she fell,
Like Herod, when the shout was in his ears,
    Struck thro' with pangs of hell.   220

Lest she should fail and perish utterly,
    God, before whom ever lie bare
The abysmal deeps of personality,
    Plagued her with sore despair.

When she would think, where'er she turn'd her sight
    The airy hand confusion wrought,

Wrote, "Mene, mene," and divided quite
    The kingdom of her thought.

Deep dread and loathing of her solitude
    Fell on her, from which mood was born   230
Scorn of herself; again, from out that mood
    Laughter at her self-scorn.

"What! is not this my place of strength," she said,
    "My spacious mansion built for me,
Whereof the strong foundation-stones were laid
    Since my first memory?"

But in dark corners of her palace stood
    Uncertain shapes; and unawares
On white-eyed phantasms weeping tears of blood,
    And horrible nightmares,   240

And hollow shades enclosing hearts of flame,
    And, with dim fretted foreheads all,
On corpses three-months-old at noon she came,
    That stood against the wall.

A spot of dull stagnation, without light
    Or power of movement, seem'd my soul,
Mid onward-sloping motions infinite
    Making for one sure goal;

A still salt pool, lock'd in with bars of sand,
    Left on the shore, that hears all night   250
The plunging seas draw backward from the land
    Their moon-led waters white;

A star that with the choral starry dance
    Join'd not, but stood, and standing saw
The hollow orb of moving Circumstance
    Roll'd round by one fix'd law.

Back on herself her serpent pride had curl'd.
    "No voice," she shriek'd in that lone hall,
"No voice breaks thro' the stillness of this world;
    One deep, deep silence all!"   260

She, mouldering with the dull earth's mouldering sod,
    Inwrapt tenfold in slothful shame,
Lay there exiled from eternal God,
    Lost to her place and name;

And death and life she hated equally,
    And nothing saw, for her despair,
But dreadful time, dreadful eternity,
    No comfort anywhere;

Remaining utterly confused with fears,
   And ever worse with growing time,   270
And ever unrelieved by dismal tears,
    And all alone in crime.

Shut up as in a crumbling tomb, girt round
   With blackness as a solid wall,
Far off she seem'd to hear the dully sound
    Of human footsteps fall:

As in strange lands a traveller walking slow,
   In doubt and great perplexity,
A little before moonrise hears the low   280
    Moan of an unknown sea;

And knows not if it be thunder, or a sound
   Of rocks thrown down, or one deep cry
Of great wild beasts; then thinketh, "I have found
    A new land, but I die."

She howl'd aloud, "I am on fire within.
   There comes no murmur of reply.
What is it that will take away my sin,
    And save me lest I die?"

So when four years were wholly finished,
   She threw her royal robes away.   290
"Make me a cottage in the vale," she said,
    "Where I may mourn and pray.

"Yet pull not down my palace towers, that are
   So lightly, beautifully built;
Perchance I may return with others there
    When I have purged my guilt."
1832, 1842

THE HESPERIDES

"Hesperus and his daughters three,
That sing about the golden tree."—*Comus.*

The North-wind fall'n, in the new-starréd night
Zidonian Hanno, voyaging beyond
The hoary promontory of Soloë
Past Thymiaterion, in calméd bays,
Between the southern and the western Horn,
Heard neither warbling of the nightingale,
Nor melody of the Libyan lotus flute
Blown seaward from the shore; but from a slope

That ran bloom-bright into the Atlantic blue,
Beneath a highland leaning down a weight   10
Of cliffs, and zoned below with cedar shade,
Came voices, like the voices in a dream,
Continuous, till he reached the outer sea.

SONG

I

The golden apple, the golden apple, the hallowed fruit,
Guard it well, guard it warily,
Singing airily,
Standing about the charmèd root.
Round about all is mute,
As the snow-field on the mountain-peaks,
As the sand-field at the mountain-foot.   20
Crocodiles in briny creeks
Sleep and stir not: all is mute.
If ye sing not, if ye make false measure,
We shall lose eternal pleasure,
Worth eternal want of rest.
Laugh not loudly: watch the treasure
Of the wisdom of the West.
In a corner wisdom whispers. Five and three
(Let it not be preached abroad) make an awful mystery.
For the blossom unto threefold music bloweth;   30
Evermore it is born anew;
And the sap to threefold music floweth,
From the root
Drawn in the dark,
Up to the fruit,
Creeping under the fragrant bark,
Liquid gold, honeysweet, thro' and thro'.
Keen-eyed Sisters, singing airily,
Looking warily
Every way,   40
Guard the apple night and day,
Lest one from the East come and take it away.

II

Father Hesper, Father Hesper, watch, watch, ever and aye,
Looking under silver hair with a silver eye.
Father, twinkle not thy steadfast sight;
Kingdoms lapse, and climates change, and races die;
Honor comes with mystery;
Hoarded wisdom brings delight.
Number, tell them over and number

How many the mystic fruit-tree holds 50
Lest the red-combed dragon slumber
Rolled together in purple folds.
Look to him, father, lest he wink, and the golden apple be stol'n
    away,
For his ancient heart is drunk with overwatchings night and day,
Round about the hallowed fruit-tree curled—
Sing away, sing aloud evermore in the wind, without stop,
Lest his scaléd eyelid drop,
For he is older than the world.
If he waken, we waken,
Rapidly levelling eager eyes. 60
If he sleep, we sleep,
Dropping the eyelid over the eyes.
If the golden apple be taken,
The world will be overwise.
Five links, a golden chain, are we,
Hesper, the dragon, and sisters three,
Bound about the golden tree.

III

Father Hesper, Father Hesper, watch, watch, night and day,
Lest the old wound of the world be healéd,
The glory unsealéd, 70
The golden apple stolén away,
And the ancient secret revealéd.
Look from west to east along:
Father, old Himala weakens, Caucasus is bold and strong.
Wandering waters unto wandering waters call;
Let them clash together, foam and fall.
Out of watchings, out of wiles,
Comes the bliss of secret smiles.
All things are not told to all.
Half-round the mantling night is drawn, 80
Purple fringéd with even and dawn.
Hesper hateth Phosphor, evening hateth morn.

IV

Every flower and every fruit the redolent breath
Of this warm sea-wind ripeneth,
Arching the billow in his sleep;
But the land-wind wandereth,
Broken by the highland-steep,
Two streams upon the violet deep;
For the western sun and the western star,
And the low west-wind, breathing afar, 90
The end of day and beginning of night

Make the apple holy and bright;
Holy and bright, round and full, bright and blest,
Mellowed in a land of rest;
Watch it warily day and night;
All good things are in the west.
Till mid noon the cool east light
Is shut out by the round of the tall hillbrow.
But when the full-faced sunset yellowly
Stays on the flowering arch of the bough,   100
The luscious fruitage clustereth mellowly,
Golden-kernelled, golden-cored,
Sunset-ripened above on the tree.
The world is wasted with fire and sword,
But the apple of gold hangs over the sea
Five links, a golden chain are we,
Hesper, the dragon, and sisters three,
Daughters three,
Bound about
All round about   110
The gnarléd bole of the charméd tree.
The golden apple, the golden apple, the hallowed fruit,
Guard it well, guard it warily,
Watch it warily,
Singing airily,
Standing about the charméd root.
1832

THE LOTOS-EATERS   Tennyson

"Courage!" he said, and pointed toward the land,
"This mounting wave will roll us shoreward soon."
In the afternoon they came unto a land
In which it seemed always afternoon.
All round the coast the languid air did swoon,
Breathing like one that hath a weary dream.
Full-faced above the valley stood the moon;
And, like a downward smoke, the slender stream
Along the cliff to fall and pause and fall did seem.

A land of streams! some, like a downward smoke,   10
Slow-dropping veils of thinnest lawn, did go;
And some thro' wavering lights and shadows broke,
Rolling a slumbrous sheet of foam below.
They saw the gleaming river seaward flow
From the inner land; far off, three mountain-tops,

Three silent pinnacles of aged snow,
Stood sunset-flush'd; and, dew'd with showery drops,
Up-clomb the shadowy pine above the woven copse.

The charmed sunset linger'd low adown
In the red West; thro' mountain clefts the dale   20
Was seen far inland, and the yellow down
Border'd with palm, and many a winding vale
And meadow, set with slender galingale;
A land where all things always seem'd the same! —
And round about the keel with faces pale,
Dark faces pale against that rosy flame,
The mild-eyed melancholy Lotos-eaters came.

Branches they bore of that enchanted stem,   Lotos-kind &
Laden with flower and fruit, whereof they gave   drug-
To each, but whoso did receive of them   30
And taste, to him the gushing of the wave
Far far away did seem to mourn and rave
On alien shores; and if his fellow spake,
His voice was thin, as voices from the grave;
And deep-asleep he seem'd, yet all awake,
And music in his ears his beating heart did make.

They sat them down upon the yellow sand,
Between the sun and moon upon the shore;
And sweet it was to dream of Fatherland,
Of child, and wife, and slave; but evermore   40
Most weary seem'd the sea, weary the oar,
Weary the wandering fields of barren foam.
Then some one said, "We will return no more;"
And all at once they sang, "Our island home
Is far beyond the wave; we will no longer roam."

CHORIC SONG

I

There is sweet music here that softer falls
Than petals from blown roses on the grass,
Or night-dews on still waters between walls
Of shadowy granite, in a gleaming pass;
Music that gentlier on the spirit lies,   50
Than tired eyelids upon tired eyes;
Music that brings sweet sleep down from the blissful skies.
Here are cool mosses deep,
And thro' the moss the ivies creep,
And in the stream the long-leaved flowers weep,
And from the craggy ledge the poppy hangs in sleep.

II

Why are we weigh'd upon with heaviness,
And utterly consumed with sharp distress,
While all things else have rest from weariness?
All things have rest: why should we toil alone,   60
We only toil, who are the first of things,
And make perpetual moan,
Still from one sorrow to another thrown;
Nor ever fold our wings,
And cease from wanderings,
Nor steep our brows in slumber's holy balm;
Nor harken what the inner spirit sings,
"There is no joy but calm!"—
Why should we only toil, the roof and crown of things?

III

Lo! in the middle of the wood,   70
The folded leaf is woo'd from out the bud
With winds upon the branch, and there
Grows green and broad, and takes no care,
Sun-steep'd at noon, and in the moon
Nightly dew-fed; and turning yellow
Falls, and floats adown the air.
Lo! sweeten'd with the summer light,
The full-juiced apple, waxing over-mellow,
Drops in a silent autumn night.
All its allotted length of days   80
The flower ripens in its place,
Ripens and fades, and falls, and hath no toil,
Fast-rooted in the fruitful soil.

IV

Hateful is the dark-blue sky,
Vaulted o'er the dark-blue sea.
Death is the end of life; ah, why
Should life all labor be?
Let us alone. Time driveth onward fast,
And in a little while our lips are dumb.
Let us alone. What is it that will last?   90
All things are taken from us, and become
Portions and parcels of the dreadful past.
Let us alone. What pleasure can we have
To war with evil? Is there any peace
In ever climbing up the climbing wave?
All things have rest, and ripen toward the grave
In silence—ripen, fall, and cease:
Give us long rest or death, dark death, or dreamful ease.

V

How sweet it were, hearing the downward stream,
With half-shut eyes ever to seem 100
Falling asleep in a half-dream!
To dream and dream, like yonder amber light,
Which will not leave the myrrh-bush on the height;
To hear each other's whisper'd speech;
Eating the Lotos day by day,
To watch the crisping ripples on the beach,
And tender curving lines of creamy spray;
To lend our hearts and spirits wholly
To the influence of mild-minded melancholy;
To muse and brood and live again in memory, 110
With those old faces of our infancy
Heap'd over with a mound of grass,
Two handfuls of white dust, shut in an urn of brass!

VI

Dear is the memory of our wedded lives,
And dear the last embraces of our wives
And their warm tears; but all hath suffer'd change;
For surely now our household hearths are cold,
Our sons inherit us, our looks are strange,
And we should come like ghosts to trouble joy.
Or else the island princes over-bold 120
Have eat our substance, and the minstrel sings
Before them of the ten years' war in Troy,
And our great deeds, as half-forgotten things.
Is there confusion in the little isle?
Let what is broken so remain.
The Gods are hard to reconcile;
'T is hard to settle order once again.
There *is* confusion worse than death,
Trouble on trouble, pain on pain,
Long labor unto aged breath, 130
Sore task to hearts worn out by many wars
And eyes grown dim with gazing on the pilot-stars.

VII

But, propt on beds of amaranth and moly,
How sweet—while warm airs lull us, blowing lowly—
With half-dropt eyelid still,
Beneath a heaven dark and holy,
To watch the long bright river drawing slowly
His waters from the purple hill—
To hear the dewy echoes calling
From cave to cave thro' the thick-twined vine— 140

To watch the emerald-color'd water falling
Thro' many a woven acanthus-wreath divine!
Only to hear and see the far-off sparkling brine,
Only to hear were sweet, stretch'd out beneath the pine.

VIII

The Lotos blooms below the barren peak,
The Lotos blows by every winding creek;
All day the wind breathes low with mellower tone;
Thro' every hollow cave and alley lone
Round and round the spicy downs the yellow Lotos-dust is blown.
We have had enough of action, and of motion we,   150
Roll'd to starboard, roll'd to larboard, when the surge was seething
   free,
Where the wallowing monster spouted his foam-fountains in the sea.
Let us swear an oath, and keep it with an equal mind,
In the hollow Lotos-land to live and lie reclined
On the hills like Gods together, careless of mankind.
For they lie beside their nectar, and the bolts are hurl'd
Far below them in the valleys, and the clouds are lightly curl'd
Round their golden houses, girdled with the gleaming world;
Where they smile in secret, looking over wasted lands,
Blight and famine, plague and earthquake, roaring deeps and fiery
   sands,   160
Clanging fights, and flaming towns, and sinking ships, and praying
   hands.
But they smile, they find a music centred in a doleful song
Steaming up, a lamentation and an ancient tale of wrong,
Like a tale of little meaning tho' the words are strong;
Chanted from an ill-used race of men that cleave the soil,
Sow the seed, and reap the harvest with enduring toil,
Storing yearly little dues of wheat, and wine and oil;
Till they perish and they suffer—some, 't is whisper'd—down in hell
Suffer endless anguish, others in Elysian valleys dwell,
Resting weary limbs at last on beds of asphodel.   170
Surely, surely, slumber is more sweet than toil, the shore
Than labor in the deep mid-ocean, wind and wave and oar;
O, rest ye, brother mariners, we will not wander more.
1832, 1842

ULYSSES

It little profits that an idle king,
By this still hearth, among these barren crags,
Match'd with an aged wife, I mete and dole
Unequal laws unto a savage race,

That hoard, and sleep, and feed, and know not me.
I cannot rest from travel; I will drink
Life to the lees. All times I have enjoy'd
Greatly, have suffer'd greatly, both with those
That loved me, and alone; on shore, and when
Thro' scudding drifts the rainy Hyades   10
Vext the dim sea. I am become a name;
For always roaming with a hungry heart
Much have I seen and known,—cities of men
And manners, climates, councils, governments,
Myself not least, but honor'd of them all,—
And drunk delight of battle with my peers,
Far on the ringing plains of windy Troy.
I am a part of all that I have met;
Yet all experience is an arch wherethro'
Gleams that untravell'd world whose margin fades   20
For ever and for ever when I move.
How dull it is to pause, to make an end,
To rust unburnish'd, not to shine in use!
As tho' to breathe were life! Life piled on life
Were all too little, and of one to me
Little remains; but every hour is saved
From that eternal silence, something more,
A bringer of new things; and vile it were
For some three suns to store and hoard myself,
And this gray spirit yearning in desire   30
To follow knowledge like a sinking star,
Beyond the utmost bound of human thought.
  This is my son, mine own Telemachus,
To whom I leave the sceptre and the isle,—
Well-loved of me, discerning to fulfil
This labor, by slow prudence to make mild
A rugged people, and thro' soft degrees
Subdue them to the useful and the good.
Most blameless is he, centred in the sphere
Of common duties, decent not to fail   40
In offices of tenderness, and pay
Meet adoration to my household gods,
When I am gone. He works his work, I mine.
  There lies the port; the vessel puffs her sail;
There gloom the dark, broad seas. My mariners,
Souls that have toil'd, and wrought, and thought with me,—
That ever with a frolic welcome took
The thunder and the sunshine, and opposed
Free hearts, free foreheads,—you and I are old;
Old age hath yet his honor and his toil.   50
Death closes all; but something ere the end,

[handwritten marginal note:] Quest that can't be fulfilled Childe Roland.

Some work of noble note, may yet be done,
Not unbecoming men that strove with Gods.
The lights begin to twinkle from the rocks;
The long day wanes; the slow moon climbs; the deep
Moans round with many voices. Come, my friends.
'T is not too late to seek a newer world.
Push off, and sitting well in order smite
The sounding furrows; for my purpose holds
To sail beyond the sunset, and the baths   60
Of all the western stars, until I die.
It may be that the gulfs will wash us down;
It may be we shall touch the Happy Isles,
And see the great Achilles, whom we knew.
Tho' much is taken, much abides; and tho'
We are not now that strength which in old days
Moved earth and heaven, that which we are, we are,—
One equal temper of heroic hearts,
Made weak by time and fate, but strong in will
To strive, to seek, to find, and not to yield.   70
1833 (1842)

TITHONUS

The woods decay, the woods decay and fall,
The vapors weep their burthen to the ground,
Man comes and tills the field and lies beneath,
And after many a summer dies the swan.
Me only cruel immortality
Consumes; I wither slowly in thine arms,
Here at the quiet limit of the world,
A white-hair'd shadow roaming like a dream
The ever-silent spaces of the East,
Far-folded mists, and gleaming halls of morn.   10
    Alas! for this gray shadow, once a man—
So glorious in his beauty and thy choice,
Who madest him thy chosen, that he seem'd
To his great heart none other than a God!
I ask'd thee, "Give me immortality."
Then didst thou grant mine asking with a smile,
Like wealthy men who care not how they give.
But thy strong Hours indignant work'd their wills,
And beat me down and marr'd and wasted me,
And tho' they could not end me, left me maim'd   20
To dwell in presence of immortal youth,
Immortal age beside immortal youth,

And all I was in ashes. Can thy love,
Thy beauty, make amends, tho' even now,
Close over us, the silver star, thy guide,
Shines in those tremulous eyes that fill with tears
To hear me? Let me go; take back thy gift.
Why should a man desire in any way
To vary from the kindly race of men,
Or pass beyond the goal of ordinance   30
Where all should pause, as is most meet for all?

    A soft air fans the cloud apart; there comes
A glimpse of that dark world where I was born.
Once more the old mysterious glimmer steals
From thy pure brows, and from thy shoulders pure,
And bosom beating with a heart renew'd.
Thy cheek begins to redden thro' the gloom,
Thy sweet eyes brighten slowly close to mine.
Ere yet they blind the stars, and the wild team
Which love thee, yearning for thy yoke, arise,   40
And shake the darkness from their loosen'd manes,
And beat the twilight into flakes of fire.

    Lo! ever thus thou growest beautiful
In silence, then before thine answer given
Departest, and thy tears are on my cheek.

    Why wilt thou ever scare me with thy tears,
And make me tremble lest a saying learnt,
In days far-off, on that dark earth, be true?
"The Gods themselves cannot recall their gifts."

    Ay me! ay me! with what another heart   50
In days far-off, and with what other eyes
I used to watch—if I be he that watch'd—
The lucid outline forming round thee; saw
The dim curls kindle into sunny rings;
Changed with thy mystic change, and felt my blood
Glow with the glow that slowly crimson'd all
Thy presence and thy portals, while I lay,
Mouth, forehead, eyelids, growing dewy-warm
With kisses balmier than half-opening buds
Of April, and could hear the lips that kiss'd   60
Whispering I knew not what of wild and sweet,
Like that strange song I heard Apollo sing,
While Ilion like a mist rose into towers.

    Yet hold me not for ever in thine East;
How can my nature longer mix with thine?
Coldly thy rosy shadows bathe me, cold
Are all thy lights, and cold my wrinkled feet
Upon thy glimmering thresholds, when the steam
Floats up from those dim fields about the homes

Of happy men that have the power to die,   70
And grassy barrows of the happier dead.
Release me, and restore me to the ground.
Thou seest all things, thou wilt see my grave;
Thou wilt renew thy beauty morn by morn,
I earth in earth forget these empty courts,
And thee returning on thy silver wheels.
1833 f. (1860)

"BREAK, BREAK, BREAK"

Break, break, break,
   On thy cold gray stones, O Sea!
And I would that my tongue could utter
   The thoughts that arise in me.

O, well for the fisherman's boy,
   That he shouts with his sister at play!
O, well for the sailor lad,
   That he sings in his boat on the bay!

And the stately ships go on
   To their haven under the hill;   10
But O for the touch of a vanish'd hand,
   And the sound of a voice that is still!

Break, break, break,
   At the foot of thy crags, O Sea!
But the tender grace of a day that is dead
   Will never come back to me.
1834? (1842)

THE EPIC

At Francis Allen's on the Christmas-eve,—
The game of forfeits done—the girls all kiss'd
Beneath the sacred bush and past away—
The parson Holmes, the poet Everard Hall,
The host, and I sat round the wassail-bowl,
Then half-way ebb'd; and there we held a talk,
How all the old honor had from Christmas gone,
Or gone or dwindled down to some odd games
In some odd nooks like this; till I, tired out
With cutting eights that day upon the pond,   10
Where, three times slipping from the outer edge,

I bump'd the ice into three several stars,
Fell in a doze; and half-awake I heard
The parson taking wide and wider sweeps,
Now harping on the church-commissioners,
Now hawking at geology and schism;
Until I woke, and found him settled down
Upon the general decay of faith
Right thro' the world: "at home was little left,
And none abroad; there was no anchor, none,   20
To hold by." Francis, laughing, clapt his hand
On Everard's shoulder, with "I hold by him."
"And I," quoth Everard, "by the wassail-bowl."
"Why yes," I said, "we knew your gift that way
At college; but another which you had—
I mean of verse (for so we held it then),
What came of that?" "You know," said Frank, "he burnt
His epic, his King Arthur, some twelve books"—
And then to me demanding why: "O, sir,
He thought that nothing new was said, or else   30
Something so said 'twas nothing—that a truth
Looks freshest in the fashion of the day;
God knows; he has a mint of reasons; ask.
It pleased *me* well enough." "Nay, nay," said Hall,
"Why take the style of those heroic times?
For nature brings not back the mastodon,
Nor we those times; and why should any man
Remodel models? these twelve books of mine
Were faint Homeric echoes, nothing-worth,
Mere chaff and draff, much better burnt." "But I,"   40
Said Francis, "pick'd the eleventh from this hearth,
And have it; keep a thing, its use will come.
I hoard it as a sugar-plum for Holmes."
He laugh'd, and I, tho' sleepy, like a horse
That hears the corn-bin open, prick'd my ears;
For I remember'd Everard's college fame
When we were Freshmen. Then at my request
He brought it; and the poet, little urged,
But with some prelude of disparagement,
Read, mouthing out his hollow oes and aes,   50
Deep-chested music, and to this result.

MORTE D'ARTHUR

So all day long the noise of battle roll'd
Among the mountains by the winter sea,
Until King Arthur's table, man by man,

Had fallen in Lyonness about their lord,
King Arthur; then, because his wound was deep,
The bold Sir Bedivere uplifted him,
Sir Bedivere, the last of all his knights,
And bore him to a chapel nigh the field,
A broken chancel with a broken cross,   60
That stood on a dark strait of barren land.
On one side lay the ocean, and on one
Lay a great water, and the moon was full.
    Then spake King Arthur to Sir Bedivere:
"The sequel of to-day unsolders all
The goodliest fellowship of famous knights
Whereof this world holds record. Such a sleep
They sleep—the men I loved. I think that we
Shall never more, at any future time,
Delight our souls with talk of knightly deeds,   70
Walking about the gardens and the halls
Of Camelot, as in the days that were.
I perish by this people which I made,—
Tho' Merlin sware that I should come again
To rule once more—but let what will be be,
I am so deeply smitten thro' the helm
That without help I cannot last till morn.
Thou therefore take my brand Excalibur,
Which was my pride; for thou rememberest how
In those old days, one summer noon, an arm   80
Rose up from out the bosom of the lake,
Clothed in white samite, mystic, wonderful,
Holding the sword—and how I row'd across
And took it, and have worn it, like a king;
And, wheresoever I am sung or told
In aftertime, this also shall be known.
But now delay not; take Excalibur,
And fling him far into the middle mere;
Watch what thou seest, and lightly bring me word."
    To him replied the bold Sir Bedivere: 90
"It is not meet, Sir King, to leave thee thus,
Aidless, alone, and smitten thro' the helm.
A little thing may harm a wounded man.
Yet I thy hest will all perform at full,
Watch what I see, and lightly bring thee word."
    So saying, from the ruin'd shrine he stept
And in the moon athwart the place of tombs,
Where lay the mighty bones of ancient men,
Old knights, and over them the sea-wind sang
Shrill, chill, with flakes of foam. He, stepping down   100
By zigzag paths and juts of pointed rock,

Came on the shining levels of the lake.
　There drew he forth the brand Excalibur,
And o'er him, drawing it, the winter moon,
Brightening the skirts of a long cloud, ran forth
And sparkled keen with frost against the hilt;
For all the haft twinkled with diamond sparks,
Myriads of topaz-lights, and jacinth-work
Of subtlest jewellery. He gazed so long
That both his eyes were dazzled, as he stood,　　　　110
This way and that dividing the swift mind,
In act to throw; but at the last it seem'd
Better to leave Excalibur conceal'd
There in the many-knotted water-flags,
That whistled stiff and dry about the marge.
So strode he back slow to the wounded king.
　Then spake King Arthur to Sir Bedivere:
"Hast thou perform'd my mission which I gave?
What is it thou hast seen, or what hast heard?"
　And answer made the bold Sir Bedivere:　　　　120
"I heard the ripple washing in the reeds,
And the wild water lapping on the crag."
　To whom replied King Arthur, faint and pale:
"Thou hast betray'd thy nature and thy name,
Not rendering true answer, as beseem'd
Thy fealty, nor like a noble knight;
For surer sign had follow'd, either hand,
Or voice, or else a motion of the mere.
This is a shameful thing for men to lie.
Yet now, I charge thee, quickly go again　　　　130
As thou art lief and dear, and do the thing
I bade thee, watch, and lightly bring me word."
　Then went Sir Bedivere the second time
Across the ridge, and paced beside the mere,
Counting the dewy pebbles, fix'd in thought;
But when he saw the wonder of the hilt,
How curiously and strangely chased, he smote
His palms together, and he cried aloud:
　"And if indeed I cast the brand away,
Surely a precious thing, one worthy note,　　　　140
Should thus be lost forever from the earth,
Which might have pleased the eyes of many men.
What good should follow this, if this were done?
What harm, undone? deep harm to disobey,
Seeing obedience is the bond of rule.
Were it well to obey then, if a king demand
An act unprofitable, against himself?
The king is sick, and knows not what he does.

What record, or what relic of my lord
Should be to aftertime, but empty breath   150
And rumors of a doubt? but were this kept,
Stored in some treasure-house of mighty kings,
Some one might show it at a joust of arms,
Saying, 'King Arthur's sword, Excalibur,
Wrought by the lonely maiden of the lake;
Nine years she wrought it, sitting in the deeps
Upon the hidden bases of the hills.'
So might some old man speak in the aftertime
To all the people, winning reverence;
But now much honor and much fame were lost."   160
    So spake he, clouded with his own conceit,
And hid Excalibur the second time,
And so strode back slow to the wounded king.
    Then spoke King Arthur, breathing heavily:
"What is it thou hast seen, or what hast heard?"
    And answer made the bold Sir Bedivere:
"I heard the water lapping on the crag,
And the long ripple washing in the reeds."
    To whom replied King Arthur, much in wrath:
"Ah, miserable and unkind, untrue,   170
Unknightly, traitor-hearted! Woe is me!
Authority forgets a dying king,
Laid widow'd of the power in his eye
That bow'd the will. I see thee what thou art,
For thou, the latest-left of all my knights,
In whom should meet the offices of all,
Thou wouldst betray me for the precious hilt;
Either from lust of gold, or like a girl
Valuing the giddy pleasure of the eyes.
Yet, for a man may fail in duty twice,   180
And the third time may prosper, get thee hence;
But, if thou spare to fling Excalibur,
I will arise and slay thee with my hands."
    Then quickly rose Sir Bedivere, and ran,
And, leaping down the ridges lightly, plunged
Among the bulrush-beds, and clutch'd the sword,
And strongly wheel'd and threw it. The great brand
Made lightnings in the splendor of the moon,
And flashing round and round, and whirl'd in an arch,
Shot like a streamer of the northern morn,   190
Seen where the moving isles of winter shock
By night, with noises of the northern sea.
So flash'd and fell the brand Excalibur;
But ere he dipt the surface, rose an arm
Cloth'd in white samite, mystic, wonderful,

And caught him by the hilt, and brandish'd him
Three times, and drew him under in the mere.
And lightly went the other to the king.
Then spoke King Arthur, drawing thicker breath:
"Now see I by thine eyes that this is done.   200
Speak out; what is it thou hast heard, or seen?"
And answer made the bold Sir Bedivere:
"Sir King, I closed mine eyelids, lest the gems
Should blind my purpose, for I never saw,
Nor shall see, here or elsewhere, till I die,
Not tho' I live three lives of mortal men,
So great a miracle as yonder hilt.
Then with both hands I flung him, wheeling him;
But when I look'd again, behold an arm,
Clothed in white samite, mystic, wonderful,   210
That caught him by the hilt, and brandish'd him
Three times, and drew him under in the mere."
And answer made King Arthur, breathing hard:
"My end draws nigh; 'tis time that I were gone.
Make broad thy shoulders to receive my weight,
And bear me to the margin; yet I fear
My wound hath taken cold, and I shall die."
So saying, from the pavement he half rose,
Slowly, with pain, reclining on his arm,
And looking wistfully with wide blue eyes   220
As in a picture. Him Sir Bedivere
Remorsefully regarded thro' his tears,
And would have spoken, but he found not words,
Then took with care, and kneeling on one knee,
O'er both his shoulders drew the languid hands,
And rising bore him thro' the place of tombs.
But, as he walk'd, King Arthur panted hard,
Like one that feels a nightmare on his bed
When all the house is mute. So sigh'd the king,
Muttering and murmuring at his ear, "Quick, quick!   230
I fear it is too late, and I shall die."
But the other swiftly strode from ridge to ridge,
Clothed with his breath, and looking, as he walk'd,
Larger than human on the frozen hills.
He heard the deep behind him, and a cry
Before. His own thought drove him like a goad.
Dry clash'd his harness in the icy caves
And barren chasms, and all to left and right
The bare black cliff clang'd round him, as he based
His feet on juts of slippery crag that rang   240
Sharp-smitten with the dint of armed heels—
And on a sudden, lo! the level lake,

And the long glories of the winter moon.
   Then saw they how there hove a dusky barge,
Dark as a funeral scarf from stem to stern,
Beneath them; and descending they were ware
That all the decks were dense with stately forms
Black-stoled, black-hooded, like a dream—by these
Three queens with crowns of gold—and from them rose
A cry that shiver'd to the tingling stars,   250
And, as it were one voice, an agony
Of lamentation, like a wind that shrills
All night in a waste land, where no one comes,
Or hath come, since the making of the world.
   Then murmur'd Arthur, "Place me in the barge,"
And to the barge they came. There those three queens
Put forth their hands, and took the king, and wept.
But she that rose the tallest of them all
And fairest laid his head upon her lap,
And loosed the shatter'd casque, and chafed his hands,   260
And call'd him by his name, complaining loud,
And dropping bitter tears against his brow
Striped with dark blood; for all his face was white
And colorless, and like the wither'd moon
Smote by the fresh beam of the springing east;
And all his greaves and cuisses dash'd with drops
Of onset; and the light and lustrous curls—
That made his forehead like a rising sun
High from the dais-throne—were parch'd with dust;
Or, clotted into points and hanging loose,   270
Mix'd with the knightly growth that fringed his lips.
So like a shatter'd column lay the king;
Not like that Arthur who, with lance in rest,
From spur to plume a star of tournament,
Shot thro' the lists at Camelot, and charged
Before the eyes of ladies and of kings.
   Then loudly cried the bold Sir Bedivere:
"Ah! my Lord Arthur, whither shall I go?
Where shall I hide my forehead and my eyes?
For now I see the true old times are dead,   280
When every morning brought a noble chance,
And every chance brought out a noble knight.
Such times have been not since the light that led
The holy Elders with the gift of myrrh.
But now the whole ROUND TABLE is dissolved
Which was an image of the mighty world;
And I, the last, go forth companionless,
And the days darken round me, and the years,
Among new men, strange faces, other minds."

And slowly answer'd Arthur from the barge: 290
"The old order changeth, yielding place to new,
And God fulfils himself in many ways,
Lest one good custom should corrupt the world.
Comfort thyself: what comfort is in me?
I have lived my life, and that which I have done
May He within himself make pure! but thou,
If thou shouldst never see my face again,
Pray for my soul. More things are wrought by prayer
Than this world dreams of. Wherefore, let thy voice
Rise like a fountain for me night and day.   300
For what are men better than sheep or goats
That nourish a blind life within the brain,
If, knowing God, they lift not hands of prayer
Both for themselves and those who call them friend?
For so the whole round earth is every way
Bound by gold chains about the feet of God.
But now farewell. I am going a long way
With these thou seest—if indeed I go—
For all my mind is clouded with a doubt—
To the island-valley of Avilion;   310
Where falls not hail, or rain, or any snow,
Nor ever wind blows loudly, but it lies
Deep-meadow'd, happy, fair with orchard lawns
And bowery hollows crown'd with summer sea,
Where I will heal me of my grievous wound."
  So said he, and the barge with oar and sail
Moved from the brink, like some full-breasted swan
That, fluting a wild carol ere her death,
Ruffles her pure cold plume, and takes the flood
With swarthy webs. Long stood Sir Bedivere   320
Revolving many memories, till the hull
Look'd one black dot against the verge of dawn,
And on the mere the wailing died away.

  Here ended Hall, and our last light, that long
Had wink'd and threaten'd darkness, flared and fell;
At which the parson, sent to sleep with sound,
And waked with silence, grunted "Good!" but we
Sat rapt: it was the tone with which he read—
Perhaps some modern touches here and there
Redeem'd it from the charge of nothingness—   330
Or else we loved the man, and prized his work;
I know not; but we sitting, as I said,
The cock crew loud, as at that time of year
The lusty bird takes every hour for dawn.
Then Francis, muttering, like a man ill-used,

"There now—that's nothing!" drew a little back,
And drove his heel into the smoulder'd log,
That sent a blast of sparkles up the flue.
And so to bed, where yet in sleep I seem'd
To sail with Arthur under looming shores,   340
Point after point; till on to dawn, when dreams
Begin to feel the truth and stir of day,
To me, methought, who waited with the crowd,
There came a bark that, blowing forward, bore
King Arthur, like a modern gentleman
Of stateliest port; and all the people cried,
"Arthur is come again: he cannot die."
Then those that stood upon the hills behind
Repeated—"Come again, and thrice as fair";
And, further inland, voices echoed—"Come   350
With all good things, and war shall be no more."
At this a hundred bells began to peal,
That with the sound I woke, and heard indeed
The clear church-bells ring in the Christmas morn.
1842

LOCKSLEY HALL

Comrades, leave me here a little, while as yet 't is early morn;
Leave me here, and when you want me, sound upon the bugle-horn.

'T is the place, and all around it, as of old, the curlews call,
Dreary gleams about the moorland flying over Locksley Hall;

Locksley Hall, that in the distance overlooks the sandy tracts,
And the hollow ocean-ridges roaring into cataracts.

Many a night from yonder ivied casement, ere I went to rest,
Did I look on great Orion sloping slowly to the west.

Many a night I saw the Pleiads, rising thro' the mellow shade,
Glitter like a swarm of fireflies tangled in a silver braid.   10

Here about the beach I wander'd, nourishing a youth sublime
With the fairy tales of science, and the long result of time;

When the centuries behind me like a fruitful land reposed;
When I clung to all the present for the promise that it closed;

When I dipt into the future far as human eye could see,
Saw the vision of the world and all the wonder that would be.—

In the spring a fuller crimson comes upon the robin's breast;
In the spring the wanton lapwing gets himself another crest;

In the spring a livelier iris changes on the burnish'd dove;
In the spring a young man's fancy lightly turns to thoughts of love. 20

Then her cheek was pale and thinner than should be for one so young,
And her eyes on all my motions with a mute observance hung.

And I said, "My cousin Amy, speak, and speak the truth to me,
Trust me, cousin, all the current of my being sets to thee."

On her pallid cheek and forehead came a color and a light,
As I have seen the rosy red flushing in the northern night.

And she turn'd—her bosom shaken with a sudden storm of sighs—
All the spirit deeply dawning in the dark of hazel eyes—

Saying, "I have hid my feelings, fearing they should do me wrong,"
Saying, "Dost thou love me, cousin?" weeping, "I have loved thee
    long." 30

Love took up the glass of Time, and turn'd it in his glowing hands;
Every moment, lightly shaken, ran itself in golden sands.

Love took up the harp of Life, and smote on all the chords with might;
Smote the chord of Self, that, trembling, past in music out of sight.

Many a morning on the moorland did we hear the copses ring,
And her whisper throng'd my pulses with the fulness of the spring.

Many an evening by the waters did we watch the stately ships,
And our spirits rush'd together at the touching of the lips.

O my cousin, shallow-hearted! O my Amy, mine no more!
O the dreary, dreary moorland! O the barren, barren shore! 40

Falser than all fancy fathoms, falser than all songs have sung,
Puppet to a father's threat, and servile to a shrewish tongue!

Is it well to wish thee happy?—having known me—to decline
On a range of lower feelings and a narrower heart than mine!

Yet it shall be; thou shalt lower to his level day by day,
What is fine within thee growing coarse to sympathize with clay.

As the husband is, the wife is; thou art mated with a clown,
And the grossness of his nature will have weight to drag thee down.

He will hold thee, when his passion shall have spent its novel force,
Something better than his dog, a little dearer than his horse. 50

What is this? his eyes are heavy; think not they are glazed with wine.
Go to him, it is thy duty; kiss him, take his hand in thine.

It may be my lord is weary, that his brain is overwrought;
Soothe him with thy finer fancies, touch him with thy lighter thought.

He will answer to the purpose, easy things to understand—
Better thou wert dead before me, tho' I slew thee with my hand!

Better thou and I were lying, hidden from the heart's disgrace,
Roll'd in one another's arms, and silent in a last embrace.

Cursed be the social wants that sin against the strength of youth!
Cursed be the social lies that warp us from the living truth! 60

Cursed be the sickly forms that err from honest Nature's rule!
Cursed be the gold that gilds the straiten'd forehead of the fool!

Well—'t is well that I should bluster!—Hadst thou less unworthy
    proved—
Would to God—for I had loved thee more than ever wife was loved.

Am I mad, that I should cherish that which bears but bitter fruit?
I will pluck it from my bosom, tho' my heart be at the root.

Never, tho' my mortal summers to such length of years should come
As the many-winter'd crow that leads the clanging rookery home.

Where is comfort? in division of the records of the mind?
Can I part her from herself, and love her, as I knew her, kind? 70

I remember one that perish'd; sweetly did she speak and move;
Such a one do I remember, whom to look at was to love.

Can I think of her as dead, and love her for the love she bore?
No—she never loved me truly; love is love for ever more.

Comfort? comfort scorn'd of devils! this is truth the poet sings,
That a sorrow's crown of sorrow is remembering happier things.

Drug thy memories, lest thou learn it, lest thy heart be put to proof,
In the dead unhappy night, and when the rain is on the roof.

Like a dog, he hunts in dreams, and thou art staring at the wall,
Where the dying night-lamp flickers, and the shadows rise and fall. 80

Then a hand shall pass before thee, pointing to his drunken sleep,
To thy widow'd marriage-pillows, to the tears that thou wilt weep.

Thou shalt hear the "Never, never," whisper'd by the phantom years,
And a song from out the distance in the ringing of thine ears;

And an eye shall vex thee, looking ancient kindness on thy pain.
Turn thee, turn thee on thy pillow; get thee to thy rest again.

Nay, but Nature brings thee solace; for a tender voice will cry.
'T is a purer life than thine, a lip to drain thy trouble dry.

Baby lips will laugh me down; my latest rival brings thee rest.
Baby fingers, waxen touches, press me from the mother's breast. 90

O, the child too clothes the father with a dearness not his due.
Half is thine and half is his; it will be worthy of the two.

O, I see thee old and formal, fitted to thy petty part,
With a little hoard of maxims preaching down a daughter's heart.

"They were dangerous guides the feelings—she herself was not
    exempt—
Truly, she herself had suffer'd"—Perish in thy self-contempt!

Overlive it—lower yet—be happy! wherefore should I care?
I myself must mix with action, lest I wither by despair.

What is that which I should turn to, lighting upon days like these?
Every door is barr'd with gold, and opens but to golden keys.   100

Every gate is throng'd with suitors, all the markets overflow.
I have but an angry fancy; what is that which I should do?

I had been content to perish, falling on the foeman's ground,
When the ranks are roll'd in vapor, and the winds are laid with sound.

But the jingling of the guinea helps the hurt that Honor feels,
And the nations do but murmur, snarling at each other's heels.

Can I but relive in sadness? I will turn that earlier page.
Hide me from my deep emotion, O thou wondrous Mother-Age!

Make me feel the wild pulsation that I felt before the strife,
When I heard my days before me, and the tumult of my life;   110

Yearning for the large excitement that the coming years would yield,
Eager-hearted as a boy when first he leaves his father's field,

And at night along the dusky highway near and nearer drawn,
Sees in heaven the light of London flaring like a dreary dawn;

And his spirit leaps within him to be gone before him then,
Underneath the light he looks at, in among the throngs of men;

Men, my brothers, men the workers, ever reaping something new;
That which they have done but earnest of the things that they shall do.

For I dipt into the future, far as human eye could see,
Saw the Vision of the world, and all the wonder that would be;   120

Saw the heavens fill with commerce, argosies of magic sails,
Pilots of the purple twilight, dropping down with costly bales;

Heard the heavens fill with shouting, and there rain'd a ghastly dew
From the nations' airy navies grappling in the central blue;

Far along the world-wide whisper of the south-wind rushing warm,
With the standards of the peoples plunging thro' the thunder-storm;

Till the war-drum throbb'd no longer, and the battle-flags were furl'd
In the Parliament of man, the Federation of the world.

There the common sense of most shall hold a fretful realm in awe,
And the kindly earth shall slumber, lapt in universal law.   130

So I triumph'd ere my passion sweeping thro' me left me dry,
Left me with the palsied heart, and left me with the jaundiced eye;

Eye, to which all order festers, all things here are out of joint.
Science moves, but slowly, slowly, creeping on from point to point;

Slowly comes a hungry people, as a lion, creeping nigher,
Glares at one that nods and winks behind a slowly-dying fire.

Yet I doubt not thro' the ages one increasing purpose runs,
And the thoughts of men are widen'd with the process of the suns.

What is that to him that reaps not harvest of his youthful joys,
Tho' the deep heart of existence beat for ever like a boy's?   140

Knowledge comes, but wisdom lingers, and I linger on the shore,
And the individual withers, and the world is more and more.

Knowledge comes, but wisdom lingers, and he bears a laden breast,
Full of sad experience, moving toward the stillness of his rest.

Hark, my merry comrades call me, sounding on the bugle-horn,
They to whom my foolish passion were a target for their scorn.

Shall it not be scorn to me to harp on such a moulder'd string?
I am shamed thro' all my nature to have loved so slight a thing.

Weakness to be wroth with weakness! woman's pleasure, woman's
        pain—
Nature made them blinder motions bounded in a shallower brain. 150

Woman is the lesser man, and all thy passions, match'd with mine,
Are as moonlight unto sunlight, and as water unto wine—

Here at least, where nature sickens, nothing. Ah, for some retreat
Deep in yonder shining Orient, where my life began to beat,

Where in wild Mahratta-battle fell my father evil-starr'd;—
I was left a trampled orphan, and a selfish uncle's ward.

Or to burst all links of habit—there to wander far away,
On from island unto island at the gateways of the day.

Larger constellations burning, mellow moons and happy skies,
Breadths of tropic shade and palms in cluster, knots of Paradise.   160

Never comes the trader, never floats an European flag,
Slides the bird o'er lustrous woodland, swings the trailer from the crag;

Droops the heavy-blossom'd bower, hangs the heavy-fruited tree—
Summer isles of Eden lying in dark-purple spheres of sea.

There methinks would be enjoyment more than in this march of mind,
In the steamship, in the railway, in the thoughts that shake mankind.

There the passions cramp'd no longer shall have scope and breathing
    space;
I will take some savage woman, she shall rear my dusky race.

Iron-jointed, supple-sinew'd, they shall dive, and they shall run,
Catch the wild goat by the hair, and hurl their lances in the sun;   170

Whistle back the parrot's call and leap the rainbows of the brooks,
Not with blinded eyesight poring over miserable books—

Fool, again the dream, the fancy! but I *know* my words are wild,
But I count the gray barbarian lower than the Christian child.

I, to herd with narrow foreheads, vacant of our glorious gains,
Like a beast with lower pleasures, like a beast with lower pains!

Mated with a squalid savage—what to me were sun or clime?
I the heir of all the ages, in the foremost files of time—

I that rather held it better men should perish one by one,
Than that earth should stand at gaze like Joshua's moon in Ajalon! 180

Not in vain the distance beacons. Forward, forward let us range,
Let the great world spin for ever down the ringing grooves of change.

Thro' the shadow of the globe we sweep into the younger day;
Better fifty years of Europe than a cycle of Cathay.

Mother-Age,—for mine I knew not,—help me as when life begun;
Rift the hills, and roll the waters, flash the lightnings, weigh the sun.

O, I see the crescent promise of my spirit hath not set.
Ancient founts of inspiration well thro' all my fancy yet.

Howsoever these things be, a long farewell to Locksley Hall!
Now for me the woods may wither, now for me the roof-tree fall.   190

Comes a vapor from the margin, blackening over heath and holt,
Cramming all the blast before it, in its breast a thunderbolt.

Let it fall on Locksley Hall, with rain or hail, or fire or snow;
For the mighty wind arises, roaring seaward, and I go.
1842

songs from THE PRINCESS

1.

Sweet and low, sweet and low,
   Wind of the western sea,
Low, low, breathe and blow,
   Wind of the western sea!
Over the rolling waters go,
Come from the dying moon, and blow,
   Blow him again to me;
While my little one, while my pretty one sleeps.

Sleep and rest, sleep and rest,
   Father will come to thee soon;   10
Rest, rest, on mother's breast,
   Father will come to thee soon;
Father will come to his babe in the nest,
Silver sails all out of the west
   Under the silver moon;
Sleep, my little one, sleep, my pretty one, sleep.

2.

The splendor falls on castle walls
   And snowy summits old in story;
The long light shakes across the lakes,
   And the wild cataract leaps in glory.
Blow, bugle, blow, set the wild echoes flying,
Blow, bugle; answer, echoes, dying, dying, dying.

O, hark, O, hear! how thin and clear,
   And thinner, clearer, farther going!
O, sweet and far from cliff and scar
   The horns of Elfland faintly blowing!   10
Blow, let us hear the purple glens replying,
Blow, bugle; answer, echoes, dying, dying, dying.

O love, they die in yon rich sky,
   They faint on hill or field or river;
Our echoes roll from soul to soul,

And grow for ever and for ever.
Blow, bugle, blow, set the wild echoes flying,
And answer, echoes, answer, dying, dying, dying.

objectiveless
Regret

"Tears, idle tears, I know not what they mean,
Tears from the depth of some divine despair
Rise in the heart, and gather to the eyes,
In looking on the happy autumn-fields,
And thinking of the days that are no more.

"Fresh as the first beam glittering on a sail,
That brings our friends up from the underworld,
Sad as the last which reddens over one
That sinks with all we love below the verge;
So sad, so fresh, the days that are no more.   10

"Ah, sad and strange as in dark summer dawns
The earliest pipe of half-awaken'd birds
To dying ears, when unto dying eyes
The casement slowly grows a glimmering square;
So sad, so strange, the days that are no more.

"Dear as remember'd kisses after death,
And sweet as those by hopeless fancy feign'd
On lips that are for others; deep as love,
Deep as first love, and wild with all regret;
O Death in Life, the days that are no more!"   20

4.

Ask me no more: the moon may draw the sea;
    The cloud may stoop from heaven and take the shape,
    With fold to fold, of mountain or of cape;
But O too fond, when have I answer'd thee?
        Ask me no more.

Ask me no more: what answer should I give?
    I love not hollow cheek or faded eye:
    Yet, O my friend, I will not have thee die!
Ask me no more, lest I should bid thee live;
        Ask me no more.   10

Ask me no more: thy fate and mine are seal'd;
    I strove against the stream and all in vain;

Let the great river take me to the main.
No more, dear love, for at a touch I yield;
        Ask me no more.

5.

"Now sleeps the crimson petal, now the white;
Nor waves the cypress in the palace walk;
Nor winks the gold fin in the porphyry font.
The fire-fly wakens; waken thou with me.

"Now droops the milk-white peacock like a ghost,
And like a ghost she glimmers on to me.

"Now lies the Earth all Danaë to the stars,
And all thy heart lies open unto me.

"Now slides the silent meteor on, and leaves
A shining furrow, as thy thoughts in me.   10

"Now folds the lily all her sweetness up,
And slips into the bosom of the lake.
So fold thyself, my dearest, thou, and slip
Into my bosom and be lost in me."

6.

"Come down, O maid, from yonder mountain height.
What pleasure lives in height (the shepherd sang),
In height and cold, the splendor of the hills?
But cease to move so near the heavens, and cease
To glide a sunbeam by the blasted pine,
To sit a star upon the sparkling spire;
And come, for Love is of the valley, come,
For love is of the valley, come thou down
And find him; by the happy threshold, he,
Or hand in hand with Plenty in the maize,   10
Or red with spirted purple of the vats,
Or foxlike in the vine; nor cares to walk
With Death and Morning on the Silver Horns.
Nor wilt thou snare him in the white ravine,
Nor find him dropt upon the firths of ice,
That huddling slant in furrow-cloven falls
To roll the torrent out of dusky doors.
But follow; let the torrent dance thee down

To find him in the valley; let the wild
Lean-headed eagles yelp alone, and leave   20
The monstrous ledges there to slope, and spill
Their thousand wreaths of dangling water-smoke,
That like a broken purpose waste in air.
So waste not thou, but come; for all the vales
Await thee; azure pillars of the hearth
Arise to thee; the children call, and I
Thy shepherd pipe, and sweet is every sound,
Sweeter thy voice, but every sound is sweet;
Myriads of rivulets hurrying thro' the lawn,
The moan of doves in immemorial elms,   30
And murmuring of innumerable bees."

IN MEMORIAM A. H. H.

OBIIT MDCCCXXXIII

Strong Son of God, immortal Love,
   Whom we, that have not seen thy face,
   By faith, and faith alone, embrace,
Believing where we cannot prove;

Thine are these orbs of light and shade;
   Thou madest Life in man and brute;
   Thou madest Death; and lo, thy foot
Is on the skull which thou hast made.

Thou wilt not leave us in the dust:
   Thou madest man, he knows not why,   10
   He thinks he was not made to die;
And thou hast made him: thou art just.

Thou seemest human and divine,
   The highest, holiest manhood, thou.
   Our wills are ours, we know not how;
Our wills are ours, to make them thine.

Our little systems have their day;
   They have their day and cease to be;
   They are but broken lights of thee,
And thou, O Lord, art more than they.   20

We have but faith: we cannot know,
   For knowledge is of things we see;
   And yet we trust it comes from thee,
A beam in darkness: let it grow.

Let knowledge grow from more to more,
    But more of reverence in us dwell;
    That mind and soul, according well,
May make one music as before,

But vaster. We are fools and slight;
    We mock thee when we do not fear: 30
    But help thy foolish ones to bear;
Help thy vain worlds to bear thy light.

Forgive what seem'd my sin in me,
    What seem'd my worth since I began;
    For merit lives from man to man,
And not from man, O Lord, to thee.

Forgive my grief for one removed,
    Thy creature, whom I found so fair.
    I trust he lives in thee, and there
I find him worthier to be loved.   40

Forgive these wild and wandering cries,
    Confusions of a wasted youth;
    Forgive them where they fail in truth,
And in thy wisdom make me wise.
1849

I

I held it truth, with him who sings
    To one clear harp in divers tones,
    That men may rise on stepping-stones
Of their dead selves to higher things.

But who shall so forecast the years
    And find in loss a gain to match?
    Or reach a hand thro' time to catch
The far-off interest of tears?

Let Love clasp Grief lest both be drown'd,
    Let darkness keep her raven gloss.   10 (54)
    Ah, sweeter to be drunk with loss,
To dance with Death, to beat the ground,

Than that the victor Hours should scorn
    The long result of love, and boast,
    "Behold the man that loved and lost,
But all he was is overworn."

II

Old yew, which graspest at the stones
    That name the underlying dead,

Thy fibres net the dreamless head,
Thy roots are wrapt about the bones.

The seasons bring the flower again,
    And bring the firstling to the flock;
    And in the dusk of thee the clock
Beats out the little lives of men.

O, not for thee the glow, the bloom,
    Who changest not in any gale,   10 (70)
    Nor branding summer suns avail
To touch thy thousand years of gloom;

And gazing on thee, sullen tree,
    Sick for thy stubborn hardihood,
    I seem to fail from out my blood
And grow incorporate into thee.

III

O Sorrow, cruel fellowship,
    O Priestess in the vaults of Death,
    O sweet and bitter in a breath,
What whispers from thy lying lip?

"The stars," she whispers, "blindly run;
    A web is woven across the sky;
    From out waste places comes a cry,
And murmurs from the dying sun;

"And all the phantom, Nature, stands—
    With all the music in her tone,   10 (86)
    A hollow echo of my own,—
A hollow form with empty hands."

And shall I take a thing so blind,
    Embrace her as my natural good;
    Or crush her, like a vice of blood,
Upon the threshold of the mind?

IV

To Sleep I give my powers away;
    My will is bondsman to the dark;
    I sit within a helmless bark,
And with my heart I muse and say:

O heart, how fares it with thee now,
    That thou shouldst fail from thy desire,
    Who scarcely darest to inquire,
"What is it makes me beat so low?"

Something it is which thou hast lost,
   Some pleasure from thine early years.   10 (102)
    Break thou deep vase of chilling tears,
That grief hath shaken into frost!

Such clouds of nameless trouble cross
   All night below the darken'd eyes;
    With morning wakes the will, and cries,
"Thou shalt not be the fool of loss."

V

I sometimes hold it half a sin
   To put in words the grief I feel:
    For words, like Nature, half reveal
And half conceal the Soul within.

But, for the unquiet heart and brain,
   A use in measured language lies;
    The sad mechanic exercise,
Like dull narcotics, numbing pain.

In words, like weeds, I 'll wrap me o'er,
   Like coarsest clothes against the cold;   10 (118)
    But that large grief which these enfold
Is given in outline and no more.

VI

One writes, that "other friends remain,"
   That "loss is common to the race"—
    And common is the commonplace,
And vacant chaff well meant for grain.

That loss is common would not make
   My own less bitter, rather more.
    Too common! Never morning wore
To evening, but some heart did break.

O father, wheresoe'er thou be,
   Who pledgest now thy gallant son,   10 (130)
    A shot, ere half thy draught be done,
Hath still'd the life that beat from thee.

O mother, praying God will save
   Thy sailor,—while thy head is bow'd,
    His heavy-shotted hammock-shroud
Drops in his vast and wandering grave.

Ye know no more than I who wrought
   At that last hour to please him well;
    Who mused on all I had to tell,
And something written, something thought;   20 (140)

Expecting still his advent home;
   And ever met him on his way
    With wishes, thinking, "here to-day,"
Or "here to-morrow will he come."

O, somewhere, meek, unconscious dove,
   That sittest ranging golden hair;
    And glad to find thyself so fair,
Poor child, that waitest for thy love!

For now her father's chimney glows
   In expectation of a guest;   30 (150)
    And thinking "this will please him best,"
She takes a riband or a rose,

For he will see them on to-night;
   And with the thought her color burns;
    And, having left the glass, she turns
Once more to set a ringlet right;

And, even when she turn'd, the curse
   Had fallen, and her future lord
    Was drown'd in passing thro' the ford,
Or kill'd in falling from his horse.   40 (160)

O, what to her shall be the end?
   And what to me remains of good?
    To her perpetual maidenhood,
And unto me no second friend.

VII

Dark house, by which once more I stand
   Here in the long unlovely street,
    Doors, where my heart was used to beat
So quickly, waiting for a hand,

A hand that can be clasp'd no more—
   Behold me, for I cannot sleep,
    And like a guilty thing I creep
At earliest morning to the door.

He is not here; but far away
   The noise of life begins again,   10 (174)
    And ghastly thro' the drizzling rain
On the bald street breaks the blank day.

VIII

A happy lover who has come
   To look on her that loves him well,
    Who 'lights and rings the gateway bell,
And learns her gone and far from home;

He saddens, all the magic light
   Dies off at once from bower and hall,
   And all the place is dark, and all
The chambers emptied of delight:

So find I every pleasant spot
   In which we two were wont to meet,   10 (186)
   The field, the chamber, and the street,
For all is dark where thou art not.

Yet as that other, wandering there
   In those deserted walks, may find
   A flower beat with rain and wind,
Which once she foster'd up with care;

So seems it in my deep regret,
   O my forsaken heart, with thee
   And this poor flower of poesy
Which, little cared for, fades not yet.   20 (196)

But since it pleased a vanish'd eye,
   I go to plant it on his tomb,
   That if it can it there may bloom,
Or, dying, there at least may die.

IX

Fair ship, that from the Italian shore
   Sailest the placid ocean-plains
   With my lost Arthur's loved remains,
Spread thy full wings, and waft him o'er.

So draw him home to those that mourn
   In vain; a favorable speed
   Ruffle thy mirror'd mast, and lead
Thro' prosperous floods his holy urn.

All night no ruder air perplex
   Thy sliding keel, till Phosphor, bright   10 (210)
   As our pure love, thro' early light
Shall glimmer on the dewy decks.

Sphere all your lights around, above;
   Sleep, gentle heavens, before the prow;
   Sleep, gentle winds, as he sleeps now,
My friend, the brother of my love;

My Arthur, whom I shall not see
   Till all my widow'd race be run;
   Dear as the mother to the son,
More than my brothers are to me.   20 (220)

X

I hear the noise about thy keel;
   I hear the bell struck in the night;
   I see the cabin-window bright;
I see the sailor at the wheel.

Thou bring'st the sailor to his wife,
   And travell'd men from foreign lands;
   And letters unto trembling hands;
And, thy dark freight, a vanish'd life.

So bring him; we have idle dreams;
   This look of quiet flatters thus   10 (230)
   Our home-bred fancies. O, to us,
The fools of habit, sweeter seems

To rest beneath the clover sod,
   That takes the sunshine and the rains,
   Or where the kneeling hamlet drains
The chalice of the grapes of God;

Than if with thee the roaring wells
   Should gulf him fathom-deep in brine,
   And hands so often clasp'd in mine,
Should toss with tangle and with shells.   20 (240)

XI

Calm is the morn without a sound,
   Calm as to suit a calmer grief,
   And only thro' the faded leaf
The chestnut pattering to the ground;

Calm and deep peace on this high wold,
   And on these dews that drench the furze,
   And all the silvery gossamers
That twinkle into green and gold;

Calm and still light on yon great plain
   That sweeps with all its autumn bowers,   10 (250)
   And crowded farms and lessening towers,
To mingle with the bounding main;

Calm and deep peace in this wide air,
   These leaves that redden to the fall,
   And in my heart, if calm at all,
If any calm, a calm despair;

Calm on the seas, and silver sleep,
   And waves that sway themselves in rest,
   And dead calm in that noble breast
Which heaves but with the heaving deep.   20 (260)

XII

Lo, as a dove when up she springs
 To bear thro' heaven a tale of woe,
 Some dolorous message knit below
The wild pulsation of her wings;

Like her I go, I cannot stay;
 I leave this mortal ark behind,
 A weight of nerves without a mind,
And leave the cliffs, and haste away

O'er ocean-mirrors rounded large,
 And reach the glow of southern skies,   10 (270)
 And see the sails at distance rise,
And linger weeping on the marge,

And saying, "Comes he thus, my friend?
 Is this the end of all my care?"
 And circle moaning in the air,
"Is this the end? Is this the end?"

And forward dart again, and play
 About the prow, and back return
 To where the body sits, and learn
That I have been an hour away.   20 (280)

XIII

Tears of the widower, when he sees
 A late-lost form that sleep reveals,
 And moves his doubtful arms, and feels
Her place is empty, fall like these;

Which weep a loss for ever new,
 A void where heart on heart reposed;
 And, where warm hands have prest and closed,
Silence, till I be silent too;

Which weep the comrade of my choice,
 An awful thought, a life removed,   10 (290)
 The human-hearted man I loved,
A Spirit, not a breathing voice.

Come, Time, and teach me, many years,
 I do not suffer in a dream;
 For now so strange do these things seem,
Mine eyes have leisure for their tears,

My fancies time to rise on wing,
 And glance about the approaching sails,
 As tho' they brought but merchants' bales,
And not the burthen that they bring.   20 (300)

XIV

If one should bring me this report,
    That thou hadst touch'd the land to-day,
    And I went down unto the quay,
And found thee lying in the port;

And standing, muffled round with woe,
    Should see thy passengers in rank
    Come stepping lightly down the plank
And beckoning unto those they know;

And if along with these should come
    The man I held as half-divine,   10 (310)
    Should strike a sudden hand in mine,
And ask a thousand things of home;

And I should tell him all my pain,
    And how my life had droop'd of late,
    And he should sorrow o'er my state
And marvel what possess'd my brain;

And I perceived no touch of change,
    No hint of death in all his frame,
    But found him all in all the same,
I should not feel it to be strange.   20 (320)

XV

To-night the winds begin to rise
    And roar from yonder dropping day;
    The last red leaf is whirl'd away,
The rooks are blown about the skies;

The forest crack'd, the waters curl'd,
    The cattle huddled on the lea;
    And wildly dash'd on tower and tree
The sunbeam strikes along the world:

And but for fancies, which aver
    That all thy motions gently pass   10 (330)
    Athwart a plane of molten glass,
I scarce could brook the strain and stir

That makes the barren branches loud;
    And but for fear it is not so,
    The wild unrest that lives in woe
Would dote and pore on yonder cloud

That rises upward always higher,
    And onward drags a laboring breast,
    And topples round the dreary west,
A looming bastion fringed with fire.   20 (340)

XVI

What words are these have fallen from me?
   Can calm despair and wild unrest
   Be tenants of a single breast,
Or Sorrow such a changeling be?

Or doth she only seem to take
   The touch of change in calm or storm,
   But knows no more of transient form
In her deep self, than some dead lake

That holds the shadow of a lark
   Hung in the shadow of a heaven?   10 (350)
   Or has the shock, so harshly given,
Confused me like the unhappy bark

That strikes by night a craggy shelf,
   And staggers blindly ere she sink?
   And stunn'd me from my power to think
And all my knowledge of myself;

And made me that delirious man
   Whose fancy fuses old and new,
   And flashes into false and true,
And mingles all without a plan?   20 (360)

XVII

Thou comest, much wept for; such a breeze
   Compell'd thy canvas, and my prayer
   Was as the whisper of an air
To breathe thee over lonely seas.

For I in spirit saw thee move
   Thro' circles of the bounding sky,
   Week after week; the days go by;
Come quick, thou bringest all I love.

Henceforth, wherever thou mayst roam,
   My blessing, like a line of light,   10 (370)
   Is on the waters day and night,
And like a beacon guards thee home.

So may whatever tempest mars
   Mid-ocean spare thee, sacred bark,
   And balmy drops in summer dark
Slide from the bosom of the stars;

So kind an office hath been done,
   Such precious relics brought by thee,
   The dust of him I shall not see
Till all my widow'd race be run.   20 (380)

XVIII

'T is well; 't is something; we may stand
    Where he in English earth is laid,
    And from his ashes may be made
The violet of his native land.

'T is little; but it looks in truth
    As if the quiet bones were blest
    Among familiar names to rest
And in the places of his youth.

Come then, pure hands, and bear the head
    That sleeps or wears the mask of sleep,   10 (390)
    And come, whatever loves to weep,
And hear the ritual of the dead.

Ah yet, even yet, if this might be,
    I, falling on his faithful heart,
    Would breathing thro' his lips impart
The life that almost dies in me;

That dies not, but endures with pain,
    And slowly forms the firmer mind,
    Treasuring the look it cannot find,
The words that are not heard again.   20 (400)

XIX

The Danube to the Severn gave
    The darken'd heart that beat no more;
    They laid him by the pleasant shore,
And in the hearing of the wave.

There twice a day the Severn fills;
    The salt sea-water passes by,
    And hushes half the babbling Wye,
And makes a silence in the hills.

The Wye is hush'd nor moved along,
    And hush'd my deepest grief of all,   10 (410)
    When fill'd with tears that cannot fall,
I brim with sorrow drowning song.

The tide flows down, the wave again
    Is vocal in its wooded walls;
    My deeper anguish also falls,
And I can speak a little then.

XX

The lesser griefs that may be said,
    That breathe a thousand tender vows,

Are but as servants in a house
Where lies the master newly dead;

Who speak their feeling as it is,
    And weep the fulness from the mind.
    "It will be hard," they say, "to find
Another service such as this."

My lighter moods are like to these,
    That out of words a comfort win;   10 (426)
    But there are other griefs within,
And tears that at their fountain freeze;

For by the hearth the children sit
    Cold in that atmosphere of death,
    And scarce endure to draw the breath,
Or like to noiseless phantoms flit;

But open converse is there none,
    So much the vital spirits sink
    To see the vacant chair, and think,
"How good! how kind! and he is gone."   20 (436)

XXI

I sing to him that rests below,
    And, since the grasses round me wave,
    I take the grasses of the grave,
And make them pipes whereon to blow.

The traveller hears me now and then,
    And sometimes harshly will he speak:
    "This fellow would make weakness weak,
And melt the waxen hearts of men."

Another answers: "Let him be,
    He loves to make parade of pain,   10 (446)
    That with his piping he may gain
The praise that comes to constancy."

A third is wroth: "Is this an hour
    For private sorrow's barren song,
    When more and more the people throng
The chairs and thrones of civil power?

"A time to sicken and to swoon,
    When Science reaches forth her arms
    To feel from world to world, and charms
Her secret from the latest moon?"   20 (456)

Behold, ye speak an idle thing;
    Ye never knew the sacred dust.

I do but sing because I must,
And pipe but as the linnets sing;

And one is glad; her note is gay,
  For now her little ones have ranged;
  And one is sad; her note is changed,
Because her brood is stolen away.

XXII

The path by which we twain did go,
  Which led by tracts that pleased us well,
  Thro' four sweet years arose and fell,
From flower to flower, from snow to snow;

And we with singing cheer'd the way,
  And, crown'd with all the season lent,
  From April on to April went,
And glad at heart from May to May.

But where the path we walk'd began
  To slant the fifth autumnal slope,   10 (474)
  As we descended following Hope,
There sat the Shadow fear'd of man;

Who broke our fair companionship,
  And spread his mantle dark and cold,
  And wrapt thee formless in the fold,
And dull'd the murmur on thy lip,

And bore thee where I could not see
  Nor follow, tho' I walk in haste,
  And think that somewhere in the waste   20 (484)
The Shadow sits and waits for me.

XXIII

Now, sometimes in my sorrow shut,
  Or breaking into song by fits,
  Alone, alone, to where he sits,
The Shadow cloak'd from head to foot,

Who keeps the keys of all the creeds,
  I wander, often falling lame,
  And looking back to whence I came,
Or on to where the pathway leads;

And crying, How changed from where it ran
  Thro' lands where not a leaf was dumb,   10 (494)
  But all the lavish hills would hum
The murmur of a happy Pan;

When each by turns was guide to each,
  And Fancy light from Fancy caught,

And Thought leapt out to wed with Thought
Ere Thought could wed itself with Speech;

And all we met was fair and good,
   And all was good that Time could bring,
   And all the secret of the Spring
Moved in the chambers of the blood;   20 (504)

And many an old philosophy
   On Argive heights divinely sang,
   And round us all the thicket rang
To many a flute of Arcady.

XXIV

And was the day of my delight
   As pure and perfect as I say?
   The very source and fount of day
Is dash'd with wandering isles of night.

If all was good and fair we met,
   This earth had been the Paradise
   It never look'd to human eyes
Since our first sun arose and set.

And is it that the haze of grief
   Makes former gladness loom so great?   10 (518)
   The lowness of the present state,
That sets the past in this relief?

Or that the past will always win
   A glory from its being far,
   And orb into the perfect star
We saw not when we moved therein?

XXV

I know that this was Life,—the track
   Whereon with equal feet we fared;
   And then, as now, the day prepared
The daily burden for the back.

But this it was that made me move
   As light as carrier-birds in air;
   I loved the weight I had to bear,
Because it needed help of Love;

Nor could I weary, heart or limb,
   When mighty Love would cleave in twain   10 (534)
   The lading of a single pain,
And part it, giving half to him.

XXVI

Still onward winds the dreary way;
    I with it, for I long to prove
    No lapse of moons can canker Love,
Whatever fickle tongues may say.

And if that eye which watches guilt
    And goodness, and hath power to see
    Within the green the moulder'd tree,
And towers fallen as soon as built—

O, if indeed that eye foresee
    Or see—in Him is no before—   10 (546)
    In more of life true life no more
And Love the indifference to be,

Then might I find, ere yet the morn
    Breaks hither over Indian seas,
    That Shadow waiting with the keys,
To shroud me from my proper scorn.

XXVII

I envy not in any moods
    The captive void of noble rage,
    The linnet born within the cage,
That never knew the summer woods;

I envy not the beast that takes
    His license in the field of time,
    Unfetter'd by the sense of crime,
To whom a conscience never wakes;

Nor, what may count itself as blest,
    The heart that never plighted troth   10 (562)
    But stagnates in the weeds of sloth:
Nor any want-begotten rest.

I hold it true, whate'er befall;
    I feel it, when I sorrow most;
    'T is better to have loved and lost
Than never to have loved at all.

XXVIII

The time draws near the birth of Christ.
    The moon is hid, the night is still;
    The Christmas bells from hill to hill
Answer each other in the mist.

Four voices of four hamlets round,
    From far and near, on mead and moor,

Swell out and fail, as if a door
Were shut between me and the sound;

Each voice four changes on the wind,
   That now dilate, and now decrease,
   Peace and goodwill, goodwill and peace,
Peace and goodwill, to all mankind.

                                               10 (578)

This year I slept and woke with pain,
   I almost wish'd no more to wake,
   And that my hold on life would break
Before I heard those bells again;

But they my troubled spirit rule,
   For they controll'd me when a boy;
   They bring me sorrow touch'd with joy,
The merry, merry bells of Yule.   20 (588)

XXIX

With such compelling cause to grieve
   As daily vexes household peace,
   And chains regret to his decease,
How dare we keep our Christmas-eve,

Which brings no more a welcome guest
   To enrich the threshold of the night
   With shower'd largess of delight
In dance and song and game and jest?

Yet go, and while the holly boughs
   Entwine the cold baptismal font,   10 (598)
   Make one wreath more for Use and Wont,
That guard the portals of the house;

Old sisters of a day gone by,
   Gray nurses, loving nothing new—
   Why should they miss their yearly due
Before their time? They too will die.

XXX

With trembling fingers did we weave
   The holly round the Christmas hearth;
   A rainy cloud possess'd the earth,
And sadly fell our Christmas-eve.

At our old pastimes in the hall
   We gamboll'd, making vain pretence
   Of gladness, with an awful sense
Of one mute Shadow watching all.

We paused: the winds were in the beech;
    We heard them sweep the winter land;   10 (614)
    And in a circle hand-in-hand
Sat silent, looking each at each.

Then echo-like our voices rang;
    We sung, tho' every eye was dim,
    A merry song we sang with him
Last year; impetuously we sang.

We ceased; a gentler feeling crept
    Upon us: surely rest is meet.
    "They rest," we said, "their sleep is sweet,"
And silence follow'd, and we wept.   20 (624)

Our voices took a higher range;
    Once more we sang: "They do not die
    Nor lose their mortal sympathy,
Nor change to us, although they change;

"Rapt from the fickle and the frail
    With gather'd power, yet the same,
    Pierces the keen seraphic flame
From orb to orb, from veil to veil."

Rise, happy morn, rise, holy morn,
    Draw forth the cheerful day from night: 30 (634)
    O Father, touch the east, and light
The light that shone when Hope was born.

XXXI

When Lazarus left his charnel-cave,
    And home to Mary's house return'd,
    Was this demanded—if he yearn'd
To hear her weeping by his grave?

"Where wert thou, brother, those four days?"
    There lives no record of reply,
    Which telling what it is to die
Had surely added praise to praise.

From every house the neighbors met,
    The streets were fill'd with joyful sound,   10 (646)
    A solemn gladness even crown'd
The purple brows of Olivet.

Behold a man raised up by Christ!
    The rest remaineth unreveal'd;
    He told it not, or something seal'd
The lips of that Evangelist.

XXXII

Her eyes are homes of silent prayer,
    Nor other thought, her mind admits
    But, he was dead, and there he sits,
And he that brought him back is there.

Then one deep love doth supersede
    All other, when her ardent gaze
    Roves from the living brother's face,
And rests upon the Life indeed.

All subtle thought, all curious fears,
    Borne down by gladness so complete,   10 (662)
    She bows, she bathes the Saviour's feet
With costly spikenard and with tears.

Thrice blest whose lives are faithful prayers,
    Whose loves in higher love endure;
    What souls possess themselves so pure,
Or is there blessedness like theirs?

XXXIII

O thou that after toil and storm
    Mayst seem to have reach'd a purer air,
    Whose faith has centre everywhere,
Nor cares to fix itself to form,

Leave thou thy sister when she prays
    Her early heaven, her happy views;
    Nor thou with shadow'd hint confuse
A life that leads melodious days.

Her faith thro' form is pure as thine,
    Her hands are quicker unto good.   10 (678)
    O, sacred be the flesh and blood
To which she links a truth divine!

See thou, that countest reason ripe
    In holding by the law within,
    Thou fail not in a world of sin,
And even for want of such a type.

XXXIV

My own dim life should teach me this,
    That life shall live for evermore,
    Else earth is darkness at the core,
And dust and ashes all that is;

This round of green, this orb of flame,
    Fantastic beauty; such as lurks

In some wild poet, when he works
Without a conscience or an aim.

What then were God to such as I?
   'T were hardly worth my while to choose   10 (694)
   Of things all mortal, or to use
A little patience ere I die;

'T were best at once to sink to peace,
   Like birds the charming serpent draws,
   To drop head-foremost in the jaws
Of vacant darkness and to cease.

XXXV

Yet if some voice that man could trust
   Should murmur from the narrow house,
   "The cheeks drop in, the body bows;
Man dies, nor is there hope in dust;"

Might I not say? "Yet even here,
   But for one hour, O Love, I strive
   To keep so sweet a thing alive."
But I should turn mine ears and hear

The moanings of the homeless sea,
   The sound of streams that swift or slow   10 (710)
   Draw down Æonian hills, and sow
The dust of continents to be;

And Love would answer with a sigh,
   "The sound of that forgetful shore
   Will change my sweetness more and more,
Half-dead to know that I shall die."

O me, what profits it to put
   An idle case? If Death were seen
   At first as Death, Love had not been,
Or been in narrowest working shut,   20 (720)

Mere fellowship of sluggish moods,
   Or in his coarsest Satyr-shape
   Had bruised the herb and crush'd the grape,
And bask'd and batten'd in the woods.

XXXVI

Tho' truths in manhood darkly join,
   Deep-seated in our mystic frame,
   We yield all blessing to the name
Of Him that made them current coin;

For Wisdom dealt with mortal powers,
   Where truth in closest words shall fail,

When truth embodied in a tale
Shall enter in at lowly doors.

And so the Word had breath, and wrought
   With human hands the creed of creeds   10 (734)
   In loveliness of perfect deeds,
More strong than all poetic thought;

Which he may read that binds the sheaf,
   Or builds the house, or digs the grave,
   And those wild eyes that watch the wave
In roarings round the coral reef.

XXXVII

Urania speaks with darken'd brow:
   "Thou pratest here where thou art least;
   This faith has many a purer priest,
And many an abler voice than thou.

"Go down beside thy native rill,
   On thy Parnassus set thy feet,
   And hear thy laurel whisper sweet
About the ledges of the hill."

And my Melpomene replies,
   A touch of shame upon her cheek: 10 (750)
   "I am not worthy even to speak
Of thy prevailing mysteries;

"For I am but an earthly Muse,
   And owning but a little art
   To lull with song an aching heart,
And render human love his dues;

"But brooding on the dear one dead,
   And all he said of things divine,—
   And dear to me as sacred wine
To dying lips is all he said,—   20 (760)

"I murmur'd, as I came along,
   Of comfort clasp'd in truth reveal'd,
   And loiter'd in the master's field,
And darken'd sanctities with song."

XXXVIII

With weary steps I loiter on,
   Tho' always under alter'd skies
   The purple from the distance dies,
My prospect and horizon gone.

No joy the blowing season gives,
 The herald melodies of spring,
 But in the songs I love to sing
A doubtful gleam of solace lives.

If any care for what is here
 Survive in spirits render'd free,   10 (774)
 Then are these songs I sing of thee
Not all ungrateful to thine ear.

XXXIX

Old warder of these buried bones,
 And answering now my random stroke
 With fruitful cloud and living smoke,
Dark yew, that graspest at the stones

And dippest toward the dreamless head,
 To thee too comes the golden hour
 When flower is feeling after flower;
But Sorrow,—fixt upon the dead,

And darkening the dark graves of men,—
 What whisper'd from her lying lips?   10 (786)
 Thy gloom is kindled at the tips,
And passes into gloom again.

XL

Could we forget the widow'd hour
 And look on Spirits breathed away,
 As on a maiden in the day
When first she wears her orange-flower!

When crown'd with blessing she doth rise
 To take her latest leave of home,
 And hopes and light regrets that come
Make April of her tender eyes;

And doubtful joys the father move,
 And tears are on the mother's face,   10 (798)
 As parting with a long embrace
She enters other realms of love;

Her office there to rear, to teach,
 Becoming as is meet and fit
 A link among the days, to knit
The generations each with each;

And, doubtless, unto thee is given
 A life that bears immortal fruit
 In those great offices that suit
The full-grown energies of heaven.   20 (808)

Ay me, the difference I discern!
  How often shall her old fireside
  Be cheer'd with tidings of the bride,
How often she herself return,

And tell them all they would have told,
  And bring her babe, and make her boast,
  Till even those that miss'd her most
Shall count new things as dear as old;

But thou and I have shaken hands,
  Till growing winters lay me low;   30 (818)
  My paths are in the fields I know,
And thine in undiscover'd lands.

XLI

Thy spirit ere our fatal loss
  Did ever rise from high to higher,
  As mounts the heavenward altar-fire,
As flies the lighter thro' the gross.

But thou art turn'd to something strange,
  And I have lost the links that bound
  Thy changes; here upon the ground,
No more partaker of thy change.

Deep folly! yet that this could be—
  That I could wing my will with might   10 (830)
  To leap the grades of life and light,
And flash at once, my friend, to thee!

For tho' my nature rarely yields
  To that vague fear implied in death,
  Nor shudders at the gulfs beneath,
The howlings from forgotten fields;

Yet oft when sundown skirts the moor
  An inner trouble I behold,
  A spectral doubt which makes me cold,
That I shall be thy mate no more,   20 (840)

Tho' following with an upward mind
  The wonders that have come to thee,
  Thro' all the secular to-be,
But evermore a life behind.

XLII

I vex my heart with fancies dim.
  He still outstript me in the race;
  It was but unity of place
That made me dream I rank'd with him.

And so may Place retain us still,
   And he the much-beloved again,
   A lord of large experience, train
To riper growth the mind and will;

And what delights can equal those
   That stir the spirit's inner deeps,   10 (854)
   When one that loves, but knows not, reaps
A truth from one that loves and knows?

XLIII

If Sleep and Death be truly one,
   And every spirit's folded bloom
   Thro' all its intervital gloom
In some long trance should slumber on;

Unconscious of the sliding hour,
   Bare of the body, might it last,
   And silent traces of the past
Be all the color of the flower:

So then were nothing lost to man;
   So that still garden of the souls   10 (866)
   In many a figured leaf enrolls
The total world since life began;

And love will last as pure and whole
   As when he loved me here in Time,
   And at the spiritual prime
Rewaken with the dawning soul.

XLIV

How fares it with the happy dead?
   For here the man is more and more;
   But he forgets the days before
God shut the doorways of his head.

The days have vanish'd, tone and tint,
   And yet perhaps the hoarding sense
   Gives out at times—he knows not whence—
A little flash, a mystic hint;

And in the long harmonious years—
   If Death so taste Lethean springs—   10 (882)
   May some dim touch of earthly things
Surprise thee ranging with thy peers.

If such a dreamy touch should fall,
   O, turn thee round, resolve the doubt;
   My guardian angel will speak out
In that high place, and tell thee all.

XLV

The baby new to earth and sky,
    What time his tender palm is prest
    Against the circle of the breast,
Has never thought that "this is I;"

But as he grows he gathers much,
    And learns the use of "I" and "me,"
    And finds "I am not what I see,
And other than the things I touch."

So rounds he to a separate mind
    From whence clear memory may begin,   10 (898)
    As thro' the frame that binds him in
His isolation grows defined.

This use may lie in blood and breath,
    Which else were fruitless of their due,
    Had man to learn himself anew
Beyond the second birth of death.

XLVI

We ranging down this lower track,
    The path we came by, thorn and flower,
    Is shadow'd by the growing hour,
Lest life should fail in looking back.

So be it: there no shade can last
    In that deep dawn behind the tomb,
    But clear from marge to marge shall bloom
The eternal landscape of the past;

A lifelong tract of time reveal'd,
    The fruitful hours of still increase;   10 (914)
    Days order'd in a wealthy peace,
And those five years its richest field.

O Love, thy province were not large,
    A bounded field, nor stretching far;
    Look also, Love, a brooding star,
A rosy warmth from marge to marge.

XLVII

That each, who seems a separate whole,
    Should move his rounds, and fusing all
    The skirts of self again, should fall
Remerging in the general Soul,

Is faith as vague as all unsweet.
    Eternal form shall still divide

The eternal soul from all beside;
And I shall know him when we meet;

And we shall sit at endless feast,
    Enjoying each the other's good.   10 (930)
    What vaster dream can hit the mood
Of Love on earth? He seeks at least

Upon the last and sharpest height,
    Before the spirits fade away,
    Some landing-place, to clasp and say,
"Farewell! We lose ourselves in light."

XLVIII

If these brief lays, of Sorrow born,
    Were taken to be such as closed
    Grave doubts and answers here proposed,
Then these were such as men might scorn.

Her care is not to part and prove;
    She takes, when harsher moods remit,
    What slender shade of doubt may flit,
And makes it vassal unto love;

And hence, indeed, she sports with words,
    But better serves a wholesome law,   10 (946)
    And holds it sin and shame to draw
The deepest measure from the chords;

Nor dare she trust a larger lay,
    But rather loosens from the lip
    Short swallow-flights of song, that dip
Their wings in tears, and skim away.

XLIX

From art, from nature, from the schools,
    Let random influences glance,
    Like light in many a shiver'd lance
That breaks about the dappled pools.

The lightest wave of thought shall lisp,
    The fancy's tenderest eddy wreathe,
    The slightest air of song shall breathe
To make the sullen surface crisp.

And look thy look, and go thy way,
    But blame not thou the winds that make   10 (962)
    The seeming-wanton ripple break,
The tender-pencill'd shadow play.

Beneath all fancied hopes and fears
    Ay me, the sorrow deepens down,

Whose muffled motions blindly drown
The bases of my life in tears.

L

Be near me when my light is low,
   When the blood creeps, and the nerves prick
   And tingle; and the heart is sick,
And all the wheels of being slow.

Be near me when the sensuous frame
   Is rack'd with pangs that conquer trust;
   And Time, a maniac scattering dust,
And Life, a Fury slinging flame.

Be near me when my faith is dry,
   And men the flies of latter spring,   10 (978)
   That lay their eggs, and sting and sing
And weave their petty cells and die.

Be near me when I fade away,
   To point the term of human strife,
   And on the low dark verge of life
The twilight of eternal day.

LI

Do we indeed desire the dead
   Should still be near us at our side?
   Is there no baseness we would hide?
No inner vileness that we dread?

Shall he for whose applause I strove,
   I had such reverence for his blame,
   See with clear eye some hidden shame
And I be lessen'd in his love?

I wrong the grave with fears untrue.
   Shall love be blamed for want of faith?   10 (994)
   There must be wisdom with great Death;
The dead shall look me thro' and thro'.

Be near us when we climb or fall;
   Ye watch, like God, the rolling hours
   With larger other eyes than ours,
To make allowance for us all.

LII

I cannot love thee as I ought,
   For love reflects the thing beloved;
   My words are only words, and moved
Upon the topmost froth of thought.

"Yet blame not thou thy plaintive song,"
   The Spirit of true love replied;
   "Thou canst not move me from thy side,
Nor human frailty do me wrong.

"What keeps a spirit wholly true
   To that ideal which he bears?   10 (1010)
   What record? not the sinless years
That breathed beneath the Syrian blue;

"So fret not, like an idle girl,
   That life is dash'd with flecks of sin.
   Abide; thy wealth is gather'd in,
When Time hath sunder'd shell from pearl."

LIII

How many a father have I seen,
   A sober man, among his boys,
   Whose youth was full of foolish noise,
Who wears his manhood hale and green;

And dare we to this fancy give,
   That had the wild oat not been sown,
   The soil, left barren, scarce had grown
The grain by which a man may live?

Or, if we held the doctrine sound
   For life outliving heats of youth,   10 (1026)
   Yet who would preach it as a truth
To those that eddy round and round?

Hold thou the good, define it well;
   For fear divine Philosophy
   Should push beyond her mark, and be
Procuress to the Lords of Hell.

LIV

O, yet we trust that somehow good
   Will be the final goal of ill,
   To pangs of nature, sins of will,
Defects of doubt, and taints of blood;

That nothing walks with aimless feet;
   That not one life shall be destroy'd,
   Or cast as rubbish to the void,
When God hath made the pile complete;

That not a worm is cloven in vain;
   That not a moth with vain desire   10 (1042)
   Is shrivell'd in a fruitless fire,
Or but subserves another's gain.

Behold, we know not anything;
   I can but trust that good shall fall
   At last—far off—at last, to all,
And every winter change to spring.

So runs my dream; but what am I?
   An infant crying in the night;
   An infant crying for the light,
And with no language but a cry.   20 (1052)

LV

The wish, that of the living whole
   No life may fail beyond the grave,
   Derives it not from what we have
The likest God within the soul?

Are God and Nature then at strife,
   That Nature lends such evil dreams?
   So careful of the type she seems,
So careless of the single life,

That I, considering everywhere
   Her secret meaning in her deeds,   10 (1062)
   And finding that of fifty seeds
She often brings but one to bear,

I falter where I firmly trod,
   And falling with my weight of cares
   Upon the great world's altar-stairs
That slope thro' darkness up to God,

I stretch lame hands of faith, and grope,
   And gather dust and chaff, and call
   To what I feel is Lord of all,
And faintly trust the larger hope.   20 (1072)

LVI

"So careful of the type?" but no.
   From scarped cliff and quarried stone
   She cries, "A thousand types are gone;
I care for nothing, all shall go.

"Thou makest thine appeal to me.
   I bring to life, I bring to death;
   The spirit does but mean the breath:
I know no more." And he, shall he,

Man, her last work, who seem'd so fair,
   Such splendid purpose in his eyes,   10 (1082)
   Who roll'd the psalm to wintry skies,
Who built him fanes of fruitless prayer,

Who trusted God was love indeed
  And love Creation's final law—
  Tho' Nature, red in tooth and claw
With ravine, shriek'd against his creed—

Who loved, who suffer'd countless ills,
  Who battled for the True, the Just,
  Be blown about the desert dust,
Or seal'd within the iron hills?   20 (1092)

No more? A monster then, a dream,
  A discord. Dragons of the prime,
  That tare each other in their slime,
Were mellow music match'd with him.

O life as futile, then, as frail!
  O for thy voice to soothe and bless!
  What hope of answer, or redress?
Behind the veil, behind the veil.

LVII

Peace; come away: the song of woe
  Is after all an earthly song.
  Peace; come away: we do him wrong
To sing so wildly: let us go.

Come; let us go: your cheeks are pale;
  But half my life I leave behind.
  Methinks my friend is richly shrined;
But I shall pass, my work will fail.

Yet in these ears, till hearing dies,
  One set slow bell will seem to toll   10 (1110)
  The passing of the sweetest soul
That ever look'd with human eyes.

I hear it now, and o'er and o'er,
  Eternal greetings to the dead;
  And "Ave, Ave, Ave," said,
"Adieu, adieu," for evermore.

LVIII

In those sad words I took farewell.
  Like echoes in sepulchral halls,
  As drop by drop the water falls
In vaults and catacombs, they fell;

And, falling, idly broke the peace
  Of hearts that beat from day to day,
  Half-conscious of their dying clay,
And those cold crypts where they shall cease.

The high Muse answer'd: "Wherefore grieve
   Thy brethren with a fruitless tear?   10 (1126)
   Abide a little longer here,
And thou shalt take a nobler leave."

LIX

O Sorrow, wilt thou live with me
   No casual mistress, but a wife,
   My bosom-friend and half of life;
As I confess it needs must be?

O Sorrow, wilt thou rule my blood,
   Be sometimes lovely like a bride,
   And put thy harsher moods aside,
If thou wilt have me wise and good?

My centred passion cannot move,
   Nor will it lessen from to-day;   10 (1138)
   But I'll have leave at times to play
As with the creature of my love;

And set thee forth, for thou art mine,
   With so much hope for years to come,
   That, howsoe'er I know thee, some
Could hardly tell what name were thine.

LX

He past, a soul of nobler tone;
   My spirit loved and loves him yet,
   Like some poor girl whose heart is set
On one whose rank exceeds her own.

He mixing with his proper sphere,
   She finds the baseness of her lot,
   Half jealous of she knows not what,
And envying all that meet him there.

The little village looks forlorn;
   She sighs amid her narrow days,   10 (1154)
   Moving about the household ways,
In that dark house where she was born.

The foolish neighbors come and go,
   And tease her till the day draws by;
   At night she weeps, "How vain am I!
How should he love a thing so low?"

LXI

If, in thy second state sublime,
   Thy ransom'd reason change replies

With all the circle of the wise,
The perfect flower of human time;

And if thou cast thine eyes below,
 How dimly character'd and slight,
 How dwarf'd a growth of cold and night,
How blanch'd with darkness must I grow!

Yet turn thee to the doubtful shore,
 Where thy first form was made a man;   10 (1170)
 I loved thee, Spirit, and love, nor can
The soul of Shakespeare love thee more.

LXII

Tho' if an eye that's downward cast
 Could make thee somewhat blench or fail,
 Then be my love an idle tale
And fading legend of the past;

And thou, as one that once declined,
 When he was little more than boy,
 On some unworthy heart with joy,
But lives to wed an equal mind,

And breathes a novel world, the while
 His other passion wholly dies,   10 (1182)
 Or in the light of deeper eyes
Is matter for a flying smile.

LXIII

Yet pity for a horse o'er-driven,
 And love in which my hound has part
 Can hang no weight upon my heart
In its assumptions up to heaven;

And I am so much more than these,
 As thou, perchance, art more than I,
 And yet I spare them sympathy,
And I would set their pains at ease.

So mayst thou watch me where I weep,
 As, unto vaster motions bound,   10 (1194)
 The circuits of thine orbit round
A higher height, a deeper deep.

LXIV

Dost thou look back on what hath been,
 As some divinely gifted man,
 Whose life in low estate began
And on a simple village green;

Who breaks his birth's invidious bar,
   And grasps the skirts of happy chance,
   And breasts the blows of circumstance,
And grapples with his evil star;

Who makes by force his merit known
   And lives to clutch the golden keys,   10 (1206)
   To mould a mighty state's decrees,
And shape the whisper of the throne;

And moving up from high to higher,
   Becomes on Fortune's crowning slope
   The pillar of a people's hope,
The centre of a world's desire;

Yet feels, as in a pensive dream,
   When all his active powers are still,
   A distant dearness in the hill,
A secret sweetness in the stream,   20 (1216)

The limit of his narrower fate,
   While yet beside its vocal springs
   He play'd at counsellors and kings,
With one that was his earliest mate;

Who ploughs with pain his native lea
   And reaps the labor of his hands,
   Or in the furrow musing stands:
"Does my old friend remember me?"

LXV

Sweet soul, do with me as thou wilt;
   I lull a fancy trouble-tost
   With "Love's too precious to be lost,
A little grain shall not be spilt."

And in that solace can I sing,
   Till out of painful phases wrought
   There flutters up a happy thought,
Self-balanced on a lightsome wing;

Since we deserved the name of friends,
   And thine effect so lives in me,   10 (1234)
   A part of mine may live in thee
And move thee on to noble ends.

LXVI

You thought my heart too far diseased;
   You wonder when my fancies play

To find me gay among the gay,
Like one with any trifle pleased.

The shade by which my life was crost,
　Which makes a desert in the mind,
　Has made me kindly with my kind,
And like to him whose sight is lost;

Whose feet are guided thro' the land,
　Whose jest among his friends is free,　　　　10 (1246)
　Who takes the children on his knee,
And winds their curls about his hand.

He plays with threads, he beats his chair
　For pastime, dreaming of the sky;
　His inner day can never die,
His night of loss is always there.

LXVII

When on my bed the moonlight falls,
　I know that in thy place of rest
　By that broad water of the west
There comes a glory on the walls:

Thy marble bright in dark appears,
　As slowly steals a silver flame
　Along the letters of thy name,
And o'er the number of thy years.

The mystic glory swims away,
　From off my bed the moonlight dies;　　　　10 (1262)
　And closing eaves of wearied eyes
I sleep till dusk is dipt in gray;

And then I know the mist is drawn
　A lucid veil from coast to coast,
　And in the dark church like a ghost
Thy tablet glimmers to the dawn.

LXVIII

When in the down I sink my head,
　Sleep, Death's twin-brother, times my breath;
　Sleep, Death's twin-brother, knows not Death,
Nor can I dream of thee as dead.

I walk as ere I walk'd forlorn,
　When all our path was fresh with dew,
　And all the bugle breezes blew
Reveillée to the breaking morn.

But what is this? I turn about,
    I find a trouble in thine eye,   10 (1278)
      Which makes me sad I know not why,
Nor can my dream resolve the doubt;

But ere the lark hath left the lea
    I wake, and I discern the truth;
      It is the trouble of my youth
That foolish sleep transfers to thee.

LXIX

I dream'd there would be Spring no more,
    That Nature's ancient power was lost;
      The streets were black with smoke and frost,
They chatter'd trifles at the door;

I wander'd from the noisy town,
    I found a wood with thorny boughs;
      I took the thorns to bind my brows,
I wore them like a civic crown;

I met with scoffs, I met with scorns
    From youth and babe and hoary hairs: 10 (1294)
      They call'd me in the public squares
The fool that wears a crown of thorns.

They call'd me fool, they call'd me child:
    I found an angel of the night;
      The voice was low, the look was bright;
He look'd upon my crown and smiled.

He reach'd the glory of a hand,
    That seem'd to touch it into leaf;
      The voice was not the voice of grief,
The words were hard to understand.   20 (1304)

LXX

I cannot see the features right,
    When on the gloom I strive to paint
      The face I know; the hues are faint
And mix with hollow masks of night;

Cloud-towers by ghostly masons wrought,
    A gulf that ever shuts and gapes,
      A hand that points, and palled shapes
In shadowy thoroughfares of thought;

And crowds that stream from yawning doors,
    And shoals of pucker'd faces drive;   10 (1314)

Dark bulks that tumble half alive,
And lazy lengths on boundless shores;

Till all at once beyond the will
   I hear a wizard music roll,
   And thro' a lattice on the soul
Looks thy fair face and makes it still.

LXXI

Sleep, kinsman thou to death and trance
   And madness, thou hast forged at last
   A night-long present of the past
In which we went thro' summer France.

Hadst thou such credit with the soul?
   Then bring an opiate trebly strong,
   Drug down the blindfold sense of wrong,
That so my pleasure may be whole;

While now we talk as once we talk'd
   Of men and minds, the dust of change,   10 (1330)
   The days that grow to something strange,
In walking as of old we walk'd

Beside the river's wooded reach,
   The fortress, and the mountain ridge,
   The cataract flashing from the bridge,
The breaker breaking on the beach.

LXXII

Risest thou thus, dim dawn, again,
   And howlest, issuing out of night,
   With blasts that blow the poplar white,
And lash with storm the streaming pane?

Day, when my crown'd estate begun
   To pine in that reverse of doom,
   Which sicken'd every living bloom,
And blurr'd the splendor of the sun;

Who usherest in the dolorous hour
   With thy quick tears that make the rose   10 (1346)
   Pull sideways, and the daisy close
Her crimson fringes to the shower;

Who mightst have heaved a windless flame
   Up the deep East, or, whispering, play'd
   A chequer-work of beam and shade
Along the hills, yet look'd the same,

As wan, as chill, as wild as now;
   Day, mark'd as with some hideous crime,
   When the dark hand struck down thro' time,
And cancell'd nature's best: but thou,   20 (1356)

Lift as thou mayst thy burthen'd brows
   Thro' clouds that drench the morning star,
   And whirl the ungarner'd sheaf afar,
And sow the sky with flying boughs,

And up thy vault with roaring sound
   Climb thy thick noon, disastrous day;
   Touch thy dull goal of joyless gray,
And hide thy shame beneath the ground.

LXXIII

So many worlds, so much to do,
   So little done, such things to be,
   How know I what had need of thee,
For thou wert strong as thou wert true?

The fame is quench'd that I foresaw,
   The head hath miss'd an earthly wreath:
   I curse not Nature, no, nor Death;
For nothing is that errs from law.

We pass; the path that each man trod
   Is dim, or will be dim, with weeds.   10 (1374)
   What fame is left for human deeds
In endless age? It rests with God.

O hollow wraith of dying fame,
   Fade wholly, while the soul exults,
   And self-infolds the large results
Of force that would have forged a name.

LXXIV

As sometimes in a dead man's face,
   To those that watch it more and more,
   A likeness, hardly seen before,
Comes out—to some one of his race;

So, dearest, now thy brows are cold,
   I see thee what thou art, and know
   Thy likeness to the wise below,
Thy kindred with the great of old.

But there is more than I can see,
   And what I see I leave unsaid,   10 (1390)

Nor speak it, knowing Death has made
His darkness beautiful with thee.

LXXV

I leave thy praises unexpress'd
    In verse that brings myself relief,
    And by the measure of my grief
I leave thy greatness to be guess'd.

What practice howsoe'er expert
    In fitting aptest words to things,
    Or voice the richest-toned that sings,
Hath power to give thee as thou wert?

I care not in these fading days
    To raise a cry that lasts not long,   10 (1402)
    And round thee with the breeze of song
To stir a little dust of praise.

Thy leaf has perish'd in the green,
    And, while we breathe beneath the sun,
    The world which credits what is done
Is cold to all that might have been.

So here shall silence guard thy fame;
    But somewhere, out of human view,
    Whate'er thy hands are set to do
Is wrought with tumult of acclaim.   20 (1412)

LXXVI

Take wings of fancy, and ascend,
    And in a moment set thy face
    Where all the starry heavens of space
Are sharpen'd to a needle's end;

Take wings of foresight; lighten thro'
    The secular abyss to come,
    And lo, thy deepest lays are dumb
Before the mouldering of a yew;

And if the matin songs, that woke
    The darkness of our planet, last,   10 (1422)
    Thine own shall wither in the vast,
Ere half the lifetime of an oak.

Ere these have clothed their branchy bowers
    With fifty Mays, thy songs are vain;
    And what are they when these remain
The ruin'd shells of hollow towers?

LXXVII

What hope is here for modern rhyme
    To him who turns a musing eye
    On songs, and deeds, and lives, that lie
Foreshorten'd in the tract of time?

These mortal lullabies of pain
    May bind a book, may line a box,
    May serve to curl a maiden's locks;
Or when a thousand moons shall wane

A man upon a stall may find,
    And, passing, turn the page that tells   10 (1438)
    A grief, then changed to something else,
Sung by a long-forgotten mind.

But what of that? My darken'd ways
    Shall ring with music all the same;
    To breathe my loss is more than fame,
To utter love more sweet than praise.

LXXVIII

Again at Christmas did we weave
    The holly round the Christmas hearth;
    The silent snow possess'd the earth,
And calmly fell our Christmas-eve.

The yule-clog sparkled keen with frost,
    No wing of wind the region swept,
    But over all things brooding slept
The quiet sense of something lost.

As in the winters left behind,
    Again our ancient games had place,   10 (1454)
    The mimic picture's breathing grace,
And dance and song and hoodman-blind.

Who show'd a token of distress?
    No single tear, no mark of pain—
    O sorrow, then can sorrow wane?
O grief, can grief be changed to less?

O last regret, regret can die!
    No—mixt with all this mystic frame,
    Her deep relations are the same,
But with long use her tears are dry.   20 (1464)

LXXIX

"More than my brothers are to me,"—
    Let this not vex thee, noble heart!

I know thee of what force thou art
To hold the costliest love in fee.

But thou and I are one in kind,
   As moulded like in Nature's mint;
   And hill and wood and field did print
The same sweet forms in either mind.

For us the same cold streamlet curl'd
   Thro' all his eddying coves, the same   10 (1474)
   All winds that roam the twilight came
In whispers of the beauteous world.

At one dear knee we proffer'd vows,
   One lesson from one book we learn'd,
   Ere childhood's flaxen ringlet turn'd
To black and brown on kindred brows.

And so my wealth resembles thine,
   But he was rich where I was poor,
   And he supplied my want the more
As his unlikeness fitted mine.   20 (1484)

LXXX

If any vague desire should rise,
   That holy Death ere Arthur died
   Had moved me kindly from his side,
And dropt the dust on tearless eyes;

Then fancy shapes, as fancy can,
   The grief my loss in him had wrought,
   A grief as deep as life or thought,
But stay'd in peace with God and man.

I make a picture in the brain;
   I hear the sentence that he speaks;   10 (1494)
   He bears the burthen of the weeks,
But turns his burthen into gain.

His credit thus shall set me free;
   And, influence-rich to soothe and save,
   Unused example from the grave
Reach out dead hands to comfort me.

LXXXI

Could I have said while he was here,
   "My love shall now no further range;
   There cannot come a mellower change,
For now is love mature in ear"?

Love, then, had hope of richer store:
   What end is here to my complaint?
   This haunting whisper makes me faint,
"More years had made me love thee more."

But Death returns an answer sweet:
   "My sudden frost was sudden gain,   10 (1510)
   And gave all ripeness to the grain
It might have drawn from after-heat."

LXXXII

I wage not any feud with Death
   For changes wrought on form and face;
   No lower life that earth's embrace
May breed with him can fright my faith.

Eternal process moving on,
   From state to state the spirit walks;
   And these are but the shatter'd stalks,
Or ruin'd chrysalis of one.

Nor blame I Death, because he bare
   The use of virtue out of earth;   10 (1522)
   I know transplanted human worth
Will bloom to profit, otherwhere.

For this alone on Death I wreak
   The wrath that garners in my heart:
   He put our lives so far apart
We cannot hear each other speak.

LXXXIII

Dip down upon the northern shore,
   O sweet new-year delaying long;
   Thou doest expectant Nature wrong;
Delaying long, delay no more.

What stays thee from the clouded noons,
   Thy sweetness from its proper place?
   Can trouble live with April days,
Or sadness in the summer moons?

Bring orchis, bring the foxglove spire,
   The little speedwell's darling blue,   10 (1538)
   Deep tulips dash'd with fiery dew,
Laburnums, dropping-wells of fire.

O thou, new-year, delaying long,
   Delayest the sorrow in my blood,

That longs to burst a frozen bud
And flood a fresher throat with song.

LXXXIV

When I contemplate all alone
    The life that had been thine below,
    And fix my thoughts on all the glow
To which thy crescent would have grown,

I see thee sitting crown'd with good,
    A central warmth diffusing bliss
    In glance and smile, and clasp and kiss,
On all the branches of thy blood;

Thy blood, my friend, and partly mine;
    For now the day was drawing on,   10 (1554)
    When thou shouldst link thy life with one
Of mine own house, and boys of thine

Had babbled "Uncle" on my knee;
    But that remorseless iron hour
    Made cypress of her orange flower,
Despair of hope, and earth of thee.

I seem to meet their least desire,
    To clap their cheeks, to call them mine.
    I see their unborn faces shine
Beside the never-lighted fire.   20 (1564)

I see myself an honor'd guest,
    Thy partner in the flowery walk
    Of letters, genial table-talk,
Or deep dispute, and graceful jest;

While now thy prosperous labor fills
    The lips of men with honest praise,
    And sun by sun the happy days
Descend below the golden hills

With promise of a morn as fair;
    And all the train of bounteous hours   30 (1574)
    Conduct, by paths of growing powers,
To reverence and the silver hair;

Till slowly worn her earthly robe,
    Her lavish mission richly wrought,
    Leaving great legacies of thought,
Thy spirit should fail from off the globe;

What time mine own might also flee,
    As link'd with thine in love and fate,

And, hovering o'er the dolorous strait
ı o the other shore, involved in thee,   40 (1584)

Arrive at last the blessed goal,
   And He that died in Holy Land
   Would reach us out the shining hand,
And take us as a single soul.

What reed was that on which I leant?
   Ah, backward fancy, wherefore wake
   The old bitterness again, and break
The low beginnings of content?

LXXXV

This truth came borne with bier and pall,
   I felt it, when I sorrow'd most,
   'T is better to have loved and lost,
Than never to have loved at all—

O true in word, and tried in deed,
   Demanding, so to bring relief
   To this which is our common grief,
What kind of life is that I lead;

And whether trust in things above
   Be dimm'd of sorrow, or sustain'd;   10 (1602)
   And whether love for him have drain'd
My capabilities of love;

Your words have virtue such as draws
   A faithful answer from the breast,
   Thro' light reproaches, half exprest,
And loyal unto kindly laws.

My blood an even tenor kept,
   Till on mine ear this message falls,
   That in Vienna's fatal walls
God's finger touch'd him, and he slept.   20 (1612)

The great Intelligences fair
   That range above our mortal state,
   In circle round the blessed gate,
Received and gave him welcome there;

And led him thro' the blissful climes,
   And show'd him in the fountain fresh
   All knowledge that the sons of flesh
Shall gather in the cycled times.

But I remain'd, whose hopes were dim,
   Whose life, whose thoughts were little worth,   30 (1622)

To wander on a darken'd earth,
Where all things round me breathed of him.

O friendship, equal-poised control,
   O heart, with kindliest motion warm,
   O sacred essence, other form,
O solemn ghost, O crowned soul!

Yet none could better know than I,
   How much of act at human hands
   The sense of human will demands
By which we dare to live or die.   40 (1632)

Whatever way my days decline,
   I felt and feel, tho' left alone,
   His being working in mine own,
The footsteps of his life in mine;

A life that all the Muses deck'd
   With gifts of grace, that might express
   All-comprehensive tenderness,
All-subtilizing intellect:

And so my passion hath not swerved
   To works of weakness, but I find   50 (1642)
   An image comforting the mind,
And in my grief a strength reserved.

Likewise the imaginative woe,
   That loved to handle spiritual strife,
   Diffused the shock thro' all my life,
But in the present broke the blow.

My pulses therefore beat again
   For other friends that once I met;
   Nor can it suit me to forget
The mighty hopes that make us men.   60 (1652)

I woo your love: I count it crime
   To mourn for any overmuch;
   I, the divided half of such
A friendship as had master'd Time;

Which masters Time indeed, and is
   Eternal, separate from fears.
   The all-assuming months and years
Can take no part away from this;

But Summer on the steaming floods,
   And Spring that swells the narrow brooks,   70 (1662)

And Autumn, with a noise of rooks,
That gather in the waning woods,

And every pulse of wind and wave
   Recalls, in change of light or gloom,
   My old affection of the tomb,
And my prime passion in the grave.

My old affection of the tomb,
   A part of stillness, yearns to speak:
   "Arise, and get thee forth and seek
A friendship for the years to come.   80 (1672)

"I watch thee from the quiet shore;
   Thy spirit up to mine can reach;
   But in dear words of human speech
We two communicate no more."

And I, "Can clouds of nature stain
   The starry clearness of the free?
   How is it? Canst thou feel for me
Some painless sympathy with pain?"

And lightly does the whisper fall:
   " 'T is hard for thee to fathom this;   90 (1682)
   I triumph in conclusive bliss,
And that serene result of all."

So hold I commerce with the dead;
   Or so methinks the dead would say;
   Or so shall grief with symbols play
And pining life be fancy-fed.

Now looking to some settled end,
   That these things pass, and I shall prove
   A meeting somewhere, love with love,
I crave your pardon, O my friend;   100 (1692)

If not so fresh, with love as true,
   I, clasping brother-hands, aver
   I could not, if I would, transfer
The whole I felt for him to you.

For which be they that hold apart
   The promise of the golden hours?
   First love, first friendship, equal powers,
That marry with the virgin heart.

Still mine, that cannot but deplore,
   That beats within a lonely place,   110 (1702)

That yet remembers his embrace,
But at his footstep leaps no more,

My heart, tho' widow'd, may not rest
   Quite in the love of what is gone,
   But seeks to beat in time with one
That warms another living breast.

Ah, take the imperfect gift I bring,
   Knowing the primrose yet is dear,
   The primrose of the later year,
As not unlike to that of Spring.   120 (1712)

LXXXVI

Sweet after showers, ambrosial air,
   That rollest from the gorgeous gloom
   Of evening over brake and bloom
And meadow, slowly breathing bare

The round of space, and rapt below
   Thro' all the dewy tassell'd wood,
   And shadowing down the horned flood
In ripples, fan my brows and blow

The fever from my cheek, and sigh
   The full new life that feeds thy breath   10 (1722)
   Throughout my frame, till Doubt and Death,
Ill brethren, let the fancy fly

From belt to belt of crimson seas
   On leagues of odor streaming far,
   To where in yonder orient star
A hundred spirits whisper "Peace."

LXXXVII

I past beside the reverend walls
   In which of old I wore the gown;
   I roved at random thro' the town,
And saw the tumult of the halls;

And heard once more in college fanes
   The storm their high-built organs make,
   And thunder-music, rolling, shake
The prophet blazon'd on the panes;

And caught once more the distant shout,
   The measured pulse of racing oars   10 (1738)
   Among the willows; paced the shores
And many a bridge, and all about

The same gray flats again, and felt
   The same, but not the same; and last
   Up that long walk of limes I past
To see the rooms in which he dwelt.

Another name was on the door.
   I linger'd; all within was noise
   Of songs, and clapping hands, and boys
That crash'd the glass and beat the floor;   20 (1748)

Where once we held debate, a band
   Of youthful friends, on mind and art,
   And labor, and the changing mart,
And all the framework of the land;

When one would aim an arrow fair,
   But send it slackly from the string;
   And one would pierce on outer ring,
And one an inner, here and there;

And last the master-bowman, he,
   Would cleave the mark. A willing ear   30 (1758)
   We lent him. Who but hung to hear
The rapt oration flowing free

From point to point, with power and grace
   And music in the bounds of law,
   To those conclusions when we saw
The God within him light his face,

And seem to lift the form, and glow
   In azure orbits heavenly-wise;
   And over those ethereal eyes
The bar of Michael Angelo?   40 (1768)

LXXXVIII

Wild bird, whose warble, liquid sweet,
   Rings Eden thro' the budded quicks,
   O, tell me where the senses mix,
O, tell me where the passions meet,

Whence radiate: fierce extremes employ
   Thy spirits in the darkening leaf,
   And in the midmost heart of grief
Thy passion clasps a secret joy;

And I—my harp would prelude woe—
   I cannot all command the strings;   10 (1778)
   The glory of the sum of things
Will flash along the chords and go.

LXXXIX

Witch-elms that counterchange the floor
    Of this flat lawn with dusk and bright;
    And thou, with all thy breadth and height
Of foliage, towering sycamore;

How often, hither wandering down,
    My Arthur found your shadows fair,
    And shook to all the liberal air
The dust and din and steam of town!

He brought an eye for all he saw;
    He mixt in all our simple sports;   10 (1790)
    They pleased him, fresh from brawling courts
And dusty purlieus of the law.

O joy to him in this retreat,
    Immantled in ambrosial dark,
    To drink the cooler air, and mark
The landscape winking thro' the heat!

O sound to rout the brood of cares,
    The sweep of scythe in morning dew,
    The gust that round the garden flew,
And tumbled half the mellowing pears!   20 (1800)

O bliss, when all in circle drawn
    About him, heart and ear were fed
    To hear him, as he lay and read
The Tuscan poets on the lawn!

Or in the all-golden afternoon
    A guest, or happy sister, sung,
    Or here she brought the harp and flung
A ballad to the brightening moon.

Nor less it pleased in livelier moods,
    Beyond the bounding hill to stray,   30 (1810)
    And break the livelong summer day
With banquet in the distant woods;

Whereat we glanced from theme to theme,
    Discuss'd the books to love or hate,
    Or touch'd the changes of the state,
Or threaded some Socratic dream;

But if I praised the busy town,
    He loved to rail against it still,
    For "ground in yonder social mill
We rub each other's angles down,   40 (1820)

"And merge," he said, "in form and gloss
   The picturesque of man and man."
   We talk'd: the stream beneath us ran,
The wine-flask lying couch'd in moss,

Or cool'd within the glooming wave;
   And last, returning from afar,
   Before the crimson-circled star
Had fallen into her father's grave,

And brushing ankle-deep in flowers,
   We heard behind the woodbine veil   50 (1830)
   The milk that bubbled in the pail,
And buzzings of the honeyed hours.

XC

He tasted love with half his mind,
   Nor ever drank the inviolate spring
   Where nighest heaven, who first could fling
This bitter seed among mankind:

That could the dead, whose dying eyes
   Were closed with wail, resume their life,
   They would but find in child and wife
An iron welcome when they rise.

'T was well, indeed, when warm with wine,
   To pledge them with a kindly tear,   10 (1842)
   To talk them o'er, to wish them here,
To count their memories half divine;

But if they came who past away,
   Behold their brides in other hands;
   The hard heir strides about their lands,
And will not yield them for a day.

Yea, tho' their sons were none of these,
   Not less the yet-loved sire would make
   Confusion worse than death, and shake
The pillars of domestic peace.   20 (1852)

Ah, dear, but come thou back to me!
   Whatever change the years have wrought,
   I find not yet one lonely thought
That cries against my wish for thee.

XCI

When rosy plumelets tuft the larch,
   And rarely pipes the mounted thrush,

Or underneath the barren bush
Flits by the sea-blue bird of March;

Come, wear the form by which I know
   Thy spirit in time among thy peers;
   The hope of unaccomplish'd years
Be large and lucid round thy brow.

When summer's hourly-mellowing change   **10 (1866)**
   May breathe, with many roses sweet,
   Upon the thousand waves of wheat
That ripple round the lowly grange,

Come; not in watches of the night,
   But where the sunbeam broodeth warm,
   Come, beauteous in thine after form,
And like a finer light in light.

XCII

If any vision should reveal
   Thy likeness, I might count in vain
   As but the canker of the brain;
Yea, tho' it spake and made appeal

To chances where our lots were cast
   Together in the days behind,
   I might but say, I hear a wind
Of memory murmuring the past.

Yea, tho' it spake and bared to view   **10 (1882)**
   A fact within the coming year;
   And tho' the months, revolving near,
 Should prove the phantom-warning true,

They might not seem thy prophecies,
   But spiritual presentiments,
   And such refraction of events
As often rises ere they rise.

XCIII

I shall not see thee. Dare I say
   No spirit ever brake the band
   That stays him from the native land
Where first he walk'd when claspt in clay?

No visual shade of some one lost,
   But he, the Spirit himself, may come
   Where all the nerve of sense is numb,
Spirit to Spirit, Ghost to Ghost.

O, therefore from thy sightless range
 With gods in unconjectured bliss,   10 (1898)
 O, from the distance of the abyss
Of tenfold-complicated change,

Descend, and touch, and enter; hear
 The wish too strong for words to name,
 That in this blindness of the frame
My Ghost may feel that thine is near.

XCIV

How pure at heart and sound in head,
 With what divine affections bold
 Should be the man whose thought would hold
An hour's communion with the dead.

In vain shalt thou, or any, call
 The spirits from their golden day,
 Except, like them, thou too canst say,
My spirit is at peace with all.

They haunt the silence of the breast,
 Imaginations calm and fair,   10 (1914)
 The memory like a cloudless air,
The conscience as a sea at rest;

But when the heart is full of din,
 And doubt beside the portal waits,
 They can but listen at the gates,
And hear the household jar within.

XCV

By night we linger'd on the lawn,
 For underfoot the herb was dry;
 And genial warmth; and o'er the sky
The silvery haze of summer drawn;

And calm that let the tapers burn
 Unwavering: not a cricket chirr'd;
 The brook alone far-off was heard,
And on the board the fluttering urn.

And bats went round in fragrant skies,
 And wheel'd or lit the filmy shapes   10 (1930)
 That haunt the dusk, with ermine capes
And woolly breasts and beaded eyes;

While now we sang old songs that peal'd
 From knoll to knoll, where, couch'd at ease,

The white kine glimmer'd, and the trees
Laid their dark arms about the field.

But when those others, one by one,
   Withdrew themselves from me and night,
   And in the house light after light
Went out, and I was all alone,   20 (1940)

A hunger seized my heart; I read
   Of that glad year which once had been,
   In those fallen leaves which kept their green,
The noble letters of the dead.

And strangely on the silence broke
   The silent-speaking words, and strange
   Was love's dumb cry defying change
To test his worth; and strangely spoke

The faith, the vigor, bold to dwell
   On doubts that drive the coward back,   30 (1950)
   And keen thro' wordy snares to track
Suggestion to her inmost cell.

So word by word, and line by line,
   The dead man touch'd me from the past,
   And all at once it seem'd at last
The living soul was flash'd on mine,

And mine in this was wound, and whirl'd
   About empyreal heights of thought,
   And came on that which is, and caught
The deep pulsations of the world,   40 (1960)

Æonian music measuring out
   The steps of Time—the shocks of Chance—
   The blows of Death. At length my trance
Was cancell'd, stricken thro' with doubt.

Vague words! but ah, how hard to frame
   In matter-moulded forms of speech,
   Or even for intellect to reach
Thro' memory that which I became;

Till now the doubtful dusk reveal'd
   The knolls once more where, couch'd at ease, 50 (1970)
   The white kine glimmer'd, and the trees
Laid their dark arms about the field;

And suck'd from out the distant gloom
   A breeze began to tremble o'er

The large leaves of the sycamore,
And fluctuate all the still perfume,

And gathering freshlier overhead,
   Rock'd the full-foliaged elms, and swung
   The heavy-folded rose, and flung
The lilies to and fro, and said,   60 (1980)

"The dawn, the dawn," and died away;
   And East and West, without a breath,
   Mixt their dim lights, like life and death,
To broaden into boundless day.

XCVI

You say, but with no touch of scorn,
   Sweet-hearted, you, whose light-blue eyes
   Are tender over drowning flies,
You tell me, doubt is Devil-born.

I know not: one indeed I knew
   In many a subtle question versed,
   Who touch'd a jarring lyre at first,
But ever strove to make it true;

Perplext in faith, but pure in deeds,
   At last he beat his music out.   10 (1994)
   There lives more faith in honest doubt,
Believe me, than in half the creeds.

He fought his doubts and gather'd strength,
   He would not make his judgment blind,
   He faced the spectres of the mind
And laid them; thus he came at length

To find a stronger faith his own,
   And Power was with him in the night,
   Which makes the darkness and the light,
And dwells not in the light alone,   20 (2004)

But in the darkness and the cloud,
   As over Sinaï's peaks of old,
   While Israel made their gods of gold,
Altho' the trumpet blew so loud.

XCVII

My love has talk'd with rocks and trees;
   He finds on misty mountain-ground
   His own vast shadow glory-crown'd;
He sees himself in all he sees.

Two partners of a married life—
　　I look'd on these and thought of thee
　　In vastness and in mystery,
And of my spirit as of a wife.

These two—they dwelt with eye on eye,
　　Their hearts of old have beat in tune,　　10　(2018)
　　Their meetings made December June,
Their every parting was to die.

Their love has never past away;
　　The days she never can forget
　　Are earnest that he loves her yet,
Whate'er the faithless people say.

Her life is lone, he sits apart;
　　He loves her yet, she will not weep,
　　Tho' rapt in matters dark and deep
He seems to slight her simple heart.　　20　(2028)

He thrids the labyrinth of the mind,
　　He reads the secret of the star,
　　He seems so near and yet so far,
He looks so cold: she thinks him kind.

She keeps the gift of years before,
　　A wither'd violet is her bliss;
　　She knows not what his greatness is,
For that, for all, she loves him more.

For him she plays, to him she sings
　　Of early faith and plighted vows;　　30　(2038)
　　She knows but matters of the house,
And he, he knows a thousand things.

Her faith is fixt and cannot move,
　　She darkly feels him great and wise,
　　She dwells on him with faithful eyes,
"I cannot understand; I love."

XCVIII

You leave us: you will see the Rhine,
　　And those fair hills I sail'd below,
　　When I was there with him; and go
By summer belts of wheat and vine

To where he breathed his latest breath,
　　That city. All her splendor seems
　　No livelier than the wisp that gleams
On Lethe in the eyes of Death.

Let her great Danube rolling fair
  Enwind her isles, unmark'd of me;   10 (2054)
  I have not seen, I will not see
Vienna; rather dream that there,

A treble darkness, Evil haunts
  The birth, the bridal; friend from friend
  Is oftener parted, fathers bend
Above more graves, a thousand wants

Gnarr at the heels of men, and prey
  By each cold hearth, and sadness flings
  Her shadow on the blaze of kings.
And yet myself have heard him say,   20 (2064)

That not in any mother town
  With statelier progress to and fro
  The double tides of chariots flow
By park and suburb under brown

Of lustier leaves; nor more content,
  He told me, lives in any crowd,
  When all is gay with lamps, and loud
With sport and song, in booth and tent,

Imperial halls, or open plain;
  And wheels the circled dance, and breaks   30 (2074)
  The rocket molten into flakes
Of crimson or in emerald rain.

XCIX

Risest thou thus, dim dawn, again,
  So loud with voices of the birds,
  So thick with lowings of the herds,
Day, when I lost the flower of men;

Who tremblest thro' thy darkling red
  On yon swollen brook that bubbles fast
  By meadows breathing of the past,
And woodlands holy to the dead;

Who murmurest in the foliage eaves
  A song that slights the coming care,   10 (2086)
  And Autumn laying here and there
A fiery finger on the leaves;

Who wakenest with thy balmy breath
  To myriads on the genial earth,
  Memories of bridal, or of birth,
And unto myriads more, of death.

O, wheresoever those may be,
   Betwixt the slumber of the poles,
   To-day they count as kindred souls;
They know me not, but mourn with me.   20 (2096)

C

I climb the hill: from end to end
   Of all the landscape underneath,
   I find no place that does not breathe
Some gracious memory of my friend;

No gray old grange, or lonely fold,
   Or low morass and whispering reed,
   Or simple stile from mead to mead,
Or sheepwalk up the windy wold;

Nor hoary knoll of ash and haw
   That hears the latest linnet trill,   10 (2106)
   Nor quarry trench'd along the hill
And haunted by the wrangling daw;

Nor runlet tinkling from the rock;
   Nor pastoral rivulet that swerves
   To left and right thro' meadowy curves,
That feed the mothers of the flock;

But each has pleased a kindred eye,
   And each reflects a kindlier day;
   And, leaving these, to pass away,
I think once more he seems to die.   20 (2116)

CI

Unwatch'd, the garden bough shall sway,
   The tender blossom flutter down,
   Unloved, that beech will gather brown,
This maple burn itself away;

Unloved, the sunflower, shining fair,
   Ray round with flames her disk of seed,
   And many a rose-carnation feed
With summer spice the humming air;

Unloved, by many a sandy bar,
   The brook shall babble down the plain,   10 (2126)
   At noon or when the Lesser Wain
Is twisting round the polar star;

Uncared for, gird the windy grove,
   And flood the haunts of hern and crake,

Or into silver arrows break
The sailing moon in creek and cove;

Till from the garden and the wild
   A fresh association blow,
   And year by year the landscape grow
Familiar to the stranger's child;   20 (2136)

As year by year the laborer tills
   His wonted glebe, or lops the glades,
   And year by year our memory fades
From all the circle of the hills.

CII

We leave the well-beloved place
   Where first we gazed upon the sky;
   The roofs that heard our earliest cry
Will shelter one of stranger race.

We go, but ere we go from home,
   As down the garden-walks I move,
   Two spirits of a diverse love
Contend for loving masterdom.

One whispers, "Here thy boyhood sung
   Long since its matin song, and heard   10 (2150)
   The low love-language of the bird
In native hazels tassel-hung."

The other answers, "Yea, but here
   Thy feet have stray'd in after hours
   With thy lost friend among the bowers,
And this hath made them trebly dear."

These two have striven half the day,
   And each prefers his separate claim,
   Poor rivals in a losing game,
That will not yield each other way.   20 (2160)

I turn to go; my feet are set
   To leave the pleasant fields and farms;
   They mix in one another's arms
To one pure image of regret.

CIII

On that last night before we went
   From out the doors where I was bred,
   I dream'd a vision of the dead,
Which left my after-morn content.

Methought I dwelt within a hall,
   And maidens with me; distant hills
   From hidden summits fed with rills
A river sliding by the wall.

The hall with harp and carol rang.
   They sang of what is wise and good   10 (2174)
   And graceful. In the centre stood
A statue veil'd, to which they sang;

And which, tho' veil'd, was known to me,
   The shape of him I loved, and love
   For ever. Then flew in a dove
And brought a summons from the sea;

And when they learnt that I must go,
   They wept and wail'd, but led the way
   To where a little shallop lay
At anchor in the flood below;   20 (2184)

And on by many a level mead,
   And shadowing bluff that made the banks,
   We glided winding under ranks
Of iris and the golden reed;

And still as vaster grew the shore
   And roll'd the floods in grander space,
   The maidens gather'd strength and grace
And presence, lordlier than before;

And I myself, who sat apart
   And watch'd them, wax'd in every limb;   30 (2194)
   I felt the thews of Anakim,
The pulses of a Titan's heart;

As one would sing the death of war,
   And one would chant the history
   Of that great race which is to be,
And one the shaping of a star;

Until the forward-creeping tides
   Began to foam, and we to draw
   From deep to deep, to where we saw
A great ship lift her shining sides.   40 (2204)

The man we loved was there on deck,
   But thrice as large as man he bent
   To greet us. Up the side I went,
And fell in silence on his neck;

Whereat those maidens with one mind
   Bewail'd their lot; I did them wrong:
     "We served thee here," they said, "so long,
And wilt thou leave us now behind?"

So rapt I was, they could not win
   An answer from my lips, but he   50 (2214)
     Replying, "Enter likewise ye
And go with us:" they enter'd in.

And while the wind began to sweep
   A music out of sheet and shroud,
     We steer'd her toward a crimson cloud
That landlike slept along the deep.

CIV

The time draws near the birth of Christ;
   The moon is hid, the night is still;
     A single church below the hill
Is pealing, folded in the mist.

A single peal of bells below,
   That wakens at this hour of rest
     A single murmur in the breast,
That these are not the bells I know.

Like strangers' voices here they sound,
   In lands where not a memory strays,   10 (2230)
     Nor landmark breathes of other days,
But all is new unhallow'd ground.

CV

To-night ungather'd let us leave
   This laurel, let this holly stand:
     We live within the stranger's land,
And strangely falls our Christmas-eve.

Our father's dust is left alone
   And silent under other snows:
     There in due time the woodbine blows,
The violet comes, but we are gone.

No more shall wayward grief abuse
   The genial hour with mask and mime;   10 (2242)
     For change of place, like growth of time,
Has broke the bond of dying use.

Let cares that petty shadows cast,
   By which our lives are chiefly proved,

A little spare the night I loved,
And hold it solemn to the past.

But let no footstep beat the floor,
   Nor bowl of wassail mantle warm;
   For who would keep an ancient form
Thro' which the spirit breathes no more?   20 (2252)

Be neither song, nor game, nor feast;
   Nor harp be touch'd, nor flute be blown;
   No dance, no motion, save alone
What lightens in the lucid East

Of rising worlds by yonder wood.
   Long sleeps the summer in the seed;
   Run out your measured arcs, and lead
The closing cycle rich in good.

CVI

Ring out, wild bells, to the wild sky,
   The flying cloud, the frosty light:
   The year is dying in the night;
Ring out, wild bells, and let him die.

Ring out the old, ring in the new,
   Ring, happy bells, across the snow:
   The year is going, let him go;
Ring out the false, ring in the true.

Ring out the grief that saps the mind,
   For those that here we see no more;   10 (2270)
   Ring out the feud of rich and poor,
Ring in redress to all mankind.

Ring out a slowly dying cause,
   And ancient forms of party strife;
   Ring in the nobler modes of life,
With sweeter manners, purer laws.

Ring out the want, the care, the sin,
   The faithless coldness of the times;
   Ring out, ring out my mournful rhymes,
But ring the fuller minstrel in.   20 (2280)

Ring out false pride in place and blood,
   The civic slander and the spite;
   Ring in the love of truth and right,
Ring in the common love of good.

Ring out old shapes of foul disease;
   Ring out the narrowing lust of gold;

Ring out the thousand wars of old,
Ring in the thousand years of peace.

Ring in the valiant man and free,
  The larger heart, the kindlier hand;   30 (2290)
  Ring out the darkness of the land,
Ring in the Christ that is to be.

CVII

It is the day when he was born,
  A bitter day that early sank
  Behind a purple-frosty bank
Of vapor, leaving night forlorn.

The time admits not flowers or leaves
  To deck the banquet. Fiercely flies
  The blast of North and East, and ice
Makes daggers at the sharpen'd eaves,

And bristles all the brakes and thorns
  To yon hard crescent, as she hangs   10 (2302)
  Above the wood which grides and clangs
Its leafless ribs and iron horns

Together, in the drifts that pass
  To darken on the rolling brine
  That breaks the coast. But fetch the wine,
Arrange the board and brim the glass;

Bring in great logs and let them lie,
  To make a solid core of heat;
  Be cheerful-minded, talk and treat
Of all things even as he were by;   20 (2312)

We keep the day. With festal cheer,
  With books and music, surely we
  Will drink to him, whate'er he be,
And sing the songs he loved to hear.

CVIII

I will not shut me from my kind,
  And, lest I stiffen into stone,
  I will not eat my heart alone,
Nor feed with sighs a passing wind:

What profit lies in barren faith,
  And vacant yearning, tho' with might
  To scale the heaven's highest height,
Or dive below the wells of death?

What find I in the highest place,
  But mine own phantom chanting hymns?   10 (2326)
  And on the depths of death there swims
The reflex of a human face.

I'll rather take what fruit may be
  Of sorrow under human skies:
  'T is held that sorrow makes us wise,
Whatever wisdom sleep with thee.

CIX

Heart-affluence in discursive talk
  From household fountains never dry;
  The critic clearness of an eye
That saw thro' all the Muses' walk;

Seraphic intellect and force
  To seize and throw the doubts of man;
  Impassion'd logic, which outran
The hearer in its fiery course;

High nature amorous of the good,
  But touch'd with no ascetic gloom;   10 (2342)
  And passion pure in snowy bloom
Thro' all the years of April blood;

A love of freedom rarely felt,
  Of freedom in her regal seat
  Of England; not the schoolboy heat,
The blind hysterics of the Celt;

And manhood fused with female grace
  In such a sort, the child would twine
  A trustful hand, unask'd, in thine,
And find his comfort in thy face;   20 (2352)

All these have been, and thee mine eyes
  Have look'd on: if thy look'd in vain,
  My shame is greater who remain,
Nor let thy wisdom make me wise.

CX

Thy converse drew us with delight,
  The men of rathe and riper years;
  The feeble soul, a haunt of fears,
Forgot his weakness in thy sight.

On thee the loyal-hearted hung,
  The proud was half disarm'd of pride,

Nor cared the serpent at thy side
To flicker with his double tongue.

The stern were mild when thou wert by,
    The flippant put himself to school   10 (2366)
    And heard thee, and the brazen fool
Was soften'd, and he knew not why;

While I, thy nearest, sat apart,
    And felt thy triumph was as mine;
    And loved them more, that they were thine,
The graceful tact, the Christian art;

Nor mine the sweetness or the skill,
    But mine the love that will not tire,
    And, born of love, the vague desire
That spurs an imitative will.   20 (2376)

CXI

The churl in spirit, up or down
    Along the scale of ranks, thro' all,
    To him who grasps a golden ball,
By blood a king, at heart a clown,—

The churl in spirit, howe'er he veil
    His want in forms for fashion's sake,
    Will let his coltish nature break
At seasons thro' the gilded pale;

For who can always act? but he,
    To whom a thousand memories call,   10 (2386)
    Not being less but more than all
The gentleness he seem'd to be,

Best seem'd the thing he was, and join'd
    Each office of the social hour
    To noble manners, as the flower
And native growth of noble mind;

Nor ever narrowness or spite,
    Or villain fancy fleeting by,
    Drew in the expression of an eye
Where God and Nature met in light;   20 (2396)

And thus he bore without abuse
    The grand old name of gentleman,
    Defamed by every charlatan,
And soil'd with all ignoble use.

CXII

High wisdom holds my wisdom less,
   That I, who gaze with temperate eyes
   On glorious insufficiencies,
Set light by narrower perfectness.

But thou, that fillest all the room
   Of all my love, art reason why
   I seem to cast a careless eye
On souls, the lesser lords of doom.

For what wert thou? some novel power
   Sprang up for ever at a touch,   10 (2410)
   And hope could never hope too much,
In watching thee from hour to hour,

Large elements in order brought,
   And tracts of calm from tempest made,
   And world-wide fluctuation sway'd
In vassal tides that follow'd thought.

CXIII

'T is held that sorrow makes us wise;
   Yet how much wisdom sleeps with thee
   Which not alone had guided me,
But served the seasons that may rise;

For can I doubt, who knew thee keen
   In intellect, with force and skill
   To strive, to fashion, to fulfil—
I doubt not what thou wouldst have been:

A life in civic action warm,
   A soul on highest mission sent,   10 (2426)
   A potent voice of Parliament,
A pillar steadfast in the storm,

Should licensed boldness gather force,
   Becoming, when the time has birth,
   A lever to uplift the earth
And roll it in another course,

With thousand shocks that come and go,
   With agonies, with energies,
   With overthrowings, and with cries,
And undulations to and fro.   20 (2436)

CXIV

Who loves not Knowledge? Who shall rail
   Against her beauty? May she mix

With men and prosper! Who shall fix
Her pillars? Let her work prevail.

But on her forehead sits a fire;
    She sets her forward countenance
    And leaps into the future chance,
Submitting all things to desire.

Half-grown as yet, a child, and vain—
    She cannot fight the fear of death.   10 (2446)
    What is she, cut from love and faith,
But some wild Pallas from the brain

Of demons? fiery-hot to burst
    All barriers in her onward race
    For power. Let her know her place;
She is the second, not the first.

A higher hand must make her mild,
    If all be not in vain, and guide
    Her footsteps, moving side by side
With Wisdom, like the younger child;   20 (2456)

For she is earthly of the mind,
    But Wisdom heavenly of the soul.
    O friend, who camest to thy goal
So early, leaving me behind,

I would the great world grew like thee,
    Who grewest not alone in power
    And knowledge, but by year and hour
In reverence and in charity.

CXV

Now fades the last long streak of snow,
    Now burgeons every maze of quick
    About the flowering squares, and thick
By ashen roots the violets blow.

Now rings the woodland loud and long,
    The distance takes a lovelier hue,
    And drown'd in yonder living blue
The lark becomes a sightless song.

Now dance the lights on lawn and lea,
    The flocks are whiter down the vale,   10 (2474)
    And milkier every milky sail
On winding stream or distant sea;

Where now the seamew pipes, or dives
    In yonder greening gleam, and fly

The happy birds, that change their sky
To build and brood, that live their lives

From land to land; and in my breast
   Spring wakens too, and my regret
   Becomes an April violet,
And buds and blossoms like the rest.   20 (2484)

CXVI

Is it, then, regret for buried time
   That keenlier in sweet April wakes,
   And meets the year, and gives and takes
The colors of the crescent prime?

Not all: the songs, the stirring air,
   The life re-orient out of dust,
   Cry thro' the sense to hearten trust
In that which made the world so fair.

Not all regret: the face will shine
   Upon me, while I muse alone,   10 (2494)
   And that dear voice, I once have known,
Still speak to me of me and mine.

Yet less of sorrow lives in me
   For days of happy commune dead,
   Less yearning for the friendship fled
Than some strong bond which is to be.

CXVII

O days and hours, your work is this,
   To hold me from my proper place,
   A little while from his embrace,
For fuller gain of after bliss;

That out of distance might ensue
   Desire of nearness doubly sweet,
   And unto meeting, when we meet,
Delight a hundredfold accrue,

For every grain of sand that runs,
   And every span of shade that steals,   10 (2510)
   And every kiss of toothed wheels,
And all the courses of the suns.

CXVIII

Contemplate all this work of Time,
   The giant laboring in his youth;
   Nor dream of human love and truth,
As dying Nature's earth and lime;

But trust that those we call the dead
   Are breathers of an ampler day
   For ever nobler ends. They say,
The solid earth whereon we tread

In tracts of fluent heat began,
   And grew to seeming-random forms,   10 (2522)
   The seeming prey of cyclic storms,
Till at the last arose the man;

Who throve and branch'd from clime to clime
   The herald of a higher race,
   And of himself in higher place,
If so he type this work of time

Within himself, from more to more;
   Or, crown'd with attributes of woe
   Like glories, move his course, and show
That life is not as idle ore,   20 (2532)

But iron dug from central gloom,
   And heated hot with burning fears,
   And dipt in baths of hissing tears,
And batter'd with the shocks of doom

To shape and use. Arise and fly
   The reeling Faun, the sensual feast;
   Move upward, working out the beast,
And let the ape and tiger die.

CXIX

Doors, where my heart was used to beat
   So quickly, not as one that weeps
   I come once more; the city sleeps;
I smell the meadow in the street;

I hear a chirp of birds; I see
   Betwixt the black fronts long-withdrawn
   A light-blue lane of early dawn,
And think of early days and thee,

And bless thee, for thy lips are bland,
   And bright the friendship of thine eye;   10 (2550)
   And in my thoughts with scarce a sigh
I take the pressure of thine hand.

CXX

I trust I have not wasted breath:
   I think we are not wholly brain,

Magnetic mockeries; not in vain,
Like Paul with beasts, I fought with Death;

Not only cunning casts in clay:
   Let Science prove we are, and then
   What matters Science unto men,
At least to me? I would not stay.

Let him, the wiser man who springs
   Hereafter, up from childhood shape   10 (2562)
   His action like the greater ape,
But I was *born* to other things.

CXXI

Sad Hesper o'er the buried sun
   And ready, thou, to die with him,
   Thou watchest all things ever dim
And dimmer, and a glory done.

The team is loosen'd from the wain,
   The boat is drawn upon the shore;
   Thou listenest to the closing door,
And life is darken'd in the brain.

Bright Phosphor, fresher for the night,
   By thee the world's great work is heard   10 (2574)
   Beginning, and the wakeful bird;
Behind thee comes the greater light.

The market boat is on the stream,
   And voices hail it from the brink;
   Thou hear'st the village hammer clink,
And see'st the moving of the team.

Sweet Hesper-Phosphor, double name
   For what is one, the first, the last,
   Thou, like my present and my past,
Thy place is changed; thou art the same.   20 (2584)

CXXII

O, wast thou with me, dearest, then,
   While I rose up against my doom,
   And yearn'd to burst the folded gloom,
To bare the eternal heavens again,

To feel once more, in placid awe,
   The strong imagination roll
   A sphere of stars about my soul,
In all her motion one with law?

If thou wert with me, and the grave
  Divide us not, be with me now,   10 (2594)
  And enter in at breast and brow,
Till all my blood, a fuller wave,

Be quicken'd with a livelier breath,
  And like an inconsiderate boy,
  As in the former flash of joy,
I slip the thoughts of life and death;

And all the breeze of Fancy blows,
  And every dewdrop paints a bow,
  The wizard lightnings deeply glow,
And every thought breaks out a rose.   20 (2604)

CXXIII

There rolls the deep where grew the tree.
  O earth, what changes hast thou seen!
  There where the long street roars hath been
The stillness of the central sea.

The hills are shadows, and they flow
  From form to form, and nothing stands;
  They melt like mist, the solid lands,
Like clouds they shape themselves and go.

But in my spirit will I dwell,
  And dream my dream, and hold it true;   10 (2614)
  For tho' my lips may breathe adieu,
I cannot think the thing farewell.

CXXIV

That which we dare invoke to bless;
  Our dearest faith; our ghastliest doubt;
  He, They, One, All; within, without;
The Power in darkness whom we guess,—

I found Him not in world or sun,
  Or eagle's wing, or insect's eye,
  Nor thro' the questions men may try,
The petty cobwebs we have spun.

If e'er when faith had fallen asleep,
  I heard a voice, "believe no more,"   10 (2626)
  And heard an ever-breaking shore
That tumbled in the Godless deep,

A warmth within the breast would melt
  The freezing reason's colder part,

And like a man in wrath the heart
Stood up and answer'd, "I have felt."

No, like a child in doubt and fear:
    But that blind clamor made me wise;
    Then was I as a child that cries,
But, crying, knows his father near;   20 (2636)

And what I am beheld again
    What is, and no man understands;
    And out of darkness came the hands
That reach thro' nature, moulding men.

CXXV

Whatever I have said or sung,
    Some bitter notes my harp would give,
    Yea, tho' there often seem'd to live
A contradiction on the tongue,

Yet Hope had never lost her youth,
    She did but look through dimmer eyes;
    Or Love but play'd with gracious lies,
Because he felt so fix'd in truth;

And if the song were full of care,
    He breathed the spirit of the song;   10 (2650)
    And if the words were sweet and strong
He set his royal signet there;

Abiding with me till I sail
    To seek thee on the mystic deeps,
    And this electric force, that keeps
A thousand pulses dancing, fail.

CXXVI

Love is and was my lord and king,
    And in his presence I attend
    To hear the tidings of my friend,
Which every hour his couriers bring.

Love is and was my king and lord,
    And will be, tho' as yet I keep
    Within the court on earth, and sleep
Encompass'd by his faithful guard,

And hear at times a sentinel
    Who moves about from place to place,   10 (2666)
    And whispers to the worlds of space,
In the deep night, that all is well.

CXXVII

And all is well, tho' faith and form
  Be sunder'd in the night of fear;
  Well roars the storm to those that hear
A deeper voice across the storm,

Proclaiming social truth shall spread,
  And justice, even tho' thrice again
  The red fool-fury of the Seine
Should pile her barricades with dead.

But ill for him that wears a crown,
  And him, the lazar, in his rags!   10 (2678)
  They tremble, the sustaining crags;
The spires of ice are toppled down,

And molten up, and roar in flood;
  The fortress crashes from on high,
  The brute earth lightens to the sky,
And the great Æon sinks in blood,

And compass'd by the fires of hell,
  While thou, dear spirit, happy star,
  O'erlook'st the tumult from afar,
And smilest, knowing all is well.   20 (2688)

CXXVIII

The love that rose on stronger wings,
  Unpalsied when he met with Death,
  Is comrade of the lesser faith
That sees the course of human things.

No doubt vast eddies in the flood
  Of onward time shall yet be made,
  And throned races may degrade;
Yet, O ye mysteries of good,

Wild Hours that fly with Hope and Fear,
  If all your office had to do   10 (2698)
  With old results that look like new—
If this were all your mission here,

To draw, to sheathe a useless sword,
  To fool the crowd with glorious lies,
  To cleave a creed in sects and cries,
To change the bearing of a word,

To shift an arbitrary power,
  To cramp the student at his desk,

To make old bareness picturesque
And tuft with grass a feudal tower,   20 (2708)

Why, then my scorn might well descend
    On you and yours. I see in part
    That all, as in some piece of art,
Is toil coöperant to an end.

CXXIX

Dear friend, far off, my lost desire,
    So far, so near in woe and weal,
    O loved the most, when most I feel
There is a lower and a higher;

Known and unknown, human, divine;
    Sweet human hand and lips and eye;
    Dear heavenly friend that canst not die,
Mine, mine, for ever, ever mine;

Strange friend, past, present, and to be;
    Loved deeplier, darklier understood;   10 (2722)
    Behold, I dream a dream of good,
And mingle all the world with thee.

CXXX

Thy voice is on the rolling air;
    I hear thee where the waters run;
    Thou standest in the rising sun,
And in the setting thou art fair.

What art thou then? I cannot guess;
    But tho' I seem in star and flower
    To feel thee some diffusive power,
I do not therefore love thee less.

My love involves the love before;
    My love is vaster passion now;   10 (2734)
    Tho' mix'd with God and Nature thou,
I seem to love thee more and more.

Far off thou art, but ever nigh;
    I have thee still, and I rejoice;
    I prosper, circled with thy voice;
I shall not lose thee tho' I die.

CXXXI

O living will that shalt endure
    When all that seems shall suffer shock,
    Rise in the spiritual rock,
Flow thro' our deeds and make them pure,

That we may lift from out of dust
  A voice as unto him that hears,
  A cry above the conquer'd years
To one that with us works, and trust,

With faith that comes of self-control,
  The truths that never can be proved   10 (2750)
  Until we close with all we loved,
And all we flow from, soul in soul.

O true and tried, so well and long,
  Demand not thou a marriage lay;
  In that it is thy marriage day
Is music more than any song.

Nor have I felt so much of bliss
  Since first he told me that he loved
  A daughter of our house, nor proved
Since that dark day a day like this;

Tho' I since then have number'd o'er
  Some thrice three years; they went and came, 10 (2762)
  Remade the blood and changed the frame,
And yet is love not less, but more;

No longer caring to embalm
  In dying songs a dead regret,
  But like a statue solid-set,
And moulded in colossal calm.

Regret is dead, but love is more
  Than in the summers that are flown,
  For I myself with these have grown
To something greater than before;   20 (2772)

Which makes appear the songs I made
  As echoes out of weaker times,
  As half but idle brawling rhymes,
The sport of random sun and shade.

But where is she, the bridal flower,
  That must be made a wife ere noon?
  She enters, glowing like the moon
Of Eden on its bridal bower.

On me she bends her blissful eyes
  And then on thee; they meet thy look   30 (2782)
  And brighten like the star that shook
Betwixt the palms of Paradise.

O, when her life was yet in bud,
    He too foretold the perfect rose.
    For thee she grew, for thee she grows
For ever, and as fair as good.

And thou art worthy, full of power;
    As gentle; liberal-minded, great,
    Consistent; wearing all that weight
Of learning lightly like a flower.   40 (2792)

But now set out: the noon is near,
    And I must give away the bride;
    She fears not, or with thee beside
And me behind her, will not fear.

For I that danced her on my knee,
    That watch'd her on her nurse's arm,
    That shielded all her life from harm,
At last must part with her to thee;

Now waiting to be made a wife,
    Her feet, my darling, on the dead;   50 (2802)
    Their pensive tablets round her head,
And the most living words of life

Breathed in her ear. The ring is on,
    The "Wilt thou?" answer'd, and again
    The "Wilt thou?" ask'd, till out of twain
Her sweet "I will" has made you one.

Now sign your names, which shall be read,
    Mute symbols of a joyful morn,
    By village eyes as yet unborn.
The names are sign'd, and overhead   60 (2812)

Begins the clash and clang that tells
    The joy to every wandering breeze;
    The blind wall rocks, and on the trees
The dead leaf trembles to the bells.

O happy hour, and happier hours
    Await them. Many a merry face
    Salutes them—maidens of the place,
That pelt us in the porch with flowers.

O happy hour, behold the bride
    With him to whom her hand I gave.   70 (2822)
    They leave the porch, they pass the grave
That has to-day its sunny side.

To-day the grave is bright for me,
    For them the light of life increased,
    Who stay to share the morning feast,
Who rest to-night beside the sea.

Let all my genial spirits advance
    To meet and greet a whiter sun;
    My drooping memory will not shun
The foaming grape of eastern France.   80 (2832)

It circles round, and fancy plays.
    And hearts are warm'd and faces bloom,
    As drinking health to bride and groom
We wish them store of happy days.

Nor count me all to blame if I
    Conjecture of a stiller guest,
    Perchance, perchance, among the rest,
And, tho' in silence, wishing joy.

But they must go, the time draws on,
    And those white-favor'd horses wait: 90 (2842)
    They rise, but linger; it is late;
Farewell, we kiss, and they are gone.

A shade falls on us like the dark
    From little cloudlets on the grass,
    But sweeps away as out we pass
To range the woods, to roam the park,

Discussing how their courtship grew,
    And talk of others that are wed,
    And how she look'd, and what he said,
And back we come at fall of dew.   100 (2852)

Again the feast, the speech, the glee,
    The shade of passing thought, the wealth
    Of words and wit, the double health,
The crowning cup, the three-times-three,

And last the dance;—till I retire.
    Dumb is that tower which spake so loud,
    And high in heaven the streaming cloud,
And on the downs a rising fire:

And rise, O moon, from yonder down,
    Till over down and over dale   110 (2862)
    All night the shining vapor sail
And pass the silent-lighted town,

The white-faced halls, the glancing rills,
   And catch at every mountain head.
   And o'er the friths that branch and spread
Their sleeping silver thro' the hills;

And touch with shade the bridal doors,
   With tender gloom the roof, the wall;
   And breaking let the splendor fall
To spangle all the happy shores   120 (2872)

By which they rest, and ocean sounds,
   And, star and system rolling past,
   A soul shall draw from out the vast
And strike his being into bounds,

And, moved thro' life of lower phase,
   Result in man, be born and think,
   And act and love, a closer link
Betwixt us and the crowning race

Of those that, eye to eye, shall look
   On knowledge; under whose command   130 (2882)
   Is Earth and Earth's, and in their hand
Is Nature like an open book;

No longer half-akin to brute,
   For all we thought and loved and did,
   And hoped, and suffer'd, is but seed
Of what in them is flower and fruit;

Whereof the man that with me trod
   This planet was a noble type
   Appearing ere the times were ripe,
That friend of mine who lives in God,   140 (2892)

That God, which ever lives and loves,
   One God, one law, one element,
   And one far-off divine event,
To which the whole creation moves.
1834–1849 (1850)

THE EAGLE

FRAGMENT

He clasps the crag with crooked hands;
Close to the sun in lonely lands,
Ring'd with the azure world, he stands.

The wrinkled sea beneath him crawls;
He watches from his mountain walls,
And like a thunderbolt he falls.
1851

THE CHARGE OF THE LIGHT BRIGADE

I

Half a league, half a league,
Half a league onward,
All in the valley of Death
    Rode the six hundred.
"Forward the Light Brigade!
Charge for the guns!" he said.
Into the valley of Death
    Rode the six hundred.

II

"Forward, the Light Brigade!"
Was there a man dismay'd?   10
Not tho' the soldier knew
    Some one had blunder'd.
Theirs not to make reply,
Theirs not to reason why,
Theirs but to do and die.
Into the valley of Death
    Rode the six hundred.

III

Cannon to right of them,
Cannon to left of them,
Cannon in front of them   20
    Volley'd and thunder'd;
Storm'd at with shot and shell,
Boldly they rode and well,
Into the jaws of Death,
Into the mouth of hell
    Rode the six hundred.

IV

Flash'd all their sabres bare,
Flash'd as they turn'd in air
Sabring the gunners there,
Charging an army, while   30
    All the world wonder'd.
Plunged in the battery-smoke

Right thro' the line they broke;
Cossack and Russian
Reel'd from the sabre-stroke
   Shatter'd and sunder'd.
Then they rode back, but not,
   Not the six hundred.

v

Cannon to right of them,
Cannon to left of them,   40
Cannon behind them
   Volley'd and thunder'd;
Storm'd at with shot and shell,
While horse and hero fell,
They that had fought so well
Came thro' the jaws of Death,
Back from the mouth of hell,
All that was left of them,
   Left of six hundred.

vi

When can their glory fade?   50
O the wild charge they made!
   All the world wonder'd.
Honor the charge they made!
Honor the Light Brigade,
   Noble six hundred!
1854

MAUD; A MONODRAMA

PART I

I

I

I hate the dreadful hollow behind the little wood;
Its lips in the field above are dabbled with blood-red heath,
The red-ribb'd ledges drip with a silent horror of blood,
And Echo there, whatever is ask'd her, answers "Death."

II

For there in the ghastly pit long since a body was found,
His who had given me life—O father! O God! was it well?—
Mangled, and flatten'd, and crush'd, and dinted into the ground;
There yet lies the rock that fell with him when he fell.

III

Did he fling himself down? who knows? for a vast speculation had fail'd,
And ever he mutter'd and madden'd, and ever wann'd with despair,
And out he walk'd when the wind like a broken worldling wail'd,   11
And the flying gold of the ruin'd woodlands drove thro' the air.

IV

I remember the time, for the roots of my hair were stirr'd
By a shuffled step, by a dead weight trail'd, by a whisper'd fright.
And my pulses closed their gates with a shock on my heart as I heard
The shrill-edged shriek of a mother divide the shuddering night.

V

Villainy somewhere! whose? One says, we are villains all.
Not he! his honest fame should at least by me be maintained;
But that old man, now lord of the broad estate and the Hall,   19
Dropt off gorged from a scheme that had left us flaccid and drain'd.

VI

Why do they prate of the blessings of peace? we have made them a curse,
Pickpockets, each hand lusting for all that is not its own;
And lust of gain, in the spirit of Cain, is it better or worse
Than the heart of the citizen hissing in war on his own hearthstone?

VII

But these are the days of advance, the works of the men of mind,
When who but a fool would have faith in a tradesman's ware or his
      word?
Is it peace or war? Civil war, as I think, and that of a kind
The viler, as underhand, not openly bearing the sword.

VIII

Sooner or later I too may passively take the print
Of the golden age—why not? I have neither hope nor trust;   30
May make my heart as a millstone, set my face as a flint,
Cheat and be cheated, and die—who knows? we are ashes and dust.

IX

Peace sitting under her olive, and slurring the days gone by,
When the poor are hovell'd and hustled together, each sex, like swine,
When only the ledger lives, and when only not all men lie;
Peace in her vineyard—yes!—but a company forges the wine.

X

And the vitriol madness flushes up in the ruffian's head,
Till the filthy by-lane rings to the yell of the trampled wife,
And chalk and alum and plaster are sold to the poor for bread,
And the spirit of murder works in the very means of life,   40

XI

And Sleep must lie down arm'd, for the villainous centre-bits
Grind on the wakeful ear in the hush of the moonless nights,
While another is cheating the sick of a few last gasps, as he sits
To pestle a poison'd poison behind his crimson lights.

XII

When a Mammonite mother kills her babe for a burial fee,
And Timour-Mammon grins on a pile of children's bones,
Is it peace or war? better, war! loud war by land and by sea,
War with a thousand battles, and shaking a hundred thrones!

XIII

For I trust if an enemy's fleet came yonder round by the hill,   49
And the rushing battle-bolt sang from the three-decker out of the foam,
That the smooth-faced, snub-nosed rogue would leap from his counter
        and till,
And strike, if he could, were it but with his cheating yardwand, home.

XIV

What! am I raging alone as my father raged in his mood?
Must *I* too creep to the hollow and dash myself down and die
Rather than hold by the law that I made, nevermore to brood
On a horror of shatter'd limbs and a wretched swindler's lie?

XV

Would there be sorrow for *me*? there was *love* in the passionate shriek,
Love for the silent thing that had made false haste to the grave—
Wrapt in a cloak, as I saw him, and thought he would rise and speak
And rave at the lie and the liar, ah God, as he used to rave.   60

XVI

I am sick of the Hall and the hill, I am sick of the moor and the main.
Why should I stay? can a sweeter chance ever come to me here?
O, having the nerves of motion as well as the nerves of pain,
Were it not wise if I fled from the place and the pit and the fear?

XVII

Workmen up at the Hall!—they are coming back from abroad;
The dark old place will be gilt by the touch of a millionaire
I have heard, I know not whence, of the singular beauty of Maud;
I play'd with the girl when a child; she promised then to be fair.

XVIII

Maud, with her venturous climbings and tumbles and childish escapes,
Maud, the delight of the village, the ringing joy of the Hall,   70
Maud, with her sweet purse-mouth when my father dangled the grapes,
Maud, the beloved of my mother, the moon-faced darling of all,—

XIX

What is she now? My dreams are bad. She may bring me a curse.
No, there is fatter game on the moor; she will let me alone.
Thanks; for the fiend best knows whether woman or man be the worse.
I will bury myself in myself, and the Devil may pipe to his own.

II

Long have I sigh'd for a calm; God grant I may find it at last!
It will never be broken by Maud; she has neither savor nor salt,
But a cold and clear-cut face, as I found when her carriage past,
Perfectly beautiful; let it be granted her; where is the fault?   80
All that I saw—for her eyes were downcast, not to be seen—
Faultily faultless, icily regular, splendidly null,
Dead perfection, no more; nothing more, if it had not been
For a chance of travel, a paleness, an hour's defect of the rose,
Or an underlip, you may call it a little too ripe, too full,
Or the least little delicate aquiline curve in a sensitive nose,
From which I escaped heart-free, with the least little touch of spleen.

III

Cold and clear-cut face, why come you so cruelly meek,
Breaking a slumber in which all spleenful folly was drown'd?
Pale with the golden beam of an eyelash dead on the cheek,   90
Passionless, pale, cold face, star-sweet on a gloom profound;
Womanlike, taking revenge too deep for a transient wrong
Done but in thought to your beauty, and ever as pale as before
Growing and fading and growing upon me without a sound,
Luminous, gemlike, ghostlike, deathlike, half the night long
Growing and fading and growing, till I could bear it no more,
But arose, and all by myself in my own dark garden ground,
Listening now to the tide in its broad-flung shipwrecking roar,
Now to the scream of a madden'd beach dragg'd down by the wave,
Walk'd in a wintry wind by a ghastly glimmer, and found   100
The shining daffodil dead, and Orion low in his grave.

IV

I

A million emeralds break from the ruby-budded lime
In the little grove where I sit—ah, wherefore cannot I be
Like things of the season gay, like the bountiful season bland,
When the far-off sail is blown by the breeze of a softer clime,
Half-lost in the liquid azure bloom of a crescent of sea,
The silent sapphire-spangled marriage ring of the land?

II

Below me, there, is the village, and looks how quiet and small!
And yet bubbles o'er like a city, with gossip, scandal, and spite;

And Jack on his ale-house bench has as many lies as a Czar;   110
And here on the landward side, by a red rock, glimmers the Hall;
And up in the high Hall-garden I see her pass like a light;
But sorrow seize me if ever that light be my leading star!

III

When have I bow'd to her father, the wrinkled head of the race?
I met her to-day with her brother, but not to her brother I bow'd;
I bow'd to his lady-sister as she rode by on the moor,
But the fire of a foolish pride flash'd over her beautiful face.
O child, you wrong your beauty, believe it, in being so proud;
Your father has wealth well-gotten, and I am nameless and poor.

IV

I keep but a man and a maid, ever ready to slander and steal;   120
I know it, and smile a hard-set smile, like a stoic, or like
A wiser epicurean, and let the world have its way.
For nature is one with rapine, a harm no preacher can heal;
The Mayfly is torn by the swallow, the sparrow spear'd by the shrike,
And the whole little wood where I sit is a world of plunder and prey.

V

We are puppets, Man in his pride, and Beauty fair in her flower;
Do we move ourselves, or are moved by an unseen hand at a game
That pushes us off from the board, and others ever succeed?
Ah yet, we cannot be kind to each other here for an hour;
We whisper, and hint, and chuckle, and grin at a brother's shame;   130
However we brave it out, we men are a little breed.

VI

A monstrous eft was of old the lord and master of earth,
For him did his high sun flame, and his river billowing ran,
And he felt himself in his force to be Nature's crowning race.
As nine months go to the shaping an infant ripe for his birth,
So many a million of ages have gone to the making of man:
He now is first, but is he the last? is he not too base?

VII

The man of science himself is fonder of glory, and vain,
An eye well-practised in nature, a spirit bounded and poor;
The passionate heart of the poet is whirl'd into folly and vice.   140
I would not marvel at either, but keep a temperate brain;
For not to desire or admire, if a man could learn it, were more
Than to walk all day like the sultan of old in a garden of spice.

VIII

For the drift of the Maker is dark, an Isis hid by the veil.
Who knows the ways of the world, how God will bring them about?

Our planet is one, the suns are many, the world is wide.
Shall I weep if a Poland fall? shall I shriek if a Hungary fail?
Or an infant civilization be ruled with rod or with knout?
I have not made the world, and He that made it will guide.

IX

Be mine a philosopher's life in the quiet woodland ways,   150
Where if I cannot be gay let a passionless peace be my lot,
Far-off from the clamor of liars belied in the hubbub of lies;
From the long-neck'd geese of the world that are ever hissing dispraise
Because their natures are little, and, whether he heed it or not,
Where each man walks with his head in a cloud of poisonous flies.

X

And most of all would I flee from the cruel madness of love
The honey of poison-flowers and all the measureless ill.
Ah, Maud, you milk-white fawn, you are all unmeet for a wife.
Your mother is mute in her grave as her image in marble above;
Your father is ever in London, you wander about at your will;   160
You have but fed on the roses and lain in the lilies of life.

V

I

A voice by the cedar tree
In the meadow under the Hall!
She is singing an air that is known to me,
A passionate ballad gallant and gay,
A martial song like a trumpet's call!
Singing alone in the morning of life,
In the happy morning of life and of May,
Singing of men that in battle array,
Ready in heart and ready in hand,   170
March with banner and bugle and fife
To the death, for their native land.

II

Maud with her exquisite face,
And wild voice pealing up to the sunny sky,
And feet like sunny gems on an English green,
Maud in the light of her youth and her grace,
Singing of Death, and of Honor that cannot die,
Till I well could weep for a time so sordid and mean,
And myself so languid and base.

III

Silence, beautiful voice!   180
Be still, for you only trouble the mind

With a joy in which I cannot rejoice,
A glory I shall not find.
Still! I will hear you no more,
For your sweetness hardly leaves me a choice
But to move to the meadow and fall before
Her feet on the meadow grass, and adore,
Not her, who is neither courtly nor kind,
Not her, not her, but a voice.

VI

I

Morning arises stormy and pale,
No sun, but a wannish glare
In fold upon fold of hueless cloud;
And the budded peaks of the wood, are bow'd,
Caught, and cuff'd by the gale:
I had fancied it would be fair.

190

II

Whom but Maud should I meet
Last night, when the sunset burn'd
On the blossom'd gable-ends
At the head of the village street,
Whom but Maud should I meet?
And she touch'd my hand with a smile so sweet,
She made me divine amends
For a courtesy not return'd.

200

III

And thus a delicate spark
Of glowing and growing light
Thro' the livelong hours of the dark
Kept itself warm in the heart of my dreams,
Ready to burst in a color'd flame;
Till at last, when the morning came
In a cloud, it faded, and seems
But an ashen-gray delight.

210

IV

What if with her sunny hair,
And smile as sunny as cold,
She meant to weave me a snare
Of some coquettish deceit,
Cleopatra-like as of old
To entangle me when we met,
To have her lion roll in a silken net
And fawn at a victor's feet.

V

Ah, what shall I be at fifty   220
Should Nature keep me alive,
If I find the world so bitter
When I am but twenty-five?
Yet, if she were not a cheat,
If Maud were all that she seem'd,
And her smile were all that I dream'd,
Then the world were not so bitter
But a smile could make it sweet.

VI

What if, tho' her eye seem'd full
Of a kind intent to me,   230
What if that dandy-despot, he,
That jewell'd mass of millinery,
That oil'd and curl'd Assyrian bull
Smelling of musk and of insolence,
Her brother, from whom I keep aloof,
Who wants the finer politic sense
To mask, tho' but in his own behoof,
With a glassy smile his brutal scorn—
What if he had told her yestermorn
How prettily for his own sweet sake   240
A face of tenderness might be feign'd,
And a moist mirage in desert eyes,
That so, when the rotten hustings shake
In another month to his brazen lies,
A wretched vote may be gain'd?

VII

For a raven ever croaks, at my side,
Keep watch and ward, keep watch and ward,
Or thou wilt prove their tool.
Yea, too, myself from myself I guard,
For often a man's own angry pride   250
Is cap and bells for a fool.

VIII

Perhaps the smile and tender tone
Came out of her pitying womanhood,
For am I not, am I not, here alone
So many a summer since she died,
My mother, who was so gentle and good?
Living alone in an empty house,
Here half-hid in the gleaming wood,
Where I hear the dead at midday moan,

And the shrieking rush of the wainscot mouse,   260
And my own sad name in corners cried,
When the shiver of dancing leaves is thrown
About its echoing chambers wide,
Till a morbid hate and horror have grown
Of a world in which I have hardly mixt,
And a morbid eating lichen fixt
On a heart half-turn'd to stone.

IX

O heart of stone, are you flesh, and caught
By that you swore to withstand?
For what was it else within me wrought   270
But, I fear, the new strong wine of love,
That made my tongue so stammer and trip
When I saw the treasured splendor, her hand,
Come sliding out of her sacred glove,
And the sunlight broke from her lip?

X

I have play'd with her when a child;
She remembers it now we meet.
Ah, well, well, well, I *may* be beguiled
By some coquettish deceit.
Yet, if she were not a cheat,   280
If Maud were all that she seem'd,
And her smile had all that I dream'd,
Then the world were not so bitter
But a smile could make it sweet.

VII

I

Did I hear it half in a doze
    Long since, I know not where?
Did I dream it an hour ago,
    When asleep in this arm-chair?

II

Men were drinking together,
    Drinking and talking of me: 290
"Well, if it prove a girl, the boy
    Will have plenty; so let it be."

III

Is it an echo of something
    Read with a boy's delight,
Viziers nodding together
    In some Arabian night?

IV

Strange, that I hear two men,
Somewhere, talking of me:
"Well, if it prove a girl, my boy
Will have plenty; so let it be."   300

VIII

She came to the village church,
And sat by a pillar alone;
An angel watching an urn
Wept over her, carved in stone;
And once, but once, she lifted her eyes,
And suddenly, sweetly, strangely blush'd
To find they were met by my own;
And suddenly, sweetly, my heart beat stronger
And thicker, until I heard no longer
The snowy-banded, dilettante,   310
Delicate-handed priest intone;
And thought, is it pride? and mused and sigh'd,
"No surely, now it cannot be pride."

IX

I was walking a mile,
More than a mile from the shore,
The sun look'd out with a smile
Betwixt the cloud and the moor;
And riding at set of day
Over the dark moor land,
Rapidly riding far away,   320
She waved to me with her hand.
There were two at her side,
Something flash'd in the sun,
Down by the hill I saw them ride,
In a moment they were gone;
Like a sudden spark
Struck vainly in the night,
Then returns the dark
With no more hope of light.

X

I

Sick, am I sick of a jealous dread?   330
Was not one of the two at her side
This new-made lord, whose splendor plucks
The slavish hat from the villager's head?
Whose old grandfather has lately died,
Gone to a blacker pit, for whom

Grimy nakedness dragging his trucks
And laying his trams in a poison'd gloom
Wrought, till he crept from a gutted mine
Master of half a servile shire,
And left his coal all turn'd into gold   340
To a grandson, first of his noble line,
Rich in the grace all women desire,
Strong in the power that all men adore,
And simper and set their voices lower,
And soften as if to a girl, and hold
Awe-stricken breaths at a work divine,
Seeing his gewgaw castle shine,
New as his title, built last year,
There amid perky larches and pine,
And over the sullen-purple moor—   350
Look at it—pricking a cockney ear.

II

What, has he found my jewel out?
For one of the two that rode at her side
Bound for the Hall, I am sure was he;
Bound for the Hall, and I think for a bride.
Blithe would her brother's acceptance be
Maud could be gracious too, no doubt,
To a lord, a captain, a padded shape,
A bought commission, a waxen face,
A rabbit mouth that is ever agape—   360
Bought? what is it he cannot buy?
And therefore splenetic, personal, base,
A wounded thing with a rancorous cry,
At war with myself and a wretched race,
Sick, sick to the heart of life, am I.

III

Last week came one to the county town,
To preach our poor little army down,
And play the game of the despot kings,
Tho' the state has done it and thrice as well.
This broad-brimm'd hawker of holy things,   370
Whose ear is cramm'd with his cotton, and rings
Even in dreams to the chink of his pence,
This huckster put down war! can he tell
Whether war be a cause or a consequence?
Put down the passions that make earth hell!
Down with ambition, avarice, pride,
Jealousy, down! cut off from the mind
The bitter springs of anger and fear!
Down too, down at your own fireside,

With the evil tongue and the evil ear,   380
For each is at war with mankind!

IV

I wish I could hear again
The chivalrous battle-song
That she warbled alone in her joy!
I might persuade myself then
She would not do herself this great wrong,
To take a wanton dissolute boy
For a man and leader of men.

V

Ah God, for a man with heart, head, hand,
Like some of the simple great ones gone   390
For ever and ever by,
One still strong man in a blatant land,
Whatever they call him—what care I?—
Aristocrat, democrat, autocrat—one
Who can rule and dare not lie!

VI

And ah for a man to arise in me,
That the man I am may cease to be!

XI

I

O, let the solid ground
    Not fail beneath my feet
Before my life has found   400
    What some have found so sweet!
Then let come what come may,
What matter if I go mad,
I shall have had my day.

II

Let the sweet heavens endure,
    Not close and darken above me
Before I am quite quite sure
    That there is one to love me!
Then let come what come may
To a life that has been so sad,   410
I shall have had my day.

XII

I

Birds in the high Hall-garden
    When twilight was falling,

Maud, Maud, Maud, Maud,
   They were crying and calling.

II

Where was Maud? in our wood;
   And I—who else?—was with her,
Gathering woodland lilies,
   Myriads blow together.

III

Birds in our wood sang   420
   Ringing thro' the valleys,
Maud is here, here, here
   In among the lilies.

IV

I kiss'd her slender hand,
   She took the kiss sedately;
Maud is not seventeen,
   But she is tall and stately.

V

I to cry out on pride.
   Who have won her favor!
O, Maud were sure of heaven   430
   If lowliness could save her!

VI

I know the way she went
   Home with her maiden posy,
For her feet have touch'd the meadows
   And left the daisies rosy.

VII

Birds in the high Hall-garden
   Were crying and calling to her,
Where is Maud, Maud, Maud?
   One is come to woo her.

VIII

Look, a horse at the door,   440
   And little King Charley snarling!
Go back, my lord, across the moor,
   You are not her darling.

XIII

I

Scorn'd, to be scorn'd by one that I scorn,
Is that a matter to make me fret?

That a calamity hard to be borne?
Well, he may live to hate me yet.
Fool that I am to be vext with his pride!
I past him, I was crossing his lands;
He stood on the path a little aside;   450
His face, as I grant, in spite of spite,
Has a broad-blown comeliness, red and white,
And six feet two, as I think, he stands;
But his essences turn'd the live air sick,
And barbarous opulence jewel-thick
Sunn'd itself on his breast and his hands.

II

Who shall call me ungentle, unfair?
I long'd so heartily then and there
To give him the grasp of fellowship;
But while I past he was humming an air,   460
Stopt, and then with a riding-whip
Leisurely tapping a glossy boot,
And curving a contumelious lip,
Gorgonized me from head to foot
With a stony British stare.

III

Why sits he here in his father's chair?
That old man never comes to his place;
Shall I believe him ashamed to be seen?
For only once, in the village street,
Last year, I caught a glimpse of his face,   470
A gray old wolf and a lean.
Scarcely, now, would I call him a cheat;
For then, perhaps, as a child of deceit,
She might by a true descent be untrue;
And Maud is as true as Maud is sweet,
Tho' I fancy her sweetness only due
To the sweeter blood by the other side;
Her mother has been a thing complete,
However she came to be so allied.
And fair without, faithful within,   480
Maud to him is nothing akin.
Some peculiar mystic grace
Made her only the child of her mother,
And heap'd the whole inherited sin
On that huge scapegoat of the race,
All, all upon the brother.

IV

Peace, angry spirit, and let him be!
Has not his sister smiled on me?

XIV

I

Maud has a garden of roses
And lilies fair on a lawn;   490
There she walks in her state
And tends upon bed and bower,
And thither I climb'd at dawn
And stood by her garden-gate.
A lion ramps at the top,
He is claspt by a passion-flower.

II

Maud's own little oak-room—
Which Maud, like a precious stone
Set in the heart of the carven gloom,
Lights with herself, when alone   500
She sits by her music and books
And her brother lingers late
With a roystering company—looks
Upon Maud's own garden-gate;
And I thought as I stood, if a hand, as white
As ocean-foam in the moon, were laid
On the hasp of the window, and my Delight
Had a sudden desire, like a glorious ghost, to glide,
Like a beam of the seventh heaven, down to my side,
There were but a step to be made.   510

III

The fancy flatter'd my mind,
And again seem'd overbold;
Now I thought that she cared for me,
Now I thought she was kind
Only because she was cold.

IV

I heard no sound where I stood
But the rivulet on from the lawn
Running down to my own dark wood,
Or the voice of the long sea-wave as it swell'd
Now and then in the dim-gray dawn;   520
But I look'd, and round, all round the house I beheld
The death-white curtain drawn,

Felt a horror over me creep,
Prickle my skin and catch my breath,
Knew that the death-white curtain meant but sleep,
Yet I shudder'd and thought like a fool of the sleep of death

XV

So dark a mind within me dwells,
   And I make myself such evil cheer,
That if *I* be dear to some one else,
   Then some one else may have much to fear;   530
But if *I* be dear to some one else,
   Then I should be to myself more dear.
Shall I not take care of all that I think,
Yea, even of wretched meat and drink,
If I be dear,
If I be dear to some one else?

XVI

I

This lump of earth has left his estate
The lighter by the loss of his weight;
And so that he find what he went to seek,
And fulsome pleasure clog him, and drown   540
His heart in the gross mud-honey of town,
He may stay for a year who has gone for a week.
But this is the day when I must speak,
And I see my Oread coming down,
O, this is the day!
O beautiful creature, what am I
That I dare to look her way?
Think I may hold dominion sweet,
Lord of the pulse that is lord of her breast,
And dream of her beauty with tender dread,   550
From the delicate Arab arch of her feet
To the grace that, bright and light as the crest
Of a peacock, sits on her shining head,
And she knows it not—O, if she knew it,
To know her beauty might half undo it!
I know it the one bright thing to save
My yet young life in the wilds of Time,
Perhaps from madness, perhaps from crime,
Perhaps from a selfish grave.

II

What, if she be fasten'd to this fool lord,   560
Dare I bid her abide by her word?
Should I love her so well if she

Had given her word to a thing so low?
Shall I love her as well if she
Can break her word were it even for me?
I trust that it is not so.

III

Catch not my breath, O clamorous heart,
Let not my tongue be a thrall to my eye,
For I must tell her before we part,
I must tell her, or die.   570

XVII

Go not, happy day,
    From the shining fields,
Go not, happy day,
    Till the maiden yields.
Rosy is the West,
    Rosy is the South,
Roses are her cheeks,
    And a rose her mouth
When the happy Yes
    Falters from her lips,   580
Pass and blush the news
    Over glowing ships;
Over blowing seas,
    Over seas at rest,
Pass the happy news,
    Blush it thro' the West;
Till the red man dance
    By his red cedar-tree,
And the red man's babe
    Leap, beyond the sea.   590
Blush from West to East,
    Blush from East to West,
Till the West is East,
    Blush it thro' the West.
Rosy is the West,
    Rosy is the South,
Roses are her cheeks,
    And a rose her mouth.

XVIII

I

I have led her home, my love, my only friend.
There is none like her, none.   600
And never yet so warmly ran my blood
And sweetly, on and on

Calming itself to the long-wish'd-for end,
Full to the banks, close on the promised good.

II

None like her, none.
Just now the dry-tongued laurels' pattering talk
Seem'd her light foot along the garden walk,
And shook my heart to think she comes once more.
But even then I heard her close the door;
The gates of heaven are closed, and she is gone.   610

III

There is none like her, none,
Nor will be when our summers have deceased.
O, art thou sighing for Lebanon
In the long breeze that streams to thy delicious East,
Sighing for Lebanon,
Dark cedar, tho' thy limbs have here increased,
Upon a pastoral slope as fair,
And looking to the South and fed
With honey'd rain and delicate air,
And haunted by the starry head   620
Of her whose gentle will has changed my fate,
And made my life a perfumed altar-flame;
And over whom thy darkness must have spread
With such delight as theirs of old, thy great
Forefathers of the thornless garden, there
Shadowing the snow-limb'd Eve from whom she came?

IV

Here will I lie, while these long branches sway,
And you fair stars that crown a happy day
Go in and out as if at merry play,
Who am no more so all forlorn   630
As when it seem'd far better to be born
To labor and the mattock-harden'd hand
Than nursed at ease and brought to understand
A sad astrology, the boundless plan
That makes you tyrants in your iron skies,
Innumerable, pitiless, passionless eyes,
Cold fires, yet with power to burn and brand
His nothingness into man.

V

But now shine on, and what care I,
Who in this stormy gulf have found a pearl   640
The countercharm of space and hollow sky,

And do accept my madness, and would die
To save from some slight shame one simple girl?—

VI

Would die, for sullen-seeming Death may give
More life to Love than is or ever was
In our low world, where yet 't is sweet to live.
Let no one ask me how it came to pass;
It seems that I am happy, that to me
A livelier emerald twinkles in the grass,
A purer sapphire melts into the sea. 650

VII

Not die, but live a life of truest breath,
And teach true life to fight with mortal wrongs.
O, why should Love, like men in drinking-songs,
Spice his fair banquet with the dust of death?
Make answer, Maud my bliss,
Maud made my Maud by that long loving kiss,
Life of my life, wilt thou not answer this?
"The dusky strand of Death inwoven here
With dear Love's tie, makes Love himself more dear."

VIII

Is that enchanted moan only the swell 660
Of the long waves that roll in yonder bay?
And hark the clock within, the silver knell
Of twelve sweet hours that past in bridal white,
And died to live, long as my pulses play;
But now by this my love has closed her sight
And given false death her hand, and stolen away
To dreamful wastes where footless fancies dwell
Among the fragments of the golden day.
May nothing there her maiden grace affright!
Dear heart, I feel with thee the drowsy spell. 670
My bride to be, my evermore delight,
My own heart's heart, my ownest own, farewell;
It is but for a little space I go.
And ye meanwhile far over moor and fell
Beat to the noiseless music of the night!
Has our whole earth gone nearer to the glow
Of your soft splendors that you look so bright?
I have climb'd nearer out of lonely hell.
Beat, happy stars, timing with things below,
Beat with my heart more blest than heart can tell, 680
Blest, but for some dark undercurrent woe
That seems to draw—but it shall not be so;
Let all be well, be well.

XIX

I

Her brother is coming back to-night,
Breaking up my dream of delight.

II

My dream? do I dream of bliss?
I have walk'd awake with Truth.
O, when did a morning shine
So rich in atonement as this
For my dark-dawning youth,   690
Darken'd watching a mother decline
And that dead man at her heart and mine;
For who was left to watch her but I?
Yet so did I let my freshness die.

III

I trust that I did not talk
To gentle Maud in our walk
For often in lonely wanderings
I have cursed him even to lifeless things—
But I trust that I did not talk,
Not touch on her father's sin.   700
I am sure I did but speak
Of my mother's faded cheek
When it slowly grew so thin
That I felt she was slowly dying
Vext with lawyers and harass'd with debt;
For how often I caught her with eyes all wet,
Shaking her head at her son and sighing
A world of trouble within!

IV

And Maud too, Maud was moved
To speak of the mother she loved   710
As one scarce less forlorn,
Dying abroad and it seems apart
From him who had ceased to share her heart,
And ever mourning over the feud,
The household Fury sprinkled with blood
By which our houses are torn.
How strange was what she said,
When only Maud and the brother
Hung over her dying bed—
That Maud's dark father and mine   720
Had bound us one to the other,
Betrothed us over their wine,

On the day when Maud was born;
Seal'd her mine from her first sweet breath!
Mine, mine by a right, from birth till death!
Mine, mine—our fathers have sworn!

v

But the true blood spilt had in it a heat
To dissolve the precious seal on a bond,
That, if left uncancell'd, had been so sweet;
And none of us thought of a something beyond,   730
A desire that awoke in the heart of the child,
As it were a duty done to the tomb,
To be friends for her sake, to be reconciled;
And I was cursing them and my doom,
And letting a dangerous thought run wild
While often abroad in the fragrant gloom
Of foreign churches—I see her there,
Bright English lily, breathing a prayer
To be friends, to be reconciled!

vi

But then what a flint is he!   740
Abroad, at Florence, at Rome,
I find whenever she touch'd on me
This brother had laugh'd her down,
And at last, when each came home,
He had darken'd into a frown,
Chid her, and forbid her to speak
To me, her friend of the years before;
And this was what had redden'd her cheek
When I bow'd to her on the moor.

vii

Yet Maud, altho' not blind   750
To the faults of his heart and mind,
I see she cannot but love him,
And says he is rough but kind,
And wishes me to approve him,
And tells me, when she lay
Sick once, with a fear of worse,
That he left his wine and horses and play,
Sat with her, read to her, night and day,
And tended her like a nurse.

viii

Kind? but the death-bed desire   760
Spurn'd by this heir of the liar—
Rough but kind? yet I know

He has plotted against me in this,
That he plots against me still.
Kind to Maud? that were not amiss.
Well, rough but kind; why, let it be so,
For shall not Maud have her will?

IX

For, Maud, so tender and true,
As long as my life endures
I feel I shall owe you a debt   770
That I never can hope to pay;
And if ever I should forget
That I owe this debt to you
And for your sweet sake to yours,
O, then, what then shall I say?—
If ever I *should* forget,
May God make me more wretched
Than ever I have been yet!

X

So now I have sworn to bury
All this dead body of hate,   780
I feel so free and so clear
By the loss of that dead weight,
That I should grow light-headed, I fear,
Fantastically merry,
But that her brother comes, like a blight
On my fresh hope, to the Hall to-night.

XX

I

Strange, that I felt so gay,
Strange, that I tried to-day
To beguile her melancholy;
The Sultan, as we name him—   790
She did not wish to blame him—
But he vext her and perplext her
With his worldly talk and folly.
Was it gentle to reprove her
For stealing out of view
From a little lazy lover
Who but claims her as his due?
Or for chilling his caresses
By the coldness of her manners,
Nay, the plainness of her dresses?   800
Now I know her but in two,
Nor can pronounce upon it

If one should ask me whether
The habit, hat, and feather,
Or the frock and gipsy bonnet
Be the neater and completer;
For nothing can be sweeter
Than maiden Maud in either.

II

But to-morrow, if we live,
Our ponderous squire will give   810
A grand political dinner
To half the squirelings near;
And Maud will wear her jewels,
And the bird of prey will hover,
And the titmouse hope to win her
With his chirrup at her ear.

III

A grand political dinner
To the men of many acres,
A gathering of the Tory,
A dinner and then a dance   820
For the maids and marriage-makers,
And every eye but mine will glance
At Maud in all her glory.

IV

For I am not invited,
But, with the Sultan's pardon,
I am all as well delighted,
For I know her own rose-garden,
And mean to linger in it
Till the dancing will be over;
And then, O, then, come out to me   830
For a minute, but for a minute,
Come out to your own true lover,
That your true lover may see
Your glory also, and render
All homage to his own darling,
Queen Maud in all her splendor.

XXI

Rivulet crossing my ground,
And bringing me down from the Hall
This garden-rose that I found,
Forgetful of Maud and me,   840
And lost in trouble and moving round
Here at the head of a tinkling fall,

And trying to pass to the sea;
O rivulet, born at the Hall,
My Maud has sent it by thee—
If I read her sweet will right—
On a blushing mission to me,
Saying in odor and color, "Ah, be
Among the roses to-night."

XXII

I

Come into the garden, Maud,   850
    For the black bat, night, has flown,
Come into the garden, Maud,
    I am here at the gate alone;
And the woodbine spices are wafted abroad,
    And the musk of the rose is blown.

II

For a breeze of morning moves,
    And the planet of Love is on high,
Beginning to faint in the light that she loves
    On a bed of daffodil sky,
To faint in the light of the sun she loves,   860
    To faint in his light, and to die.

III

All night have the roses heard
    The flute, violin, bassoon;
All night has the casement jessamine stirr'd
    To the dancers dancing in tune;
Till a silence fell with the waking bird,
    And a hush with the setting moon.

IV

I said to the lily, "There is but one,
    With whom she has heart to be gay.
When will the dancers leave her alone?   870
    She is weary of dance and play."
Now half to the setting moon are gone,
    And half to the rising day;
Low on the sand and loud on the stone
    The last wheel echoes away.

V

I said to the rose, "The brief night goes
    In babble and revel and wine.
O young lord-lover, what sighs are those,

For one that will never be thine?
But mine, but mine," so I sware to the rose,   880
   "For ever and ever, mine."

VI

And the soul of the rose went into my blood,
   As the music clash'd in the hall;
And long by the garden lake I stood,
   For I heard your rivulet fall
From the lake to the meadow and on to the wood,
   Our wood, that is dearer than all;

VII

From the meadow your walks have left so sweet
   That whenever a March-wind sighs
He sets the jewel-print of your feet   890
   In violets blue as your eyes,
To the woody hollows in which we meet
   And the valleys of Paradise.

VIII

The slender acacia would not shake
   One long milk-bloom on the tree;
The white lake-blossom fell into the lake
   As the pimpernel dozed on the lea;
But the rose was awake all night for your sake,
   Knowing your promise to me;
The lilies and roses were all awake,   900
   They sigh'd for the dawn and thee.

IX

Queen rose of the rosebud garden of girls,
   Come hither, the dances are done,
In gloss of satin and glimmer of pearls,
   Queen lily and rose in one;
Shine out, little head, sunning over with curls,
   To the flowers, and be their sun.

X

There has fallen a splendid tear
   From the passion-flower at the gate.
She is coming, my dove, my dear;   910
   She is coming, my life, my fate.
The red rose cries, "She is near, she is near;"
   And the white rose weeps, "She is late;"
The larkspur listens, "I hear, I hear;"
   And the lily whispers, "I wait."

XI

She is coming, my own, my sweet;
    Were it ever so airy a tread,
My heart would hear her and beat,
    Were it earth in an earthy bed;
My dust would hear her and beat,   920
    Had I lain for a century dead,
Would start and tremble under her feet,
    And blossom in purple and red.

PART II

I

I

"The fault was mine, the fault was mine"—
Why am I sitting here so stunn'd and still,
Plucking the harmless wild-flower on the hill?—
It is this guilty hand!—
And there rises ever a passionate cry
From underneath in the darkening land—
What is it, that has been done?
O dawn of Eden bright over earth and sky,
The fires of hell brake out of thy rising sun,
The fires of hell and of hate;   10
For she, sweet soul, had hardly spoken a word,
When her brother ran in his rage to the gate,
He came with the babe-faced lord,
Heap'd on her terms of disgrace;
And while she wept, and I strove to be cool,
He fiercely gave me the lie,
Till I with as fierce an anger spoke,
And he struck me, madman, over the face,
Struck me before the languid fool,
Who was gaping and grinning by;   20
Struck for himself an evil stroke,
Wrought for his house an irredeemable woe.
For front to front in an hour we stood,
And a million horrible bellowing echoes broke
From the red-ribb'd hollow behind the wood,
And thunder'd up into heaven the Christless code
That must have life for a blow.
Ever and ever afresh they seem'd to grow.
Was it he lay there with a fading eye?
"The fault was mine," he whisper'd, "fly!"   30
Then glided out of the joyous wood
The ghastly Wraith of one that I know,
And there rang on a sudden a passionate cry,

A cry for a brother's blood;
It will ring in my heart and my ears, till I die, till I die.

II

Is it gone? my pulses beat—
What was it? a lying trick of the brain?
Yet I thought I saw her stand,
A shadow there at my feet,
High over the shadowy land.   40
It is gone; and the heavens fall in a gentle rain,
When they should burst and drown with deluging storms
The feeble vassals of wine and anger and lust,
The little hearts that know not how to forgive.
Arise, my God, and strike, for we hold Thee just,
Strike dead the whole weak race of venomous worms,
That sting each other here in the dust;
We are not worthy to live.

II

I

See what a lovely shell,
Small and pure as a pearl,   50
Lying close to my foot,
Frail, but a work divine,
Made so fairly well
With delicate spire and whorl,
How exquisitely minute,
A miracle of design!

II

What is it? a learned man
Could give it a clumsy name.
Let him name it who can,
The beauty would be the same.   60

III

The tiny cell is forlorn,
Void of the little living will
That made it stir on the shore.
Did he stand at the diamond door
Of his house in a rainbow frill?
Did he push, when he was uncurl'd,
A golden foot or a fairy horn
Thro' his dim water-world?

IV

Slight, to be crush'd with a tap
Of my finger-nail on the sand,   70

Small, but a work divine,
Frail, but of force to withstand,
Year upon year, the shock
Of cataract seas that snap
The three-decker's oaken spine
Athwart the ledges of rock,
Here on the Breton strand!

V

Breton, not Briton; here
Like a shipwreck'd man on a coast
Of ancient fable and fear—   80
Plagued with a flitting to and fro,
A disease, a hard mechanic ghost
That never came from on high
Nor ever arose from below,
But only moves with the moving eye,
Flying along the land and the main—
Why should it look like Maud?
Am I to be overawed
By what I cannot but know
'Is a juggle born of the brain?   90

VI

Back from the Breton coast,
Sick of a nameless fear,
Back to the dark sea-line
Looking, thinking of all I have lost;
An old song vexes my ear,
But that of Lamech is mine.

VII

For years, a measureless ill,
For years, for ever, to part—
But she, she would love me still;
And as long, O God, as she   100
Have a grain of love for me,
So long, no doubt, no doubt,
Shall I nurse in my dark heart,
However weary, a spark of will
Not to be trampled out.

VIII

Strange, that the mind, when fraught
With a passion so intense
One would think that it well
Might drown all life in the eye,—
'That it should, by being so overwrought,   110

Suddenly strike on a sharper sense
For a shell, or a flower, little things
Which else would have been past by!
And now I remember, I,
When he lay dying there,
I noticed one of his many rings—
For he had many, poor worm—and thought,
It is his mother's hair.

IX

Who knows if he be dead?
Whether I need have fled?   120
Am I guilty of blood?
However this may be,
Comfort her, comfort her, all things good,
While I am over the sea!
Let me and my passionate love go by,
But speak to her all things holy and high,
Whatever happen to me!
Me and my harmful love go by;
But come to her waking, find her asleep,
Powers of the height, Powers of the deep,   130
And comfort her tho' I die!

III

Courage, poor heart of stone!
I will not ask thee why
Thou canst not understand
That thou art left for ever alone;
Courage, poor stupid heart of stone!—
Or if I ask thee why,
Care not thou to reply:
She is but dead, and the time is at hand   140
When thou shalt more than die.

IV

I

O that 't were possible
After long grief and pain
To find the arms of my true love
Round me once again!

II

When I was wont to meet her
In the silent woody places
By the home that gave me birth,
We stood tranced in long embraces

Mixt with kisses sweeter, sweeter
Than anything on earth.   150

III

A shadow flits before me,
Not thou, but like to thee.
Ah, Christ, that it were possible
For one short hour to see
The souls we loved, that they might tell us
What and where they be!

IV

It leads me forth at evening,
It lightly winds and steals
In a cold white robe before me,
When all my spirit reels   160
At the shouts, the leagues of lights,
And the roaring of the wheels.

V

Half the night I waste in sighs,
Half in dreams I sorrow after
The delight of early skies;
In a wakeful doze I sorrow
For the hand, the lips, the eyes,
For the meeting of the morrow,
The delight of happy laughter,
The delight of low replies.   170

VI

'T is a morning pure and sweet,
And a dewy splendor falls
On the little flower that clings
To the turrets and the walls;
'T is a morning pure and sweet,
And the light and shadow fleet.
She is walking in the meadow,
And the woodland echo rings;
In a moment we shall meet.
She is singing in the meadow,   180
And the rivulet at her feet
Ripples on in light and shadow
To the ballad that she sings.

VII

Do I hear her sing as of old,
My bird with the shining head,
My own dove with the tender eye?

But there rings on a sudden a passionate cry,
There is some one dying or dead,
And a sullen thunder is roll'd;
For a tumult shakes the city,   190
And I wake, my dream is fled.
In the shuddering dawn, behold,
Without knowledge, without pity,
By the curtains of my bed
That abiding phantom cold!

VIII

Get thee hence, nor come again,
Mix not memory with doubt,
Pass, thou deathlike type of pain,
Pass and cease to move about!
'T is the blot upon the brain   200
That *will* show itself without.

IX

Then I rise, the eave-drops fall,
And the yellow vapors choke
The great city sounding wide;
The day comes, a dull red ball
Wrapt in drifts of lurid smoke
On the misty river-tide.

X

Thro' the hubbub of the market
I steal, a wasted frame;
It crosses here, it crosses there,   210
Thro' all that crowd confused and loud,
The shadow still the same;
And on my heavy eyelids
My anguish hangs like shame.

XI

Alas for her that met me,
That heard me softly call,
Came glimmering thro' the laurels
At the quiet evenfall,
In the garden by the turrets
Of the old manorial hall!   220

XII

Would the happy spirit descend
From the realms of light and song,
In the chamber or the street,
As she looks among the blest,

Should I fear to greet my friend
Or to say "Forgive the wrong,"
Or to ask her, "Take me, sweet,
To the regions of thy rest"?

XIII

But the broad light glares and beats,
And the shadow flits and fleets   230
And will not let me be;
And I loathe the squares and streets,
And the faces that one meets,
Hearts with no love for me.
Always I long to creep
Into some still cavern deep,
There to weep, and weep, and weep
My whole soul out to thee.

V

I

Dead, long dead,
Long dead!   240
And my heart is a handful of dust,
And the wheels go over my head,
And my bones are shaken with pain,
For into a shallow grave they are thrust,
Only a yard beneath the street,
And the hoofs of the horses beat, beat,
The hoofs of the horses beat,
Beat into my scalp and my brain,
With never an end to the stream of passing feet,
Driving, hurrying, marrying, burying,   250
Clamor and rumble, and ringing and clatter;
And here beneath it is all as bad,
For I thought the dead had peace, but it is not so.
To have no peace in the grave, is that not sad?
But up and down and to and fro,
Ever about me the dead men go;
And then to hear a dead man chatter
Is enough to drive one mad.

II

Wretchedest age, since Time began,
They cannot even bury a man;   260
And tho' we paid our tithes in the days that are gone,
Not a bell was rung, not a prayer was read.
It is that which makes us loud in the world of the dead;
There is none that does his work, not one.

A touch of their office might have sufficed,
But the churchmen fain would kill their church,
As the churches have kill'd their Christ.

III

See, there is one of us sobbing,
No limit to his distress;
And another, a lord of all things, praying   270
To his own great self, as I guess;
And another, a statesman there, betraying
His party-secret, fool, to the press;
And yonder a vile physician, blabbing
The case of his patient—all for what?
To tickle the maggot born in an empty head,
And wheedle a world that loves him not,
For it is but a world of the dead.

IV

Nothing but idiot gabble!
For the prophecy given of old   280
And then not understood,
Has come to pass as foretold;
Not let any man think for the public good,
But babble, merely for babble.
For I never whisper'd a private affair
Within the hearing of cat or mouse,
No, not to myself in the closet alone,
But I heard it shouted at once from the top of the house;
Everything came to be known.
Who told *him* we were there?   290

V

Not that gray old wolf, for he came not back
From the wilderness, full of wolves, where he used to lie;
He has gather'd the bones for his o'ergrown whelp to crack—
Crack them now for yourself, and howl, and die.

VI

Prophet, curse me the blabbing lip,
And curse me the British vermin, the rat;
I know not whether he came in the Hanover ship,
But I know that he lies and listens mute
In an ancient mansion's crannies and holes.
Arsenic, arsenic, sure, would do it,   300
Except that now we poison our babes, poor souls!
It is all used up for that.

VII

Tell him now: she is standing here at my head;
Not beautiful now, not even kind;
He may take her now; for she never speaks her mind,
But is ever the one thing silent here.
She is not *of* us, as I divine;
She comes from another stiller world of the dead,
Stiller, not fairer than mine.

VIII

But I know where a garden grows,   310
Fairer than aught in the world beside,
All made up of the lily and rose
That blow by night, when the season is good,
To the sound of dancing music and flutes:
It is only flowers, they had no fruits,
And I almost fear they are not roses, but blood;
For the keeper was one, so full of pride,
He linkt a dead man there to a spectral bride;
For he, if he had not been a Sultan of brutes,
Would he have that hole in his side?   320

IX

But what will the old man say?
He laid a cruel snare in a pit
To catch a friend of mine one stormy day;
Yet now I could even weep to think of it;
For what will the old man say
When he comes to the second corpse in the pit?

X

Friend, to be struck by the public foe,
Then to strike him and lay him low,
That were a public merit, far,
Whatever the Quaker holds, from sin;   330
But the red life spilt for a private blow—
I swear to you, lawful and lawless war
Are scarcely even akin.

XI

O me, why have they not buried me deep enough?
Is it kind to have made me a grave so rough,
Me, that was never a quiet sleeper?
Maybe still I am but half-dead;
Then I cannot be wholly dumb.
I will cry to the steps above my head
And somebody, surely, some kind heart will come   340

To bury me, bury me
Deeper, ever so little deeper.

PART III

I

My life has crept so long on a broken wing
Thro' cells of madness, haunts of horror and fear,
That I come to be grateful at last for a little thing.
My mood is changed, for it fell at a time of year
When the face of night is fair on the dewy downs,
And the shining daffodil dies, and the Charioteer
And starry Gemini hang like glorious crowns
Over Orion's grave low down in the west,
That like a silent lightning under the stars
She seem'd to divide in a dream from a band of the blest,   10
And spoke of a hope for the world in the coming wars—
"And in that hope, dear soul, let trouble have rest,
Knowing I tarry for thee," and pointed to Mars
As he glow'd like a ruddy shield on the Lion's breast.

II

And it was but a dream, yet it yielded a dear delight
To have look'd tho' but in a dream, upon eyes so fair,
That had been in a weary world my one thing bright;
And it was but a dream, yet it lighten'd my despair
When I thought that a war would arise in defence of the right,
That an iron tyranny now should bend or cease,   20
The glory of manhood stand on his ancient height,
Nor Britain's one sole God be the millionaire.
No more shall commerce be all in all, and Peace
Pipe on her pastoral hillock a languid note,
And watch her harvest ripen, her herd increase,
Nor the cannon-bullet rust on a slothful shore,
And the cobweb woven across the cannon's throat
Shall shake its threaded tears in the wind no more.

III

And as months ran on and rumor of battle grew,
"It is time, it is time, O passionate heart," said I,—   30
For I cleaved to a cause that I felt to be pure and true,—
"It is time, O passionate heart and morbid eye,
That old hysterical mock-disease should die."
And I stood on a giant deck and mixt my breath
With a loyal people shouting a battlecry,
Till I saw the dreary phantom arise and fly
Far into the North, and battle, and seas of death.

IV

Let it go or stay, so I wake to the higher aims
Of a land that has lost for a little her lust of gold,
And love of a peace that was full of wrongs and shames,   40
Horrible, hateful, monstrous, not to be told;
And hail once more to the banner of battle unroll'd!
Tho' many a light shall darken, and many shall weep
For those that are crush'd in the clash of jarring claims
Yet God's just wrath shall be wreak'd on a giant liar,
And many a darkness into the light shall leap,
And shine in the sudden making of splendid names,
And noble thought be freer under the sun,
And the heart of a people beat with one desire;
For the peace, that I deem'd no peace, is over and done,   50
And now by the side of the Black and the Baltic deep,
And deathful-grinning mouths of the fortress, flames
The blood-red blossom of war with a heart of fire.

V

Let it flame or fade, and the war roll down like a wind,
We have proved we have hearts in a cause, we are noble still,
And myself have awaked, as it seems, to the better mind.
It is better to fight for the good than to rail at the ill;
I have felt with my native land, I am one with my kind,
I embrace the purpose of God, and the doom assign'd.
1855, 1856

LUCRETIUS

Lucilia, wedded to Lucretius, found
Her master cold; for when the morning flush
Of passion and the first embrace had died
Between them, tho' he loved her none the less,
Yet often when the woman heard his foot
Return from pacings in the field, and ran
To greet him with a kiss, the master took
Small notice, or austerely, for—his mind
Half buried in some weightier argument,
Or fancy-borne perhaps upon the rise   10
And long roll of the hexameter—he past
To turn and ponder those three hundred scrolls
Left by the Teacher, whom he held divine.
She brook'd it not, but wrathful, petulant,
Dreaming some rival, sought and found a witch
Who brew'd the philtre which had power, they said,

To lead an errant passion home again.
And this, at times, she mingled with his drink,
And this destroy'd him; for the wicked broth
Confused the chemic labor of the blood,   20
And tickling the brute brain within the man's
Made havoc among those tender cells, and check'd
His power to shape. He loathed himself, and once
After a tempest woke upon a morn
That mock'd him with returning calm, and cried:

   "Storm in the night! for thrice I heard the rain
Rushing; and once the flesh of a thunderbolt—
Methought I never saw so fierce a fork—
Struck out the streaming mountain-side, and show'd
A riotous confluence of watercourses   30
Blanching and billowing in a hollow of it,
Where all but yester-eve was dusty-dry.

   "Storm, and what dreams, ye holy Gods, what dreams!
For thrice I waken'd after dreams. Perchance
We do but recollect the dreams that come
Just ere the waking. Terrible: for it seem'd
A void was made in Nature; all her bonds
Crack'd; and I saw the flaring atom-streams
And torrents of her myriad universe,
Ruining along the illimitable inane,   40
Fly on to clash together again, and make
Another and another frame of things
For ever. That was mine, my dream, I knew it—
Of and belonging to me, as the dog
With inward yelp and restless forefoot plies
His function of the woodland; but the next!
I thought that all the blood by Sylla shed
Came driving rainlike down again on earth,
And where it dash'd the reddening meadow, sprang
No dragon warriors from Cadmean teeth,   50
For these I thought my dream would show to me,
But girls, Hetairai, curious in their art,
Hired animalisms, vile as those that made
The mulberry-faced Dictator's orgies worse
Than aught they fable of the quiet Gods.
And hands they mixt, and yell'd and round me drove
In narrowing circles till I yell'd again
Half-suffocated, and sprang up, and saw—
Was it the first beam of my latest day?

   "Then, then, from utter gloom stood out the breasts,   60
The breasts of Helen, and hoveringly a sword

Now over and now under, now direct,
Pointed itself to pierce, but sank down shamed
At all that beauty; and as I stared, a fire,
The fire that left a roofless Ilion,
Shot out of them, and scorch'd me that I woke.

"Is this thy vengeance, holy Venus, thine,
Because I would not one of thine own doves,
Not even a rose, were offer'd to thee? thine,
Forgetful how my rich procemion makes   70
Thy glory fly along the Italian field,
In lays that will outlast thy deity?

"Deity? nay, thy worshippers. My tongue
Trips, or I speak profanely. Which of these
Angers thee most, or angers thee at all?
Not if thou be'st of those who, far aloof
From envy, hate and pity, and spite and scorn,
Live the great life which all our greatest fain
Would follow, centred in eternal calm.

"Nay, if thou canst, O Goddess, like ourselves   80
Touch, and be touch'd, then would I cry to thee
To kiss thy Mavors, roll thy tender arms
Round him, and keep him from the lust of blood
That makes a steaming slaughter-house of Rome.

"Ay, but I meant not thee; I meant not her
Whom all the pines of Ida shook to see
Slide from that quiet heaven of hers, and tempt
The Trojan, while his neatherds were abroad;
Nor her that o'er her wounded hunter wept
Her deity false in human-amorous tears;   90
Nor whom her beardless apple-arbiter
Decided fairest. Rather, O ye Gods,
Poet-like, as the great Sicilian called
Calliope to grace his golden verse—
Ay, and this Kypris also—did I take
That popular name of thine to shadow forth
The all-generating powers and genial heat
Of Nature, when she strikes thro' the thick blood
Of cattle, and light is large, and lambs are glad
Nosing the mother's udder, and the bird   100
Makes his heart voice amid the blaze of flowers;
Which things appear the work of mighty Gods.

"The Gods! and if I go *my* work is left
Unfinish'd—*if* I go. The Gods, who haunt
The lucid interspace of world and world,

Where never creeps a cloud, or moves a wind,
Nor ever falls the least white star of snow,
Nor ever lowest roll of thunder moans,
Nor sound of human sorrow mounts to mar
Their sacred everlasting calm! and such,   110
Not all so fine, nor so divine a calm,
Not such, nor all unlike it, man may gain
Letting his own life go. The Gods, the Gods!
If all be atoms, how then should the Gods
Being atomic not be dissoluble,
Not follow the great law? My master held
That Gods there are, for all men so believe.
I prest my footsteps into his, and meant
Surely to lead my Memmius in a train
Of flowery clauses onward to the proof   120
That Gods there are, and deathless. Meant? I meant?
I have forgotten what I meant; my mind
Stumbles, and all my faculties are lamed.

  "Look where another of our Gods, the Sun,
Apollo, Delius, or of older use
All-seeing Hyperion—what you will—
Has mounted yonder; since he never sware,
Except his wrath were wreak'd on wretched man,
That he would only shine among the dead
Hereafter—tales! for never yet on earth   130
Could dead flesh creep, or bits of roasting ox
Moan round the spit—nor knows he what he sees;
King of the East altho' he seem, and girt
With song and flame and fragrance, slowly lifts
His golden feet on those empurpled stairs
That climb into the windy halls of heaven
And here he glances on an eye new-born,
And gets for greeting but a wail of pain;
And here he stays upon a freezing orb
That fain would gaze upon him to the last;   140
And here upon a yellow eyelid fallen
And closed by those who mourn a friend in vain,
Not thankful that his troubles are no more.
And me, altho' his fire is on my face
Blinding, he sees not, nor at all can tell
Whether I mean this day to end myself.
Or lend an ear to Plato where he says,
That men like soldiers may not quit the post
Allotted by the Gods. But he that holds
The Gods are careless, wherefore need he care   150
Greatly for them, nor rather plunge at once,

Being troubled, wholly out of sight, and sink
Past earthquake—ay, and gout and stone, that break
Body toward death, and palsy, death-in-life,
And wretched age—and worst disease of all,
These prodigies of myriad nakednesses,
And twisted shapes of lust, unspeakable,
Abominable, strangers at my hearth
Not welcome, harpies miring every dish,
The phantom husks of something foully done,⁣   160
And fleeting thro' the boundless universe,
And blasting the long quiet of my breast
With animal heat and dire insanity?

"How should the mind, except it loved them, clasp
These idols to herself? or do they fly
Now thinner, and now thicker, like the flakes
In a fall of snow, and so press in, perforce
Of multitude, as crowds that in an hour
Of civic tumult jam the doors, and bear
The keepers down, and throng, their rags and they   170
The basest, far into that council-hall
Where sit the best and stateliest of the land?

"Can I not fling this horror off me again,
Seeing with how great ease Nature can smile,
Balmier and nobler from her bath of storm,
At random ravage? and how easily
The mountain there has cast his cloudy slough,
Now towering o'er him in serenest air,
A mountain o'er a mountain,—ay, and within
All hollow as the hopes and fears of men?   180

"But who was he that in the garden snared
Picus and Faunus, rustic Gods? a tale
To laugh at—more to laugh at in myself—
For look! what is it? there? yon arbutus
Totters; a noiseless riot underneath
Strikes through the wood, sets all the tops quivering—
The mountain quickens into Nymph and Faun,
And here an Oread—how the sun delights
To glance and shift about her slippery sides,
And rosy knees and supple roundedness,   190
And budded bosom-peaks—who this way runs
Before the rest!—a satyr, a satyr, see,
Follows; but him I proved impossible;
Twy-natured is no nature. Yet he draws
Nearer and nearer, and I scan him now
Beastlier than any phantom of his kind

That ever butted his rough brother-brute
For lust or lusty blood or provender.
I hate, abhor, spit, sicken at him; and she
Loathes him as well; such a precipitate heel,   200
Fledged as it were with Mercury's ankle-wing,
Whirls her to me—but will she fling herself
Shameless upon me? Catch her, goatfoot! nay,
Hide, hide them, million-myrtled wilderness,
And cavern-shadowing laurels, hide! do I wish—
What?—that the bush were leafless? or to whelm
All of them in one massacre? O ye Gods,
I know you careless, yet, behold, to you
From childly wont and ancient use I call—
I thought I lived securely as yourselves—   210
No lewdness, narrowing envy, monkey-spite,
No madness of ambition, avarice, none;
No larger feast than under plane or pine
With neighbors laid along the grass, to take
Only such cups as left us friendly-warm,
Affirming each his own philosophy—
Nothing to mar the sober majesties
Of settled, sweet, Epicurean life.
But now it seems some unseen monster lays
His vast and filthy hands upon my will,   220
Wrenching it backward into his, and spoils
My bliss in being; and it was not great,
For save when shutting reasons up in rhythm,
Or Heliconian honey in living words,
To make a truth less harsh, I often grew
Tired of so much within our little life,
Or of so little in our little life—
Poor little life that toddles half an hour
Crown'd with a flower or two, and there an end—
And since the nobler pleasure seems to fade,   230
Why should I, beastlike as I find myself,
Not manlike end myself?—our privilege—
What beast has heart to do it? And what man,
What Roman would be dragg'd in triumph thus?
Not I; not he, who bears one name with her
Whose death-blow struck the dateless doom of kings,
When, brooking not the Tarquin in her veins,
She made her blood in sight of Collatine
And all his peers, flushing the guiltless air,
Spout from the maiden fountain in her heart.   240
And from it sprang the Commonwealth, which breaks
As I am breaking now!

"And therefore now
Let her, that is the womb and tomb of all,
Great Nature, take, and forcing far apart
Those blind beginnings that have made me man,
Dash them anew together at her will
Thro' all her cycles—into man once more,
Or beast or bird or fish, or opulent flower.
But till this cosmic order everywhere
Shatter'd into one earthquake in one day   250
Cracks all to pieces,—and that hour perhaps
Is not so far when momentary man
Shall seem no more a something to himself,
But he, his hopes and hates, his homes and fanes,
And even his bones long laid within the grave,
The very sides of the grave itself shall pass,
Vanishing, atom and void, atom and void,
Into the unseen for ever,—till that hour,
My golden work in which I told a truth
That stays the rolling Ixionian wheel,   260
And numbs the Fury's ringlet-snake, and plucks
The mortal soul from out immortal hell,
Shall stand. Ay, surely; then it fails at last
And perishes as I must; for O Thou,
Passionless bride, divine Tranquillity,
Yearn'd after by the wisest of the wise,
Who fail to find thee, being as thou art
Without one pleasure and without one pain,
Howbeit I know thou surely must be mine
Or soon or late, yet out of season, thus   270
I woo thee roughly, for thou carest not
How roughly men may woo thee so they win—
Thus—thus—the soul flies out and dies in the air."

    With that he drove the knife into his side.
She heard him raging, heard him fall, ran in,
Beat breast, tore hair, cried out upon herself
As having fail'd in duty to him, shriek'd
That she but meant to win him back, fell on him,
Clasp'd, kiss'd him, wail'd. He answer'd, "Care not thou!
Thy duty? What is duty? Fare thee well!"   280
1868

from IDYLLS OF THE KING

"Flos Regum Arthurus."—JOSEPH OF EXETER

THE COMING OF ARTHUR

Leodogran, the king of Cameliard,
Had one fair daughter, and none other child;
And she was fairest of all flesh on earth,
Guinevere, and in her his one delight.

   For many a petty king ere Arthur came
Ruled in this isle and, ever waging war
Each upon other, wasted all the land;
And still from time to time the heathen host
Swarm'd over-seas, and harried what was left.
And so there grew great tracts of wilderness,   10
Wherein the beast was ever more and more,
But man was less and less, till Arthur came.
For first Aurelius lived and fought and died,
And after him King Uther fought and died,
But either fail'd to make the kingdom one.
And after these King Arthur for a space,
And thro' the puissance of his Table Round,
Drew all their petty princedoms under him,
Their king and head, and made a realm and reign'd.

   And thus the land of Cameliard was waste,   20
Thick with wet woods, and many a beast therein,
And none or few to scare or chase the beast;
So that wild dog and wolf and boar and bear
Came night and day, and rooted in the fields,
And wallow'd in the gardens of the King.
And ever and anon the wolf would steal
The children and devour, but now and then,
Her own brood lost or dead, lent her fierce teat
To human sucklings; and the children, housed
In her foul den, there at their meat would growl,   30
And mock their foster-mother on four feet,
Till, straighten'd, they grew up to wolf-like men,
Worse than the wolves. And King Leodogran

Groan'd for the Roman legions here again
And Cæsar's eagle. Then his brother king,
Urien, assail'd him; last a heathen horde,
Reddening the sun with smoke and earth with blood,
And on the spike that split the mother's heart
Spitting the child, brake on him, till, amazed,
He knew not whither he should turn for aid.   40

But—for he heard of Arthur newly crown'd,
Tho' not without an uproar made by those
Who cried, "He is not Uther's son"—the King
Sent to him, saying, "Arise, and help us thou!
For here between the man and beast we die."

And Arthur yet had done no deed of arms,
But heard the call and came; and Guinevere
Stood by the castle walls to watch him pass;
But since he neither wore on helm or shield
The golden symbol of his kinglihood,   50
But rode a simple knight among his knights,
And many of these in richer arms than he,
She saw him not, or mark'd not, if she saw,
One among many, tho' his face was bare.
But Arthur, looking downward as he past,
Felt the light of her eyes into his life
Smite on the sudden, yet rode on, and pitch'd
His tents beside the forest. Then he drave
The heathen; after, slew the beast, and fell'd
The forest, letting in the sun, and made   60
Broad pathways for the hunter and the knight,
And so return'd.

                    For while he linger'd there,
A doubt that ever smoulder'd in the hearts
Of those great lords and barons of his realm
Flash'd forth and into war; for most of these,
Colleaguing with a score of petty kings,
Made head against him, crying: "Who is he
That he should rule us? who hath proven him
King Uther's son? for lo! we look at him,
And find nor face nor bearing, limbs nor voice,   70
Are like to those of Uther whom we knew.
This is the son of Gorloïs, not the King;
This is the son of Anton, not the King."

And Arthur, passing thence to battle, felt
Travail, and throes and agonies of the life,
Desiring to be join'd with Guinevere,

And thinking as he rode: "Her father said
That there between the man and beast they die.
Shall I not lift her from this land of beasts
Up to my throne and side by side with me?   80
What happiness to reign a lonely king,
Vext—O ye stars that shudder over me,
O earth that soundest hollow under me,
Vext with waste dreams? For saving I be join'd
To her that is the fairest under heaven,
I seem as nothing in the mighty world,
And cannot will my will nor work my work
Wholly, nor make myself in mine own realm
Victor and lord. But were I join'd with her,
Then might we live together as one life,   90
And reigning with one will in everything
Have power on this dark land to lighten it,
And power on this dead world to make it live."

    Thereafter—as he speaks who tells the tale—
When Arthur reach'd a field of battle bright
With pitch'd pavilions of his foe, the world
Was all so clear about him that he saw
The smallest rock far on the faintest hill,
And even in high day the morning star.
So when the King had set his banner broad,   100
At once from either side, with trumpet-blast,
And shouts, and clarions shrilling unto blood,
The long-lanced battle let their horses run.
And now the barons and the kings prevail'd,
And now the King, as here and there that war
Went swaying; but the Powers who walk the world
Made lightnings and great thunders over him,
And dazed all eyes, till Arthur by main might,
And mightier of his hands with every blow,
And leading all his knighthood threw the kings,   110
Carádos, Urien, Cradlemont of Wales,
Claudius, and Clariance of Northumberland,
The King Brandagoras of Latangor,
With Anguisant of Erin, Morganore,
And lot of Orkney. Then, before a voice
As dreadful as the shout of one who sees
To one who sins, and deems himself alone
And all the world asleep, they swerved and brake
Flying, and Arthur call'd to stay the brands
That hack'd among the flyers, "Ho! they yield!"   120
So like a painted battle the war stood
Silenced, the living quiet as the dead,

And in the heart of Arthur joy was lord.
He laugh'd upon his warrior whom he loved
And honor'd most. "Thou dost not doubt me King,
So well thine arm hath wrought for me today."
"Sir and my liege," he cried, "the fire of God
Descends upon thee in the battle-field.
I know thee for my King!" Whereat the two,
For each had warded either in the fight,   130
Sware on the field of death a deathless love.
And Arthur said, "Man's word is God in man;
Let chance what will, I trust thee to the death."

    Then quickly from the foughten field he sent
Ulfius, and Brastias, and Bedivere,
His new-made knights, to King Leodogran,
Saying, "If I in aught have served thee well,
Give me thy daughter Guinevere to wife."

    Whom when he heard, Leodogran in heart
Debating—"How should I that am a king,   140
However much he holp me at my need,
Give my one daughter saving to a king,
And a king's son?"—lifted his voice, and call'd
A hoary man, his chamberlain, to whom
He trusted all things, and of him required
His counsel: "Knowest thou aught of Arthur's birth?"

    Then spake the hoary chamberlain and said:
"Sir King, there be but two old men that know;
And each is twice as old as I; and one
Is Merlin, the wise man that ever served   150
King Uther thro' his magic art, and one
Is Merlin's master—so they call him—Bleys,
Who taught him magic; but the scholar ran
Before the master, and so far that Bleys
Laid magic by, and sat him down, and wrote
All things and whatsoever Merlin did
In one great annal-book, where after-years
Will learn the secret of our Arthur's birth."

    To whom the King Leodogran replied:
"O friend, had I been holpen half as well   160
By this King Arthur as by thee to-day,
Then beast and man had had their share of me;
But summon here before us yet once more
Ulfius, and Brastias, and Bedivere."

    Then, when they came before him, the king said:
"I have seen the cuckoo chased by lesser fowl,

And reason in the chase; but wherefore now
Do these your lords stir up the heat of war,
Some calling Arthur born of Gorloïs,
Others of Anton? Tell me, ye yourselves,   170
Hold ye this Arthur for King Uther's son?"

    And Ulfius and Brastias answer'd, "Ay."
Then Bedivere, the first of all his knights
Knighted by Arthur at his crowning, spake—
For bold in heart and act and word was he,
Whenever slander breathed against the King—

    "Sir, there be many rumors on this head;
For there be those who hate him in their hearts,
Call him baseborn, and since his ways are sweet,
And theirs are bestial, hold him less than man;   180
And there be those who deem him more than man,
And dream he dropt from heaven. But my belief
In all this matter—so ye care to learn—
Sir, for ye know that in King Uther's time
The prince and warrior Gorloïs, he that held
Tintagil castle by the Cornish sea,
Was wedded with a winsome wife, Ygerne.
And daughters had she borne him,—one whereof,
Lot's wife, the Queen of Orkney, Bellicent,
Hath ever like a loyal sister cleaved   190
To Arthur,—but a son she had not borne.
And Uther cast upon her eyes of love;
But she, a stainless wife to Gorloïs,
So loathed the bright dishonor of his love
That Gorloïs and King Uther went to war,
And overthrown was Gorloïs and slain.
Then Uther in his wrath and heat besieged
Ygerne within Tintagil, where her men,
Seeing the mighty swarm about their walls,
Left her and fled, and Uther enter'd in,   200
And there was none to call to but himself.
So, compass'd by the power of the king,
Enforced she was to wed him in her tears,
And with a shameful swiftness; afterward
Not many moons, King Uther died himself,
Moaning and wailing for an heir to rule
After him, lest the realm should go to wrack.
And that same night, the night of the new year,
By reason of the bitterness and grief
That vext his mother, all before his time   210
Was Arthur born, and all as soon as born

Deliver'd at a secret postern-gate
To Merlin, to be holden far apart
Until his hour should come, because the lords
Of that fierce day were as the lords of this,
Wild beasts, and surely would have torn the child
Piecemeal among them, had they known; for each
But sought to rule for his own self and hand,
And many hated Uther for the sake
Of Gorloïs. Wherefore Merlin took the child,   220
And gave him to Sir Anton, an old knight
And ancient friend of Uther; and his wife
Nursed the young prince, and rear'd him with her own;
And no man knew. And ever since the lords
Have foughten like wild beasts among themselves,
So that the realm has gone to wrack; but now,
This year, when Merlin—for his hour had come—
Brought Arthur forth, and set him in the hall,
Proclaiming, 'Here is Uther's heir, your king,'
A hundred voices cried: 'Away with him!   230
No king of ours! a son of Gorloïs he,
Or else the child of Anton, and no king,
Or else baseborn.' Yet Merlin thro' his craft,
And while the people clamor'd for a king,
Had Arthur crown'd; but after, the great lords
Banded, and so brake out in open war."

    Then while the king debated with himself
If Arthur were the child of shamefulness,
Or born the son of Gorloïs after death,
Or Uther's son and born before his time.   240
Or whether there were truth in anything
Said by these three, there came to Cameliard,
With Gawain and young Modred, her two sons,
Lot's wife, the Queen of Orkney, Bellicent;
Whom as he could, not as he would, the king
Made feast for, saying, as they sat at meat:
"A doubtful throne is ice on summer seas.
Ye come from Arthur's court. Victor his men
Report him! Yea, but ye—think ye this king—
So many those that hate him, and so strong,   250
So few his knights, however brave they be—
Hath body enow to hold his foemen down?"

    "O King," she cried, "and I will tell thee: few,
Few, but all brave, all of one mind with him;
For I was near him when the savage yells
Of Uther's peerage died, and Arthur sat
Crowned on the daïs, and his warriors cried,

'Be thou the king, and we will work thy will
Who love thee.' Then the King in low deep tones,
And simple words of great authority,   260
Bound them by so strait vows to his own self
That when they rose, knighted from kneeling, some
Were pale as at the passing of a ghost,
Some flush'd, and others dazed, as one who wakes
Half-blinded at the coming of a light.

    "But when he spake, and cheer'd his Table Round
With large, divine, and comfortable words,
Beyond my tongue to tell thee—I beheld
From eye to eye thro' all their Order flash
A momentary likeness of the King;   270
And ere it left their faces, thro' the cross
And those around it and the Crucified,
Down from the casement over Arthur smote
Flame-color, vert, and azure, in three rays,
One falling upon each of three fair queens
Who stood in silence near his throne, the friends
Of Arthur, gazing on him, tall, with bright
Sweet faces, who will help him at his need.

    "And there I saw mage Merlin, whose vast wit
And hundred winters are but as the hands   280
Of loyal vassals toiling for their liege.

    "And near him stood the Lady of the Lake,
Who knows a subtler magic than his own—
Clothed in white samite, mystic, wonderful.
She gave the King his huge cross-hilted sword,
Whereby to drive the heathen out. A mist
Of incense curl'd about her, and her face
Wellnigh was hidden in the minster gloom;
But there was heard among the holy hymns
A voice as of the waters, for she dwells   290
Down in a deep—calm, whatsoever storms
May shake the world—and when the surface rolls,
Hath power to walk the waters like our Lord.

    "There likewise I beheld Excalibur
Before him at his crowning borne, the sword
That rose from out the bosom of the lake,
And Arthur row'd across and took it—rich
With jewels, elfin Urim, on the hilt,
Bewildering heart and eye—the blade so bright
That men are blinded by it—on one side,   300
Graven in the oldest tongue of all this world,
'Take me,' but turn the blade and ye shall see,

And written in the speech ye speak yourself,
'Cast me away!' And sad was Arthur's face
Taking it, but old Merlin counsell'd him,
'Take thou and strike! the time to cast away
Is yet far-off.' So this great brand the king
Took, and by this will beat his foemen down."

    Thereat Leodogran rejoiced, but thought
To sift his doubtings to the last, and ask'd,   310
Fixing full eyes of question on her face,
"The swallow and the swift are near akin,
But thou art closer to this noble prince,
Being his own dear sister;" and she said,
"Daughter of Gorloïs and Ygerne am I;"
"And therefore Arthur's sister?" ask'd the king.
She answer'd, "These be secret things," and sign'd
To those two sons to pass, and let them be.
And Gawain went, and breaking into song
Sprang out, and follow'd by his flying hair   320
Ran like a colt, and leapt at all he saw;
But Modred laid his ear beside the doors,
And there half-heard—the same that afterward
Struck for the throne, and striking found his doom.

    And then the Queen made answer: "What know I?
For dark my mother was in eyes and hair,
And dark in hair and eyes am I; and dark
Was Gorloïs; yea, and dark was Uther too,
Wellnigh to blackness; but this king is fair
Beyond the race of Britons and of men.   330
Moreover, always in my mind I hear
A cry from out the dawning of my life,
A mother weeping, and I hear her say,
'O that ye had some brother, pretty one,
To guard thee on the rough ways of the world.' "

    "Ay," said the king, "and hear ye such a cry?
But when did Arthur chance upon thee first?"

    "O King!" she cried, "and I will tell thee true.
He found me first when yet a little maid.
Beaten I had been for a little fault   340
Whereof I was not guilty; and out I ran
And flung myself down on a bank of heath,
And hated this fair world and all therein,
And wept, and wish'd that I were dead; and he—
I know not whether of himself he came,
Or brought by Merlin, who, they say, can walk
Unseen at pleasure—he was at my side,

And spake sweet words, and comforted my heart,
And dried my tears, being a child with me.
And many a time he came, and evermore   350
As I grew greater grew with me; and sad
At times he seem'd, and sad with him was I,
Stern too at times, and then I loved him not,
But sweet again, and then I loved him well.
And now of late I see him less and less,
But those first days had golden hours for me,
For then I surely thought he would be king.

    "But let me tell thee now another tale:
For Bleys, our Merlin's master, as they say,
Died but of late, and sent his cry to me,   360
To hear him speak before he left his life.
Shrunk like a fairy changeling lay the mage;
And when I enter'd told me that himself
And Merlin ever served about the king,
Uther, before he died; and on the night
When Uther in Tintagil past away
Moaning and wailing for an heir, the two
Left the still king, and passing forth to breathe,
Then from the castle gateway by the chasm
Descending thro' the dismal night—a night   370
In which the bounds of heaven and earth were lost—
Beheld, so high upon the dreary deeps
It seem'd in heaven, a ship, the shape thereof
A dragon wing'd, and all from stem to stern
Bright with a shining people on the decks,
And gone as soon as seen. And then the two
Dropt to the cove, and watch'd the great sea fall,
Wave after wave, each mightier than the last,
Till last, a ninth one, gathering half the deep
And full of voices, slowly rose and plunged   380
Roaring, and all the wave was in a flame;
And down the wave and in the flame was borne
A naked babe, and rode to Merlin's feet,
Who stoopt and caught the babe, and cried, 'The King!
Here is an heir for Uther!' And the fringe
Of that great breaker, sweeping up the strand,
Lash'd at the wizard as he spake the word,
And all at once all round him rose in fire,
So that the child and he were clothed in fire.
And presently thereafter follow'd calm,   390
Free sky and stars. 'And this same child,' he said,
'Is he who reigns; nor could I part in peace
Till this were told.' And saying this the seer

Went thro' the strait and dreadful pass of death,
Not ever to be question'd any more
Save on the further side; but when I met
Merlin, and ask'd him if these things were truth—
The shining dragon and the naked child
Descending in the glory of the seas—
He laugh'd as is his wont, and answer'd me   400
In riddling triplets of old time, and said:—

    " 'Rain, rain, and sun! a rainbow in the sky!
A young man will be wiser by and by;
An old man's wit may wander ere he die.

    " 'Rain, rain, and sun! a rainbow on the lea!
And truth is this to me and that to thee;
And truth or clothed or naked let it be.

    " 'Rain, sun, and rain! and the free blossom blows;
Sun, rain, and sun! and where is he who knows?
From the great deep to the great deep he goes.'   410

  "So Merlin riddling anger'd me; but thou
Fear not to give this King thine only child,
Guinevere; so great bards of him will sing
Hereafter, and dark sayings from of old
Ranging and ringing thro' the minds of men,
And echo'd by old folk beside their fires
For comfort after their wage-work is done,
Speak of the King; and Merlin in our time
Hath spoken also, not in jest, and sworn
Tho' men may wound him that he will not die,   420
But pass, again to come, and then or now
Utterly smite the heathen underfoot,
Till these and all men hail him for their king."

   She spake and King Leodogran rejoiced,
But musing "Shall I answer yea or nay?"
Doubted, and drowsed, nodded and slept, and saw,
Dreaming, a slope of land that ever grew,
Field after field, up to a height, the peak
Haze-hidden, and thereon a phantom king,
Now looming, and now lost; and on the slope   430
The sword rose, the hind fell, the herd was driven,
Fire glimpsed; and all the land from roof and rick,
In drifts of smoke before a rolling wind,
Stream'd to the peak, and mingled with the haze
And made it thicker; while the phantom king
Sent out at times a voice; and here or there
Stood one who pointed toward the voice, the rest
Slew on and burnt, crying, "No king of ours,
No son of Uther, and no king of ours;"
Till with a wink his dream was changed, the haze   440

Descended, and the solid earth became
As nothing, but the King stood out in heaven,
Crown'd. And Leodogran awoke, and sent
Ulfius, and Brastias, and Bedivere,
Back to the court of Arthur answering yea.

Then Arthur charged his warrior whom he loved
And honor'd most, Sir Lancelot, to ride forth
And bring the Queen, and watch'd him from the gates;
And Lancelot past away among the flowers—
For then was latter April—and return'd   450
Among the flowers, in May, with Guinevere.
To whom arrived, by Dubric the high saint,
Chief of the church in Britain, and before
The stateliest of her altar-shrines, the King
That morn was married, while in stainless white,
The fair beginners of a nobler time,
And glorying in their vows and him, his knights
Stood round him, and rejoicing in his joy.
Far shone the fields of May thro' open door,
The sacred altar blossom'd white with May,   460
The sun of May descended on their King,
They gazed on all earth's beauty in their Queen,
Roll'd incense, and there past along the hymns
A voice as of the waters, while the two
Sware at the shrine of Christ a deathless love.
And Arthur said, "Behold, thy doom is mine.
Let chance what will, I love thee to the death!"
To whom the Queen replied with drooping eyes,
"King and my lord, I love thee to the death!"
And holy Dubric spread his hands and spake: 470
"Reign ye, and live and love, and make the world
Other, and may thy Queen be one with thee,
And all this Order of thy Table Round
Fulfil the boundless purpose of their King!"

So Dubric said; but when they left the shrine
Great lords from Rome before the portal stood,
In scornful stillness gazing as they past;
Then while they paced a city all on fire
With sun and cloth of gold, the trumpets blew,
And Arthur's knighthood sang before the King:—   480

"Blow trumpet, for the world is white with May!
Blow trumpet, the long night hath roll'd away!
Blow thro' the living world—'Let the King reign!'

"Shall Rome or Heathen rule in Arthur's realm?
Flash brand and lance, fall battle-axe upon helm,
Fall battle-axe, and flash brand! Let the King reign!

"Strike for the King and live! his knights have heard
That God hath told the King a secret word.
Fall battle-axe, and flash brand! Let the King reign!

"Blow trumpet! he will lift us from the dust.   490
Blow trumpet! live the strength, and die the lust!
Clang battle-axe, and clash brand! Let the King reign!

"Strike for the King and die! and if thou diest,
The King is king, and ever wills the highest.
Clang battle-axe, and clash brand! Let the King reign!

"Blow, for our Sun is mighty in his May!
Blow, for our Sun is mightier day by day!
Clang battle-axe, and clash brand! Let the King reign!

"The King will follow Christ, and we the King,
In whom high God hath breathed a secret thing.   500
Fall battle-axe, and clash brand! Let the King reign!"

So sang the knighthood, moving to their hall.
There at the banquet those great lords from Rome,
The slowly-fading mistress of the world,
Strode in and claim'd their tribute as of yore.
But Arthur spake: "Behold, for these have sworn
To wage my wars, and worship me their King;
The old order changeth, yielding place to new,
And we that fight for our fair father Christ,
Seeing that ye be grown too weak and old   510
To drive the heathen from your Roman wall,
No tribute will we pay." So those great lords
Drew back in wrath, and Arthur strove with Rome.

And Arthur and his knighthood for a space
Were all one will, and thro' that strength the King
Drew in the petty princedoms under him,
Fought, and in twelve great battles overcame
The heathen hordes, and made a realm and reign'd.
1869

THE HOLY GRAIL

From noiseful arms, and acts of prowess done
In tournament or tilt, Sir Percivale
Whom Arthur and his knighthood call'd the Pure,
Had past into the silent life of prayer,
Praise, fast, and alms; and leaving for the cowl
The helmet in an abbey far away
From Camelot, there, and not long after, died.

And one, a fellow-monk among the rest,
Ambrosius, loved him much beyond the rest,

And honor'd him, and wrought into his heart   10
A way by love that waken'd love within,
To answer that which came; and as they sat
Beneath a world-old yew-tree, darkening half
The cloisters, on a gustful April morn
That puff'd the swaying branches into smoke
Above them, ere the summer when he died,
The monk Ambrosius question'd Percivale:

"O brother, I have seen this yew-tree smoke,
Spring after spring, for half a hundred years;
For never have I known the world without,   20
Nor ever stray'd beyond the pale. But thee,
When first thou camest—such a courtesy
Spake thro' the limbs and in the voice—I knew
For one of those who eat in Arthur's hall;
For good ye are and bad, and like to coins,
Some true, some light, but every one of you
Stamp'd with the image of the King; and now
Tell me, what drove thee from the Table Round,
My brother? was it earthly passion crost?"

"Nay," said the knight; "for no such passion mine.   30
But the sweet vision of the Holy Grail
Drove me from all vainglories, rivalries,
And earthly heats that spring and sparkle out
Among us in the jousts, while women watch
Who wins, who falls, and waste the spiritual strength
Within us, better offer'd up to heaven."

To whom the monk: "The Holy Grail!—I trust
We are green in Heaven's eyes; but here too much
We moulder—as to things without I mean—
Yet one of your own knights, a guest of ours,   40
Told us of this in our refectory,
But spake with such a sadness and so low
We heard not half of what he said. What is it?
The phantom of a cup that comes and goes?"

"Nay, monk! what phantom?" answer'd Percivale.
"The cup, the cup itself, from which our Lord
Drank at the last sad supper with his own.
This, from the blessed land of Aromat—
After the day of darkness, when the dead
Went wandering o'er Moriah—the good saint   50
Arimathæan Joseph, journeying brought
To Glastonbury, where the winter thorn
Blossoms at Christmas, mindful of our Lord.

And there awhile it bode; and if a man
Could touch or see it, he was heal'd at once,
By faith, of all his ills. But then the times
Grew to such evil that the holy cup
Was caught away to heaven, and disappear'd."

To whom the monk: "From our old books I know
That Joseph came of old to Glastonbury,   60
And there the heathen Prince, Arviragus,
Gave him an isle of marsh whereon to build;
And there he built with wattles from the marsh
A little lonely church in days of yore,
For so they say, these books of ours, but seem
Mute of this miracle, far as I have read.
But who first saw the holy thing to-day?"

"A woman," answer'd Percivale, "a nun,
And one no further off in blood from me
Than sister; and if ever holy maid   70
With knees of adoration wore the stone,
A holy maid; tho' never maiden glow'd,
But that was in her earlier maidenhood,
With such a fervent flame of human love,
Which, being rudely blunted, glanced and shot
Only to holy things; to prayer and praise
She gave herself, to fast and alms. And yet,
Nun as she was, the scandal of the Court,
Sin against Arthur and the Table Round,
And the strange sound of an adulterous race,   80
Across the iron grating of her cell
Beat, and she pray'd and fasted all the more.

"And he to whom she told her sins, or what
Her all but utter whiteness held for sin,
A man wellnigh a hundred winters old,
Spake often with her of the Holy Grail,
A legend handed down thro' five or six,
And each of these a hundred winters old,
From our Lord's time. And when King Arthur made
His Table Round, and all men's hearts became   90
Clean for a season, surely he had thought
That now the Holy Grail would come again;
But sin broke out. Ah, Christ, that it would come,
And heal the world of all their wickedness!
'O Father!' ask'd the maiden, 'might it come
To me by prayer and fasting?' 'Nay,' said he,
'I know not, for thy heart is pure as snow.'

And so she pray'd and fasted, till the sun
Shone, and the wind blew, thro' her, and I thought
She might have risen and floated when I saw her.   100

  "For on a day she sent to speak with me.
And when she came to speak, behold her eyes
Beyond my knowing of them, beautiful,
Beyond all knowing of them, wonderful,
Beautiful in the light of holiness!
And 'O my brother Percivale,' she said,
'Sweet brother, I have seen the Holy Grail;
For, waked at dead of night, I heard a sound
As of a silver horn from o'er the hills
Blown, and I thought, "It is not Arthur's use   110
To hunt by moonlight." And the slender sound
As from a distance beyond distance grew
Coming upon me—O never harp nor horn,
Nor aught we blow with breath, or touch with hand,
Was like that music as it came; and then
Stream'd thro' my cell a cold and silver beam,
And down the long beam stole the Holy Grail,
Rose-red with beatings in it, as if alive,
Till all the white walls of my cell were dyed
With rosy colors leaping on the wall;   120
And then the music faded, and the Grail
Past, and the beam decay'd, and from the walls
The rosy quiverings died into the night.
So now the Holy Thing is here again
Among us, brother, fast thou too and pray,
And tell thy brother knights to fast and pray,
That so perchance the vision may be seen
By thee and those, and all the world be heal'd.'

  "Then leaving the pale nun, I spake of this
To all men; and myself fasted and pray'd   130
Always, and many among us many a week
Fasted and pray'd even to the uttermost,
Expectant of the wonder that would be.

  "And one there was among us, ever moved
Among us in white armor, Galahad.
'God make thee good as thou art beautiful!'
Said Arthur, when he dubb'd him knight, and none
In so young youth was ever made a knight
Till Galahad; and this Galahad, when he heard
My sister's vision, fill'd me with amaze;   140
His eyes became so like her own, they seem'd
Hers, and himself her brother more than I.

"Sister or brother none had he; but some
Call'd him a son of Lancelot, and some said
Begotten by enchantment—chatterers they,
Like birds of passage piping up and down,
That gape for flies—we know not whence they come;
For when was Lancelot wanderingly lewd?

"But she, the wan sweet maiden, shore away
Clean from her forehead all that wealth of hair   150
Which made a silken mat-work for her feet;
And out of this she plaited broad and long
A strong sword-belt, and wove with silver thread
And crimson in the belt a strange device,
A crimson grail within a silver beam;
And saw the bright boy-knight, and bound it on him,
Saying: 'My knight, my love, my knight of heaven,
O thou, my love, whose love is one with mine,
I, maiden, round thee, maiden, bind my belt.
Go forth, for thou shalt see what I have seen,   160
And break thro' all, till one will crown thee king
Far in the spiritual city;' and as she spake
She sent the deathless passion in her eyes
Thro' him, and made him hers, and laid her mind
On him, and he believed in her belief.

"Then came a year of miracle. O brother,
In our great hall there stood a vacant chair,
Fashion'd by Merlin ere he past away,
And carven with strange figures; and in and out
The figures, like a serpent, ran a scroll   170
Of letters in a tongue no man could read.
And Merlin call'd it 'the Siege Perilous,'
Perilous for good and ill; 'for there,' he said,
'No man could sit but he should lose himself.'
And once by misadvertence Merlin sat
In his own chair, and so was lost; but he,
Galahad, when he heard of Merlin's doom,
Cried, 'If I lose myself, I save myself!'

"Then on a summer night it came to pass,
While the great banquet lay along the hall,   180
That Galahad would sit down in Merlin's chair.

"And all at once, as there we sat, we heard
A cracking and a riving of the roofs,
And rending, and a blast, and overhead
Thunder and in the thunder was a cry.
And in the blast there smote along the hall
A beam of light seven times more clear than day;

And down the long beam stole the Holy Grail
All over cover'd with a luminous cloud,
And none might see who bare it, and it past.   190
But every knight beheld his fellow's face
As in a glory, and all the knights arose,
And staring each at other like dumb men
Stood, till I found a voice and sware a vow.

"I sware a vow before them all, that I,
Because I had not seen the Grail, would ride
A twelvemonth and a day in quest of it,
Until I found and saw it, as the nun
My sister saw it; and Galahad sware the vow,
And good Sir Bors, our Lancelot's cousin, sware,   200
And Lancelot sware, and many among the knights,
And Gawain sware, and louder than the rest."

Then spake the monk Ambrosius, asking him,
"What said the King? Did Arthur take the vow?"

"Nay, for my lord," said Percivale, "the King,
Was not in hall; for early that same day,
Scaped thro' a cavern from a bandit bold,
An outraged maiden sprang into the hall
Crying on help; for all her shining hair
Was smear'd with earth, and either milky arm   210
Red-rent with hooks of bramble, and all she wore
Torn as a sail that leaves the rope is torn
In tempest. So the King arose and went
To smoke the scandalous hive of those wild bees
That made such honey in his realm. Howbeit
Some little of this marvel he too saw,
Returning o'er the plain that then began
To darken under Camelot; whence the King
Look'd up, calling aloud, 'Lo, there! the roofs
Of our great hall are roll'd in thunder-smoke!   220
Pray heaven, they be not smitten by the bolt!'
For dear to Arthur was that hall of ours,
As having there so oft with all his knights
Feasted, and as the stateliest under heaven.

"O brother, had you known our mighty hall,
Which Merlin built for Arthur long ago!
For all the sacred mount of Camelot,
And all the dim rich city, roof by roof,
Tower after tower, spire beyond spire,
By grove, and garden-lawn, and rushing brook,   230
Climbs to the mighty hall that Merlin built.
And four great zones of sculpture, set betwixt

With many a mystic symbol, gird the hall;
And in the lowest beasts are slaying men,
And in the second men are slaying beasts,
And on the third are warriors, perfect men,
And on the fourth are men with growing wings,
And over all one statue in the mould
Of Arthur, made by Merlin, with a crown,
And peak'd wings pointed to the Northern Star.   240
And eastward fronts the statue, and the crown
And both the wings are made of gold, and flame
At sunrise till the people in far fields,
Wasted so often by the heathen hordes,
Behold it, crying 'We have still a king.'

    "And, brother had you known our hall within,
Broader and higher than any in all the lands!
Where twelve great windows blazon Arthur's wars,
And all the light that falls upon the board
Streams thro' the twelve great battles of our King.   250
Nay, one there is, and at the eastern end,
Wealthy with wandering lines of mount and mere,
Where Arthur finds the brand Excalibur.
And also one to the west, and counter to it,
And blank; and who shall blazon it? when and how?—
O, there, perchance, when all our wars are done,
The brand Excalibur will be cast away!

    "So to this hall full quickly rode the King,
In horror lest the work by Merlin wrought,
Dreamlike, should on the sudden vanish, wrapt   260
In unremorseful folds of rolling fire.
And in he rode, and up I glanced, and saw
The golden dragon sparkling over all;
And many of those who burnt the hold, their arms
Hack'd, and their foreheads grimed with smoke and sear'd,
Follow'd, and in among bright faces, ours,
Full of the vision, prest; and then the King
Spake to me, being nearest, 'Percivale,'—
Because the hall was all in tumult—some
Vowing, and some protesting,—'what is this?'   270

    "O brother, when I told him what had chanced,
My sister's vision and the rest, his face
Darken'd, as I have seen it more than once,
When some brave deed seem'd to be done in vain,
Darken; and 'Woe is me, my knights,' he cried,
'Had I been here, ye had not sworn the vow.'
Bold was mine answer, 'Had thyself been here,

My King, thou wouldst have sworn.' 'Yea, yea,' said he,
'Art thou so bold and hast not seen the Grail?'

   " 'Nay, lord, I heard the sound, I saw the light,   280
But since I did not see the holy thing,
I sware a vow to follow it till I saw.'

   "Then when he ask'd us, knight by knight, if any
Had seen it, all their answers were as one:
'Nay, lord, and therefore have we sworn our vows.'

   " 'Lo, now,' said Arthur, 'have ye seen a cloud?
What go ye into the wilderness to see?'

   "Then Galahad on the sudden, and in a voice
Shrilling along the hall to Arthur, call'd,
'But I, Sir Arthur, saw the Holy Grail,   290
I saw the Holy Grail and heard a cry—
"O Galahad, and O Galahad, follow me!" ' "

   " 'Ah, Galahad, Galahad,' said the King, 'for such
As thou art is the vision, not for these.
Thy holy nun and thou have seen a sign—
Holier is none, my Percivale, than she—
A sign to maim this Order which I made.
But ye that follow but the leader's bell,'—
Brother, the King was hard upon his knights,—
'Taliessin is our fullest throat of song,   300
And one hath sung and all the dumb will sing.
Lancelot is Lancelot, and hath overborne
Five knights at once, and every younger knight,
Unproven, holds himself as Lancelot,
Till overborne by one, he learns—and ye,
What are ye? Galahads?—no, nor Percivales'—
For thus it pleased the King to range me close
After Sir Galahad;—'nay,' said he, 'but men
With strength and will to right the wrong'd, of power
To lay the sudden heads of violence flat,   310
Knights that in twelve great battles splash'd and dyed
The strong White Horse in his own heathen blood—
But one hath seen, and all the blind will see.
Go, since your vows are sacred, being made.
Yet—for ye know the cries of all my realm
Pass thro' this hall—how often, O my knights,
Your places being vacant at my side,
This chance of noble deeds will come and go
Unchallenged, while ye follow wandering fires
Lost in the quagmire! Many of you, yea most,   320
Return no more. Ye think I show myself

Too dark a prophet. Come now, let us meet
The morrow morn once more in one full field
Of gracious pastime, that once more the King,
Before ye leave him for this quest, may count
The yet-unbroken strength of all his knights,
Rejoicing in that Order which he made.'

"So when the sun broke next from underground,
All the great Table of our Arthur closed
And clash'd in such a tourney and so full,   330
So many lances broken—never yet
Had Camelot seen the like since Arthur came;
And I myself and Galahad, for a strength
Was in us from the vision, overthrew
So many knights that all the people cried,
And almost burst the barriers in their heat,
Shouting, 'Sir Galahad and Sir Percivale!'

"But when the next day brake from underground—
O brother, had you known our Camelot,
Built by old kings, age after age, so old   340
The King himself had fears that it would fall,
So strange, and rich, and dim; for where the roofs
Totter'd toward each other in the sky,
Met foreheads all along the street of those
Who watch'd us pass; and lower, and where the long
Rich galleries, lady-laden, weigh'd the necks
Of dragons clinging to the crazy walls,
Thicker than drops from thunder, showers of flowers
Fell as we past; and men and boys astride
On wyvern, lion, dragon, griffin, swan,   350
At all the corners, named us each by name,
Calling 'God speed!' but in the ways below
The knights and ladies wept, and rich and poor
Wept, and the King himself could hardly speak
For grief, and all in middle street the Queen,
Who rode by Lancelot, wail'd and shriek'd aloud,
'This madness has come on us for our sins.'
So to the Gate of the Three Queens we came,
Where Arthur's wars are render'd mystically,
And thence departed every one his way.   360

"And I was lifted up in heart, and thought
Of all my late-shown prowess in the lists,
How my strong lance had beaten down the knights,
So many and famous names; and never yet
Had heaven appear'd so blue, nor earth so green,
For all my blood danced in me, and I knew
That I should light upon the Holy Grail.

"Thereafter, the dark warning of our King,
That most of us would follow wandering fires,
Came like a driving gloom across my mind.   370
Then every evil word I had spoken once,
And every evil thought I had thought of old,
And every evil deed I ever did,
Awoke and cried, 'This quest is not for thee.'
And lifting up mine eyes, I found myself
Alone, and in a land of sand and thorns,
And I was thirsty even unto death;
And I, too, cried, 'This quest is not for thee.'

"And on I rode, and when I thought my thirst
Would slay me, saw deep lawns, and then a brook,   380
With one sharp rapid, where the crisping white
Play'd ever back upon the sloping wave
And took both ear and eye; and o'er the brook
Were apple-trees, and apples by the brook
Fallen, and on the lawns. 'I will rest here,'
I said, 'I am not worthy of the quest;'
But even while I drank the brook, and ate
The goodly apples, all these things at once
Fell into dust, and I was left alone
And thirsting in a land of sand and thorns.   390

"And then behold a woman at a door
Spinning; and fair the house whereby she sat.
And kind the woman's eyes and innocent,
And all her bearing gracious; and she rose
Opening her arms to meet me, as who should say,
'Rest here;' but when I touch'd her, lo! she, too,
Fell into dust and nothing, and the house
Became no better than a broken shed,
And in it a dead babe; and also this
Fell into dust, and I was left alone.   400

"And on I rode, and greater was my thirst.
Then flash'd a yellow gleam across the world,
And where it smote the plowshare in the field
The plowman left his plowing and fell down
Before it; where it glitter'd on her pail
The milkmaid left her milking and fell down
Before it, and I knew not why, but thought
'The sun is rising,' tho' the sun had risen.
Then was I ware of one that on me moved
In golden armor with a crown of gold   410
About a casque all jewels, and his horse
In golden armor jewelled everywhere;

And on the splendor came, flashing me blind,
And seem'd to me the lord of all the world,
Being so huge. But when I thought he meant
To crush me, moving on me, lo! he, too,
Open'd his arms to embrace me as he came,
And up I went and touch'd him, and he, too,
Fell into dust, and I was left alone
And wearying in a land of sand and thorns.   420

"And I rode on and found a mighty hill,
And on the top a city wall'd; the spires
Prick'd with incredible pinnacles into heaven.
And by the gateway stirr'd a crowd; and these
Cried to me climbing, 'Welcome, Percivale!
Thou mightiest and thou purest among men!'
And glad was I and clomb, but found at top
No man, nor any voice. And thence I past
Far thro' a ruinous city, and I saw
That man had once dwelt there; but there I found   430
Only one man of an exceeding age.
'Where is that goodly company,' and I,
'That so cried out upon me?' and he had
Scarce any voice to answer, and yet gasp'd,
'Whence and what art thou?' and even as he spoke
Fell into dust and disappear'd, and I
Was left alone once more and cried in grief,
'Lo, if I find the Holy Grail itself
And touch it, it will crumble into dust!'

"And thence I dropt into a lowly vale,   440
Low as the hill was high, and where the vale
Was lowest found a chapel, and thereby
A holy hermit in a hermitage,
To whom I told my phantoms, and he said:

" 'O son, thou hast not true humility,
The highest virtue, mother of them all;
For when the Lord of all things made Himself
Naked of glory for His mortal change,
"Take thou my robe," she said, "for all is thine,"
And all her form shone forth with sudden light   450
So that the angels were amazed, and she
Follow'd Him down, and like a flying star
Led on the gray-hair'd wisdom of the east.
But her thou hast not known; for what is this
Thou thoughtest of thy prowess and thy sins?
Thou hast not lost thyself to save thyself
As Galahad.' When the hermit made an end,

In silver armor suddenly Galahad shone
Before us, and against the chapel door
Laid lance and enter'd, and we knelt in prayer.   460
And there the hermit slaked my burning thirst,
And at the sacring of the mass I saw
The holy elements alone; but he,
'Saw ye no more? I, Galahad, saw the Grail,
The Holy Grail, descend upon the shrine.
I saw the fiery face as of a child
That smote itself into the bread and went;
And hither am I come; and never yet
Hath what thy sister taught me first to see,
This holy thing, fail'd from my side, nor come   470
Cover'd, but moving with me night and day,
Fainter by day, but always in the night
Blood-red, and sliding down the blacken'd marsh
Blood-red, and on the naked mountain top
Blood-red, and in the sleeping mere below
Blood-red. And in the strength of this I rode,
Shattering all evil customs everywhere,
And past thro' Pagan realms, and made them mine,
And clash'd with Pagan hordes, and bore them down,
And broke thro' all, and in the strength of this   480
Come victor. But my time is hard at hand,
And hence I go, and one will crown me king
Far in the spiritual city; and come thou, too,
For thou shalt see the vision when I go.'

   "While thus he spake, his eye, dwelling on mine,
Drew me, with power upon me, till I grew
One with him, to believe as he believed.
Then, when the day began to wane, we went.

   "There rose a hill that none but man could climb,
Scarr'd with a hundred wintry watercourses—   490
Storm at the top, and when we gain'd it, storm
Round us and death; for every moment glanced
His silver arms and gloom'd, so quick and thick
The lightnings here and there to left and right
Struck, till the dry old trunks about us, dead,
Yea, rotten with a hundred years of death,
Sprang into fire. And at the base we found
On either hand, as far as eye could see,
A great black swamp and of an evil smell,
Part black, part whiten'd with the bones of men,   500
Not to be crost, save that some ancient king
Had built a way, where, link'd with many a bridge,
A thousand piers ran into the great Sea.

And Galahad fled along them bridge by bridge,
And every bridge as quickly as he crost
Sprang into fire and vanish'd, tho' I yearn'd
To follow; and thrice above him all the heavens
Open'd and blazed with thunder such as seem'd
Shoutings of all the sons of God. And first
At once I saw him far on the great Sea,   510
In silver-shining armor starry-clear;
And o'er his head the Holy Vessel hung
Clothed in white samite or a luminous cloud.
And with exceeding swiftness ran the boat,
If boat it were—I saw not whence it came.
And when the heavens open'd and blazed again
Roaring, I saw him like a silver star—
And had he set the sail, or had the boat
Become a living creature clad with wings?
And o'er his head the Holy Vessel hung   520
Redder than any rose, a joy to me,
For now I knew the veil had been withdrawn.
Then in a moment when they blazed again
Opening, I saw the least of little stars
Down on the waste, and straight beyond the star
I saw the spiritual city and all her spires
And gateways in a glory like one pearl—
No larger, tho' the goal of all the saints—
Strike from the sea; and from the star there shot
A rose-red sparkle to the city, and there   530
Dwelt, and I knew it was the Holy Grail,
Which never eyes on earth again shall see.
Then fell the floods of heaven drowning the deep,
And how my feet recrost the deathful ridge
No memory in me lives; but that I touch'd
The chapel-doors at dawn I know, and thence
Taking my war-horse from the holy man,
Glad that no phantom vext me more, return'd
To whence I came, the gate of Arthur's wars."

    "O brother," ask'd Ambrosius,—"for in sooth   540
These ancient books—and they would win thee—teem,
Only I find not there this Holy Grail,
With miracles and marvels like to these,
Not all unlike; which oftentime I read,
Who read but on my breviary with ease,
Till my head swims, and then go forth and pass
Down to the little thorpe that lies so close,
And almost plaster'd like a martin's nest
To these old walls—and mingle with our folk;

And knowing every honest face of theirs 550
As well as ever shepherd knew his sheep,
And every homely secret in their hearts,
Delight myself with gossip and old wives,
And ills and aches, and teethings, lyings-in,
And mirthful sayings, children of the place,
That have no meaning half a league away;
Or lulling random squabbles when they rise,
Chafferings and chatterings at the market-cross,
Rejoice, small man, in this small world of mine,
Yea, even in their hens and in their eggs— 560
O brother, saving this Sir Galahad,
Came ye on none but phantoms in your quest,
No man, no woman?"

    Then Sir Percivale:
"All men, to one so bound by such a vow,
And women were as phantoms. O, my brother,
Why wilt thou shame me to confess to thee
How far I falter'd from my quest and vow?
For after I had lain so many nights,
A bed-mate of the snail and eft and snake,
In grass and burdock, I was changed to wan 570
And meagre, and the vision had not come;
And then I chanced upon a goodly town
With one great dwelling in the middle of it.
Thither I made, and there was I disarm'd
By maidens each as fair as any flower;
But when they led me into hall, behold,
The princess of that castle was the one,
Brother, and that one only, who had ever
Made my heart leap; for when I moved of old
A slender page about her father's hall, 580
And she a slender maiden, all my heart
Went after her with longing, yet we twain
Had never kiss'd a kiss or vow'd a vow.
And now I came upon her once again,
And one had wedded her, and he was dead,
And all his land and wealth and state were hers.
And while I tarried, every day she set
A banquet richer than the day before
By me, for all her longing and her will
Was toward me as of old; till one fair morn, 590
I walking to and fro beside a stream
That flash'd across her orchard underneath
Her castle-walls, she stole upon my walk,
And calling me the greatest of all knights,

Embraced me, and so kiss'd me the first time,
And gave herself and all her wealth to me.
Then I remember'd Arthur's warning word,
That most of us would follow wandering fires,
And the quest faded in my heart. Anon,
The heads of all her people drew to me,   600
With supplication both of knees and tongue:
'We have heard of thee; thou art our greatest knight,
Our Lady says it, and we well believe.
Wed thou our Lady, and rule over us,
And thou shalt be as Arthur in our land.'
O me, my brother! but one night my vow
Burnt me within, so that I rose and fled,
But wail'd and wept, and hated mine own self,
And even the holy quest, and all but her;
Then after I was join'd with Galahad   610
Cared not for her nor anything upon earth."

    Then said the monk: "Poor men, when yule is cold,
Must be content to sit by little fires.
And this am I, so that ye care for me
Ever so little; yea, and blest be heaven
That brought thee here to this poor house of ours
Where all the brethren are so hard, to warm
My cold heart with a friend; but O the pity
To find thine own first love once more—to hold,
Hold her a wealthy bride within thine arms,   620
Or all but hold, and then—cast her aside,
Foregoing all her sweetness, like a weed!
For we that want the warmth of double life,
We that are plagued with dreams of something sweet
Beyond all sweetness in a life so rich,—
Ah, blessed Lord, I speak too earthly-wise,
Seeing I never stray'd beyond the cell,
But live like an old badger in his earth,
With earth about him everywhere, despite
All fast and penance. Saw ye none beside,   630
None of your knights?"

               "Yea, so," said Percivale:
"One night my pathway swerving east, I saw
The pelican on the casque of our Sir Bors
All in the middle of the rising moon,
And toward him spurr'd, and hail'd him, and he me,
And each made joy of either. Then he ask'd:
Where is he? hast thou seen him—Lancelot?—Once,'
Said good Sir Bors, 'he dash'd across me—mad,
And maddening what he rode; and when I cried,

"Ridest thou then so hotly on a quest 640
So holy?" Lancelot shouted, "Stay me not!
I have been the sluggard, and I ride apace,
For now there is a lion in the way!"
So vanish'd.'

"Then Sir Bors had ridden on
Softly, and sorrowing for our Lancelot,
Because his former madness, once the talk
And scandal of our table, had return'd;
For Lancelot's kith and kin so worship him
That ill to him is ill to them, to Bors
Beyond the rest. He well had been content 650
Not to have seen, so Lancelot might have seen,
The Holy Cup of healing; and, indeed,
Being so clouded with his grief and love,
Small heart was his after the holy quest.
If God would send the vision, well; if not,
The quest and he were in the hands of Heaven.

"And then, with small adventure met, Sir Bors
Rode to the lonest tract of all the realm,
And found a people there among their crags,
Our race and blood, a remnant that were left 660
Paynim amid their circles, and the stones
They pitch up straight to heaven; and their wise men
Were strong in that old magic which can trace
The wandering of the stars, and scoff'd at him
And this high quest as at a simple thing,
Told him he follow'd—almost Arthur's words—
A mocking fire: 'what other fire than he
Whereby the blood beats, and the blossom blows,
And the sea rolls, and all the world is warm'd?'
And when his answer chafed them, the rough crowd, 670
Hearing he had a difference with their priests,
Seized him, and bound and plunged him into a cell
Of great piled stones; and lying bounden there
In darkness thro' innumerable hours
He heard the hollow-ringing heavens sweep
Over him till by miracle—what else?—
Heavy as it was, a great stone slipt and fell,
Such as no wind could move; and thro' the gap
Glimmer'd the streaming scud. Then came a night
Still as the day was loud, and thro' the gap 680
The seven clear stars of Arthur's Table Round—
For, brother, so one night, because they roll
Thro' such a round in heaven, we named the stars,
Rejoicing in ourselves and in our King—

And these, like bright eyes of familiar friends,
In on him shone: 'And then to me, to me,'
Said good Sir Bors, 'beyond all hopes of mine,
Who scarce had pray'd or ask'd it for myself—
Across the seven clear stars—O grace to me!—
In color like the fingers of a hand   690
Before a burning taper, the sweet Grail
Glided and past, and close upon it peal'd
A sharp quick thunder.' Afterwards, a maid,
Who kept our holy faith among her kin
In secret, entering, loosed and let him go."

To whom the monk: "And I remember now
That pelican on the casque. Sir Bors it was
Who spake so low and sadly at our board,
And mighty reverent at our grace was he;
A square-set man and honest, and his eyes,   700
An outdoor sign of all the warmth within,
Smiled with his lips—a smile beneath a cloud,
But heaven had meant it for a sunny one.
Ay, ay, Sir Bors, who else? But when ye reach'd
The city, found ye all your knights return'd,
Or was there sooth in Arthur's prophecy,
Tell me, and what said each, and what the King?"

Then answer'd Percivale: "And that can I,
Brother, and truly; since the living words
Of so great men as Lancelot and our King   710
Pass not from door to door and out again,
But sit within the house. O, when we reach'd
The city, our horses stumbling as they trode
On heaps of ruin, hornless unicorns,
Crack'd basilisks, and splinter'd cockatrices,
And shatter'd talbots, which had left the stones
Raw that they fell from, brought us to the hall.

"And there sat Arthur on the dais-throne,
And those that had gone out upon the quest,
Wasted and worn, and but a tithe of them,   720
And those that had not, stood before the King,
Who, when he saw me, rose and bade me hail,
Saying: 'A welfare in thine eyes reproves
Our fear of some disastrous chance for thee
On hill or plain, at sea or flooding ford.
So fierce a gale made havoc here of late
Among the strange devices of our kings,
Yea, shook this newer, stronger hall of ours,
And from the statue Merlin moulded for us

Half-wrench'd a golden wing; but now—the quest,   730
This vision—hast thou seen the Holy Cup
That Joseph brought of old to Glastonbury?'

"So when I told him all thyself hast heard,
Ambrosius, and my fresh but fixt resolve
To pass away into the quiet life,
He answer'd not, but, sharply turning, ask'd
Of Gawain, 'Gawain, was this quest for thee?'

"'Nay, lord,' said Gawain, 'not for such as I.
Therefore I communed with a saintly man,
Who made me sure the quest was not for me;   740
For I was much a-wearied of the quest,
But found a silk pavilion in a field,
And merry maidens in it; and then this gale
Tore my pavilion from the tenting-pin,
And blew my merry maidens all about
With all discomfort; yea, and but for this,
My twelvemonth and a day were pleasant to me.'

"He ceased; and Arthur turn'd to whom at first
He saw not, for Sir Bors, on entering, push'd
Athwart the throng to Lancelot, caught his hand,   750
Held it, and there, half-hidden by him, stood,
Until the King espied him, saying to him,
'Hail, Bors! if ever loyal man and true
Could see it, thou hast seen the Grail;' and Bors,
'Ask me not, for I may not speak of it;
I saw it;' and the tears were in his eyes.

"Then there remain'd but Lancelot, for the rest
Spake but of sundry perils in the storm.
Perhaps, like him of Cana in Holy Writ,
Our Arthur kept his best until the last;   760
'Thou, too, my Lancelot,' ask'd the King, 'my friend,
Our mightiest, hath this quest avail'd for thee?'

"'Our mightiest!' answer'd Lancelot, with a groan;
'O King!'—and when he paused methought I spied
A dying fire of madness in his eyes—
'O King, my friend, if friend of thine I be,
Happier are those that welter in their sin,
Swine in the mud, that cannot see for slime,
Slime of the ditch; but in me lived a sin
So strange, of such a kind, that all of pure,   770
Noble, and knightly in me twined and clung
Round that one sin, until the wholesome flower
And poisonous grew together, each as each,

Not to be pluck'd asunder; and when thy knights
Sware, I sware with them only in the hope
That could I touch or see the Holy Grail
They might be pluck'd asunder. Then I spake
To one most holy saint, who wept and said
That, save they could be pluck'd asunder, all
My quest were but in vain; to whom I vow'd   780
That I would work according as he will'd.
And forth I went, and while I yearn'd and strove
To tear the twain asunder in my heart,
My madness came upon me as of old,
And whipt me into waste fields far away.
There was I beaten down by little men,
Mean knights, to whom the moving of my sword
And shadow of my spear had been enow
To scare them from me once; and then I came
All in my folly to the naked shore,   790
Wide flats, where nothing but coarse grasses grew;
But such a blast, my King, began to blow,
So loud a blast along the shore and sea,
Ye could not hear the waters for the blast,
Tho' heapt in mounds and ridges all the sea
Drove like a cataract, and all the sand
Swept like a river, and the clouded heavens
Were shaken with the motion and the sound.
And blackening in the sea-foam sway'd a boat,
Half-swallow'd in it, anchor'd with a chain;   800
And in my madness to myself I said,
"I will embark and I will lose myself,
And in the great sea wash away my sin."
I burst the chain, I sprang into the boat.
Seven days I drove along the dreary deep,
And with me drove the moon and all the stars;
And the wind fell, and on the seventh night
I heard the shingle grinding in the surge,
And felt the boat shock earth, and looking up,
Behold, the enchanted towers of Carbonek,   810
A castle like a rock upon a rock,
With chasm-like portals open to the sea,
And steps that met the breaker! There was none
Stood near it but a lion on each side
That kept the entry, and the moon was full.
Then from the boat I leapt, and up the stairs,
There drew my sword. With sudden-flaring manes
Those two great beasts rose upright like a man,
Each gript a shoulder, and I stood between,
And, when I would have smitten them, heard a voice,   820

"Doubt not, go forward; if thou doubt, the beasts
Will tear thee piecemeal." Then with violence
The sword was dash'd from out my hand, and fell.
And up into the sounding hall I past;
But nothing in the sounding hall I saw,
No bench nor table, painting on the wall
Or shield of knight, only the rounded moon
Thro' the tall oriel on the rolling sea.
But always in the quiet house I heard,
Clear as a lark, high o'er me as a lark,   830
A sweet voice singing in the topmost tower
To the eastward. Up I climb'd a thousand steps
With pain; as in a dream I seem'd to climb
For ever; at the last I reach'd a door,
A light was in the crannies, and I heard,
"Glory and joy and honor to our Lord
And to the Holy Vessel of the Grail!"
Then in my madness I essay'd the door;
It gave, an thro' a stormy glare, a heat
As from a seven-times-heated furnace, I,   840
Blasted and burnt, and blinded as I was,
With such a fierceness that I swoon'd away—
O, yet methought I saw the Holy Grail,
All pall'd in crimson samite, and around
Great angels, awful shapes, and wings and eyes!
And but for all my madness and my sin,
And then my swooning, I had sworn I saw
That which I saw; but what I saw was veil'd
And cover'd, and this quest was not for me.'

   "So speaking, and here ceasing, Lancelot left   850
The hall long silent, till Sir Gawain—nay,
Brother, I need not tell thee foolish words,—
A reckless and irreverent knight was he,
Now bolden'd by the silence of his King,—
Well, I will tell thee: 'O King, my liege,' he said,
'Hath Gawain fail'd in any quest of thine?
When have I stinted stroke in foughten field?
But as for thine, my good friend Percivale,
Thy holy nun and thou have driven men mad,
Yea, made our mightiest madder than our least.   860
But by mine eyes and by mine ears I swear,
I will be deafer than the blue-eyed cat,
And thrice as blind as any noonday owl,
To holy virgins in their ecstasies,
Henceforward.'

" 'Deafer,' said the blameless King,
'Gawain, and blinder unto holy things,
Hope not to make thyself by idle vows,
Being too blind to have desire to see.
But if indeed there came a sign from heaven,
Blessed are Bors, Lancelot, and Percivale,   870
For these have seen according to their sight.
For every fiery prophet in old times,
And all the sacred madness of the bard,
When God made music thro' them, could but speak
His music by the framework and the chord;
And as ye saw it ye have spoken truth.

 " 'Nay—but thou errest, Lancelot; never yet
Could all of true and noble in knight and man
Twine round one sin, whatever it might be,
With such a closeness but apart there grew,   880
Save that he were the swine thou spakest of,
Some root of knighthood and pure nobleness;
Whereto see thou, that it may bear its flower.

 " 'And spake I not too truly, O my knights?
Was I too dark a prophet when I said
To those who went upon the Holy Quest,
That most of them would follow wandering fires,
Lost in the quagmire?—lost to me and gone,
And left me gazing at a barren board,
And a lean Order—scarce return'd a tithe—   890
And out of those to whom the vision came
My greatest hardly will believe he saw.
Another hath beheld it afar off,
And, leaving human wrongs to right themselves,
Cares but to pass into the silent life.
And one hath had the vision face to face,
And now his chair desires him here in vain,
However they may crown him otherwhere.

 " 'And some among you held that if the King
Had seen the sight he would have sworn the vow.   900
Not easily, seeing that the King must guard
That which he rules, and is but as the hind
To whom a space of land is given to plow,
Who may not wander from the allotted field
Before his work be done, but, being done,
Let visions of the night or of the day
Come as they will; and many a time they come,
Until this earth he walks on seems not earth,
This light that strikes his eyeball is not light,

This air that smites his forehead is not air   910
But vision—yea, his very hand and foot—
In moments when he feels he cannot die,
And knows himself no vision to himself,
Nor the high God a vision, nor that One
Who rose again. Ye have seen what ye have seen.'

  "So spake the King; I knew not all he meant."
1869

THE LAST TOURNAMENT

Dagonet, the fool, whom Gawain in his mood
Had made mock-knight of Arthur's Table Round,
At Camelot, high above the yellowing woods,
Danced like a wither'd leaf before the hall.
And toward him from the hall, with harp in hand,
And from the crown thereof a carcanet
Of ruby swaying to and fro, the prize
Of Tristram in the jousts of yesterday,
Came Tristram, saying, "Why skip ye so, Sir Fool?"

  For Arthur and Sir Lancelot riding once   10
Far down beneath a winding wall of rock
Heard a child wail. A stump of oak half-dead,
From roots like some black coil of carven snakes,
Clutch'd at the crag, and started thro' mid air
Bearing an eagle's nest; and thro' the tree
Rush'd ever a rainy wind, and thro' the wind
Pierced ever a child's cry; and crag and tree
Scaling, Sir Lancelot from the perilous nest,
This ruby necklace thrice around her neck,
And all unscarr'd from beak or talon, brought   20
A maiden babe, which Arthur pitying took,
Then gave it to his Queen to rear. The Queen,
But coldly acquiescing, in her white arms
Received, and after loved it tenderly,
And named it Nestling; so forgot herself
A moment, and her cares; till that young life
Being smitten in mid heaven with mortal cold
Past from her, and in time the carcanet
Vext her with plaintive memories of the child.
So she, delivering it to Arthur, said,   30
"Take thou the jewels of this dead innocence,
And make them, an thou wilt, a tourney-prize."

To whom the King: "Peace to thine eagle-borne
Dead nestling, and this honor after death,
Following thy will! but, O my Queen, I muse
Why ye not wear on arm, or neck, or zone
Those diamonds that I rescued from the tarn,
And Lancelot won, methought, for thee to wear."

"Would rather you had let them fall," she cried,
"Plunge and be lost—ill-fated as they were,   40
A bitterness to me!—ye look amazed,
Not knowing they were lost as soon as given—
Slid from my hands when I was lerning out
Above the river—that unhappy child
Past in her barge; but rosier luck will go
With these rich jewels, seeing that they came
Not from the skeleton of a brother-slayer,
But the sweet body of a maiden babe.
Perchance—who knows?—the purest of thy knights
May win them for the purest of my maids."   50

She ended, and the cry of a great jousts
With trumpet-blowings ran on all the ways
From Camelot in among the faded fields
To furthest towers; and everywhere the knights
Arm'd for a day of glory before the King.

But on the hither side of that loud morn
Into the hall stagger'd, his visage ribb'd
From ear to ear with dogwhip-weals, his nose
Bridge-broken, one eye out, and one hand off,
And one with shatter'd fingers dangling lame,   60
A churl, to whom indignantly the King:

"My churl, for whom Christ died, what evil beast
Hath drawn his claws athwart thy face? or fiend?
Man was it who marr'd heaven's image in thee thus?"

Then, sputtering thro' the hedge of splinter'd teeth,
Yet strangers to the tongue, and with blunt stump
Pitch-blacken'd sawing the air, said the maim'd churl:

"He took them and he drave them to his tower—
Some hold he was a table-knight of thine—
A hundred goodly ones—the Red Knight, he—   70
Lord, I was tending swine, and the Red Knight
Brake in upon me and drave them to his tower;
And when I call'd upon thy name as one
That doest right by gentle and by churl,
Maim'd me and maul'd, and would outright have slain,
Save that he sware me to a message, saying:

'Tell thou the King and all his liars that I
Have founded my Round Table in the North,
And whatsoever his own knights have sworn
My knights have sworn the counter to it—and say   80
My tower is full of harlots, like his court,
But mine are worthier, seeing they profess
To be none other than themselves—and say
My knights are all adulterers like his own,
But mine are truer, seeing they profess
To be none other; and say his hour is come,
The heathen are upon him, his long lance
Broken, and his Excalibur a straw.' "

　　Then Arthur turn'd to Kay the seneschal:
"Take thou my churl, and tend him curiously   90
Like a king's heir, till all his hurts be whole.
The heathen—but that ever-climbing wave,
Hurl'd back again so often in empty foam,
Hath lain for years at rest—and renegades,
Thieves, bandits, leavings of confusion, whom
The wholesome realm is purged of otherwhere,
Friends, thro' your manhood and your fealty,—now
Make their last head like Satan in the North.
My younger knights, new-made, in whom your flower
Waits to be solid fruit of golden deeds,   100
Move with me toward their quelling, which achieved,
The loneliest ways are safe from shore to shore.
But thou, Sir Lancelot, sitting in my place
Enchair'd to-morrow, arbitrate the field;
For wherefore shouldst thou care to mingle with it,
Only to yield my Queen her own again?
Speak, Lancelot, thou art silent; is it well?"

　　Thereto Sir Lancelot answer'd: "It is well;
Yet better if the King abide, and leave
The leading of his younger knights to me.   110
Else, for the King has will'd it, it is well."

　　Then Arthur rose and Lancelot follow'd him,
And while they stood without the doors, the King
Turn'd to him saying: "Is it then so well?
Or mine the blame that oft I seem as he
Of whom was written, 'A sound is in his ears'?
The foot that loiters, bidden go,—the glance
That only seems half-loyal to command,—
A manner somewhat fallen from reverence—
Or have I dream'd the bearing of our knights   120
Tells of a manhood ever less and lower?

Or whence the fear lest this my realm, uprear'd,
By noble deeds at one with noble vows,
From flat confusion and brute violences,
Reel back into the beast, and be no more?"

He spoke, and taking all his younger knights,
Down the slope city rode, and sharply turn'd
North by the gate. In her high bower the Queen,
Working a tapestry, lifted up her head,
Watch'd her lord pass, and knew not that she sigh'd.   130
Then ran across her memory the strange rhyme
Of bygone Merlin, "Where is he who knows?
From the great deep to the great deep he goes."

But when the morning of a tournament,
By these in earnest those in mockery call'd
The Tournament of the Dead Innocence,
Brake with a wet wind blowing, Lancelot,
Round whose sick head all night, like birds of prey,
The words of Arthur flying shriek'd, arose,
And down a streetway hung with folds of pure   140
White samite, and by fountains running wine,
Where children sat in white with cups of gold,
Moved to the lists, and there, with slow sad steps
Ascending, fill'd his double-dragon'd chair.

He glanced and saw the stately galleries,
Dame, damsel, each thro' worship of their Queen
White-robed in honor of the stainless child,
And some with scatter'd jewels, like a bank
Of maiden snow mingled with sparks of fire.
He look'd but once, and vail'd his eyes again.   150

The sudden trumpet sounded as in a dream
To ears but half-awaked, then one low roll
Of Autumn thunder, and the jousts began;
And ever the wind blew, and yellowing leaf,
And gloom and gleam, and shower and shorn plume
Went down it. Sighing weariedly, as one
Who sits and gazes on a faded fire,
When all the goodlier guests are past away,
Sat their great umpire looking o'er the lists.
He saw the laws that ruled the tournament   160
Broken, but spake not; once, a knight cast down
Before his throne of arbitration cursed
The dead babe and the follies of the King;
And once the laces of a helmet crack'd,
And show'd him, like a vermin in its hole,
Modred, a narrow face. Anon he heard

The voice that billow'd round the barriers roar
An ocean-sounding welcome to one knight,
But newly-enter'd, taller than the rest,
And armor'd all in forest green, whereon   170
There tript a hundred tiny silver deer,
And wearing but a holly-spray for crest,
With ever-scattering berries, and on shield
A spear, a harp, a bugle—Tristram—late
From over-seas in Brittany return'd,
And marriage with a princess of that realm,
Isolt the White—Sir Tristram of the Woods—
Whom Lancelot knew, had held sometime with pain
His own against him, and now yearn'd to shake
The burthen off his heart in one full shock   180
With Tristram even to death. His strong hands gript
And dinted the gilt dragons right and left,
Until he groan'd for wrath—so many of those
That ware their ladies' colors on the casque
Drew from before Sir Tristram to the bounds,
And there with gibes and flickering mockeries
Stood, while he mutter'd, "Craven crests! O shame!
What faith have these in whom they sware to love?
The glory of our Round Table is no more."

   So Tristram won, and Lancelot gave, the gems,   190
Not speaking other word than, "Hast thou won?
Art thou the purest, brother? See, the hand
Wherewith thou takest this is red!" to whom
Tristram, half plagued by Lancelot's languorous mood,
Made answer: "Ay, but wherefore toss me this
Like a dry bone cast to some hungry hound?
Let be thy fair Queen's fantasy. Strength of heart
And might of limb, but mainly use and skill,
Are winners in this pastime of our King.
My hand—belike the lance hath dript upon it—   200
No blood of mine, I trow; but O chief knight,
Right arm of Arthur in the battle-field,
Great brother, thou nor I have made the world;
Be happy in thy fair Queen as I in mine."

   And Tristram round the gallery made his horse
Caracole; then bow'd his homage, bluntly saying,
"Fair damsels, each to him who worships each
Sole Queen of Beauty and of love, behold
This day my Queen of Beauty is not here."
And most of these were mute, some anger'd, one   210
Murmuring, "All courtesy is dead," and one,
"The glory of our Round Table is no more."

Then fell thick rain, plume droopt and mantle clung,
And pettish cries awoke, and the wan day
Went glooming down in wet and weariness;
But under her black brows a swarthy one
Laugh'd shrilly, crying: "Praise the patient saints,
Our one white day of Innocence hath past,
Tho' somewhat draggled at the skirt. So be it.
The snowdrop only, flowering thro' the year,   220
Would make the world as blank as winter-tide.
Come—let us gladden their sad eyes, our Queen's
And Lancelot's, at this night's solemnity
With all the kindlier colors of the field."

So dame and damsel glitter'd at the feast
Variously gay; for he that tells the tale
Liken'd them, saying, as when an hour of cold
Falls on the mountain in midsummer snows,
And all the purple slopes of mountain flowers
Pass under white, till the warm hour returns   230
With veer of wind and all are flowers again,
So dame and damsel cast the simple white,
And glowing in all colors, the live grass,
Rose-campion, bluebell, kingcup, poppy, glanced
About the revels, and with mirth so loud
Beyond all use, that, half-amazed, the Queen,
And wroth at Tristram and the lawless jousts,
Brake up their sports, then slowly to her bower
Parted, and in her bosom pain was lord.

And little Dagonet on the morrow morn,   240
High over all the yellowing autumn-tide,
Danced like a wither'd leaf before the hall.
Then Tristram saying, "Why skip ye so, Sir Fool?"
Wheel'd round on either heel, Dagonet replied,
"Belike for lack of wiser company;
Or being fool, and seeing too much wit
Makes the world rotten, why, belike I skip
To know myself the wisest knight of all."
"Ay, fool," said Tristram, "but 't is eating dry
To dance without a catch, a roundelay   250
To dance to." Then he twangled on his harp,
And while he twangled little Dagonet stood
Quiet as any water-sodden log
Stay'd in the wandering warble of a brook,
But when the twangling ended, skipt again;
And being ask'd, "Why skipt ye not, Sir Fool?"
Made answer, "I had liefer twenty years
Skip to the broken music of my brains

Than any broken music thou canst make."
Then Tristram, waiting for the quip to come,   260
"Good now, what music have I broken, fool?"
And little Dagonet, skipping, "Arthur, the King's;
For when thou playest that air with Queen Isolt,
Thou makest broken music with thy bride,
Her daintier namesake down in Brittany—
And so thou breakest Arthur's music too."
"Save for that broken music in thy brains,
Sir Fool," said Tristram, "I would break thy head.
Fool, I came late, the heathen wars were o'er,
The life had flown, we sware but by the shell—   270
I am but a fool to reason with a fool—
Come, thou art crabb'd and sour; but lean me down,
Sir Dagonet, one of thy long asses' ears,
And harken if my music be not true.

     " 'Free love—free field—we love but while we may.
    The woods are hush'd, their music is no more;
    The leaf is dead, the yearning past away.
    New leaf, new life—the days of frost are o'er;
    New life, new love, to suit the newer day;
    New loves are sweet as those that went before.   280
    Free love—free field—we love but while we may.'

"Ye might have moved slow-measure to my tune,
Not stood stock-still. I made it in the woods,
And heard it ring as true as tested gold."

But Dagonet with one foot poised in his hand:
"Friend, did ye mark that fountain yesterday,
Made to run wine?—but this had run itself
All out like a long life to a sour end—
And them that round it sat with golden cups
To hand the wine to whosoever came—   290
The twelve small damosels white as Innocence,
In honor of poor Innocence the babe,
Who left the gems which Innocence the Queen
Lent to the King, and Innocence the King
Gave for a prize—and one of those white slips
Handed her cup and piped, the pretty one,
'Drink, drink, Sir Fool,' and thereupon I drank,
Spat—pish—the cup was gold, the draught was mud."

And Tristram: "Was it muddier than thy gibes?
Is all the laughter gone dead out of thee?—   300
Not marking how the knighthood mock thee, fool—
'Fear God: honor the King—his one true knight—
Sole follower of the vows'—for here be they
Who knew thee swine enow before I came,

Smuttier than blasted grain. But when the King
Had made thee fool, thy vanity so shot up
It frighted all free fool from out thy heart;
Which left thee less than fool, and less than swine,
A naked aught—yet swine I hold thee still,
For I have flung thee pearls and find thee swine."   310

    And little Dagonet mincing with his feet:
"Knight, an ye fling those rubies round my neck
In lieu of hers, I 'll hold thou hast some touch
Of music, since I care not for thy pearls.
Swine? I have wallow'd, I have wash'd—the world
Is flesh and shadow—I have had my day.
The dirty nurse, Experience, in her kind
Hath foul'd me—an I wallow'd, then I wash'd—
I have had my day and my philosophies—
And thank the Lord I am King Arthur's fool.   320
Swine, say ye? swine, goats, asses, rams, and geese
Troop'd round a Paynim harper once, who thrumm'd
On such a wire as musically as thou
Some such fine song—but never a king's fool."

    And Tristram, "Then were swine, goats, asses, geese
The wiser fools, seeing thy Paynim bard
Had such a mastery of his mystery
That he could harp his wife up out of hell."

    Then Dagonet, turning on the ball of his foot,
"And whither harp'st thou thine? down! and thyself   330
Down! and two more; a helpful harper thou,
That harpest downward! Dost thou know the star
We call the Harp of Arthur up in heaven?"

    And Tristram, "Ay, Sir Fool, for when our King
Was victor wellnigh day by day, the knights,
Glorying in each new glory, set his name
High on all hills and in the signs of heaven."

    And Dagonet answer'd: "Ay, and when the land
Was freed, and the Queen false, ye set yourself
To babble about him, all to show your wit—   340
And whether he were king by courtesy,
Or king by right—and so went harping down
The black king's highway, got so far and grew
So witty that ye play'd at ducks and drakes
With Arthur's vows on the great lake of fire.
Tuwhoo! do ye see it? do ye see the star?"

    "Nay, fool," said Tristram, "not in open day."
And Dagonet: "Nay, nor will; I see it and hear.

It makes a silent music up in heaven,
And I and Arthur and the angels hear, 350
And then we skip." "Lo, fool," he said, "ye talk
Fool's treason; is the King thy brother fool?"
Then little Dagonet clapt his hands and shrill'd:
"Ay, ay, my brother fool, the king of fools!
Conceits himself as God that he can make
Figs out of thistles, silk from bristles, milk
From burning spurge, honey from hornet-combs,
And men from beasts—Long live the king of fools!"

And down the city Dagonet danced away;
But thro' the slowly-mellowing avenues 360
And solitary passes of the wood
Rode Tristram toward Lyonnesse and the west.
Before him fled the face of Queen Isolt
With ruby-circled neck, but evermore
Past, as a rustle or twitter in the wood
Made dull his inner, keen his outer eye
For all that walk'd, or crept, or perch'd, or flew.
Anon the face, as, when a gust hath blown,
Unruffling waters re-collect the shape
Of one that in them sees himself, return'd; 370
But at the slot or fewmets of a deer,
Or even a fallen feather, vanish'd again.

So on for all that day from lawn to lawn
Thro' many a league-long bower he rode. At length
A lodge of intertwisted beechen-boughs,
Furze-cramm'd and bracken-rooft, the which himself
Built for a summer day with Queen Isolt
Against a shower, dark in the golden grove
Appearing, sent his fancy back to where
She lived a moon in that low lodge with him; 380
Till Mark her lord had past, the Cornish King,
With six or seven, when Tristram was away,
And snatch'd her thence, yet, dreading worse than shame
Her warrior Tristram, spake not any word,
But bode his hour, devising wretchedness.

And now that desert lodge to Tristram lookt
So sweet that, halting, in he past and sank
Down on a drift of foliage random-blown;
But could not rest for musing how to smooth
And sleek his marriage over to the queen. 390
Perchance in lone Tintagil far from all
The tonguesters of the court she had not heard.
But then what folly had sent him over-seas

After she left him lonely here? a name?
Was it the name of one in Brittany,
Isolt, the daughter of the king? "Isolt
Of the White Hands" they call'd her: the sweet name
Allured him first, and then the maid herself,
Who served him well with those white hands of hers,
And loved him well, until himself had thought   400
He loved her also, wedded easily,
But left her all as easily, and return'd.
The black-blue Irish hair and Irish eyes
Had drawn him home—what marvel? then he laid
His brows upon the drifted leaf and dream'd.

    He seem'd to pace the strand of Brittany
Between Isolt of Britain and his bride,
And show'd them both the ruby-chain, and both
Began to struggle for it, till his queen
Graspt it so hard that all her hand was red.   410
Then cried the Breton, "Look, her hand is red!
These be no rubies, this is frozen blood,
And melts within her hand—her hand is hot
With ill desires, but this I gave thee, look,
Is all as cool and white as any flower."
Follow'd a rush of eagle's wings, and then
A whimpering of the spirit of the child,
Because the twain had spoil'd her carcanet.

    He dream'd; but Arthur with a hundred spears
Rode far, till o'er the illimitable reed,   420
And many a glancing plash and sallowy isle,
The wide-wing'd sunset of the misty marsh
Glared on a huge machicolated tower
That stood with open doors, whereout was roll'd
A roar of riot, as from men secure
Amid their marshes, ruffians at their ease
Among their harlot-brides, an evil song.
"Lo there," said one of Arthur's youth, for there,
High on a grim dead tree before the tower,
A goodly brother of the Table Round   430
Swung by the neck; and on the boughs a shield
Showing a shower of blood in a field noir,
And therebeside a horn, inflamed the knights
At that dishonor done the gilded spur,
Till each would clash the shield and blow the horn.
But Arthur waved them back. Alone he rode.
Then at the dry harsh roar of the great horn,
That sent the face of all the marsh aloft
An ever upward-rushing storm and cloud

Of shriek and plume, the Red Knight heard, and all,   440
Even to tipmost lance and topmost helm,
In blood-red armor sallying, howl'd to the King:

"The teeth of Hell flay bare and gnash thee flat!—
Lo! art thou not that eunuch-hearted king
Who fain had clipt free manhood from the world—
The woman-worshipper? Yea, God's curse, and I,
Slain was the brother of my paramour
By a knight of thine, and I that heard her whine
And snivel, being eunuch-hearted too,
Sware by the scorpion-worm that twists in hell   450
And stings itself to everlasting death,
To hang whatever knight of thine I fought
And tumbled. Art thou king?—Look to thy life!"

He ended. Arthur knew the voice; the face
Wellnigh was helmet-hidden, and the name
Went wandering somewhere darkling in his mind.
And Arthur deign'd not use of word or sword,
But let the drunkard, as he stretch'd from horse
To strike him, overbalancing his bulk,
Down from the causeway heavily to the swamp   460
Fall, as the crest of some slow-arching wave,
Heard in dead night along that table-shore,
Drops flat, and after the great waters break
Whitening for half a league, and thin themselves,
Far over sands marbled with moon and cloud,
From less and less to nothing; thus he fell
Head-heavy. Then the knights, who watch'd him, roar'd
And shouted and leapt down upon the fallen,
There trampled out his face from being known,
And sank his head in mire, and slimed themselves;   470
Nor heard the King for their own cries, but sprang
Thro' open doors, and swording right and left
Men, women, on their sodden faces, hurl'd
The tables over and the wines, and slew
Till all the rafters rang with woman-yells,
And all the pavement stream'd with massacre.
Then, echoing yell with yell, they fired the tower,
Which half that autumn night, like the live North,
Red-pulsing up thro' Alioth and Alcor,
Made all above it, and a hundred meres   480
About it, as the water Moab saw
Come round by the east, and out beyond them flush'd
The long low dune and lazy-plunging sea.

So all the ways were safe from shore to shore,
But in the heart of Arthur pain was lord.

Then, out of Tristram waking, the red dream
Fled with a shout, and that low lodge return'd,
Mid-forest, and the wind among the boughs.
He whistled his good war-horse left to graze
Among the forest greens, vaulted upon him,   490
And rode beneath an ever-showering leaf,
Till one lone woman, weeping near a cross,
Stay'd him. "Why weep ye?" "Lord," she said, "my man
Hath left me or is dead;" whereon he thought—
"What, if she hate me now? I would not this.
What, if she love me still? I would not that.
I know not what I would"—but said to her,
"Yet weep not thou, lest, if thy mate return,
He find thy favor changed and love thee not"—
Then pressing day by day thro' Lyonnesse   500
Last in a roky hollow, belling, heard
The hounds of Mark, and felt the goodly hounds
Yelp at his heart, but, turning, past and gain'd
Tintagil, half in sea and high on land,
A crown of towers.

                    Down in a casement sat,
A low sea-sunset glorying round her hair
And glossy-throated grace, Isolt the queen.
And when she heard the feet of Tristram grind
The spiring stone that scaled about her tower,
Flush'd, started, met him at the doors, and there   510
Belted his body with her white embrace,
Crying aloud: "Not Mark—not Mark, my soul!
The footstep flutter'd me at first—not he!
Catlike thro' his own castle steals my Mark,
But warrior-wise thou stridest thro' his halls
Who hates thee, as I him—even to the death.
My soul, I felt my hatred for my Mark
Quicken within me, and knew that thou wert nigh."
To whom Sir Tristram smiling, "I am here;
Let by thy Mark, seeing he is not thine."   520

And drawing somewhat backward she replied:
"Can he be wrong'd who is not even his own,
But save for dread of thee had beaten me,
Scratch'd, bitten, blinded, marr'd me somehow—Mark?
What rights are his that dare not strike for them?
Not lift a hand—not, tho' he found me thus!
But harken! have ye met him? hence he went
To-day for three days' hunting—as he said—
And so returns belike within an hour.
Mark's way, my soul!—but eat not thou with Mark,   530

Because he hates thee even more than fears,
Nor drink; and when thou passest any wood
Close vizor, lest an arrow from the bush
Should leave me all alone with Mark and hell.
My God, the measure of my hate for Mark
Is as the measure of my love for thee!"

So, pluck'd one way by hate and one by love,
Drain'd of her force, again she sat, and spake
To Tristram, as he knelt before her, saying:
"O hunter, and O blower of the horn,   540
Harper, and thou hast been a rover too,
For, ere I mated with my shambling king,
Ye twain had fallen out about the bride
Of one—his name is out of me—the prize,
If prize she were—what marvel?—she could see—
Thine, friend; and ever since my craven seeks
To wreck thee villainously—but, O Sir Knight,
What dame or damsel have ye kneel'd to last?"

And Tristram, "Last to my Queen Paramount,
Here now to my queen paramount of love   550
And loveliness—ay, lovelier than when first
Her light feet fell on our rough Lyonnesse,
Sailing from Ireland."

         Softly laugh'd Isolt:
"Flatter me not, for hath not our great Queen
My dole of beauty trebled?" and he said:
"Her beauty is her beauty, and thine thine,
And thine is more to me—soft, gracious, kind—
Save when thy Mark is kindled on thy lips
Most gracious; but she, haughty, even to him,
Lancelot; for I have seen him wan enow   560
To make one doubt if ever the great Queen
Have yielded him her love."

         To whom Isolt:
"Ah, then, false hunter and false harper, thou
Who brakest thro' the scruple of my bond,
Calling me thy white hind, and saying to me
That Guinevere had sinn'd against the highest,
And I—misyoked with such a want of man—
That I could hardly sin against the lowest."

He answer'd: "O my soul, be comforted!
If this be sweet, to sin in leading-strings,   570
If here be comfort, and if ours be sin,
Crown'd warrant had we for the crowning sin

That made us happy; but how ye greet me—fear
And fault and doubt—no word of that fond tale—
Thy deep heart-yearnings, thy sweet memories
Of Tristram in that year he was away."

And, saddening on the sudden, spake Isolt:
"I had forgotten all in my strong joy
To see thee—yearnings?—ay! for, hour by hour,
Here in the never-ended afternoon,   580
O, sweeter than all memories of thee,
Deeper than any yearnings after thee
Seem'd those far-rolling, westward-smiling seas,
Watch'd from this tower. Isolt of Britain dash'd
Before Isolt of Brittany on the strand,
Would that have chill'd her bride-kiss? Wedded her?
Fought in her father's battles? wounded there?
The King was all fulfill'd with gratefulness,
And she, my namesake of the hands, that heal'd
Thy hurt and heart with unguent and caress—   590
Well—can I wish her any huger wrong
Than having known thee? her too hast thou left
To pine and waste in those sweet memories.
O, were I not my Mark's, by whom all men
Are noble, I should hate thee more than love."

And Tristram, fondling her light hands, replied:
"Grace, queen, for being loved; she loved me well.
Did I love her? the name at least I loved.
Isolt?—I fought his battles, for Isolt!
The night was dark; the true star set. Isolt!   600
The name was ruler of the dark—Isolt?
Care not for her! patient, and prayerful, meek,
Pale-blooded, she will yield herself to God."

And Isolt answer'd: "Yea, and why not I?
Mine is the larger need, who am not meek,
Pale-blooded, prayerful. Let me tell thee now.
Here one black, mute midsummer night I sat,
Lonely, but musing on thee, wondering where,
Murmuring a light song I had heard thee sing,
And once or twice I spake thy name aloud.   610
Then flash'd a levin-brand; and near me stood,
In fuming sulphur blue and green, a fiend—
Mark's way to steal behind one in the dark—
For there was Mark: 'He has wedded her,' he said,
Not said, but hiss'd it; then this crown of towers
So shook to such a roar of all the sky,
That here in utter dark I swoon'd away,

And woke again in utter dark, and cried,
'I will flee hence and give myself to God'—
And thou wert lying in thy new leman's arms."   620

   Then Tristram, ever dallying with her hand,
"May God be with thee, sweet, when old and gray,
And past desire!" a saying that anger'd her.
" 'May God be with thee, sweet, when thou art old,
And sweet no more to me!' I need Him now.
For when had Lancelot utter'd aught so gross
Even to the swineherd's malkin in the mast?
The greater man the greater courtesy.
Far other was the Tristram, Arthur's knight!
But thou, thro' ever harrying thy wild beasts—   630
Save that to touch a harp, tilt with a lance
Becomes thee well—art grown wild beast thyself.
How darest thou, if lover, push me even
In fancy from thy side, and set me far
In the gray distance, half a life away.
Her to be loved no more? Unsay it, unswear!
Flatter me rather, seeing me so weak,
Broken with Mark and hate and solitude,
Thy marriage and mine own, that I should suck
Lies like sweet wines. Lie to me; I believe.   640
Will ye not lie? not swear, as there ye kneel,
And solemnly as when ye sware to him,
The man of men, our King—My God, the power
Was once in vows when men believed the King!
They lied not then who sware, and thro' their vows
The King prevailing made his realm—I say,
Swear to me thou wilt love me even when old,
Gray-hair'd, and past desire, and in despair."

   Then Tristram, pacing moodily up and down:
"Vows! did you keep the vow you made to Mark   650
More than I mine? Lied, say ye? Nay, but learnt,
The vow that binds too strictly snaps itself—
My knighthood taught me this—ay, being snapt—
We run more counter to the soul thereof
Than had we never sworn. I swear no more.
I swore to the great King, and am forsworn.
For once—even to the height—I honor'd him.
'Man, is he man at all?' methought, when first
I rode from our rough Lyonnesse, and beheld
That victor of the Pagan throned in hall—   660
His hair, a sun that ray'd from off a brow
Like hill-snow high in heaven, the steel-biue eyes,
The golden beard that clothed his lips with light—

Moreover, that weird legend of his birth,
With Merlin's mystic babble about his end
Amazed me; then, his foot was on a stool
Shaped as a dragon; he seem'd to me no man,
But Michael trampling Satan; so I sware,
Being amazed. But this went by—The vows!
O, ay—the wholesome madness of an hour— 670
They served their use, their time; for every knight
Believed himself a greater than himself,
And every follower eyed him as a God;
Till he, being lifted up beyond himself,
Did mightier deeds than elsewise he had done,
And so the realm was made. But then their vows—
First mainly thro' that sullying of our Queen—
Began to gall the knighthood, asking whence
Had Arthur right to bind them to himself?
Dropt down from heaven? wash'd up from out the deep? 680
They fail'd to trace him thro' the flesh and blood
Of our old kings. Whence then? a doubtful lord
To bind them by inviolable vows,
Which flesh and blood perforce would violate;
For feel this arm of mine—the tide within
Red with free chase and heather-scented air,
Pulsing full man. Can Arthur make me pure
As any maiden child? lock up my tongue
From uttering freely what I freely hear?
Bind me to one? The wide world laughs at it. 690
And worldling of the world am I, and know
The ptarmigan that whitens ere his hour
Woos his own end; we are not angels here
Nor shall be. Vows—I am woodman of the woods,
And hear the garnet-headed yaffingale
Mock them—my soul, we love but while we may;
And therefore is my love so large for thee,
Seeing it is not bounded save by love."

Here ending, he moved toward her, and she said:
"Good; an I turn'd away my love for thee 700
To some one thrice as courteous as thyself—
For courtesy wins woman all as well
As valor may, but he that closes both
Is perfect, he is Lancelot—taller indeed,
Rosier and comelier, thou—but say I loved
This knightliest of all knights, and cast thee back
Thine own small saw, 'We love but while we may,'
Well then, what answer?"

He that while she spake,

Mindful of what he brought to adorn her with,
The jewels, had let one finger lightly touch   710
The warm white apple of her throat, replied,
"Press this a little closer, sweet, until—
Come, I am hunger'd and half-anger'd—meat,
Wine, wine—and I will love thee to the death,
And out beyond into the dream to come."

So then, when both were brought to full accord,
She rose, and set before him all he will'd;
And after these had comforted the blood
With meats and wines, and satiated their hearts—
Now talking of their woodland paradise,   720
The deer, the dews, the fern, the founts, the lawns;
Now mocking at the much ungainliness,
And craven shifts, and long crane legs of Mark—
Then Tristram laughing caught the harp and sang:

"Ay, ay, O, ay—the winds that bend the brier!
A star in heaven, a star within the mere!
Ay, ay, O, ay—a star was my desire,
And one was far apart and one was near.
Ay, ay, O, ay—the winds that bow the grass!
And one was water and one star was fire,   730
And one will ever shine and one will pass.
Ay, ay, O, ay—the winds that move the mere!"

Then in the light's last glimmer Tristram show'd
And swung the ruby carcanet. She cried,
"The collar of some Order, which our King
Hath newly founded, all for thee, my soul,
For thee, to yield thee grace beyond thy peers."

"Not so, my queen," he said, "but the red fruit
Grown on a magic oak-tree in mid-heaven,
And won by Tristram as a tourney-prize,   740
And hither brought by Tristram for his last
Love-offering and peace-offering unto thee."

He spoke, he turn'd, then, flinging round her neck,
Claspt it, and cried, "Thine Order, O my queen!"
But, while he bow'd to kiss the jewell'd throat,
Out of the dark, just as the lips had touch'd,
Behind him rose a shadow and a shriek—
"Mark's way," said Mark, and clove him thro' the brain.

That night came Arthur home, and while he climb'd,
All in a death-dumb autumn-dripping gloom,   750
The stairway to the hall, and look'd and saw

The great Queen's bower was dark,—about his feet
A voice clung sobbing till he question'd it,
"What art thou?" and the voice about his feet
Sent up an answer, sobbing, "I am thy fool,
And I shall never make thee smile again."
1871

TO THE QUEEN

O loyal to the royal in thyself,
And loyal to thy land, as this to thee—
Bear witness, that rememberable day,
When, pale as yet and fever-worn, the Prince
Who scarce had pluck'd his flickering life again
From halfway down the shadow of the grave
Past with thee thro' thy people and their love,
And London roll'd one tide of joy thro' all
Her trebled millions, and loud leagues of man
And welcome! witness, too, the silent cry,   10
The prayer of many a race and creed, and clime—
Thunderless lightnings striking under sea
From sunset and sunrise of all thy realm,
And that true North, whereof we lately heard
A strain to shame us, "Keep you to yourselves;
So loyal is too costly! friends—your love
Is but a burthen; loose the bond, and go."
Is this the tone of empire? here the faith
That made us rulers? this, indeed, her voice
And meaning whom the roar of Hougoumont   20
Left mightiest of all peoples under heaven?
What shock has fool'd her since, that she should speak
So feebly? wealthier—wealthier—hour by hour!
The voice of Britain, or a sinking land,
Some third-rate isle half-lost among her seas?
There rang her voice, when the full city peal'd
Thee and thy Prince! The loyal to their crown
Are loyal to their own far sons, who love
Our ocean-empire with her boundless homes
For ever-broadening England, and her throne   30
In our vast Orient, and one isle, one isle,
That knows not her own greatness; if she knows
And dreads it we are fallen.—But thou, my Queen,
Not for itself, but thro' thy living love
For one to whom I made it o'er his grave
Sacred, accept this old imperfect tale,

New-old, and shadowing Sense at war with Soul,
Ideal manhood closed in real man,
Rather than that gray king whose name, a ghost,
Streams like a cloud, man-shaped, from mountain peak,   40
And cleaves to cairn and cromlech still; or him
Of Geoffrey's book, or him of Malleor's, one
Touch'd by the adulterous finger of a time
That hover'd between war and wantonness,
And crownings and dethronements. Take withal
Thy poet's blessing, and his trust that Heaven
Will blow the tempest in the distance back
From thine and ours; for some are scared, who mark,
Or wisely or unwisely, signs of storm,
Waverings of every vane with every wind,   50
And wordy trucklings to the transient hour,
And fierce or careless looseners of the faith,
And Softness breeding scorn of simple life,
Or Cowardice, the child of lust for gold,
Or Labor, with a groan and not a voice,
Or Art with poisonous honey stolen from France,
And that which knows, but careful for itself,
And that which knows not, ruling that which knows
To its own harm. The goal of this great world
Lies beyond sight; yet—if our slowly-grown   60
And crown'd Republic's crowning common-sense,
That sav'd her many times, not fail—their fears
Are morning shadows huger than the shapes
That cast them, not those gloomier which forego
The darkness of that battle in the west
Where all of high and holy dies away.
1872

THE VOYAGE OF MAELDUNE

FOUNDED ON AN IRISH LEGEND A.D. 700

I

I was the chief of the race—he had stricken my father dead—
But I gather'd my fellows together, I swore I would strike off his head
Each of them look'd like a king, and was noble in birth as in worth,
And each of them boasted he sprang from the oldest race upon earth.
Each was as brave in the fight as the bravest hero of song,
And each of them liefer had died than have done one another a wrong
He lived on an isle in the ocean—we sail'd on a Friday morn—
He that had slain my father the day before I was born.

II

And we came to the isle in the ocean, and there on the shore was he.
But a sudden blast blew us out and away thro' a boundless sea.   10

III

And we came to the Silent Isle that we never had touch'd at before,
Where a silent ocean always broke on a silent shore,
And the brooks glitter'd on in the light without sound, and the long
  waterfalls
Pour'd in a thunderless plunge to the base of the mountain walls,
And the poplar and cypress unshaken by storm flourish'd up beyond
  sight,
And the pine shot aloft from the crag to an unbelievable height,
And high in the heaven above it there flicker'd a songless lark,
And the cock could n't crow, and the bull could n't low, and the dog
  could n't bark.
And round it we went, and thro' it, but never a murmur, a breath—
It was all of it fair as life, it was all of it quiet as death,   20
And we hated the beautiful isle, for whenever we strove to speak
Our voices were thinner and fainter than any flittermouse-shriek;
And the men that were mighty of tongue and could raise such a battle-
  cry
That a hundred who heard it would rush on a thousand lances and
  die—
O, they to be dumb'd by the charm!—so fluster'd with anger were they
They almost fell on each other; but after we sail'd away.

IV

And we came to the Isle of Shouting; we landed, a score of wild birds
Cried from the topmost summit with human voices and words.
Once in an hour they cried, and whenever their voices peal'd
The steer fell down at the plow and the harvest died from the field,   30
And the men dropt dead in the valleys and half of the cattle went lame,
And the roof sank in on the hearth, and the dwelling broke into flame;
And the shouting of these wild birds ran into the hearts of my crew,
Till they shouted along with the shouting and seized one another and
  slew.
But I drew them the one from the other; I saw that we could not stay,
And we left the dead to the birds, and we sail'd with our wounded
  away.

V

And we came to the Isle of Flowers; their breath met us out on the seas,
For the Spring and the middle Summer sat each on the lap of the
  breeze;
And the red passion-flower to the cliffs, and the dark-blue clematis,
  clung,

And starr'd with a myriad blossom the long convolvulus hung;   40
And the topmost spire of the mountain was lilies in lieu of snow,
And the lilies like glaciers winded down, running out below
Thro' the fire of the tulip and poppy, the blaze of gorse, and the blush
Of millions of roses that sprang without leaf or a thorn from the bush;
And the whole isle-side flashing down from the peak without ever a
    tree
Swept like a torrent of gems from the sky to the blue of the sea.
And we roll'd upon capes of crocus and vaunted our kith and our kin,
And we wallow'd in beds of lilies, and chanted the triumph of Finn,
Till each like a golden image was pollen'd from head to feet
And each was as dry as a cricket, with thirst in the middle-day heat.
Blossom and blossom, and promise of blossom, but never a fruit!   51
And we hated the Flowering Isle, as we hated the isle that was mute,
And we tore up the flowers by the million and flung them in bight and
    bay,
And we left but a naked rock, and in anger we sail'd away.

VI

And we came to the Isle of Fruits; all round from the cliffs and the
    capes,
Purple or amber, dangled a hundred fathom of grapes,
And the warm melon lay like a little sun on the tawny sand,
And the fig ran up from the beach and rioted over the land,
And the mountain arose like a jewell'd throne thro' the fragrant air,
Glowing with all-color'd plums and with golden masses of pear,   60
And the crimson and scarlet of berries that flamed upon bine and vine,
But in every berry and fruit was the poisonous pleasure of wine;
And the peak of the mountain was apples, the hugest that ever were
    seen,
And they prest, as they grew, on each other, with hardly a leaflet be-
    tween,
And all of them redder than rosiest health or than utterest shame,
And setting, when Even descended, the very sunset aflame.
And we stay'd three days, and we gorged and we madden'd, till every
    one drew
His sword on his fellow to slay him, and ever they struck and they slew;
And myself, I had eaten but sparely, and fought till I sunder'd the fray,
Then I bade them remember my father's death, and we sail'd away.   70

VII

And we came to the Isle of Fire; we were lured by the light from afar,
For the peak sent up one league of fire to the Northern Star;
Lured by the glare and the blare, but scarcely could stand upright,
For the whole isle shudder'd and shook like a man in a mortal affright.
We were giddy besides with the fruits we had gorged, and so crazed
    that at last

There were some leap'd into the fire; and away we sail'd, and we past
Over that undersea isle, where the water is clearer than air.
Down we look'd—what a garden! O bliss, what a Paradise there!
Towers of a happier time, low down in a rainbow deep
Silent palaces, quiet fields of eternal sleep!   80
And three of the gentlest and best of my people, whate'er I could say,
Plunged head-down in the sea, and the Paradise trembled away.

VIII

And we came to the Bounteous Isle, where the heavens lean low on the
    land,
And ever at dawn from the cloud glitter'd o'er us a sun-bright hand,
Then it open'd and dropt at the side of each man, as he rose from his
    rest,
Bread enough for his need till the laborless day dipt under the west;
And we wander'd about it and thro' it. O, never was time so good!
And we sang of the triumphs of Finn, and the boast of our ancient
    blood,
And we gazed at the wandering wave as we sat by the gurgle of
    springs,   89
And we chanted the songs of the Bards and the glories of fairy kings.
But at length we began to be weary, to sigh, and to stretch and yawn,
Till we hated the Bounteous Isle and the sun-bright hand of the dawn,
For there was not an enemy near, but the whole green isle was our own,
And we took to playing at ball, and we took to throwing the stone,
And we took to playing at battle, but that was a perilous play,
For the passion of battle was in us, we slew and we sail'd away.

IX

And we came to the Isle of Witches and heard their musical cry—
"Come to us, O, come, come!" in the stormy red of a sky
Dashing the fires and the shadows of dawn on the beautiful shapes,
For a wild witch naked as heaven stood on each of the loftiest capes,
And a hundred ranged on the rock like white sea-birds in a row,   101
And a hundred gamboll'd and pranced on the wrecks in the sand below,
And a hundred splash'd from the ledges, and bosom'd the burst of the
    spray;
But I knew we should fall on each other, and hastily sail'd away.

X

And we came in an evil time to the Isle of the Double Towers,
One was of smooth-cut stone, one carved all over with flowers,
But an earthquake always moved in the hollows under the dells,
And they shock'd on each other and butted each other with clashing
    of bells,   108
And the daws flew out of the towers and jangled and wrangled in vain,
And the clash and boom of the bells rang into the heart and the brain,

Till the passion of battle was on us, and all took sides with the towers,
There were some for the clean-cut stone, there were more for the carven
    flowers,
And the wrathful thunder of God peal'd over us all the day,
For the one half slew the other, and after we sail'd away.

XI

And we came to the Isle of a Saint who had sail'd with Saint Brendan
    of yore,
He had lived ever since on the isle and his winters were fifteen score,
And his voice was low as from other worlds, and his eyes were sweet,
And his white hair sank to his heels, and his white beard fell to his feet,
And he spake to me: "O Maeldune, let be this purpose of thine!
Remember the words of the Lord when he told us, 'Vengeance is
    mine!'   120
His fathers have slain thy fathers in war or in single strife,
Thy fathers have slain his fathers, each taken a life for a life,
Thy father had slain his father, how long shall the murder last?
Go back to the Isle of Finn and suffer the Past to be Past."
And we kiss'd the fringe of his beard, and we pray'd as we heard him
    pray,
And the holy man he assoil'd us, and sadly we sail'd away.

XII

And we came to the isle we were blown from, and there on the shore
    was he,
The man that had slain my father. I saw him and let him be.
O, weary was I of the travel, the trouble, the strife, and the sin,
When I landed again with a tithe of my men, on the Isle of Finn!   130
1880

RIZPAH

17—

I

Wailing, wailing, wailing, the wind over land and sea—
And Willy's voice in the wind, "O mother, come out to me!"
Why should he call me to-night, when he knows that I cannot go?
For the downs are as bright as day, and the full moon stares at the
    snow.

II

We should be seen, my dear; they would spy us out of the town.
The loud black nights for us, and the storm rushing over the down,

When I cannot see my own hand, but am led by the creak of the
 chain,
And grovel and grope for my son till I find myself drenched with the
 rain.

III

Anything fallen again? nay—what was there left to fall?
I have taken them home, I have number'd the bones, I have hidden
 them all.   10
What am I saying? and what are *you*? do you come as a spy?
Falls? what falls? who knows? As the tree falls so must it lie.

IV

Who let her in? how long has she been? you—what have you heard?
Why did you sit so quiet? you never have spoken a word.
O—to pray with me—yes—a lady—none of their spies—
But the night has crept into my heart, and begun to darken my eyes.

V

Ah—you, that have lived so soft, what should *you* know of the night,
The blast and the burning shame and the bitter frost and the fright?
I have done it, while you were asleep—you were only made for the day.
I have gather'd my baby together—and now you may go your way.   20

VI

Nay—for it 's kind of you, madam, to sit by an old dying wife.
But say nothing hard of my boy, I have only an hour of life.
I kiss'd my boy in the prison, before he went out to die.
"They dared me to do it," he said, and he never has told me a lie.
I whipt him for robbing an orchard once when he was but a child—
"The farmer dared me to do it," he said; he was always so wild—
And idle—and could n't be idle—my Willy—he never could rest.
The King should have made him a soldier, he would have been one of
 his best.

VII

But he lived with a lot of wild mates, and they never would let him
 be good;
They swore that he dare not rob the mail, and he swore that he
 would;   30
And he took no life, but he took one purse, and when all was done
He flung it among his fellows—"I 'll none of it," said my son.

VIII

I came into court to the judge and the lawyers. I told them my tale,
God's own truth—but they kill'd him, they kill'd him for robbing the
 mail.

They hang'd him in chains for a show—we had always borne a good
  name—
To be hang'd for a thief—and then put away—is n't that enough
  shame?
Dust to dust—low down—let us hide! but they set him so high
That all the ships of the world could stare at him, passing by.
God 'ill pardon the hell-black raven and horrible fowls of the air,
But not the black heart of the lawyer who kill'd him and hang'd him
  there.   40

IX

And the jailer forced me away. I had bid him my last good-bye;
They had fasten'd the door of his cell. "O mother!" I heard him cry.
I could n't get back tho' I tried, he had something further to say,
And now I never shall know it. The jailer forced me away.

X

Then since I could n't but hear that cry of my boy that was dead,
They seized me and shut me up: they fasten'd me down on my bed.
"Mother, O mother!"—he call'd in the dark to me year after year—
They beat me for that, they beat me—you know that I could n't but
  hear;
And then at the last they found I had grown so stupid and still
They let me abroad again—but the creatures had worked their will. 50

XI

Flesh of my flesh was gone, but bone of my bone was left—
I stole them all from the lawyers—and you, will you call it a theft?—
My baby, the bones that had suck'd me, the bones that had laughed
  and had cried—
Theirs? O, no! they are mine—not theirs—they had moved in my side.

XII

Do you think I was scared by the bones? I kiss'd 'em, I buried 'em all—
I can't dig deep, I am old—in the night by the churchyard wall.
My Willy 'ill rise up whole when the trumpet of judgment 'ill sound,
But I charge you never to say that I laid him in holy ground.

XIII

They would scratch him up—they would hang him again on the cursed
  tree.
Sin? O, yes, we are sinners, I know—let all that be,   60
And read me a Bible verse of the Lord's goodwill toward men—
"Full of compassion and mercy, the Lord"—let me hear it again;
"Full of compassion and mercy—long-suffering." Yes, O, yes!
For the lawyer is born but to murder—the Saviour lives but to bless.
He 'll never put on the black cap except for the worst of the worst,

And the first may be last—I have heard it in church—and the last may
    be first.
Suffering—O, long-suffering—yes, as the Lord must know,
Year after year in the mist and the wind and the shower and the snow.

XIV

Heard, have you? what? they have told you he never repented his sin.
How do they know it? are *they* his mother? are *you* of his kin?   70
Heard! have you ever heard, when the storm on the downs began,
The wind that 'ill wail like a child and the sea that 'ill moan like a
    man?

XV

Election, Election, and Reprobation—it 's all very well.
But I go to-night to my boy, and I shall not find him in hell.
For I cared so much for my boy that the Lord has look'd into my care,
And He means me I'm sure to be happy with Willy, I know not where.

XVI

And if *he* be lost—but to save *my* soul, that is all your desire—
Do you think that I care for *my* soul if my boy be gone to the fire?
I have been with God in the dark—go, go, you may leave me alone—
You never have borne a child—you are just as hard as a stone.   80

XVII

Madam, I beg your pardon! I think that you mean to be kind,
But I cannot hear what you say for my Willy's voice in the wind—
The snow and the sky so bright—he used but to call in the dark,
And he calls to me now from the church and not from the gibbet—
    for hark!
Nay—you can hear it yourself—it is coming—shaking the walls—
Willy—the moon 's in a cloud——Good-night. I am going. He calls.
1880

DEMETER AND PERSEPHONE

(IN ENNA)

Faint as a climate-changing bird that flies
All night across the darkness, and at dawn
Falls on the threshold of her native land,
And can no more, thou camest, O my child,
Led upward by the God of ghosts and dreams,
Who laid thee at Eleusis, dazed and dumb
With passing thro' at once from state to state,
Until I brought thee hither, that the day,
When here thy hands let fall the gather'd flower,

Might break thro' clouded memories once again 10
On thy lost self. A sudden nightingale
Saw thee, and flash'd into a frolic of song
And welcome; and a gleam as of the moon,
When first she peers along the tremulous deep,
Fled wavering o'er thy face, and chased away
That shadow of a likeness to the king
Of shadows, thy dark mate. Persephone!
Queen of the dead no more—my child! Thine eyes
Again were human-godlike, and the Sun
Burst from a swimming fleece of winter gray, 20
And robed thee in his day from head to feet—
"Mother!" and I was folded in thine arms.

    Child, those imperial, disimpassion'd eyes
Awed even me at first, thy mother—eyes
That oft had seen the serpent-wanded power
Draw downward into Hades with his drift
Of flickering spectres, lighted from below
By the red race of fiery Phlegethon;
But when before have Gods or men beheld
The Life that had descended re-arise, 30
And lighted from above him by the Sun?
So mighty was the mother's childless cry,
A cry that rang thro' Hades, Earth, and Heaven!

    So in this pleasant vale we stand again,
The field of Enna, now once more ablaze
With flowers that brighten as thy footstep falls,
All flowers—but for one black blur of earth
Left by that closing chasm, thro' which the car
Of dark Aïdoneus rising rapt thee hence.
And here, my child, tho' folded in thine arms, 40
I feel the deathless heart of motherhood
Within me shudder, lest the naked glebe
Should yawn once more into the gulf, and thence
The shrilly whinnyings of the team of Hell,
Ascending, pierce the glad and songful air,
And all at once their arch'd necks, midnight-maned,
Jet upward thro' the midday blossom. No!
For, see, thy foot has touch'd it; all the space
Of blank earth-baldness clothes itself afresh,
And breaks into the crocus-purple hour 50
That saw thee vanish.

            Child, when thou wert gone,
I envied human wives, and nested birds,
Yea, the cubb'd lioness; went in search of thee

Thro' many a palace, many a cot, and gave
Thy breast to ailing infants in the night,
And set the mother waking in a maze
To find her sick one whole; and forth again
Among the wail of midnight winds, and cried,
"Where is my loved one? Wherefore do ye wail?"
And out from all the night an answer shrill'd,   60
"We know not, and we know not why we wail."
I climb'd on all the cliffs of all the seas,
And ask'd the waves that moan about the world,
"Where? do ye make your moaning for my child?"
And round from all the world the voices came,
"We know not, and we know not why we moan."
"Where?" and I stared from every eagle-peak,
I thridded the black heart of all the woods,
I peer'd thro' tomb and cave, and in the storms
Of autumn swept across the city, and heard   70
The murmur of their temples chanting me,
Me, me, the desolate mother! "Where?"—and turn'd,
And fled by many a waste, forlorn of man,
And grieved for man thro' all my grief for thee,—
The jungle rooted in his shatter'd hearth,
The serpent coil'd about his broken shaft,
The scorpion crawling over naked skulls;—
I saw the tiger in the ruin'd fane
Spring from his fallen God, but trace of thee
I saw not; and far on, and, following out   80
A league of labyrinthine darkness, came
On three gray heads beneath a gleaming rift.
"Where?" and I heard one voice from all the three,
"We know not, for we spin the lives of men,
And not of Gods, and know not why we spin!
There is a Fate beyond us." Nothing knew.

    Last as the likeness of a dying man,
Without his knowledge, from him flits to warn
A far-off friendship that he comes no more,
So he, the God of dreams, who heard my cry,   90
Drew from thyself the likeness of thyself
Without thy knowledge, and thy shadow past
Before me, crying, "The Bright one in the highest
Is brother of the Dark one in the lowest,
And Bright and Dark have sworn that I, the child
Of thee, the great Earth-Mother, thee, the Power
That lifts her buried life from gloom to bloom,
Should be for ever and for evermore
The Bride of Darkness."

So the Shadow wail'd.
Then I, Earth-Goddess, cursed the Gods of heaven.　　　100
I would not mingle with their feasts; to me
Their nectar smack'd of hemlock on the lips,
Their rich ambrosia tasted aconite.
That man, that only lives and loves an hour,
Seem'd nobler than their hard eternities.
My quick tears kill'd the flower, my ravings hush'd
The bird, and lost in utter grief I fail'd
To send my life thro' olive-yard and vine
And golden-grain, my gift to helpless man.
Rain-rotten died the wheat, the barley-spears　　　110
Were hollow-husk'd, the leaf fell, and the Sun,
Pale at my grief, drew down before his time
Sickening, and Ætna kept her winter snow.

Then He, the brother of this Darkness, He
Who still is highest, glancing from his height
On earth a fruitless fallow, when he miss'd
The wonted steam of sacrifice, the praise
And prayer of men, decreed that thou shouldst dwell
For nine white moons of each whole year with me,
Three dark ones in the shadow with thy king.　　　120

Once more the reaper in the gleam of dawn
Will see me by the landmark far away,
Blessing his field, or seated in the dusk
Of even, by the lonely threshing-floor,
Rejoicing in the harvest and the grange.

Yet I, Earth-Goddess, am but ill-content
With them who still are highest. Those gray heads,
What meant they by their "Fate beyond the Fates"
But younger kindlier Gods to bear us down,
As we bore down the Gods before us? Gods,　　　130
To quench, not hurl the thunderbolt, to stay,
Not spread the plague, the famine; Gods indeed,
To send the noon into the night and break
The sunless halls of Hades into Heaven?
Till thy dark lord accept and love the Sun,
And all the Shadow die into the Light,
When thou shalt dwell the whole bright year with me,
And souls of men, who grew beyond their race,
And made themselves as Gods against the fear
Of Death and Hell; and thou that hast from men,　　　140
As Queen of Death, that worship which is Fear,
Henceforth, as having risen from out the dead,
Shalt ever send thy life along with mine

From buried grain thro' springing blade, and bless
Their garner'd autumn also, reap with me,
Earth-mother, in the harvest hymns of Earth
The worship which is Love, and see no more
The Stone, the Wheel, the dimly-glimmering lawns
Of that Elysium, all the hateful fires
Of torment, and the shadowy warrior glide   150
Along the silent field of Asphodel.
1887 (1889)

MERLIN AND THE GLEAM

I

O young Mariner,
You from the haven
Under the sea-cliff,
You that are watching
The gray Magician
With eyes of wonder,
I am Merlin,
And I am dying,
I am Merlin
Who follow the Gleam.   10

II

Mighty the Wizard
Who found me at sunrise
Sleeping, and woke me
And learn'd me Magic!
Great the Master,
And sweet the Magic,
When over the valley,
In early summers,
Over the mountain,
On human faces,   20
And all around me,
Moving to melody,
Floated the Gleam.

III

Once at the croak of a Raven who crost it
A barbarous people,
Blind to the magic
And deaf to the melody,
Snarl'd at and cursed me,
A demon vext me,

The light retreated, 30
The landskip darken'd,
The melody deaden'd,
The Master whisper'd,
"Follow the Gleam."

IV

Then to the melody,
Over a wilderness
Gliding, and glancing at
Elf of the woodland,
Gnome of the cavern,
Griffin and Giant, 40
And dancing of Fairies
In desolate hollows,
And wraiths of the mountain,
And rolling of dragons
By warble of water,
Or cataract music
Of falling torrents,
Flitted the Gleam.

V

Down from the mountain
And over the level, 50
And streaming and shining on
Silent river,
Silvery willow,
Pasture and plowland,
Innocent maidens,
Garrulous children,
Homestead and harvest,
Reaper and gleaner,
And rough-ruddy faces
Of lowly labor, 60
Slided the Gleam—

VI

Then, with a melody
Stronger and statelier,
Led me at length
To the city and palace
Of Arthur the King;
Touch'd at the golden
Cross of the churches,
Flash'd on the tournament,
Flicker'd and bicker'd 70
From helmet to helmet,

And last on the forehead
Of Arthur the blameless
Rested the Gleam.

VII

Clouds and darkness
Closed upon Camelot;
Arthur had vanish'd
I knew not whither,
The king who loved me,
And cannot die;   80
For out of the darkness
Silent and slowly
The Gleam, that had waned to a wintry glimmer
On icy fallow
And faded forest,
Drew to the valley
Named of the shadow,
And slowly brightening
Out of the glimmer,
And slowly moving again to a melody   90
Yearningly tender,
Fell on the shadow,
No longer a shadow,
But clothed with the Gleam.

VIII

And broader and brighter
The Gleam flying onward,
Wed to the melody,
Sang thro' the world;
And slower and fainter,
Old and weary,   100
But eager to follow,
I saw, whenever
In passing it glanced upon
Hamlet or city,
That under the Crosses
The dead man's garden,
The mortal hillock,
Would break into blossom;
And so to the land's
Last limit I came—   110
And can no longer,
But die rejoicing,
For thro' the Magic
Of Him the Mighty,
Who taught me in childhood,

There on the border
Of boundless Ocean,
And all but in Heaven
Hovers the Gleam.

IX

Not of the sunlight,   **120**
Not of the moonlight,
Not of the starlight!
O young Mariner,
Down to the haven,
Call your companions,
Launch your vessel
And crowd your canvas,
And, ere it vanishes
Over the margin,
After it, follow it,   **130**
Follow the Gleam.
1889

CROSSING THE BAR

Sunset and evening star,
   And one clear call for me!
And may there be no moaning of the bar,
   When I put out to sea,

But such a tide as moving seems asleep,
   Too full for sound and foam,
When that which drew from out the boundless deep
   Turns again home.

Twilight and evening bell,
   And after that the dark!   **10**
And may there be no sadness of farewell,
   When I embark;

For tho' from out our bourne of Time and Place
   The flood may bear me far,
I hope to see my Pilot face to face
   When I have crost the bar.
1889

Robert Browning
May 7, 1812—December 12, 1889

A BIOGRAPHICAL SKETCH

Apparently Browning did not suffer from the personal anxieties and domestic tensions that contributed to the many nightmare moments in the youth of Tennyson. The Brownings' home circle was small, secure, and urbane. His father was a successful official in the Bank of England, an amateur artist, an avid book collector and reader, with few if any "thou shalt" and "thou shalt not" hang-ups. His intellectual interests were broad and nondogmatic and his literary appreciation of a peculiarly experiential kind: according to Browning his father "seemed to have known Paracelsus, Faustus, and even Talmudic personages, personally." Browning's mother was gentle, musically accomplished, and supportive. When he discovered Shelley's *Queen Mab* at the age of fourteen, his mother helped him acquire the complete works of the late poet. The foundation and much of the superstructure of Browning's massive erudition were built in this home in the London suburbs with its serenity and its six thousand volumes.

Browning's thoughts of a career ran in many directions: art, music, poetry, fiction, drama, and diplomacy. He had the means to travel; in the winter of 1833 he visited Russia and in the late 1830's spent two years in Italy. The expansiveness of his spirit marked his early poems with a high degree of virtuosity. *Pauline* (1833), *Paracelsus* (1835), *Strafford* (1837, a drama), and *Sordello* (1840) are all long, brilliant, and unsuccessful. Many of the elements identifiable in the mature work of Browning can be traced in these early ones: the influence of Shelley; a fascination with and acute knowledge of the value conflicts that emerged with the Renaissance; the plight and moral seriousness of grand but crisis-oriented characters; lyricism; a keen apprehension of the dramatic; and a persistent, thematic probing of the artist's dilemma in a spiritually turbulent society. But Browning had not yet mastered his medium. In fact he merely succeeded in gaining a reputation for caprice and obscurity that clung to him for decades.

The crucial years in the shaping of Browning's poetry were 1841–1846. During those years he published a series of experiments in "sound and sense" entitled *Bells and Pomegranates*. The eight pamphlets contained not only his final efforts to produce drama for the closet and the stage (*The Return of the Druses* (1843), A *Blot in the 'Scutcheon* (1843), *Colombe's Birthday* (1844), *Luria* and A *Soul's Tragedy* (1846)) but also a dramatic poem, *Pippa Passes* (1841) and a series of "dramatic lyrics" and "dramatic romances and lyrics." Some of these have become touchstones in the Browning canon, e.g., *My Last Duchess, Soliloquy of the Spanish Cloister, Johannes Agricola in Meditation, Porphyria's Lover* (all in 1842) and *Pictor Ignotus, The Italian in England, The Englishman in Italy, The Bishop Orders His Tomb at Saint Praxed's Church,* an incomplete version of *Saul* (all in 1845).

On the personal side, Browning first wrote to Elizabeth Barrett on January 10, 1845, praising her two volumes of *Poems* published late the year before. Thus began the correspondence and courtship which climaxed in their marriage on September 12, 1846. A few days later they traveled to Florence, where they made their home at Casa Guidi until her death on June 29, 1861.

In 1855 Browning published *Men and Women*. The fifty-one poems contained in the two volumes signaled Browning's mastery of his complex perceptions and of the variety of dramatic and lyric forms through which he gave them distinctive expression. The imaginary voices, the action in character, the crucial moment in the history of a soul—in short, the mix of essential elements was present, brilliant with life and fully functioning. This new level of excellence Browning maintained during the next decade and a half, through *Dramatis Personae* (1864) to a different but equally brilliant climax in *The Ring and the Book* (1868–1869), his chief work and the test by which his stature must ultimately be measured.

Except for his last volume, *Asolando: Fancies and Facts* (1889), little that Browning wrote after *The Ring and the Book* is read by anyone but specialists. His devotion (and that of Mrs. Browning) to the Greek dramatists is reflected in *Balaustion's Adventure: Including a Transcript from Euripides* (1871), *Aristophanes' Apology: Including a Transcript from Euripides, Being the Last Adventure of Balaustion* (1875), and *The Agamemnon of Aeschylus* (1877). *Prince Hohenstiel-Schwangau, Saviour of Society* (1871) presents a disguised version of Napoleon III defending his policy of political expediency and realism; and *Parleyings with Certain People of Importance in Their Day* (1887) has been carefully studied by W. C. DeVane as "notes for Browning's mental autobiography."

Titles of other volumes of Browning are these: *Fifine at the Fair* (1872), *Red Cotton Night-Cap Country* (1873), *The Inn Album* (1875), *Pacchiarotto, and How He Worked in Distemper, with Other Poems* (1876), *La Saisiaz* and *The Two Poets of Croisic* (1878), *Dramatic Idyls* (1879), *Dramatic Idyls: Second Series* (1880), *Jocoseria* (1883), and *Ferishtah's Fancies* (1884).

Browning was amused, flattered, and embarrassed by the establishment of the Browning Society and affiliated clubs in England and America from 1881 on. In 1882 he was awarded the honorary degree of D. C. L. by Oxford. He spent his last two years in Italy at Asolo, the scene of *Pippa Passes,* and at Venice, the home of his son, where he died on December 12, 1889. He was buried in Westminster Abbey.

A BIBLIOGRAPHICAL NOTE

The standard editions of Browning's poetry are the Florentine Edition, edited by Charlotte Porter and Helen A. Clarke (twelve volumes, London: Smith, Elder, 1910) and the Centenary Edition, edited by F. G. Kenyon (ten volumes, New York: Crowell, 1912). The standard biography is still that by W. H. Griffin and H. C. Minchin, *The Life of Robert Browning* (London: Methuen, 1910; third edition, revised, 1938). William Clyde DeVane's *A Browning Handbook* (second edition, New York: Appleton-Century-Crofts, 1955) is encyclopedic, and Philip Drew's edition of *Critical Essays on the Poetry of Browning* (Boston: Houghton Mifflin, 1966) provides a useful critical introduction.

The shorter poems in this text are based on the Florentine Edition, the selections from *The Ring and the Book* on the Kenyon Edition. The numbering of lines has been standardized by counting two half-lines between verse-paragraphs as one line.

MY LAST DUCHESS

FERRARA

That's my last Duchess painted on the wall,
Looking as if she were alive. I call
That piece a wonder, now: Frà Pandolf's hands
Worked busily a day, and there she stands.
Will't please you sit and look at her? I said
"Frà Pandolf" by design, for never read
Strangers like you that pictured countenance,
The depth and passion of its earnest glance,
But to myself they turned (since none puts by
The curtain I have drawn for you, but I)   10

And seemed as they would ask me, if they durst,
How such a glance came there; so, not the first
Are you to turn and ask thus. Sir, 'twas not
Her husband's presence only, called that spot
Of joy into the Duchess' cheek: perhaps
Frà Pandolf chanced to say "Her mantle laps
Over my lady's wrist too much," or "Paint
Must never hope to reproduce the faint
Half-flush that dies along her throat:" such stuff
Was courtesy, she thought, and cause enough   20
For calling up that spot of joy. She had
A heart—how shall I say?—too soon made glad,
Too easily impressed; she liked whate'er
She looked on, and her looks went everywhere.
Sir, 'twas all one! My favor at her breast,
The dropping of the daylight in the West,
The bough of cherries some officious fool
Broke in the orchard for her, the white mule
She rode with round the terrace—all and each
Would draw from her alike the approving speech,   30
Or blush, at least. She thanked men,—good! but thanked
Somehow—I know not how—as if she ranked
My gift of a nine-hundred-years-old name
With anybody's gift. Who'd stoop to blame
This sort of trifling? Even had you skill
In speech—(which I have not)—to make your will
Quite clear to such an one, and say, "Just this
Or that in you disgusts me; here you miss,
Or there exceed the mark"—and if she let
Herself be lessoned so, nor plainly set   40
Her wits to yours, forsooth, and made excuse,
—E'en then would be some stooping; and I choose
Never to stoop. Oh sir, she smiled, no doubt,
Whene'er I passed her; but who passed without
Much the same smile? This grew; I gave commands;
Then all smiles stopped together. There she stands
As if alive. Will't please you rise? We'll meet
The company below, then. I repeat,
The Count your master's known munificence
Is ample warrant that no just pretense   50
Of mine for dowry will be disallowed;
Though his fair daughter's self, as I avowed
At starting, is my object. Nay, we'll go
Together down, sir. Notice Neptune, though,
Taming a sea-horse, thought a rarity,
Which Claus of Innsbruck cast in bronze for me!
1842

COUNT GISMOND

AIX IN PROVENCE

I

Christ God who savest man, save most
    Of men Count Gismond who saved me!
Count Gauthier, when he chose his post,
    Chose time and place and company
To suit it; when he struck at length
My honor, 'twas with all his strength.

II

And doubtlessly ere he could draw
    All points to one, he must have schemed!
That miserable morning saw
    Few half so happy as I seemed,   10
While being dressed in queen's array
To give our tourney prize away.

III

I thought they loved me, did me grace
    To please themselves; 'twas all their deed;
God makes, or fair or foul, our face;
    If showing mine so caused to bleed
My cousins' hearts, they should have dropped
A word, and straight the play had stopped.

IV

They, too, so beauteous! Each a queen
    By virtue of her brow and breast;   20
Not needing to be crowned, I mean,
    As I do. E'en when I was dressed,
Had either of them spoke, instead
Of glancing sideways with still head!

V

But no: they let me laugh, and sing
    My birthday song quite through, adjust
The last rose in my garland, fling
    A last look on the mirror, trust
My arms to each an arm of theirs,
And so descend the castle-stairs—   30

VI

And come out on the morning-troop
    Of merry friends who kissed my cheek,
And called me queen, and made me stoop
    Under the canopy—(a streak
That pierced it, of the outside sun,
Powdered with gold its gloom's soft dun)—

VII

And they could let me take my state
    And foolish throne amid applause
Of all come there to celebrate
    My queen's-day—Oh I think the cause   40
Of much was, they forgot no crowd
Makes up for parents in their shroud!

VIII

However that be, all eyes were bent
    Upon me, when my cousins cast
Theirs down; 'twas time I should present
    The victor's crown, but . . . there, 'twill last
No long time . . . the old mist again
Blinds me as then it did. How vain!

IX

See! Gismond's at the gate, in talk
    With his two boys: I can proceed.   50
Well, at that moment, who should stalk
    Forth boldly—to my face, indeed—
But Gauthier, and he thundered "Stay!"
And all stayed. "Bring no crowns, I say!

X

"Bring torches! Wind the penance-sheet
    About her! Let her shun the chaste,
Or lay herself before their feet!
    Shall she whose body I embraced
A night long, queen it in the day?
For honor's sake no crowns, I say!"   60

XI

I? What I answered? As I live,
    I never fancied such a thing
As answer possible to give.
    What says the body when they spring
Some monstrous torture-engine's whole
Strength on it? No more says the soul.

XII

Till out strode Gismond; then I knew
    That I was saved. I never met
His face before, but, at first view,
    I felt quite sure that God had set   70
Himself to Satan; who would spend
A minute's mistrust on the end?

XIII

He strode to Gauthier, in his throat
    Gave him the lie, then struck his mouth
With one back-handed blow that wrote
    In blood men's verdict there. North, South,
East, West, I looked. The lie was dead,
And damned, and truth stood up instead.

XIV

This glads me most, that I enjoyed
    The heart of the joy, with my content   80
In watching Gismond unalloyed
    By any doubt of the event:
God took that on him—I was bid
Watch Gismond for my part: I did.

XV

Did I not watch him while he let
    His armorer just brace his greaves,
Rivet his hauberk, on the fret
    The while! His foot . . . my memory leaves
No least stamp out, nor how anon
He pulled his ringing gauntlets on.   90

XVI

And e'en before the trumpet's sound
    Was finished, prone lay the false knight,
Prone as his lie, upon the ground:
    Gismond flew at him, used no sleight
O' the sword, but open-breasted drove,
Cleaving till out the truth he clove.

XVII

Which done, he dragged him to my feet
    And said "Here die, but end thy breath
In full confession, lest thou fleet
    From my first, to God's second death!   100
Say, hast thou lied?" And, "I have lied
To God and her," he said, and died.

XVIII

Then Gismond, kneeling to me, asked
　　—What safe my heart holds, though no word
Could I repeat now, if I tasked
　　My powers forever, to a third
Dear even as you are. Pass the rest
Until I sank upon his breast.

XIX

Over my head his arm he flung
　　Against the world; and scarce I felt　　　　　110
His sword (that dripped by me and swung)
　　A little shifted in its belt:
For he began to say the while
How South our home lay many a mile.

XX

So 'mid the shouting multitude
　　We two walked forth to never more
Return. My cousins have pursued
　　Their life, untroubled as before
I vexed them. Gauthier's dwelling-place
God lighten! May his soul find grace!　　　　　120

XXI

Our elder boy has got the clear
　　Great brow; tho' when his brother's black
Full eye shows scorn, it . . . Gismond here?
　　And have you brought my tercel back?
I just was telling Adela
How many birds it struck since May.
1842

SOLILOQUY OF THE SPANISH CLOISTER

I

Gr-r-r—there go, my heart's abhorrence!
　　Water your damned flower-pots, do!
If hate killed men, Brother Lawrence,
　　God's blood, would not mine kill you!
What? your myrtle-bush wants trimming?
　　Oh, that rose has prior claims—
Needs its leaden vase filled brimming?
　　Hell dry you up with its flames!

II

At the meal we sit together:
    Salve tibi! I must hear   10
Wise talk of the kind of weather,
    Sort of season, time of year:
Not a plenteous cork-crop: scarcely
    Dare we hope oak-galls, I doubt:
What's the Latin name for "parsley"?
    What's the Greek name for Swine's Snout?

III

Whew! We'll have our platter burnished,
    Laid with care on our own shelf!
With a fire-new spoon we're furnished,
    And a goblet for ourself,   20
Rinsed like something sacrificial
    Ere 'tis fit to touch our chaps—
Marked with L. for our initial!
    (He-he! There his lily snaps!)

IV

Saint, forsooth! While brown Dolores
    Squats outside the Convent bank
With Sanchicha, telling stories,
    Steeping tresses in the tank,
Blue-black, lustrous, thick like horsehairs,
    —Can't I see his dead eye glow,   30
Bright as 'twere a Barbary corsair's?
    (That is, if he'd let it show!)

V

When he finishes refection,
    Knife and fork he never lays
Cross-wise, to my recollection,
    As do I, in Jesu's praise.
I the Trinity illustrate,
    Drinking watered orange-pulp—
In three sips the Arian frustrate;
    While he drains his at one gulp.   40

VI

Oh, those melons? If he's able
    We're to have a feast! so nice!
One goes to the Abbot's table,
    All of us get each a slice.
How go on your flowers? None double?
    Not one fruit-sort can you spy?

Strange!—And I, too, at such trouble,
    Keep them close-nipped on the sly!

VII

There's a great text in Galatians,
    Once you trip on it, entails   50
Twenty-nine distinct damnations,
    One sure, if another fails:
If I trip him just a-dying,
    Sure of heaven as sure can be,
Spin him round and send him flying
    Off to hell, a Manichee?

VIII

Or, my scrofulous French novel
    On gray paper with blunt type!
Simply glance at it, you grovel
    Hand and foot in Belial's gripe: 60
If I double down its pages
    At the woeful sixteenth print,
When he gathers his greengages,
    Ope a sieve and slip it in't?

IX

Or, there's Satan!—one might venture
    Pledge one's soul to him, yet leave
Such a flaw in the indenture
    As he'd miss till, past retrieve,
Blasted lay that rose-acacia
    We're so proud of! *Hy, Zy, Hine.*   70
'St, there's Vespers! *Plena gratiâ*
    Ave, Virgo! Gr-r-r—you swine!
1842

JOHANNES AGRICOLA IN MEDITATION

There's heaven above, and night by night
    I look right through its gorgeous roof;
No suns and moons though e'er so bright
    Avail to stop me; splendor-proof
    I keep the broods of stars aloof:
For I intend to get to God,
    For 'tis to God I speed so fast,
For in God's breast, my own abode.
    Those shoals of dazzling glory, past,
    I lay my spirit down at last.   10

I lie where I have always lain,
    God smiles as he has always smiled;
Ere suns and moons could wax and wane,
     Ere stars were thundergirt, or piled
     The heavens, God thought on me his child;
Ordained a life for me, arrayed
    Its circumstances, every one
To the minutest; ay, God said
    This head this hand should rest upon
    Thus, ere he fashioned star or sun.   20
And having thus created me,
    Thus rooted me, he bade me grow,
Guiltless forever, like a tree
    That buds and blooms, nor seeks to know
    The law by which it prospers so:
But sure that thought and word and deed
    All go to swell his love for me,
Me, made because that love had need
    Of something irreversibly
    Pledged solely its content to be.   30
Yes, yes, a tree which must ascend,
    No poison-gourd foredoomed to stoop!
I have God's warrant, could I blend
    All hideous sins, as in a cup,
    To drink the mingled venoms up;
Secure my nature will convert
    The draught to blossoming gladness fast:
While sweet dews turn to the gourd's hurt,
    And bloat, and while they bloat it, blast,
    As from the first its lot was cast.   40
For as I lie, smiled on, full-fed
    By unexhausted power to bless,
I gaze below on hell's fierce bed,
    And those its waves of flame oppress,
    Swarming in ghastly wretchedness;
Whose life on earth aspired to be
    One altar-smoke, so pure!—to win
If not love like God's love for me,
    At least to keep his anger in;
    And all their striving turned to sin.   50
Priest, doctor, hermit, monk grown white
    With prayer, the broken-hearted nun,
The martyr, the wan acolyte,
    The incense-swinging child,—undone
    Before God fashioned star or sun!
God, whom I praise; how could I praise,
    If such as I might understand,

Make out and reckon on his ways,
  And bargain for his love, and stand,
Paying a price, at his right hand?   60
1842

PORPHYRIA'S LOVER

The rain set early in to-night,
  The sullen wind was soon awake,
It tore the elm-tops down for spite,
  And did its worst to vex the lake:
  I listened with heart fit to break.
When glided in Porphyria; straight
  She shut the cold out and the storm,
And kneeled and made the cheerless grate
  Blaze up, and all the cottage warm;
  Which done, she rose, and from her form   10
Withdrew the dripping cloak and shawl,
  And laid her soiled gloves by, untied
Her hat and let the damp hair fall,
  And, last, she sat down by my side
  And called me. When no voice replied,
She put my arm about her waist,
  And made her smooth white shoulder bare,
And all her yellow hair displaced,
  And, stooping, made my cheek lie there,
  And spread, o'er all, her yellow hair,   20
Murmuring how she loved me—she
  Too weak, for all her heart's endeavor,
To set its struggling passion free
  From pride, and vainer ties dissever,
  And give herself to me forever.
But passion sometimes would prevail,
  Nor could to-night's gay feast restrain
A sudden thought of one so pale
  For love of her, and all in vain:
  So, she was come through wind and rain.   30
Be sure I looked up at her eyes
  Happy and proud; at last I knew
Porphyria worshipped me: surprise
  Made my heart swell, and still it grew
  While I debated what to do.
That moment she was mine, mine, fair,
  Perfectly pure and good: I found
A thing to do, and all her hair

In one long yellow string I wound
    Three times her little throat around,   40
And strangled her. No pain felt she;
    I am quite sure she felt no pain.
As a shut bud that holds a bee,
    I warily oped her lids: again
    Laughed the blue eyes without a stain.
And I untightened next the tress
    About her neck; her cheek once more
Blushed bright beneath my burning kiss:
    I propped her head up as before,
    Only, this time my shoulder bore   50
Her head, which droops upon it still:
    The smiling rosy little head,
So glad it has its utmost will,
    That all it scorned at once is fled,
    And I, its love, am gained instead!
Porphyria's love: she guessed not how
    Her darling one wish would be heard.
And thus we sit together now,
    And all night long we have not stirred,
    And yet God has not said a word!   60
1842

PICTOR IGNOTUS

FLORENCE, 15—

I could have painted pictures like that youth's
    Ye praise so. How my soul springs up! No bar
Stayed me—ah, thought which saddens while it soothes!
    —Never did fate forbid me, star by star,
To outburst on your night with all my gift
    Of fires from God: nor would my flesh have shrunk
From seconding my soul, with eyes uplift
    And wide to heaven, or, straight like thunder, sunk
To the centre, of an instant; or around
    Turned calmly and inquisitive, to scan   10
The license and the limit, space and bound,
    Allowed to truth made visible in man.
And, like that youth ye praise so, all I saw,
    Over the canvas could my hand have flung,
Each face obedient to its passion's law,
    Each passion clear proclaimed without a tongue;

Whether Hope rose at once in all the blood,
    A-tiptoe for the blessing of embrace,
Or Rapture drooped the eyes, as when her brood
    Pull down the nesting dove's heart to its place;   20
Or Confidence lit swift the forehead up,
    And locked the mouth fast, like a castle braved,—
O human faces, hath it spilt, my cup?
    What did ye give me that I have not saved?
Nor will I say I have not dreamed (how well!)
    Of going—I, in each new picture,—forth,
As, making new hearts beat and bosoms swell,
    To Pope or Kaiser, East, West, South, or North,
Bound for the calmly-satisfied great State,
    Or glad aspiring little burgh, it went,   30
Flowers cast upon the car which bore the freight,
    Through old streets named afresh from the event,
Till it reached home, where learned age should greet
    My face, and youth, the star not yet distinct
Above his hair, lie learning at my feet!—
    Oh, thus to live, I and my picture, linked
With love about, and praise, till life should end,
    And then not go to heaven, but linger here,
Here on my earth, earth's every man my friend,—
    The thought grew frightful, 'twas so wildly dear!   40
But a voice changed it. Glimpses of such sights
    Have scared me, like the revels through a door
Of some strange house of idols at its rites!
    This world seemed not the world it was before:
Mixed with my loving trusting ones, there trooped
    . . . Who summoned those cold faces that begun
To press on me and judge me? Though I stooped
    Shrinking, as from the soldiery a nun,
They drew me forth, and spite of me . . . enough!
    These buy and sell our pictures, take and give,   50
Count them for garniture and household-stuff,
    And where they live needs must our pictures live
And see their faces, listen to their prate,
    Partakers of their daily pettiness,
Discussed of,—"This I love, or this I hate,
    This likes me more, and this affects me less!"
Wherefore I chose my portion. If at whiles
    My heart sinks, as monotonous I paint
These endless cloisters and eternal aisles
    With the same series, Virgin, Babe and Saint,   60
With the same cold calm beautiful regard,—
    At least no merchant traffics in my heart;

The sanctuary's gloom at least shall ward
  Vain tongues from where my pictures stand apart:
Only prayer breaks the silence of the shrine
  While, blackening in the daily candle-smoke,
They moulder on the damp wall's travertine,
  'Mid echoes the light footstep never woke.
So, die my pictures! surely, gently die!
  O youth, men praise so—holds their praise its worth?   70
Blown harshly, keeps the trump its golden cry?
  Tastes sweet the water with such specks of earth?
1845

THE ENGLISHMAN IN ITALY

PIANO DI SORRENTO

Fortù, Fortù, my beloved one,
  Sit here by my side,
On my knees put up both little feet!
  I was sure, if I tried,
I could make you laugh spite of Scirocco.
  Now, open your eyes,
Let me keep you amused till he vanish
  In black from the skies,
With telling my memories over
  As you tell your beads;   10
All the Plain saw me gather, I garland
  —The flowers or the weeds.

Time for rain! for your long hot dry Autumn
  Had net-worked with brown
The white skin of each grape on the bunches,
  Marked like a quail's crown,
Those creatures you make such account of,
  Whose heads,—speckled white
Over brown like a great spider's back,
  As I told you last night,—   20
Your mother bites off for her supper.
  Red-ripe as could be,
Pomegranates were chapping and splitting
  In halves on the tree:
And betwixt the loose walls of great flint stone,
  Or in the thick dust
On the path, or straight out of the rock-side,
  Wherever could thrust

Some burnt sprig of bold hardy rock-flower
    Its yellow face up,   30
For the prize were great butterflies fighting,
    Some five for one cup.
So, I guessed, ere I got up this morning,
    What change was in store,
By the quick rustle-down of the quail-nets
    Which woke me before
I could open my shutter, made fast
    With a bough and a stone,
And looked thro' the twisted dead vine-twigs,
    Sole lattice that's known.   40
Quick and sharp rang the rings down the net-poles,
    While, busy beneath,
Your priest and his brother tugged at them,
    The rain in their teeth.
And out upon all the flat house-roofs
    Where split figs lay drying,
The girls took the frails under cover:
    Nor use seemed in trying
To get out the boats and go fishing,
    For, under the cliff,   50
Fierce the black water frothed o'er the blind-rock.
    No seeing our skiff
Arrive about noon from Amalfi,
    —Our fisher arrive,
And pitch down his basket before us,
    All trembling alive
With pink and gray jellies, your sea-fruit;
    You touch the strange lumps,
And mouths gape there, eyes open, all manner
    Of horns and of humps,   60
Which only the fisher looks grave at,
    While round him like imps
Cling screaming the children as naked
    And brown as his shrimps;
Himself too as bare to the middle
    —You see round his neck
The string and its brass coin suspended,
    That saves him from wreck.
But to-day not a boat reached Salerno,
    So back, to a man,   70
Came our friends, with whose help in the vineyards
    Grape-harvest began.
In the vat, halfway up in our house-side,
    Like blood the juice spins,
While your brother all bare-legged is dancing

Till breathless he grins
Dead-beaten in effort on effort
  To keep the grapes under,
Since still when he seems all but master,
  In pours the fresh plunder   80
From girls who keep coming and going
  With basket on shoulder,
And eyes shut against the rain's driving;
  Your girls that are older,—
For under the hedges of aloe,
  And where, on its bed
Of the orchard's black mould, the love-apple
  Lies pulpy and red,
All the young ones are kneeling and filling
  Their laps with the snails   90
Tempted out by this first rainy weather,—
  Your best of regales,
As to-night will be proved to my sorrow,
  When, supping in state,
We shall feast our grape-gleaners (two dozen,
  Three over one plate)
With lasagne so tempting to swallow
  In slippery ropes,
And gourds fried in great purple slices,
  That color of popes.   100
Meantime, see the grape bunch they've brought you:
  The rain-water slips
O'er the heavy blue bloom on each globe
  Which the wasp to your lips
Still follows with fretful persistence:
  Nay, taste, while awake,
This half of a curd-white smooth cheese-ball
  That peels, flake by flake,
Like an onion, each smoother and whiter;
  Next, sip this weak wine   110
From the thin green glass flask, with its stopper,
  A leaf of the vine;
And end with the prickly-pear's red flesh
  That leaves thro' its juice
The stony black seeds on your pearl-teeth.
  Scirocco is loose!
Hark, the quick, whistling pelt of the olives
  Which, thick in one's track,
Tempt the stranger to pick up and bite them,
  Tho' not yet half black!   120
How the old twisted olive trunks shudder,
  The medlars let fall

Their hard fruit, and the brittle great fig-trees
    Snap off, figs and all,
For here comes the whole of the tempest!
    No refuge, but creep
Back again to my side and my shoulder,
    And listen or sleep.
O how will your country show next week,
    When all the vine-boughs   130
Have been stripped of their foliage to pasture
    The mules and the cows?
Last eve, I rode over the mountains:
    Your brother, my guide,
Soon left me, to feast on the myrtles
    That offered, each side,
Their fruit-balls, black, glossy and luscious,—
    Or strip from the sorbs
A treasure, or, rosy and wondrous,
    Those hairy gold orbs!   140
But my mule picked his sure sober path out,
    Just stopping to neigh
When he recognized down in the valley
    His mates on their way
With the faggots and barrels of water;
    And soon we emerged
From the plain, where the woods could scarce follow;
    And still as we urged
Our way, the woods wondered, and left us,
    As up still we trudged   150
Though the wild path grew wilder each instant,
    And place was e'en grudged
'Mid the rock-chasms and piles of loose stones
    Like the loose broken teeth
Of some monster which climbed there to die
    From the ocean beneath—
Place was grudged to the silver-gray fume-weed
    That clung to the path,
And dark rosemary ever a-dying
    That, 'spite the wind's wrath,   160
So loves the salt rock's face to seaward,
    And lentisks as staunch
To the stone where they root and bear berries,
    And . . . what shows a branch
Coral-colored, transparent, with circlets
    Of pale seagreen leaves;
Over all trod my mule with the caution
    Of gleaners o'er sheaves,
Still, foot after foot like a lady,

Till, round after round,   170
He climbed to the top of Calvano,
    And God's own profound
Was above me, and round me the mountains,
    And under, the sea,
And within me my heart to bear witness
    What was and shall be.
Oh, heaven and the terrible crystal!
    No rampart excludes
Your eye from the life to be lived
    In the blue solitudes.   180
Oh, those mountains, their infinite movement!
    Still moving with you;
For, ever some new head and breast of them
    Thrusts into view
To observe the intruder; you see it
    If quickly you turn
And, before they escape you surprise them.
    They grudge you should learn
How the soft plains they look on, lean over
    And love (they pretend)   190
—Cower beneath them, the flat sea-pine crouches,
    The wild fruit-trees bend,
E'en the myrtle-leaves curl, shrink and shut:
    All is silent and grave:
'Tis a sensual and timorous beauty,
    How fair! but a slave.
So, I turned to the sea; and there slumbered
    As greenly as ever
Those isles of the siren, your Galli;
    No ages can sever   200
The Three, nor enable their sister
    To join them,—halfway
On the voyage, she looked at Ulysses—
    No farther to-day,
Tho' the small one, just launched in the wave,
    Watches breast-high and steady
From under the rock, her bold sister
    Swum halfway already.
Fortù, shall we sail there together
    And see from the sides   210
Quite new rocks show their faces, new haunts
    Where the siren abides?
Shall we sail round and round them, close over
    The rocks, tho' unseen,
That ruffle the gray glassy water
    To glorious green?

Then scramble from splinter to splinter,
    Reach land and explore,
On the largest, the strange square black turret
    With never a door,   220
Just a loop to admit the quick lizards;
    Then, stand there and hear
The birds' quiet singing, that tells us
    What life is, so clear?
—The secret they sang to Ulysses
    When, ages ago,
He heard and he knew this life's secret
    I hear and I know.

Ah, see! The sun breaks o'er Calvano;
    He strikes the great gloom   230
And flutters it o'er the mount's summit
    In airy gold fume.
All is over. Look out, see the gipsy,
    Our tinker and smith,
Has arrived, set up bellows and forge,
    And down-squatted forthwith
To his hammering, under the wall there;
    One eye keeps aloof
The urchins that itch to be putting
    His jews'-harps to proof,   240
While the other, thro' locks of curled wire,
    Is watching how sleek
Shines the hog, come to share in the windfall
    —Chew, abbot's own cheek!
All is over. Wake up and come out now,
    And down let us go,
And see the fine things got in order
    At church for the show
Of the Sacrament, set forth this evening.
    To-morrow's the Feast   250
Of the Rosary's Virgin, by no means
    Of Virgins the least,
As you'll hear in the off-hand discourse
    Which (all nature, no art)
The Dominican brother, these three weeks,
    Was getting by heart.
Not a pillar nor post but is dizened
    With red and blue papers;
All the roof waves with ribbons, each altar
    A-blaze with long tapers;   260
But the great masterpiece is the scaffold
    Rigged glorious to hold

All the fiddlers and fifers and drummers
    And trumpeters bold,
Not afraid of Bellini nor Auber,
    Who, when the priest's hoarse,
Will strike us up something that's brisk
    For the feast's second course.
And then will the flaxen-wigged Image
    Be carried in pomp   2 '0
Thro' the plain, while in gallant procession
    The priests mean to stomp.
All round the glad church lie old bottles
    With gunpowder stopped,
Which will be, when the Image re-enters,
    Religiously popped;
And at night from the crest of Calvano
    Great bonfires will hang,
On the plain will the trumpets join chorus,
    And more poppers bang.   **280**
At all events, come—to the garden
    As far as the wall;
See me tap with a hoe on the plaster
    Till out there shall fall
A scorpion with wide angry nippers!

    —"Such trifles!" you say?
Fortù, in my England at home,
    Men meet gravely to-day
And debate, if abolishing Corn-laws
    Be righteous and wise   290
—If't were proper, Scirocco should vanish
    In black from the skies!
1845

HOME-THOUGHTS, FROM ABROAD

I

Oh, to be in England
Now that April's there,
And whoever wakes in England
Sees, some morning, unaware,
That the lowest boughs and the brushwood sheaf
Round the elm-tree bole are in tiny leaf,
While the chaffinch sings on the orchard bough
In England—now!

II

And after April, when May follows,
And the whitethroat builds, and all the swallows!   10
Hark, where my blossomed pear-tree in the hedge
Leans to the field and scatters on the clover
Blossoms and dewdrops—at the bent spray's edge—
That's the wise thrush; he sings each song twice over,
Lest you should think he never could recapture
The first fine careless rapture!
And though the fields look rough with hoary dew,
All will be gay when noontide wakes anew
The buttercups, the little children's dower
—Far brighter than this gaudy melon-flower!   20
1845

THE BISHOP ORDERS HIS TOMB AT SAINT PRAXED'S CHURCH

ROME, 15—

Vanity, saith the preacher, vanity!
Draw round my bed: is Anselm keeping back?
Nephews—sons mine . . . ah God, I know not! Well—
She, men would have to be your mother once,
Old Gandolf envied me, so fair she was!
What's done is done, and she is dead beside,
Dead long ago, and I am Bishop since,
And as she died so must we die ourselves,
And thence ye may perceive the world's a dream.
Life, how and what is it? As here I lie   10
In this state-chamber, dying by degrees,
Hours and long hours in the dead night, I ask
"Do I live, am I dead?" Peace, peace seems all.
Saint Praxed's ever was the church for peace;
And so, about this tomb of mine. I fought
With tooth and nail to save my niche, ye know:
—Old Gandolf cozened me, despite my care;
Shrewd was that snatch from out the corner South
He graced his carrion with, God curse the same!
Yet still my niche is not so cramped but thence   20
One sees the pulpit o' the epistle-side,
And somewhat of the choir, those silent seats,
And up into the aery dome where live
The angels, and a sunbeam's sure to lurk:
And I shall fill my slab of basalt there,

And 'neath my tabernacle take my rest,
With those nine columns round me, two and two,
The odd one at my feet where Anselm stands:
Peach-blossom marble all, the rare, the ripe
As fresh-poured red wine of a mighty pulse.   30
—Old Gandolf with his paltry onion-stone,
Put me where I may look at him! True peach,
Rosy and flawless: how I earned the prize!
Draw close: that conflagration of my church
—What then? So much was saved if aught were missed!
My sons, ye would not be my death? Go dig
The white-grape vineyard where the oil-press stood,
Drop water gently till the surface sink,
And if ye find . . . Ah God, I know not, I! . . .
Bedded in store of rotten fig-leaves soft,   40
And corded up in a tight olive-frail,
Some lump, ah God, of *lapis lazuli*,
Big as a Jew's head cut off at the nape,
Blue as a vein o'er the Madonna's breast . . .
Sons, all have I bequeathed you, villas, all,
That brave Frascati villa with its bath,
So, let the blue lump poise between my knees,
Like God the Father's globe on both his hands
Ye worship in the Jesu Church so gay,
For Gandolf shall not choose but see and burst!   50
Swift as a weaver's shuttle fleet our years:
Man goeth to the grave, and where is he?
Did I say basalt for my slab, sons? Black—
'Twas ever antique-black I meant! How else
Shall ye contrast my frieze to come beneath?
The bas-relief in bronze ye promised me,
Those Pans and Nymphs ye wot of, and perchance
Some tripod, thyrsus, with a vase or so,
The Saviour at his sermon on the mount,
Saint Praxed in a glory, and one Pan   60
Ready to twitch the Nymph's last garment off,
And Moses with the tables . . . but I know
Ye mark me not! What do they whisper thee,
Child of my bowels, Anselm? Ah, ye hope
To revel down my villas while I gasp
Bricked o'er with beggar's mouldy travertine
Which Gandolf from his tomb-top chuckles at,
Nay, boys, ye love me—all of jasper, then!
'Tis jasper ye stand pledged to, lest I grieve
My bath must needs be left behind, alas!   70
One block, pure green as a pistachio-nut,
There's plenty jasper somewhere in the world—

And have I not Saint Praxed's ear to pray
Horses for ye, and brown Greek manuscripts,
And mistresses with great smooth marbly limbs?
—That's if ye carve my epitaph aright,
Choice Latin, picked phrase, Tully's every word,
No gaudy ware like Gandolf's second line—
Tully, my masters? Ulpian serves his need!
And then how I shall lie through centuries,   80
And hear the blessed mutter of the mass,
And see God made and eaten all day long,
And feel the steady candle-flame, and taste
Good strong thick stupefying incense-smoke!
For as I lie here, hours of the dead night,
Dying in state and by such slow degrees,
I fold my arms as if they clasped a crook,
And stretch my feet forth straight as stone can point,
And let the bedclothes, for a mortcloth, drop
Into great laps and folds of sculptor's-work: 90
And as yon tapers dwindle, and strange thoughts
Grow, with a certain humming in my ears,
About the life before I lived this life,
And this life too, popes, cardinals and priests,
Saint Praxed at his sermon on the mount,
Your tall pale mother with her talking eyes,
And new-found agate urns as fresh as day,
And marble's language, Latin pure, discreet,
—Aha, ELUCESCEBAT quoth our friend?
No Tully, said I, Ulpian at the best!   100
Evil and brief hath been my pilgrimage.
All *lapis*, all, sons! Else I give the Pope
My villas! Will ye ever eat my heart?
Ever your eyes were as a lizard's quick,
They glitter like your mother's for my soul,
Or ye would heighten my impoverished frieze,
Piece out its starved design, and fill my vase
With grapes, and add a vizor and a Term,
And to the tripod ye would tie a lynx
That in his struggle throws the thyrsus down,   110
To comfort me on my entablature
Whereon I am to lie till I must ask
"Do I live, am I dead?" There, leave me, there!
For ye have stabbed me with ingratitude
To death—ye wish it—God, ye wish it! Stone—
Gritstone, a-crumble! Clammy squares which sweat
As if the corpse they keep were oozing through—
And no more *lapis* to delight the world!
Well go! I bless ye. Fewer tapers there,

But in a row: and, going, turn your backs   120
—ay, like departing altar-ministrants,
And leave me in my church, the church for peace,
That I may watch at leisure if he leers—
Old Gandolf, at me, from his onion-stone,
As still he envied me, so fair she was!
1845

FRA LIPPO LIPPI

I am poor brother Lippo, by your leave!
You need not clap your torches to my face.
Zooks, what's to blame? you think you see a monk!
What, 'tis past midnight, and you go the rounds,
And here you catch me at an alley's end
Where sportive ladies leave their doors ajar?
The Carmine's my cloister: hunt it up,
Do,—harry out, if you must show your zeal,
Whatever rat, there, haps on his wrong hole,
And nip each softling of a wee white mouse,   10
Weke, weke, that's crept to keep him company!
Aha, you know your betters! Then, you'll take
Your hand away that's fiddling on my throat,
And please to know me likewise. Who am I?
Why, one, sir, who is lodging with a friend
Three streets off—he's a certain . . . how d'ye call?
Master—a . . . Cosimo of the Medici,
I' the house that caps the corner. Boh! you were best!
Remember and tell me, the day you're hanged,
How you affected such a gullet's-gripe!   20
But you, sir, it concerns you that your knaves
Pick up a manner nor discredit you:
Zooks, are we pilchards, that they sweep the streets
And count fair prize what comes into their net?
He's Judas to a tittle, that man is!
Just such a face! Why, sir, you make amends.
Lord, I'm not angry! Bid your hangdogs go
Drink out this quarter-florin to the health
Of the munificent House that harbors me
(And many more beside, lads! more beside!)   30
And all's come square again. I'd like his face—
His, elbowing on his comrade in the door
With the pike and lantern,—for the slave that holds
John Baptist's head a-dangle by the hair
With one hand ("Look you, now," as who should say)
And his weapon in the other, yet unwiped!

It's not your chance to have a bit of chalk,
A wood-coal or the like? or you should see!
Yes, I'm the painter, since you style me so.
What, brother Lippo's doings, up and down,　　　　40
You know them and they take you? like enough!
I saw the proper twinkle in your eye—
'Tell you, I liked your looks at very first.
Let's sit and set things straight now, hip to haunch.
Here's spring come, and the nights one makes up bands
To roam the town and sing out carnival,
And I've been three weeks shut within my mew,
A-painting for the great man, saints and saints
And saints again. I could not paint all night—
Ouf! I leaned out of window for fresh air.　　　　50
There came a hurry of feet and little feet,
A sweep of lute-strings, laughs, and whiffs of song,—
Flower o' the broom,
Take away love, and our earth is a tomb!
Flower o' the quince,
I let Lisa go, and what good in life since?
Flower o' the thyme—and so on. Round they went.
Scarce had they turned the corner when a titter
Like the skipping of rabbits by moonlight,—three slim shapes,
And a face that looked up . . . zooks, sir, flesh and blood,　　60
That's all I'm made of! Into shreds it went,
Curtain and counterpane and coverlet,
All the bed-furniture—a dozen knots,
There was a ladder! Down I let myself,
Hands and feet, scrambling somehow, and so dropped,
And after them. I came up with the fun
Hard by Saint Laurence, hail fellow, well met,—
Flower o' the rose,
If I've been merry, what matter who knows?
And so as I was stealing back again　　　　70
To get to bed and have a bit of sleep
Ere I rise up to-morrow and go work
On Jerome knocking at his poor old breast
With his great round stone to subdue the flesh,
You snap me of the sudden. Ah, I see!
Though your eye twinkles still, you shake your head—
Mine's shaved—a monk, you say—the sting's in that!
If Master Cosimo announced himself,
Mum's the word naturally; but a monk!
Come, what am I a beast for? tell us, now!　　　　80
I was a baby when my mother died
And father died and left me in the street.
I starved there, God knows how, a year or two

On fig-skins, melon-parings, rinds and shucks,
Refuse and rubbish. One fine frosty day,
My stomach being empty as your hat,
The wind doubled me up and down I went.
Old Aunt Lapaccia trussed me with one hand,
(Its fellow was a stinger as I knew)
And so along the wall, over the bridge,   90
By the straight cut to the convent. Six words there,
While I stood munching my first bread that month:
"So, boy, you're minded," quoth the good fat father
Wiping his own mouth, 'twas refection-time,—
"To quit this very miserable world?
Will you renounce" . . . "the mouthful of bread?" thought I;
By no means! Brief, they made a monk of me;
I did renounce the world, its pride and greed,
Palace, farm, villa, shop and banking-house,
Trash, such as these poor devils of Medici   100
Have given their hearts to—all at eight years old.
Well, sir, I found in time, you may be sure,
'Twas not for nothing—the good bellyful,
The warm serge and the rope that goes all round,
And day-long blessed idleness beside!
"Let's see what the urchin's fit for"—that came next.
Not overmuch their way, I must confess.
Such a to-do! They tried me with their books:
Lord, they'd have taught me Latin in pure waste!
Flower o' the clove,   110
All the Latin I construe is, "amo" I love!
But, mind you, when a boy starves in the streets
Eight years together, as my fortune was,
Watching folk's faces to know who will fling
The bit of half-stripped grape-bunch he desires,
And who will curse or kick him for his pains,—
Which gentleman processional and fine,
Holding a candle to the Sacrament,
Will wink and let him lift a plate and catch
The droppings of the wax to sell again,   120
Or holla for the Eight and have him whipped,—
How say I?—nay, which dog bites, which lets drop
His bone from the heap of offal in the street,—
Why, soul and sense of him grow sharp alike,
He learns the look of things, and none the less
For admonition from the hunger-pinch.
I had a store of such remarks, be sure,
Which, after I found leisure, turned to use.
I drew men's faces on my copy-books,
Scrawled them within the antiphonary's marge,   130

Joined legs and arms to the long music-notes,
Found eyes and nose and chin for A's and B's,
And made a string of pictures of the world
Betwixt the ins and outs of verb and noun,
On the wall, the bench, the door. The monks looked black.
"Nay," quoth the Prior, "turn him out, d' ye say?
In no wise. Lose a crow and catch a lark.
What if at last we get our man of parts,
We Carmelites, like those Camaldolese
And Preaching Friars, to do our church up fine   140
And put the front on it that ought to be!"
And hereupon he bade me daub away.
Thank you! my head being crammed, the walls a blank,
Never was such prompt disemburdening.
First, every sort of monk, the black and white,
I drew them, fat and lean: then, folk at church,
From good old gossips waiting to confess
Their cribs of barrel-droppings, candle-ends,—
To the breathless fellow at the altar-foot,
Fresh from his murder, safe and sitting there   150
With the little children round him in a row
Of admiration, half for his beard and half
For that white anger of his victim's son
Shaking a fist at him with one fierce arm,
Signing himself with the other because of Christ
(Whose sad face on the cross sees only this
After the passion of a thousand years)
Till some poor girl, her apron o'er her head,
(Which the intense eyes looked through) came at eve
On tiptoe, said a word, dropped in a loaf,   160
Her pair of earrings and a bunch of flowers
(The brute took growling), prayed, and so was gone.
I painted all, then cried " 'Tis ask and have;
Choose, for more's ready!"—laid the ladder flat,
And showed my covered bit of cloister-wall.
The monks closed in a circle and praised loud
Till checked, taught what to see and not to see,
Being simple bodies,—"That's the very man!
Look at the boy who stoops to pat the dog!
That woman's like the Prior's niece who comes   170
To care about his asthma: it's the life!"
But there my triumph's straw-fire flared and funked;
Their betters took their turn to see and say:
The Prior and the learned pulled a face
And stopped all that in no time. "How? what's here?
Quite from the mark of painting, bless us all!
Faces, arms, legs and bodies like the true

As much as pea and pea! it's devil's-game!
Your business is not to catch men with show,
With homage to the perishable clay,   180
But lift them over it, ignore it all,
Make them forget there's such a thing as flesh.
Your business is to paint the souls of men—
Man's soul, and it's a fire, smoke . . . no, it's not . . .
It's vapor done up like a new-born babe—
(In that shape when you die it leaves your mouth)
It's . . . well, what matters talking, it's the soul!
Give us no more of body than shows soul!
Here's Giotto, with his Saint a-praising God,
That sets us praising,—why not stop with him?   190
Why put all thoughts of praise out of our head
With wonder at lines, colors, and what not?
Paint the soul, never mind the legs and arms!
Rub all out, try at it a second time.
Oh, that white smallish female with the breasts,
She's just my niece . . . Herodias, I would say,—
Who went and danced and got men's heads cut off!
Have it all out!" Now, is this sense, I ask?
A fine way to paint soul, by painting body
So ill, the eye can't stop there, must go further   200
And can't fare worse! Thus, yellow does for white
When what you put for yellow's simply black,
And any sort of meaning looks intense
When all beside itself means and looks naught.
Why can't a painter lift each foot in turn,
Left foot and right foot, go a double step,
Make his flesh liker and his soul more like,
Both in their order? Take the prettiest face,
The Prior's niece . . . patron-saint—is it so pretty
You can't discover if it means hope, fear,   210
Sorrow or joy? won't beauty go with these?
Suppose I've made her eyes all right and blue,
Can't I take breath and try to add life's flash,
And then add soul and heighten them three-fold?
Or say there's beauty with no soul at all—
(I never saw it—put the case the same—)
If you get simple beauty and naught else,
You get about the best thing God invents:
That's somewhat: and you'll find the soul you have missed,
Within yourself, when you return him thanks.   220
"Rub all out!" Well, well, there's my life, in short,
And so the thing has gone on ever since.
I'm grown a man no doubt, I've broken bounds:
You should not take a fellow eight years old

And make him swear to never kiss the girls.
I'm my own master, paint now as I please—
Having a friend, you see, in the Corner-house!
Lord, it's fast holding by the rings in front—
Those great rings serve more purposes than just
To plant a flag in, or tie up a horse!   230
And yet the old schooling sticks, the old grave eyes
Are peeping o'er my shoulder as I work,
The heads shake still—"It's art's decline, my son!
You're not of the true painters, great and old;
Brother Angelico's the man, you'll find;
Brother Lorenzo stands his single peer:
Fag on at flesh, you'll never make the third!"
Flower o' the pine,
You keep your mistr . . . manners, and I'll stick to mine!
I'm not the third, then: bless us, they must know!   240
Don't you think they're the likeliest to know,
They with their Latin? So, I swallow my rage,
Clench my teeth, suck my lips in tight, and paint
To please them—sometimes do and sometimes don't;
For, doing most, there's pretty sure to come
A turn, some warm eve finds me at my saints—
A laugh, a cry, the business of the world—
(*Flower o' the peach,*
Death for us all, and his own life for each!)
And my whole soul revolves, the cup runs over,   250
The world and life's too big to pass for a dream,
And I do these wild things in sheer despite,
And play the fooleries you catch me at,
In pure rage! The old mill-horse, out at grass
After hard years, throws up his stiff heels so,
Although the miller does not preach to him
The only good of grass is to make chaff.
What would men have? Do they like grass or no—
May they or mayn't they? all I want's the thing
Settled forever one way. As it is,   260
You tell too many lies and hurt yourself:
You don't like what you only like too much,
You do like what, if given you at your word,
You find abundantly detestable.
For me, I think I speak as I was taught;
I always see the garden and God there
A-making man's wife: and, my lesson learned,
The value and significance of flesh,
I can't unlearn ten minutes afterwards.

     You understand me: I'm a beast, I know.   270
But see, now—why, I see as certainly

As that the morning-star's about to shine,
What will hap some day. We've a youngster here
Comes to our convent, studies what I do,
Slouches and stares and lets no atom drop:
His name is Guidi—he'll not mind the monks—
They call him Hulking Tom, he lets them talk—
He picks my practice up—he'll paint apace,
I hope so—though I never live so long,
I know what's sure to follow. You be judge!   280
You speak no Latin more than I, belike;
However, you're my man, you've seen the world
—The beauty and the wonder and the power,
The shapes of things, their colors, lights and shades,
Changes, surprises,—and God made it all!
—For what? Do you feel thankful, ay or no,
For this fair town's face, yonder river's line,
The mountain round it and the sky above,
Much more the figures of man, woman, child,
These are the frame to? What's it all about?   290
To be passed over, despised? or dwelt upon,
Wondered at? oh, this last of course!—you say.
But why not do as well as say,—paint these
Just as they are, careless what comes of it?
God's works—paint any one, and count it crime
To let a truth slip. Don't object, "His works
Are here already; nature is complete:
Suppose you reproduce her—(which you can't)
There's no advantage! You must beat her, then."
For, don't you mark? we're made so that we love   300
First when we see them painted, things we have passed
Perhaps a hundred times nor cared to see;
And so they are better, painted—better to us,
Which is the same thing. Art was given for that;
God uses us to help each other so,
Lending our minds out. Have you noticed, now,
Your cullion's hanging face? A bit of chalk,
And trust me but you should, though! How much more,
If I drew higher things with the same truth!
That were to take the Prior's pulpit-place,   310
Interpret God to all of you! Oh, oh,
It makes me mad to see what men shall do
And we in our graves! This world's no blot for us,
Nor blank; it means intensely, and means good:
To find its meaning is my meat and drink.
"Ay, but you don't so instigate to prayer!"
Strikes in the Prior: "when your meaning's plain
It does not say to folk—remember matins,
Or, mind you fast next Friday!" Why, for this

What need of art at all? A skull and bones, 320
Two bits of stick nailed crosswise, or, what's best,
A bell to chime the hour with, does as well.
I painted a Saint Laurence six months since
At Prato, splashed the fresco in fine style:
"How looks my painting, now the scaffold's down?"
I ask a brother: "Hugely," he returns—
"Already not one phiz of your three slaves
Who turn the Deacon off his toasted side,
But's scratched and prodded to our heart's content,
The pious people have so eased their own 330
With coming to say prayers there in a rage:
We get on fast to see the bricks beneath.
Expect another job this time next year,
For pity and religion grow i' the crowd—
Your painting serves its purpose!" Hang the fools!

      —That is—you'll not mistake an idle word
Spoke in a huff by a poor monk, God wot,
Tasting the air this spicy night which turns
The unaccustomed head like Chianti wine!
Oh, the church knows! don't misreport me, now! 340
It's natural a poor monk out of bounds
Should have his apt word to excuse himself:
And hearken how I plot to make amends.
I have bethought me: I shall paint a piece
. . . There's for you! Give me six months, then go, see
Something in Sant' Ambrogio's! Bless the nuns!
They want a cast o' my office. I shall paint
God in the midst, Madonna and her babe,
Ringed by a bowery flowery angel-brood,
Lilies and vestments and white faces, sweet 350
As puff on puff of grated orris-root
When ladies crowd to Church at midsummer.
And then i' the front, of course a saint or two—
Saint John, because he saves the Florentines,
Saint Ambrose, who puts down in black and white
The convent's friends and gives them a long day,
And Job, I must have him there past mistake,
The man of Uz (and Us without the z,
Painters who need his patience). Well, all these
Secured at their devotion, up shall come 360
Out of a corner when you least expect,
As one by a dark stair into a great light,
Music and talking, who but Lippo! I!—
Mazed, motionless and moonstruck—I'm the man!
Back I shrink—what is this I see and hear?
I, caught up with my monk's-things by mistake,

My old serge gown and rope that goes all round,
I, in this presence, this pure company!
Where's a hole, where's a corner for escape?
Then steps a sweet angelic slip of a thing   370
Forward, puts out a soft palm—"Not so fast!"
—Addresses the celestial presence, "nay—
He made you and devised you, after all,
Though he's none of you! Could Saint John there draw—
His camel-hair make up a painting-brush?
We come to brother Lippo for all that,
Iste perfecit opus!" So, all smile—
I shuffle sideways with my blushing face
Under the cover of a hundred wings
Thrown like a spread of kirtles when you're gay   380
And play hot cockles, all the doors being shut,
Till, wholly unexpected, in there pops
The hothead husband! Thus I scuttle off
To some safe bench behind, not letting go
The palm of her, the little lily thing
That spoke the good word for me in the nick,
Like the Prior's niece . . . Saint Lucy, I would say.
And so all's saved for me, and for the church
A pretty picture gained. Go, six months hence!
Your hand, sir, and good-bye: no lights, no lights!   390
The street's hushed, and I know my own way back,
Don't fear me! There's the gray beginning. Zooks!
1855

A TOCCATA OF GALUPPI'S

I

Oh, Galuppi, Baldassaro, this is very sad to find!
I can hardly misconceive you; it would prove me deaf and blind;
But although I take your meaning, 'tis with such a heavy mind!

II

Here you come with your old music, and here's all the good it brings.
What, they lived once thus at Venice where the merchants were the
    kings,
Where Saint Mark's is, where the Doges used to wed the sea with
    rings?

III

Ay, because the sea's the street there; and 'tis arched by . . . what you
    call
. . . Shylock's bridge with houses on it, where they kept the carnival:
I was never out of England—it's as if I saw it all.

IV

Did young people take their pleasure when the sea was warm in May?
Balls and masks begun at midnight, burning ever to mid-day,   11
When they made up fresh adventures for the morrow, do you say?

V

Was a lady such a lady, cheeks so round and lips so red,—
On her neck the small face buoyant, like a bell-flower on its bed,
O'er the breast's superb abundance where a man might base his head?

VI

Well, and it was graceful of them—they'd break talk off and afford
—She, to bite her mask's black velvet—he, to finger on his sword,
While you sat and played Toccatas, stately at the clavichord?

VII

What? Those lesser thirds so plaintive, sixths diminished, sigh on sigh,
Told them something? Those suspensions, those solutions—"Must we
    die?"   20
Those commiserating sevenths—"Life might last! we can but try!"

VIII

"Were you happy?"—"Yes."—"And are you still as happy?"—"Yes.
    And you?"
—"Then, more kisses!"—"Did *I* stop them, when a million seemed so
    few?"
Hark, the dominant's persistence till it must be answered to!

IX

So, an octave struck the answer. Oh, they praised you, I dare say!
"Brave Galuppi! that was music; good alike at grave and gay!
I can always leave off talking when I hear a master play!"

X

Then they left you for their pleasure: till in due time, one by one,
Some with lives that came to nothing, some with deeds as well undone,
Death stepped tacitly and took them where they never see the sun.   30

XI

But when I sit down to reason, think to take my stand nor swerve,
While I triumph o'er a secret wrung from nature's close reserve,
In you come with your cold music till I creep thro' every nerve.

XII

Yes, you, like a ghostly cricket, creaking where a house was burned:
"Dust and ashes, dead and done with, Venice spent what Venice
    earned.
The soul, doubtless, is immortal—where a soul can be discerned.

XIII

"Yours for instance: you know physics, something of geology,
Mathematics are your pastime; souls shall rise in their degree;
Butterflies may dread extinction,—you'll not die, it cannot be!

XIV

"As for Venice and her people, merely born to bloom and drop,   40
Here on earth they bore their fruitage, mirth and folly were the crop:
What of soul was left, I wonder, when the kissing had to stop?

XV

"Dust and ashes!" So you creak it, and I want the heart to scold.
Dear dead women, with such hair, too—what's become of all the gold
Used to hang and brush their bosoms? I feel chilly and grown old.
1855

AN EPISTLE

CONTAINING THE STRANGE MEDICAL EXPERIENCE OF KARSHISH, THE ARAB PHYSICIAN

Karshish, the picker-up of learning's crumbs,
The not-incurious in God's handiwork
(This man's-flesh he hath admirably made,
Blown like a bubble, kneaded like a paste,
To coop up and keep down on earth a space
That puff of vapor from his mouth, man's soul)
—To Abib, all-sagacious in our art,
Breeder in me of what poor skill I boast,
Like me inquisitive how pricks and cracks
Befall the flesh through too much stress and strain,   10
Whereby the wily vapor fain would slip
Back and rejoin its source before the term,—
And aptest in contrivance (under God)
To baffle it by deftly stopping such:—
The vagrant Scholar to his Sage at home
Sends greeting (health and knowledge, fame with peace)
Three samples of true snakestone—rarer still,
One of the other sort, the melon-shaped,
(But fitter, pounded fine, for charms than drugs)
And writeth now the twenty-second time.   20

My journeyings were brought to Jericho:
Thus I resume. Who studious in our art
Shall count a little labor unrepaid?

I have shed sweat enough, left flesh and bone
On many a flinty furlong of this land.
Also, the country-side is all on fire
With rumors of a marching hitherward:
Some say Vespasian cometh, some, his son.
A black lynx snarled and pricked a tufted ear;
Lust of my blood inflamed his yellow balls: 30
I cried and threw my staff and he was gone.
Twice have the robbers stripped and beaten me,
And once a town declared me for a spy;
But at the end, I reach Jerusalem,
Since this poor covert where I pass the night,
This Bethany, lies scarce the distance thence
A man with plague-sores at the third degree
Runs till he drops down dead. Thou laughest here!
'Sooth, it elates me, thus reposed and safe,
To void the stuffing of my travel-scrip   40
And share with thee whatever Jewry yields.
A viscid choler is observable
In tertians, I was nearly bold to say;
And falling-sickness hath a happier cure
Than our school wots of: there's a spider here
Weaves no web, watches on the ledge of tombs,
Sprinkled with mottles on an ash-gray back;
Take five and drop them . . . but who knows his mind,
The Syrian runagate I trust this to?
His service payeth me a sublimate   50
Blown up his nose to help the ailing eye.
Best wait: I reach Jerusalem at morn,
There set in order my experiences,
Gather what most deserves, and give thee all—
Or I might add, Judæa's gum-tragacanth
Scales off in purer flakes, shines clearer-grained,
Cracks 'twixt the pestle and the porphyry,
In fine exceeds our produce. Scalp-disease
Confounds me, crossing so with leprosy—
Thou hadst admired one sort I gained at Zoar—   60
But zeal outruns discretion. Here I end.

       Yet stay: my Syrian blinketh gratefully,
Protesteth his devotion is my price—
Suppose I write what harms not, though he steal?
I half resolve to tell thee, yet I blush,
What set me off a-writing first of all.
An itch I had, a sting to write, a tang!
For, be it this town's barrenness—or else
The Man had something in the look of him—

His case has struck me far more than 'tis worth. 70
So, pardon if—(lest presently I lose
In the great press of novelty at hand
The care and pains this somehow stole from me)
I bid thee take the thing while fresh in mind,
Almost in sight—for, wilt thou have the truth?
The very man is gone from me but now,
Whose ailment is the subject of discourse.
Thus then, and let thy better wit help all!

     'Tis but a case of mania—subinduced
By epilepsy, at the turning-point 80
Of trance prolonged unduly some three days:
When, by the exhibition of some drug
Or spell, exorcisation, stroke of art
Unknown to me and which 'twere well to know,
The evil thing out-breaking all at once
Left the man whole and sound of body indeed,—
But, flinging (so to speak) life's gates too wide,
Making a clear house of it too suddenly,
The first conceit that entered might inscribe
Whatever it was minded on the wall 90
So plainly at that vantage, as it were,
(First come, first served) that nothing subsequent
Attaineth to erase those fancy-scrawls
The just-returned and new-established soul
Hath gotten now so thoroughly by heart
That henceforth she will read or these or none.
And first—the man's own firm conviction rests
That he was dead (in fact they buried him)
—That he was dead and then restored to life
By a Nazarene physician of his tribe: 100
—'Sayeth, the same bade "Rise," and he did rise.
"Such cases are diurnal," thou wilt cry.
Not so this figment!—not, that such a fume,
Instead of giving way to time and health,
Should eat itself into the life of life,
As saffron tingeth flesh, blood, bones and all!
For see, how he takes up the after-life.
The man—it is one Lazarus a Jew,
Sanguine, proportioned, fifty years of age,
The body's habit wholly laudable, 110
As much, indeed, beyond the common health
As he were made and put aside to show.
Think, could we penetrate by any drug
And bathe the wearied soul and worried flesh,
And bring it clear and fair, by three days' sleep!

Whence has the man the balm that brightens all?
This grown man eyes the world now like a child.
Some elders of his tribe, I should premise,
Led in their friend, obedient as a sheep,
To bear my inquisition. While they spoke,   120
Now sharply, now with sorrow,—told the case,—
He listened not except I spoke to him,
But folded his two hands and let them talk,
Watching the flies that buzzed: and yet no fool.
And that's a sample how his years must go.
Look, if a beggar, in fixed middle-life,
Should find a treasure,—can he use the same
With straitened habits and with tastes starved small,
And take at once to his impoverished brain
The sudden element that changes things,   130
That sets the undreamed-of rapture at his hand
And puts the cheap old joy in the scorned dust?
Is he not such an one as moves to mirth—
Warily parsimonious, when no need,
Wasteful as drunkenness at undue times?
All prudent counsel as to what befits
The golden mean, is lost on such an one:
The man's fantastic will is the man's law.
So here—we call the treasure knowledge, say,
Increased beyond the fleshly faculty—   140
Heaven opened to a soul while yet on earth,
Earth forced on a soul's use while seeing heaven:
The man is witless of the size, the sum,
The value in proportion of all things,
Or whether it be little or be much.
Discourse to him of prodigious armaments
Assembled to besiege his city now,
And of the passing of a mule with gourds—
'Tis one! Then take it on the other side,
Speak of some trifling fact,—he will gaze rapt   150
With stupor at its very littleness,
(Far as I see) as if in that indeed
He caught prodigious import, whole results;
And so will turn to us the bystanders
In ever the same stupor (note this point)
That we too see not with his opened eyes.
Wonder and doubt come wrongly into play,
Preposterously, at cross purposes.
Should his child sicken unto death,—why, look
For scarce abatement of his cheerfulness,   160
Or pretermission of the daily craft!
While a word, gesture, glance from that same child

At play or in the school or laid asleep,
Will startle him to an agony of fear,
Exasperation, just as like. Demand
The reason why—" 'tis but a word," object—
"A gesture"—he regards thee as our lord
Who lived there in the pyramid alone,
Looked at us (dost thou mind?) when, being young,
We both would unadvisedly recite 170
Some charm's beginning, from that book of his,
Able to bid the sun throb wide and burst
All into stars, as suns grown old are wont.
Thou and the child have each a veil alike
Thrown o'er your heads, from under which ye both
Stretch your blind hands and trifle with a match
Over a mine of Greek fire, did ye know!
He holds on firmly to some thread of life—
(It is the life to lead perforcedly)
Which runs across some vast distracting orb 180
Of glory on either side that meagre thread,
Which, conscious of, he must not enter yet—
The spiritual life around the earthly life:
The law of that is known to him as this,
His heart and brain move there, his feet stay here.
So is the man perplext with impulses
Sudden to start off crosswise, not straight on,
Proclaiming what is right and wrong across,
And not along, this black thread through the blaze—
"It should be" balked by "here it cannot be." 190
And oft the man's soul springs into his face
As if he saw again and heard again
His sage that bade him "Rise" and he did rise.
Something, a word, a tick o' the blood within
Admonishes: then back he sinks at once
To ashes, who was very fire before,
In sedulous recurrence to his trade
Whereby he earneth him the daily bread;
And studiously the humbler for that pride,
Professedly the faultier that he knows 200
God's secret, while he holds the thread of life.
Indeed the especial marking of the man
Is prone submission to the heavenly will—
Seeing it, what it is, and why it is.
'Sayeth, he will wait patient to the last
For that same death which must restore his being
To equilibrium, body loosening soul
Divorced even now by premature full growth:

He will live, nay, it pleaseth him to live
So long as God please, and just how God please.   210
He even seeketh not to please God more
(Which meaneth, otherwise) than as God please.
Hence, I perceive not he affects to preach
The doctrine of his sect whate'er it be,
Make proselytes as madmen thirst to do:
How can he give his neighbor the real ground,
His own conviction? Ardent as he is—
Call his great truth a lie, why, still the old
"Be it as God please" reassureth him.
I probed the sore as thy disciple should: 220
"How, beast," said I, "this stolid carelessness
Sufficeth thee, when Rome is on her march
To stamp out like a little spark thy town,
Thy tribe, thy crazy tale and thee at once?"
He merely looked with his large eyes on me.
The man is apathetic, you deduce?
Contrariwise, he loves both old and young,
Able and weak, affects the very brutes
And birds—how say I? flowers of the field—
As a wise workman recognizes tools   230
In a master's workshop, loving what they make.
Thus is the man as harmless as a lamb:
Only impatient, let him do his best,
At ignorance and carelessness and sin—
An indignation which is promptly curbed:
As when in certain travel I have feigned
To be an ignoramus in our art
According to some preconceived design,
And happed to hear the land's practitioners
Steeped in conceit sublimed by ignorance,   240
Prattle fantastically on disease,
Its cause and cure—and I must hold my peace!

          Thou wilt object—why have I not ere this
Sought out the sage himself, the Nazarene
Who wrought this cure, inquiring at the source,
Conferring with the frankness that befits?
Alas! it grieveth me, the learned leech
Perished in a tumult many years ago,
Accused,—our learning's fate,—of wizardry,
Rebellion, to the setting up a rule   250
And creed prodigious as described to me.
His death, which happened when the earthquake fell
(Prefiguring, as soon appeared, the loss

To occult learning in our lord the sage
Who lived there in the pyramid alone)
Was wrought by the mad people—that's their wont!
On vain recourse, as I conjecture it,
To his tried virtue, for miraculous help—
How could he stop the earthquake? That's their way!
The other imputations must be lies;   260
But take one, though I loathe to give it thee,
In mere respect for any good man's fame.
(And after all, our patient Lazarus
Is stark mad; should we count on what he says?
Perhaps not: though in writing to a leech
'Tis well to keep back nothing of a case.)
This man so cured regards the curer, then,
As—God forgive me! who but God himself,
Creator and sustainer of the world,
That came and dwelt in flesh on it awhile!   270
—'Sayeth that such an one was born and lived,
Taught, healed the sick, broke bread at his own house,
Then died, with Lazarus by, for aught I know,
And yet was . . . what I said nor choose repeat,
And must have so avouched himself, in fact,
In hearing of this very Lazarus
Who saith—but why all this of what he saith?
Why write of trivial matters, things of price
Calling at every moment for remark?
I noticed on the margin of a pool   280
Blue-flowering borage, the Aleppo sort,
Aboundeth, very nitrous. It is strange!

        Thy pardon for this long and tedious case,
Which, now that I review it, needs must seem
Unduly dwelt on, prolixly set forth!
Nor I myself discern in what is writ
Good cause for the peculiar interest
And awe indeed this man has touched me with.
Perhaps the journey's end, the weariness
Had wrought upon me first. I met him thus: 290
I crossed a ridge of short sharp broken hills
Like an old lion's cheek teeth. Out there came
A moon made like a face with certain spots
Multiform, manifold and menacing:
Then a wind rose behind me. So we met
In this old sleepy town at unaware,
The man and I. I send thee what is writ.
Regard it as a chance, a matter risked
To this ambiguous Syrian—he may lose,
Or steal, or give it thee with equal good.   300

Jerusalem's repose shall make amends
For time this letter wastes, thy time and mine;
Till when, once more thy pardon and farewell!

    The very God! think, Abib; dost thou think?
So, the All-Great, were the All-Loving too—
So, through the thunder comes a human voice
Saying, "O heart I made, a heart beats here!
Face, my hands fashioned, see it in myself!
Thou hast no power nor mayst conceive of mine,
But love I gave thee, with myself to love,   310
And thou must love me who have died for thee!"
The madman saith He said so: it is strange.
1855

"CHILDE ROLAND TO THE DARK TOWER CAME"

(See Edgar's song in *Lear*)

I

My first thought was, he lied in every word,
    That hoary cripple, with malicious eye
    Askance to watch the working of his lie
On mine, and mouth scarce able to afford
Suppression of the glee, that pursed and scored
    Its edge, at one more victim gained thereby.

II

What else should he be set for, with his staff?
    What, save to waylay with his lies, ensnare
    All travellers who might find him posted there,
And ask the road? I guessed what skull-like laugh   10
Would break, what crutch 'gin write my epitaph
    For pastime in the dusty thoroughfare,

III

If at his counsel I should turn aside
    Into that ominous tract which, all agree,
    Hides the Dark Tower. Yet acquiescingly
I did turn as he pointed: neither pride
Nor hope rekindling at the end descried,
    So much as gladness that some end might be.

IV

For, what with my whole world-wide wandering,
    What with my search drawn out thro' years, my hope   20
    Dwindled into a ghost not fit to cope

With that obstreperous joy success would bring,
I hardly tried now to rebuke the spring
    My heart made, finding failure in its scope.

V

As when a sick man very near to death
    Seems dead indeed, and feels begin and end
    The tears and takes the farewell of each friend,
And hears one bid the other go, draw breath
Freelier outside, ("since all is o'er," he saith,
    "And the blow fallen no grieving can amend;")   30

VI

While some discuss if near the other graves
    Be room enough for this, and when a day
    Suits best for carrying the corpse away,
With care about the banners, scarves and staves:
And still the man hears all, and only craves
    He may not shame such tender love and stay.

VII

Thus, I had so long suffered in this quest,
    Heard failure prophesied so oft, been writ
    So many times among "The Band"—to wit,
The knights who to the Dark Tower's search addressed   40
Their steps—that just to fail as they, seemed best,
    And all the doubt was now—should I be fit?

VIII

So, quiet as despair, I turned from him,
    That hateful cripple, out of his highway
    Into the path he pointed. All the day
Had been a dreary one at best, and dim
Was settling to its close, yet shot one grim
    Red leer to see the plain catch its estray.

IX

For mark! no sooner was I fairly found
    Pledged to the plain, after a pace or two,   50
    Than, pausing to throw backward a last view
O'er the safe road, 'twas gone; gray plain all round:
Nothing but plain to the horizon's bound.
    I might go on; naught else remained to do.

X

So, on I went. I think I never saw
    Such starved ignoble nature; nothing throve:
    For flowers—as well expect a cedar grove!

But cockle, spurge, according to their law
   Might propagate their kind, with none to awe,
      You'd think; a burr had been a treasure-trove.   60

XI

No! penury, inertness and grimace,
   In some strange sort, were the land's portion. "See
   Or shut your eyes," said Nature peevishly,
"It nothing skills: I cannot help my case:
'Tis the Last Judgment's fire must cure this place,
   Calcine its clods and set my prisoners free."

XII

If there pushed any ragged thistle-stalk
   Above its mates, the head was chopped; the bents
   Were jealous else. What made those holes and rents
In the dock's harsh swarth leaves, bruised as to balk   70
All hope of greenness? 'tis a brute must walk
   Pashing their life out, with a brute's intents.

XIII

As for the grass, it grew as scant as hair
   In leprosy; thin dry blades pricked the mud
   Which underneath looked kneaded up with blood.
One stiff blind horse, his every bone a-stare,
Stood stupefied, however he came there:
   Thrust out past service from the devil's stud!

XIV

Alive? he might be dead for aught I know,
   With that red gaunt and colloped neck a-strain,   80
   And shut eyes underneath the rusty mane;
Seldom went such grotesqueness with such woe;
I never saw a brute I hated so;
   He must be wicked to deserve such pain.

XV

I shut my eyes and turned them on my heart.
   As a man calls for wine before he fights,
   I asked one draught of earlier, happier sights,
Ere fitly I could hope to play my part.
Think first, fight afterwards—the soldier's art:
   One taste of the old time sets all to rights.   90

XVI

Not it! I fancied Cuthbert's reddening face
   Beneath its garniture of curly gold,
   Dear fellow, till I almost felt him fold

An arm in mine to fix me to the place,
That way he used. Alas, one night's disgrace!
    Out went my heart's new fire and left it cold.

XVII

Giles then, the soul of honour—there he stands
    Frank as ten years ago when knighted first.
    What honest man should dare (he said) he durst.
Good—but the scene shifts—faugh! what hangman hands   100
Pin to his breast a parchment? His own bands
    Read it. Poor traitor, spit upon and curst!

XVIII

Better this present than a past like that;
    Back therefore to my darkening path again!
    No sound, no sight as far as eye could strain.
Will the night send a howlet or a bat?
I asked: when something on the dismal flat
    Came to arrest my thoughts and change their train.

XIX

A sudden little river crossed my path
    As unexpected as a serpent comes.   110
    No sluggish tide congenial to the glooms;
This, as it frothed by, might have been a bath
For the fiend's glowing hoof—to see the wrath
    Of its black eddy bespate with flakes and spumes.

XX

So petty yet so spiteful! All along,
    Low scrubby alders kneeled down over it;
    Drenched willows flung them headlong in a fit
Of mute despair, a suicidal throng:
The river which had done them all the wrong,
    Whate'er that was, rolled by, deterred no whit.   120

XXI

Which, while I forded,—good saints, how I feared
    To set my foot upon a dead man's cheek,
    Each step, or feel the spear I thrust to seek
For hollows, tangled in his hair or beard!
—It may have been a water-rat I speared,
    But, ugh! it sounded like a baby's shriek.

XXII

Glad was I when I reached the other bank.
    Now for a better country. Vain presage!
    Who were the strugglers, what war did they wage

Whose savage trample thus could pad the dank   130
Soil to a plash? Toads in a poisoned tank,
   Or wild cats in a red-hot iron cage—

XXIII

The fight must so have seemed in that fell cirque.
   What penned them there, with all the plain to choose?
   No foot-print leading to that horrid mews,
None out of it. Mad brewage set to work
Their brains, no doubt, like galley-slaves the Turk
   Pits for his pastime, Christians against Jews.

XXIV

And more than that—a furlong on—why, there!
   What bad use was that engine for, that wheel,   140
   Or brake, not wheel—that harrow fit to reel
Men's bodies out like silk? with all the air
Of Tophet's tool, on earth left unaware,
   Or brought to sharpen its rusty teeth of steel.

XXV

Then came a bit of stubbed ground, once a wood,
   Next a marsh, it would seem, and now mere earth
   Desperate and done with; (so a fool finds mirth,
Makes a thing and then mars it, till his mood
Changes and off he goes!) within a rood—
   Bog, clay and rubble, sand and stark black dearth.   150

XXVI

Now blotches rankling, colored gay and grim,
   Now patches where some leanness of the soil's
   Broke into moss or substances like boils;
Then came some palsied oak, a cleft in him
Like a distorted mouth that splits its rim
   Gaping at death, and dies while it recoils.

XXVII

And just as far as ever from the end!
   Naught in the distance but the evening, naught
   To point my footstep further! At the thought,
A great black bird, Apollyon's bosom-friend,   160
Sailed past, nor beat his wide wing dragon-penned
   That brushed my cap—perchance the guide I sought.

XXVIII

For, looking up, aware I somehow grew,
   'Spite of the dusk, the plain had given place
   All round to mountains—with such name to grace

Mere ugly heights and heaps now stolen in view.
How thus they had surprised me,—solve it, you!
    How to get from them was no clearer case.

XXIX

Yet half I seemed to recognize some trick
    Of mischief happened to me, God knows when—   170
    In a bad dream perhaps. Here ended, then,
Progress this way. When, in the very nick
Of giving up, one time more, came a click
    As when a trap shuts—you're inside the den!

XXX

Burningly it came on me all at once,
    This was the place! those two hills on the right,
    Crouched like two bulls locked horn in horn in fight;
While to the left, a tall scalped mountain . . . Dunce,
Dotard, a-dozing at the very nonce,
    After a life spent training for the sight!   180

XXXI

What in the midst lay but the Tower itself?
    The round squat turret, blind as the fool's heart,
    Built of brown stone, without a counterpart
In the whole world. The tempest's mocking elf
Points to the shipman thus the unseen shelf
    He strikes on, only when the timbers start.

XXXII

Not see? because of night perhaps?—why, day
    Came back again for that! before it left,
    The dying sunset kindled through a cleft:
The hills, like giants at a hunting, lay,   190
Chin upon hand, to see the game at bay,—
    "Now stab and end the creature—to the heft!"

XXXIII

Not hear? when noise was everywhere! it tolled
    Increasing like a bell. Names in my ears
    Of all the lost adventurers my peers,—
How such a one was strong, and such was bold,
And such was fortunate, yet each of old
    Lost, lost! one moment knelled the woe of years.

XXXIV

There they stood, ranged along the hill-sides, met
    To view the last of me, a living frame   200
    For one more picture! in a sheet of flame
I saw them and I knew them all. And yet

Dauntless the slug-horn to my lips I set,
    And blew. "*Childe Roland to the Dark Tower came.*"
1855

BISHOP BLOUGRAM'S APOLOGY

No more wine? then we'll push back chairs and talk.
A final glass for me, though: cool, i' faith!
We ought to have our Abbey back, you see.
It's different, preaching in basilicas,
And doing duty in some masterpiece   5
Like this of brother Pugin's, bless his heart!
I doubt if they're half baked, those chalk rosettes,
Ciphers and stucco-twiddlings everywhere;
It's just like breathing in a lime-kiln: eh?
These hot long ceremonies of our church   10
Cost us a little—oh, they pay the price,
You take me—amply pay it! Now, we'll talk.

So, you despise me, Mr. Gigadibs.
No deprecation,—nay, I beg you, sir!
Beside 'tis our engagement: don't you know,   15
I promised, if you'd watch a dinner out,
We'd see truth dawn together?—truth that peeps
Over the glasses' edge when dinner's done,
And body gets its sop and holds its noise
And leaves soul free a little. Now's the time: 20
Truth's break of day! You do despise me then.
And if I say, "despise me,"—never fear!
I know you do not in a certain sense—
Not in my arm-chair, for example: here,
I well imagine you respect my place   25
(*Status, entourage*, worldly circumstance)
Quite to its value—very much indeed:
—Are up to the protesting eyes of you
In pride at being seated here for once—
You'll turn it to such capital account!   30
When somebody, through years and years to come,
Hints of the bishop,—names me—that's enough:
"Blougram? I knew him"—(into it you slide)
"Dined with him once, a Corpus Christi Day,
All alone, we two; he's a clever man: 35
And after dinner,—why, the wine you know,—
Oh, there was wine, and good!—what with the wine . . .
'Faith, we began upon all sorts of talk!
He's no bad fellow, Blougram; he had seen
Something of mine he relished, some review: 40

He's quite above their humbug in his heart,
Half-said as much, indeed—the thing's his trade.
I warrant, Blougram's sceptical at times:
How otherwise? I liked him, I confess!"
Che che, my dear sir, as we say at Rome,   45
Don't you protest now! It's fair give and take;
You have had your turn and spoken your home-truths:
The hand's mine now, and here you follow suit.

    Thus much conceded, still the first fact stays—
You do despise me; your ideal of life   50
Is not the bishop's: you would not be I.
You would like better to be Goethe, now,
Or Buonaparte, or bless me, lower still,
Count D'Orsay,—so you did what you preferred,
Spoke as you thought, and, as you cannot help,   55
Believed or disbelieved, no matter what,
So long as on that point, whate'er it was,
You loosed your mind, were whole and sole yourself.
—That, my ideal never can include,
Upon that element of truth and worth   60
Never be based! for say they make me Pope—
(They can't—suppose it for our argument!)
Why, there I'm at my tether's end, I've reached
My height, and not a height which pleases you:
An unbelieving Pope won't do, you say.   65
It's like those eerie stories nurses tell,
Of how some actor on a stage played Death,
With pasteboard crown, sham orb and tinselled dart,
And called himself the monarch of the world;
Then, going in the tire-room afterward,   70
Because the play was done, to shift himself,
Got touched upon the sleeve familiarly,
The moment he had shut the closet door,
By Death himself. Thus God might touch a Pope
At unawares, ask what his baubles mean,   75
And whose part he presumed to play just now.
Best be yourself, imperial, plain and true!

    So, drawing comfortable breath again,
You weigh and find, whatever more or less
I boast of my ideal realized   80
Is nothing in the balance when opposed
To your ideal, your grand simple life,
Of which you will not realize one jot.
I am much, you are nothing; you would be all,
I would be merely much: you beat me there.   85

No, friend, you do not beat me: harken why!
The common problem, yours, mine, every one's,
Is—not to fancy what were fair in life
Provided it could be,—but, finding first
What may be, then find how to make it fair   90
Up to our means: a very different thing!
No abstract intellectual plan of life
Quite irrespective of life's plainest laws,
But one, a man, who is man and nothing more,
May lead within a world which (by your leave)   95
Is Rome or London, not Fool's-paradise.
Embellish Rome, idealize away,
Make paradise of London if you can,
You're welcome, nay, you're wise.

                 A simile!
We mortals cross the ocean of this world   100
Each in his average cabin of a life;
The best's not big, the worst yields elbow-room.
Now for our six months' voyage—how prepare?
You come on shipboard with a landsman's list
Of things he calls convenient: so they are!   105
An India screen is pretty furniture,
A piano-forte is a fine resource,
All Balzac's novels occupy one shelf,
The new edition fifty volumes long;
And little Greek books, with the funny type   110
They get up well at Leipsic, fill the next:
Go on! slabbed marble, what a bath it makes!
And Parma's pride, the Jerome, let us add!
'Twere pleasant could Correggio's fleeting glow
Hang full in face of one where'er one roams,   115
Since he more than the others brings with him
Italy's self,—the marvellous Modenese!—
Yet was not on your list before, perhaps.
—Alas, friend, here's the agent . . . is't the name?
The captain, or whoever's master here—   120
You see him screw his face up; what's his cry
Ere you set foot on shipboard? "Six feet square!"
If you won't understand what six feet mean,
Compute and purchase stores accordingly—
And if, in pique because he overhauls   125
Your Jerome, piano, bath, you come on board
Bare—why, you cut a figure at the first
While sympathetic landsmen see you off;
Not afterward, when long ere half seas over,
You peep up from your utterly naked boards   130
Into some snug and well-appointed berth,

Like mine for instance (try the cooler jug—
Put back the other, but don't jog the ice!)
And mortified you mutter "Well and good;
He sits enjoying his sea-furniture;   135
'Tis stout and proper, and there's store of it:
Though I've the better notion, all agree,
Of fitting rooms up. Hang the carpenter,
Neat ship-shape fixings and contrivances—
I would have brought my Jerome, frame and all!"   140
And meantime you bring nothing: never mind—
You've proved your artist-nature: what you don't
You might bring, so despise me, as I say.

    Now come, let's backward to the starting-place.
See my way: we're two college friends, suppose.   145
Prepare together for our voyage, then;
Each note and check the other in his work,—
Here's mine, a bishop's outfit; criticise!
What's wrong? why won't you be a bishop too?

    Why first, you don't believe, you don't and can't,   150
(Not statedly, that is, and fixedly
And absolutely and exclusively)
In any revelation called divine.
No dogmas nail your faith; and what remains
But say so, like the honest man you are?   155
First, therefore, overhaul theology!
Nay, I too, not a fool, you please to think,
Must find believing every whit as hard:
And if I do not frankly say as much,
The ugly consequence is clear enough.   160

    Now wait, my friend: well, I do not believe—
If you'll accept no faith that is not fixed,
Absolute and exclusive, as you say.
You're wrong—I mean to prove it in due time.
Meanwhile, I know where difficulties lie   165
I could not, cannot solve, nor ever shall,
So give up hope accordingly to solve—
(To you, and over the wine). Our dogmas then
With both of us, though in unlike degree,
Missing full credence—overboard with them!   170
I mean to meet you on your own premise:
Good, there go mine in company with yours!

    And now what are we? unbelievers both,
Calm and complete, determinately fixed
To-day, to-morrow and forever, pray?   175
You'll guarantee me that? Not so, I think!

In no wise! all we've gained is, that belief,
As unbelief before, shakes us by fits,
Confounds us like its predecessor. Where's
The gain? how can we guard our unbelief,   180
Make it bear fruit to us?—the problem here.
Just when we are safest, there's a sunset-touch,
A fancy from a flower-bell, some one's death,
A chorus-ending from Euripides,—
And that's enough for fifty hopes and fears   185
As old and new at once as nature's self,
To rap and knock and enter in our soul,
Take hands and dance there, a fantastic ring,
Round the ancient idol, on his base again,—
The grand Perhaps! We look on helplessly.   190
There the old misgivings, crooked questions are—
This good God,—what he could do, if he would,
Would, if he could—then must have done long since:
If so, when, where and how? some way must be,—
Once feel about, and soon or late you hit   195
Some sense, in which it might be, after all.
Why not, "The Way, the Truth, the Life?"

                                                —That way
Over the mountain, which who stands upon
Is apt to doubt if it be meant for a road;
While, if he views it from the waste itself,   200
Up goes the line there, plain from base to brow,
Not vague, mistakable! what's a break or two
Seen from the unbroken desert either side?
And then (to bring in fresh philosophy)
What if the breaks themselves should prove at last   205
The most consummate of contrivances
To train a man's eye, teach him what is faith?
And so we stumble at truth's very test!
All we have gained then by our unbelief
Is a life of doubt diversified by faith,   210
For one of faith diversified by doubt:
We called the chess-board white,—we call it black.

    "Well," you rejoin, "the end's no worse, at least;
We've reason for both colors on the board:
Why not confess then, where I drop the faith   215
And you the doubt, that I'm as right as you?"

    Because, friend, in the next place, this being so,
And both things even,—faith and unbelief
Left to a man's choice,—we'll proceed a step,
Returning to our image, which I like.   220

A man's choice, yes—but a cabin-passenger's—
The man made for the special life o' the world—
Do you forget him? I remember though!
Consult our ship's conditions and you find
One and but one choice suitable to all;   225
The choice, that you unluckily prefer,
Turning things topsy-turvy—they or it
Going to the ground. Belief or unbelief
Bears upon life, determines its whole course,
Begins at its beginning. See the world   230
Such as it is,—you made it not, nor I;
I mean to take it as it is,—and you,
Not so you'll take it,—though you get naught else.
I know the special kind of life I like,
What suits the most my idiosyncrasy,   235
Brings out the best of me and bears me fruit
In power, peace, pleasantness and length of days.
I find that positive belief does this
For me, and unbelief, no whit of this.
—For you, it does, however?—that, we'll try!   240
'Tis clear, I cannot lead my life, at least,
Induce the world to let me peaceably,
Without declaring at the outset, "Friends,
I absolutely and peremptorily
Believe!"—I say, faith is my waking life: 245
One sleeps, indeed, and dreams at intervals,
We know, but waking's the main point with us,
And my provision's for life's waking part.
Accordingly, I use heart, head and hand
All day, I build, scheme, study, and make friends;   250
And when night overtakes me, down I lie,
Sleep, dream a little, and get done with it,
The sooner the better, to begin afresh.
What's midnight doubt before the dayspring's faith?
You, the philosopher, that disbelieve,   255
That recognize the night, give dreams their weight—
To be consistent you should keep your bed,
Abstain from healthy acts that prove you man,
For fear you drowse perhaps at unawares!
And certainly at night you'll sleep and dream,   260
Live through the day and bustle as you please.
And so you live to sleep as I to wake,
To unbelieve as I to still believe?
Well, and the common sense o' the world calls you
Bed-ridden,—and its good things come to me.   265
Its estimation, which is half the fight,
That's the first-cabin comfort I secure:

The next . . . but you perceive with half an eye!
Come, come, it's best believing, if we may;
You can't but own that!

                 Next, concede again,   270
If once we choose belief, on all accounts
We can't be too decisive in our faith,
Conclusive and exclusive in its terms,
To suit the world which gives us the good things.
In every man's career are certain points   275
Whereon he dares not be indifferent;
The world detects him clearly, if he dare,
As baffled at the game, and losing life.
He may care little or he may care much
For riches, honor, pleasure, work, repose,   280
Since various theories of life and life's
Success are extant which might easily
Comport with either estimate of these;
And whoso chooses wealth or poverty,
Labor or quiet, is not judged a fool   285
Because his fellow would choose otherwise:
We let him choose upon his own account
So long as he's consistent with his choice.
But certain points, left wholly to himself,
When once a man has arbitrated on,   290
We say he must succeed there or go hang.
Thus, he should wed the woman he loves most
Or needs most, whatsoe'er the love or need—
For he can't wed twice. Then, he must avouch,
Or follow, at the least, sufficiently,   295
The form of faith his conscience holds the best.
Whate'er the process of conviction was:
For nothing can compensate his mistake
On such a point, the man himself being judge:
He cannot wed twice, nor twice lose his soul.   300

     Well now, there's one great form of Christian faith
I happened to be born in—which to teach
Was given me as I grew up, on all hands,
As best and readiest means of living by;
The same on examination being proved   305
The most pronounced moreover, fixed, precise
And absolute form of faith in the whole world—
Accordingly, most potent of all forms
For working on the world. Observe, my friend!
Such as you know me, I am free to say,   310
In these hard latter days which hamper one,
Myself—by **no** immoderate exercise

Of intellect and learning, but the tact
To let external forces work for me,
—Bid the street's stones be bread and they are bread;   315
Big Peter's creed, or rather, Hildebrand's,
Exalt me o'er my fellows in the world
And make my life an ease and joy and pride;
It does so,—which for me's a great point gained,
Who have a soul and body that exact   320
A comfortable care in many ways.
There's power in me and will to dominate
Which I must exercise, they hurt me else:
In many ways I need mankind's respect,
Obedience, and the love that's born of fear: 325
While at the same time, there's a taste I have,
A toy of soul, a titillating thing,
Refuses to digest these dainties crude.
The naked life is gross till clothed upon:
I must take what men offer, with a grace   330
As though I would not, could I help it, take!
An uniform I wear though over-rich—
Something imposed on me, no choice of mine;
No fancy-dress worn for pure fancy's sake
And despicable therefore! now folk kneel   335
And kiss my hand—of course the Church's hand.
Thus I am made, thus life is best for me,
And thus that it should be I have procured;
And thus it could not be another way,
I venture to imagine.

        You'll reply,   340
So far my choice, no doubt, is a success;
But were I made of better elements,
With nobler instincts, purer tastes, like you,
I hardly would account the thing success
Though it did all for me I say.

          But, friend,   345
We speak of what is; not of what might be,
And how 'twere better if 'twere otherwise.
I am the man you see here plain enough:
Grant I'm a beast, why, beasts must lead beasts' lives!
Suppose I own at once to tail and claws;   350
The tailless man exceeds me: but being tailed
I'll lash out lion fashion, and leave apes
To dock their stump and dress their haunches up.
My business is not to remake myself,
But make the absolute best of what God made.   355
Or—our first simile—though you prove me doomed

To a viler berth still, to the steerage-hole,
The sheep-pen or the pig-stye, I should strive
To make what use of each were possible;
And as this cabin gets upholstery,   360
That hutch should rustle with sufficient straw.

    But, friend, I don't acknowledge quite so fast
I fail of all your manhood's lofty tastes
Enumerated so complacently,
On the mere ground that you forsooth can find   365
In this particular life I choose to lead
No fit provision for them. Can you not?
Say you, my fault is I address myself
To grosser estimators than should judge?
And that's no way of holding up the soul,   370
Which, nobler, needs men's praise perhaps, yet knows
One wise man's verdict outweighs all the fools'—
Would like the two, but, forced to choose, takes that.
I pine among my million imbeciles
(You think) aware some dozen men of sense   375
Eye me and know me, whether I believe
In the last winking Virgin, as I vow,
And am a fool, or disbelieve in her
And am a knave,—approve in neither case,
Withhold their voices though I look their way: 380
Like Verdi when, at his worst opera's end
(The thing they gave at Florence,—what's its name?)
While the mad houseful's plaudits near outbang
His orchestra of salt-box, tongs and bones,
He looks through all the roaring and the wreaths   385
Where sits Rossini patient in his stall.

    Nay, friend, I meet you with an answer here—
That even your prime men who appraise their kind
Are men still, catch a wheel within a wheel,
See more in a truth than the truth's simple self,   390
Confuse themselves. You see lads walk the street
Sixty the minute; what's to note in that?
You see one lad o'erstride a chimney-stack;
Him you must watch—he's sure to fall, yet stands!
Our interest's on the dangerous edge of things.   395
The honest thief, the tender murderer,
The superstitious atheist, demirep
That loves and saves her soul in new French books—
We watch while these in equilibrium keep
The giddy line midway: one step aside,   400
They're classed and done with. I, then, keep the line
Before your sages,—just the men to shrink

From the gross weights, coarse scales and labels broad
You offer their refinement. Fool or knave?
Why needs a bishop be a fool or knave   405
When there's a thousand diamond weights between?
So, I enlist them. Your picked twelve, you'll find,
Profess themselves indignant, scandalized
At thus being held unable to explain
How a superior man who disbelieves   410
May not believe as well: that's Schelling's way!
It's through my coming in the tail of time,
Nicking the minute with a happy tact.
Had I been born three hundred years ago
They'd say, "What's strange? Blougram of course believes"; 415
And, seventy years since, "disbelieves of course."
But now, "He may believe; and yet, and yet
How can he?" All eyes turn with interest.
Whereas, step off the line on either side—
You, for example, clever to a fault,   420
The rough and ready man who write apace,
Read somewhat seldomer, think perhaps even less—
You disbelieve! Who wonders and who cares?
Lord So-and-so—his coat bedropped with wax,
All Peter's chains about his waist, his back   425
Brave with the needlework of Noodledom—
Believes! Again, who wonders and who cares?
But I, the man of sense and learning too,
The able to think yet act, the this, the that,
I, to believe at this late time of day!   430
Enough; you see, I need not fear contempt.

  —Except it's yours! Admire me as these may,
You don't. But whom at least do you admire?
Present your own perfection, your ideal,
Your pattern man for a minute—oh, make haste,   435
Is it Napoleon you would have us grow?
Concede the means; allow his head and hand,
(A large concession, clever as you are)
Good! In our common primal element
Of unbelief (we can't believe, you know—   440
We're still at that admission, recollect!)
Where do you find—apart from, towering o'er
The secondary temporary aims
Which satisfy the gross taste you despise—
Where do you find his star?—his crazy trust   445
God knows through what or in what? it's alive
And shines and leads him, and that's all we want.
Have we aught in our sober night shall point
Such ends as his were, and direct the means

Of working out our purpose straight as his,   450
Nor bring a moment's trouble on success
With after-care to justify the same?
—Be a Napoleon, and yet disbelieve—
Why, the man's mad, friend, take his light away!
What's the vague good o' the world, for which you dare   455
With comfort to yourself blow millions up?
We neither of us see it! we do see
The blown-up millions—spatter of their brains
And writhing of their bowels and so forth,
In that bewildering entanglement   460
Of horrible eventualities
Past calculation to the end of time!
Can I mistake for some clear word of God
(Which were my ample warrant for it all)
His puff of hazy instinct, idle talk,   465
"The State, that's I," quack-nonsense about crowns,
And (when one beats the man to his last hold)
A vague idea of setting things to rights,
Policing people efficaciously,
More to their profit, most of all to his own;   470
The whole to end that dismallest of ends
By an Austrian marriage, cant to us the Church,
And resurrection of the old *régime?*
Would I, who hope to live a dozen years,
Fight Austerlitz for reasons such and such?   475
No: for, concede me but the merest chance
Doubt may be wrong—there's judgment, life to come!
With just that chance, I dare not. Doubt proves right?
This present life is all?—you offer me
Its dozen noisy years, without a chance   480
That wedding an archduchess, wearing lace,
And getting called by divers new-coined names,
Will drive off ugly thoughts and let me dine,
Sleep, read and chat in quiet as I like!
Therefore I will not.

              Take another case;   485
Fit up the cabin yet another way.
What say you to the poets? shall we write
Hamlet, Othello—make the world our own,
Without a risk to run of either sort?
I can't!—to put the strongest reason first.   490
"But try," you urge, "the trying shall suffice;
The aim, if reached or not, makes great the life:
Try to be Shakespeare, leave the rest to fate!"
Spare my self-knowledge—there's no fooling me!

If I prefer remaining my poor self,   495
I say so not in self-dispraise but praise.
If I'm a Shakespeare, let the well alone;
Why should I try to be what now I am?
If I'm no Shakespeare, as too probable,—
His power and consciousness and self-delight   500
And all we want in common, shall I find—
Trying forever? while on points of taste
Wherewith, to speak it humbly, he and I
Are dowered alike—I'll ask you, I or he,
Which in our two lives realizes most?   505
Much, he imagined—somewhat, I possess.
He had the imagination; stick to that!
Let him say, "In the face of my soul's works
Your world is worthless and I touch it not
Lest I should wrong them"—I'll withdraw my plea.   510
But does he say so? look upon his life!
Himself, who only can, gives judgment there.
He leaves his towers and gorgeous palaces
To build the trimmest house in Stratford town;
Saves money, spends it, owns the worth of things,   515
Giulio Romano's pictures, Dowland's lute;
Enjoys a show, respects the puppets, too,
And none more, had he seen its entry once,
Than "Pandulph, of fair Milan cardinal."
Why then should I who play that personage,   520
The very Pandulph Shakespeare's fancy made,
Be told that had the poet chanced to start
From where I stand now (some degree like mine
Being just the goal he ran his race to reach)
He would have run the whole race back, forsooth,   525
And left being Pandulph, to begin write plays?
Ah, the earth's best can be but the earth's best!
Did Shakespeare live, he could but sit at home
And get himself in dreams the Vatican,
Greek busts, Venetian paintings, Roman walls,   530
And English books, none equal to his own,
Which I read, bound in gold (he never did).
—Terni's fall, Naple's bay and Gothard's top—
Eh, friend? I could not fancy one of these;
But, as I pour this claret, there they are: 535
I've gained them—crossed St. Gothard last July
With ten mules to the carriage and a bed
Slung inside; is my hap the worse for that?
We want the same things, Shakespeare and myself,
And what I want, I have: he, gifted more,   540
Could fancy he too had them when he liked,

But not so thoroughly that, if fate allowed,
He would not have them also in my sense.
We play one game; I send the ball aloft
No less adroitly that of fifty strokes   545
Scarce five go o'er the wall so wide and high
Which sends them back to me: I wish and get.
He struck balls higher and with better skill,
But at a poor fence level with his head,
And hit—his Stratford house, a coat of arms,   550
Successful dealings in his grain and wool,—
While I receive heaven's incense in my nose
And style myself the cousin of Queen Bess.
Ask him, if this life's all, who wins the game?

    Believe—and our whole argument breaks up.   555
Enthusiasm's the best thing, I repeat;
Only, we can't command it; fire and life
Are all, dead matter's nothing, we agree:
And be it a mad dream or God's very breath,
The fact's the same,—belief's fire, once in us,   560
Makes of all else mere stuff to show itself:
We penetrate our life with such a glow
As fire lends wood and iron—this turns steel,
That burns to ash—all's one, fire proves its power
For good or ill, since men call flare success.   565
But paint a fire, it will not therefore burn.
Light one in me, I'll find it food enough!
Why, to be Luther—that's a life to lead,
Incomparably better than my own.
He comes, reclaims God's earth for God, he says,   570
Sets up God's rule again by simple means,
Re-opens a shut book, and all is done.
He flared out in the flaring of mankind;
Such Luther's luck was: how shall such be mine?
If he succeeded, nothing's left to do: 575
And if he did not altogether—well,
Strauss is the next advance. All Strauss should be
I might be also. But to what result?
He looks upon no future: Luther did.
What can I gain on the denying side?   580
Ice makes no conflagration. State the facts,
Read the text right, emancipate the world—
The emancipated world enjoys itself
With scarce a thank-you: Blougram told it first
It could not owe a farthing,—not to him   585
More than Saint Paul! 'twould press its pay, you think?
Then add there's still that plaguy hundredth chance

Strauss may be wrong. And so a risk is run—
For what gain? not for Luther's, who secured
A real heaven in his heart throughout his life,   590
Supposing death a little altered things.

    "Ay, but since really you lack faith," you cry,
"You run the same risk really on all sides,
In cool indifference as bold unbelief.
As well be Strauss as swing 'twixt Paul and him.   595
It's not worth having, such imperfect faith,
No more available to do faith's work
Than unbelief like mine. Whole faith, or none!"

    Softly, my friend! I must dispute that point.
Once own the use of faith, I'll find you faith.   600
We're back on Christian ground. You call for faith:
I show you doubt, to prove that faith exists.
The more of doubt, the stronger faith, I say,
If faith o'ercomes doubt. How I know it does?
By life and man's free will, God gave for that!   605
To mould life as we choose it, shows our choice:
That's our one act, the previous work's his own.
You criticise the soul? it reared this tree—
This broad life and whatever fruit it bears!
What matter though I doubt at every pore,   610
Head-doubts, heart-doubts, doubts at my fingers' ends,
Doubts in the trivial work of every day,
Doubts at the very bases of my soul
In the grand moments when she probes herself—
If finally I have a life to show,   615
The thing I did, brought out in evidence
Against the thing done to me underground
By hell and all its brood, for aught I know?
I say, whence sprang this? shows it faith or doubt?
All's doubt in me; where's break of faith in this?   620
It is the idea, the feeling and the love,
God means mankind should strive for and show forth
Whatever be the process to that end,—
And not historic knowledge, logic sound,
And metaphysical acumen, sure!   625
"What think ye of Christ," friend? when all's done and said,
Like you this Christianity or not?
It may be false, but will you wish it true?
Has it your vote to be so if it can?
Trust you an instinct silenced long ago   630
That will break silence and enjoin you love
What mortified philosophy is hoarse,
And all in vain, with bidding you despise?

If you desire faith—then you've faith enough:
What else seeks God—nay, what else seek ourselves?   635
You form a notion of me, we'll suppose,
On hearsay: it's a favorable one:
"But still" (you add), "there was no such good man,
Because of contradiction in the facts.
One proves, for instance, he was born in Rome,   640
This Blougram; yet throughout the tales of him
I see he figures as an Englishman."
Well, the two things are reconcilable.
But would I rather you discovered that,
Subjoining—"Still, what matter though they be?   645
Blougram concerns me naught, born here or there."

Pure faith indeed—you know not what you ask!
Naked belief in God the Omnipotent,
Omniscient, Omnipresent, sears too much
The sense of conscious creatures to be borne.   650
It were the seeing him, no flesh shall dare.
Some think, Creation's meant to show him forth:
I say it's meant to hide him all it can,
And that's what all the blessed evil's for.
Its use in Time is to environ us,   655
Our breath, our drop of dew, with shield enough
Against that sight till we can bear its stress.
Under a vertical sun, the exposed brain
And lidless eye and disemprisoned heart
Less certainly would wither up at once   660
Than mind, confronted with the truth of him.
But time and earth case-harden us to live;
The feeblest sense is trusted most; the child
Feels God a moment, ichors o'er the place,
Plays on and grows to be a man like us.   665
With me, faith means perpetual unbelief
Kept quiet like the snake 'neath Michael's foot
Who stands calm just because he feels it writhe.
Or, if that's too ambitious,—here's my box—
I need the excitation of a pinch   670
Threatening the torpor of the inside-nose
Nigh on the imminent sneeze that never comes.
"Leave it in peace" advise the simple folk:
Make it aware of peace by itching-fits,
Say I—let doubt occasion still more faith!   675

You'll say, once all believed, man, woman, child,
In that dear middle-age these noodles praise.
How you'd exult if I could put you back
Six hundred years, blot out cosmogony,

Geology, ethnology, what not,   680
(Greek endings, each the little passing-bell
That signifies some faith's about to die),
And set you square with Genesis again,—
When such a traveller told you his last news,
He saw the ark a-top of Ararat   685
But did not climb there since 'twas getting dusk
And robber-bands infest the mountain's foot!
How should you feel, I ask, in such an age,
How act? As other people felt and did;
With soul more blank than this decanter's knob,   690
Believe—and yet lie, kill, rob, fornicate
Full in belief's face, like the beast you'd be!

No, when the fight begins within himself,
A man's worth something. God stoops o'er his head,
Satan looks up between his feet—both tug—   695
He's left, himself, i' the middle: the soul wakes
And grows. Prolong that battle through his life!
Never leave growing till the life to come!
Here, we've got callous to the Virgin's winks
That used to puzzle people wholesomely: 700
Men have outgrown the shame of being fools.
What are the laws of nature, not to bend
If the Church bid them?—brother Newman asks.
Up with the Immaculate Conception, then—
On to the rack with faith!—is my advice.   705
Will not that hurry us upon our knees,
Knocking our breasts, "It can't be—yet it shall!
Who am I, the worm, to argue with my Pope?
Low things confound the high things!" and so forth.
That's better than acquitting God with grace   710
As some folk do. He's tried—no case is proved,
Philosophy is lenient—he may go!

You'll say, the old system's not so obsolete
But men believe still: ay, but who and where?
King Bomba's lazzaroni foster yet   715
The sacred flame, so Antonelli writes;
But even of these, what ragamuffin-saint
Believes God watches him continually,
As he believes in fire that it will burn,
Or rain that it will drench him? Break fire's law,   720
Sin against rain, although the penalty
Be just a singe or soaking? "No," he smiles;
"Those laws are laws that can enforce themselves."

The sum of all is—yes, my doubt is great,
My faith's still greater, then my faith's enough.   725

I have read much, thought much, experienced much,
Yet would die rather than avow my fear
The Naples' liquefaction may be false,
When set to happen by the palace-clock
According to the clouds or dinner-time.   730
I hear you recommend, I might at least
Eliminate, decrassify my faith
Since I adopt it; keeping what I must
And leaving what I can—such points as this.
I won't—that is, I can't throw one away.   735
Supposing there's no truth in what I hold
About the need of trial to man's faith,
Still, when you bid me purify the same,
To such a process I discern no end.
Clearing off one excrescence to see two,   740
There's ever a next in size, now grown as big,
That meets the knife: I cut and cut again!
First cut the Liquefaction, what comes last
But Fichte's clever cut at God himself?
Experimentalize on sacred things!   745
I trust nor hand nor eye nor heart nor brain
To stop betimes: they all get drunk alike.
The first step, I am master not to take.

  You'd find the cutting-process to your taste
As much as leaving growths of lies unpruned,   750
Nor see more danger in it,—you retort.
Your taste's worth mine; but my taste proves more wise
When we consider that the steadfast hold
On the extreme end of the chain of faith
Gives all the advantage, makes the difference   755
With the rough purblind mass we seek to rule:
We are their lords, or they are free of us,
Just as we tighten or relax our hold.
So, other matters equal, we'll revert
To the first problem—which, if solved my way   760
And thrown into the balance, turns the scale—
How we may lead a comfortable life,
How suit our luggage to the cabin's size.

  Of course you are remarking all this time
How narrowly and grossly I view life,   765
Respect the creature-comforts, care to rule
The masses, and regard complacently
"The cabin," in our old phrase. Well, I do.
I act for, talk for, live for this world now,
As this world prizes action, life and talk: 770
No prejudice to what next world may prove,

Whose new laws and requirements, my best pledge
To observe then, is that I observe these now,
Shall do hereafter what I do meanwhile.
Let us concede (gratuitously though)   775
Next life relieves the soul of body, yields
Pure spiritual enjoyment: well, my friend,
Why lose this life i' the meantime, since its use
May be to make the next life more intense?

Do you know, I have often had a dream   780
(Work it up in your next month's article)
Of man's poor spirit in its progress, still
Losing true life forever and a day
Through ever trying to be and ever being—
In the evolution of successive spheres—   785
Before its actual sphere and place of life,
Halfway into the next, which having reached,
It shoots with corresponding foolery
Halfway into the next still, on and off!
As when a traveller, bound from North to South,   790
Scouts fur in Russia: what's its use in France?
In France spurns flannel: where's its need in Spain?
In Spain drops cloth, too cumbrous for Algiers!
Linen goes next, and last the skin itself,
A superfluity at Timbuctoo.   795
When, through his journey, was the fool at ease?
I'm at ease now, friend; worldly in this world,
I take and like its way of life; I think
My brothers, who administer the means,
Live better for my comfort—that's good too;   800
And God, if he pronounce upon such life,
Approves my service, which is better still.
If he keep silence,—why, for you or me
Or that brute beast pulled-up in to-day's "Times,"
What odds is't, save to ourselves, what life we lead?   805

You meet me at this issue: you declare,—
All special-pleading done with—truth is truth,
And justifies itself by undreamed ways.
You don't fear but it's better, if we doubt.
To say so, act up to our truth perceived   810
However feebly. Do then,—act away!
'Tis there I'm on the watch for you. How one acts
Is, both of us agree, our chief concern:
And how you'll act is what I fain would see.
If, like the candid person you appear,   815
You dare to make the most of your life's scheme
As I of mine, live up to its full law

Since there's no higher law that counterchecks.
Put natural religion to the test
You've just demolished the revealed with—quick,   820
Down to the root of all that checks your will,
All prohibition to lie, kill and thieve,
Or even to be an atheistic priest!
Suppose a pricking to incontinence—
Philosophers deduce you chastity   825
Or shame, from just the fact that at the first
Whoso embraced a woman in the field,
Threw club down and forewent his brains beside,
So, stood a ready victim in the reach
Of any brother savage, club in hand;   830
Hence saw the use of going out of sight
In wood or cave to prosecute his loves:
I read this in a French book t'other day.
Does law so analyzed coerce you much?
Oh, men spin clouds of fuzz where matters end,   835
But you who reach where the first thread begins,
You'll soon cut that!—which means you can, but won't,
Through certain instincts, blind, unreasoned-out,
You dare not set aside, you can't tell why,
But there they are, and so you let them rule.   840
Then, friend, you seem as much a slave as I,
A liar, conscious coward and hypocrite,
Without the good the slave expects to get,
In case he has a master after all!
You own your instincts? why, what else do I,   845
Who want, am made for, and must have a God
Ere I can be aught, do aught?—no mere name
Want, but the true thing with what proves its truth,
To wit, a relation from that thing to me,
Touching from head to foot—which touch I feel,   850
And with it take the rest, this life of ours!
I live my life here; yours you dare not live.

    —Not as I state it, who (you please subjoin)
Disfigure such a life and call it names.
While, to your mind, remains another way   855
For simple men: knowledge and power have rights,
But ignorance and weakness have rights too.
There needs no crucial effort to find truth
If here or there or anywhere about:
We ought to turn each side, try hard and see,   860
And if we can't, be glad we've earned at least
The right, by one laborious proof the more,
To graze in peace earth's pleasant pasturage.
Men are not angels, neither are they brutes:

Something we may see, all we cannot see.   865
What need of lying? I say, I see all,
And swear to each detail the most minute
In what I think a Pan's face—you, mere cloud:
I swear I hear him speak and see him wink,
For fear, if once I drop the emphasis,   870
Mankind may doubt there's any cloud at all.
You take the simple life—ready to see,
Willing to see (for no cloud's worth a face)—
And leaving quiet what no strength can move,
And which, who bids you move? who has the right?   875
I bid you; but you are God's sheep, not mine:
"*Pastor est tui Dominus.*" You find
In this the pleasant pasture of our life
Much you may eat without the least offence,
Much you don't eat because your maw objects,   880
Much you would eat but that your fellow-flock
Open great eyes at you and even butt,
And thereupon you like your mates so well
You cannot please yourself, offending them;
Though when they seem exorbitantly sheep,   885
You weigh your pleasure with their butts and bleats
And strike the balance. Sometimes certain fears
Restrain you, real checks since you find them so;
Sometimes you please yourself and nothing checks:
And thus you graze through life with not one lie,   890
And like it best.

             But do you, in truth's name?
If so, you beat—which means you are not I—
Who needs must make earth mine and feed my fill
Not simply unbutted at, unbickered with,
But motioned to the velvet of the sward   895
By those obsequious wethers' very selves.
Look at me, sir; my age is double yours:
At yours, I knew beforehand, so enjoyed,
What now I should be—as, permit the word,
I pretty well imagine your whole range   900
And stretch of tether twenty years to come.
We both have minds and bodies much alike:
In truth's name, don't you want my bishopric,
My daily bread, my influence and my state?
You're young. I'm old; you must be old one day;   905
Will you find then, as I do hour by hour,
Women their lovers kneel to, who cut curls
From your fat lap-dog's ear to grace a brooch—
Dukes, who petition just to kiss your ring—

With much beside you know or may conceive?   910
Suppose we die to-night: well, here am I,
Such were my gains, life bore this fruit to me,
While writing all the same my articles
On music, poetry, the fictile vase
Found at Albano, chess, Anacreon's Greek.   915
But you—the highest honor in your life,
The things you'll crown yourself with, all your days,
Is—dining here and drinking this last glass
I pour you out in sign of amity
Before we part forever. Of your power   920
And social influence, worldly worth in short,
Judge what's my estimation by the fact,
I do not condescend to enjoin, beseech,
Hint secrecy on one of all these words!
You're shrewd and know that should you publish one   925
The world would brand the lie—my enemies first,
Who'd sneer—"the bishop's an arch-hypocrite
And knave perhaps, but not so frank a fool."
Whereas I should not dare for both my ears
Breathe one such syllable, smile one such smile,   930
Before the chaplain who reflects myself—
My shade's so much more potent than your flesh.
What's your reward, self-abnegating friend?
Stood you confessed of those exceptional
And privileged great natures that dwarf mine—   935
A zealot with a mad ideal in reach,
A poet just about to print his ode,
A statesman with a scheme to stop this war,
An artist whose religion is his art—
I should have nothing to object: such men   940
Carry the fire, all things grow warm to them,
Their drugget's worth my purple, they beat me.
But you,—you're just as little those as I—
You, Gigadibs, who, thirty years of age,
Write stately for Blackwood's Magazine,   945
Believe you see two points in Hamlet's soul
Unseized by the Germans yet—which view you'll print—
Meantime the best you have to show being still
That lively lightsome article we took
Almost for the true Dickens,—what's its name?   950
"The Slum and Cellar, or Whitechapel life
Limned after dark!" it made me laugh, I know,
And pleased a month, and brought you in ten pounds.
—Success I recognize and compliment,
And therefore give you, if you choose, three words   955
(The card and pencil-scratch is quite enough)

Which whether here, in Dublin or New York,
Will get you, prompt as at my eyebrow's wink,
Such terms as never you aspired to get
In all our own reviews and some not ours.   960
Go write your lively sketches! be the first
"Blougram, or The Eccentric Confidence"—
Or better simply say, "The Outward-bound."
Why, men as soon would throw it in my teeth
As copy and quote the infamy chalked broad   965
About me on the church-door opposite.
You will not wait for that experience though,
I fancy, howsoever you decide,
To discontinue—not detesting, not
Defaming, but at least—despising me!   970

    Over his wine so smiled and talked his hour
Sylvester Blougram, styled *in partibus*
Episcopus, nec non—(the deuce knows what
It's changed to by our novel hierarchy)
With Gigadibs the literary man,   975
Who played with spoons, explored his plate's design,
And ranged the olive-stones about its edge,
While the great bishop rolled him out a mind
Long crumpled, till creased consciousness lay smooth.

    For Blougram, he believed, say, half he spoke.   980
The other portion, as he shaped it thus
For argumentatory purposes,
He felt his foe was foolish to dispute.
Some arbitrary accidental thoughts
That crossed his mind, amusing because new,   985
He chose to represent as fixtures there,
Invariable convictions (such they seemed
Beside his interlocutor's loose cards
Flung daily down, and not the same way twice)
While certain hell-deep instincts, man's weak tongue   990
Is never bold to utter in their truth
Because styled hell-deep ('tis an old mistake
To place hell at the bottom of the earth)
He ignored these,—not having in readiness
Their nomenclature and philosophy: 995
He said true things, but called them by wrong names.
"On the whole," he thought, "I justify myself
On every point where cavillers like this
Oppugn my life: he tries one kind of fence,
I close, he's worsted, that's enough for him.   1000
He's on the ground: if ground should break away
I take my stand on, there's a firmer yet

Beneath it, both of us may sink and reach.
His ground was over mine and broke the first:
So, let him sit with me this many a year!" 1005

He did not sit five minutes. Just a week
Sufficed his sudden healthy vehemence.
Something had struck him in the "Outward-bound"
Another way than Blougram's purpose was:
And having bought, not cabin-furniture 1010
But settler's-implements (enough for three)
And started for Australia—there, I hope,
By this time he has tested his first plough,
And studied his last chapter of St. John.
1855

ANDREA DEL SARTO

(CALLED "THE FAULTLESS PAINTER")

But do not let us quarrel any more,
No, my Lucrezia; bear with me for once:
Sit down and all shall happen as you wish.
You turn your face, but does it bring your heart?
I'll work then for your friend's friend, never fear,
Treat his own subject after his own way,
Fix his own time, accept too his own price,
And shut the money into this small hand
When next it takes mine. Will it? tenderly?
Oh, I'll content him,—but to-morrow, Love! 10
I often am much wearier than you think,
This evening more than usual, and it seems
As if—forgive now—should you let me sit
Here by the window with your hand in mine
And look a half-hour forth on Fiesole,
Both of one mind, as married people use,
Quietly, quietly the evening through,
I might get up to-morrow to my work
Cheerful and fresh as ever. Let us try.
To-morrow, how you shall be glad for this! 20
Your soft hand is a woman of itself,
And mine the man's bared breast she curls inside.
Don't count the time lost, neither; you must serve
For each of the five pictures we require:
It saves a model. So! keep looking so—
My serpentining beauty, rounds on rounds!
—How could you ever prick those perfect ears,

Even to put the pearl there! oh, so sweet—
My face, my moon, my everybody's moon,
Which everybody looks on and calls his, 30
And, I suppose, is looked on by in turn,
While she looks—no one's: very dear, no less.
You smile? why, there's my picture ready made,
There's what we painters call our harmony!
A common grayness silvers everything,—
All in a twilight, you and I alike
—You, at the point of your first pride in me
(That's gone you know),—but I, at every point;
My youth, my hope, my art, being all toned down
To yonder sober pleasant Fiesole. 40
There's the bell clinking from the chapel-top;
That length of convent-wall across the way
Holds the trees safer, huddled more inside;
The last monk leaves the garden; days decrease,
And autumn grows, autumn in everything.
Eh? the whole seems to fall into a shape
As if I saw alike my work and self
And all that I was born to be and do,
A twilight-piece. Love, we are in God's hand.
How strange now, looks the life he makes us lead; 50
So free we seem, so fettered fast we are!
I feel he laid the fetter: let it lie!
This chamber for example—turn your head—
All that's behind us! You don't understand
Nor care to understand about my art,
But you can hear at least when people speak:
And that cartoon, the second from the door
—It is the thing, Love! so such things should be—
Behold Madonna!—I am bold to say.
I can do with my pencil what I know, 60
What I see, what at bottom of my heart
I wish for, if I ever wish so deep—
Do easily, too—when I say, perfectly,
I do not boast, perhaps: yourself are judge,
Who listened to the Legate's talk last week,
And just as much they used to say in France.
At any rate 'tis easy, all of it!
No sketches first, no studies, that's long past:
I do what many dream of, all their lives,
—Dream? strive to do, and agonize to do, 70
And fail in doing. I could count twenty such
On twice your fingers, and not leave this town,
Who strive—you don't know how the others strive
To paint a little thing like that you smeared

Carelessly passing with your robes afloat,—
Yet do much less, so much less, Someone says,
(I know his name, no matter)—so much less!
Well, less is more, Lucrezia: I am judged.
There burns a truer light of God in them,
In their vexed beating stuffed and stopped-up brain,   80
Heart, or whate'er else, than goes on to prompt
This low-pulsed forthright craftsman's hand of mine.
Their works drop groundward, but themselves, I know,
Reach many a time a heaven that's shut to me,
Enter and take their place there sure enough,
Though they come back and cannot tell the world.
My works are nearer heaven, but I sit here.
The sudden blood of these men! at a word—
Praise them, it boils, or blame them, it boils too.
I, painting from myself and to myself,   90
Know what I do, am unmoved by men's blame
Or their praise either. Somebody remarks
Morello's outline there is wrongly traced,
His hue mistaken; what of that? or else,
Rightly traced and well ordered; what of that?
Speak as they please, what does the mountain care?
Ah, but a man's reach should exceed his grasp,
Or what's a heaven for? All is silver-gray
Placid and perfect with my art: the worse!
I know both what I want and what might gain,   100
And yet how profitless to know, to sigh
"Had I been two, another and myself,
Our head would have o'erlooked the world!" No doubt.
Yonder's a work now, of that famous youth
The Urbinate who died five years ago.
('Tis copied, George Vasari sent it me.)
Well, I can fancy how he did it all,
Pouring his soul, with kings and popes to see,
Reaching, that heaven might so replenish him,
Above and through his art—for it gives way;   110
That arm is wrongly put—and there again—
A fault to pardon in the drawing's lines,
Its body, so to speak: its soul is right,
He means right—that, a child may understand.
Still, what an arm! and I could alter it:
But all the play, the insight and the stretch—
Out of me, out of me! And wherefore out?
Had you enjoined them on me, given me soul,
We might have risen to Rafael, I and you!
Nay, Love, you did give all I asked, I think—   120
More than I merit, yes, by many times.

But had you—oh, with the same perfect brow,
And perfect eyes, and more than perfect mouth,
And the low voice my soul hears, as a bird
The fowler's pipe, and follows to the snare—
Had you, with these the same, but brought a mind!
Some women do so. Had the mouth there urged
"God and the glory! never care for gain.
The present by the future, what is that?
Live for fame, side by side with Agnolo!   130
Rafael is waiting: up to God, all three!"
I might have done it for you. So it seems:
Perhaps not. All is as God over-rules.
Beside, incentives come from the soul's self;
The rest avail not. Why do I need you?
What wife had Rafael, or has Agnolo?
In this world, who can do a thing, will not;
And who would do it, cannot, I perceive:
Yet the will's somewhat—somewhat, too, the power—
And thus we half-men struggle. At the end,   140
God, I conclude, compensates, punishes.
'Tis safer for me, if the award be strict,
That I am something underrated here.
Poor this long while, despised, to speak the truth.
I dared not, do you know, leave home all day,
For fear of chancing on the Paris lords.
The best is when they pass and look aside;
But they speak sometimes; I must bear it all.
Well may they speak! That Francis, that first time,
And that long festal year at Fontainebleau!   150
I surely then could sometimes leave the ground,
Put on the glory, Rafael's daily wear,
In that humane great monarch's golden look,—
One finger in his beard or twisted curl
Over his mouth's good mark that made the smile,
One arm about my shoulder, round my neck,
The jingle of his gold chain in my ear,
I painting proudly with his breath on me,
All his court round him, seeing with his eyes,
Such frank French eyes, and such a fire of souls   160
Profuse, my hand kept plying by those hearts,—
And, best of all, this, this, this face beyond,
This in the background, waiting on my work,
To crown the issue with a last reward!
A good time, was it not, my kingly days?
And had you not grown restless . . . but I know—
'Tis done and past; 'twas right, my instinct said;
Too live the life grew, golden and not gray,

And I'm the weak-eyed bat no sun should tempt
Out of the grange whose four walls make his world.   170
How could it end in any other way?
You called me, and I came home to your heart.
The triumph was—to reach and stay there; since
I reached it ere the triumph, what is lost?
Let my hands frame your face in your hair's gold,
You beautiful Lucrezia that are mine!
"Rafael did this, Andrea painted that;
The Roman's is the better when you pray,
But still the other's Virgin was his wife—"
Men will excuse me. I am glad to judge   180
Both pictures in your presence; clearer grows
My better fortune, I resolve to think.
For, do you know, Lucrezia, as God lives,
Said one day Agnolo, his very self,
To Rafael . . . I have known it all these years . . .
(When the young man was flaming out his thoughts
Upon a palace-wall for Rome to see,
Too lifted up in heart because of it)
"Friend, there's a certain sorry little scrub
Goes up and down our Florence, none cares how,   190
Who, were he set to plan and execute
As you are, pricked on by your popes and kings,
Would bring the sweat into that brow of yours!"
To Rafael's!—And indeed the arm is wrong.
I hardly dare . . . yet, only you to see,
Give the chalk here—quick, thus the line should go!
Ay, but the soul! he's Rafael! rub it out!
Still, all I care for, if he spoke the truth,
(What he? why, who but Michel Agnolo?
Do you forget already words like those?)   200
If really there was such a chance, so lost,—
Is, whether you're—not grateful—but more pleased.
Well, let me think so. And you smile indeed!
This hour has been an hour! Another smile?
If you would sit thus by me every night
I should work better, do you comprehend?
I mean that I should earn more, give you more.
See, it is settled dusk now; there's a star;
Morello's gone, the watch-lights show the wall,
The cue-owls speak the name we call them by.   210
Come from the window, love,—come in, at last,
Inside the melancholy little house
We built to be so gay with. God is just.
King Francis may forgive me: oft at nights
When I look up from painting, eyes tired out,

The walls become illumined, brick from brick
Distinct, instead of mortar, fierce bright gold,
That gold of his I did cement them with!
Let us but love each other. Must you go?
That Cousin here again? he waits outside? 220
Must see you—you, and not with me? Those loans?
More gaming debts to pay? you smiled for that?
Well, let smiles buy me! have you more to spend?
While hand and eye and something of a heart
Are left me, work's my ware, and what's it worth?
I'll pay my fancy. Only let me sit
The gray remainder of the evening out,
Idle, you call it, and muse perfectly
How I could paint, were I but back in France,
One picture, just one more—the Virgin's face, 230
Not yours this time! I want you at my side
To hear them—that is, Michel Agnolo—
Judge all I do and tell you of its worth.
Will you? To-morrow, satisfy your friend.
I take the subjects for his corridor,
Finish the portrait out of hand—there, there,
And throw him in another thing or two
If he demurs; the whole should prove enough
To pay for this same Cousin's freak. Beside,
What's better and what's all I care about, 240
Get you the thirteen scudi for the ruff!
Love, does that please you? Ah, but what does he,
The Cousin! What does he to please you more?

I am grown peaceful as old age to-night.
I regret little, I would change still less.
Since there my past life lies, why alter it?
The very wrong to Francis!—it is true
I took his coin, was tempted and complied,
And built this house and sinned, and all is said.
My father and my mother died of want. 250
Well, had I riches of my own? you see
How one gets rich! Let each one bear his lot.
They were born poor, lived poor, and poor they died:
And I have labored somewhat in my time
And not been paid profusely. Some good son
Paint my two hundred pictures—let him try!
No doubt, there's something strikes a balance. Yes,
You loved me quite enough, it seems to-night.
This must suffice me here. What would one have?
In heaven, perhaps, new chances, one more chance— 260
Four great walls in the New Jerusalem,

Meted on each side by the angel's reed,
For Leonard, Rafael, Agnolo and me
To cover—the three first without a wife,
While I have mine! So—still they overcome
Because there's still Lucrezia,—as I choose.

Again the Cousin's whistle! Go, my Love.
1855

SAUL

I

Said Abner, "At last thou art come! Ere I tell, ere thou speak,
Kiss my cheek, wish me well!" Then I wished it, and did kiss his
    cheek.
And he, "Since the King, O my friend, for thy countenance sent,
Neither drunken nor eaten have we; nor until from his tent
Thou return with the joyful assurance the King liveth yet,
Shall our lip with the honey be bright, with the water be wet.
For out of the black mid-tent's silence, a space of three days,
Not a sound hath escaped to thy servants, of prayer nor of praise,
To betoken that Saul and the Spirit have ended their strife,
And that, faint in his triumph, the monarch sings back upon life.   10

II

"Yet now my heart leaps, O beloved! God's child with his dew
On thy gracious gold hair, and those lilies still living and blue
Just broken to twine round thy harp-strings, as if no wild heat
Were now raging to torture the desert!"

III

                        Then I, as was meet,
Knelt down to the God of my fathers, and rose on my feet,
And ran o'er the sand burnt to powder. The tent was unlooped;
I pulled up the spear that obstructed, and under I stooped;
Hands and knees on the slippery grass-patch, all withered and gone,
That extends to the second enclosure, I groped my way on
Till I felt where the foldskirts fly open. Then once more I prayed,   20
And opened the foldskirts and entered, and was not afraid
But spoke, "Here is David, thy servant!" And no voice replied.
At the first I saw naught but the blackness; but soon I descried
A something more black than the blackness—the vast, the upright
Main prop which sustains the pavilion: and slow into sight
Grew a figure against it, gigantic and blackest of all.
Then a sunbeam, that burst thro' the tent-roof, showed Saul.

IV

He stood as erect as that tent-prop, both arms stretched out wide
On the great cross-support in the centre, that goes to each side;
He relaxed not a muscle, but hung there as, caught in his pangs   30
And waiting his change, the king-serpent all heavily hangs,
Far away from his kind, in the pine, till deliverance come
With the spring-time,—so agonized Saul, drear and stark, blind and
    dumb.

V

Then I tuned my harp,—took off the lilies we twine round its chords
Lest they snap 'neath the stress of the noon-tide—those sunbeams
    like swords!
And I first played the tune all our sheep know, as, one after one,
So docile they come to the pen-door till folding be done.
They are white and untorn by the bushes, for lo, they have fed
Where the long grasses stifle the water within the stream's bed;
And now one after one seeks its lodging, as star follows star   40
Into eve and the blue far above us,—so blue and so far!

VI

—Then the tune, for which quails on the cornland will each leave
    his mate
To fly after the player; then, what makes the crickets elate
Till for boldness they fight one another; and then, what has weight
To set the quick jerboa a-musing outside his sand house—
There are none such as he for a wonder, half bird and half mouse!
God made all the creatures and gave them our love and our fear,
To give sign, we and they are his children, one family here.

VII

Then I played the help-tune of our reapers, their wine-song, when
    hand
Grasps at hand, eye lights eye in good friendship, and great hearts
    expand   50
And grow one in the sense of this world's life.—And then, the last
    song
When the dead man is praised on his journey—"Bear, bear him along
With his few faults shut up like dead flowerets! Are balm-seeds not
    here
To console us? The land has none left such as he on the bier.
Oh, would we might keep thee, my brother!"—And then, the glad
    chaunt
Of the marriage,—first go the young maidens, next, she whom we
    vaunt
As the beauty, the pride of our dwelling.—And then, the great march
Wherein man runs to man to assist him and buttress an arch

Naught can break; who shall harm them, our friends?—Then, the
    chorus intoned
As the Levites go up to the altar in glory enthroned.   60
But I stopped here: for here in the darkness Saul groaned.

VIII

And I paused, held my breath in such silence, and listened apart;
And the tent shook, for mighty Saul shuddered: and sparkles 'gan
    dart
From the jewels that woke in his turban, at once with a start,
All its lordly male-sapphires, and rubies courageous at heart.
So the head: but the body still moved not, still hung there erect.
And I bent once again to my playing, pursued it unchecked,
As I sang,—

IX

      "Oh, our manhood's prime vigor! No spirit feels waste,
Not a muscle is stopped in its playing nor sinew unbraced.
Oh, the wild joys of living! the leaping from rock up to rock,   70
The strong rending of boughs from the fir-tree, the cool silver shock
Of the plunge in a pool's living water, the hunt of the bear,
And the sultriness showing the lion is couched in his lair.
And the meal, the rich dates yellowed over with gold dust divine,
And the locust-flesh steeped in the pitcher, the full draught of wine,
And the sleep in the dried river-channel where bulrushes tell
That the water was wont to go warbling so softly and well.
How good is man's life, the mere living! how fit to employ
All the heart and the soul and the senses forever in joy!
Hast thou loved the white locks of thy father, whose sword thou didst
    guard   80
When he trusted thee forth with the armies, for glorious reward?
Didst thou see the thin hands of thy mother, held up as men sung
The low song of the nearly-departed, and hear her faint tongue
Joining in while it could to the witness, 'Let one more attest,
I have lived, seen God's hand thro' a lifetime, and all was for best'?
Then they sung thro' their tears in strong triumph, not much, but
    the rest.
And thy brothers, the help and the contest, the working whence
    grew
Such result as, from seething grape-bundles, the spirit strained true:
And the friends of thy boyhood—that boyhood of wonder and hope,
Present promise and wealth of the future beyond the eye's scope,—
Till lo, thou art grown to a monarch; a people is thine;   91
And all gifts, which the world offers singly, on one head combine!
On one head, all the beauty and strength, love and rage (like the
    throe
That, a-work in the rock, helps its labor and lets the gold go)

High ambition and deeds which surpass it, fame crowning them,—
   all
Brought to blaze on the head of one creature—King Saul!"

X

And lo, with that leap of my spirit,—heart, hand, harp and voice,
Each lifting Saul's name out of sorrow, each bidding rejoice
Saul's fame in the light it was made for—as when, dare I say,
The Lord's army, in rapture of service, strains through its array,   100
And upsoareth the cherubim-chariot—"Saul!" cried I, and stopped,
And waited the thing that should follow. Then Saul, who hung
   propped
By the tent's cross-support in the centre, was struck by his name.
Have ye seen when Spring's arrowy summons goes right to the aim,
And some mountain, the last to withstand her, that held (he alone,
While the vale laughed in freedom and flowers) on a broad bust of
   stone
A year's snow bound about for a breastplate,—leaves grasp of the
   sheet?
Fold on fold all at once it crowds thunderously down to his feet,
And there fronts you, stark, black, but alive yet, your mountain of
   old,
With his rents, the successive bequeathings of ages untold—   110
Yea, each harm got in fighting your battles, each furrow and scar
Of his head thrust 'twixt you and the tempest—all hail, there they
   are!
—Now again to be softened with verdure, again hold the nest
Of the dove, tempt the goat and its young to the green on his crest
For their food in the ardors of summer. One long shudder thrilled
All the tent till the very air tingled, then sank and was stilled
At the King's self left standing before me, released and aware.
What was gone, what remained? All to traverse, 'twixt hope and
   despair;
Death was past, life not come: so he waited. Awhile his right hand
Held the brow, helped the eyes left too vacant forthwith to remand
To their place what new objects should enter: 'twas Saul as before.
I looked up and dared gaze at those eyes, nor was hurt any more   122
Than by slow pallid sunsets in autumn, ye watch from the shore,
At their sad level gaze o'er the ocean—a sun's slow decline
Over hills which, resolved in stern silence, o'erlap and entwine
Base with base to knit strength more intensely: so, arm folded arm
O'er the chest whose slow heavings subsided.

XI

                              What spell or what charm,
(For, awhile there was trouble within me) what next should I urge
To sustain him where song had restored him?—Song filled to the
   verge

His cup with the wine of this life, pressing all that it yields   130
Of mere fruitage, the strength and the beauty: beyond, on what
    fields,
Glean a vintage more potent and perfect to brighten the eye
And bring blood to the lip, and commend them the cup they put
    by?
He saith, "It is good;" still he drinks not: he lets me praise life,
Gives assent, yet would die for his own part.

XII

                          Then fancies grew rife
Which had come long ago on the pasture, when round me the sheep
Fed in silence—above, the one eagle wheeled slow as in sleep;
And I lay in my hollow and mused on the world that might lie
'Neath his ken, though I saw but the strip 'twixt the hill and the
    sky:
And I laughed—"Since my days are ordained to be passed with my
    flocks,   140
Let me people at least, with my fancies, the plains and the rocks,
Dream the life I am never to mix with, and image the show
Of mankind as they live in those fashions I hardly shall know!
Schemes of life, its best rules and right uses, the courage that gains,
And the prudence that keeps what men strive for." And now these
    old trains
Of vague thought came again; I grew surer; so, once more the string
Of my harp made response to my spirit, as thus—

XIII

                              "Yea, my King,"
I began—"thou dost well in rejecting mere comforts that spring
From the mere mortal life held in common by man and by brute:
In our flesh grows the branch of this life, in our soul it bears fruit.
Thou hast marked the slow rise of the tree,—how its stem trembled
    first   151
Till it passed the kid's lip, the stag's antler; then safely outburst
The fan-branches all round; and thou mindest when these too, in
    turn
Broke a-bloom and the palm-tree seemed perfect: yet more was to
    learn,
E'en the good that comes in with the palm-fruit. Our dates shall we
    slight,
When their juice brings a cure for all sorrow? or care for the plight
Of the palm's self whose slow growth produced them? Not so! stem
    and branch
Shall decay, nor be known in their place, while the palm-wine shall
    staunch
Every wound of man's spirit in winter. I pour thee such wine.

Leave the flesh to the fate it was fit for! the spirit be thine!   160
By the spirit, when age shall o'ercome thee, thou still shalt enjoy
More indeed, than at first when inconscious, the life of a boy.
Crush that life, and behold its wine running! Each deed thou hast
  done
Dies, revives, goes to work in the world; until e'en as the sun
Looking down on the earth, though clouds spoil him, though
  tempests efface,
Can find nothing his own deed produced not, must everywhere trace
The results of his past summer-prime,—so, each ray of thy will,
Every flash of thy passion and prowess, long over, shall thrill
Thy whole people, the countless, with ardor, till they too give forth
A like cheer to their sons, who in turn, fill the South and the North
With the radiance thy deed was the germ of. Carouse in the past!
But the license of age has its limit; thou diest at last: 172
As the lion when age dims his eyeball, the rose at her height,
So with man—so his power and his beauty forever take flight.
No! Again a long draught of my soul-wine! Look forth o'er the years!
Thou hast done now with eyes for the actual; begin with the seer's!
Is Saul dead? In the depth of the vale make his tomb—bid arise
A gray mountain of marble heaped four-square, till, built to the
  skies,
Let it mark where the great First King slumbers: whose fame would
  ye know?
Up above see the rock's naked face, where the record shall go   180
In great characters cut by the scribe,—Such was Saul, so he did;
With the sages directing the work, by the populace chid,—
For not half, they'll affirm, is comprised there! Which fault to amend,
In the grove with his kind grows the cedar, whereon they shall spend
(See, in tablets 'tis level before them) their praise, and record
With the gold of the graver, Saul's story,—the statesman's great
  word
Side by side with the poet's sweet comment. The river's a-wave
With smooth paper-reeds grazing each other when prophet-winds
  rave:
So the pen gives unborn generations their due and their part   189
In thy being! Then, first of the mighty, thank God that thou art!"

XIV

And behold while I sang . . . but O Thou who didst grant me that
  day,
And before it not seldom hast granted thy help to essay,
Carry on and complete an adventure,—my shield and my sword
In that act where my soul was thy servant, thy word was my word,—
Still be with me, who then at the summit of human endeavor
And scaling the highest, man's thought could, gazed hopeless as ever
On the new stretch of heaven above me—till, mighty to save,

Just one lift of thy hand cleared that distance—God's throne from
    man's grave!
Let me tell out my tale to its ending—my voice to my heart
Which can scarce dare believe in what marvels last night I took part,
As this morning I gather the fragments, alone with my sheep,   201
And still fear lest the terrible glory evanish like sleep!
For I wake in the gray dewy covert, while Hebron upheaves
The dawn struggling with night on his shoulder, and Kidron retrieves
Slow the damage of yesterday's sunshine.

XV

                            I say then,—my song
While I sang thus, assuring the monarch, and ever more strong
Made a proffer of good to console him—he slowly resumed
His old motions and habitudes kingly. The right-hand replumed
His black locks to their wonted composure, adjusted the swathes
Of his turban, and see—the huge sweat that his countenance bathes,
He wipes off with the robe; and he girds now his loins as of yore,   211
And feels slow for the armlets of price, with the clasp set before.
He is Saul, ye remember in glory,—ere error had bent
The broad brow from the daily communion; and still, though much
    spent
Be the life and the bearing that front you, the same, God did choose,
To receive what a man may waste, desecrate, never quite lose.
So sank he along by the tent-prop till, stayed by the pile
Of his armor and war-cloak and garments, he leaned there awhile,
And sat out my singing,—one arm round the tent-prop, to raise
His bent head, and the other hung slack—till I touched on the
    praise   220
I foresaw from all men in all time, to the man patient there;
And thus ended, the harp falling forward. Then first I was 'ware
That he sat, as I say, with my head just above his vast knees
Which were thrust out on each side around me, like oak-roots which
    please
To encircle a lamb when it slumbers. I looked up to know
If the best I could do had brought solace: he spoke not, but slow
Lifted up the hand slack at his side, till he laid it with care
Soft and grave, but in mild settled will, on my brow: thro' my hair
The large fingers were pushed, and he bent back my head, with kind
    power—
All my face back, intent to peruse it, as men do a flower.   230
Thus held he me there with his great eyes that scrutinized mine—
And oh, all my heart how it loved him! but where was the sign?
I yearned—"Could I help thee, my father, inventing a bliss,
I would add, to that life of the past, both the future and this;
I would give thee new life altogether, as good, ages hence,
As this moment,—had love but the warrant, love's heart to dispense!"

XVI

Then the truth came upon me. No harp more—no song more! outbroke—

XVII

"I have gone the whole round of creation: I saw and I spoke:
I, a work of God's hand for that purpose, received in my brain
And pronounced on the rest of his handwork—returned him again
His creation's approval or censure: I spoke as I saw: 241
I report, as a man may of God's work—all's love, yet all's law.
Now I lay down the judgeship he lent me. Each faculty tasked
To perceive him, has gained an abyss, where a dewdrop was asked.
Have I knowledge? confounded it shrivels at Wisdom laid bare.
Have I forethought? how purblind, how blank, to the Infinite Care!
Do I task any faculty highest, to image success?
I but open my eyes,—and perfection, no more and no less,
In the kind I imagined, full-fronts me, and God is seen God
In the star, in the stone, in the flesh, in the soul and the clod.   250
And thus looking within and around me, I ever renew
(With that stoop of the soul which in bending upraises it too)
The submission of man's nothing-perfect to God's all-complete,
As by each new obeisance in spirit, I climb to his feet.
Yet with all this abounding experience, this deity known,
I shall dare to discover some province, some gift of my own.
There's a faculty pleasant to exercise, hard to hoodwink,
I am fain to keep still in abeyance, (I laugh as I think)
Lest, insisting to claim and parade in it, wot ye, I worst
E'en the Giver in one gift.—Behold, I could love if I durst!   260
But I sink the pretension as fearing a man may o'ertake
God's own speed in the one way of love: I abstain for love's sake.
—What, my soul? see thus far and no farther? when doors great and
small,
Nine-and-ninety flew ope at our touch, should the hundredth appall?
In the least things have faith, yet distrust in the greatest of all?
Do I find love so full in my nature, God's ultimate gift,
That I doubt his own love can compete with it? Here, the parts shift?
Here, the creature surpass the Creator,—the end, what Began?
Would I fain in my impotent yearning do all for this man,
And dare doubt he alone shall not help him, who yet alone can?   270
Would it ever have entered my mind, the bare will, much less
power,
To bestow on this Saul what I sang of, the marvellous dower
Of the life he was gifted and filled with? to make such a soul,
Such a body, and then such an earth for insphering the whole?
And doth it not enter my mind (as my warm tears attest)
These good things being given, to go on, and give one more, the
best?

Ay, to save and redeem and restore him, maintain at the height
This perfection,—succeed with life's day-spring, death's minute of
    night?
Interpose at the difficult minute, snatch Saul the mistake,
Saul the failure, the ruin he seems now,—and bid him awake   280
From the dream, the probation, the prelude, to find himself set
Clear and safe in new light and new life,—a new harmony yet
To be run, and continued, and ended—who knows?—or endure!
The man taught enough, by life's dream, of the rest to make sure;
By the pain-throb, triumphantly winning intensified bliss,
And the next world's reward and repose, by the struggles in this.

XVIII

"I believe it! 'Tis thou, God, that givest, 'tis I who receive:
In the first is the last, in thy will is my power to believe.
All's one gift: thou canst grant it moreover, as prompt to my prayer
As I breathe out this breath, as I open these arms to the air.   290
From thy will, stream the worlds, life and nature, thy dread Sabaoth:
I will?—the mere atoms despise me! Why am I not loth
To look that, even that in the face too? Why is it I dare
Think but lightly of such impuissance? What stops my despair?
This;—'tis not what man Does which exalts him, but what man
    Would do!
See the King—I would help him but cannot, the wishes fall through.
Could I wrestle to raise him from sorrow, grow poor to enrich,
To fill up his life, starve my own out, I would—knowing which,
I know that my service is perfect. Oh, speak through me now!
Would I suffer for him that I love? So wouldst thou—so wilt thou!
So shall crown thee the topmost, ineffablest, uttermost crown—   301
And thy love fill infinitude wholly, nor leave up nor down
One spot for the creature to stand in! It is by no breath,
Turn of eye, wave of hand, that salvation joins issue with death!
As thy Love is discovered almighty, almighty be proved
Thy power, that exists with and for it, of being Beloved!
He who did most, shall bear most; the strongest shall stand the most
    weak.
'Tis the weakness in strength, that I cry for! my flesh, that I seek
In the Godhead! I seek and I find it. O Saul, it shall be
A Face like my face that receives thee; a Man like to me,   310
Thou shalt love and be loved by, forever: a Hand like this hand
Shall throw open the gates of new life to thee! See the Christ stand!"

XIX

I know not too well how I found my way home in the night.
There were witnesses, cohorts about me, to left and to right,
Angels, powers, the unuttered, unseen, the alive, the aware:
I repressed, I got through them as hardly, as strugglingly there,
As a runner beset by the populace famished for news—

Life or death. The whole earth was awakened, hell loosed with her
   crews;
And the stars of night beat with emotion, and tingled and shot
Out in fire the strong pain of pent knowledge: but I fainted not,   320
For the Hand still impelled me at once and supported, suppressed
All the tumult, and quenched it with quiet, and holy behest,
Till the rapture was shut in itself, and the earth sank to rest.
Anon at the dawn, all that trouble had withered from earth—
Not so much, but I saw it die out in the day's tender birth;
In the gathered intensity brought to the gray of the hills;
In the shuddering forests' held breath; in the sudden wind-thrills;
In the startled wild beasts that bore off, each with eye sidling still
Though averted with wonder and dread; in the birds stiff and chill
That rose heavily, as I approached them, made stupid with awe: 330
E'en the serpent that slid away silent,—he felt the new law.
The same stared in the white humid faces upturned by the flowers;
The same worked in the heart of the cedar and moved the vine-
   bowers:
And the little brooks witnessing murmured, persistent and low,
With their obstinate, all but hushed voices—"E'en so, it is so!"
1855

CLEON

"As certain also of your own poets have said"—

Cleon the poet (from the sprinkled isles,
Lily on lily, that o'erlace the sea,
And laugh their pride when the light wave lisps "Greece")—
To Protus in his Tyranny: much health!

      They give thy letter to me, even now:
I read and seem as if I heard thee speak.
The master of thy galley still unlades
Gift after gift; they block my court at last
And pile themselves along its portico
Royal with sunset, like a thought of thee: 10
And one white she-slave from the group dispersed
Of black and white slaves (like the chequer-work
Pavement, at once my nation's work and gift,
Now covered with this settle-down of doves),
One lyric woman, in her crocus vest
Woven of sea-wools, with her two white hands
Commends to me the strainer and the cup
Thy lip hath bettered ere it blesses mine.

Well-counselled, king, in thy munificence!
For so shall men remark, in such an act   20
Of love for him whose song gives life its joy,
Thy recognition of the use of life;
Nor call thy spirit barely adequate
To help on life in straight ways, broad enough
For vulgar souls, by ruling and the rest.
Thou, in the daily building of thy tower,—
Whether in fierce and sudden spasms of toil,
Or through dim lulls of unapparent growth,
Or when the general work 'mid good acclaim
Climbed with the eye to cheer the architect,—   30
Didst ne'er engage in work for mere work's sake—
Hadst ever in thy heart the luring hope
Of some eventual rest a-top of it,
Whence, all the tumult of the building hushed,
Thou first of men mightst look out to the East:
The vulgar saw thy tower, thou sawest the sun.
For this, I promise on thy festival
To pour libation, looking o'er the sea,
Making this slave narrate thy fortunes, speak
Thy great words, and describe thy royal face—   40
Wishing thee wholly where Zeus lives the most,
Within the eventual element of calm.

      Thy letter's first requirement meets me here.
It is as thou hast heard: in one short life
I, Cleon, have effected all those things
Thou wonderingly dost enumerate.
That epos on thy hundred plates of gold
Is mine,—and also mine the little chant,
So sure to rise from every fishing-bark
When, lights at prow, the seamen haul their net.   50
The image of the sun-god on the phare,
Men turn from the sun's self to see, is mine;
The Pœcile, o'er-storied its whole length,
As thou didst hear, with painting, is mine too.
I know the true proportions of a man
And woman also, not observed before;
And I have written three books on the soul,
Proving absurd all written hitherto,
And putting us to ignorance again.
For music,—why, I have combined the moods,   60
Inventing one. In brief, all arts are mine;
Thus much the people know and recognize,
Throughout our seventeen islands. Marvel not.

We of these latter days, with greater mind
Than our forerunners, since more composite,
Look not so great, beside their simple way,
To a judge who only sees one way at once,
One mind-point and no other at a time,—
Compares the small part of a man of us
With some whole man of the heroic age,   70
Great in his way—not ours, nor meant for ours.
And ours is greater, had we skill to know:
For, what we call this life of men on earth,
This sequence of the soul's achievements here
Being, as I find much reason to conceive,
Intended to be viewed eventually
As a great whole, not analyzed to parts,
But each part having reference to all,—
How shall a certain part, pronounced complete,
Endure effacement by another part?   80
Was the thing done?—then, what's to do again?
See, in the chequered pavement opposite,
Suppose the artist made a perfect rhomb,
And next a lozenge, then a trapezoid—
He did not overlay them, superimpose
The new upon the old and blot it out,
But laid them on a level in his work,
Making at last a picture; there it lies
So, first the perfect separate forms were made,
The portions of mankind; and after, so,   90
Occurred the combination of the same.
For where had been a progress, otherwise?
Mankind, made up of all the single men,—
In such a synthesis the labor ends.
Now mark me! those divine men of old time
Have reached, thou sayest well, each at one point
The outside verge that rounds our faculty;
And where they reached, who can do more than reach?
It takes but little water just to touch
At some one point the inside of a sphere,   100
And, as we turn the sphere, touch all the rest
In due succession: but the finer air
Which not so palpably nor obviously,
Though no less universally, can touch
The whole circumference of that emptied sphere,
Fills it more fully than the water did,
Holds thrice the weight of water in itself
Resolved into a subtler element.
And yet the vulgar call the sphere first full
Up to the visible height—and after, void;   110

Not knowing air's more hidden properties.
And thus our soul, misknown, cries out to Zeus
To vindicate his purpose in our life:
Why stay we on the earth unless to grow?
Long since, I imaged, wrote the fiction out,
That he or other god descended here
And, once for all, showed simultaneously
What, in its nature, never can be shown,
Piecemeal or in succession;—showed, I say,
The worth both absolute and relative   120
Of all his children from the birth of time,
His instruments for all appointed work.
I now go on to image,—might we hear
The judgment which should give the due to each,
Show where the labor lay and where the ease,
And prove Zeus' self, the latent everywhere!
This is a dream:—but no dream, let us hope,
That years and days, the summers and the springs,
Follow each other with unwaning powers.
The grapes which dye thy wine are richer far,   130
Through culture, than the wild wealth of the rock;
The suave plum than the savage-tasted drupe;
The pastured honey-bee drops choicer sweet;
The flowers turn double, and the leaves turn flowers;
That young and tender crescent-moon, thy slave,
Sleeping above her robe as buoyed by clouds,
Refines upon the women of my youth.
What, and the soul alone deteriorates?
I have not chanted verse like Homer, no—
Nor swept string like Terpander, no—nor carved   140
And painted men like Phidias and his friend:
I am not great as they are, point by point.
But I have entered into sympathy
With these four, running these into one soul,
Who, separate, ignored each other's art.
Say, is it nothing that I know them all?
The wild flower was the larger; I have dashed
Rose-blood upon its petals, pricked its cup's
Honey with wine, and driven its seed to fruit,
And show a better flower if not so large: 150
I stand myself. Refer this to the gods
Whose gift alone it is! which, shall I dare
(All pride apart) upon the absurd pretext
That such a gift by chance lay in my hand,
Discourse of lightly or depreciate?
It might have fallen to another's hand: what then?
I pass too surely: let at least truth stay!

And next, of what thou followest on to ask.
This being with me as I declare, O king,
My works, in all these varicolored kinds,   160
So done by me, accepted so by men—
Thou askest, if (my soul thus in men's hearts)
I must not be accounted to attain
The very crown and proper end of life?
Inquiring thence how, now life closeth up,
I face death with success in my right hand:
Whether I fear death less than dost thyself
The fortunate of men? "For" (writest thou)
"Thou leavest much behind, while I leave naught.
Thy life stays in the poems men shall sing,   170
The pictures men shall study; while my life,
Complete and whole now in its power and joy,
Dies altogether with my brain and arm,
Is lost indeed; since, what survives myself?
The brazen statue to o'erlook my grave,
Set on the promontory which I named.
And that—some supple courtier of my heir
Shall use its robed and sceptred arm, perhaps,
To fix the rope to, which best drags it down.
I go then: triumph thou, who dost not go!"   180

Nay, thou art worthy of hearing my whole mind.
Is this apparent, when thou turn'st to muse
Upon the scheme of earth and man in chief,
That admiration grows as knowledge grows?
That imperfection means perfection hid,
Reserved in part, to grace the after-time?
If, in the morning of philosophy,
Ere aught had been recorded, nay perceived,
Thou, with the light now in thee, couldst have looked
On all earth's tenantry, from worm to bird,   190
Ere man, her last, appeared upon the stage—
Thou wouldst have seen them perfect, and deduced
The perfectness of others yet unseen.
Conceding which,—had Zeus then questioned thee
"Shall I go on a step, improve on this,
Do more for visible creatures than is done?"
Thou wouldst have answered, "Ay, by making each
Grow conscious in himself—by that alone.
All's perfect else: the shell sucks fast the rock,
The fish strikes through the sea, the snake both swims   200
And slides, forth range the beasts, the birds take flight,
Till life's mechanics can no further go—
And all this joy in natural life is put

Like fire from off thy finger into each,
So exquisitely perfect is the same.
But 'tis pure fire, and they mere matter are;
It has them, not they it: and so I choose.
For man, thy last premeditated work
(If I might add a glory to the scheme)
That a third thing should stand apart from both,   210
A quality arise within his soul,
Which, intro-active, made to supervise
And feel the force it has, may view itself,
And so be happy." Man might live at first
The animal life: but is there nothing more?
In due time, let him critically learn
How he lives; and, the more he gets to know
Of his own life's adaptabilities,
The more joy-giving will his life become.
Thus man, who hath this quality, is best.   220

        But thou, king, hadst more reasonably said:
"Let progress end at once,—man make no step
Beyond the natural man, the better beast,
Using his senses, not the sense of sense."
In man there's failure, only since he left
The lower and inconscious forms of life.
We called it an advance, the rendering plain
Man's spirit might grow conscious of man's life,
And, by new lore so added to the old,
Take each step higher over the brute's head.   230
This grew the only life, the pleasure-house,
Watch-tower and treasure-fortress of the soul,
Which whole surrounding flats of natural life
Seemed only fit to yield subsistence to;
A tower that crowns a country. But alas,
The soul now climbs it just to perish there!
For thence we have discovered ('tis no dream—
We know this, which we had not else perceived)
That there's a world of capability
For joy, spread round about us, meant for us,   240
Inviting us; and still the soul craves all,
And still the flesh replies, "Take no jot more
Than ere thou clombst the tower to look abroad!
Nay, so much less as that fatigue has brought
Deduction to it." We struggle, fain to enlarge
Our bounded physical recipiency,
Increase our power, supply fresh oil to life,
Repair the waste of age and sickness: no,
It skills not! life's inadequate to joy,

As the soul sees joy, tempting life to take.   250
They praise a fountain in my garden here
Wherein a Naiad sends the water-bow
Thin from her tube; she smiles to see it rise.
What if I told her, it is just a thread
From that great river which the hills shut up,
And mock her with my leave to take the same?
The artificer has given her one small tube
Past power to widen or exchange—what boots
To know she might spout oceans if she could?
She cannot lift beyond her first thin thread: 260
And so a man can use but a man's joy
While he sees God's. Is it for Zeus to boast,
"See, man, how happy I live, and despair—
That I may be still happier—for thy use!"
If this were so, we could not thank our Lord,
As hearts beat on to doing; 'tis not so—
Malice it is not. Is it carelessness?
Still, no. If care—where is the sign? I ask,
And get no answer, and agree in sum,
O king, with thy profound discouragement,   270
Who seest the wider but to sigh the more.
Most progress is most failure: thou sayest well.

     The last point now:—thou dost except a case—
Holding joy not impossible to one
With artist-gifts—to such a man as I
Who leave behind me living works indeed;
For, such a poem, such a painting lives.
What? dost thou verily trip upon a word,
Confound the accurate view of what joy is
(Caught somewhat clearer by my eyes than thine)   280
With feeling joy? confound the knowing how
And showing how to live (my faculty)
With actually living?—Otherwise
Where is the artist's vantage o'er the king?
Because in my great epos I display
How divers men young, strong, fair, wise, can act—
Is this as though I acted? if I paint,
Carve the young Phœbus, am I therefore young?
Methinks I'm older that I bowed myself
The many years of pain that taught me art!   290
Indeed, to know is something, and to prove
How all this beauty might be enjoyed, is more:
But, knowing naught, to enjoy is something too.
Yon rower, with the moulded muscles there,
Lowering the sail, is nearer it than I.

I can write love-odes: thy fair slave's an ode.
I get to sing of love, when grown too gray
For being beloved· she turns to that young man,
The muscles all a-ripple on his back.
I know the joy of kingship: well, thou art king!   300

    "But," sayest thou—(and I marvel, I repeat,
To find thee trip on such a mere word) "what
Thou writest, paintest, stays; that does not die:
Sappho survives, because we sing her songs,
And Æschylus, because we read his plays!"
Why, if they live still, let them come and take
Thy slave in my despite, drink from thy cup,
Speak in my place. Thou diest while I survive?
Say rather that my fate is deadlier still,
In this, that every day my sense of joy   310
Grows more acute, my soul (intensified
By power and insight) more enlarged, more keen;
While every day my hairs fall more and more,
My hand shakes, and the heavy years increase—
The horror quickening still from year to year,
The consummation coming past escape
When I shall know most, and yet least enjoy—
When all my works wherein I prove my worth,
Being present still to mock me in men's mouths,
Alive still, in the praise of such as thou,   320
I, I the feeling, thinking, acting man,
The man who loved his life so over-much,
Sleep in my urn. It is so horrible,
I dare at times imagine to my need
Some future state revealed to us by Zeus,
Unlimited in capability
For joy, as this is in desire for joy,
—To seek which, the joy-hunger forces us:
That, stung by straitness of our life, made strait
On purpose to make prized the life at large—   330
Freed by the throbbing impulse we call death,
We burst there as the worm into the fly,
Who, while a worm still, wants his wings. But no!
Zeus has not yet revealed it; and alas,
He must have done so, were it possible!

    Live long and happy, and in that thought die:
Glad for what was! Farewell. And for the rest,
I cannot tell thy messenger aright
Where to deliver what he bears of thine
To one called Paulus; we have heard his fame   340
Indeed, if Christus be not one with him—

I know not, nor am troubled much to know.
Thou canst not think a mere barbarian Jew,
As Paulus proves to be, one circumcised,
Hath access to a secret shut from us?
Thou wrongest our philosophy, O king,
In stooping to inquire of such an one,
As if his answer could impose at all!
He writeth, doth he? well, and he may write.
Oh, the Jew findeth scholars! certain slaves   350
Who touched on this same isle, preached him and Christ;
And (as I gathered from a bystander)
Their doctrine could be held by no sane man.
1855

A GRAMMARIAN'S FUNERAL

SHORTLY AFTER THE REVIVAL OF LEARNING IN EUROPE

Let us begin and carry up this corpse,
    Singing together.
Leave we the common crofts, the vulgar thorpes
    Each in its tether
Sleeping safe on the bosom of the plain,
    Cared-for till cock-crow:
Look out if yonder be not day again
    Rimming the rock-row!
That's the appropriate country; there, man's thought,
    Rarer, intenser,   10
Self-gathered for an outbreak, as it ought,
    Chafes in the censer.
Leave we the unlettered plain its herd and crop;
    Seek we sepulture
On a tall mountain, cited to the top,
    Crowded with culture!
All the peaks soar, but one the rest excels;
    Clouds overcome it;
No! yonder sparkle is the citadel's
    Circling its summit.   20
Thither our path lies; wind we up the heights:
    Wait ye the warning?
Our low life was the level's and the night's;
    He's for the morning.
Step to a tune, square chests, erect each head,
    'Ware the beholders!

This is our master, famous calm and dead,
    Borne on our shoulders.
Sleep, crop and herd! sleep, darkling thorpe and croft,
    Safe from the weather! 30
He, whom we convoy to his grave aloft,
    Singing together,
He was a man born with thy face and throat,
    Lyric Apollo!
Long he lived nameless: how should spring take note
    Winter would follow?
Till lo, the little touch, and youth was gone!
    Cramped and diminished,
Moaned he, "New measures, other feet anon!
    My dance is finished?" 40
No, that's the world's way: (keep the mountain-side,
    Make for the city!)
He knew the signal, and stepped on with pride
    Over men's pity;
Left play for work, and grappled with the world
    Bent on escaping:
"What's in the scroll," quoth he, "thou keepest furled?
    Show me their shaping,
Theirs who most studied man, the bard and sage,—
    Give!"—So, he gowned him, 50
Straight got by heart that book to its last page:
    Learned, we found him.
Yea, but we found him bald too, eyes like lead,
    Accents uncertain:
"Time to taste life," another would have said,
    "Up with the curtain!"
This man said rather, "Actual life comes next?
    Patience a moment!
Grant I have mastered learning's crabbed text,
    Still there's the comment. 60
Let me know all! Prate not of most or least,
    Painful or easy!
Even to the crumbs I'd fain eat up the feast,
    Ay, nor feel queasy."
Oh, such a life as he resolved to live,
    When he had learned it,
When he had gathered all books had to give!
    Sooner, he spurned it.
Image the whole, then execute the parts—
    Fancy the fabric 70
Quite, ere you build, ere steel strike fire from quartz,
    Ere mortar dab brick!

(Here's the town-gate reached: there's the market-place
    Gaping before us.)
Yea, this in him was the peculiar grace
    (Hearten our chorus!)
That before living he'd learn how to live—
    No end to learning:
Earn the means first—God surely will contrive
    Use for our earning.   80
Others mistrust and say, "But time escapes:
    Live now or never!"
He said, "What's time? Leave Now for dogs and apes!
    Man has Forever."
Back to his book then: deeper drooped his head:
    Calculus racked him:
Leaden before, his eyes grew dross of lead:
    Tussis attacked him.
"Now, master, take a little rest!"—not he!
    (Caution redoubled,   90
Step two abreast, the way winds narrowly!)
    Not a whit troubled
Back to his studies, fresher than at first,
    Fierce as a dragon
He (soul-hydroptic with a sacred thirst)
    Sucked at the flagon.
Oh, if we draw a circle premature,
    Heedless of far gain,
Greedy for quick returns of profit, sure
    Bad is our bargain!   100
Was it not great? did not he throw on God,
    (He loves the burthen)—
God's task to make the heavenly period
    Perfect the earthen?
Did not he magnify the mind, show clear
    Just what it all meant?
He would not discount life, as fools do here,
    Paid by instalment.
He ventured neck or nothing—heaven's success
    Found, or earth's failure: 110
"Wilt thou trust death or not?" He answered "Yes:
    Hence with life's pale lure!"
That low man seeks a little thing to do,
    Sees it and does it:
This high man, with a great thing to pursue,
    Dies ere he knows it.
That low man goes on adding one to one,
    His hundred's soon hit:
This high man, aiming at a million,
    Misses an unit.   120

That, has the world here—should he need the next,
    Let the world mind him!
This, throws himself on God, and unperplexed
    Seeking shall find him.
So, with the throttling hands of death at strife,
    Ground he at grammar;
Still, thro' the rattle, parts of speech were rife:
    While he could stammer
He settled *Hoti's* business—let it be!—
    Properly based *Oun*—   **130**
Gave us the doctrine of the enclitic *De*,
    Dead from the waist down.
Well, here's the platform, here's the proper place:
    Hail to your purlieus,
All ye highfliers of the feathered race,
    Swallows and curlews!
Here's the top-peak; the multitude below
    Live, for they can, there:
This man decided not to Live but Know—
    Bury this man there?   **140**
Here—here's his place, where meteors shoot, clouds form,
    Lightnings are loosened,
Stars come and go! Let joy break with the storm,
    Peace let the dew send!
Lofty designs must close in like effects:
    Loftily lying,
Leave him—still loftier than the world suspects,
    Living and dying.
1855

ABT VOGLER

(AFTER HE HAS BEEN EXTEMPORIZING UPON THE MUSICAL INSTRUMENT OF HIS INVENTION)

I

Would that the structure brave, the manifold music I build,
    Bidding my organ obey, calling its keys to their work,
Claiming each slave of the sound, at a touch, as when Solomon willed
    Armies of angels that soar, legions of demons that lurk,
Man, brute, reptile, fly,—alien of end and of aim,
    Adverse, each from the other heaven-high, hell-deep removed,—
Should rush into sight at once as he named the ineffable Name,
    And pile him a palace straight, to pleasure the princess he loved!

II

Would it might tarry like his, the beautiful building of mine,
    This which my keys in a crowd pressed and importuned to raise!
Ah, one and all, how they helped, would dispart now and now com-
        bine,   11
    Zealous to hasten the work, heighten their master his praise!
And one would bury his brow with a blind plunge down to hell,
    Burrow awhile and build, broad on the roots of things,
Then up again swim into sight, having based me my palace well,
    Founded it, fearless of flame, flat on the nether springs.

III

And another would mount and march, like the excellent minion he
        was,
    Ay, another and yet another, one crowd but with many a crest,
Raising my rampired walls of gold as transparent as glass,
    Eager to do and die, yield each his place to the rest: 20
For higher still and higher (as a runner tips with fire,
    When a great illumination surprises a festal night—
Outlining round and round Rome's dome from space to spire)
    Up, the pinnacled glory reached, and the pride of my soul was
        in sight.

IV

In sight? Not half! for it seemed, it was certain, to match man's
        birth,
    Nature in turn conceived, obeying an impulse as I;
And the emulous heaven yearned down, made effort to reach the
        earth,
    As the earth had done her best, in my passion, to scale the sky:
Novel splendors burst forth, grew familiar and dwelt with mine,
    Not a point nor peak but found and fixed its wandering star;   30
Meteor-moons, balls of blaze: and they did not pale nor pine,
    For earth had attained to heaven, there was no more near nor
        far.

V

Nay more; for there wanted not who walked in the glare and glow,
    Presences plain in the place; or, fresh from the Protoplast,
Furnished for ages to come, when a kindlier wind should blow,
    Lured now to begin and live, in a house to their liking at last;
Or else the wonderful Dead who have passed through the body and
        gone,
    But were back once more to breathe in an old world worth their
        new:
What never had been, was now; what was, as it shall be anon;
    And what is,—shall I say, matched both? for I was made perfect
        too.   40

VI

All through my keys that gave their sounds to a wish of my soul,
    All through my soul that praised as its wish flowed visibly forth,
All through music and me! For think, had I painted the whole,
    Why, there it had stood, to see, nor the process so wonder-
      worth:
Had I written the same, made verse—still, effect proceeds from
    cause,
    Ye know why the forms are fair, ye hear how the tale is told;
It is all triumphant art, but art in obedience to laws,
    Painter and poet are proud in the artist-list enrolled:—

VII

But here is the finger of God, a flash of the will that can,
    Existent behind all laws, that made them and, lo, they are!   50
And I know not if, save in this, such gift be allowed to man,
    That out of three sounds he frame, not a fourth sound, but a
      star.
Consider it well: each tone of our scale in itself is naught;
    It is everywhere in the world—loud, soft, and all is said:
Give it to me to use! I mix it with two in my thought:
    And, there! Ye have heard and seen: consider and bow the head!

VIII

Well, it is gone at last, the palace of music I reared;
    Gone! and the good tears start, the praises that come too slow;
For one is assured at first, one scarce can say that he feared,
    That he even gave it a thought, the gone thing was to go.   60
Never to be again! But many more of the kind
    As good, nay, better perchance: is this your comfort to me?
To me, who must be saved because I cling with my mind
    To the same, same self, same love, same God: ay, what was, shall
      be.

IX

Therefore to whom turn I but to thee, the ineffable Name?
    Builder and maker, thou, of houses not made with hands!
What, have fear of change from thee who art ever the same?
    Doubt that thy power can fill the heart that thy power expands?
There shall never be one lost good! What was, shall live as before;
    The evil is null, is naught, is silence implying sound;   70
What was good shall be good, with, for evil, so much good more;
    On the earth the broken arcs; in the heaven, a perfect round.

X

All we have willed or hoped or dreamed of good shall exist;
    Not its semblance, but itself; no beauty, nor good, nor power
Whose voice has gone forth, but each survives for the melodist

When eternity affirms the conception of an hour.
The high that proved too high, the heroic for earth too hard,
    The passion that left the ground to lose itself in the sky,
Are music sent up to God by the lover and the bard;
    Enough that he heard it once: we shall hear it by-and-by.   80

XI

And what is our failure here but a triumph's evidence
    For the fulness of the days? Have we withered or agonized?
Why else was the pause prolonged but that singing might issue
    thence?
    Why rushed the discords in but that harmony should be prized?
Sorrow is hard to bear, and doubt is slow to clear,
    Each sufferer says his say, his scheme of the weal and woe:
But God has a few of us whom he whispers in the ear;
    The rest may reason and welcome: 'tis we musicians know.

XII

Well, it is earth with me; silence resumes her reign:
    I will be patient and proud, and soberly acquiesce.   90
Give me the keys. I feel for the common chord again,
    Sliding my semitones, till I sink to the minor,—yes,
And I blunt it into a ninth, and I stand on alien ground,
    Surveying awhile the heights I rolled from into the deep;
Which, hark, I have dared and done, for my resting-place is found,
    The C Major of this life: so, now I will try to sleep.
1864

RABBI BEN EZRA

I

    Grow old along with me!
    The best is yet to be,
The last of life, for which the first was made:
    Our times are in His hand
    Who saith "A whole I planned,
Youth shows but half; trust God: see all nor be afraid!"

II

    Not that, amassing flowers,
    Youth sighed "Which rose make ours,
Which lily leave and then as best recall?"
    Not that, admiring stars,   10
    It yearned "Nor Jove, nor Mars;
Mine be some figured flame which blends, transcends them all!"

III

Not for such hopes and fears
Annulling youth's brief years,
Do I remonstrate: folly wide the mark!
Rather I prize the doubt
Low kinds exist without,
Finished and finite clods, untroubled by a spark.

IV

Poor vaunt of life indeed,
Were man but formed to feed   20
On joy, to solely seek and find and feast:
Such feasting ended, then
As sure an end to men;
Irks care the crop-full bird? Frets doubt the maw-crammed beast?

V

Rejoice we are allied
To That which doth provide
And not partake, effect and not receive!
A spark disturbs our clod;
Nearer we hold of God
Who gives, than of His tribes that take, I must believe.   30

VI

Then, welcome each rebuff
That turns earth's smoothness rough,
Each sting that bids nor sit nor stand but go!
Be our joys three-parts pain!
Strive, and hold cheap the strain;
Learn, nor account the pang; dare, never grudge the throe!

VII

For thence,—a paradox
Which comforts while it mocks,—
Shall life succeed in that it seems to fail:
What I aspired to be,   40
And was not, comforts me:
A brute I might have been, but would not sink i' the scale.

VIII

What is he but a brute
Whose flesh has soul to suit,
Whose spirit works lest arms and legs want play?
To man, propose this test—
Thy body at its best,
How far can that project thy soul on its lone way?

IX

Yet gifts should prove their use:
I own the Past profuse   50
Of power each side, perfection every turn:
Eyes, ears took in their dole,
Brain treasured up the whole;
Should not the heart beat once "How good to live and learn"?

X

Not once beat "Praise be Thine!
I see the whole design,
I, who saw power, see now love perfect too:
Perfect I call Thy plan:
Thanks that I was a man!
Maker, remake, complete,—I trust what Thou shalt do!"   60

XI

For pleasant is this flesh;
Our soul, in its rose-mesh
Pulled ever to the earth, still yearns for rest;
Would we some prize might hold
To match those manifold
Possessions of the brute,—gain most, as we did best!

XII

Let us not always say
"Spite of this flesh to-day
I strove, made head, gained ground upon the whole!"
As the bird wings and sings,   70
Let us cry "All good things
Are ours, nor soul helps flesh more, now, than flesh helps soul!"

XIII

Therefore I summon age
To grant youth's heritage,
Life's struggle having so far reached its term:
Thence shall I pass, approved
A man, for aye removed
From the developed brute; a god though in the germ.

XIV

And I shall thereupon
Take rest, ere I be gone   80
Once more on my adventure brave and new:
Fearless and unperplexed,
When I wage battle next,
What weapons to select, what armor to indue.

XV

Youth ended, I shall try
My gain or loss thereby;
Leave the fire ashes, what survives is gold:
And I shall weigh the same,
Give life its praise or blame:
Young, all lay in dispute; I shall know, being old.   90

XVI

For note, when evening shuts,
A certain moment cuts
The deed off, calls the glory from the gray:
A whisper from the west
Shoots—"Add this to the rest,
Take it and try its worth: here dies another day."

XVII

So, still within this life,
Though lifted o'er its strife,
Let me discern, compare, pronounce at last,
"This rage was right i' the main,
That acquiescence vain:
The Future I may face now I have proved the Past."   100

XVIII

For more is not reserved
To man, with soul just nerved
To act to-morrow what he learns to-day:
Here, work enough to watch
The Master work, and catch
Hints of the proper craft, tricks of the tool's true play.

XIX

As it was better, youth
Should strive, through acts uncouth,   110
Toward making, than repose on aught found made:
So, better, age, exempt
From strife, should know, than tempt
Further. Thou waitedest age: wait death nor be afraid!

XX

Enough now, if the Right
And Good and Infinite
Be named here, as thou callest thy hand thine own,
With knowledge absolute,
Subject to no dispute
From fools that crowded youth, nor let thee feel alone.   120

XXI

Be there, for once and all,
Severed great minds from small,
Announced to each his station in the Past!
Was I, the world arraigned,
Were they, my soul disdained,
Right? Let age speak the truth and give us peace at last!

XXII

Now, who shall arbitrate?
Ten men love what I hate,
Shun what I follow, slight what I receive;
Ten, who in ears and eyes   130
Match me: we all surmise,
They this thing, and I that: whom shall my soul believe?

XXIII

Not on the vulgar mass
Called "work," must sentence pass,
Things done, that took the eye and had the price;
O'er which, from level stand,
The low world laid its hand,
Found straightway to its mind, could value in a trice:

XXIV

But all, the world's coarse thumb
And finger failed to plumb,   140
So passed in making up the main account;
All instincts immature,
All purposes unsure,
That weighed not as his work, yet swelled the man's amount:

XXV

Thoughts hardly to be packed
Into a narrow act,
Fancies that broke through language and escaped;
All I could never be,
All, men ignored in me,
This, I was worth to God, whose wheel the pitcher shaped.   150

XXVI

Ay, note that Potter's wheel,
That metaphor! and feel
Why time spins fast, why passive lies our clay,—
Thou, to whom fools propound,
When the wine makes its round,
"Since life fleets, all is change; the Past gone, seize to-day!"

XXVII

Fool! All that is, at all,
Lasts ever, past recall;
Earth changes, but thy soul and God stand sure:
What entered into thee, 160
That was, is, and shall be:
Time's wheel runs back or stops: Potter and clay endure.

XXVIII

He fixed thee 'mid this dance
Of plastic circumstance,
This Present, thou, forsooth, wouldst fain arrest:
Machinery just meant
To give thy soul its bent,
Try thee and turn thee forth, sufficiently impressed.

XXIX

What though the earlier grooves
Which ran the laughing loves 170
Around thy base, no longer pause and press?
What though, about thy rim,
Skull-things in order grim
Grow out, in graver mood, obey the sterner stress?

XXX

Look not thou down but up!
To uses of a cup,
The festal board, lamp's flash and trumpet's peal,
The new wine's foaming flow,
The Master's lips a-glow!
Thou, heaven's consummate cup, what need'st thou with earth's
wheel? 180

XXXI

But I need, now as then,
Thee, God, who mouldest men;
And since, not even while the whirl was worst,
Did I,—to the wheel of life
With shapes and colors rife,
Bound dizzily,—mistake my end, to slake Thy thirst:

XXXII

So, take and use Thy work:
Amend what flaws may lurk,
What strain o' the stuff, what warpings past the aim!
My times be in Thy hand! 190
Perfect the cup as planned!
Let age approve of youth, and death complete the same!
1864

from THE RING AND THE BOOK

V

COUNT GUIDO FRANCESCHINI

Thanks, Sir, but, should it please the reverend Court,
I feel I can stand somehow, half sit down
Without help, make shift to even speak, you see,
Fortified by the sip of . . . why, 't is wine,
Velletri,—and not vinegar and gall,
So changed and good the times grow! Thanks, kind Sir!
Oh, but one sip 's enough! I want my head
To save my neck, there 's work awaits me still.
How cautious and considerate . . . aie, aie, aie,
Nor your fault, sweet Sir! Come, you take to heart   10
An ordinary matter. Law is law.
Noblemen were exempt, the vulgar thought,
From racking; but, since law thinks otherwise,
I have been put to the rack: all 's over now,
And neither wrist—what men style, out of joint:
If any harm be, 't is the shoulder-blade,
The left one, that seems wrong i' the socket,—Sirs,
Much could not happen, I was quick to faint,
Being past my prime of life, and out of health.
In short I thank you,—yes, and mean the word.   20
Needs must the Court be slow to understand
How this quite novel form of taking pain,
This getting tortured merely in the flesh,
Amounts to almost an agreeable change
In my case, me fastidious, plied too much
With opposite treatment, used (forgive the joke)
To the rasp-tooth toying with this brain of mine,
And, in and out my heart, the play o' the probe.
Four years have I been operated on
I' the soul, do you see—its tense or tremulous part—   30
My self-respect, my care for a good name,
Pride in an old one, love of kindred—just
A mother, brothers, sisters, and the like,
That looked up to my face when days were dim,
And fancied they found light there—no one spot,

Foppishly sensitive, but has paid its pang.
That, and not this you now oblige me with,
That was the Vigil-torment, if you please!
The poor old noble House that drew the rags
O' the Franceschini's once superb array   **40**
Close round her, hoped to slink unchallenged by,—
Pluck off these! Turn the drapery inside out
And teach the tittering town how scarlet wears!
Show men the lucklessness, the improvidence
Of the easy-natured Count before this Count,
The father I have some slight feeling for,
Who let the world slide, nor foresaw that friends
Then proud to cap and kiss their patron's shoe,
Would, when the purse he left held spider-webs,
Properly push his child to wall one day!   **50**
Mimic the tetchy humor, furtive glance,
And brow where half was furious, half fatigued,
O' the same son got to be of middle age,
Sour, saturnine,—your humble servant here,—
When things go cross and the young wife, he finds
Take to the window at a whistle's bid,
And yet demurs thereon, preposterous fool!—
Whereat the worthies judge he wants advice
And beg to civilly ask what 's evil here,
Perhaps remonstrate on the habit they deem   **60**
He 's given unduly to, of beating her:
. . . Oh, sure he beats her—why says John so else,
Who is cousin to George who is sib to Tecla's self
Who cooks the meal and combs the lady's hair?
What! 'T is my wrist you merely dislocate
For the future when you mean me martyrdom?
—Let the old mother's economy alone,
How the brocade-strips saved o' the seamy side
O' the wedding-gown buy raiment for a year?
—How she can dress and dish up—lordly dish   **70**
Fit for a duke, lamb's head and purtenance—
With her proud hands, feast household so a week?
No word o' the wine rejoicing God and man,
The less when three-parts water? Then, I say,
A trifle of torture to the flesh, like yours,
While soul is spared such foretaste of hell-fire,
Is naught. But I curtail the catalogue
Through policy,—a rhetorician's trick,—
Because I would reserve some choicer points
O' the practice, more exactly parallel   **80**
(Having an eye to climax) with what gift,
Eventual grace the Court may have in store

I' the way of plague—what crown of punishments.
When I am hanged or headed, time enough
To prove the tenderness of only that,
Mere heading, hanging,—not their counterpart,
Not demonstration public and precise
That I, having married the mongrel of a drab,
Am bound to grant that mongrel-brat, my wife,
Her mother's birthright-license as is just,—   90
Let her sleep undisturbed, i' the family style,
Her sleep out in the embraces of a priest,
Nor disallow their bastard as my heir!
Your sole mistake,—dare I submit so much
To the reverend Court?—has been in all this pains
To make a stone roll down hill,—rack and wrench
And rend a man to pieces, all for what?
Why—make him ope mouth in his own defence,
Show cause for what he has done, the irregular deed,
(Since that he did it, scarce dispute can be)   100
And clear his fame a little, beside the luck
Of stopping even yet, if possible,
Discomfort to his flesh from noose or axe—
For that, out come the implements of law!
May it content my lords the gracious Court
To listen only half so patient-long
As I will in that sense profusely speak,
And—fie, they shall not call in screws to help!
I killed Pompilia Franceschini, Sirs;
Killed too the Comparini, husband, wife,   110
Who called themselves, by a notorious lie,
Her father and her mother to ruin me.
There 's the irregular deed: you want no more
Than right interpretation of the same,
And truth so far—am I to understand?
To that then, with convenient speed,—because
Now I consider,—yes, despite my boast,
There is an ailing in this omoplat
May clip my speech all too abruptly short,
Whatever the good-will in me. Now for truth!   120

I' the name of the indivisible Trinity!
Will my lords, in the plenitude of their light,
Weigh well that all this trouble has come on me
Through my persistent treading in the paths
Where I was trained to go,—wearing that yoke
My shoulder was predestined to receive,
Born to the hereditary stoop and crease?
Noble, I recognized my nobler still,

The Church, my suzerain; no mock-mistress, she;
The secular owned the spiritual: mates of mine   130
Have thrown their careless hoofs up at her call
"Forsake the clover and come drag my wain!"
There they go cropping: I protruded nose
To halter, bent my back of docile beast,
And now am whealed, one wide wound all of me,
For being found at the eleventh hour o' the day
Padding the mill-track, not neck-deep in grass:
—My one fault, I am stiffened by my work,
—My one reward, I help the Court to smile!

I am representative of a great line,   140
One of the first of the old families
In Arezzo, ancientest of Tuscan towns.
When my worst foe is fain to challenge this,
His worst exception runs—not first in rank
But second, noble in the next degree
Only; not malice' self maligns me more.
So, my lord opposite has composed, we know,
A marvel of a book, sustains the point
That Francis boasts the primacy 'mid saints;
Yet not inaptly hath his argument   150
Obtained response from yon my other lord
In thesis published with the world's applause
—Rather 't is Dominic such post befits:
Why, at the worst, Francis stays Francis still,
Second in rank to Dominic it may be,
Still, very saintly, very like our Lord;
And I at least descend from Guido once
Homager to the Empire, nought below—
Of which account as proof that, none o' the line
Having a single gift beyond brave blood,   160
Or able to do aught but give, give, give
In blood and brain, in house and land and cash,
Not get and garner as the vulgar may,
We became poor as Francis or our Lord.
Be that as it likes you, Sirs,—whenever it chanced
Myself grew capable anyway of remark,
(Which was soon—penury makes wit premature)
This struck me, I was poor who should be rich
Or pay that fault to the world which trifles not
When lineage lacks the flag yet lifts the pole: 170
On, therefore, I must move forthwith, transfer
My stranded self, born fish with gill and fin
Fit for the deep sea, now left flap bare-backed
In slush and sand, a show to crawlers vile

Reared of the low-tide and aright therein.
The enviable youth with the old name,
Wide chest, stout arms, sound brow and pricking veins,
A heartful of desire, man's natural load,
A brainful of belief, the noble's lot,—
All this life, cramped and gasping, high and dry   180
I' the wave's retreat,—the misery, good my lords,
Which made you merriment at Rome of late,—
It made me reason, rather—muse, demand
—Why our bare dropping palace, in the street
Where such-an-one whose grandfather sold tripe
Was adding to his purchased pile a fourth
Tall tower, could hardly show a turret sound?
Why Countess Beatrice, whose son I am,
Cowered in the winter-time as she spun flax,
Blew on the earthen basket of live ash,   190
Instead of jaunting forth in coach and six
Like such-another widow who ne'er was wed?
I asked my fellows, how came this about?
"Why, Jack, the sutler's child, perhaps the camp's,
Went to the wars, fought sturdily, took a town
And got rewarded as was natural.
She of the coach and six—excuse me there!
Why, don't you know the story of her friend?
A clown dressed vines on somebody's estate,
His boy recoiled from muck, liked Latin more,   200
Stuck to his pen and got to be a priest,
Till one day . . . don't you mind that telling tract
Against Molinos, the old Cardinal wrote?
He penned and dropped it in the patron's desk,
Who, deep in thought and absent much of mind,
Licensed the thing, allowed it for his own;
Quick came promotion,—*suum cuique*, Count!
Oh, he can pay for coach and six, be sure!"
"—Well, let me go, do likewise: war 's the word—
That way the Franceschini worked at first,   210
I'll take my turn, try soldiership."—"What, you?
The eldest son and heir and prop o' the house,
So do you see your duty? Here 's your post,
Hard by the hearth and altar. (Roam from roof,
This youngster, play the gypsy out of doors,
And who keeps kith and kin that fall on us?)
Stand fast, stick tight, conserve your gods at home!"
"—Well then, the quiet course, the contrary trade!
We had a cousin amongst us once was Pope,
And minor glories manifold. Try the Church,   220
The tonsure, and,—since heresy 's but half-slain

Even by the Cardinal's tract he thought he wrote,—
Have at Molinos!"—"Have at a fool's head!
You a priest? How were marriage possible?
There must be Franceschini till time ends—
That 's your vocation. Make your brothers priests,
Paul shall be porporate, and Girolamo step
Red-stockinged in the presence when you choose,
But save one Franceschini for the age!
Be not the vine but dig and dung its root,   230
Be not a priest but gird up priesthood's loins,
With one foot in Arezzo stride to Rome,
Spend yourself there and bring the purchase back!
Go hence to Rome, be guided!"

           So I was.
I turned alike from the hillside zigzag thread
Of way to the table-land a soldier takes,
Alike from the low-lying pasture-place
Where churchmen graze, recline and ruminate,
—Ventured to mount no platform like my lords
Who judge the world, bear brain I dare not brag—   240
But stationed me, might thus the expression serve,
As who should fetch and carry, come and go,
Meddle and make i' the cause my lords love most—
The public weal, which hangs to the law, which holds
By the Church, which happens to be through God himself.
Humbly I helped the Church till here I stand,—
Or would stand but for the omoplat, you see!
Bidden qualify for Rome, I, having a field,
Went, sold it, laid the sum at Peter's foot:
Which means—I settled home-accounts with speed,   250
Set apart just a modicum should suffice
To hold the villa's head above the waves
Of weed inundating its oil and wine,
And prop roof, stanchion wall o' the palace so
As to keep breath i' the body, out of heart
Amid the advance of neighboring loftiness—
(People like building where they used to beg)—
Till succored one day,—shared the residue
Between my mother and brothers and sisters there,
Black-eyed babe Donna This and Donna That,   260
As near to starving as might decently be,
—Left myself journey-charges, change of suit,
A purse to put i' the pocket of the Groom
O' the Chamber of the patron, and a glove
With a ring to it for the digits of the niece
Sure to be helpful in his household,—then

Started for Rome, and led the life prescribed.
Close to the Church, though clean of it, I assumed
Three or four orders of no consequence,
—They cast out evil spirits and exorcise,   270
For example; bind a man to nothing more,
Give clerical savor to his layman's-salt,
Facilitate his claim to loaf and fish
Should miracle leave, beyond what feeds the flock,
Fragments to brim the basket of a friend—
While, for the world's sake, I rode, danced and gamed,
Quitted me like a courtier, measured mine
With whatsoever blade had fame in fence,
—Ready to let the basket go its round
Even though my turn was come to help myself,   280
Should Dives count on me at dinner-time
As just the understander of a joke
And not immoderate in repartee.
Utrique sic paratus, Sirs, I said,
"Here," (in the fortitude of years fifteen,
So good a pedagogue is penury)
"Here wait, do service,—serving and to serve!
And, in due time, I nowise doubt at all,
The recognition of my service comes.
Next year I 'm only sixteen. I can wait."   290

I waited thirty years, may it please the Court:
Saw meanwhile many a denizen o' the dung
Hop, skip, jump o'er my shoulder, make him wings
And fly aloft,—succeed, in the usual phrase.
Every one soon or late comes round by Rome:
Stand still here, you 'll see all in turn succeed.
Why, look you, so and so, the physician here,
My father's lacquey's son we sent to school,
Doctored and dosed this Eminence and that,
Salved the last Pope his certain obstinate sore,   300
Soon bought land as became him, names it now:
I grasp bell at his griffin-guarded gate,
Traverse the half-mile avenue,—a term,
A cypress, and a statue, three and three,—
Deliver message from my Monsignor,
With varletry at lounge i' the vestibule
I 'm barred from, who bear mud upon my shoe.
My father's chaplain's nephew, Chamberlain,—
Nothing less, please you!—courteous all the same,
—He does not see me though I wait an hour   310
At his staircase-landing 'twixt the brace of busts,
A noseless Sylla, Marius maimed to match,

My father gave him for a hexastich
Made on my birthday,—but he sends me down,
To make amends, that relic I prize most—
The unburnt end o' the very candle, Sirs,
Purfled with paint so prettily round and round,
He carried in such state last Peter's-day,—
In token I, his gentleman and squire,
Had held the bridle, walked his managed mule   320
Without a tittup the procession through.
Nay, the official,—one you know, sweet lords!—
Who drew the warrant for my transfer late
To the New Prisons from Tordinona,—he
Graciously had remembrance—"Francesc . . . ha?
His sire, now—how a thing shall come about!—
Paid me a dozen florins above the fee,
For drawing deftly up a deed of sale
When troubles fell so thick on him, good heart,
And I was prompt and pushing! By all means!   330
At the New Prisons be it his son shall lie,—
Anything for an old friend!" and thereat
Signed name with triple flourish underneath.
These were my fellows, such their fortunes now,
While I—kept fasts and feasts innumerable,
Matins and vespers, functions to no end
I' the train of Monsignor and Eminence,
As gentleman-squire, and for my zeal's reward
Have rarely missed a place at the table-foot
Except when some Ambassador, or such like,   340
Brought his own people. Brief, one day I felt
The tick of time inside me, turning-point
And slight sense there was now enough of this:
That I was near my seventh climacteric,
Hard upon, if not over, the middle life,
And, although fed by the east-wind, fulsome-fine
With foretaste of the Land of Promise, still
My gorge gave symptom it might play me false;
Better not press it further,—be content
With living and dying only a nobleman,   350
Who merely had a father great and rich,
Who simply had one greater and richer yet,
And so on back and back till first and best
Began i' the night; I finish in the day.
"The mother must be getting old," I said;
"The sisters are well wedded away, our name
Can manage to pass a sister off, at need,
And do for dowry: both my brothers thrive—
Regular priests they are, nor, bat-like, 'bide

'Twixt flesh and fowl with neither privilege.   360
My spare revenue must keep me and mine.
I am tired: Arezzo's air is good to breathe;
Vittiano,—one limes flocks of thrushes there;
A leathern coat costs little and lasts long:
Let me bid hope good-bye, content at home!"
Thus, one day, I disbosomed me and bowed.
Whereat began the little buzz and thrill
O' the gazers round me; each face brightened up:
As when at your Casino, deep in dawn,
A gamester says at last, "I play no more,   370
Forego gain, acquiesce in loss, withdraw
Anyhow:" and the watchers of his ways,
A trifle struck compunctious at the word,
Yet sensible of relief, breathe free once more,
Break up the ring, venture polite advice—
"How, Sir? So scant of heart and hope indeed?
Retire with neither cross nor pile from play?—
So incurious, so short-casting?—give your chance
To a younger, stronger, bolder spirit belike,
Just when luck turns and the fine throw sweeps all?"   380
Such was the chorus: and its goodwill meant—
"See that the loser leave door handsomely!
There 's an ill look,—it 's sinister, spoils sport,
When an old bruised and battered year-by-year
Fighter with fortune, not a penny in poke,
Reels down the steps of our establishment
And staggers on broad daylight and the world,
In shagrag beard and doleful doublet, drops
And breaks his heart on the outside: people prate
'Such is the profit of a trip upstairs!'   390
Contrive he sidle forth, balked of the blow
Best dealt by way of moral, bidding down
No curse but blessings rather on our heads
For some poor prize he bears at tattered breast,
Some palpable sort of kind of good to set
Over and against the grievance: give him quick!"
Whereon protested Paul, "Go hang yourselves!
Leave him to me. Count Guido and brother of mine,
A word in your ear! Take courage, since faint heart
Ne'er won . . . aha, fair lady, don't men say?   400
There 's a sors, there 's a right Virgilian dip!
Do you see the happiness o' the hint? At worst,
If the Church want no more of you, the Court
No more, and the Camp as little, the ingrates,—come,
Count you are counted: still you 've coat to back,
Not cloth of gold and tissue, as we hoped,

But cloth with sparks and spangles on its frieze
From Camp, Court, Church, enough to make a shine,
Entitle you to carry home a wife
With the proper dowry, let the worst betide!   410
Why, it was just a wife you meant to take!"

Now, Paul's advice was weighty: priests should know:
And Paul apprised me, ere the week was out,
That Pietro and Violante, the easy pair,
The cits enough, with stomach to be more,
Had just the daughter and exact the sum
To truck for the quality of myself: "She's young,
Pretty and rich: you're noble, classic, choice.
Is it to be a match?"—"A match," said I.
Done! He proposed all, I accepted all,   420
And we performed all. So I said and did
Simply. As simply followed, not at first,
But with the outbreak of misfortune, still
One comment on the saying and doing—"What?
No blush at the avowal you dared buy
A girl of age beseems your granddaughter,
Like ox or ass? Are flesh and blood a ware?
Are heart and soul a chattel?"
                  Softly, Sirs!
Will the Court of its charity teach poor me
Anxious to learn, of any way i' the world,   430
Allowed by custom and convenience, save
This same which, taught from my youth up, I trod?
Take me along with you; where was the wrong step?
If what I gave in barter, style and state
And all that hangs to Franceschinihood,
Were worthless,—why, society goes to ground,
Its rules are idiot's-rambling. Honor of birth,—
If that thing has no value, cannot buy
Something with value of another sort,
You've no reward nor punishment to give   440
I' the giving or the taking honor; straight
Your social fabric, pinnacle to base,
Comes down a-clatter like a house of cards.
Get honor, and keep honor free from flaw,
Aim at still higher honor,—gabble o' the goose!
Go bid a second blockhead like myself
Spend fifty years in guarding bubbles of breath,
Soapsuds with air i' the belly, gilded brave,
Guarded and guided, all to break at touch
O' the first young girl's hand and first old fool's purse!   450
All my privation and endurance, all

Love, loyalty and labor dared and did,
Fiddle-de-dee!—why, doer and darer both,—
Count Guido Franceschini had hit the mark
Far better, spent his life with more effect,
As a dancer or a prizer, trades that pay!
On the other hand, bid this buffoonery cease,
Admit that honor is a privilege,
The question follows, privilege worth what?
Why, worth the market-price,—now up, now down,   460
Just so with this as with all other ware:
Therefore essay the market, sell your name,
Style and condition to who buys them best!
"Does my name purchase," had I dared inquire,
"Your niece, my lord?" there would have been rebuff
Though courtesy, your Lordship cannot else—
"Not altogether! Rank for rank may stand:
But I have wealth beside, you—poverty;
Your scale flies up there: bid a second bid,
Rank too and wealth too!" Reasoned like yourself!   470
But was it to you I went with goods to sell?
This time 't was my scale quietly kissed the ground,
Mere rank against mere wealth—some youth beside,
Some beauty too, thrown into the bargain, just
As the buyer likes or lets alone. I thought
To deal o' the square: others find fault, it seems:
The thing is, those my offer most concerned,
Pietro, Violante, cried they fair or foul?
What did they make o' the terms? Preposterous terms?
Why then accede so promptly, close with such   480
Nor take a minute to chaffer? Bargain struck,
They straight grew bilious, wished their money back,
Repented them, no doubt: why, so did I,
So did your Lordship, if town-talk be true,
Of paying a full farm's worth for that piece
By Pietro of Cortona—probably
His scholar Ciro Ferri may have retouched—
You caring more for color than design—
Getting a little tired of cupids too.
That 's incident to all the folk who buy!   490
I am charged, I know, with gilding fact by fraud;
I falsified and fabricated, wrote
Myself down roughly richer than I prove,
Rendered a wrong revenue,—grant it all!
Mere grace, mere coquetry such fraud, I say:
A flourish round the figures of a sum
For fashion's sake, that deceives nobody.
The veritable back-bone, understood

Essence of this same bargain, blank and bare,
Being the exchange of quality for wealth,—   500
What may such fancy-flights be? Flecks of oil
Flirted by chapmen where plain dealing grates.
I may have dripped a drop—"My name I sell;
Not but that I too boast my wealth"—as they,
"—We bring you riches; still our ancestor
Was hardly the rapscallion, folk saw flogged,
But heir to we know who, were rights of force!"
They knew and I knew where the back-bone lurked
I' the writhings of the bargain, lords, believe!
I paid down all engaged for, to a doit,   510
Delivered them just that which, their life long,
They hungered in the hearts of them to gain—
Incorporation with nobility thus
In word and deed: for that they gave me wealth.
But when they came to try their gain, my gift,
Quit Rome and qualify for Arezzo, take
The tone o' the new sphere that absorbed the old,
Put away gossip Jack and goody Joan
And go become familiar with the Great,
Greatness to touch and taste and handle now,—   520
Why, then,—they found that all was vanity,
Vexation, and what Solomon describes!
The old abundant city-fare was best,
The kindly warmth o' the commons, the glad clap
Of the equal on the shoulder, the frank grin
Of the underling at all so many spoons
Fire-new at neighborly treat,—best, best and best
Beyond compare!—down to the loll itself
O' the pot-house settle,—better such a bench
Than the stiff crucifixion by my dais   530
Under the piecemeal damask canopy
With the coroneted coat-of-arms a-top!
Poverty and privation for pride's sake,
All they engaged to easily brave and bear,—
With the fit upon them and their brains a-work,—
Proved unendurable to the sobered sots.
A banished prince, now, will exude a juice
And salamander-like support the flame:
He dines on chestnuts, chucks the husks to help
The broil o' the brazier, pays the due baioc,   540
Goes off light-hearted: his grimace begins
At the funny humors of the christening-feast
Of friend the money-lender,—then he 's touched
By the flame and frizzles at the babe to kiss!
Here was the converse trial, opposite mind:

Here did a petty nature split on rock
Of vulgar wants predestinate for such—
One dish at supper and weak wine to boot!
The prince had grinned and borne: the citizen shrieked,
Summoned the neighborhood to attest the wrong,   550
Made noisy protest he was murdered,—stoned
And burned and drowned and hanged,—then broke away,
He and his wife, to tell their Rome the rest.
And this you admire, you men o' the world, my lords?
This moves compassion, makes you doubt my faith?
Why, I appeal to . . . sun and moon? Not I!
Rather to Plautus, Terence, Boccaccio's Book,
My townsman, frank Ser Franco's merry Tales,—
To all who strip a vizard from a face,
A body from its padding, and a soul   560
From froth and ignorance it styles itself,—
If this be other than the daily hap
Of purblind greed that dog-like still drops bone,
Grasps shadow, and then howls the case is hard!

So much for them so far: now for myself,
My profit or loss i' the matter: married am I:
Text whereon friendly censors burst to preach.
Ay, at Rome even, long ere I was left
To regulate her life for my young bride
Alone at Arezzo, friendliness outbroke   570
(Sifting my future to predict its fault)
"Purchase and sale being thus so plain a point,
How of a certain soul bound up, maybe,
I' the barter with the body and money-bags?
From the bride's soul what is it you expect?"
Why, loyalty and obedience,—wish and will
To settle and suit her fresh and plastic mind
To the novel, not disadvantageous mould!
Father and mother shall the woman leave,
Cleave to the husband, be it for weal or woe: 580
There is the law: what sets this law aside
In my particular case? My friends submit
"Guide, guardian, benefactor,—fee, faw, fum,
The fact is you are forty-five years old,
Nor very comely even for that age:
Girls must have boys." Why, let girls say so then,
Nor call the boys and men, who say the same,
Brute this and beast the other as they do!
Come, cards on table! When you chant us next
Epithalamium full to overflow   590
With praise and glory of white womanhood,
The chaste and pure—troll no such lies o'er lip!

Put in their stead a crudity or two,
Such short and simple statement of the case
As youth chalks on our walls at spring of year!
No! I shall still think nobler of the sex,
Believe a woman still may take a man
For the short period that his soul wears flesh,
And, for the soul's sake, understand the fault
Of armor frayed by fighting. Tush, it tempts   600
One's tongue too much! I 'll say—the law 's the law:
With a wife I look to find all wifeliness,
As when I buy, timber and twig, a tree—
I buy the song o' the nightingale inside.

Such was the pact: Pompilia from the first
Broke it, refused from the beginning day
Either in body or soul to cleave to mine,
And published it forthwith to all the world.
No rupture,—you must join ere you can break,—
Before we had cohabited a month   610
She found I was a devil and no man,—
Made common cause with those who found as much,
Her parents, Pietro and Violante,—moved
Heaven and earth to the rescue of all three.
In four months' time, the time o' the parents' stay,
Arezzo was a-ringing, bells in a blaze,
With the unimaginable story rife
I' the mouth of man, woman and child—to wit
My misdemeanor. First the lighter side,
Ludicrous face of things,—how very poor   620
The Franceschini had become at last,
The meanness and the misery of each shift
To save a soldo, stretch and make ends meet.
Next, the more hateful aspect,—how myself
With cruelty beyond Caligula's
Had stripped and beaten, robbed and murdered them,
The good old couple, I decoyed, abused,
Plundered and then cast out, and happily so,
Since,—in due course the abominable comes,—
Woe worth the poor young wife left lonely here!   630
Repugnant in my person as my mind,
I sought,—was ever heard of such revenge?
—To lure and bind her to so cursed a couch,
Such co-embrace with sulphur, snake and toad,
That she was fain to rush forth, call the stones
O' the common street to save her, not from hate
Of mine merely, but . . . must I burn my lips
With the blister of the lie? . . . the satyr-love
Of who but my own brother, the young priest,

Too long enforced to lenten fare belike,   640
Now tempted by the morsel tossed him full
I' the trencher where lay bread and herbs at best.
Mark, this yourselves say!—this, none disallows,
Was charged to me by the universal voice
At the instigation of my four-months' wife!—
And then you ask, "Such charges so preferred,
(Truly or falsely, here concerns us not)
Pricked you to punish now if not before?—
Did not the harshness double itself, the hate
Harden?" I answer, "Have it your way and will!"   650
Say my resentment grew apace: what then?
Do you cry out on the marvel? When I find
That pure smooth egg which, laid within my nest,
Could not but hatch a comfort to us all,
Issues a cockatrice for me and mine,
Do you stare to see me stamp on it? Swans are soft:
Is it not clear that she you call my wife,
That any wife of any husband, caught
Whetting a sting like this against his breast,—
Speckled with fragments of the fresh-broke shell,   660
Married a month and making outcry thus,—
Proves a plague-prodigy to God and man?
She married: what was it she married for,
Counted upon and meant to meet thereby?
"Love," suggests some one, "love, a little word
Whereof we have not heard one syllable."
So, the Pompilia, child, girl, wife, in one,
Wanted the beating pulse, the rolling eye,
The frantic gesture, the devotion due
From Thyrsis to Neæra! Guido's love—   670
Why not Provençal roses in his shoe,
Plume to his cap, and trio of guitars
At casement, with a bravo close beside?
Good things all these are, clearly claimable
When the fit price is paid the proper way.
Had it been some friend's wife, now, threw her fan
At my foot, with just this pretty scrap attached,
"Shame, death, damnation—fall these as they may,
So I find you, for a minute! Come this eve!"
—Why, at such sweet self-sacrifice,—who knows?   680
I might have fired up, found me at my post,
Ardent from head to heel, nor feared catch cough.
Nay, had some other friend's . . . say, daughter, tripped
Upstairs and tumbled flat and frank on me,
Bareheaded and barefooted, with loose hair
And garments all at large,—cried "Take me thus!

Duke So-and-So, the greatest man in Rome—
To escape his hand and heart have I broke bounds,
Traversed the town and reached you!"—Then, indeed,
The lady had not reached a man of ice!   690
I would have rummaged, ransacked at the word
Those old odd corners of an empty heart
For remnants of dim love the long disused,
And dusty crumblings of romance! But here,
We talk of just a marriage, if you please—
The every-day conditions and no more;
Where do these bind me to bestow one drop
Of blood shall dye my wife's true-love-knot pink?
Pompilia was no pigeon, Venus' pet,
That shuffled from between her pressing paps   700
To sit on my rough shoulder,—but a hawk,
I bought at a hawk's price and carried home
To do hawk's service—at the Rotunda, say,
Where, six o' the callow nestlings in a row,
You pick and choose and pay the price for such.
I have paid my pound, await my penny's worth,
So, hoodwink, starve and properly train my bird,
And, should she prove a haggard,—twist her neck!
Did I not pay my name and style, my hope
And trust, my all? Through spending these amiss   710
I am here! 'T is scarce the gravity of the Court
Will blame me that I never piped a tune,
Treated my falcon-gentle like my finch.
The obligation I incurred was just
To practise mastery, prove my mastership:—
Pompilia's duty was—submit herself,
Afford me pleasure, perhaps cure my bile.
Am I to teach my lords what marriage means,
What God ordains thereby and man fulfils
Who, docile to the dictate, treads the house?   720
My lords have chosen the happier part with Paul
And neither marry nor burn,—yet priestliness
Can find a parallel to the marriage-bond
In its own blessed special ordinance
Whereof indeed was marriage made the type:
The Church may show her insubordinate,
As marriage her refractory. How of the Monk
Who finds the claustral regimen too sharp
After the first month's essay? What 's the mode
With the Deacon who supports indifferently   730
The rod o' the Bishop when he tastes its smart
Full four weeks? Do you straightway slacken hold
Of the innocents, the all-unwary ones

Who, eager to profess, mistook their mind?—
Remit a fast-day's rigor to the Monk
Who fancied Francis' manna meant roast quails,—
Concede the Deacon sweet society,
He never thought the Levite-rule renounced,—
Or rather prescribe short chain and sharp scourge
Corrective of such peccant humors? This—   740
I take to be the Church's mode, and mine.
If I was over-harsh,—the worse i' the wife
Who did not win from harshness as she ought,
Wanted the patience and persuasion, lore
Of love, should cure me and console herself.
Put case that I mishandle, flurry and fright
My hawk through clumsiness in sportsmanship,
Twitch out five pens where plucking one would serve—
What, shall she bite and claw to mend the case?
And, if you find I pluck five more for that,   750
Shall you weep "How he roughs the turtle there"?

Such was the starting; now of the further step.
In lieu of taking penance in good part,
The Monk, with hue and cry, summons a mob
To make a bonfire of the convent, say,—
And the Deacon's pretty piece of virtue (save
The ears o' the Court! I try to save my head)
Instructed by the ingenuous postulant,
Taxes the Bishop with adultery, (mud
Needs must pair off with mud, and filth with filth)—   760
Such being my next experience. Who knows not—
The couple, father and mother of my wife,
Returned to Rome, published before my lords,
Put into print, made circulate far and wide
That they had cheated me who cheated them?
Pompilia, I supposed their daughter, drew
Breath first 'mid Rome's worst rankness, through the deed
Of a drab and a rogue, was by-blow bastard-babe
Of a nameless strumpet, passed off, palmed on me
As the daughter with the dowry. Daughter? Dirt   770
O' the kennel! Dowry? Dust o' the street! Nought more
Nought less, nought else but—oh—ah—assuredly
A Franceschini and my very wife!
Now take this charge as you will, for false or true,—
This charge, preferred before your very selves
Who judge me now,—I pray you, adjudge again,
Classing it with the cheats or with the lies,
By which category I suffer most!
But of their reckoning, theirs who dealt with me

In either fashion,—I reserve my word,   780
Justify that in its place; I am now to say,
Whichever point o' the charge might poison most,
Pompilia's duty was no doubtful one.
You put the protestation in her mouth,
"Henceforward and forevermore, avaunt
Ye fiends, who drop disguise and glare revealed
In your own shape, no longer father mine
Nor mother mine! Too nakedly you hate
Me whom you looked as if you loved once,—me
Whom, whether true or false, your tale now damns,   790
Divulged thus to my public infamy,
Private perdition, absolute overthrow.
For, hate my husband to your hearts' content,
I, spoil and prey of you from first to last,
I who have done you the blind service, lured
The lion to your pitfall,—I, thus left
To answer for my ignorant bleating there,
I should have been remembered and withdrawn
From the first o' the natural fury, not flung loose
A proverb and a byword men will mouth   800
At the cross-way, in the corner, up and down
Rome and Arezzo,—there, full in my face,
If my lord, missing them and finding me,
Content himself with casting his reproach
To drop i' the street where such impostors die.
Ah, but—that husband, what the wonder were!—
If, far from casting thus away the rag
Smeared with the plague, his hand had chanced upon,
Sewn to his pillow by Locusta's wile,—
Far from abolishing, root, stem and branch,   810
The misgrowth of infectious mistletoe
Foisted into his stock for honest graft,—
If he repudiate not, renounce nowise,
But, guarding, guiding me, maintain my cause
By making it his own, (what other way?)
—To keep my name for me, he call it his,
Claim it of who would take it by their lie,—
To save my wealth for me—or babe of mine
Their lie was framed to beggar at the birth—
He bid them loose grasp, give our gold again: 820
If he become no partner with the pair
Even in a game which, played adroitly, gives
Its winner life's great wonderful new chance,—
Of marrying, to wit, a second time,—
Ah, if he did thus, what a friend were he!
Anger he might show,—who can stamp out flame

Yet spread no black o' the brand?—yet, rough albeit
In the act, as whose bare feet feel embers scorch,
What grace were his, what gratitude were mine!"
Such protestation should have been my wife's.   830
Looking for this, do I exact too much?
Why, here 's the—word for word so much, no more—
Avowal she made, her pure spontaneous speech
To my brother the Abate at first blush,
Ere the good impulse had begun to fade:
So did she make confession for the pair,
So pour forth praises in her own behalf.
"Ay, the false letter," interpose my lords—
"The simulated writing,—'t was a trick:
You traced the signs, she merely marked the same,   840
The product was not hers but yours.'' Alack,
I want no more impulsion to tell truth
From the other trick, the torture inside there!
I confess all—let it be understood—
And deny nothing! If I baffle you so,
Can so fence, in the plenitude of right,
That my poor lathen dagger puts aside
Each pass o' the Bilboa, beats you all the same,—
What matters inefficiency of blade?
Mine and not hers the letter,—conceded, lords!   850
Impute to me that practice!—take as proved
I taught my wife her duty, made her see
What it behoved her see and say and do,
Feel in her heart and with her tongue declare,
And, whether sluggish or recalcitrant,
Forced her to take the right step, I myself
Was marching in marital rectitude!
Why, who finds fault here, say the tale be true?
Would not my lords commend the priest whose zeal
Seized on the sick, morose or moribund,   860
By the palsy-smitten finger, made it cross
His brow correctly at the critical time?
—Or answered for the inarticulate babe
At baptism, in its stead declared the faith,
And saved what else would perish unprofessed?
True, the incapable hand may rally yet,
Renounce the sign with renovated strength,—
The babe may grow up man and Molinist,—
And so Pompilia, set in the good path
And left to go alone there, soon might see   870
That too frank-forward, all too simple-strait
Her step was, and decline to tread the rough,
When here lay, tempting foot, the meadow-side,

And there the coppice rang with singing-birds!
Soon she discovered she was young and fair,
That many in Arezzo knew as much,—
Yes, this next cup of bitterness, my lords,
Had to begin go filling, drop by drop,
Its measure up of full disgust for me,
Filtered into by every noisome drain—   880
Society's sink toward which all moisture runs.
Would not you prophesy—"She on whose brow is stamped
The note of the imputation that we know,—
Rightly or wrongly mothered with a whore,—
Such an one, to disprove the frightful charge,
What will she but exaggerate chastity,
Err in excess of wifehood, as it were,
Renounce even levities permitted youth,
Though not youth struck to age by a thunderbolt?
Cry 'wolf' i' the sheepfold, where 's the sheep dares bleat,   890
Knowing the shepherd listens for a growl?"
So you expect. How did the devil decree?
Why, my lords, just the contrary of course!
It was in the house from the window, at the church
From the hassock,—where the theatre lent its lodge,
Or staging for the public show left space,—
That still Pompilia needs must find herself
Launching her looks forth, letting looks reply
As arrows to a challenge; on all sides
Ever new contribution to her lap,   900
Till one day, what is it knocks at my clenched teeth
But the cup full, curse-collected all for me?
And I must needs drink, drink this gallant's praise,
That minion's prayer, the other fop's reproach,
And come at the dregs to—Caponsacchi! Sirs,
I,—chin deep in a marsh of misery,
Struggling to extricate my name and fame
And fortune from the marsh would drown them all,
My face the sole unstrangled part of me,—
I must have this new gad-fly in that face,   910
Must free me from the attacking lover too!
Men say I battled ungracefully enough—
Was harsh, uncouth and ludicrous beyond
The proper part o' the husband: have it so!
Your lordships are considerate at least—
You order me to speak in my defence
Plainly, expect no quavering tuneful trills
As when you bid a singer solace you,—
Nor look that I shall give it, for a grace,
Stans pede in uno:—you remember well   920

In the one case, 't is a plainsong too severe,
This story of my wrongs,—and that I ache
And need a chair, in the other. Ask you me
Why, when I felt this trouble flap my face,
Already pricked with every shame could perch,—
When, with her parents, my wife plagued me too,—
Why I enforced not exhortation mild
To leave whore's-tricks and let my brows alone,
With mulct of comfits, promise of perfume?

"Far from that! No, you took the opposite course,   930
Breathed threatenings, rage and slaughter!" What you will!
And the end has come, the doom is verily here,
Unhindered by the threatening. See fate's flare
Full on each face of the dead guilty three!
Look at them well, and now, lords, look at this!
Tell me: if on that day when I found first
That Caponsacchi thought the nearest way
To his church was some half-mile round by my door,
And that he so admired, shall I suppose,
The manner of the swallows' come-and-go   940
Between the props o' the window overhead,—
That window happening to be my wife's,—
As to stand gazing by the hour on high,
Of May-eves, while she sat and let him smile,—
If I,—instead of threatening, talking big,
Showing hair-powder, a prodigious pinch,
For poison in a bottle,—making believe
At desperate doings with a bauble-sword,
And other bugaboo-and-baby-work,—
Had, with the vulgarest household implement,   950
Calmly and quietly cut off, clean through bone,
But one joint of one finger of my wife,
Saying, "For listening to the serenade,
Here 's your ring-finger shorter a full third:
Be certain I will slice away next joint,
Next time that anybody underneath
Seems somehow to be sauntering as he hoped
A flower would eddy out of your hand to his,
While you please fidget with the branch above
O' the rose-tree in the terrace!"—had I done so,   960
Why, there had followed a quick sharp scream, some pain,
Much calling for plaister, damage to the dress,
A somewhat sulky countenance next day,
Perhaps reproaches,—but reflections too!
I don't hear much of harm that Malchus did
After the incident of the ear, my lords!

Saint Peter took the efficacious way;
Malchus was sore but silenced for his life:
He did not hang himself i' the Potter's Field
Like Judas, who was trusted with the bag   970
And treated to sops after he proved a thief.
So, by this time, my true and obedient wife
Might have been telling beads with a gloved hand;
Awkward a little at pricking hearts and darts
On sampler possibly, but well otherwise:
Not where Rome shudders now to see her lie.
I give that for the course a wise man takes;
I took the other however, tried the fool's,
The lighter remedy, brandished rapier dread
With cork-ball at the tip, boxed Malchus' ear   980
Instead of severing the cartilage,
Called her a terrible nickname, and the like,
And there an end: and what was the end of that?
What was the good effect o' the gentle course?
Why, one night I went drowsily to bed,
Dropped asleep suddenly, not suddenly woke,
But did wake with rough rousing and loud cry,
To find noon in my face, a crowd in my room,
Fumes in my brain, fire in my throat, my wife
Gone God knows whither,—rifled vesture-chest,   990
And ransacked money-coffer. "What does it mean?"
The servants had been drugged too, stared and yawned
"It must be that our lady has eloped!"
—"Whither and with whom?"—"With whom but the Canon's self?
One recognizes Caponsacchi there!"—
(By this time the admiring neighborhood
Joined chorus round me while I rubbed my eyes)
" 'T is months since their intelligence began,—
A comedy the town was privy to,—
He wrote and she wrote, she spoke, he replied,   1000
And going in and out your house last night
Was easy work for one . . . to be plain with you . . .
Accustomed to do both, at dusk and dawn
When you were absent,—at the villa, you know,
Where husbandry required the master-mind.
Did not you know? Why, we all knew, you see!"
And presently, bit by bit, the full and true
Particulars of the tale were volunteered
With all the breathless zeal of friendship—"Thus
Matters were managed: at the seventh hour of night" . . .   1010
—"Later, at daybreak" . . . "Caponsacchi came" . . .
—"While you and all your household slept like death,
Drugged as your supper was with drowsy stuff" . . .

—"And your own cousin Guillichini too—
Either or both entered your dwelling-place,
Plundered it at their pleasure, made prize of all,
Including your wife" . . . —"Oh, your wife led the way,
Out of doors, on to the gate" . . . —"But gates are shut,
In a decent town, to darkness and such deeds:
They climbed the wall—your lady must be lithe—   1020
At the gap, the broken bit" . . . —"Torrione, true!
To escape the questioning guard at the proper gate,
Clemente, where at the inn, hard by, 'the Horse,'
Just outside, a calash in readiness
Took the two principals, all alone at last,
To gate San Spirito, which o'erlooks the road,
Leads to Perugia, Rome and liberty."
Bit by bit thus made-up mosaic-wise,
Flat lay my fortune,—tessellated floor,
Imperishable tracery devils should foot   1030
And frolic it on, around my broken gods,
Over my desecrated hearth.
          So much
For the terrible effect of threatening, Sirs!

Well, this way I was shaken wide awake,
Doctored and drenched, somewhat unpoisoned so.
Then, set on horseback and bid seek the lost,
I started alone, head of me, heart of me
Fire, and each limb as languid . . . ah, sweet lords,
Bethink you!—poison-torture, try persuade
The next refractory Molinist with that! . . .   1040
Floundered through day and night, another day
And yet another night, and so at last,
As Lucifer kept falling to find hell,
Tumbled into the court-yard of an inn
At the end, and fell on whom I thought to find,
Even Caponsacchi,—what part once was priest,
Cast to the winds now with the cassock-rags:
In cape and sword a cavalier confessed,
There stood he chiding dilatory grooms,
Chafing that only horseflesh and no team   1050
Of eagles would supply the last relay,
Whirl him along the league, the one post more
Between the couple and Rome and liberty.
'T was dawn, the couple were rested in a sort,
And though the lady, tired,—the tenderer sex,—
Still lingered in her chamber,—to adjust
The limp hair, look for any blush astray,—
She would descend in a twinkling,—"Have you out

The horses therefore!"
               So did I find my wife.
Is the case complete? Do your eyes here see with mine?   1060
Even the parties dared deny no one
Point out of all these points.
                 What follows next?
"Why, that then was the time," you interpose,
"Or then or never, while the fact was fresh,
To take the natural vengeance: there and thus
They and you,—somebody had stuck a sword
Beside you while he pushed you on your horse,—
'T was requisite to slay the couple, Count!"
Just so my friends say—"Kill!" they cry in a breath,
Who presently, when matters grow to a head   1070
And I do kill the offending ones indeed,—
When crime of theirs, only surmised before,
Is patent, proved indisputably now,—
When remedy for wrong, untried at the time,
Which law professes shall not fail a friend,
Is thrice tried now, found threefold worse than null,—
When what might turn to transient shade, who knows?
Solidifies into a blot which breaks
Hell's black off in pale flakes for fear of mine,—
Then, when I claim and take revenge—"So rash?"   1080
They cry—"so little reverence for the law?"

Listen, my masters, and distinguish here!
At first, I called in law to act and help:
Seeing I did so, "Why, 't is clear," they cry,
"You shrank from gallant readiness and risk,
Were coward: the thing 's inexplicable else."
Sweet my lords, let the thing be! I fall flat,
Play the reed, not the oak, to breath of man.
Only, inform my ignorance! Say I stand
Convicted of the having been afraid,   1090
Proved a poltroon, no lion but a lamb,—
Does that deprive me of my right of lamb
And give my fleece and flesh to the first wolf?
Are eunuchs, women, children, shieldless quite
Against attack their own timidity tempts?
Cowardice were misfortune and no crime!
—Take it that way, since I am fallen so low
I scarce dare brush the fly that blows my face,
And thank the man who simply spits not there,—
Unless the Court be generous, comprehend   1100
How one brought up at the very feet of law
As I, awaits the grave Gamaliel's nod

Ere he clench fist at outrage,—much less, stab!
—How, ready enough to rise at the right time,
I still could recognize no time mature
Unsanctioned by a move o' the judgment-seat,
So, mute in misery, eyed my masters here
Motionless till the authoritative word
Pronounced amercement. There 's the riddle solved:
This is just why I slew nor her nor him,   1110
But called in law, law's delegate in the place,
And bade arrest the guilty couple, Sirs!
We had some trouble to do so—you have heard
They braved me,—he with arrogance and scorn,
She, with a volubility of curse,
A conversancy in the skill of tooth
And claw to make suspicion seem absurd,
Nay, an alacrity to put to proof
At my own throat my own sword, teach me so
To try conclusions better the next time,—   1120
Which did the proper service with the mob.
They never tried to put on mask at all:
Two avowed lovers forcibly torn apart,
Upbraid the tyrant as in a playhouse scene,
Ay, and with proper clapping and applause
From the audience that enjoys the bold and free.
I kept still, said to myself, "There 's law!" Anon
We searched the chamber where they passed the night,
Found what confirmed the worst was feared before,
However needless confirmation now—   1130
The witches' circle intact, charms undisturbed
That raised the spirit and succubus,—letters, to wit,
Love-laden, each the bag o' the bee that bore
Honey from lily and rose to Cupid's hive,—
Now, poetry in some rank blossom-burst,
Now, prose,—"Come here, go there, wait such a while,
He 's at the villa, now he 's back again:
We are saved, we are lost, we are lovers all the same!"
All in order, all complete,—even to a clue
To the drowsiness that happed so opportune—   1140
No mystery, when I read, "Of all things, find
What wine Sir Jealousy decides to drink—
Red wine? Because a sleeping-potion, dust
Dropped into white, discolors wine and shows."

—"Oh, but we did not write a single word!
Somebody forged the letters in our name!—"
Both in a breath protested presently.
Aha, Sacchetti again!—"Dame,"—quoth the Duke,

"What meaneth this epistle, counsel me,
I pick from out thy placket and peruse, 1150
Wherein my page averreth thou art white
And warm and wonderful 'twixt pap and pap?"
"Sir," laughed the Lady, " 't is a counterfeit!
Thy page did never stroke but Dian's breast,
The pretty hound I nurture for thy sake:
To lie were losel,—by my fay, no more!"
And no more say I too, and spare the Court.

Ah, the Court! yes, I come to the Court's self;
Such the case, so complete in fact and proof,
I laid at the feet of law,—there sat my lords, 1160
Here sit they now, so may they ever sit
In easier attitude than suits my haunch!
In this same chamber did I bare my sores
O' the soul and not the body,—shun no shame,
Shrink from no probing of the ulcerous part,
Since confident in Nature,—which is God,—
That she who, for wise ends, concocts a plague,
Curbs, at the right time, the plague's virulence too
Law renovates even Lazarus,—cures me!
Cæsar thou seekest? To Cæsar thou shalt go! 1170
Cæsar 's at Rome: to Rome accordingly!

The case was soon decided: both weights, cast
I' the balance, vibrate, neither kicks the beam,
Here away, there away, this now and now that.
To every one o' my grievances law gave
Redress, could purblind eye but see the point.
The wife stood a convicted runagate
From house and husband,—driven to such a course
By what she somehow took for cruelty,
Oppression and imperilment of life— 1180
Not that such things were, but that so they seemed:
Therefore, the end conceded lawful, (since
To save life there 's no risk should stay our leap)
It follows that all means to the lawful end
Are lawful likewise,—poison, theft and flight.
As for the priest's part, did he meddle or make,
Enough that he too thought life jeopardized;
Concede him then the color charity
Casts on a doubtful course,—if blackish white
Or whitish black, will charity hesitate? 1190
What did he else but act the precept out,
Leave, like a provident shepherd, his safe flock
To follow the single lamb and strayaway?
Best hope so and think so,—that the ticklish time

I' the carriage, the tempting privacy, the last
Somewhat ambiguous accident at the inn,
—All may bear explanation: may? then, must!
The letters,—do they so incriminate?
But what if the whole prove a prank o' the pen,
Flight of the fancy, none of theirs at all,   1200
Bred of the vapors of my brain belike,
Or at worst mere exercise of scholar's-wit
In the courtly Caponsacchi: verse, convict?
Did not Catullus write less seemly once?
Yet *doctus* and unblemished he abides.
Wherefore so ready to infer the worst?
Still, I did righteously in bringing doubts
For the law to solve,—take the solution now!
"Seeing that the said associates, wife and priest,
Bear themselves not without some touch of blame   1210
—Else why the pother, scandal and outcry
Which trouble our peace and require chastisement?
We for complicity in Pompilia's flight
And deviation, and carnal intercourse
With the same, do set aside and relegate
The Canon Caponsacchi for three years
At Civita in the neighborhood of Rome:
And we consign Pompilia to the care
Of a certain Sisterhood of penitents
I' the city's self, expert to deal with such.   1220
Word for word, there 's your judgment! Read it, lords,
Re-utter your deliberate penalty
For the crime yourselves establish! Your award—
Who chop a man's right-hand off at the wrist
For tracing with forefinger words in wine
O' the table of a drinking-booth that bear
Interpretation as they mocked the Church!
—Who brand a woman black between the breasts
For sinning by connection with a Jew:
While for the Jew's self—pudency be dumb!—   1230
You mete out punishment such and such, yet so
Punish the adultery of wife and priest!
Take note of that, before the Molinists do,
And read me right the riddle, since right must be!
While I stood rapt away with wonderment,
Voices broke in upon my mood and muse.
"Do you sleep?" began the friends at either ear,
"The case is settled,—you willed it should be so—
None of our counsel, always recollect!
With law's award, budge! Back into your place!   1240
Your betters shall arrange the rest for you.

We 'll enter a new action, claim divorce:
Your marriage was a cheat themselves allow:
You erred i' the person,—might have married thus
Your sister or your daughter unaware.
We 'll gain you, that way, liberty at least,
Sure of so much by law's own showing. Up
And off with you and your unluckiness—
Leave us to bury the blunder, sweep things smooth!"
I was in humble frame of mind, be sure!   1250
I bowed, betook me to my place again.
Station by station I retraced the road,
Touched at this hostel, passed this post-house by,
Where, fresh-remembered yet, the fugitives
Had risen to the heroic stature: still—
"That was the bench they sat on,—there 's the board
They took the meal at,—yonder garden-ground
They leaned across the gate of,"—ever a word
O' the Helen and the Paris, with "Ha! you 're he.
The . . . much-commiserated husband?" Step   1260
By step, across the pelting, did I reach
Arezzo, underwent the archway's grin,
Traversed the length of sarcasm in the street,
Found myself in my horrible house once more,
And after a colloquy . . . no word assists!
With the mother and the brothers, stiffened me
Straight out from head to foot as dead man does,
And, thus prepared for life as he for hell,
Marched to the public Square and met the world.
Apologize for the pincers, palliate screws?   1270
Ply me with such toy-trifles, I entreat!
Trust who has tried both sulphur and sops-in-wine!

I played the man as I best might, bade friends
Put non-essentials by and face the fact.
"What need to hang myself as you advise?
The paramour is banished,—the ocean's width,
Or the suburb's length,—to Ultima Thule, say,
Or Proxima Civitas, what 's the odds of name
And place? He 's banished, and the fact 's the thing.
Why should law banish innocence an inch?   1280
Here 's guilt then, what else do I care to know?
The adulteress lies imprisoned,—whether in a well
With bricks above and a snake for company,
Or tied by a garter to a bedpost,—much
I mind what 's little,—least 's enough and to spare!
The little fillip on the coward's cheek
Serves as though crab-tree cudgel broke his pate.

Law has pronounced there 's punishment, less or more:
And I take note o' the fact and use it thus—
For the first flaw in the original bond,   1290
I claim release. My contract was to wed
The daughter of Pietro and Violante. Both
Protest they never had a child at all.
Then I have never made a contract: good!
Cancel me quick the thing pretended one.
I shall be free. What matter if hurried over
The harbor-boom by a great favoring tide,
Or the last of a spent ripple that lifts and leaves?
The Abate is about it. Laugh who wins!
You shall not laugh me out of faith in law!   1300
I listen, through all your noise, to Rome!"

                                          Rome spoke
In three months letters thence admonished me,
"Your plan for the divorce is all mistake.
It would hold, now, had you, taking thought to wed
Rachel of the blue eye and golden hair,
Found swarth-skinned Leah cumber couch next day:
But Rachel, blue-eyed golden-haired aright,
Proving to be only Laban's child, not Lot's,
Remains yours all the same forevermore.
No whit to the purpose is your plea: you err   1310
I' the person and the quality—nowise
In the individual,—that 's the case in point!
You go to the ground,—are met by a cross-suit
For separation, of the Rachel here,
From bed and board,—she is the injured one,
You did the wrong and have to answer it.
As for the circumstance of imprisonment
And color it lends to this your new attack,
Never fear, that point is considered too!
The durance is already at an end;   1320
The convent-quiet preyed upon her health,
She is transferred now to her parents' house
—No-parents, when that cheats and plunders you,
But parentage again confessed in full,
When such confession pricks and plagues you more—
As now—for, this their house is not the house
In Via Vittoria wherein neighbors' watch
Might incommode the freedom of your wife,
But a certain villa smothered up in vines
At the town's edge by the gate i' the Pauline way,   1330
Out of eye-reach, out of ear-shot, little and lone,
Whither a friend,—at Civita, we hope,
A good half-dozen-hours' ride off,—might, some eve,

Betake himself, and whence ride back, some morn,
Nobody the wiser: but be that as it may,
Do not afflict your brains with trifles now.
You have still three suits to manage, all and each
Ruinous truly should the event play false.
It is indeed the likelier so to do,
That brother Paul, your single prop and stay,   1340
After a vain attempt to bring the Pope
To set aside procedures, sit himself
And summarily use prerogative,
Afford us the infallible finger's tact
To disentwine your tangle of affairs,
Paul,—finding it moreover past his strength
To stem the irruption, bear Rome's ridicule
Of . . . since friends must speak . . . to be round with you . . .
Of the old outwitted husband, wronged and wroth,
Pitted against a brace of juveniles—   1350
A brisk priest who is versed in Ovid's art
More than his "Summa," and a gamesome wife
Able to act Corinna without book,
Beside the waggish parents who played dupes
To dupe the duper—(and truly divers scenes
Of the Arezzo palace, tickle rib
And tease eye till the tears come, so we laugh;
Nor wants the shock at the inn its comic force,
And then the letters and poetry—*merum sal!*)
—Paul, finally, in such a state of things,   1360
After a brief temptation to go jump
And join the fishes in the Tiber, drowns
Sorrow another and a wiser way:
House and goods, he has sold all off, is gone,
Leaves Rome,—whether for France or Spain, who knows?
Or Britain almost divided from our orb.
You have lost him anyhow."
                          Now,—I see my lords
Shift in their seat,—would I could do the same!
They probably please expect my bile was moved
To purpose, nor much blame me: now, they judge,   1370
The fiery titillation urged my flesh
Break through the bonds. By your pardon, no, sweet Sirs!
I got such missives in the public place;
When I sought home,—with such news, mounted stair
And sat at last in the sombre gallery,
('T was Autumn, the old mother in bed betimes,
Having to bear that cold, the finer frame
Of her daughter-in-law had found intolerable—
The brother, walking misery away

O' the mountain-side with dog and gun belike,)   1380
As I supped, ate the coarse bread, drank the wine
Weak once, now acrid with the toad's-head-squeeze,
My wife's bestowment,—I broke silence thus:
"Let me, a man, manfully meet the fact,
Confront the worst o' the truth, end, and have peace!
I am irremediably beaten here,—
The gross illiterate vulgar couple,—bah!
Why, they have measured forces, mastered mine,
Made me their spoil and prey from first to last.
They have got my name,—'t is nailed now fast to theirs,   1390
The child or changeling is anyway my wife;
Point by point as they plan they execute,
They gain all, and I lose all—even to the lure
That led to loss,—they have the wealth again
They hazarded awhile to hook me with,
Have caught the fish and find the bait entire:
They even have their child or changeling back
To trade with, turn to account a second time.
The brother, presumably might tell a tale
Or give a warning,—he, too, flies the field,   1400
And with him vanish help and hope of help.
They have caught me in the cavern where I fell,
Covered my loudest cry for human aid
With this enormous paving-stone of shame.
Well, are we demigods or merely clay?
Is success still attendant on desert?
Is this, we live on, heaven and the final state,
Or earth which means probation to the end?
Why claim escape from man's predestined lot
Of being beaten and baffled?—God's decree,   1410
In which I, bowing bruised head, acquiesce.
One of us Franceschini fell long since
I' the Holy Land, betrayed, tradition runs,
To Paynims by the feigning of a girl
He rushed to free from ravisher, and found
Lay safe enough with friends in ambuscade
Who flayed him while she clapped her hands and laughed:
Let me end, falling by a like device.
It will not be so hard. I am the last
O' my line which will not suffer any more.   1420
I have attained to my full fifty years,
(About the average of us all, 't is said,
Though it seems longer to the unlucky man)
—Lived through my share of life; let all end here,
Me and the house and grief and shame at once.
Friends my informants,—I can bear your blow!"

And I believe 't was in no unmeet match
For the stoic's mood, with something like a smile,
That, when morose December roused me next,
I took into my hand, broke seal to read   1430
The new epistle from Rome. "All to no use!
Whate'er the turn next injury take," smiled I,
"Here 's one has chosen his part and knows his cue.
I am done with, dead now; strike away, good friends!
Are the three suits decided in a trice?
Against me,—there 's no question! How does it go?
Is the parentage of my wife demonstrated
Infamous to her wish? Parades she now
Loosed of the cincture that so irked the loin?
Is the last penny extracted from my purse   1440
To mulct me for demanding the first pound
Was promised in return for value paid?
Has the priest, with nobody to court beside,
Courted the Muse in exile, hitched my hap
Into a rattling ballad-rhyme which, bawled
At tavern-doors, wakes rapture everywhere,
And helps cheap wine down throat this Christmas time,
Beating the bagpipes? Any or all of these!
As well, good friends, you cursed my palace here
To its old cold stone face,—stuck your cap for crest   1450
Over the shield that 's extant in the Square,—
Or spat on the statue's cheek, the impatient world
Sees cumber tomb-top in our family church:
Let him creep under covert as I shall do,
Half below-ground already indeed. Good-bye!
My brothers are priests, and childless so; that 's well—
And, thank God most for this, no child leave I—
None after me to bear till his heart break
The being a Franceschini and my son!"

"Nay," said the letter, "but you have just that!   1460
A babe, your veritable son and heir—
Lawful,—'t is only eight months since your wife
Left you,—so, son and heir, your babe was born
Last Wednesday in the villa,—you see the cause
For quitting Convent without beat of drum,
Stealing a hurried march to this retreat
That 's not so savage as the Sisterhood
To slips and stumbles: Pietro's heart is soft,
Violante leans to pity's side,—the pair
Ushered you into life a bouncing boy: 1470
And he 's already hidden away and safe
From any claim on him you mean to make—

They need him for themselves,—don't fear, they know
The use o' the bantling,—the nerve thus laid bare
To nip at, new and nice, with finger-nail!"

Then I rose up like fire, and fire-like roared.
What, all is only beginning not ending now?
The worm which wormed its way from skin through flesh
To the bone and there lay biting, did its best,—
What, it goes on to scrape at the bone's self,   1480
Will wind to inmost marrow and madden me?
There 's to be yet my representative,
Another of the name shall keep displayed
The flag with the ordure on it, brandish still
The broken sword has served to stir a jakes?
Who will he be, how will you call the man?
A Franceschini,—when who cut my purse,
Filched my name, hemmed me round, hustled me hard
As rogues at a fair some fool they strip i' the midst,
When these count gains, vaunt pillage presently:—   1490
But a Caponsacchi, oh, be very sure!
When what demands its tribute of applause
Is the cunning and impudence o' the pair of cheats,
The lies and lust o' the mother, and the brave
Bold carriage of the priest, worthily crowned
By a witness to his feat i' the following age,—
And how this threefold cord could hook and fetch
And land leviathan that king of pride!
Or say, by some mad miracle of chance,
Is he indeed my flesh and blood, this babe?   1500
Was it because fate forged a link at last
Betwixt my wife and me, and both alike
Found we had henceforth some one thing to love,
Was it when she could damn my soul indeed
She unlatched door, let all the devils o' the dark
Dance in on me to cover her escape?
Why then, the surplusage of disgrace, the spilth
Over and above the measure of infamy,
Failing to take effect on my coarse flesh
Seasoned with scorn now, saturate with shame,—   1510
Is saved to instil on and corrode the brow,
The baby-softness of my first-born child—
The child I had died to see though in a dream,
The child I was bid strike out for, beat the wave
And baffle the tide of troubles where I swam,
So I might touch shore, lay down life at last
At the feet so dim and distant and divine
Of the apparition, as 't were Mary's babe

Had held, through night and storm, the torch aloft,—
Born now in very deed to bear this brand   1520
On forehead and curse me who could not save!
Rather be the town-talk true, Square's jest, street's jeer
True, my own inmost heart's confession true,
And he the priest's bastard and none of mine!
Ay, there was cause for flight, swift flight and sure!
The husband gets unruly, breaks all bounds
When he encounters some familiar face,
Fashion of feature, brow and eyes and lips
Where he least looked to find them,—time to fly!
This bastard then, a nest for him is made,   1530
As the manner is of vermin, in my flesh—
Shall I let the filthy pest buzz, flap and sting,
Busy at my vitals and, nor hand nor foot
Lift, but let be, lie still and rot resigned?
No, I appeal to God,—what says Himself,
How lessons Nature when I look to learn?
Why, that I am alive, and still a man
With brain and heart and tongue and right-hand too—
Nay, even with friends, in such a cause as this,
To right me if I fail to take my right.   1540
No more of law; a voice beyond the law
Enters my heart, *Quis est pro Domino?*

Myself, in my own Vittiano, told the tale
To my own serving-people summoned there:
Told the first half of it, scarce heard to end
By judges who got done with judgment quick
And clamored to go execute her 'hest—
Who cried, "Not one of us that dig your soil
And dress your vineyard, prune your olive-trees,
But would have brained the man debauched our wife,   1550
And staked the wife whose lust allured the man,
And paunched the Duke, had it been possible,
Who ruled the land, yet barred us such revenge!"
I fixed on the first whose eyes caught mine, some four
Resolute youngsters with the heart still fresh,
Filled my purse with the residue o' the coin
Uncaught-up by my wife whom haste made blind,
Donned the first rough and rural garb I found,
Took whatsoever weapon came to hand,
And out we flung and on we ran or reeled   1560
Romeward. I have no memory of our way,
Only that, when at intervals the cloud
Of horror about me opened to let in life,
I listened to some song in the ear, some snatch

Of a legend, relic of religion, stray
Fragment of record very strong and old
Of the first conscience, the anterior right,
The God's-gift to mankind, impulse to quench
The antagonistic spark of hell and tread
Satan and all his malice into dust,   1570
Declare to the world the one law, right is right.
Then the cloud re-encompassed me, and so
I found myself, as on the wings of winds,
Arrived: I was at Rome on Christmas Eve.
Festive bells—everywhere the Feast o' the Babe,
Joy upon earth, peace and good will to man!
I am baptized. I started and let drop
The dagger. "Where is it, His promised peace?"
Nine days o' the Birth-Feast did I pause and pray
To enter into no temptation more.   1580
I bore the hateful house, my brother's once,
Deserted,—let the ghost of social joy
Mock and make mouths at me from empty room
And idle door that missed the master's step,—
Bore the frank wonder of incredulous eyes,
As my own people watched without a word,
Waited, from where they huddled round the hearth
Black like all else, that nod so slow to come.
I stopped my ears even to the inner call
Of the dread duty, only heard the song   1590
"Peaee upon earth," saw nothing but the face
O' the Holy Infant and the halo there
Able to cover yet another face
Behind it, Satan's, which I else should see.
But, day by day, joy waned and withered off:
The Babe's face, premature with peak and pine,
Sank into wrinkled ruinous old age,
Suffering and death, then mist-like disappeared,
And showed only the Cross at end of all,
Left nothing more to interpose 'twixt me   1600
And the dread duty,—for the angels' song,
"Peace upon earth," louder and louder pealed,
"O Lord, how long, how long be unavenged?"
On the ninth day, this grew too much for man.
I started up—"Some end must be!" At once,
Silence: then, scratching like a death-watch-tick,
Slowly within my brain was syllabled,
"One more concession, one decisive way
And but one, to determine thee the truth,—
This way, in fine, I whisper in thy ear: 1610
Now doubt, anon decide, thereupon act!"

"That is a way, thou whisperest in my ear!
I doubt, I will decide, then act," said I—
Then beckoned my companions: "Time is come!"

And so, all yet uncertain save the will
To do right, and the daring aught save leave
Right undone, I did find myself at last
I' the dark before the villa with my friends,
And made the experiment, the final test,
Ultimate chance that ever was to be   1620
For the wretchedness inside. I knocked—pronounced
The name, the predetermined touch for truth,
"What welcome for the wanderer? Open straight—"
To the friend, physician, friar upon his rounds,
Traveller belated, beggar lame and blind?
No, but—"to Caponsacchi!" And the door
Opened.
      And then,—why, even then, I think,
I' the minute that confirmed my worst of fears,
Surely,—I pray God that I think aright!—
Had but Pompilia's self, the tender thing   1630
Who once was good and pure, was once my lamb
And lay in my bosom, had the well-known shape
Fronted me in the doorway,—stood there faint
With the recent pang, perhaps, of giving birth
To what might, though by miracle, seem my child,—
Nay more, I will say, had even the aged fool
Pietro, the dotard, in whom folly and age
Wrought, more than enmity or malevolence,
To practise and conspire against my peace,—
Had either of these but opened, I had paused.   1640
But it was she the hag, she that brought hell
For a dowry with her to her husband's house,
She the mock-mother, she that made the match
And married me to perdition, spring and source
O' the fire inside me that boiled up from heart
To brain and hailed the Fury gave it birth,—
Violante Comparini, she it was,
With the old grin amid the wrinkles yet,
Opened: as if in turning from the Cross,
With trust to keep the sight and save my soul,   1650
I had stumbled, first thing, on the serpent's head
Coiled with a leer at foot of it.
             There was the end!
Then was I rapt away by the impulse, one
Immeasurable everlasting wave of a need
To abolish that detested life. 'T was done:

You know the rest and how the folds o' the thing,
Twisting for help, involved the other two
More or less serpent-like: how I was mad,
Blind, stamped on all, the earth-worms with the asp,
And ended so.

        You came on me that night,   1660
Your officers of justice,—caught the crime
In the first natural frenzy of remorse?
Twenty miles off, sound sleeping as a child
On a cloak i' the straw which promised shelter first,
With the bloody arms beside me,—was it not so?
Wherefore not? Why, how else should I be found?
I was my own self, had my sense again,
My soul safe from the serpents. I could sleep:
Indeed and, dear my lords, I shall sleep now,
Spite of my shoulder, in five minutes' space,   1670
When you dismiss me, having truth enough!
It is but a few days are passed, I find,
Since this adventure. Do you tell me, four?
Then the dead are scarce quiet where they lie,
Old Pietro, old Violante, side by side
At the church Lorenzo,—oh, they know it well!
So do I. But my wife is still alive,
Has breath enough to tell her story yet,
Her way, which is not mine, no doubt, at all.
And Caponsacchi, you have summoned him,—   1680
Was he so far to send for? Not at hand?
I thought some few o' the stabs were in his heart,
Or had not been so lavish: less had served.
Well, he too tells his story,—florid prose
As smooth as mine is rough. You see, my lords,
There will be a lying intoxicating smoke
Born of the blood,—confusion probably,—
For lies breed lies—but all that rests with you!
The trial is no concern of mine; with me
The main of the care is over: I at least   1690
Recognize who took that huge burden off,
Let me begin to live again. I did
God's bidding and man's duty, so, breathe free;
Look you to the rest! I heard Himself prescribe,
That great Physician, and dared lance the core
Of the bad ulcer; and the rage abates,
I am myself and whole now: I prove cured
By the eyes that see, the ears that hear again,
The limbs that have relearned their youthful play,
The healthy taste of food and feel of clothes   1700
And taking to our common life once more,

All that now urges my defence from death.
The willingness to live, what means it else?
Before,—but let the very action speak!
Judge for yourselves, what life seemed worth to me
Who, not by proxy but in person, pitched
Head-foremost into danger as a fool
That never cares if he can swim or no—
So he but find the bottom, braves the brook.
No man omits precaution, quite neglects   1710
Secrecy, safety, schemes not how retreat,
Having schemed he might advance. Did I so scheme?
Why, with a warrant which 't is ask and have,
With horse thereby made mine without a word,
I had gained the frontier and slept safe that night.
Then, my companions,—call them what you please,
Slave or stipendiary,—what need of one
To me whose right-hand did its owner's work?
Hire an assassin yet expose yourself?
As well buy glove and then thrust naked hand   1720
I' the thorn-bush. No, the wise man stays at home,
Sends only agents out, with pay to earn:
At home, when they come back,—he straight discards
Or else disowns. Why use such tools at all
When a man's foes are of his house, like mine,
Sit at his board, sleep in his bed? Why noise,
When there 's the *acquetta* and the silent way?
Clearly my life was valueless.

                                        But now
Health is returned, and sanity of soul
Nowise indifferent to the body's harm.   1730
I find the instinct bids me save my life;
My wits, too, rally round me; I pick up
And use the arms that strewed the ground before,
Unnoticed or spurned aside: I take my stand,
Make my defence. God shall not lose a life
May do Him further service, while I speak
And you hear, you my judges and last hope!
You are the law: 't is to the law I look.
I began life by hanging to the law,
To the law it is I hang till life shall end.   1740
My brother made appeal to the Pope, 't is true,
To stay proceedings, judge my cause himself
Nor trouble law,—some fondness of conceit
That rectitude, sagacity sufficed
The investigator in a case like mine,
Dispensed with the machine of law. The Pope

Knew better, set aside my brother's plea
And put me back to law,—referred the cause
Ad judices meos,—doubtlessly did well.
Here, then, I clutch my judges,—I claim law—   1750
Cry, by the higher law whereof your law
O' the land is humbly representative,—
Cry, on what point is it, where either accuse,
I fail to furnish you defence? I stand
Acquitted, actually or virtually,
By every intermediate kind of court
That takes account of right or wrong in man,
Each unit in the series that begins
With God's throne, ends with the tribunal here.
God breathes, not speaks, his verdicts, felt not heard   1760
Passed on successively to each court I call
Man's conscience, custom, manners, all that make
More and more effort to promulgate, mark
God's verdict in determinable words,
Till last come human jurists—solidify
Fluid result,—what 's fixable lies forged,
Statute,—the residue escapes in fume,
Yet hangs aloft, a cloud, as palpable
To the finer sense as word the legist welds.
Justinian's Pandects only make precise   1770
What simply sparkled in men's eyes before,
Twitched in their brow or quivered on their lip,
Waited the speech they called but would not come.
These courts then, whose decree your own confirms,—
Take my whole life, not this last act alone,
Look on it by the light reflected thence!
What has Society to charge me with?
Come, unreservedly,—favor none nor fear,—
I am Guido Franceschini, am I not?
You know the courses I was free to take?   1780
I took just that which let me serve the Church,
I gave it all my labor in body and soul
Till these broke down i' the service. "Specify?"
Well, my last patron was a Cardinal.
I left him unconvicted of a fault—
Was even helped, by way of gratitude,
Into the new life that I left him for,
This very misery of the marriage,—he
Made it, kind soul, so far as in him lay—
Signed the deed where you yet may see his name.   1790
He is gone to his reward,—dead, being my friend
Who could have helped here also,—that, of course!
So far, there 's my acquittal, I suppose.

Then comes the marriage itself—no question, lords,
Of the entire validity of that!
In the extremity of distress, 't is true,
For after-reasons, furnished abundantly,
I wished the thing invalid, went to you
Only some months since, set you duly forth
My wrong and prayed your remedy, that a cheat   1800
Should not have force to cheat my whole life long.
"Annul a marriage? 'T is impossible!
Though ring about your neck be brass not gold,
Needs must it clasp, gangrene you all the same!"
Well, let me have the benefit, just so far,
O' the fact announced,—my wife then is my wife,
I have allowance for a husband's right.
I am charged with passing right's due bound,—such acts
As I thought just, my wife called cruelty,
Complained of in due form,—convoked no court   1810
Of common gossipry, but took her wrongs—
And not once, but so long as patience served—
To the town's top, jurisdiction's pride of place,
To the Archbishop and the Governor.
These heard her charge with my reply, and found
That futile, this sufficient: they dismissed
The hysteric querulous rebel, and confirmed
Authority in its wholesome exercise,
They, with directest access to the facts.
"—Ay, for it was their friendship favored you,   1820
Hereditary alliance against a breach
I' the social order: prejudice for the name
Of Franceschini!"—So I hear it said:
But not here. You, lords, never will you say
"Such is the nullity of grace and truth,
Such the corruption of the faith, such lapse
Of law, such warrant have the Molinists
For daring reprehend us as they do,—
That we pronounce it just a common case,
Two dignitaries, each in his degree   1830
First, foremost, this the spiritual head, and that
The secular arm o' the body politic,
Should, for mere wrongs' love and injustice' sake,
Side with, aid and abet in cruelty
This broken beggarly noble,—bribed perhaps
By his watered wine and mouldy crust of bread—
Rather than that sweet tremulous flower-like wife
Who kissed their hands and curled about their feet
Looking the irresistible loveliness
In tears that takes man captive, turns" . . . enough!   1840

Do you blast your predecessors? What forbids
Posterity to trebly blast yourselves
Who set the example and instruct their tongue?
You dreaded the crowd, succumbed to the popular cry,
Or else, would nowise seem defer thereto
And yield to public clamor though i' the right!
You ridded your eye of my unseemliness,
The noble whose misfortune wearied you,—
Or, what 's more probable, made common cause
With the cleric section, punished in myself   1850
Maladroit uncomplaisant laity,
Defective in behavior to a priest
Who claimed the customary partnership
I' the house and the wife. Lords, any lie will serve!
Look to it,—or allow me freed so far!

Then I proceed a step, come with clean hands
Thus far, re-tell the tale told eight months since.
The wife, you allow so far, I have not wronged,
Has fled my roof, plundered me and decamped
In company with the priest her paramour: 1860
And I gave chase, came up with, caught the two
At the wayside inn where both had spent the night,
Found them in flagrant fault, and found as well,
By documents with name and plan and date,
The fault was furtive then that 's flagrant now,
Their intercourse a long established crime.
I did not take the license law's self gives
To slay both criminals o' the spot at the time,
But held my hand,—preferred play prodigy
Of patience which the world calls cowardice,   1870
Rather than seem anticipate the law
And cast discredit on its organs,—you.
So, to your bar I brought both criminals,
And made my statement: heard their counter-charge,
Nay,—their corroboration of my tale,
Nowise disputing its allegements, not
I' the main, not more than nature's decency
Compels men to keep silence in this kind,—
Only contending that the deeds avowed
Would take another color and bear excuse.   1880
You were to judge between us; so you did.
You disregard the excuse, you breathe away
The color of innocence and leave guilt black;
"Guilty" is the decision of the court,
And that I stand in consequence untouched,
One white integrity from head to heel.

Not guilty? Why then did you punish them?
True, punishment has been inadequate—
'T is not I only, not my friends that joke,
My foes that jeer, who echo "inadequate"—   1890
For, by a chance that comes to help for once,
The same case simultaneously was judged
At Arezzo, in the province of the Court
Where the crime had its beginning but not end
They then, deciding on but half o' the crime,
The effraction, robbery,—features of the fault
I never cared to dwell upon at Rome,—
What was it they adjudged as penalty
To Pompilia,—the one criminal o' the pair
Amenable to their judgment, not the priest   1900
Who is Rome's? Why, just imprisonment for life
I' the Stinche. There was Tuscany's award
To a wife that robs her husband: you at Rome—
Having to deal with adultery in a wife
And, in a priest, breach of the priestly vow—
Give gentle sequestration for a month
In a manageable Convent, then release,
You call imprisonment, in the very house
O' the very couple, which the aim and end
Of the culprits' crime was—just to reach and rest   1910
And there take solace and defy me: well,—
This difference 'twixt their penalty and yours
Is immaterial: make your penalty less—
Merely that she should henceforth wear black gloves
And white fan, she who wore the opposite—
Why, all the same the fact o' the thing subsists.
Reconcile to your conscience as you may,
Be it on your own heads, you pronounced but half
O' the penalty for heinousness like hers
And his, that pays a fault at Carnival   1920
Of comfit-pelting past discretion's law,
Or accident to handkerchief in Lent
Which falls perversely as a lady kneels
Abruptly, and but half conceals her neck!
I acquiesce for my part: punished, though
By a pin-point scratch, means guilty: guilty means
—What have I been but innocent hitherto?
Anyhow, here the offence, being punished, ends.

Ends?—for you deemed so, did you not, sweet lords?
That was throughout the veritable aim   1930
O' the sentence light or heavy,—to redress
Recognized wrong? You righted me, I think?

Well then,—what if I, at this last of all,
Demonstrate you, as my whole pleading proves,
No particle of wrong received thereby
One atom of right?—that cure grew worse disease?
That in the process you call "justice done"
All along you have nipped away just inch
By inch the creeping climbing length of plague
Breaking my tree of life from root to branch,   1940
And left me, after all and every act
Of your interference,—lightened of what load?
At liberty wherein? Mere words and wind!
"Now I was saved, now I should feel no more
The hot breath, find a respite from fixed eye
And vibrant tongue!" Why, scarce your back was turned,
There was the reptile, that feigned death at first,
Renewing its detested spire and spire
Around me, rising to such heights of hate
That, so far from mere purpose now to crush   1950
And coil itself on the remains of me,
Body and mind, and there flesh fang content,
Its aim is now to evoke life from death,
Make me anew, satisfy in my son
The hunger I may feed but never sate,
Tormented on to perpetuity,—
My son, whom, dead, I shall know, understand,
Feel, hear, see, never more escape the sight
In heaven that 's turned to hell, or hell returned
(So, rather, say) to this same earth again,—   1960
Moulded into the image and made one,
Fashioned of soul as featured like in face,
First taught to laugh and lisp and stand and go
By that thief, poisoner and adulteress
I call Pompilia, he calls . . . sacred name,
Be unpronounced, be unpolluted here!
And last led up to the glory and prize of hate
By his . . . foster-father, Caponsacchi's self,
The perjured priest, pink of conspirators,
Tricksters and knaves, yet polished, superfine,   1970
Manhood to model adolescence by!
Lords, look on me, declare,—when, what I show,
Is nothing more nor less than what you deemed
And doled me out for justice,—what did you say?
For reparation, restitution and more,—
Will you not thank, praise, bid me to your breasts
For having done the thing you thought to do,
And thoroughly trampled out sin's life at last?
I have heightened phrase to make your soft speech serve,

Doubled the blow you but essayed to strike,   1980
Carried into effect your mandate here
That else had fallen to ground: mere duty done,
Oversight of the master just supplied
By zeal i' the servant. I, being used to serve,
Have simply . . . what is it they charge me with?
Blackened again, made legible once more
Your own decree, not permanently writ,
Rightly conceived but all too faintly traced.
It reads efficient, now, comminatory,
A terror to the wicked, answers so   1990
The mood o' the magistrate, the mind of law.
Absolve, then, me, law's mere executant!
Protect your own defender,—save me, Sirs!
Give me my life, give me my liberty,
My good name and my civic rights again!
It would be too fond, too complacent play
Into the hands o' the devil, should we lose
The game here, I for God: a soldier-bee
That yields his life, exenterate with the stroke
O' the sting that saves the hive. I need that life.   2000
Oh, never fear! I 'll find life plenty use
Though it should last five years more, aches and all!
For, first thing, there 's the mother's age to help—
Let her come break her heart upon my breast,
Not on the blank stone of my nameless tomb!
The fugitive brother has to be bidden back
To the old routine, repugnant to the tread,
Of daily suit and service to the Church,—
Through gibe and jest, those stones that Shimei flung!
Ay, and the spirit-broken youth at home,   2010
The awe-struck altar-ministrant, shall make
Amends for faith now palsied at the source,
Shall see truth yet triumphant, justice yet
A victor in the battle of this world!
Give me—for last, best gift—my son again,
Whom law makes mine,—I take him at your word,
Mine be he, by miraculous mercy, lords!
Let me lift up his youth and innocence
To purify my palace, room by room
Purged of the memories, lend from his bright brow   2020
Light to the old proud paladin my sire
Shrunk now for shame into the darkest shade
O' the tapestry, showed him once and shrouds him now!
Then may we,—strong from that rekindled smile,—
Go forward, face new times, the better day.
And when, in times made better through your brave

Decision now,—might but Utopia be!—
Rome rife with honest women and strong men,
Manners reformed, old habits back once more,
Customs that recognize the standard worth,—   2030
The wholesome household rule in force again,
Husbands once more God's representative,
Wives like the typical Spouse once more, and Priests
No longer men of Belial, with no aim
At leading silly women captive, but
Of rising to such duties as yours now,—
Then will I set my son at my right-hand
And tell his father's story to this point,
Adding, "The task seemed superhuman, still
I dared and did it, trusting God and law: 2040
And they approved of me: give praise to both!"
And if, for answer, he shall stoop to kiss
My hand, and peradventure start thereat,—
I engage to smile, "That was an accident
I' the necessary process,—just a trip
O' the torture-irons in their search for truth,—
Hardly misfortune, and no fault at all."

VI

GIUSEPPE CAPONSACCHI

Answer you, Sirs? Do I understand aright?
Have patience! In this sudden smoke from hell,—
So things disguise themselves,—I cannot see
My own hand held thus broad before my face
And know it again. Answer you? Then that means
Tell over twice what I, the first time, told
Six months ago: 't was here, I do believe,
Fronting you same three in this very room,
I stood and told you: yet now no one laughs,
Who then . . . nay, dear my lords, but laugh you did,   10
As good as laugh, what in a judge we style
Laughter—no levity, nothing indecorous, lords!
Only,—I think I apprehend the mood:
There was the blameless shrug, permissible smirk,
The pen's pretence at play with the pursed mouth,
The titter stifled in the hollow palm
Which rubbed the eyebrow and caressed the nose,
When I first told my tale: they meant, you know,
"The sly one, all this we are bound believe!
Well, he can say no other than what he says.   20

We have been young, too,—come, there 's greater guilt!
Let him but decently disembroil himself,
Scramble from out the scrape nor move the mud,—
We solid ones may risk a finger-stretch!"
And now you sit as grave, stare as aghast
As if I were a phantom: now 't is—"Friend,
Collect yourself!"—no laughing matter more—
"Counsel the Court in this extremity,
Tell us again!"—tell that, for telling which,
I got the jocular piece of punishment,   30
Was sent to lounge a little in the place
Whence now of a sudden here you summon me
To take the intelligence from just—your lips!
You, Judge Tommati, who then tittered most,—
That she I helped eight months since to escape
Her husband, was retaken by the same,
Three days ago, if I have seized your sense,—
(I being disallowed to interfere,
Meddle or make in a matter none of mine,
For you and law were guardians quite enough   40
O' the innocent, without a pert priest's help)
And that he has butchered her accordingly,
As she foretold and as myself believed,—
And, so foretelling and believing so,
We were punished, both of us, the merry way:
Therefore, tell once again the tale! For what?
Pompilia is only dying while I speak!
Why does the mirth hang fire and miss the smile?
My masters, there 's an old book, you should con
For strange adventures, applicable yet,   50
'T is stuffed with. Do you know that there was once
This thing: a multitude of worthy folk
Took recreation, watched a certain group
Of soldiery intent upon a game,—
How first they wrangled, but soon fell to play,
Threw dice,—the best diversion in the world.
A word in your ear,—they are now casting lots,
Ay, with that gesture quaint and cry uncouth,
For the coat of One murdered an hour ago!
I am a priest,—talk of what I have learned.   60
Pompilia is bleeding out her life belike,
Gasping away the latest breath of all,
This minute, while I talk—not while you laugh.

Yet, being sobered now, what is it you ask
By way of explanation? There 's the fact!
It seems to fill the universe with sight

And sound,—from the four corners of this earth
Tells itself over, to my sense at least.
But you may want it lower set i' the scale,—
Too vast, too close it clangs in the ear, perhaps;   70
You 'd stand back just to comprehend it more.
Well then, let me, the hollow rock, condense
The voice o' the sea and wind, interpret you
The mystery of this murder. God above!
It is too paltry, such a transference
O' the storm's roar to the cranny of the stone!

This deed, you saw begin—why does its end
Surprise you? Why should the event enforce
The lesson, we ourselves learned, she and I,
From the first o' the fact, and taught you, all in vain?   80
This Guido from whose throat you took my grasp,
Was this man to be favored, now, or feared,
Let do his will, or have his will restrained,
In the relation with Pompilia?—say!
Did any other man need interpose
—Oh, though first comer, though as strange at the work
As fribble must be, coxcomb, fool that 's near
To knave as, say, a priest who fears the world—
Was he bound brave the peril, save the doomed,
Or go on, sing his snatch and pluck his flower,   90
Keep the straight path and let the victim die?
I held so; you decided otherwise,
Saw no such peril, therefore no such need
To stop song, loosen flower, and leave path. Law,
Law was aware and watching, would suffice,
Wanted no priest's intrusion, palpably
Pretence, too manifest a subterfuge!
Whereupon I, priest, coxcomb, fribble and fool,
Ensconced me in my corner, thus rebuked,
A kind of culprit, over-zealous hound   100
Kicked for his pains to kennel; I gave place
To you, and let the law reign paramount:
I left Pompilia to your watch and ward,
And now you point me—there and thus she lies!

Men, for the last time, what do you want with me?
Is it,—you acknowledge, as it were, a use,
A profit in employing me?—at length
I may conceivably help the august law?
I am free to break the blow, next hawk that swoops
On next dove, nor miss much of good repute?   110
Or what if this your summons, after all,

Be but the form of mere release, no more,
Which turns the key and lets the captive go?
I have paid enough in person at Civita,
Am free,—what more need I concern me with?
Thank you! I am rehabilitated then,
A very reputable priest. But she—
The glory of life, the beauty of the world,
The splendor of heaven, . . . well, Sirs, does no one move?
Do I speak ambiguously? The glory, I say,   120
And the beauty, I say, and splendor, still say I,
Who, priest and trained to live my whole life long
On beauty and splendor, solely at their source,
God,—have thus recognized my food in her,
You tell me, that 's fast dying while we talk,
Pompilia! How does lenity to me
Remit one death-bed pang to her? Come, smile!
The proper wink at the hot-headed youth
Who lets his soul show, through transparent words,
The mundane love that 's sin and scandal too!   130
You are all struck acquiescent now, it seems:
It seems the oldest, gravest signor here,
Even the redoubtable Tommati, sits
Chopfallen,—understands how law might take
Service like mine, of brain and heart and hand,
In good part. Better late than never, law!
You understand of a sudden, gospel too
Has a claim here, may possibly pronounce
Consistent with my priesthood, worthy Christ,
That I endeavored to save Pompilia?

                        Then,   140
You were wrong, you see: that 's well to see, though late:
That 's all we may expect of man, this side
The grave: his good is—knowing he is bad:
Thus will it be with us when the books ope
And we stand at the bar on judgment-day.
Well then, I have a mind to speak, see cause
To relume the quenched flax by this dreadful light,
Burn my soul out in showing you the truth.
I heard, last time I stood here to be judged,
What is priest's-duty,—labor to pluck tares   150
And weed the corn of Molinism; let me
Make you hear, this time, how, in such a case,
Man, be he in the priesthood or at plough,
Mindful of Christ or marching step by step
With . . . what 's his style, the other potentate

Who bids have courage and keep honor safe,
Nor let minuter admonition tease?—
How he is bound, better or worse, to act.
Earth will not end through this misjudgment, no!
For you and the others like you sure to come, 160
Fresh work is sure to follow,—wickedness
That wants withstanding. Many a man of blood,
Many a man of guile will clamor yet,
Bid you redress his grievance,—as he clutched
The prey, forsooth a stranger stepped between,
And there 's the good gripe in pure waste! My part
Is done; i' the doing it, I pass away
Out of the world. I want no more with earth.
Let me, in heaven's name, use the very snuff
O' the taper in one last spark shall show truth 170
For a moment, show Pompilia who was true!
Not for her sake, but yours: if she is dead,
Oh, Sirs, she can be loved by none of you
Most or least priestly! Saints, to do us good,
Must be in heaven, I seem to understand:
We never find them saints before, at least.
Be her first prayer then presently for you—
She has done the good to me . . .
                              What is all this?
There, I was born, have lived, shall die, a fool!
This is a foolish outset:—might with cause 180
Give color to the very lie o' the man,
The murderer,—make as if I loved his wife
In the way he called love. He is the fool there!
Why, had there been in me the touch of taint,
I had picked up so much of knaves'-policy
As hide it, keep one hand pressed on the place
Suspected of a spot would damn us both.
Or no, not her!—not even if any of you
Dares think that I, i' the face of death, her death
That 's in my eyes and ears and brain and heart, 190
Lie,—if he does, let him! I mean to say,
So he stop there, stay thought from smirching her
The snow-white soul that angels fear to take
Untenderly. But, all the same, I know
I too am taintless, and I bare my breast.
You can't think, men as you are, all of you,
But that, to hear thus suddenly such an end
Of such a wonderful white soul, that comes
Of a man and murderer calling the white black,
Must shake me, trouble and disadvantage. Sirs, 200
Only seventeen!

Why, good and wise you are!
You might at the beginning stop my mouth:
So, none would be to speak for her, that knew.
I talk impertinently, and you bear,
All the same. This it is to have to do
With honest hearts: they easily may err,
But in the main they wish well to the truth.
You are Christians; somehow, no one ever plucked
A rag, even, from the body of the Lord,
To wear and mock with, but, despite himself,   210
He looked the greater and was the better. Yes,
I shall go on now. Does she need or not
I keep calm? Calm I 'll keep as monk that croons
Transcribing battle, earthquake, famine, plague,
From parchment to his cloister's chronicle.
Not one word more from the point now!

                                    I begin.
Yes, I am one of your body and a priest.
Also I am a younger son o' the House
Oldest now, greatest once, in my birth-town
Arezzo, I recognize no equal there—   220
(I want all arguments, all sorts of arms
That seem to serve,—use this for a reason, wait!)
Not therefore thrust into the Church, because
O' the piece of bread one gets there. We were first
Of Fiesole, that rings still with the fame
Of Capo-in-Sacco our progenitor:
When Florence ruined Fiesole, our folk
Migrated to the victor-city, and there
Flourished,—our palace and our tower attest,
In the Old Mercato,—this was years ago,   230
Four hundred, full,—no, it wants fourteen just.
Our arms are those of Fiesole itself,
The shield quartered with white and red: a branch
Are the Salviati of us, nothing more.
That were good help to the Church? But better still—
Not simply for the advantage of my birth
I' the way of the world, was I proposed for priest;
But because there 's an illustration, late
I' the day, that 's loved and looked to as a saint
Still in Arezzo, he was bishop of,   240
Sixty years since: he spent to the last doit
His bishop's-revenue among the poor,
And used to tend the needy and the sick,
Barefoot, because of his humility.
He it was,—when the Granduke Ferdinand

Swore he would raze our city, plough the place
And sow it with salt, because we Aretines
Had tied a rope about the neck, to hale
The statue of his father from its base
For hate's sake,—he availed by prayers and tears   250
To pacify the Duke and save the town.
This was my father's father's brother. You see,
For his sake, how it was I had a right
To the selfsame office, bishop in the egg,
So, grew i' the garb and prattled in the school,
Was made expect, from infancy almost,
The proper mood o' the priest; till time ran by
And brought the day when I must read the vows,
Declare the world renounced, and undertake
To become priest and leave probation,—leap   260
Over the ledge into the other life,
Having gone trippingly hitherto up to the height
O'er the wan water. Just a vow to read!

I stopped short awe-struck. "How shall holiest flesh
Engage to keep such vow inviolate,
How much less mine? I know myself too weak,
Unworthy! Choose a worthier stronger man!"
And the very Bishop smiled and stopped my mouth
In its mid-protestation. "Incapable?
Qualmish of conscience? Thou ingenuous boy!   270
Clear up the clouds and cast thy scruples far!
I satisfy thee there 's an easier sense
Wherein to take such vow than suits the first
Rough rigid reading. Mark what makes all smooth,
Nay, has been even a solace to myself!
The Jews who needs must, in their synagogue,
Utter sometimes the holy name of God,
A thing their superstition boggles at,
Pronounce aloud the ineffable sacrosanct,—
How does their shrewdness help them? In this wise;   280
Another set of sounds they substitute,
Jumble so consonants and vowels—how
Should I know?—that there grows from out the old
Quite a new word that means the very same—
And o'er the hard place slide they with a smile.
Giuseppe Maria Caponsacchi mine,
Nobody wants you in these latter days
To prop the Church by breaking your backbone,—
As the necessary way was once, we know,
When Diocletian flourished and his like.   290
That building of the buttress-work was done

By martyrs and confessors: let it bide,
Add not a brick, but, where you see a chink,
Stick in a sprig of ivy or root a rose
Shall make amends and beautify the pile!
We profit as you were the painfullest
O' the martyrs, and you prove yourself a match
For the cruellest confessor ever was,
If you march boldly up and take your stand
Where their blood soaks, their bones yet strew the soil,   300
And cry 'Take notice, I the young and free
And well-to-do i' the world, thus leave the world,
Cast in my lot thus with no gay young world
But the grand old Church: she tempts me of the two!'
Renounce the world? Nay, keep and give it us!
Let us have you, and boast of what you bring.
We want the pick o' the earth to practise with,
Not its offscouring, halt and deaf and blind
In soul and body. There 's a rubble-stone
Unfit for the front o' the building, stuff to stow   310
In a gap behind and keep us weather-tight;
There 's porphyry for the prominent place. Good lack!
Saint Paul has had enough and to spare, I trow,
Of ragged run-away Onesimus:
He wants the right-hand with the signet-ring
Of King Agrippa, now, to shake and use.
I have a heavy scholar cloistered up,
Close under lock and key, kept at his task
Of letting Fénelon know the fool he is,
In a book I promise Christendom next Spring.   320
Why, if he covets so much meat, the clown,
As a lark's wing next Friday, or, any day,
Diversion beyond catching his own fleas,
He shall be properly swinged, I promise him.
But you, who are so quite another paste
Of a man,—do you obey me? Cultivate
Assiduous, that superior gift you have
Of making madrigals—(who told me? Ah!)
Get done a Marinesque Adoniad straight
With a pulse o' the blood a-pricking, here and there,   330
That I may tell the lady, 'And he 's ours!' "

So I became a priest: those terms changed all,
I was good enough for that, nor cheated so;
I could live thus and still hold head erect.
Now you see why I may have been before
A fribble and coxcomb, yet, as priest, break word
Nowise, to make you disbelieve me now.

I need that you should know my truth. Well, then,
According to prescription did I live,
—Conformed myself, both read the breviary   340
And wrote the rhymes, was punctual to my place
I' the Pieve, and as diligent at my post
Where beauty and fashion rule. I throve apace,
Sub-deacon, Canon, the authority
For delicate play at tarocs, and arbiter
O' the magnitude of fan-mounts: all the while
Wanting no whit the advantage of a hint
Benignant to the promising pupil,—thus:
"Enough attention to the Countess now,
The young one; 't is her mother rules the roast,   350
We know where, and puts in a word: go pay
Devoir to-morrow morning after mass!
Break that rash promise to preach, Passion-week!
Has it escaped you the Archbishop grunts
And snuffles when one grieves to tell his Grace
No soul dares treat the subject of the day
Since his own masterly handling it (ha, ha!)
Five years ago,—when somebody could help
And touch up an odd phrase in time of need,
(He, he!)—and somebody helps you, my son!   360
Therefore, don't prove so indispensable
At the Pieve, sit more loose i' the seat, nor grow
A fixture by attendance morn and eve!
Arezzo 's just a haven midway Rome—
Rome 's the eventual harbor,—make for port,
Crowd sail, crack cordage! And your cargo be
A polished presence, a genteel manner, wit
At will, and tact at every pore of you!
I sent our lump of learning, Brother Clout,
And Father Slouch, our piece of piety,   370
To see Rome and try suit the Cardinal.
Thither they clump-clumped, beads and book in hand,
And ever since 't is meat for man and maid
How both flopped down, prayed blessing on bent pate
Bald many an inch beyond the tonsure's need,
Never once dreaming, the two moony dolts,
There 's nothing moves his Eminence so much
As—far from all this awe at sanctitude—
Heads that wag, eyes that twinkle, modified mirth
At the closet-lectures on the Latin tongue   380
A lady learns so much by, we know where.
Why, body o' Bacchus, you should crave his rule
For pauses in the elegiac couplet, chasms
Permissible only to Catullus! There!
Now go to duty: brisk, break Priscian's head

By reading the day's office—there 's no help.
You 've Ovid in your poke to plaster that;
Amen 's at the end of all: then sup with me!"

Well, after three or four years of this life,   390
In prosecution of my calling, I
Found myself at the theatre one night
With a brother Canon, in a mood and mind
Proper enough for the place, amused or no:
When I saw enter, stand, and seat herself
A lady, young, tall, beautiful, strange and sad.
It was as when, in our cathedral once,
As I got yawningly through matin-song,
I saw *facchini* bear a burden up,
Base it on the high-altar, break away
A board or two, and leave the thing inside   400
Lofty and lone: and lo, when next I looked,
There was the Rafael! I was still one stare,
When—"Nay, I 'll make her give you back your gaze"—
Said Canon Conti; and at the word he tossed
A paper-twist of comfits to her lap,
And dodged and in a trice was at my back
Nodding from over my shoulder. Then she turned,
Looked our way, smiled the beautiful sad strange smile.
"Is not she fair? 'T is my new cousin," said he:
"The fellow lurking there i' the black o' the box   410
Is Guido, the old scapegrace: she 's his wife,
Married three years since: how his Countship sulks!
He has brought little back from Rome beside,
After the bragging, bullying. A fair face,
And—they do say—a pocket-full of gold
When he can worry both her parents dead.
I don't go much there, for the chamber 's cold
And the coffee pale. I got a turn at first
Paying my duty: I observed they crouched
—The two old frightened family spectres—close   420
In a corner, each on each like mouse on mouse
I' the cat's cage: ever since, I stay at home.
Hallo, there 's Guido, the black, mean and small,
Bends his brows on us—please to bend your own
On the shapely nether limbs of Light-skirts there
By way of a diversion! I was a fool
To fling the sweetmeats. Prudence, for God's love!
To-morrow I 'll make my peace, e'en tell some fib,
Try if I can't find means to take you there."

That night and next day did the gaze endure,   430
Burnt to my brain, as sunbeam through shut eyes,
And not once changed the beautiful sad strange smile.

At vespers Conti leaned beside my seat
I' the choir,—part said, part sung—"*In ex-cel-sis*—
All 's to no purpose: I have louted low,
But he saw you staring—*quia sub*—don't incline
To know you nearer: him we would not hold
For Hercules,—the man would lick your shoe
If you and certain efficacious friends
Managed him warily,—but there 's the wife: 440
Spare her, because he beats her, as it is,
She 's breaking her heart quite fast enough—*jam tu*—
So, be you rational and make amends
With little Light-skirts yonder—*in secula*
Secu-lo-o-o-o-rum. Ah, you rogue! Every one knows
What great dame she makes jealous: one against one,
Play, and win both!"
           Sirs, ere the week was out,
I saw and said to myself, "Light-skirts hides teeth
Would make a dog sick,—the great dame shows spite
Should drive a cat mad: 't is but poor work this—   450
Counting one's fingers till the sonnet 's crowned.
I doubt much if Marino really be
A better bard than Dante after all.
'T is more amusing to go pace at eve
I' the Duomo,—watch the day's last gleam outside
Turn, as into a skirt of God's own robe,
Those lancet-windows' jewelled miracle,—
Than go eat the Archbishop's ortolans,
Digest his jokes. Luckily Lent is near:
Who cares to look will find me in my stall   460
At the Pieve, constant to this faith at least—
Never to write a canzonet any more."

So, next week, 't was my patron spoke abrupt,
In altered guise, "Young man, can it be true
That after all your promise of sound fruit,
You have kept away from Countess young or old
And gone play truant in church all day long?
Are you turning Molinist?" I answered quick:
"Sir, what if I turned Christian? It might be.
The fact is, I am troubled in my mind,   470
Beset and pressed hard by some novel thoughts.
This your Arezzo is a limited world;
There 's a strange Pope,—'t is said, a priest who thinks.
Rome is the port, you say: to Rome I go.
I will live alone, one does so in a crowd,
And look into my heart a little." "Lent
Ended,"—I told friends,—"I shall go to Rome."

One evening I was sitting in a muse
Over the opened "Summa," darkened round
By the mid-March twilight, thinking how my life   480
Had shaken under me,—broke short indeed
And showed the gap 'twixt what is, what should be,—
And into what abysm the soul may slip,
Leave aspiration here, achievement there,
Lacking omnipotence to connect extremes—
Thinking moreover . . . oh, thinking, if you like,
How utterly dissociated was I
A priest and celibate, from the sad strange wife
Of Guido,—just as an instance to the point,
Nought more,—how I had a whole store of strengths   490
Eating into my heart, which craved employ,
And she, perhaps, need of a finger's help,—
And yet there was no way in the wide world
To stretch out mine and so relieve myself,—
How when the page o' the "Summa" preached its best,
Her smile kept glowing out of it, as to mock
The silence we could break by no one word,—
There came a tap without the chamber-door,
And a whisper, when I bade who tapped speak out,
And, in obedience to my summons, last   500
In glided a masked muffled mystery,
Laid lightly a letter on the opened book,
Then stood with folded arms and foot demure,
Pointing as if to mark the minutes' flight.

I took the letter, read to the effect
That she, I lately flung the comfits to,
Had a warm heart to give me in exchange,
And gave it,—loved me and confessed it thus,
And bade me render thanks by word of mouth,
Going that night to such a side o' the house   510
Where the small terrace overhangs a street
Blind and deserted, not the street in front:
Her husband being away, the surly patch,
At his villa of Vittiano.

                    "And you?"—I asked:
"What may you be?" "Count Guido's kind of maid—
Most of us have two functions in his house.
We all hate him, the lady suffers much,
'T is just we show compassion, furnish help,
Specially since her choice is fixed so well.
What answer may I bring to cheer the sweet   520
Pompilia?"

Then I took a pen and wrote.
"No more of this! That you are fair, I know:
But other thoughts now occupy my mind.
I should not thus have played thee insensible
Once on a time. What made you,—may one ask,—
Marry your hideous husband? 'T was a fault,
And now you taste the fruit of it. Farewell."

"There!" smiled I as she snatched it and was gone—
"There, let the jealous miscreant,—Guido's self,
Whose mean soul grins through this transparent trick,—   530
Be balked so far, defrauded of his aim!
What fund of satisfaction to the knave,
Had I kicked this his messenger down stairs,
Trussed to the middle of her impudence,
And set his heart at ease so! No, indeed!
There 's the reply which he shall turn and twist
At pleasure, snuff at till his brain grow drunk,
As the bear does when he finds a scented glove
That puzzles him,—a hand and yet no hand,
Of other perfume than his own foul paw!   540
Last month, I had doubtless chosen to play the dupe,
Accepted the mock-invitation, kept
The sham appointment, cudgel beneath cloak,
Prepared myself to pull the appointer's self
Out of the window from his hiding-place
Behind the gown of this part-messenger
Part-mistress who would personate the wife.
Such had seemed once a jest permissible:
Now, I am not i' the mood."
                              Back next morn brought
The messenger, a second letter in hand.   550
"You are cruel, Thyrsis, and Myrtilla moans
Neglected but adores you, makes request
For mercy: why is it you dare not come?
Such virtue is scarce natural to your age:
You must love some one else; I hear you do,
The Baron's daughter or the Advocate's wife,
Or both,—all 's one, would you make me the third—
I take the crumbs from table gratefully
Nor grudge who feasts there. 'Faith, I blush and blaze!
Yet if I break all bounds, there 's reason sure.   560
Are you determinedly bent on Rome?
I am wretched here, a monster tortures me:
Carry me with you! Come and say you will!
Concert this very evening! Do not write!
I am ever at the window of my room
Over the terrace, at the *Ave*. Come!"

I questioned—lifting half the woman's mask
To let her smile loose. "So, you gave my line
To the merry lady?" "She kissed off the wax,
And put what paper was not kissed away, 570
In her bosom to go burn: but merry, no!
She wept all night when evening brought no friend,
Alone, the unkind missive at her breast;
Thus Philomel, the thorn at her breast too,
Sings" . . . "Writes this second letter?" "Even so!
Then she may peep at vespers forth?"—"What risk
Do we run o' the husband?"—"Ah,—no risk at all!
He is more stupid even than jealous. Ah—
That was the reason? Why, the man 's away!
Beside, his bugbear is that friend of yours, 580
Fat little Canon Conti. He fears him—
How should he dream of you? I told you truth:
He goes to the villa at Vittiano—'t is
The time when Spring-sap rises in the vine—
Spends the night there. And then his wife 's a child:
Does he think a child outwits him? A mere child:
Yet so full-grown, a dish for any duke.
Don't quarrel longer with such cates, but come!"

I wrote, "In vain do you solicit me.
I am a priest: and you are wedded wife, 590
Whatever kind of brute your husband prove.
I have scruples, in short. Yet should you really show
Sign at the window . . . but nay, best be good!
My thoughts are elsewhere."—"Take her that!"

                              —"Again

Let the incarnate meanness, cheat and spy,
Mean to the marrow of him, make his heart
His food, anticipate hell's worm once more!
Let him watch shivering at the window—ay,
And let this hybrid, this his light-of-love
And lackey-of-lies,—a sage economy,— 600
Paid with embracings for the rank brass coin,—
Let her report and make him chuckle o'er
The breakdown of my resolution now,
And lour at disappointment in good time!
—So tantalize and so enrage by turns,
Until the two fall each on the other like
Two famished spiders, as the coveted fly
That toys long, leaves their net and them at last!"

And so the missives followed thick and fast
For a month, say,—I still came at every turn 610
On the soft sly adder, endlong 'neath my tread.

I was met i' the street, made sign to in the church,
A slip was found i' the door-sill, scribbled word
'Twixt page and page o' the prayer-book in my place.
A crumpled thing dropped even before my feet,
Pushed through the blind, above the terrace-rail,
As I passed, by day, the very window once.
And ever from corners would be peering up
The messenger, with the selfsame demand,
"Obdurate still, no flesh but adamant?   620
Nothing to cure the wound, assuage the throe
O' the sweetest lamb that ever loved a bear?"
And ever my one answer in one tone—
"Go your ways, temptress! Let a priest read, pray,
Unplagued of vain talk, visions not for him!
In the end, you 'll have your will and ruin me!"

One day, a variation: thus I read:
"You have gained little by timidity.
My husband has found out my love at length,
Sees cousin Conti was the stalking-horse,   630
And you the game he covered, poor fat soul!
My husband is a formidable foe,
Will stick at nothing to destroy you. Stand
Prepared, or better, run till you reach Rome!
I bade you visit me, when the last place
My tyrant would have turned suspicious at,
Or cared to seek you in, was . . . why say, where?
But now all 's changed: beside, the season 's past
At the villa,—wants the master's eye no more.
Anyhow, I beseech you, stay away   640
From the window! He might well be posted there."

I wrote—"You raise my courage, or call up
My curiosity, who am but man.
Tell him he owns the palace, not the street
Under—that 's his and yours and mine alike.
If it should please me had the path this eve,
Guido will have two troubles, first to get
Into a rage and then get out again.
Be cautious, though: at the *Ave!*"
                          You of the court!
When I stood question here and reached this point   650
O' the narrative,—search notes and see and say
If some one did not interpose with smile
And sneer, "And prithee why so confident
That the husband must, of all needs, not the wife,
Fabricate thus,—what if the lady loved?
What if she wrote the letters?"
                          Learned Sir,

I told you there 's a picture in our church.
Well, if a low-browed verger sidled up
Bringing me, like a blotch, on his prod's point,
A transfixed scorpion, let the reptile writhe,   660
And then said, "See a thing that Rafael made—
This venom issued from Madonna's mouth!"
I should reply, "Rather, the soul of you
Has issued from your body, like from like,
By way of the ordure-corner!"

                 But no less,
I tired of the same long black teasing lie
Obtruded thus at every turn; the pest
Was far too near the picture, anyhow:
One does Madonna service, making clowns
Remove their dung-heap from the sacristy.   670
"I will to the window, as he tempts," said I:
"Yes, whom the easy love has failed allure,
This new bait of adventure tempts,—thinks he.
Though the imprisoned lady keeps afar,
There will they lie in ambush, heads alert,
Kith, kin, and Count mustered to bite my heel.
No mother nor brother viper of the brood
Shall scuttle off without the instructive bruise!"

So, I went: crossed street and street: "The next street's turn,
I stand beneath the terrace, see, above,   680
The black of the ambush-window. Then, in place
Of hand's throw of soft prelude over lute,
And cough that clears way for the ditty last,"—
I began to laugh already—"he will have
'Out of the hole you hide in, on to the front,
Count Guido Franceschini, show yourself!
Hear what a man thinks of a thing like you,
And after, take this foulness in your face!' "

The words lay living on my lip, I made
The one turn more—and there at the window stood,   690
Framed in its black square length, with lamp in hand,
Pompilia; the same great, grave, griefful air
As stands i' the dusk, on altar that I know,
Left alone with one moonbeam in her cell,
Our Lady of all the Sorrows. Ere I knelt—
Assured myself that she was flesh and blood—
She had looked one look and vanished.

                 I thought—"Just so:
It was herself, they have set her there to watch—
Stationed to see some wedding-band go by,
On fair pretence that she must bless the bride,   700
Or wait some funeral with friends wind past,

And crave peace for the corpse that claims its due.
She never dreams they used her for a snare,
And now withdraw the bait has served its turn.
Well done, the husband, who shall fare the worse!"
And on my lip again was—"Out with thee,
Guido!" When all at once she reappeared;
But, this time, on the terrace overhead,
So close above me, she could almost touch
My head if she bent down; and she did bend,   710
While I stood still as stone, all eye, all ear.

She began—"You have sent me letters, Sir:
I have read none, I can neither read nor write;
But she you gave them to, a woman here,
One of the people in whose power I am,
Partly explained their sense, I think, to me
Obliged to listen while she inculcates
That you, a priest, can dare love me, a wife,
Desire to live or die as I shall bid,
(She makes me listen if I will or no)   720
Because you saw my face a single time.
It cannot be she says the thing you mean;
Such wickedness were deadly to us both:
But good true love would help me now so much—
I tell myself, you may mean good and true.
You offer me, I seem to understand,
Because I am in poverty and starve,
Much money, where one piece would save my life.
The silver cup upon the altar-cloth
Is neither yours to give nor mine to take;   730
But I might take one bit of bread therefrom,
Since I am starving, and return the rest,
Yet do no harm: this is my very case.
I am in that strait, I may not dare abstain
From so much of assistance as would bring
The guilt of theft on neither you nor me;
But no superfluous particle of aid.
I think, if you will let me state my case,
Even had you been so fancy-fevered here,
Not your sound self, you must grow healthy now—   740
Care only to bestow what I can take.
That it is only you in the wide world,
Knowing me nor in thought nor word nor deed,
Who, all unprompted save by your own heart,
Come proffering assistance now,—were strange
But that my whole life is so strange: as strange
It is, my husband whom I have not wronged

Should hate and harm me. For his own soul's sake,
Hinder the harm! But there is something more,
And that the strangest: it has got to be   750
Somehow for my sake too, and yet not mine,
—This is a riddle—for some kind of sake
Not any clearer to myself than you,
And yet as certain as that I draw breath,—
I would fain live, not die—oh no, not die!
My case is, I was dwelling happily
At Rome with those dear Comparini, called
Father and mother to me; when at once
I found I had become Count Guido's wife:
Who then, not waiting for a moment, changed   760
Into a fury of fire, if once he was
Merely a man: his face threw fire at mine,
He laid a hand on me that burned all peace,
All joy, all hope, and last all fear away,
Dipping the bough of life, so pleasant once,
In fire which shrivelled leaf and bud alike,
Burning not only present life but past,
Which you might think was safe beyond his reach.
He reached it, though, since that beloved pair,
My father once, my mother all those years,   770
That loved me so, now say I dreamed a dream
And bid me wake, henceforth no child of theirs,
Never in all the time their child at all.
Do you understand? I cannot: yet so it is.
Just so I say of you that proffer help:
I cannot understand what prompts your soul,
I simply needs must see that it is so,
Only one strange and wonderful thing more.
They came here with me, those two dear ones, kept
All the old love up, till my husband, till   780
His people here so tortured them, they fled.
And now, is it because I grow in flesh
And spirit one with him their torturer,
That they, renouncing him, must cast off me?
If I were graced by God to have a child,
Could I one day deny God graced me so?
Then, since my husband hates me, I shall break
No law that reigns in this fell house of hate,
By using—letting have effect so much
Of hate as hides me from that whole of hate   790
Would take my life which I want and must have—
Just as I take from your excess of love
Enough to save my life with, all I need.
The Archbishop said to murder me were sin:

My leaving Guido were a kind of death
With no sin,—more death, he must answer for.
Hear now what death to him and life to you
I wish to pay and owe. Take me to Rome!
You go to Rome, the servant makes me hear.
Take me as you would take a dog, I think,   800
Masterless left for strangers to maltreat:
Take me home like that—leave me in the house
Where the father and the mother are; and soon
They 'll come to know and call me by my name,
Their child once more, since child I am, for all
They now forget me, which is the worst o' the dream—
And the way to end dreams is to break them, stand,
Walk, go: then help me to stand, walk and go!
The Governor said the strong should help the weak:
You know how weak the strongest women are.   810
How could I find my way there by myself?
I cannot even call out, make them hear—
Just as in dreams: I have tried and proved the fact.
I have told this story and more to good great men,
The Archbishop and the Governor: they smiled.
'Stop your mouth, fair one!'—presently they frowned,
'Get you gone, disengage you from our feet!'
I went in my despair to an old priest,
Only a friar, no great man like these two,
But good, the Augustinian, people name   820
Romano,—he confessed me two months since:
He fears God, why then needs he fear the world?
And when he questioned how it came about
That I was found in danger of a sin—
Despair of any help from providence,—
'Since, though your husband outrage you,' said he,
'That is a case too common, the wives die
Or live, but do not sin so deep as this'—
Then I told—what I never will tell you—
How, worse than husband's hate, I had to bear   830
The love,—soliciting to shame called love,—
Of his brother,—the young idle priest i' the house
With only the devil to meet there. 'This is grave—
Yes, we must interfere: I counsel,—write
To those who used to be your parents once,
Of dangers here, bid them convey you hence!'
'But,' said I, 'when I neither read nor write?'
Then he took pity and promised 'I will write.'
If he did so,—why, they are dumb or dead:
Either they give no credit to the tale,   840
Or else, wrapped wholly up in their own joy

Of such escape, they care not who cries, still
I' the clutches. Anyhow, no word arrives.
All such extravagance and dreadfulness
Seems incident to dreaming, cured one way,—
Wake me! The letter I received this morn,
Said—if the woman spoke your very sense—
'You would die for me:' I can believe it now:
For now the dream gets to involve yourself.
First of all, you seemed wicked and not good,   850
In writing me those letters; you came in
Like a thief upon me. I this morning said
In my extremity, entreat the thief!
Try if he have in him no honest touch!
A thief might save me from a murderer.
'T was a thief said the last kind word to Christ:
Christ took the kindness and forgave the theft:
And so did I prepare what I now say.
But now, that you stand and I see your face,
Though you have never uttered word yet,—well, I know,   860
Here too has been dream-work, delusion too,
And that at no time, you with the eyes here,
Ever intended to do wrong by me,
Nor wrote such letters therefore. It is false,
And you are true, have been true, will be true.
To Rome then,—when is it you take me there?
Each minute lost is mortal. When?—I ask."

I answered, "It shall be when it can be.
I will go hence and do your pleasure, find
The sure and speedy means of travel, then   870
Come back and take you to your friends in Rome.
There wants a carriage, money and the rest,—
A day's work by to-morrow at this time.
How shall I see you and assure escape?"

She replied, "Pass, to-morrow at this hour.
If I am at the open window, well:
If I am absent, drop a handkerchief
And walk by! I shall see from where I watch,
And know that all is done. Return next eve,
And next, and so till we can meet and speak!"   880
"To-morrow at this hour I pass," said I.
She was withdrawn.
                    Here is another point
I bid you pause at. When I told thus far,
Some one said, subtly, "Here at least was found
Your confidence in error,—you perceived
The spirit of the letters, in a sort,

Had been the lady's, if the body should be
Supplied by Guido: say, he forged them all!
Here was the unforged fact—she sent for you,
Spontaneously elected you to help,   890
—What men call, loved you: Guido read her mind,
Gave it expression to assure the world
The case was just as he foresaw: he wrote,
She spoke."
        Sirs, that first simile serves still,—
That falsehood of a scorpion hatched, I say,
Nowhere i' the world but in Madonna's mouth.
Go on! Suppose, that falsehood foiled, next eve
Pictured Madonna raised her painted hand,
Fixed the face Rafael bent above the Babe,
On my face as I flung me at her feet: 900
Such miracle vouchsafed and manifest,
Would that prove the first lying tale was true?
Pompilia spoke, and I at once received,
Accepted my own fact, my miracle
Self-authorized and self-explained,—she chose
To summon me and signify her choice.
Afterward,—oh! I gave a passing glance
To a certain ugly cloud-shape, goblin-shred
Of hell-smoke hurrying past the splendid moon
Out now to tolerate no darkness more,   910
And saw right through the thing that tried to pass
For truth and solid, not an empty lie:
"So, he not only forged the words for her
But words for me, made letters he called mine:
What I sent, he retained, gave these in place,
All by the mistress-messenger! As I
Recognized her, at potency of truth,
So she, by the crystalline soul, knew me,
Never mistook the signs. Enough of this—
Let the wraith go to nothingness again,   920
Here is the orb, have only thought for her!"
"Thought?" nay, Sirs, what shall follow was not thought:
I have thought sometimes, and thought long and hard.
I have stood before, gone round a serious thing,
Tasked my whole mind to touch and clasp it close,
As I stretch forth my arm to touch this bar.
God and man, and what duty I owe both,—
I dare to say I have confronted these
In thought: but no such faculty helped here.
I put forth no thought,—powerless, all that night   930
I paced the city: it was the first Spring.
By the invasion I lay passive to,

In rushed new things, the old were rapt away;
Alike abolished—the imprisonment
Of the outside air, the inside weight o' the world
That pulled me down. Death meant, to spurn the ground
Soar to the sky,—die well and you do that.
The very immolation made the bliss;
Death was the heart of life, and all the harm
My folly had crouched to avoid, now proved a veil   940
Hiding all gain my wisdom strove to grasp:
As if the intense centre of the flame
Should turn a heaven to that devoted fly
Which hitherto, sophist alike and sage,
Saint Thomas with his sober gray goose-quill,
And sinner Plato by Cephisian reed,
Would fain, pretending just the insect's good,
Whisk off, drive back, consign to shade again.
Into another state, under new rule
I knew myself was passing swift and sure;   950
Whereof the initiatory pang approached,
Felicitous annoy, as bitter-sweet
As when the virgin-band, the victors chaste,
Feel at the end the earthly garments drop,
And rise with something of a rosy shame
Into immortal nakedness: so I
Lay, and let come the proper throe would thrill
Into the ecstasy and outthrob pain.

I' the gray of dawn it was I found myself
Facing the pillared front o' the Pieve—mine,   960
My church: it seemed to say for the first time,
"But am not I the Bride, the mystic love
O' the Lamb, who took thy plighted troth, my priest,
To fold thy warm heart on my heart of stone
And freeze thee nor unfasten any more?
This is a fleshly woman,—let the free
Bestow their life-blood, thou art pulseless now!"
See! Day by day I had risen and left this church
At the signal waved me by some foolish fan,
With half a curse and half a pitying smile   970
For the monk I stumbled over in my haste,
Prostrate and corpse-like at the altar-foot
Intent on his *corona:* then the church
Was ready with her quip, if word conduced,
To quicken my pace nor stop for prating—"There!
Be thankful you are no such ninny, go
Rather to teach a black-eyed novice cards
Than gabble Latin and protrude that nose

Smoothed to a sheep's through no brains and much faith!"
That sort of incentive! Now the church changed tone—   980
Now, when I found out first that life and death
Are means to an end, that passion uses both,
Indisputably mistress of the man
Whose form of worship is self-sacrifice:
Now, from the stone lungs sighed the scrannel voice,
"Leave that live passion, come be dead with me!"
As if, i' the fabled garden, I had gone
On great adventure, plucked in ignorance
Hedge-fruit, and feasted to satiety,
Laughing at such high fame for hips and haws,   990
And scorned the achievement: then come all at once
O' the prize o' the place, the thing of perfect gold,
The apple's self: and, scarce my eye on that,
Was 'ware as well o' the seven-fold dragon's watch.

Sirs, I obeyed. Obedience was too strange,—
This new thing that had been struck into me
By the look o' the lady,—to dare disobey
The first authoritative word. 'T was God's.
I had been lifted to the level of her,
Could take such sounds into my sense. I said,   1000
"We two are cognizant o' the Master now;
She it is bids me bow the head: how true,
I am a priest! I see the function here;
I thought the other way self-sacrifice:
This is the true, seals up the perfect sum.
I pay it, sit down, silently obey."

So, I went home. Dawn broke, noon broadened, I—
I sat stone-still, let time run over me.
The sun slanted into my room, had reached
The west. I opened book,—Aquinas blazed   1010
With one black name only on the white page.
I looked up, saw the sunset: vespers rang:
"She counts the minutes till I keep my word
And come say all is ready. I am a priest.
Duty to God is duty to her: I think
God, who created her, will save her too
Some new way, by one miracle the more,
Without me. Then, prayer may avail perhaps."
I went to my own place i' the Pieve, read
The office: I was back at home again   1020
Sitting i' the dark. "Could she but know—but know
That, were there good in this distinct from God's,
Really good as it reached her, though procured
By a sin of mine,—I should sin: God forgives.

She knows it is no fear withholds me: fear?
Of what? Suspense here is the terrible thing.
If she should, as she counts the minutes, come
On the fantastic notion that I fear
The world now, fear the Archbishop, fear perhaps
Count Guido, he who, having forged the lies,   1030
May wait the work, attend the effect,—I fear
The sword of Guido! Let God see to that—
Hating lies, let not her believe a lie!"

Again the morning found me. "I will work,
Tie down my foolish thoughts. Thank God so far!
I have saved her from a scandal, stopped the tongues
Had broken else into a cackle and hiss
Around the noble name. Duty is still
Wisdom: I have been wise." So the day wore.

At evening—"But, achieving victory,   1040
I must not blink the priest's peculiar part,
Nor shrink to counsel, comfort: priest and friend—
How do we discontinue to be friends?
I will go minister, advise her seek
Help at the source,—above all, not despair:
There may be other happier help at hand.
I hope it,—wherefore then neglect to say?"

There she stood—leaned there, for the second time,
Over the terrace, looked at me, then spoke:
"Why is it you have suffered me to stay   1050
Breaking my heart two days more than was need?
Why delay help, your own heart yearns to give?
You are again here, in the selfsame mind,
I see here, steadfast in the face of you,—
You grudge to do no one thing that I ask.
Why then is nothing done? You know my need.
Still, through God's pity on me, there is time
And one day more: shall I be saved or no?"
I answered—"Lady, waste no thought, no word
Even to forgive me! Care for what I care—   1060
Only! Now follow me as I were fate!
Leave this house in the dark to-morrow night,
Just before daybreak:—there 's new moon this eve—
It sets, and then begins the solid black.
Descend, proceed to the Torrione, step
Over the low dilapidated wall,
Take San Clemente, there 's no other gate
Unguarded at the hour: some paces thence
An inn stands; cross to it; I shall be there."

She answered, "If I can but find the way.　　　　　1070
But I shall find it. Go now!"

　　　　　　　　　　I did go,
Took rapidly the route myself prescribed,
Stopped at Torrione, climbed the ruined place,
Proved that the gate was practicable, reached
The inn, no eye, despite the dark, could miss,
Knocked there and entered, made the host secure:
"With Caponsacchi it is ask and have;
I know my betters. Are you bound for Rome?
I get swift horse and trusty man," said he.

Then I retraced my steps, was found once more　　　1080
In my own house for the last time: there lay
The broad pale opened "Summa." "Shut his book,
There 's other showing! 'T was a Thomas too
Obtained,—more favored than his namesake here,—
A gift, tied faith fast, foiled the tug of doubt,--
Our Lady's girdle; down he saw it drop
As she ascended into heaven, they say:
He kept that safe and bade all doubt adieu.
I too have seen a lady and hold a grace."

I know not how the night passed: morning broke,　　1090
Presently came my servant. "Sir, this eve—
Do you forget?" I started. "How forget?
What is it you know?" "With due submission, Sir,
This being last Monday in the month but one,
And a vigil, since to-morrow is Saint George,
And feast-day, and moreover day for copes,
And Canon Conti now away a month,
And Canon Crispi sour because, forsooth,
You let him sulk in stall and bear the brunt
Of the octave. . . . Well, Sir, 't is important!"
　　　　　　　　　　　　　　　　"True!　　1100

Hearken, I have to start for Rome this night.
No word, lest Crispi overboil and burst!
Provide me with a laic dress! Throw dust
I' the Canon's eye, stop his tongue's scandal so!
See there 's a sword in case of accident."
I knew the knave, the knave knew me.

　　　　　　　　　　　　　And thus
Through each familiar hindrance of the day
Did I make steadily for its hour and end,—
Felt time's old barrier-growth of right and fit
Give way through all its twines, and let me go.　　1110
Use and wont recognized the excepted man,

Let speed the special service,—and I sped
Till, at the dead between midnight and morn,
There was I at the goal, before the gate,
With a tune in the ears, low leading up to loud,
A light in the eyes, faint that would soon be flare,
Ever some spiritual witness new and new
In faster frequence, crowding solitude
To watch the way o' the warfare,—till, at last,
When the ecstatic minute must bring birth,   1120
Began a whiteness in the distance, waxed
Whiter and whiter, near grew and more near,
Till it was she: there did Pompilia come:
The white I saw shine through her was her soul's,
Certainly, for the body was one black,
Black from head down to foot. She did not speak,
Glided into the carriage,—so a cloud
Gathers the moon up. "By San Spirito,
To Rome, as if the road burned underneath!
Reach Rome, then hold my head in pledge, I pay   1130
The run and the risk to heart's content!" Just that,
I said,—then, in another tick of time,
Sprang, was beside her, she and I alone.

So it began, our flight through dusk to clear,
Through day and night and day again to night
Once more, and to last dreadful dawn of all.
Sirs, how should I lie quiet in my grave
Unless you suffer me wring, drop by drop,
My brain dry, make a riddance of the drench
Of minutes with a memory in each,   1140
Recorded motion, breath or look of hers,
Which poured forth would present you one pure glass,
Mirror you plain,—as God's sea, glassed in gold,
His saints,—the perfect soul Pompilia? Men,
You must know that a man gets drunk with truth
Stagnant inside him! Oh, they 've killed her, Sirs!
Can I be calm?
                      Calmly! Each incident
Proves, I maintain, that action of the flight
For the true thing it was. The first faint scratch
O' the stone will test its nature, teach its worth   1150
To idiots who name Parian—coprolite.
After all, I shall give no glare—at best
Only display you certain scattered lights
Lamping the rush and roll of the abyss:
Nothing but here and there a fire-point pricks
Wavelet from wavelet: well!
                      For the first hour

We both were silent in the night, I know:
Sometimes I did not see nor understand.
Blackness engulfed me,—partial stupor, say—
Then I would break way, breathe through the surprise,   1160
And be aware again, and see who sat
In the dark vest with the white face and hands.
I said to myself—"I have caught it, I conceive
The mind o' the mystery: 't is the way they wake
And wait, two martyrs somewhere in a tomb
Each by each as their blessing was to die;
Some signal they are promised and expect,—
When to arise before the trumpet scares:
So, through the whole course of the world they wait
The last day, but so fearless and so safe!   1170
No otherwise, in safety and not fear,
I lie, because she lies too by my side."
You know this is not love, Sirs,—it is faith,
The feeling that there 's God, he reigns and rules
Out of this low world: that is all; no harm!
At times she drew a soft sigh—music seemed
Always to hover just above her lips,
Not settle,—break a silence music too.

In the determined morning, I first found
Her head erect, her face turned full to me,   1180
Her soul intent on mine through two wide eyes.
I answered them. "You are saved hitherto.
We have passed Perugia,—gone round by the wood,
Not through, I seem to think,—and opposite
I know Assisi; this is holy ground."
Then she resumed. "How long since we both left
Arezzo?"—"Years—and certain hours beside."

It was at . . . ah, but I forget the names!
'T is a mere post-house and a hovel or two;
I left the carriage and got bread and wine   1190
And brought it her.—"Does it detain to eat?"
"—They stay perforce, change horses,—therefore eat!
We lose no minute: we arrive, be sure!"
This was—I know not where—there 's a great hill
Close over, and the stream has lost its bridge,
One fords it. She began—"I have heard say
Of some sick body that my mother knew,
'T was no good sign when in a limb diseased
All the pain suddenly departs,—as if
The guardian angel discontinued pain   1200
Because the hope of cure was gone at last:
The limb will not again exert itself,

It needs be pained no longer: so with me,
—My soul whence all the pain is past at once:
All pain must be to work some good in the end.
True, this I feel now, this may be that good,
Pain was because of,—otherwise, I fear!"

She said,—a long while later in the day,
When I had let the silence be,—abrupt—
"Have you a mother?" "She died, I was born."   1210
"A sister then?" "No sister." "Who was it—
What woman were you used to serve this way,
Be kind to, till I called you and you came?"
I did not like that word. Soon afterward—
"Tell me, are men unhappy, in some kind
Of mere unhappiness at being men,
As women suffer, being womanish?
Have you, now, some unhappiness, I mean,
Born of what may be man's strength overmuch,
To match the undue susceptibility,   1220
The sense at every pore when hate is close?
It hurts us if a baby hides its face
Or child strikes at us punily, calls names
Or makes a mouth,—much more if stranger men
Laugh or frown,—just as that were much to bear!
Yet rocks split,—and the blow-ball does no more,
Quivers to featLery nothing at a touch;
And strength may have its drawback, weakness 'scapes."

Once she asked, "What is it that made you smile,
At the great gate with the eagles and the snakes,   1230
Where the company entered, 't is a long time since?"
"—Forgive—I think you would not understand:
Ah, but you ask me,—therefore, it was this.
That was a certain bishop's villa-gate,
I knew it by the eagles,—and at once
Remembered this same bishop was just he
People of old were wont to bid me please
If I would catch preferment: so, I smiled
Because an impulse came to mé, a whim—
What if I prayed the prelate leave to speak,   1240
Began upon him in his presence-hall
—'What, still at work so gray and obsolete?
Still rocheted and mitred more or less?
Don't you feel all that out of fashion now?
I find out when the day of things is done!' "

At eve we heard the *angelus:* she turned—
"I told you I can neither read nor write.

My life stopped with the play-time; I will learn,
If I begin to live again: but you—
Who are a priest—wherefore do you not read   1250
The service at this hour? Read Gabriel's song,
The lesson, and then read the little prayer
To Raphael, proper for us travellers!"
I did not like that, neither, but I read.

When we stopped at Foligno it was dark.
The people of the post came out with lights:
The driver said, "This time to-morrow, may
Saints only help, relays continue good,
Nor robbers hinder, we arrive at Rome."
I urged,—"Why tax your strength a second night?   1260
Trust me, alight here and take brief repose!
We are out of harm's reach, past pursuit: go sleep
If but an hour! I keep watch, guard the while
Here in the doorway." But her whole face changed,
The misery grew again about her mouth,
The eyes burned up from faintness, like the fawn's
Tired to death in the thicket, when she feels
The probing spear o' the huntsman. "Oh, no stay!"
She cried, in the fawn's cry, "On to Rome, on, on—
Unless 't is you who fear,—which cannot be!"   1270

We did go on all night; but at its close
She was troubled, restless, moaned low, talked at whiles
To herself, her brow on quiver with the dream:
Once, wide awake, she menaced, at arms' length
Waved away something—"Never again with you!
My soul is mine, my body is my soul's:
You and I are divided ever more
In soul and body: get you gone!" Then I—
"Why, in my whole life I have never prayed!
Oh, if the God, that only can, would help!   1280
Am I his priest with power to cast out fiends?
Let God arise and all his enemies
Be scattered!" By morn, there was peace, no sigh
Out of the deep sleep.

                        When she woke at last,
I answered the first look—"Scarce twelve hours more,
Then, Rome! There probably was no pursuit,
There cannot now be peril: bear up brave!
Just some twelve hours to press through to the prize:
Then, no more of the terrible journey!" "Then,
No more o' the journey: if it might but last!   1290
Always, my life-long, thus to journey still!

It is the interruption that I dread,—
With no dread, ever to be here and thus!
Never to see a face nor hear a voice!
Yours is no voice; you speak when you are dumb;
Nor face, I see it in the dark. I want
No face nor voice that change and grow unkind."
That I liked, that was the best thing she said.

In the broad day, I dared entreat, "Descend!"
I told a woman, at the garden-gate   1300
By the post-house, white and pleasant in the sun,
"It is my sister,—talk with her apart!
She is married and unhappy, you perceive;
I take her home because her head is hurt;
Comfort her as you women understand!"
So, there I left them by the garden-wall,
Paced the road, then bade put the horses to,
Came back, and there she sat: close to her knee,
A black-eyed child still held the bowl of milk,
Wondered to see how little she could drink,   1310
And in her arms the woman's infant lay.
She smiled at me, "How much good this has done!
This is a whole night's rest and how much more!
I can proceed now, though I wish to stay.
How do you call that tree with the thick top
That holds in all its leafy green and gold
The sun now like an immense egg of fire?"
(It was a million-leaved mimosa.) "Take
The babe away from me and let me go!"
And in the carriage, "Still a day, my friend!   1320
And perhaps half a night, the woman fears.
I pray it finish since it cannot last.
There may be more misfortune at the close,
And where will you be? God suffice me then!"
And presently—for there was a roadside-shrine—
"When I was taken first to my own church
Lorenzo in Lucina, being a girl,
And bid confess my faults, I interposed
'But teach me what fault to confess and know!'
So, the priest said—'You should bethink yourself: 1330
Each human being needs must have done wrong!'
Now, be you candid and no priest but friend—
Were I surprised and killed here on the spot,
A runaway from husband and his home,
Do you account it were in sin I died?
My husband used to seem to harm me, not . . .
Not on pretence he punished sin of mine,

Nor for sin's sake and lust of cruelty,
But as I heard him bid a farming-man
At the villa take a lamb once to the wood   1340
And there ill-treat it, meaning that the wolf
Should hear its cries, and so come, quick be caught,
Enticed to the trap: he practised thus with me
That so, whatever were his gain thereby,
Others than I might become prey and spoil.
Had it been only between our two selves,—
His pleasure and my pain,—why, pleasure him
By dying, nor such need to make a coil!
But this was worth an effort, that my pain
Should not become a snare, prove pain threefold   1350
To other people—strangers—or unborn—
How should I know? I sought release from that—
I think, or else from,—dare I say, some cause
Such as is put into a tree, which turns
Away from the north wind with what nest it holds,—
The woman said that trees so turn: now, friend,
Tell me, because I cannot trust myself!
You are a man: what have I done amiss?"
You must conceive my answer,—I forget—
Taken up wholly with the thought, perhaps,   1360
This time she might have said,—might, did not say—
"You are a priest." She said, "my friend."

                                        Day wore,
We passed the places, somehow the calm went,
Again the restless eyes began to rove
In new fear of the foe mine could not see.
She wandered in her mind,—addressed me once
"Gaetano!"—that is not my name: whose name?
I grew alarmed, my head seemed turning too.
I quickened pace with promise now, now threat:
Bade drive and drive, nor any stopping more.   1370
"Too deep i' the thick of the struggle, struggle through!
Then drench her in repose though death's self pour
The plenitude of quiet,—help us, God,
Whom the winds carry!"

                        Suddenly I saw
The old tower, and the little white-walled clump
Of buildings and the cypress-tree or two,—
"Already Castelnuovo—Rome!" I cried,
"As good as Rome,—Rome is the next stage, think!
This is where travellers' hearts are wont to beat.
Say you are saved, sweet lady!" Up she woke   1380
The sky was fierce with color from the sun

Setting. She screamed out, "No, I must not die!
Take me no farther, I should die: stay here!
I have more life to save than mine!"

She swooned.
We seemed safe: what was it foreboded so?
Out of the coach into the inn I bore
The motionless and breathless pure and pale
Pompilia,—bore her through a pitying group
And laid her on a couch, still calm and cured
By deep sleep of all woes at once. The host   1390
Was urgent, "Let her stay an hour or two!
Leave her to us, all will be right by morn!"
Oh, my foreboding! But I could not choose.

I paced the passage, kept watch all night long.
I listened,—not one movement, not one sigh.
"Fear not: she sleeps so sound!" they said: but I
Feared, all the same, kept fearing more and more,
Found myself throb with fear from head to foot,
Filled with a sense of such impending woe,
That, at first pause of night, pretence of gray,   1400
I made my mind up it was morn.—"Reach Rome,
Lest hell reach her! A dozen miles to make,
Another long breath, and we emerge!" I stood
I' the courtyard, roused the sleepy grooms. "Have out
Carriage and horse, give haste, take gold!" said I.
While they made ready in the doubtful morn,—
'T was the last minute,—needs must I ascend
And break her sleep; I turned to go.

And there
Faced me Count Guido, there posed the mean man
As master,—took the field, encamped his rights,   1410
Challenged the world: there leered new triumph, there
Scowled the old malice in the visage bad
And black o' the scamp. Soon triumph suppled the tongue
A little, malice glued to his dry throat,
And he part howled, part hissed . . . oh, how he kept
Well out o' the way, at arm's length and to spare!—
"My salutation to your priestship! What?
Matutinal, busy with book so soon
Of an April day that 's damp as tears that now
Deluge Arezzo at its darling's flight?—   1420
'T is unfair, wrongs feminity at large,
To let a single dame monopolize
A heart the whole sex claims, should share alike:
Therefore I overtake you, Canon! Come!
The lady,—could you leave her side so soon?

You have not yet experienced at her hands
My treatment, you lay down undrugged, I see!
Hence this alertness—hence no death-in-life
Like what held arms fast when she stole from mine.
To be sure, you took the solace and repose   1430
That first night at Foligno!—news abound
O' the road by this time,—men regaled me much,
As past them I came halting after you,
Vulcan pursuing Mars, as poets sing,—
Still at the last here pant I, but arrive,
Vulcan—and not without my Cyclops too,
The Commissary and the unpoisoned arm
O' the Civil Force, should Mars turn mutineer.
Enough of fooling: capture the culprits, friend!
Here is the lover in the smart disguise   1440
With the sword,—he is a priest, so mine lies still.
There upstairs hides my wife the runaway,
His leman: the two plotted, poisoned first,
Plundered me after, and eloped thus far
Where now you find them. Do your duty quick!
Arrest and hold him! That 's done: now catch her!"
During this speech of that man,—well, I stood
Away, as he managed,—still, I stood as near
The throat of him,—with these two hands, my own,—
As now I stand near yours, Sir,—one quick spring,   1450
One great good satisfying gripe, and lo!
There had he lain abolished with his lie,
Creation purged o' the miscreate, man redeemed,
A spittle wiped off from the face of God!
I, in some measure, seek a poor excuse
For what I left undone, in just this fact
That my first feeling at the speech I quote
Was—not of what a blasphemy was dared,
Not what a bag of venomed purulence
Was split and noisome,—but how splendidly   1460
Mirthful, how ludicrous a lie was launched!
Would Molière's self wish more than hear such man
Call, claim such woman for his own, his wife,
Even though, in due amazement at the boast,
He had stammered, she moreover was divine?
She to be his,—were hardly less absurd
Than that he took her name into his mouth,
Licked, and then let it go again, the beast,
Signed with his slaver. Oh, she poisoned him,
Plundered him, and the rest! Well, what I wished   1470
Was, that he would but go on, say once more
So to the world, and get his meed of men,

The fist's reply to the filth. And while I mused,
The minute, oh the misery, was gone!
On either idle hand of me there stood
Really an officer, nor laughed i' the least:
They rendered justice to his reason, laid
Logic to heart, as 't were submitted them
"Twice two makes four."
                    "And now, catch her!"—he cried.
That sobered me. "Let myself lead the way—   1480
Ere you arrest me, who am somebody,
Being, as you hear, a priest and privileged,—
To the lady's chamber! I presume you—men
Expert, instructed how to find out truth,
Familiar with the guise of guilt. Detect
Guilt on her face when it meets mine, then judge
Between us and the mad dog howling there!"
Up we all went together, in they broke
O' the chamber late my chapel. There she lay,
Composed as when I laid her, that last eve,   1490
O' the couch, still breathless, motionless, sleep's self,
Wax-white, seraphic, saturate with the sun
O' the morning that now flooded from the front
And filled the window with a light like blood.
"Behold the poisoner, the adulteress,
—And feigning sleep too! Seize, bind!" Guido hissed.

She started up, stood erect, face to face
With the husband: back he fell, was buttressed there
By the window all aflame with morning-red,
He the black figure, the opprobrious blur   1500
Against all peace and joy and light and life.
"Away from between me and hell!" she cried:
"Hell for me, no embracing any more!
I am God's, I love God, God—whose knees I clasp,
Whose utterly most just award I take,
But bear no more love-making devils: hence!"
I may have made an effort to reach her side
From where I stood i' the doorway,—anyhow
I found the arms, I wanted, pinioned fast,
Was powerless in the clutch to left and right   1510
O' the rabble pouring in, rascality
Enlisted, rampant on the side of hearth,
Home and the husband,—pay in prospect too!
They heaped themselves upon me. "Ha!—and him
Also you outrage? Him, too, my sole friend,
Guardian and savior? That I balk you of,
Since—see how God can help at last and worst!"

She sprang at the sword that hung beside him, seized,
Drew, brandished it, the sunrise burned for joy
O' the blade, "Die," cried she, "devil, in God's name!"   1520
Ah, but they all closed round her, twelve to one
—The unmanly men, no woman-mother made,
Spawned somehow! Dead-white and disarmed she lay.
No matter for the sword, her word sufficed
To spike the coward through and through: he shook,
Could only spit between the teeth—"You see?
You hear? Bear witness, then! Write down . . . but no—
Carry these criminals to the prison-house,
For first thing! I begin my search meanwhile
After the stolen effects, gold, jewels, plate,   1530
Money and clothes, they robbed me of and fled,
With no few amorous pieces, verse and prose,
I have much reason to expect to find."

When I saw that—no more than the first mad speech,
Made out the speaker mad and a laughing-stock,
So neither did this next device explode
One listener's indignation,—that a scribe
Did sit down; set himself to write indeed,
While sundry knaves began to peer and pry
In corner and hole,—that Guido, wiping brow   1540
And getting him a countenance, was fast
Losing his fear, beginning to strut free
O' the stage of his exploit, snuff here, sniff there,—
Then I took truth in, guessed sufficiently
The service for the moment. "What I say,
Slight at your peril! We are aliens here,
My adversary and I, called noble both;
I am the nobler, and a name men know.
I could refer our cause to our own court
In our own country, but prefer appeal   1550
To the nearer jurisdiction. Being a priest,
Though in a secular garb,—for reasons good
I shall adduce in due time to my peers,—
I demand that the Church I serve, decide
Between us, right the slandered lady there.
A Tuscan noble, I might claim the Duke:
A priest, I rather choose the Church,—bid Rome
Cover the wronged with her inviolate shield."

There was no refusing this: they bore me off,
They bore her off, to separate cells o' the same   1560
Ignoble prison, and, separate, thence to Rome.
Pompilia's face, then and thus, looked on me
The last time in this life: not one sight since,

Never another sight to be! And yet
I thought I had saved her. I appealed to Rome:
It seems I simply sent her to her death.
You tell me she is dying now, or dead;
I cannot bring myself to quite believe
This is a place you torture people in:
What if this your intelligence were just   1570
A subtlety, an honest wile to work
On a man at unawares? 'T were worthy you.
No, Sirs, I cannot have the lady dead!
That erect form, flashing brow, fulgurant eye,
That voice immortal (oh, that voice of hers!)
That vision in the blood-red daybreak—that
Leap to life of the pale electric sword
Angels go armed with,—that was not the last
O' the lady! Come, I see through it, you find—
Know the manœuvre! Also herself said   1580
I had saved her: do you dare say she spoke false?
Let me see for myself if it be so!
Though she were dying, a Priest might be of use,
The more when he 's a friend too,—she called me
Far beyond "friend." Come, let me see her—indeed
It is my duty, being a priest: I hope
I stand confessed, established, proved a priest?
My punishment had motive that, a priest
I, in a laic garb, a mundane mode,
Did what were harmlessly done otherwise.   1590
I never touched her with my finger-tip
Except to carry her to the couch, that eve,
Against my heart, beneath my head, bowed low,
As we priests carry the paten: that is why
—To get leave and go see her of your grace—
I have told you this whole story over again.
Do I deserve grace? For I might lock lips,
Laugh at your jurisdiction: what have you
To do with me in the matter? I suppose
You hardly think I donned a bravo's dress   1600
To have a hand in the new crime; on the old,
Judgment 's delivered, penalty imposed,
I was chained fast at Civita hand and foot—
She had only you to trust to, you and Rome,
Rome and the Church, and no pert meddling priest
Two days ago, when Guido, with the right,
Hacked her to pieces. One might well be wroth;
I have been patient, done my best to help:
I come from Civita and punishment
As friend of the court—and for pure friendship's sake   1610

Have told my tale to the end,—nay, not the end—
For, wait—I 'll end—not leave you that excuse!

When we were parted,—shall I go on there?
I was presently brought to Rome—yes, here I stood
Opposite yonder very crucifix—
And there sat you and you, Sirs, quite the same.
I heard charge, and bore question, and told tale
Noted down in the book there,—turn and see
If, by one jot or tittle, I vary now!
I' the color the tale takes, there 's change perhaps;   1620
'T is natural, since the sky is different,
Eclipse in the air now; still, the outline stays.
I showed you how it came to be my part
To save the lady. Then your clerk produced
Papers, a pack of stupid and impure
Banalities called letters about love—
Love, indeed,—I could teach who styled them so,
Better, I think, though priest and loveless both!
"—How was it that a wife, young, innocent,
And stranger to your person, wrote this page?"—   1630
"—She wrote it when the Holy Father wrote
The bestiality that posts through Rome,
Put in his mouth by Pasquin." "Nor perhaps
Did you return these answers, verse and prose,
Signed, sealed and sent the lady? There 's your hand!"
"—This precious piece of verse, I really judge,
Is meant to copy my own character,
A clumsy mimic; and this other prose,
Not so much even; both rank forgery:
Verse, quotha? Bembo's verse! When Saint John wrote   1640
The tract 'De Tribus,' I wrote this to match."
"—How came it, then, the documents were found
At the inn on your departure?"—"I opine,
Because there were no documents to find
In my presence,—you must hide before you find.
Who forged them hardly practised in my view;
Who found them waited till I turned my back."
"—And what of the clandestine visits paid,
Nocturnal passage in and out the house
With its lord absent? 'T is alleged you climbed" . .   1650
"—Flew on a broomstick to the man i' the moon!
Who witnessed or will testify this trash?"
"—The trusty servant, Margherita's self,
Even she who brought you letters, you confess,
And, you confess, took letters in reply:
Forget not we have knowledge of the facts!"

"—Sirs, who have knowledge of the facts, defray
The expenditure of wit I waste in vain,
Trying to find out just one fact of all!
She who brought letters from who could not write,   1660
And took back letters to who could not read,—
Who was that messenger, of your charity?"
"—Well, so far favors you the circumstance
That this same messenger . . . how shall we say? . . .
Sub imputatione meretricis
Laborat,—which makes accusation null:
We waive this woman's:—nought makes void the next.
Borsi, called Venerino, he who drove,
O' the first night when you fled away, at length
Deposes to your kissings in the coach,   1670
—Frequent, frenetic" . . . "When deposed he so?"
"After some weeks of sharp imprisonment" . . .
"—Granted by friend the Governor, I engage"—
"—For his participation in your flight!
At length his obduracy melting made
The avowal mentioned" . . . "Was dismissed forthwith
To liberty, poor knave, for recompense.
Sirs, give what credit to the lie you can!
For me, no word in my defence I speak,
And God shall argue for the lady!"

                              So   1680
Did I stand question, and make answer, still
With the same result of smiling disbelief,
Polite impossibility of faith
In such affected virtue in a priest;
But a showing fair play, an indulgence, even,
To one no worse than others after all—
Who had not brought disgrace to the order, played
Discreetly, ruffled gown nor ripped the cloth
In a bungling game at romps: I have told you, Sirs—
If I pretended simply to be pure   1690
Honest and Christian in the case,—absurd!
As well go boast myself above the needs
O' the human nature, careless how meat smells,
Wine tastes,—a saint above the smack! But once
Abate my crest, own flaws i' the flesh, agree
To go with the herd, be hog no more nor less,
Why, hogs in common herd have common rights:
I must not be unduly borne upon,
Who just romanced a little, sowed wild oats,
But 'scaped without a scandal, flagrant fault.   1700
My name helped to a mirthful circumstance:

"Joseph" would do well to amend his plea:
Undoubtedly—some toying with the wife,
But as for ruffian violence and rape,
Potiphar pressed too much on the other side!
The intrigue, the elopement, the disguise,—well charged!
The letters and verse looked hardly like the truth.
Your apprehension was—of guilt enough
To be compatible with innocence,
So, punished best a little and not too much.   1710
Had I struck Guido Franceschini's face,
You had counselled me withdraw for my own sake,
Balk him of bravo-hiring. Friends came round,
Congratulated, "Nobody mistakes!
The pettiness o' the forfeiture defines
The peccadillo: Guido gets his share:
His wife is free of husband and hook-nose,
The mouldy viands and the mother-in-law.
To Civita with you and amuse the time,
Travesty us 'De Raptu Helenæ!'   1720
A funny figure must the husband cut
When the wife makes him skip,—too ticklish, eh?
Do it in Latin, not the Vulgar, then!
Scazons—we 'll copy and send his Eminence.
Mind—one iambus in the final foot!
He 'll rectify it, be your friend for life!"
Oh, Sirs, depend on me for much new light
Thrown on the justice and religion here
By this proceeding, much fresh food for thought!

And I was just set down to study these   1730
In relegation, two short days ago,
Admiring how you read the rules, when, clap,
A thunder comes into my solitude—
I am caught up in a whirlwind and cast here,
Told of a sudden, in this room where so late
You dealt out law adroitly, that those scales,
I meekly bowed to, took my allotment from,
Guido has snatched at, broken in your hands,
Metes to himself the murder of his wife,
Full measure, pressed down, running over now!   1740
Can I assist to an explanation?—Yes,
I rise in your esteem, sagacious Sirs,
Stand up a renderer of reasons, not
The officious priest would personate Saint George
For a mock Princess in undragoned days.
What, the blood startles you? What, after all
The priest who needs must carry sword on thigh

May find imperative use for it? Then, there was
A Princess, was a dragon belching flame,
And should have been a Saint George also? Then,   1750
There might be worse schemes than to break the bonds
At Arezzo, lead her by the little hand,
Till she reached Rome, and let her try to live?
But you were law and gospel,—would one please
Stand back, allow your faculty elbow-room?
You blind guides who must needs lead eyes that see!
Fools, alike ignorant of man and God!
What was there here should have perplexed your wit
For a wink of the owl-eyes of you? How miss, then,
What 's now forced on you by this flare of fact—   1760
As if Saint Peter failed to recognize
Nero as no apostle, John or James,
Till some one burned a martyr, made a torch
O' the blood and fat to show his features by!
Could you fail read this cartulary aright
On head and front of Franceschini there,
Large-lettered like hell's masterpiece of print,—
That he, from the beginning pricked at heart
By some lust, letch of hate against his wife,
Plotted to plague her into overt sin   1770
And shame, would slay Pompilia body and soul,
And save his mean self—miserably caught
I' the quagmire of his own tricks, cheats and lies?
—That himself wrote those papers,—from himself
To himself,—which, i' the name of me and her,
His mistress-messenger gave her and me,
Touching us with such pustules of the soul
That she and I might take the taint, be shown
To the world and shuddered over, speckled so?
—That the agent put her sense into my words,   1780
Made substitution of the thing she hoped,
For the thing she had and held, its opposite,
While the husband in the background bit his lips
At each fresh failure of his precious plot?
—That when at the last we did rush each on each,
By no chance but because God willed it so—
The spark of truth was struck from out our souls—
Made all of me, descried in the first glance,
Seem fair and honest and permissible love
O' the good and true—as the first glance told me   1790
There was no duty patent in the world
Like daring try be good and true myself,
Leaving the shows of things to the Lord of Show
And Prince o' the Power of the Air. Our very flight,

Even to its most ambiguous circumstance,
Irrefragably proved how futile, false . . .
Why, men—men and not boys—boys and not babes—
Babes and not beasts—beasts and not stocks and stones!—
Had the liar's lie been true one pin-point speck,
Were I the accepted suitor, free o' the place,   1800
Disposer of the time, to come at a call
And go at a wink as who should say me nay,—
What need of flight, what were the gain therefrom
But just damnation, failure or success?
Damnation pure and simple to her the wife
And me the priest—who bartered private bliss
For public reprobation, the safe shade
For the sunshine which men see to pelt me by:
What other advantage—we who led the days
And nights alone i' the house—was flight to find?   1810
In our whole journey did we stop an hour,
Diverge a foot from strait road till we reached
Or would have reached—but for that fate of ours—
The father and mother, in the eye of Rome,
The eye of yourselves we made aware of us
At the first fall of misfortune? And indeed
You did so far give sanction to our flight,
Confirm its purpose, as lend helping hand,
Deliver up Pompilia not to him
She fled, but those the flight was ventured for.   1820
Why then could you, who stopped short, not go on
One poor step more, and justify the means,
Having allowed the end?—not see and say
"Here 's the exceptional conduct that should claim
To be exceptionally judged on rules
Which, understood, make no exception here"—
Why play instead into the devil's hands
By dealing so ambiguously as gave
Guido the power to intervene like me,
Prove one exception more? I saved his wife   1830
Against law: against law he slays her now:
Deal with him!

                    I have done with being judged.
I stand here guiltless in thought, word and deed,
To the point that I apprise you,—in contempt
For all misapprehending ignorance
O' the human heart, much more the mind of Christ,—
That I assuredly did bow, was blessed
By the revelation of Pompilia. There!
Such is the final fact I fling you, Sirs,

To mouth and mumble and misinterpret: there!   1840
"The priest 's in love," have it the vulgar way!
Unpriest me, rend the rags o' the vestment, do—
Degrade deep, disenfranchise all you dare—
Remove me from the midst, no longer priest
And fit companion for the like of you—
Your gay Abati with the well-turned leg
And rose i' the hat-rim, Canons, cross at neck
And silk mask in the pocket of the gown,
Brisk bishops with the world's musk still unbrushed
From the rochet; I 'll no more of these good things: 1850
There 's a crack somewhere, something that 's unsound
I' the rattle!

       For Pompilia—be advised,
Build churches, go pray! You will find me there,
I know, if you come,—and you will come, I know.
Why, there 's a Judge weeping! Did not I say
You were good and true at bottom? You see the truth—
I am glad I helped you: she helped me just so.

But for Count Guido,—you must counsel there!
I bow my head, bend to the very dust,
Break myself up in shame of faultiness.   1860
I had him one whole moment, as I said—
As I remember, as will never out
O' the thoughts of me,—I had him in arm's reach
There,—as you stand, Sir, now you cease to sit,—
I could have killed him ere he killed his wife,
And did not: he went off alive and well
And then effected this last feat—through me!
Me—not through you—dismiss that fear! 'T was you
Hindered me staying here to save her,—not
From leaving you and going back to him   1870
And doing service in Arezzo. Come,
Instruct me in procedure! I conceive—
In all due self-abasement might I speak—
How you will deal with Guido: oh, not death!
Death, if it let her life be: otherwise
Not death,—your lights will teach you clearer! I
Certainly have an instinct of my own
I' the matter: bear with me and weigh its worth!
Let us go away—leave Guido all alone
Back on the world again that knows him now!   1880
I think he will be found (indulge so far!)
Not to die so much as slide out of life,
Pushed by the general horror and common hate
Low, lower,—left o' the very ledge of things,

I seem to see him catch convulsively
One by one at all honest forms of life,
At reason, order, decency and use—
To cramp him and get foothold by at least;
And still they disengage them from his clutch.
"What, you are he, then, had Pompilia once   1890
And so forewent her? Take not up with us!"
And thus I see him slowly and surely edged
Off all the table-land whence life upsprings
Aspiring to be immortality,
As the snake, hatched on hill-top by mischance,
Despite his wriggling, slips, slides, slidders down
Hillside, lies low and prostrate on the smooth
Level of the outer place, lapsed in the vale:
So I lose Guido in the loneliness,
Silence and dusk, till at the doleful end,   1900
At the horizontal line, creation's verge,
From what just is to absolute nothingness—
Whom is it, straining onward still, he meets?
What other man deep further in the fate,
Who, turning at the prize of a footfall
To flatter him and promise fellowship,
Discovers in the act a frightful face—
Judas, made monstrous by much solitude!
The two are at one now! Let them love their love
That bites and claws like hate, or hate their hate   1910
That mops and mows and makes as it were love!
There, let them each tear each in devil's-fun,
Or fondle this the other while malice aches—
Both teach, both learn detestability!
Kiss him the kiss, Iscariot! Pay that back,
That smatch o' the slaver blistering on your lip,
By the better trick, the insult he spared Christ—
Lure him the lure o' the letters, Aretine!
Lick him o'er slimy-smooth with jelly-filth
O' the verse-and-prose pollution in love's guise!   1920
The cockatrice is with the basilisk!
There let them grapple, denizens o' the dark,
Foes or friends, but indissolubly bound,
In their one spot out of the ken of God
Or care of man, forever and evermore!

Why, Sirs, what's this? Why, this is sorry and strange!
Futility, divagation: this from me
Bound to be rational, justify an act
Of sober man!—whereas, being moved so much,
I give you cause to doubt the lady's mind: 1930

A pretty sarcasm for the world! I fear
You do her wit injustice,—all through me!
Like my fate all through,—ineffective help!
A poor rash advocate I prove myself.
You might be angry with good cause: but sure
At the advocate,—only at the undue zeal
That spoils the force of his own plea, I think?
My part was just to tell you how things stand,
State facts and not be flustered at their fume.
But then 't is a priest speaks: as for love,—no!   1940
If you let buzz a vulgar fly like that
About your brains, as if I loved, forsooth,
Indeed, Sirs, you do wrong! We had no thought
Of such infatuation, she and I:
There are many points that prove it: do be just!
I told you,—at one little roadside-place
I spent a good half-hour, paced to and fro
The garden; just to leave her free awhile,
I plucked a handful of Spring herb and bloom:
I might have sat beside her on the bench   1950
Where the children were: I wish the thing had been,
Indeed: the event could not be worse, you know:
One more half-hour of her saved! She 's dead now, Sirs!
While I was running on at such a rate,
Friends should have plucked me by the sleeve: I went
Too much o' the trivial outside of her face
And the purity that shone there—plain to me,
Not to you, what more natural? Nor am I
Infatuated,—oh, I saw, be sure!
Her brow had not the right line, leaned too much.   1960
Painters would say; they like the straight-up Greek:
This seemed bent somewhat with an invisible crown
Of martyr and saint, not such as art approves.
And how the dark orbs dwelt deep underneath,
Looked out of such a sad sweet heaven on me!
The lips, compressed a little, came forward too,
Careful for a whole world of sin and pain.
That was the face, her husband makes his plea,
He sought just to disfigure,—no offence
Beyond that! Sirs, let us be rational!   1970
He needs must vindicate his honor,—ay,
Yet shirks, the coward, in a clown's disguise,
Away from the scene, endeavors to escape.
Now, had he done so, slain and left no trace
O' the slayer,—what were vindicated, pray?
You had found his wife disfigured or a corpse,
For what and by whom? It is too palpable!

Then, here 's another point involving law:
I use this argument to show you meant
No calumny against us by that title   1980
O' the sentence,—liars try to twist it so:
What penalty it bore, I had to pay
Till further proof should follow of innocence—
Probationis ob defectum,—proof?
How could you get proof without trying us?
You went through the preliminary form,
Stopped there, contrived this sentence to amuse
The adversary. If the title ran
For more than fault imputed and not proved,
That was a simple penman's error, else   1990
A slip i' the phrase,—as when we say of you
"Charged with injustice"—which may either be
Or not be,—'t is a name that sticks meanwhile.
Another relevant matter: fool that I am!
Not what I wish true, yet a point friends urge:
It is not true,—yet, since friends think it helps,—
She only tried me when some others failed—
Began with Conti, whom I told you of,
And Guillichini, Guido's kinsfolk both,
And when abandoned by them, not before,   2000
Turned to me. That 's conclusive why she turned.
Much good they got by the happy cowardice!
Conti is dead, poisoned a month ago:
Does that much strike you as a sin? Not much,
After the present murder,—one mark more
On the Moor's skin,—what is black by blacker still?
Conti had come here and told truth. And so
With Guillichini; he 's condemned of course
To the galleys, as a friend in this affair,
Tried and condemned for no one thing i' the world,   2010
A fortnight since by who but the Governor?—
The just judge, who refused Pompilia help
At first blush, being her husband's friend, you know.
There are two tales to suit the separate courts,
Arezzo and Rome: he tells you here, we fled
Alone, unhelped,—lays stress on the main fault,
The spiritual sin, Rome looks to: but elsewhere
He likes best we should break in, steal, bear off,
Be fit to brand and pillory and flog—
That 's the charge goes to the heart of the Governor: 2020
If these unpriest me, you and I may yet
Converse, Vincenzo Marzi-Medici!
Oh, Sirs, there are worse men than you, I say!
More easily duped, I mean; this stupid lie,
Its liar never dared propound in Rome,

He gets Arezzo to receive,—nay more,
Gets Florence and the Duke to authorize!
This is their Rota's sentence, their Granduke
Signs and seals! Rome for me henceforward—Rome,
Where better men are,—most of all, that man   2030
The Augustinian of the Hospital,
Who writes the letter,—he confessed, he says,
Many a dying person, never one
So sweet and true and pure and beautiful.
A good man! Will you make him Pope one day?
Not that he is not good too, this we have—
But old,—else he would have his word to speak,
His truth to teach the world: I thirst for truth,
But shall not drink it till I reach the source.

Sirs, I am quiet again. You see, we are   2040
So very pitiable, she and I,
Who had conceivably been otherwise.
Forget distemperature and idle heat!
Apart from truth's sake, what 's to move so much?
Pompilia will be presently with God;
I am, on earth, as good as out of it,
A relegated priest; when exile ends,
I mean to do my duty and live long.
She and I are mere strangers now: but priests
Should study passion; how else cure mankind,   2050
Who come for help in passionate extremes?
I do but play with an imagined life
Of who, unfettered by a vow, unblessed
By the higher call,—since you will have it so,—
Leads it companioned by the woman there.
To live, and see her learn, and learn by her,
Out of the low obscure and petty world—
Or only see one purpose and one will
Evolve themselves i' the world, change wrong to right:
To have to do with nothing but the true,   2060
The good, the eternal—and these, not alone
In the main current of the general life,
But small experiences of every day,
Concerns of the particular hearth and home:
To learn not only by a comet's rush
But a rose's birth,—not by the grandeur, God—
But the comfort, Christ. All this, how far away!
Mere delectation, meet for a minute's dream!—
Just as a drudging student trims his lamp,
Opens his Plutarch, puts him in the place   2070
Of Roman, Grecian; draws the patched gown close,
Dreams, "Thus should I fight, save or rule the world!"—

Then smilingly, contentedly, awakes
To the old solitary nothingness.
So I, from such communion, pass content . . .

O great, just, good God! Miserable me!

VII

POMPILIA

I am just seventeen years and five months old,
And, if I lived one day more, three full weeks;
'T is writ so in the church's register,
Lorenzo in Lucina, all my names
At length, so many names for one poor child,
—Francesca Camilla Vittoria Angela
Pompilia Comparini,—laughable!
Also 't is writ that I was married there
Four years ago: and they will add, I hope,
When they insert my death, a word or two,—   10
Omitting all about the mode of death,—
This, in its place, this which one cares to know,
That I had been a mother of a son
Exactly two weeks. It will be through grace
O' the Curate, not through any claim I have;
Because the boy was born at, so baptized
Close to, the Villa, in the proper church:
A pretty church, I say no word against,
Yet stranger-like,—while this Lorenzo seems
My own particular place, I always say.   20
I used to wonder, when I stood scarce high
As the bed here, what the marble lion meant,
With half his body rushing from the wall,
Eating the figure of a prostrate man—
(To the right, it is, of entry by the door)—
An ominous sign to one baptized like me,
Married, and to be buried there, I hope.
And they should add, to have my life complete,
He is a boy and Gaetan by name—
Gaetano, for a reason,—if the friar   30
Don Celestine will ask this grace for me
Of Curate Ottoboni: he it was
Baptized me: he remembers my whole life
As I do his gray hair.

        All these few things
I know are true,—will you remember them?

Because time flies. The surgeon cared for me,
To count my wounds,—twenty-two dagger-wounds,
Five deadly, but I do not suffer much—
Or too much pain,—and am to die to-night.

Oh how good God is that my babe was born,   40
—Better than born, baptized and hid away
Before this happened, safe from being hurt!
That had been sin God could not well forgive:
He was too young to smile and save himself.
When they took, two days after he was born,
My babe away from me to be baptized
And hidden awhile, for fear his foe should find,—
The country-woman, used to nursing babes,
Said, "Why take on so? where is the great loss?
These next three weeks he will but sleep and feed,   50
Only begin to smile at the month's end;
He would not know you, if you kept him here,
Sooner than that; so, spend three merry weeks
Snug in the Villa, getting strong and stout,
And then I bring him back to be your own,
And both of you may steal to—we know where!"
The month—there wants of it two weeks this day!
Still, I half fancied when I heard the knock
At the Villa in the dusk, it might prove she—
Come to say, "Since he smiles before the time,   60
Why should I cheat you out of one good hour?
Back I have brought him; speak to him and judge!"
Now I shall never see him; what is worse,
When he grows up and gets to be my age,
He will seem hardly more than a great boy;
And if he asks, "What was my mother like?"
People may answer, "Like girls of seventeen"—
And how can he but think of this and that,
Lucias, Marias, Sofias, who titter or blush
When he regards them as such boys may do?   70
Therefore I wish some one will please to say
I looked already old though I was young;
Do I not . . . say, if you are by to speak . . .
Look nearer twenty? No more like, at least,
Girls who look arch or redden when boys laugh,
Than the poor Virgin that I used to know
At our street-corner in a lonely niche,—
The babe, that sat upon her knees, broke off,—
Then white glazed clay, you pitied her the more:
She, not the gay ones, always got my rose.   80
How happy those are who know how to write!
Such could write what their son should read in time,

Had they a whole day to live out like me.
Also my name is not a common name,
"Pompilia," and may help to keep apart
A little the thing I am from what girls are.
But then how far away, how hard to find
Will anything about me have become,
Even if the boy bethink himself and ask!
No father that he ever knew at all,   90
Nor ever had—no, never had, I say!
That is the truth,—nor any mother left,
Out of the little two weeks that she lived,
Fit for such memory as might assist:
As good too as no family, no name,
Not even poor old Pietro's name, nor hers,
Poor kind unwise Violante, since it seems
They must not be my parents any more.
That is why something put it in my head
To call the boy "Gaetano"—no old name   100
For sorrow's sake; I looked up to the sky
And took a new saint to begin anew.
One who has only been made saint—how long?
Twenty-five years: so, carefuller, perhaps,
To guard a namesake than those old saints grow,
Tired out by this time,—see my own five saints!

On second thoughts, I hope he will regard
The history of me as what some one dreamed,
And get to disbelieve it at the last:
Since to myself it dwindles fast to that,   110
Sheer dreaming and impossibility,—
Just in four days too! All the seventeen years,
Not once did a suspicion visit me
How very different a lot is mine
From any other woman's in the world.
The reason must be, 't was by step and step
It got to grow so terrible and strange.
These strange woes stole on tiptoe, as it were,
Into my neighborhood and privacy,
Sat down where I sat, laid them where I lay;   120
And I was found familiarized with fear,
When friends broke in, held up a torch and cried,
"Why, you Pompilia in the cavern thus,
How comes that arm of yours about a wolf?
And the soft length,—lies in and out your feet
And laps you round the knee,—a snake it is!"
And so on.

        Well, and they are right enough,

By the torch they hold up now: for first, observe,
I never had a father,—no, nor yet
A mother: my own boy can say at least, 130
"I had a mother whom I kept two weeks!"
Not I, who little used to doubt . . . I doubt
Good Pietro, kind Violante, gave me birth?
They loved me always as I love my babe
(—Nearly so, that is—quite so could not be—)
Did for me all I meant to do for him,
Till one surprising day, three years ago,
They both declared, at Rome, before some judge
In some court where the people flocked to hear,
That really I had never been their child, 140
Was a mere castaway, the careless crime
Of an unknown man, the crime and care too much
Of a woman known too well,—little to these,
Therefore, of whom I was the flesh and blood:
What then to Pietro and Violante, both
No more my relatives than you or you?
Nothing to them! You know what they declared.

So with my husband,—just such a surprise,
Such a mistake, in that relationship!
Every one says that husbands love their wives, 150
Guard them and guide them, give them happiness;
'T is duty, law, pleasure, religion: well,
You see how much of this comes true in mine!
People indeed would fain have somehow proved
He was no husband: but he did not hear,
Or would not wait, and so has killed us all.
Then there is . . . only let me name one more!
There is the friend,—men will not ask about,
But tell untruths of, and give nicknames to,
And think my lover, most surprise of all! 160
Do only hear, it is the priest they mean,
Giuseppe Caponsacchi: a priest—love,
And love me! Well, yet people think he did.
I am married, he has taken priestly vows,
They know that, and yet go on, say, the same,
"Yes, how he loves you!" "That was love"—they say,
When anything is answered that they ask:
Or else "No wonder you love him"—they say.
Then they shake heads, pity much, scarcely blame—
As if we neither of us lacked excuse, 170
And anyhow are punished to the full,
And downright love atones for everything!
Nay, I heard read out in the public court
Before the judge, in presence of my friends,
Letters 't was said the priest had sent to me,

And other letters sent him by myself,
We being lovers!

        Listen what this is like!
When I was a mere child, my mother . . . that's
Violante, you must let me call her so,
Nor waste time, trying to unlearn the word, . . .   180
She brought a neighbor's child of my own age
To play with me of rainy afternoons;
And, since there hung a tapestry on the wall,
We two agreed to find each other out
Among the figures. "Tisbe, that is you,
With half-moon on your hair-knot, spear in hand,
Flying, but no wings, only the great scarf
Blown to a bluish rainbow at your back:
Call off your hound and leave the stag alone!"
"—And there are you, Pompilia, such green leaves   190
Flourishing out of your five finger-ends,
And all the rest of you so brown and rough:
Why is it you are turned a sort of tree?"
You know the figures never were ourselves
Though we nicknamed them so. Thus, all my life,—
As well what was, as what, like this, was not,—
Looks old, fantastic and impossible:
I touch a fairy thing that fades and fades.
—Even to my babe! I thought, when he was born,
Something began for once that would not end,   200
Nor change into a laugh at me, but stay
Forevermore, eternally quite mine.
Well, so he is,—but yet they bore him off,
The third day, lest my husband should lay traps
And catch him, and by means of him catch me.
Since they have saved him so, it was well done:
Yet thence comes such confusion of what was
With what will be,—that late seems long ago,
And, what years should bring round, already come,
Till even he withdraws into a dream   210
As the rest do: I fancy him grown great,
Strong, stern, a tall young man who tutors me,
Frowns with the others, "Poor imprudent child!
Why did you venture out of the safe street?
Why go so far from help to that lone house?
Why open at the whisper and the knock?"

Six days ago when it was New Year's day,
We bent above the fire and talked of him,
What he should do when he was grown and great.
Violante, Pietro, each had given the arm   220

I leant on, to walk by, from couch to chair
And fireside,—laughed, as I lay safe at last,
"Pompilia's march from bed to board is made,
Pompilia back again and with a babe,
Shall one day lend his arm and help her walk!"
Then we all wished each other more New Years.
Pietro began to scheme—"Our cause is gained;
The law is stronger than a wicked man:
Let him henceforth go his way, leave us ours!
We will avoid the city, tempt no more   230
The greedy ones by feasting and parade,—
Live at the other villa, we know where,
Still farther off, and we can watch the babe
Grow fast in the good air; and wood is cheap
And wine sincere outside the city gate.
I still have two or three old friends will grope
Their way along the mere half-mile of road,
With staff and lantern on a moonless night
When one needs talk: they'll find me, never fear,
And I'll find them a flask of the old sort yet!"   240
Violante said, "You chatter like a crow:
Pompilia tires o' the tattle, and shall to bed:
Do not too much the first day,—somewhat more
To-morrow, and, the next, begin the cape
And hood and coat! I have spun wool enough."
Oh what a happy friendly eve was that!

And, next day, about noon, out Pietro went—
He was so happy and would talk so much,
Until Violante pushed and laughed him forth
Sight-seeing in the cold,—"So much to see   250
I' the churches! Swathe your throat three times!" she cried,
"And, above all, beware the slippery ways,
And bring us all the news by supper-time!"
He came back late, laid by cloak, staff and hat,
Powdered so thick with snow it made us laugh,
Rolled a great log upon the ash o' the hearth,
And bade Violante treat us to a flask,
Because he had obeyed her faithfully,
Gone sight-see through the seven, and found no church
To his mind like San Giovanni—"There's the fold,   260
And all the sheep together, big as cats!
And such a shepherd, half the size of life,
Starts up and hears the angel"—when, at the door,
A tap: we started up: you know the rest.

Pietro at least had done no harm, I know;
Nor even Violante, so much harm as makes

Such revenge lawful. Certainly she erred—
Did wrong, how shall I dare say otherwise?—
In telling that first falsehood, buying me
From my poor faulty mother at a price,   270
To pass off upon Pietro as his child.
If one should take my babe, give him a name,
Say he was not Gaetano and my own,
But that some other woman made his mouth
And hands and feet,—how very false were that!
No good could come of that; and all harm did.
Yet if a stranger were to represent
"Needs must you either give your babe to me
And let me call him mine forevermore,
Or let your husband get him"—ah, my God,   280
That were a trial I refuse to face!
Well, just so here: it proved wrong but seemed right
To poor Violante—for there lay, she said,
My poor real dying mother in her rags,
Who put me from her with the life and all,
Poverty, pain, shame and disease at once,
To die the easier by what price I fetched—
Also (I hope) because I should be spared
Sorrow and sin,—why may not that have helped?
My father,—he was no one, any one,—   290
The worse, the likelier,—call him,—he who came,
Was wicked for his pleasure, went his way,
And left no trace to track by; there remained
Nothing but me, the unnecessary life,
To catch up or let fall,—and yet a thing
She could make happy, be made happy with,
This poor Violante,—who would frown thereat?

Well, God, you see! God plants us where we grow.
It is not that, because a bud is born
At a wild brier's end, full i' the wild beast's way,   300
We ought to pluck and put it out of reach
On the oak-tree top,—say, "There the bud belongs!"
She thought, moreover, real lies were lies told
For harm's sake; whereas this had good at heart,
Good for my mother, good for me, and good
For Pietro who was meant to love a babe,
And needed one to make his life of use,
Receive his house and land when he should die.
Wrong, wrong, and always wrong! how plainly wrong!
For see, this fault kept pricking, as faults do,   310
All the same at her heart: this falsehood hatched,
She could not let it go nor keep it fast.
She told me so,—the first time I was found

Locked in her arms once more after the pain,
When the nuns let me leave them and go home,
And both of us cried all the cares away,—
This it was set her on to make amends,
This brought about the marriage—simply this!
Do let me speak for her you blame so much!
When Paul, my husband's brother, found me out,   320
Heard there was wealth for who should marry me,
So, came and made a speech to ask my hand
For Guido,—she, instead of piercing straight
Through the pretence to the ignoble truth,
Fancied she saw God's very finger point,
Designate just the time for planting me
(The wild-brier slip she plucked to love and wear)
In soil where I could strike real root, and grow,
And get to be the thing I called myself:
For, wife and husband are one flesh, God says,   330
And I, whose parents seemed such and were none,
Should in a husband have a husband now,
Find nothing, this time, but was what it seemed,
—All truth and no confusion any more.
I know she meant all good to me, all pain
To herself,—since how could it be aught but pain,
To give me up, so, from her very breast,
The wilding flower-tree-branch that, all those years,
She had got used to feel for and find fixed?
She meant well: has it been so ill i' the main?   340
That is but fair to ask: one cannot judge
Of what has been the ill or well of life,
The day that one is dying;—sorrows change
Into not altogether sorrow-like;
I do see strangeness but scarce misery,
Now it is over, and no danger more.
My child is safe; there seems not so much pain.
It comes, most like, that I am just absolved,
Purged of the past, the foul in me, washed fair,—
One cannot both have and not have, you know,—   350
Being right now, I am happy and color things.
Yes, everybody that leaves life sees all
Softened and bettered: so with other sights:
To me at least was never evening yet
But seemed far beautifuller than its day,
For past is past.

             There was a fancy came,
When somewhere, in the journey with my friend,
We stepped into a hovel to get food;
And there began a yelp here, a bark there,—

Misunderstanding creatures that were wroth   360
And vexed themselves and us till we retired.
The hovel is life: no matter what dogs bit
Or cats scratched in the hovel I break from,
All outside is lone field, moon and such peace—
Flowing in, filling up as with a sea
Whereon comes Someone, walks fast on the white,
Jesus Christ's self, Don Celestine declares,
To meet me and calm all things back again.

Beside, up to my marriage, thirteen years
Were, each day, happy as the day was long: 370
This may have made the change too terrible.
I know that when Violante told me first
The cavalier—she meant to bring next morn,
Whom I must also let take, kiss my hand—
Would be at San Lorenzo the same eve
And marry me,—which over, we should go
Home both of us without him as before,
And, till she bade speak, I must hold my tongue,
Such being the correct way with girl-brides,
From whom one word would make a father blush,—   380
I know, I say, that when she told me this,
—Well, I no more saw sense in what she said
Than a lamb does in people clipping wool;
Only lay down and let myself be clipped.
And when next day the cavalier who came
(Tisbe had told me that the slim young man
With wings at head, and wings at feet, and sword
Threatening a monster, in our tapestry,
Would eat a girl else,—was a cavalier)—
When he proved Guido Franceschini,—old   390
And nothing like so tall as I myself,
Hook-nosed and yellow in a bush of beard,
Much like a thing I saw on a boy's wrist,
He called an owl and used for catching birds,—
And when he took my hand and made a smile—
Why, the uncomfortableness of it all
Seemed hardly more important in the case
Than—when one gives you, say, a coin to spend—
Its newness or its oldness; if the piece
Weigh properly and buy you what you wish,   400
No matter whether you get grime or glare!
Men take the coin, return you grapes and figs.
Here, marriage was the coin, a dirty piece
Would purchase me the praise of those I loved:
About what else should I concern myself?

So, hardly knowing what a husband meant,
I supposed this or any man would serve,
No whit the worse for being so uncouth:
For I was ill once and a doctor came
With a great ugly hat, no plume thereto,   410
Black jerkin and black buckles and black sword,
And white sharp beard over the ruff in front,
And oh so lean, so sour-faced and austere!—
Who felt my pulse, made me put out my tongue,
Then oped a phial, dripped a drop or two
Of a black bitter something,—I was cured!
What mattered the fierce beard or the grim face?
It was the physic beautified the man,
Master Malpichi,—never met his match
In Rome, they said,—so ugly all the same!   420

However, I was hurried through a storm,
Next dark eve of December's deadest day—
How it rained!—through our street and the Lion's-mouth
And the bit of Corso,—cloaked round, covered close,
I was like something strange or contraband,—
Into blank San Lorenzo, up the aisle,
My mother keeping hold of me so tight,
I fancied we were come to see a corpse
Before the altar which she pulled me toward.
There we found waiting an unpleasant priest   430
Who proved the brother, not our parish friend,
But one with mischief-making mouth and eye,
Paul, whom I know since to my cost. And then
I heard the heavy church-door lock out help
Behind us: for the customary warmth,
Two tapers shivered on the altar. "Quick—
Lose no time!" cried the priest. And straightway down
From . . . what 's behind the altar where he hid—
Hawk-nose and yellowness and bush and all,
Stepped Guido, caught my hand, and there was I   440
O' the chancel, and the priest had opened book,
Read here and there, made me say that and this,
And after, told me I was now a wife,
Honored indeed, since Christ thus weds the Church,
And therefore turned he water into wine,
To show I should obey my spouse like Christ.
Then the two slipped aside and talked apart,
And I, silent and scared, got down again
And joined my mother, who was weeping now.
Nobody seemed to mind us any more,   450
And both of us on tiptoe found our way

To the door which was unlocked by this, and wide.
When we were in the street, the rain had stopped,
All things looked better. At our own house-door,
Violante whispered, "No one syllable
To Pietro! Girl-brides never breathe a word!"
"—Well treated to a wetting, draggle-tails!"
Laughed Pietro as he opened—"Very near
You made me brave the gutter's roaring sea
To carry off from roost old dove and young,   460
Trussed up in church, the cote, by me, the kite!
What do these priests mean, praying folk to death
On stormy afternoons, with Christmas close
To wash our sins off nor require the rain?"
Violante gave my hand a timely squeeze,
Madonna saved me from immodest speech,
I kissed him and was quiet, being a bride.

When I saw nothing more, the next three weeks,
Of Guido—"Nor the Church sees Christ" thought I:
"Nothing is changed however, wine is wine   470
And water only water in our house.
Nor did I see that ugly doctor since
That cure of the illness: just as I was cured,
I am married,—neither scarecrow will return."

Three weeks, I chuckled—"How would Giulia stare,
And Tecla smile and Tisbe laugh outright,
Were it not impudent for brides to talk!"—
Until one morning, as I sat and sang
At the broidery-frame alone i' the chamber,—loud
Voices, too, three together, sobbings too,   480
And my name, "Guido," "Paolo," flung like stones
From each to the other! In I ran to see.
There stood the very Guido and the priest
With sly face,—formal but nowise afraid,—
While Pietro seemed all red and angry, scarce
Able to stutter out his wrath in words;
And this it was that made my mother sob,
As he reproached her—"You have murdered us,
Me and yourself and this our child beside!"
Then Guido interposed, "Murdered or not,   490
Be it enough your child is now my wife!
I claim and come to take her." Paul put in,
"Consider—kinsman, dare I term you so?—
What is the good of your sagacity
Except to counsel in a strait like this?
I guarantee the parties man and wife
Whether you like or loathe it, bless or ban.

May spilt milk be put back within the bowl—
The done thing, undone? You, it is, we look
For counsel to, you fitliest will advise!   500
Since milk, though spilt and spoilt, does marble good,
Better we down on knees and scrub the floor,
Than sigh, 'the waste would make a syllabub!'
Help us so turn disaster to account,
So predispose the groom, he needs shall grace
The bride with favor from the very first,
Not begin marriage an embittered man!"
He smiled,—the game so wholly in his hands!
While fast and faster sobbed Violante—"Ay,
All of us murdered, past averting now!   510
O my sin, O my secret!" and such like.

Then I began to half surmise the truth;
Something had happened, low, mean, underhand,
False, and my mother was to blame, and I
To pity, whom all spoke of, none addressed:
I was the chattel that had caused a crime.
I stood mute,—those who tangled must untie
The embroilment. Pietro cried, "Withdraw, my child!
She is not helpful to the sacrifice
At this stage,—do you want the victim by   520
While you discuss the value of her blood?
For her sake, I consent to hear you talk:
Go, child, and pray God help the innocent!"
I did go and was praying God, when came
Violante, with eyes swollen and red enough,
But movement on her mouth for make-believe
Matters were somehow getting right again.
She bade me sit down by her side and hear.
"You are too young and cannot understand,
Nor did your father understand at first.   530
I wished to benefit all three of us,
And when he failed to take my meaning,—why,
I tried to have my way at unaware—
Obtained him the advantage he refused.
As if I put before him wholesome food
Instead of broken victual,—he finds change
I' the viands, never cares to reason why,
But falls to blaming me, would fling the plate
From window, scandalize the neighborhood,
Even while he smacks his lips,—men's way, my child!   540
But either you have prayed him unperverse
Or I have talked him back into his wits:
And Paolo was a help in time of need,—

Guido, not much—my child, the way of men!
A priest is more a woman than a man,
And Paul did wonders to persuade. In short,
Yes, he was wrong, your father sees and says;
My scheme was worth attempting: and bears fruit,
Gives you a husband and a noble name,
A palace and no end of pleasant things.   550
What do you care about a handsome youth?
They are so volatile, and tease their wives!
This is the kind of man to keep the house.
We lose no daughter,—gain a son, that's all:
For 't is arranged we never separate,
Nor miss, in our gray time of life, the tints
Of you that color eve to match with morn.
In good or ill, we share and share alike,
And cast our lots into a common lap,
And all three die together as we lived!   560
Only, at Arezzo,—that's a Tuscan town,
Not so large as this noisy Rome, no doubt,
But older far and finer much, say folk,—
In a great palace where you will be queen,
Know the Archbishop and the Governor,
And we see homage done you ere we die.
Therefore, be good and pardon!"—"Pardon what?
You know things, I am very ignorant:
All is right if you only will not cry!"
And so an end! Because a blank begins   570
From when, at the word, she kissed me hard and hot,
And took me back to where my father leaned
Opposite Guido—who stood eying him,
As eyes the butcher the cast panting ox
That feels his fate is come, nor struggles more,—
While Paul looked archly on, pricked brow at whiles
With the pen-point as to punish triumph there,—
And said, "Count Guido, take your lawful wife
Until death part you!"

                   All since is one blank,
Over and ended; a terrific dream.   580
It is the good of dreams—so soon they go!
Wake in a horror of heart-beats, you may—
Cry, "The dread thing will never from my thoughts!"
Still, a few daylight doses of plain life,
Cock-crow and sparrow-chirp, or bleat and bell
Of goats that trot by, tinkling, to be milked;
And when you rub your eyes awake and wide,
Where is the harm o' the horror? Gone! So here.

I know I wake,—but from what? Blank, I say!
This is the note of evil: for good lasts. 590
Even when Don Celestine bade "Search and find!
For your soul's sake, remember what is past,
The better to forgive it,"—all in vain!
What was fast getting indistinct before,
Vanished outright. By special grace perhaps,
Between that first calm and this last, four years
Vanish,—one quarter of my life, you know.
I am held up, amid the nothingness,
By one or two truths only—thence I hang,
And there I live,—the rest is death or dream, 600
All but those points of my support. I think
Of what I saw at Rome once in the Square
O' the Spaniards, opposite the Spanish House:
There was a foreigner had trained a goat,
A shuddering white woman of a beast,
To climb up, stand straight on a pile of sticks
Put close, which gave the creature room enough:
When she was settled there, he, one by one,
Took away all the sticks, left just the four
Whereon the little hoofs did really rest, 610
There she kept firm, all underneath was air.
So, what I hold by, are my prayer to God,
My hope, that came in answer to the prayer,
Some hand would interpose and save me—hand
Which proved to be my friend's hand: and,—blest bliss,—
That fancy which began so faint at first,
That thrill of dawn's suffusion through my dark,
Which I perceive was promise of my child,
The light his unborn face sent long before,—
God's way of breaking the good news to flesh. 620
That is all left now of those four bad years.
Don Celestine urged, "But remember more!
Other men's faults may help me find your own.
I need the cruelty exposed, explained,
Or how can I advise you to forgive?"
He thought I could not properly forgive
Unless I ceased forgetting,—which is true:
For, bringing back reluctantly to mind
My husband's treatment of me,—by a light
That's later than my lifetime, I review 630
And comprehend much and imagine more,
And have but little to forgive at last.
For now,—be fair and say,—is it not true
He was ill-used and cheated of his hope
To get enriched by marriage? Marriage gave

Me and no money, broke the compact so:
He had a right to ask me on those terms,
As Pietro and Violante to declare
They would not give me: so the bargain stood:
They broke it, and he felt himself aggrieved,   640
Became unkind with me to punish them.
They said 't was he began deception first,
Nor, in one point whereto he pledged himself,
Kept promise: what of that, suppose it were?
Echoes die off, scarcely reverberate
Forever,—why should ill keep echoing ill,
And never let our ears have done with noise?
Then my poor parents took the violent way
To thwart him,—he must needs retaliate,—wrong,
Wrong, and all wrong,—better say, all blind!   65(
As I myself was, that is sure, who else
Had understood the mystery: for his wife
Was bound in some sort to help somehow there.
It seems as if I might have interposed,
Blunted the edge of their resentment so,
Since he vexed me because they first vexed him;
"I will entreat them to desist, submit,
Give him the money and be poor in peace,—
Certainly not go tell the world: perhaps
He will grow quiet with his gains."
                        Yes, say   660
Something to this effect and you do well!
But then you have to see first: I was blind.
That is the fruit of all such wormy ways,
The indirect, the unapproved of God:
You cannot find their author's end and aim,
Not even to substitute your good for bad,
Your straight for the irregular; you stand
Stupefied, profitless, as cow or sheep
That miss a man's mind; anger him just twice
By trial at repairing the first fault.   670
Thus, when he blamed me, "You are a coquette,
A lure-owl posturing to attract birds,
You look love-lures at theatre and church,
In walk, at window!"—that, I knew, was false:
But why he charged me falsely, whither sought
To drive me by such charge,—how could I know?
So, unaware, I only made things worse.
I tried to soothe him by abjuring walk,
Window, church, theatre, for good and all,
As if he had been in earnest: that, you know,   680
Was nothing like the object of his charge.

Yes, when I got my maid to supplicate
The priest, whose name she read when she would read
Those feigned false letters I was forced to hear
Though I could read no word of,—he should cease
Writing,—nay, if he minded prayer of mine,
Cease from so much as even pass the street
Whereon our house looked,—in my ignorance
I was just thwarting Guido's true intent;
Which was, to bring about a wicked change   690
Of sport to earnest, tempt a thoughtless man
To write indeed, and pass the house, and more,
Till both of us were taken in a crime.
He ought not to have wished me thus act lies,
Simulate folly: but—wrong or right, the wish—
I failed to apprehend its drift. How plain
It follows,—if I fell into such fault,
He also may have overreached the mark,
Made mistake, by perversity of brain,
I' the whole sad strange plot, the grotesque intrigue   700
To make me and my friend unself ourselves,
Be other man and woman than we were!
Think it out, you who have the time! for me,—
I cannot say less; more I will not say.
Leave it to God to cover and undo!
Only, my dulness should not prove too much!
—Not prove that in a certain other point
Wherein my husband blamed me,—and you blame,
If I interpret smiles and shakes of head,—
I was dull too. Oh, if I dared but speak!   710
Must I speak? I am blamed that I forewent
A way to make my husband's favor come.
That is true: I was firm, withstood, refused . . .
—Women as you are, how can I find the words?

I felt there was just one thing Guido claimed
I had no right to give nor he to take;
We being in estrangement, soul from soul:
Till, when I sought help, the Archbishop smiled,
Inquiring into privacies of life,
—Said I was blamable—(he stands for God)   720
Nowise entitled to exemption there.
Then I obeyed,—as surely had obeyed
Were the injunction "Since your husband bids,
Swallow the burning coal he proffers you!"
But I did wrong, and he gave wrong advice
Though he were thrice Archbishop,—that, I know!—
Now I have got to die and see things clear.

Remember I was barely twelve years old—
A child at marriage: I was let alone
For weeks, I told you, lived my child-life still   730
Even at Arezzo, when I woke and found
First . . . but I need not think of that again—
Over and ended! Try and take the sense
Of what I signify, if it must be so.
After the first, my husband, for hate's sake,
Said one eve, when the simpler cruelty
Seemed somewhat dull at edge and fit to bear,
"We have been man and wife six months almost:
How long is this your comedy to last?
Go this night to my chamber, not your own!"   740
At which word, I did rush—most true the charge—
And gain the Archbishop's house—he stands for God—
And fall upon my knees and clasp his feet,
Praying him hinder what my estranged soul
Refused to bear, though patient of the rest:
"Place me within a convent," I implored—
"Let me henceforward lead the virgin life
You praise in Her you bid me imitate!"
What did he answer? "Folly of ignorance!
Know, daughter, circumstances make or mar   750
Virginity,—'t is virtue or 't is vice.
That which was glory in the Mother of God
Had been, for instance, damnable in Eve
Created to be mother of mankind.
Had Eve, in answer to her Maker's speech
'Be fruitful, multiply, replenish earth'—
Pouted 'But I choose rather to remain
Single'—why, she had spared herself forthwith
Further probation by the apple and snake,
Been pushed straight out of Paradise! For see—   760
If motherhood be qualified impure,
I catch you making God command Eve sin!
—A blasphemy so like these Molinists',
I must suspect you dip into their books.'
Then he pursued " 'T was in your covenant!"

No! There my husband never used deceit.
He never did by speech nor act imply
"Because of our souls' yearning that we meet
And mix in soul through flesh, which yours and mine
Wear and impress, and make their visible selves,   770
—All which means, for the love of you and me,
Let us become one flesh, being one soul!"
He only stipulated for the wealth;

Honest so far. But when he spoke as plain—
Dreadfully honest also—"Since our souls
Stand each from each, a whole world's width between,
Give me the fleshly vesture I can reach
And rend and leave just fit for hell to burn!"—
Why, in God's name, for Guido's soul's own sake
Imperilled by polluting mine,—I say,   780
I did resist; would I had overcome!

My heart died out at the Archbishop's smile;
—It seemed so stale and worn a way o' the world,
As though 't were nature frowning—"Here is Spring,
The sun shines as he shone at Adam's fall,
The earth requires that warmth reach everywhere:
What, must your patch of snow be saved forsooth
Because you rather fancy snow than flowers?"
Something in this style he began with me.
Last he said, savagely for a good man,   790
"This explains why you call your husband harsh,
Harsh to you, harsh to whom you love. God's Bread!
The poor Count has to manage a mere child
Whose parents leave untaught the simplest things
Their duty was and privilege to teach,—
Goodwives' instruction, gossips' lore: they laugh
And leave the Count the task,—or leave it me!"
Then I resolved to tell a frightful thing.
"I am not ignorant,—know what I say,
Declaring this is sought for hate, not love.   800
Sir, you may hear things like almighty God.
I tell you that my housemate, yes—the priest
My husband's brother, Canon Girolamo—
Has taught me what depraved and misnamed love
Means, and what outward signs denote the sin,
For he solicits me and says he loves,
The idle young priest with nought else to do.
My husband sees this, knows this, and lets be.
Is it your counsel I bear this beside?"
"—More scandal, and against a priest this time!   810
What, 't is the Canon now?"—less snappishly—
"Rise up, my child, for such a child you are,
The rod were too advanced a punishment!
Let 's try the honeyed cake. A parable!
'Without a parable spake He not to them.'

There was a ripe round long black toothsome fruit,
Even a flower-fig, the prime boast of May:
And, to the tree, said . . . either the spirit o' the fig.

Or, if we bring in men, the gardener,
Archbishop of the orchard—had I time   820
To try o' the two which fits in best: indeed
It might be the Creator's self, but then
The tree should bear an apple, I suppose,—
Well, anyhow, one with authority said,
'Ripe fig, burst skin, regale the fig-pecker—
The bird whereof thou art a perquisite!'
'Nay,' with a flounce, replied the restif fig,
'I much prefer to keep my pulp myself:
He may go breakfastless and dinnerless,
Supperless of one crimson seed, for me!'   830
So, back she flopped into her bunch of leaves.
He flew off, left her,—did the natural lord,—
And lo, three hundred thousand bees and wasps
Found her out, feasted on her to the shuck:
Such gain the fig's that gave its bird no bite!
The moral,—fools elude their proper lot,
Tempt other fools, get ruined all alike.
Therefore go home, embrace your husband quick!
Which if his Canon brother chance to see,
He will the sooner back to book again."   840
So, home I did go; so, the worst befell:
So, I had proof the Archbishop was just man,
And hardly that, and certainly no more.
For, miserable consequence to me,
My husband's hatred waxed nor waned at all,
His brother's boldness grew effrontery soon,
And my last stay and comfort in myself
Was forced from me: henceforth I looked to God
Only, nor cared my desecrated soul
Should have fair walls, gay windows for the world.   850
God's glimmer, that came through the ruin-top,
Was witness why all lights were quenched inside·
Henceforth I asked God counsel, not mankind.

So, when I made the effort, freed myself,
They said—"No care to save appearance here!
How cynic,—when, how wanton, were enough!"
—Adding, it all came of my mother's life—
My own real mother, whom I never knew,
Who did wrong (if she needs must have done wrong)
Through being all her life, not my four years,   860
At mercy of the hateful: every beast
O' the field was wont to break that fountain-fence,
Trample the silver into mud so murk
Heaven could not find itself reflected there.

Now they cry, "Out on her, who, plashy pool,
Bequeathed turbidity and bitterness
To the daughter-stream where Guido dipt and drank!"

Well, since she had to bear this brand—let me!
The rather do I understand her now,—
From my experience of what hate calls love,—   870
Much love might be in what their love called hate.
If she sold . . . what they call, sold . . . me her child—
I shall believe she hoped in her poor heart
That I at least might try be good and pure,
Begin to live untempted, not go doomed
And done with ere once found in fault, as she.
Oh and, my mother, it all came to this?
Why should I trust those that speak ill of you,
When I mistrust who speaks even well of them?
Why, since all bound to do me good, did harm,   880
May not you, seeming as you harmed me most,
Have meant to do most good—and feed your child
From bramble-bush, whom not one orchard-tree
But drew bough back from, nor let one fruit fall?
This it was for you sacrificed your babe?
Gained just this, giving your heart's hope away
As I might give mine, loving it as you,
If . . . but that never could be asked of me!

There, enough! I have my support again,
Again the knowledge that my babe was, is,   890
Will be mine only. Him, by death, I give
Outright to God, without a further care,—
But not to any parent in the world,—
So to be safe: why is it we repine?
What guardianship were safer could we choose?
All human plans and projects come to nought:
My life, and what I know of other lives,
Prove that: no plan nor project! God shall care!

And now you are not tired? How patient then
All of you,—Oh yes, patient this long while   900
Listening, and understanding, I am sure!
Four days ago, when I was sound and well
And like to live, no one would understand.
People were kind, but smiled, "And what of him,
Your friend, whose tonsure, the rich dark-brown hides?
There, there!—your lover, do we dream he was?
A priest too—never were such naughtiness!
Still, he thinks many a long think, never fear,
After the shy pale lady,—lay so light

For a moment in his arms, the lucky one!" 910
And so on: wherefore should I blame you much?
So we are made, such difference in minds,
Such difference too in eyes that see the minds!
That man, you misinterpret and misprise—
The glory of his nature, I had thought,
Shot itself out in white light, blazed the truth
Through every atom of his act with me:
Yet where I point you, through the crystal shrine,
Purity in quintessence, one dew-drop,
You all descry a spider in the midst. 920
One says, "The head of it is plain to see,"
And one, "They are the feet by which I judge,"
All say, "Those films were spun by nothing else."

Then, I must lay my babe away with God,
Nor think of him again for gratitude.
Yes, my last breath shall wholly spend itself
In one attempt more to disperse the stain,
The mist from other breath fond mouths have made,
About a lustrous and pellucid soul:
So that, when I am gone but sorrow stays, 930
And people need assurance in their doubt
If God yet have a servant, man a friend,
The weak a savior, and the vile a foe,—
Let him be present, by the name invoked,
Giuseppe-Maria Caponsacchi!

There,
Strength comes already with the utterance!
I will remember once more for his sake
The sorrow: for he lives and is belied.
Could he be here, how he would speak for me!

I had been miserable three drear years 940
In that dread palace and lay passive now,
When I first learned there could be such a man.
Thus it fell: I was at a public play,
In the last days of Carnival last March,
Brought there I knew not why, but now know well.
My husband put me where I sat, in front;
Then crouched down, breathed cold through me from behind,
Stationed i' the shadow,—none in front could see,—
I, it was, faced the stranger-throng beneath,
The crowd with upturned faces, eyes one stare, 950
Voices one buzz. I looked but to the stage,
Whereon two lovers sang and interchanged

"True life is only love, love only bliss:
I love thee—thee I love!" then they embraced.
I looked thence to the ceiling and the walls,—
Over the crowd, those voices and those eyes,—
My thoughts went through the roof and out, to Rome
On wings of music, waft of measured words,—
Set me down there, a happy child again,
Sure that to-morrow would be festa-day,   960
Hearing my parents praise past festas more,
And seeing they were old if I was young,
Yet wondering why they still would end discourse
With "We must soon go, you abide your time,
And,—might we haply see the proper friend
Throw his arm over you and make you safe!"

Sudden I saw him; into my lap there fell
A foolish twist of comfits, broke my dream
And brought me from the air and laid me low,
As ruined as the soaring bee that 's reached   970
(So Pietro told me at the Villa once)
By the dust-handful. There the comfits lay:
I looked to see who flung them, and I faced
This Caponsacchi, looking up in turn.
Ere I could reason out why, I felt sure,
Whoever flung them, his was not the hand,—
Up rose the round face and good-natured grin
Of one who, in effect, had played the prank,
From covert close beside the earnest face,—
Fat waggish Conti, friend of all the world.   980
He was my husband's cousin, privileged
To throw the thing: the other, silent, grave,
Solemn almost, saw me, as I saw him.

There is a psalm Don Celestine recites,
"Had I a dove's wings, how I fain would flee!"
The psalm runs not "I hope, I pray for wings,"—
Not "If wings fall from heaven, I fix them fast,"—
Simply "How good it were to fly and rest,
Have hope now, and one day expect content!
How well to do what I shall never do!"   990
So I said, "Had there been a man like that,
To lift me with his strength out of all strife
Into the calm, how I could fly and rest!
I have a keeper in the garden here
Whose sole employment is to strike me low
If ever I, for solace, seek the sun.
Life means with me successful feigning death,

Lying stone-like, eluding notice so,
Foregoing here the turf and there the sky.
Suppose that man had been instead of this!"   1000

Presently Conti laughed into my ear,
—Had tripped up to the raised place where I sat—
"Cousin, I flung them brutishly and hard!
Because you must be hurt, to look austere
As Caponsacchi yonder, my tall friend
A-gazing now. Ah, Guido, you so close?
Keep on your knees, do! Beg her to forgive!
My cornet battered like a cannon-ball.
Good-bye, I 'm gone!"—nor waited the reply.

That night at supper, out my husband broke,   1010
"Why was that throwing, that buffoonery?
Do you think I am your dupe? What man would dare
Throw comfits in a stranger lady's lap?
'T was knowledge of you bred such insolence
In Caponsacchi; he dared shoot the bolt,
Using that Conti for his stalking-horse.
How could you see him this once and no more,
When he is always haunting hereabout
At the street-corner or the palace-side,
Publishing my shame and your impudence?   1020
You are a wanton,—I a dupe, you think?
O Christ, what hinders that I kill her quick?"
Whereat he drew his sword and feigned a thrust.

All this, now,—being not so strange to me,
Used to such misconception day by day
And broken-in to bear,—I bore, this time,
More quietly than woman should perhaps;
Repeated the mere truth and held my tongue.

Then he said, "Since you play the ignorant,
I shall instruct you. This amour,—commenced   1030
Or finished or midway in act, all 's one,—
'T is the town-talk; so my revenge shall be.
Does he presume because he is a priest?
I warn him that the sword I wear shall pink
His lily-scented cassock through and through,
Next time I catch him underneath your eaves!"
But he had threatened with the sword so oft
And, after all, not kept his promise. All
I said was, "Let God save the innocent!
Moreover, death is far from a bad fate.   1040
I shall go pray for you and me, not him;.

And then I look to sleep, come death or, worse,
Life." So, I slept.

There may have elapsed a week,
When Margherita,—called my waiting-maid,
Whom it is said my husband found too fair—
Who stood and heard the charge and the reply,
Who never once would let the matter rest
From that night forward, but rang changes still
On this the thrust and that the shame, and how
Good cause for jealousy cures jealous fools,   1050
And what a paragon was this same priest
She talked about until I stopped my ears,—
She said, "A week is gone; you comb your hair,
Then go mope in a corner, cheek on palm,
Till night comes round again,—so, waste a week
As if your husband menaced you in sport.
Have not I some acquaintance with his tricks?
Oh no, he did not stab the serving-man
Who made and sang the rhymes about me once!
For why? They sent him to the wars next day.   1060
Nor poisoned he the foreigner, my friend,
Who wagered on the whiteness of my breast,—
The swarth skins of our city in dispute:
For, though he paid me proper compliment,
The Count well knew he was besotted with
Somebody else, a skin as black as ink,
(As all the town knew save my foreigner)—
He found and wedded presently,—'Why need
Better revenge?'—the Count asked. But what 's here?
A priest that does not fight, and cannot wed,   1070
Yet must be dealt with! If the Count took fire
For the poor pastime of a minute,—me—
What were the conflagration for yourself,
Countess and lady-wife and all the rest?
The priest will perish; you will grieve too late:
So shall the city-ladies' handsomest
Frankest and liberalest gentleman
Die for you, to appease a scurvy dog
Hanging 's too good for. Is there no escape?
Were it not simple Christian charity   1080
To warn the priest be on his guard,—save him
Assured death, save yourself from causing it?
I meet him in the street. Give me a glove,
A ring to show for token! Mum 's the word!"

I answered, "If you were, as styled, my maid,
I would command you: as you are, you say,

My husband's intimate,—assist his wife
Who can do nothing but entreat 'Be still!'
Even if you speak truth and a crime is planned,
Leave help to God as I am forced to do!   1090
There is no other help or we should craze,
Seeing such evil with no human cure.
Reflect that God, who makes the storm desist,
Can make an angry violent heart subside.
Why should we venture teach Him governance?
Never address me on this subject more!"

Next night she said, "But I went, all the same,
—Ay, saw your Caponsacchi in his house,
And come back stuffed with news I must outpour.
I told him, 'Sir, my mistress is a stone: 1100
Why should you harm her for no good you get?
For you do harm her—prowl about our place
With the Count never distant half the street,
Lurking at every corner, would you look!
'T is certain she has witched you with a spell.
Are there not other beauties at your beck?
We all know, Donna This and Monna That
Die for a glance of yours, yet here you gaze!
Go make them grateful, leave the stone its cold!'
And he—oh, he turned first white and then red,   1110
And then—'To her behest I bow myself,
Whom I love with my body and my soul:
Only a word i' the bowing! See, I write
One little word, no harm to see or hear!
Then, fear no further!' This is what he wrote.
I know you cannot read,—therefore, let me!
'My idol!' " . . .

                    But I took it from her hand
And tore it into shreds. "Why, join the rest
Who harm me? Have I ever done you wrong?
People have told me 't is you wrong myself: 1120
Let it suffice I either feel no wrong
Or else forgive it,—yet you turn my foe!
The others hunt me and you throw a noose!"

She muttered, "Have your wilful way!" I slept.

Whereupon . . . no, I leave my husband out!
It is not to do him more hurt, I speak.
Let it suffice, when misery was most,
One day, I swooned and got a respite so.
She stooped as I was slowly coming to,

This Margherita, ever on my trace,   1130
And whispered—"Caponsacchi!"

                If I drowned,
But woke afloat i' the wave with upturned eyes,
And found their first sight was a star! I turned—
For the first time, I let her have her will,
Heard passively,—"The imposthume at such head,
One touch, one lancet-puncture would relieve,—
And still no glance the good physician's way
Who rids you of the torment in a trice!
Still he writes letters you refuse to hear.
He may prevent your husband, kill himself,   1140
So desperate and all fordone is he!
Just hear the pretty verse he made to-day!
A sonnet from Mirtillo. '*Peerless fair. . . .*'
All poetry is difficult to read,
—The sense of it is, anyhow, he seeks
Leave to contrive you an escape from hell,
And for that purpose asks an interview.
I can write, I can grant it in your name,
Or, what is better, lead you to his house.
Your husband dashes you against the stones;   1150
This man would place each fragment in a shrine:
You hate him, love your husband!"
                    I returned,
"It is not true I love my husband,—no,
Nor hate this man. I listen while you speak,
—Assured that what you say is false, the same:
Much as when once, to me a little child,
A rough gaunt man in rags, with eyes on fire,
A crowd of boys and idlers at his heels,
Rushed as I crossed the Square, and held my head
In his two hands, 'Here 's she will let me speak!   1160
You little girl, whose eyes do good to mine,
I am the Pope, am Sextus, now the Sixth;
And that Twelfth Innocent, proclaimed to-day,
Is Lucifer disguised in human flesh!
The angels, met in conclave, crowned me!'—thus
He gibbered and I listened; but I knew
All was delusion, ere folk interposed,
'Unfasten him, the maniac!' Thus I know
All your report of Caponsacchi false,
Folly or dreaming; I have seen so much   1170
By that adventure at the spectacle,
The face I fronted that one first, last time:
He would belie it by such words and thoughts.

Therefore while you profess to show him me,
I ever see his own face. Get you gone!"

"—That will I, nor once open mouth again,—
No, by Saint Joseph and the Holy Ghost!
On your head be the damage, so adieu!"

And so more days, more deeds I must forget,
Till . . . what a strange thing now is to declare!   1180
Since I say anything, say all if true!
And how my life seems lengthened as to serve!
It may be idle or inopportune,
But, true?—why, what was all I said but truth,
Even when I found that such as are untrue
Could only take the truth in through a lie?
Now—I am speaking truth to the Truth's self:
God will lend credit to my words this time.

It had got half through April. I arose
One vivid daybreak,—who had gone to bed   1190
In the old way my wont those last three years,
Careless until, the cup drained, I should die.
The last sound in my ear, the over-night,
Had been a something let drop on the sly
In prattle by Margherita, "Soon enough
Gayeties end, now Easter 's past: a week,
And the Archbishop gets him back to Rome,—
Every one leaves the town for Rome, this Spring,—
Even Caponsacchi, out of heart and hope,
Resigns himself and follows with the flock."   1200
I heard this drop and drop like rain outside
Fast-falling through the darkness while she spoke:
So had I heard with like indifference,
"And Michael's pair of wings will arrive first
At Rome, to introduce the company,
And bear him from our picture where he fights
Satan,—expect to have that dragon loose
And never a defender!"—my sole thought
Being still, as night came, "Done, another day!
How good to sleep and so get nearer death!"—   1210
When, what, first thing at daybreak, pierced the sleep
With a summons to me? Up I sprang alive,
Light in me, light without me, everywhere
Change! A broad yellow sunbeam was let fall
From heaven to earth,—a sudden drawbridge lay,
Along which marched a myriad merry motes,
Mocking the flies that crossed them and recrossed
In rival dance, companions new-born too.

On the house-eaves, a dripping shag of weed
Shook diamonds on each dull gray lattice-square,   1220
As first one, then another bird leapt by,
And light was off, and lo was back again,
Always with one voice,—where are two such joys?—
The blessed building-sparrow! I stepped forth,
Stood on the terrace,—o'er the roofs, such sky!
My heart sang, "I too am to go away,
I too have something I must care about,
Carry away with me to Rome, to Rome!
The bird brings hither sticks and hairs and wool,
And nowhere else i' the world; what fly breaks rank,   1230
Falls out of the procession that befits,
From window here to window there, with all
The world to choose,—so well he knows his course?
I have my purpose and my motive too,
My march to Rome, like any bird or fly!
Had I been dead! How right to be alive!
Last night I almost prayed for leave to die,
Wished Guido all his pleasure with the sword
Or the poison,—poison, sword, was but a trick,
Harmless, may God forgive him the poor jest!   1240
My life is charmed, will last till I reach Rome!
Yesterday, but for the sin,—ah, nameless be
The deed I could have dared against myself!
Now—see if I will touch an unripe fruit,
And risk the health I want to have and use!
Not to live, now, would be the wickedness,—
For life means to make haste and go to Rome
And leave Arezzo, leave all woes at once!"

Now, understand here, by no means mistake!
Long ago had I tried to leave that house   1250
When it seemed such procedure would stop sin;
And still failed more the more I tried—at first
The Archbishop, as I told you,—next, our lord
The Governor,—indeed I found my way,
I went to the great palace where he rules,
Though I knew well 't was he who,—when I gave
A jewel or two, themselves had given me,
Back to my parents,—since they wanted bread,
They who had never let me want a nosegay,—he
Spoke of the jail for felons, if they kept   1260
What was first theirs, then mine, so doubly theirs,
Though all the while my husband's most of all!
I knew well who had spoke the word wrought this:
Yet, being in extremity, I fled

To the Governor, as I say,—scarce opened lip
When—the cold cruel snicker close behind—
Guido was on my trace, already there,
Exchanging nod and wink for shrug and smile,
And I—pushed back to him and, for my pains,
Paid with . . . but why remember what is past? 1270
I sought out a poor friar the people call
The Roman, and confessed my sin which came
Of their sin,—that fact could not be repressed,—
The frightfulness of my despair in God:
And feeling, through the grate, his horror shake,
Implored him, "Write for me who cannot write,
Apprise my parents, make them rescue me!
You bid me be courageous and trust God:
Do you in turn dare somewhat, trust and write,
'Dear friends, who used to be my parents once, 1280
And now declare you have no part in me,
This is some riddle I want wit to solve,
Since you must love me with no difference.
Even suppose you altered,—there's your hate,
To ask for: hate of you two dearest ones
I shall find liker love than love found here,
If husbands love their wives. Take me away
And hate me as you do the gnats and fleas,
Even the scorpions! How I shall rejoice!'
Write that and save me!" And he promised—wrote 1290
Or did not write; things never changed at all:
He was not like the Augustinian here!
Last, in a desperation I appealed
To friends, whoever wished me better days,
To Guillichini, that's of kin,—"What, I—
Travel to Rome with you? A flying gout
Bids me deny my heart and mind my leg!"
Then I tried Conti, used to brave—laugh back
The louring thunder when his cousin scowled
At me protected by his presence: "You— 1300
Who well know what you cannot save me from,—
Carry me off! What frightens you, a priest?"
He shook his head, looked grave—"Above my strength!
Guido has claws that scratch, shows feline teeth;
A formidabler foe than I dare fret:
Give me a dog to deal with, twice the size!
Of course I am a priest and Canon too,
But . . . by the bye . . . though both, not quite so bold
As he, my fellow-Canon, brother-priest,
The personage in such ill odor here 1310
Because of the reports—pure birth o' the brain!

Our Caponsacchi, he's your true Saint George
To slay the monster, set the Princess free,
And have the whole High-Altar to himself:
I always think so when I see that piece
I' the Pieve, that's his church and mine, you know:
Though you drop eyes at mention of his name!"
That name had got to take a half-grotesque
Half-ominous, wholly enigmatic sense,
Like any by-word, broken bit of song   1320
Born with a meaning, changed by mouth and mouth
That mix it in a sneer or smile, as chance
Bids, till it now means nought but ugliness
And perhaps shame.

      —All this intends to say,
That, over-night, the notion of escape
Had seemed distemper, dreaming; and the name,—
Not the man, but the name of him, thus made
Into a mockery and disgrace,—why, she
Who uttered it persistently, had laughed,
"I name his name, and there you start and wince   1330
As criminal from the red tongs' touch!"—yet now,
Now, as I stood letting morn bathe me bright,
Choosing which butterfly should bear my news,—
The white, the brown one, or that tinier blue,—
The Margherita, I detested so,
In she came—"The fine day, the good Spring time!
What, up and out at window? That is best.
No thought of Caponsacchi?—who stood there
All night on one leg, like the sentry crane,
Under the pelting of your water-spout—   1340
Looked last look at your lattice ere he leave
Our city, bury his dead hope at Rome.
Ay, go to looking-glass and make you fine,
While he may die ere touch one least loose hair
You drag at with the comb in such a rage!"

I turned—"Tell Caponsacchi he may come!"

"Tell him to come? Ah, but, for charity,
A truce to fooling! Come? What,—come this eve?
Peter and Paul! But I see through the trick!
Yes, come, and take a flower-pot on his head,   1350
Flung from your terrace! No joke, sincere truth?"

How plainly I perceived hell flash and fade
O' the face of her,—the doubt that first paled joy,
Then, final reassurance I indeed
Was caught now, never to be free again!

What did I care?—who felt myself of force
To play with silk, and spurn the horsehair-springe.
"But—do you know that I have bade him come,
And in your own name? I presumed so much,
Knowing the thing you needed in your heart.   1360
But somehow—what had I to show in proof?
He would not come: half-promised, that was all,
And wrote the letters you refused to read.
What is the message that shall move him now?"

"After the Ave Maria, at first dark,
I will be standing on the terrace, say!"
"I would I had a good long lock of hair
Should prove I was not lying! Never mind!"

Off she went—"May he not refuse, that's all—
Fearing a trick!"

        I answered, "He will come."   1370
And, all day, I sent prayer like incense up
To God the strong, God the beneficent,
God ever mindful in all strife and strait,
Who, for our own good, makes the need extreme,
Till at the last He puts forth might and saves.
An old rhyme came into my head and rang
Of how a virgin, for the faith of God,
Hid herself, from the Paynims that pursued,
In a cave's heart; until a thunderstone,
Wrapped in a flame, revealed the couch and prey: 1380
And they laughed—"Thanks to lightning, ours at last!"
And she cried, "Wrath of God, assert His love!
Servant of God, thou fire, befriend His child!"
And lo, the fire she grasped at, fixed its flash,
Lay in her hand a calm cold dreadful sword
She brandished till pursuers strewed the ground.
So did the souls within them die away,
As o'er the prostrate bodies, sworded, safe,
She walked forth to the solitudes and Christ:
So should I grasp the lightning and be saved!   1390

And still, as the day wore, the trouble grew
Whereby I guessed there would be born a star,
Until at an intense throe of the dusk,
I started up, was pushed, I dare to say,
Out on the terrace, leaned and looked at last
Where the deliverer waited me: the same
Silent and solemn face, I first descried
At the spectacle, confronted mine once more.
So was that minute twice vouchsafed me, so

The manhood, wasted then, was still at watch   1400
To save me yet a second time: no change
Here, though all else changed in the changing world!

I spoke on the instant, as my duty bade,
In some such sense as this, whatever the phrase.
"Friend, foolish words were borne from you to me;
Your soul behind them is the pure strong wind,
Not dust and feathers which its breath may bear:
These to the witless seem the wind itself,
Since proving thus the first of it they feel.
If by mischance you blew offence my way,   1410
The straws are dropt, the wind desists no whit,
And how such strays were caught up in the street
And took a motion from you, why inquire?
I speak to the strong soul, no weak disguise.
If it be truth,—why should I doubt it truth?—
You serve God specially, as priests are bound,
And care about me, stranger as I am,
So far as wish my good.—that miracle
I take to intimate He wills you serve
By saving me,—what else can He direct?   1420
Here is the service. Since a long while now,
I am in course of being put to death:
While death concerned nothing but me, I bowed
The head and bade, in heart, my husband strike.
Now I imperil something more, it seems,
Something that 's trulier me than this myself,
Something I trust in God and you to save.
You go to Rome, they tell me: take me there,
Put me back with my people!"

                  He replied—
The first word I heard ever from his lips,   1430
All himself in it,—an eternity
Of speech, to match the immeasurable depth
O' the soul that then broke silence—"I am yours."

So did the star rise, soon to lead my step,
Lead on, nor pause before it should stand still
Above the House o' the Babe,—my babe to be,
That knew me first and thus made me know him,
That had his right of life and claim on mine,
And would not let me die till he was born,
But pricked me at the heart to save us both,   1440
Saying, "Have you the will? Leave God the way!"
And the way was Caponsacchi—"mine," thank God!
He was mine, he is mine, he will be mine.

No pause i' the leading and the light! I know.
Next night there was a cloud came, and not he:
But I prayed through the darkness till it broke
And let him shine. The second night, he came.

"The plan is rash; the project desperate:
In such a flight needs must I risk your life,
Give food for falsehood, folly or mistake,   1450
Ground for your husband's rancor and revenge"—
So he began again, with the same face.
I felt that, the same loyalty—one star
Turning now red that was so white before—
One service apprehended newly: just
A word of mine and there the white was back!

"No, friend, for you will take me! 'T is yourself
Risk all, not I,—who let you, for I trust
In the compensating great God: enough!
I know you: when is it that you will come?"   1460

"To-morrow at the day's dawn." Then I heard
What I should do: how to prepare for flight
And where to fly.

                    That night my husband bade,
"—You, whom I loathe, beware you break my sleep
This whole night! Couch beside me like the corpse
I would you were!" The rest you know, I think—
How I found Caponsacchi and escaped.

And this man, men call sinner? Jesus Christ!
Of whom men said, with mouths Thyself mad'st once,
"He hath a devil"—say he was Thy saint,   1470
My Caponsacchi! Shield and show—unshroud
In Thine own time the glory of the soul
If aught obscure,—if ink-spot, from vile pens
Scribbling a charge against him—(I was glad
Then, for the first time, that I could not write)—
Flirted his way, have flecked the blaze!

                                    For me,
'T is otherwise: let men take, sift my thoughts
—Thoughts I throw like the flax for sun to bleach!
I did pray, do pray, in the prayer shall die,
"Oh, to have Caponsacchi for my guide!"   1480
Ever the face upturned to mine, the hand
Holding my hand across the world,—a sense
That reads, as only such can read, the mark
God sets on woman, signifying so
She should—shall peradventure—be divine;

Yet 'ware, the while, how weakness mars the print
And makes confusion, leaves the thing men see,
—Not this man sees,—who from his soul, re-writes
The obliterated charter,—love and strength
Mending what 's marred. "So kneels a votarist,   1490
Weeds some poor waste traditionary plot
Where shrine once was, where temple yet may be,
Purging the place but worshipping the while,
By faith and not by sight, sight clearest so,—
Such way the saints work,"—says Don Celestine.
But I, not privileged to see a saint
Of old when such walked earth with crown and palm,
If I call "saint" what saints call something else—
The saints must bear with me, impute the fault
To a soul i' the bud, so starved by ignorance,   1500
Stinted of warmth, it will not blow this year
Nor recognize the orb which Spring-flowers know.
But if meanwhile some insect with a heart
Worth floods of lazy music, spendthrift joy—
Some fire-fly renounced Spring for my dwarfed cup,
Crept close to me, brought lustre for the dark,
Comfort against the cold,—what though excess
Of comfort should miscall the creature—sun?
What did the sun to hinder while harsh hands
Petal by petal, crude and colorless,   1510
Tore me? This one heart gave me all the Spring!

Is all told? There 's the journey: and where 's time
To tell you how that heart burst out in shine?
Yet certain points do press on me too hard.
Each place must have a name, though I forget:
How strange it was—there where the plain begins
And the small river mitigates its flow—
When eve was fading fast, and my soul sank,
And he divined what surge of bitterness,
In overtaking me, would float me back   1520
Whence I was carried by the striding day—
So,—"This gray place was famous once," said he—
And he began that legend of the place
As if in answer to the unspoken fear,
And told me all about a brave man dead,
Which lifted me and let my soul go on!
How did he know too—at that town's approach
By the rock-side—that in coming near the signs
Of life, the house-roofs and the church and tower,
I saw the old boundary and wall o' the world   1530
Rise plain as ever round me, hard and cold,

As if the broken circlet joined again,
Tightened itself about me with no break,—
As if the town would turn Arezzo's self,—
The husband there,—the friends my enemies,
All ranged against me, not an avenue
To try, but would be blocked and drive me back
On him,—this other, . . . oh the heart in that!
Did not he find, bring, put into my arms
A new-born babe?—and I saw faces beam   1540
Of the young mother proud to teach me joy,
And gossips round expecting my surprise
At the sudden hole through earth that lets in heaven.
I could believe himself by his strong will
Had woven around me what I thought the world
We went along in, every circumstance,
Towns, flowers and faces, all things helped so well!
For, through the journey, was it natural
Such comfort should arise from first to last?
As I look back, all is one milky way;   1550
Still bettered more, the more remembered, so
Do new stars bud while I but search for old,
And fill all gaps i' the glory, and grow him—
Him I now see make the shine everywhere.
Even at the last when the bewildered flesh,
The cloud of weariness about my soul
Clogging too heavily, sucked down all sense,—
Still its last voice was, "He will watch and care;
Let the strength go, I am content: he stays!"
I doubt not he did stay and care for all—   1560
From that sick minute when the head swam round,
And the eyes looked their last and died on him,
As in his arms he caught me, and, you say,
Carried me in, that tragical red eve,
And laid me where I next returned to life
In the other red of morning, two red plates
That crushed together, crushed the time between,
And are since then a solid fire to me,—
When in, my dreadful husband and the world
Broke,—and I saw him, master, by hell's right,   1570
And saw my angel helplessly held back
By guards that helped the malice—the lamb prone,
The serpent towering and triumphant—then
Came all the strength back in a sudden swell,
I did for once see right, do right, give tongue
The adequate protest: for a worm must turn
If it would have its wrong observed by God.
I did spring up, attempt to thrust aside

That ice-block 'twixt the sun and me, lay low
The neutralizer of all good and truth. 1580
If I sinned so,—never obey voice more
O' the Just and Terrible, who bids us—"Bear!"
Not—"Stand by, bear to see my angels bear!"
I am clear it was on impulse to serve God
Not save myself,—no—nor my child unborn!
Had I else waited patiently till now?—
Who saw my old kind parents, silly-sooth
And too much trustful, for their worst of faults,
Cheated, browbeaten, stripped and starved, cast out
Into the kennel: I remonstrated, 1590
Then sank to silence, for,—their woes at end,
Themselves gone,—only I was left to plague.
If only I was threatened and belied,
What matter? I could bear it and did bear;
It was a comfort, still one lot for all:
They were not persecuted for my sake
And I, estranged, the single happy one.
But when at last, all by myself I stood
Obeying the clear voice which bade me rise,
Not for my own sake but my babe unborn, 1600
And take the angel's hand was sent to help—
And found the old adversary athwart the path—
Not my hand simply struck from the angel's, but
The very angel's self made foul i' the face
By the fiend who struck there,—that I would not bear,
That only I resisted! So, my first
And last resistance was invincible.
Prayers move God; threats, and nothing else, move men!
I must have prayed a man as he were God
When I implored the Governor to right 1610
My parents' wrongs: the answer was a smile.
The Archbishop,—did I clasp his feet enough,
Hide my face hotly on them, while I told
More than I dared make my own mother know?
The profit was—compassion and a jest.
This time, the foolish prayers were done with, right
Used might, and solemnized the sport at once.
All was against the combat: vantage, mine?
The runaway avowed, the accomplice-wife,
In company with the plan-contriving priest? 1620
Yet, shame thus rank and patent, I struck, bare,
At foe from head to foot in magic mail,
And off it withered, cobweb-armory
Against the lightning! 'T was truth singed the lies
And saved me, not the vain sword nor weak speech!

You see, I will not have the service fail!
I say, the angel saved me: I am safe!
Others may want and wish, I wish nor want
One point o' the circle plainer, where I stand
Traced round about with white to front the world.   1630
What of the calumny I came across,
What o' the way to the end?—the end crowns all.
The judges judged aright i' the main, gave me
The uttermost of my heart's desire, a truce
From torture and Arezzo, balm for hurt,
With the quiet nuns,—God recompense the good!
Who said and sang away the ugly past.
And, when my final fortune was revealed,
What safety, while, amid my parents' arms,
My babe was given me! Yes, he saved my babe: 1640
It would not have peeped forth, the bird-like thing,
Through that Arezzo noise and trouble: back
Had it returned nor ever let me see!
But the sweet peace cured all, and let me live
And give my bird the life among the leaves
God meant him! Weeks and months of quietude,
I could lie in such peace and learn so much—
Begin the task, I see how needful now,
Of understanding somewhat of my past,—
Know life a little, I should leave so soon.   1650
Therefore, because this man restored my soul,
All has been right; I have gained my gain, enjoyed
As well as suffered,—nay, got foretaste too
Of better life beginning where this ends—
All through the breathing-while allowed me thus,
Which let good premonitions reach my soul
Unthwarted, and benignant influence flow
And interpenetrate and change my heart,
Uncrossed by what was wicked,—nay, unkind.
For, as the weakness of my time drew nigh,   1660
Nobody did me one disservice more,
Spoke coldly or looked strangely, broke the love
I lay in the arms of, till my boy was born,
Born all in love, with nought to spoil the bliss
A whole long fortnight: in a life like mine
A fortnight filled with bliss is long and much.
All women are not mothers of a boy,
Though they live twice the length of my whole life,
And, as they fancy, happily all the same.
There I lay, then, all my great fortnight long,   1670
As if it would continue, broaden out
Happily more and more, and lead to heaven:

Christmas before me,—was not that a chance?
I never realized God's birth before—
How He grew likest God in being born.
This time I felt like Mary, had my babe
Lying a little on my breast like hers.
So all went on till, just four days ago—
The night and the tap.

          O it shall be success
To the whole of our poor family! My friends   1680
. . . Nay, father and mother,—give me back my word!
They have been rudely stripped of life, disgraced
Like children who must needs go clothed too fine,
Carry the garb of Carnival in Lent.
If they too much affected frippery,
They have been punished and submit themselves,
Say no word: all is over, they see God
Who will not be extreme to mark their fault
Or He had granted respite: they are safe.

For that most woeful man my husband once,   1690
Who, needing respite, still draws vital breath,
I—pardon him? So far as lies in me,
I give him for his good the life he takes,
Praying the world will therefore acquiesce.
Let him make God amends,—none, none to me
Who thank him rather that, whereas strange fate
Mockingly styled him husband and me wife,
Himself this way at least pronounced divorce,
Blotted the marriage-bond: this blood of mine
Flies forth exultingly at any door,   1700
Washes the parchment white, and thanks the blow.
We shall not meet in this world nor the next,
But where will God be absent? In His face
Is light, but in His shadow healing too:
Let Guido touch the shadow and be healed!
And as my presence was importunate,—
My earthly good, temptation and a snare,—
Nothing about me but drew somehow down
His hate upon me,—somewhat so excused
Therefore, since hate was thus the truth of him,—   1710
May my evanishment forevermore
Help further to relieve the heart that cast
Such object of its natural loathing forth!
So he was made; he nowise made himself:
I could not love him, but his mother did.
His soul has never lain beside my soul;
But for the unresisting body,—thanks!

He burned that garment spotted by the flesh.
Whatever he touched is rightly ruined: plague
It caught, and disinfection it had craved   1720
Still but for Guido; I am saved through him
So as by fire; to him—thanks and farewell!

Even for my babe, my boy, there 's safety thence—
From the sudden death of me, I mean: we poor
Weak souls, how we endeavor to be strong!
I was already using up my life,—
This portion, now, should do him such a good,
This other go to keep off such an ill!
The great life; see, a breath and it is gone!
So is detached, so left all by itself   1730
The little life, the fact which means so much.
Shall not God stoop the kindlier to His work,
His marvel of creation, foot would crush,
Now that the hand He trusted to receive
And hold it, lets the treasure fall perforce?
The better; He shall have in orphanage
His own way all the clearlier: if my babe
Outlived the hour—and he has lived two weeks—
It is through God who knows I am not by.
Who is it makes the soft gold hair turn black,   1740
And sets the tongue, might lie so long at rest,
Trying to talk? Let us leave God alone!
Why should I doubt He will explain in time
What I feel now, but fail to find the words?
My babe nor was, nor is, nor yet shall be
Count Guido Franceschini's child at all—
Only his mother's, born of love not hate!
So shall I have my rights in after-time.
It seems absurd, impossible to-day;
So seems so much else, not explained but known!   1750

Ah! Friends, I thank and bless you every one!
No more now: I withdraw from earth and man
To my own soul, compose myself for God.

Well, and there is more! Yes, my end of breath
Shall bear away my soul in being true!
He is still here, not outside with the world,
Here, here, I have him in his rightful place!
'T is now, when I am most upon the move,
I feel for what I verily find—again
The face, again the eyes, again, through all,   1760
The heart and its immeasurable love
Of my one friend, my only, all my own,

Who put his breast between the spears and me.
Ever with Caponsacchi! Otherwise
Here alone would be failure, loss to me—
How much more loss to him, with life debarred
From giving life, love locked from love's display,
The day-star stopped its task that makes night morn!
O lover of my life, O soldier-saint,
No work begun shall ever pause for death!   1770
Love will be helpful to me more and more
I' the coming course, the new path I must tread—
My weak hand in thy strong hand, strong for that!
Tell him that if I seem without him now,
That 's the world's insight! Oh, he understands!
He is at Civita—do I once doubt
The world again is holding us apart?
He had been here, displayed in my behalf
The broad brow that reverberates the truth,
And flashed the word God gave him, back to man!   1780
I know where the free soul is flown! My fate
Will have been hard for even him to bear:
Let it confirm him in the trust of God,
Showing how holily he dared the deed!
And, for the rest,—say, from the deed, no touch
Of harm came, but all good, all happiness,
Not one faint fleck of failure! Why explain?
What I see, oh, he sees and how much more!
Tell him,—I know not wherefore the true word
Should fade and fall unuttered at the last—   1790
It was the name of him I sprang to meet
When came the knock, the summons and the end.
"My great heart, my strong hand are back again!"
I would have sprung to these, beckoning across
Murder and hell gigantic and distinct
O' the threshold, posted to exclude me heaven:
He is ordained to call and I to come!
Do not the dead wear flowers when dressed for God?
Say,—I am all in flowers from head to foot!
Say,—not one flower of all he said and did,   1800
Might seem to flit unnoticed, fade unknown,
But dropped a seed, has grown a balsam-tree
Whereof the blossoming perfumes the place
At this supreme of moments! He is a priest;
He cannot marry therefore, which is right:
I think he would not marry if he could.
Marriage on earth seems such a counterfeit,
Mere imitation of the inimitable:
In heaven we have the real and true and sure.

'T is there they neither marry nor are given   1810
In marriage but are as the angels: right,
Oh how right that is, how like Jesus Christ
To say that! Marriage-making for the earth,
With gold so much,—birth, power, repute so much,
Or beauty, youth so much, in lack of these!
Be as the angels rather, who, apart,
Know themselves into one, are found at length
Married, but marry never, no, nor give
In marriage; they are man and wife at once
When the true time is: here we have to wait   1820
Not so long neither! Could we by a wish
Have what we will and get the future now,
Would we wish aught done undone in the past?
So, let him wait God's instant men call years;
Meantime hold hard by truth and his great soul,
Do out the duty! Through such souls alone
God stooping shows sufficient of His light
For us i' the dark to rise by. And I rise.

X

THE POPE

Like to Ahasuerus, that shrewd prince,
I will begin,—as is, these seven years now,
My daily wont,—and read a History
(Written by one whose deft right hand was dust
To the last digit, ages ere my birth)
Of all my predecessors, Popes of Rome:
For though mine ancient early dropped the pen,
Yet others picked it up and wrote it dry,
Since of the making books there is no end.
And so I have the Papacy complete   10
From Peter first to Alexander last;
Can question each and take instruction so.
Have I to dare?—I ask, how dared this Pope?
To suffer? Such-an-one, how suffered he?
Being about to judge, as now, I seek
How judged once, well or ill, some other Pope;
Study some signal judgment that subsists
To blaze on, or else blot, the page which seals
The sum up of what gain or loss to God
Came of His one more Vicar in the world.   20
So, do I find example, rule of life;

So, square and set in order the next page,
Shall be stretched smooth o'er my own funeral cyst.

Eight hundred years exact before the year
I was made Pope, men made Formosus Pope,
Say Sigebert and other chroniclers.
Ere I confirm or quash the Trial here
Of Guido Franceschini and his friends,
Read,—How there was a ghastly Trial once
Of a dead man by a live man, and both, Popes: 30
Thus—in the antique penman's very phrase.

"Then Stephen, Pope and seventh of the name,
Cried out, in synod as he sat in state,
While choler quivered on his brow and beard,
'Come into court, Formosus, thou lost wretch,
That claimedst to be late Pope as even I!'

"And at the word, the great door of the church
Flew wide, and in they brought Formosus' self,
The body of him, dead, even as embalmed
And buried duly in the Vatican   40
Eight months before, exhumed thus for the nonce.
They set it, that dead body of a Pope,
Clothed in pontific vesture now again,
Upright on Peter's chair as if alive.

"And Stephen, springing up, cried furiously,
'Bishop of Porto, wherefore didst presume
To leave that see and take this Roman see,
Exchange the lesser for the greater see,
—A thing against the canons of the Church?'

"Then one—(a Deacon who, observing forms,   50
Was placed by Stephen to repel the charge,
Be advocate and mouthpiece of the corpse)—
Spoke as he dared, set stammeringly forth
With white lips and dry tongue,—as but a youth,
For frightful was the corpse-face to behold,—
How nowise lacked there precedent for this.

"But when, for his last precedent of all,
Emboldened by the Spirit, out he blurts,
'And, Holy Father, didst not thou thyself
Vacate the lesser for the greater see,   60
Half a year since change Arago for Rome?'
'—Ye have the sin's defence now, synod mine!'
Shrieks Stephen in a beastly froth of rage:
'Judge now betwixt him dead and me alive!

Hath he intruded, or do I pretend?
Judge, judge!'—breaks wavelike one whole foam of wrath.

"Whereupon they, being friends and followers,
Said, 'Ay, thou art Christ's Vicar, and not he!
Away with what is frightful to behold!
This act was uncanonic and a fault.'   70

"Then, swallowed up in rage, Stephen exclaimed,
'So, guilty! So, remains I punish guilt!
He is unpoped, and all he did I damn:
The Bishop, that ordained him, I degrade:
Depose to laics those he raised to priests:
What they have wrought is mischief nor shall stand,
It is confusion, let it vex no more!
Since I revoke, annul and abrogate
All his decrees in all kinds: they are void!
In token whereof and warning to the world,   80
Strip me yon miscreant of those robes usurped,
And clothe him with vile serge befitting such!
Then hale the carrion to the market-place;
Let the town-hangman chop from his right hand
Those same three fingers which he blessed withal;
Next cut the head off, once was crowned forsooth:
And last go fling them, fingers, head and trunk,
To Tiber that my Christian fish may sup!'
—Either because of ΙΧΘΥΣ which means Fish
And very aptly symbolizes Christ,   90
Or else because the Pope is Fisherman,
And seals with Fisher's-signet.

                              "Anyway,
So said, so done: himself, to see it done,
Followed the corpse they trailed from street to street
Till into Tiber wave they threw the thing.
The people, crowded on the banks to see,
Were loud or mute, wept or laughed, cursed or jeered,
According as the deed addressed their sense;
A scandal verily: and out spake a Jew,
'Wot ye your Christ had vexed our Herod thus?'   100

"Now when, Formosus being dead a year,
His judge Pope Stephen tasted death in turn,
Made captive by the mob and strangled straight,
Romanus, his successor for a month,
Did make protest Formosus was with God,
Holy, just, true in thought and word and deed.
Next Theodore, who reigned but twenty days,
Therein convoked a synod, whose decree

Did reinstate, repope the late unpoped,
And do away with Stephen as accursed.   110
So that when presently certain fisher-folk
(As if the queasy river could not hold
Its swallowed Jonas, but discharged the meal)
Produced the timely product of their nets,
The mutilated man, Formosus,—saved
From putrefaction by the embalmer's spice,
Or, as some said, by sanctity of flesh,—
'Why, lay the body again,' bade Theodore,
'Among his predecessors, in the church
And burial-place of Peter!' which was done.   120
'And,' addeth Luitprand, 'many of repute,
Pious and still alive, avouch to me
That, as they bore the body up the aisle,
The saints in imaged row bowed each his head
For welcome to a brother-saint come back.'
As for Romanus and this Theodore,
These two Popes, through the brief reign granted each,
Could but initiate what John came to close
And give the final stamp to: he it was
Ninth of the name, (I follow the best guides)   130
Who,—in full synod at Ravenna held
With Bishops seventy-four, and present too
Eude King of France with his Archbishopry,—
Did condemn Stephen, anathematize
The disinterment, and make all blots blank.
'For,' argueth here Auxilius in a place
De Ordinationibus, 'precedents
Had been, no lack, before Formosus long,
Of Bishops so transferred from see to see,—
Marinus, for example:' read the tract.   140

"But, after John, came Sergius, reaffirmed
The right of Stephen, cursed Formosus, nay
Cast out, some say, his corpse a second time.
And here,—because the matter went to ground,
Fretted by new griefs, other cares of the age,—
Here is the last pronouncing of the Church,
Her sentence that subsists unto this day.
Yet constantly opinion hath prevailed
I' the Church, Formosus was a holy man."

Which of the judgments was infallible?   150
Which of my predecessors spoke for God?
And what availed Formosus that this cursed,
That blessed, and then this other cursed again?
"Fear ye not those whose power can kill the body

And not the soul," saith Christ, "but rather those
Can cast both soul and body into hell!"

John judged thus in Eight Hundred Ninety Eight,
Exact eight hundred years ago to-day
When, sitting in his stead, Vicegerent here,
I must give judgment on my own behoof.   160
So worked the predecessor: now, my turn!
In God's name! Once more on this earth of God's,
While twilight lasts and time wherein to work,
I take His staff with my uncertain hand,
And stay my six and fourscore years, my due
Labor and sorrow, on His judgment-seat,
And forthwith think, speak, act, in place of Him—
The Pope for Christ. Once more appeal is made
From man's assize to mine: I sit and see
Another poor weak trembling human wretch   170
Pushed by his fellows, who pretend the right,
Up to the gulf which, where I gaze, begins
From this world to the next,—gives way and way,
Just on the edge over the awful dark:
With nothing to arrest him but my feet.
He catches at me with convulsive face,
Cries "Leave to live the natural minute more!"
While hollowly the avengers echo "Leave?
None! So has he exceeded man's due share
In man's fit license, wrung by Adam's fall,   180
To sin and yet not surely die,—that we,
All of us sinful, all with need of grace,
All chary of our life,—the minute more
Or minute less of grace which saves a soul,—
Bound to make common cause with who craves time,
—We yet protest against the exorbitance
Of sin in this one sinner, and demand
That his poor sole remaining piece of time
Be plucked from out his clutch: put him to death!
Punish him now! As for the weal or woe   190
Hereafter, God grant mercy! Man be just,
Nor let the felon boast he went scot-free!"
And I am bound, the solitary judge,
To weigh the worth, decide upon the plea,
And either hold a hand out, or withdraw
A foot and let the wretch drift to the fall.
Ay, and while thus I dally, dare perchance
Put fancies for a comfort 'twixt this calm
And yonder passion that I have to bear,—
As if reprieve were possible for both   200

Prisoner and Pope,—how easy were reprieve!
A touch o' the hand-bell here, a hasty word
To those who wait, and wonder they wait long,
I' the passage there, and I should gain the life!—
Yea, though I flatter me with fancy thus,
I know it is but Nature's craven-trick.
The case is over, judgment at an end,
And all things done now and irrevocable:
A mere dead man is Franceschini here,
Even as Formosus centuries ago.   210
I have worn through this sombre wintry day,
With winter in my soul beyond the world's,
Over these dismalest of documents
Which drew night down on me ere eve befell,—
Pleadings and counter-pleadings, figure of fact
Beside fact's self, these summaries, to wit,—
How certain three were slain by certain five:
I read here why it was, and how it went,
And how the chief o' the five preferred excuse,
And how law rather chose defence should lie,—   220
What argument he urged by wary word
When free to play off wile, start subterfuge,
And what the unguarded groan told, torture's feat
When law grew brutal, outbroke, overbore
And glutted hunger on the truth, at last,—
No matter for the flesh and blood between.
All 's a clear rede and no more riddle now.
Truth, nowhere, lies yet everywhere in these—
Not absolutely in a portion, yet
Evolvible from the whole: evolved at last   230
Painfully, held tenaciously by me.
Therefore there is not any doubt to clear
When I shall write the brief word presently
And chink the hand-bell, which I pause to do.
Irresolute? Not I, more than the mound
With the pine-trees on it yonder! Some surmise,
Perchance, that since man's wit is fallible,
Mine may fail here? Suppose it so,—what then?
Say,—Guido, I count guilty, there 's no babe
So guiltless, for I misconceive the man!   240
What 's in the chance should move me from my mind?
If, as I walk in a rough country-side,
Peasants of mine cry, "Thou art he can help,
Lord of the land and counted wise to boot:
Look at our brother, strangling in his foam,
He fell so where we find him,—prove thy worth!"
I may presume, pronounce, "A frenzy-fit,

A falling-sickness or a fever-stroke!
Breathe a vein, copiously let blood at once!"
So perishes the patient, and anon   250
I hear my peasants—"All was error, lord!
Our story, thy prescription: for there crawled
In due time from our hapless brother's breast
The serpent which had stung him: bleeding slew
Whom a prompt cordial had restored to health."
What other should I say than "God so willed:
Mankind is ignorant, a man am I:
Call ignorance my sorrow not my sin!"
So and not otherwise, in after-time,
If some acuter wit, fresh probing, sound   260
This multifarious mass of words and deeds
Deeper, and reach through guilt to innocence,
I shall face Guido's ghost nor blench a jot.
"God who set me to judge thee, meted out
So much of judging faculty, no more:
Ask Him if I was slack in use thereof!"
I hold a heavier fault imputable
Inasmuch as I changed a chaplain once,
For no cause,—no, if I must bare my heart,—
Save that he snuffled somewhat saying mass.   270
For I am 'ware it is the seed of act,
God holds appraising in His hollow palm,
Not act grown great thence on the world below,
Leafage and branchage, vulgar eyes admire.
Therefore I stand on my integrity,
Nor fear at all: and if I hesitate,
It is because I need to breathe awhile,
Rest, as the human right allows, review
Intent the little seeds of act, my tree,—
The thought, which, clothed in deed, I give the world   280
At chink of bell and push of arrased door.

O pale departure, dim disgrace of day!
Winter 's in wane, his vengeful worst art thou,
To dash the boldness of advancing March!
Thy chill persistent rain has purged our streets
Of gossipry; pert tongue and idle ear
By this, consort 'neath archway, portico.
But wheresoe'er Rome gathers in the gray,
Two names now snap and flash from mouth to mouth—
(Sparks, flint and steel strike)—Guido and the Pope.   290
By this same hour to-morrow eve—aha,
How do they call him?—the sagacious Swede
Who finds by figures how the chances prove,

Why one comes rather than another thing,
As, say, such dots turn up by throw of dice.
Or, if we dip in Virgil here and there
And prick for such a verse, when such shall point.
Take this Swede, tell him, hiding name and rank,
Two men are in our city this dull eve;
One doomed to death,—but hundreds in such plight   300
Slip aside, clean escape by leave of law
Which leans to mercy in this latter time;
Moreover in the plenitude of life
Is he, with strength of limb and brain adroit,
Presumably of service here: beside,
The man is noble, backed by nobler friends:
Nay, they so wish him well, the city's self
Makes common cause with who—house-magistrate,
Patron of hearth and home, domestic lord—
But ruled his own, let aliens cavil. Die?   310
He 'll bribe a jailer or break prison first!
Nay, a sedition may be helpful, give
Hint to the mob to batter wall, burn gate,
And bid the favorite malefactor march.
Calculate now these chances of escape!
"It is not probable, but well may be."
Again, there is another man, weighed now
By twice eight years beyond the seven-times-ten,
Appointed overweight to break our branch.
And this man's loaded branch lifts, more than snow,   320
All the world's cark and care, though a bird's-nest
Were a superfluous burden: notably
Hath he been pressed, as if his age were youth,
From to-day's dawn till now that day departs,
Trying one question with true sweat of soul,
"Shall the said doomed man fitlier die or live?"
When a straw swallowed in his posset, stool
Stumbled on where his path lies, any puff
That 's incident to such a smoking flax,
Hurries the natural end and quenches him!   330
Now calculate, thou sage, the chances here,
Say, which shall die the sooner, this or that?
"That, possibly, this in all likelihood."
I thought so: yet thou tripp'st, my foreign friend!
No, it will be quite otherwise,—to-day
Is Guido's last: my term is yet to run.

But say the Swede were right, and I forthwith
Acknowledge a prompt summons and lie dead:
Why, then I stand already in God's face

And hear, "Since by its fruit a tree is judged,   340
Show me thy fruit, the latest act of thine!
For in the last is summed the first and all,—
What thy life last put heart and soul into,
There shall I taste thy product." I must plead
This condemnation of a man to-day.

Not so! Expect nor question nor reply
At what we figure as God's judgment-bar!
None of this vile way by the barren words
Which, more than any deed, characterize
Man as made subject to a curse: no speech—   350
That still bursts o'er some lie which lurks inside,
As the split skin across the coppery snake,
And most denotes man! since, in all beside,
In hate or lust or guile or unbelief,
Out of some core of truth the excrescence comes,
And, in the last resort, the man may urge
"So was I made, a weak thing that gave way
To truth, to impulse only strong since true,
And hated, lusted, used guile, forewent faith."
But when man walks the garden of this world   360
For his own solace, and, unchecked by law,
Speaks or keeps silence as himself sees fit,
Without the least incumbency to lie,
—Why, can he tell you what a rose is like,
Or how the birds fly, and not slip to false
Though truth serve better? Man must tell his mate
Of you, me and himself, knowing he lies,
Knowing his fellow knows the same,—will think
"He lies, it is the method of a man!"
And yet will speak for answer "It is truth"   370
To him who shall rejoin "Again a lie!"
Therefore these filthy rags of speech, this coil
Of statement, comment, query and response,
Tatters all too contaminate for use,
Have no renewing: He, the Truth, is, too,
The Word. We men, in our degree, may know
There, simply, instantaneously, as here
After long time and amid many lies,
Whatever we dare think we know indeed
—That I am I, as He is He,—what else?   380
But be man's method for man's life at least!
Wherefore, Antonio Pignatelli, thou
My ancient self, who wast no Pope so long
But studied God and man, the many years
I' the school, i' the cloister, in the diocese
Domestic, legate-rule in foreign lands,—

Thou other force in those old busy days
Than this gray ultimate decrepitude,—
Yet sensible of fires that more and more
Visit a soul, in passage to the sky,   390
Left nakeder than when flesh-robe was new—
Thou, not Pope but the mere old man o' the world,
Supposed inquisitive and dispassionate,
Wilt thou, the one whose speech I somewhat trust,
Question the after-me, this self now Pope,
Hear his procedure, criticise his work?
Wise in its generation is the world.

This is why Guido is found reprobate.
I see him furnished forth for his career,
On starting for the life-chance in our world,   400
With nearly all we count sufficient help:
Body and mind in balance, a sound frame,
A solid intellect: the wit to seek,
Wisdom to choose, and courage wherewithal
To deal in whatsoever circumstance
Should minister to man, make life succeed.
Oh, and much drawback! what were earth without?
Is this our ultimate stage, or starting-place
To try man's foot, if it will creep or climb,
'Mid obstacles in seeming, points that prove   410
Advantage for who vaults from low to high
And makes the stumbling-block a stepping-stone?
So, Guido, born with appetite, lacks food:
Is poor, who yet could deftly play-off wealth:
Straitened, whose limbs are restless till at large.
He, as he eyes each outlet of the cirque
And narrow penfold for probation, pines
After the good things just outside its grate,
With less monition, fainter conscience-twitch,
Rarer instinctive qualm at the first feel   ·420
Of greed unseemly, prompting grasp undue,
Than nature furnishes her main mankind,—
Making it harder to do wrong than right
The first time, careful lest the common ear
Break measure, miss the outstep of life's march.
Wherein I see a trial fair and fit
For one else too unfairly fenced about,
Set above sin, beyond his fellows here:
Guarded from the arch-tempter all must fight,
By a great birth, traditionary name,   430
Diligent culture, choice companionship,
Above all, conversancy with the faith
Which puts forth for its base of doctrine just,

"Man is born nowise to content himself,
But please God." He accepted such a rule,
Recognized man's obedience; and the Church,
Which simply is such rule's embodiment,
He clave to, he held on by,—nay, indeed,
Near pushed inside of, deep as layman durst,
Professed so much of priesthood as might sue   440
For priest's-exemption where the layman sinned,—
Got his arm frocked which, bare, the law would bruise.
Hence, at this moment, what 's his last resource,
His extreme stay and utmost stretch of hope
But that,—convicted of such crime as law
Wipes not away save with a worldling's blood,—
Guido, the three-parts consecrate, may 'scape?
Nay, the portentous brothers of the man
Are veritably priests, protected each
May do his murder in the Church's pale,   450
Abate Paul, Canon Girolamo!
This is the man proves irreligiousest
Of all mankind religion's parasite!
This may forsooth plead dinned ear, jaded sense,
The vice o' the watcher who bides near the bell,
Sleeps sound because the clock is vigilant,
And cares not whether it be shade or shine,
Doling out day and night to all men else!
Why was the choice o' the man to niche himself
Perversely 'neath the tower where Time's own tongue   460
Thus undertakes to sermonize the world?
Why, but because the solemn is safe too,
The belfry proves a fortress of a sort,
Has other uses than to teach the hour:
Turns sunscreen, paravent and ombrifuge
To whoso seeks a shelter in its pale,
—Ay, and attractive to unwary folk
Who gaze at storied portal, statued spire,
And go home with full head but empty purse,
Nor dare suspect the sacristan the thief!   470
Shall Judas—hard upon the donor's heel,
To filch the fragments of the basket—plead
He was too near the preacher's mouth, nor sat
Attent with fifties in a company?
No,—closer to promulgated decree,
Clearer the censure of default. Proceed!

I find him bound, then, to begin life well;
Fortified by propitious circumstance,
Great birth, good breeding, with the Church for guide,

How lives he? Cased thus in a coat of proof, 480
Mailed like a man-at-arms, though all the while
A puny starveling,—does the breast pant big,
The limb swell to the limit, emptiness
Strive to become solidity indeed?
Rather, he shrinks up like the ambiguous fish,
Detaches flesh from shell and outside show,
And steals by moonlight (I have seen the thing)
In and out, now to prey and now to skulk.
Armor he boasts when a wave breaks on beach,
Or bird stoops for the prize: with peril nigh,— 490
The man of rank, the much-befriended man,
The man almost affiliate to the Church,
Such is to deal with, let the world beware!
Does the world recognize, pass prudently?
Do tides abate and sea-fowl hunt i' the deep?
Already is the slug from out its mew,
Ignobly faring with all loose and free,
Sand-fly and slush-worm at their garbage-feast,
A naked blotch no better than they all:
Guido has dropped nobility, slipped the Church, 500
Plays trickster if not cut-purse, body and soul
Prostrate among the filthy feeders—faugh!
And when Law takes him by surprise at last,
Catches the foul thing on its carrion-prey,
Behold, he points to shell left high and dry,
Pleads "But the case out yonder is myself!"
Nay, it is thou, Law prongs amid thy peers,
Congenial vermin; that was none of thee,
Thine outside,—give it to the soldier-crab!

For I find this black mark impinge the man, 510
That he believes in just the vile of life.
Low instinct, base pretension, are these truth?
Then, that aforesaid armor, probity,
He figures in, is falsehood scale on scale;
Honor and faith,—a lie and a disguise,
Probably for all livers in this world,
Certainly for himself! All say good words
To who will hear, all do thereby bad deeds
To who must undergo; so thrive mankind!
See this habitual creed exemplified 520
Most in the last deliberate act; as last,
So, very sum and substance of the soul
Of him that planned and leaves one perfect piece,
The sin brought under jurisdiction now,
Even the marriage of the man: this act

I sever from his life as sample, show
For Guido's self, intend to test him by,
As, from a cup filled fairly at the fount,
By the components we decide enough
Or to let flow as late, or stanch the source.   530

He purposes this marriage, I remark,
On no one motive that should prompt thereto—
Farthest, by consequence, from ends alleged
Appropriate to the action; so they were:
The best, he knew and feigned, the worst he took.
Not one permissible impulse moves the man,
From the mere liking of the eye and ear,
To the true longing of the heart that loves,
No trace of these: but all to instigate,
Is what sinks man past level of the brute,   540
Whose appetite if brutish is a truth.
All is the lust for money: to get gold,—
Why, lie, rob, if it must be, murder! Make
Body and soul wring gold out, lured within
The clutch of hate by love, the trap's pretence!
What good else get from bodies and from souls?
This got, there were some life to lead thereby,
—What, where or how, appreciate those who tell
How the toad lives: it lives,—enough for me!
To get this good—with but a groan or so.   550
Then, silence of the victims—were the feat.
He foresaw, made a picture in his mind,—
Of father and mother stunned and echoless
To the blow, as they lie staring at fate's jaws
Their folly danced into, till the woe fell;
Edged in a month by strenuous cruelty
From even the poor nook whence they watched the wolf
Feast on their heart, the lamb-like child his prey;
Plundered to the last remnant of their wealth,
(What daily pittance pleased the plunderer dole,)   560
Hunted forth to go hide head, starve and die,
And leave the pale awe-stricken wife, past hope
Of help i' the world now, mute and motionless,
His slave, his chattel, to first use, then destroy.
All this, he bent mind how to bring about,
Put plain in act and life, as painted plain,
So have success, reach crown of earthly good,
In this particular enterprise of man,
By marriage—undertaken in God's face
With all these lies so opposite God's truth,   570
For end so other than man's end.

Thus schemes
Guido, and thus would carry out his scheme:
But when an obstacle first blocks the path,
When he finds none may boast monopoly
Of lies and trick i' the tricking lying world,—
That sorry timid natures, even this sort
O' the Comparini, want nor trick nor lie
Proper to the kind,—that as the gor-crow treats
The bramble-finch so treats the finch the moth,
And the great Guido is minutely matched   580
By this same couple,—whether true or false
The revelation of Pompilia's birth,
Which in a moment brings his scheme to nought,—
Then, he is piqued, advances yet a stage,
Leaves the low region to the finch and fly,
Soars to the zenith whence the fiercer fowl
May dare the inimitable swoop. I see.
He draws now on the curious crime, the fine
Felicity and flower of wickedness;
Determines, by the utmost exercise   590
Of violence, made safe and sure by craft,
To satiate malice, pluck one last arch-pang
From the parents, else would triumph out of reach,
By punishing their child, within reach yet,
Who, by thought, word or deed, could nowise wrong
I' the matter that now moves him. So plans he,
Always subordinating (note the point!)
Revenge, the manlier sin, to interest
The meaner,—would pluck pang forth, but unclench
No gripe in the act, let fall no money-piece.   600
Hence a plan for so plaguing, body and soul,
His wife, so putting, day by day, hour by hour,
The untried torture to the untouched place,
As must precipitate an end foreseen,
Goad her into some plain revolt, most like
Plunge upon patent suicidal shame,
Death to herself, damnation by rebound
To those whose hearts he, holding hers, holds still:
Such plan as, in its bad completeness, shall
Ruin the three together and alike,   610
Yet leave himself in luck and liberty,
No claim renounced, no right a forfeiture,
His person unendangered, his good fame
Without a flaw, his pristine worth intact,—
While they, with all their claims and rights that cling,
Shall forthwith crumble off him every side,
Scorched into dust, a plaything for the winds.

As when, in our Campagna, there is fired
The nest-like work that overruns a hut;
And, as the thatch burns here, there, everywhere,   620
Even to the ivy and wild vine, that bound
And blessed the home where men were happy once,
There rises gradual, black amid the blaze,
Some grim and unscathed nucleus of the nest,—
Some old malicious tower, some obscene tomb
They thought a temple in their ignorance,
And clung about and thought to lean upon—
There laughs it o'er their ravage,—where are they?
So did his cruelty burn life about,
And lay the ruin bare in dreadfulness,   630
Try the persistency of torment so
Upon the wife, that, at extremity,
Some crisis brought about by fire and flame,
The patient frenzy-stung must needs break loose,
Fly anyhow, find refuge anywhere,
Even in the arms of who should front her first,
No monster but a man—while nature shrieked
"Or thus escape, or die!" The spasm arrived,
Not the escape by way of sin,—O God,
Who shall pluck sheep Thou holdest, from Thy hand?   640
Therefore she lay resigned to die,—so far
The simple cruelty was foiled. Why then,
Craft to the rescue, let craft supplement
Cruelty and show hell a masterpiece!
Hence this consummate lie, this love-intrigue,
Unmanly simulation of a sin,
With place and time and circumstance to suit—
These letters false beyond all forgery—
Not just handwriting and mere authorship,
But false to body and soul they figure forth—   650
As though the man had cut out shape and shape
From fancies of that other Aretine,
To paste below—incorporate the filth
With cherub faces on a missal-page!

Whereby the man so far attains his end
That strange temptation is permitted,—see!
Pompilia, wife, and Caponsacchi, priest,
Are brought together as nor priest nor wife
Should stand, and there is passion in the place,
Power in the air for evil as for good,   660
Promptings from heaven and hell, as if the stars
Fought in their courses for a fate to be.
Thus stand the wife and priest, a spectacle,

I doubt not, to unseen assemblage there.
No lamp will mark that window for a shrine,
No tablet signalize the terrace, teach
New generations which succeed the old,
The pavement of the street is holy ground;
No bard describe in verse how Christ prevailed
And Satan fell like lightning! Why repine?   670
What does the world, told truth, but lie the more?

A second time the plot is foiled; nor, now,
By corresponding sin for countercheck,
No wile and trick that baffle trick and wile,—
The play o' the parents! Here the blot is blanched
By God's gift of a purity of soul
That will not take pollution, ermine-like
Armed from dishonor by its own soft snow.
Such was this gift of God who showed for once
How He would have the world go white: it seems   680
As a new attribute were born of each
Champion of truth, the priest and wife I praise,—
As a new safeguard sprang up in defence
Of their new noble nature: so a thorn
Comes to the aid of and completes the rose—
Courage, to wit, no woman's gift nor priest's,
I' the crisis; might leaps vindicating right.
See how the strong aggressor, bad and bold,
With every vantage, preconcerts surprise,
Leaps of a sudden at his victim's throat   690
In a byway,—how fares he when face to face
With Caponsacchi? Who fights, who fears now?
There quails Count Guido, armed to the chattering teeth,
Cowers at the steadfast eye and quiet word
O' the Canon of the Pieve! There skulks crime
Behind law called in to back cowardice!
While out of the poor trampled worm the wife,
Springs up a serpent!

                 But anon of these!
Him I judge now,—of him proceed to note,
Failing the first, a second chance befriends   700
Guido, gives pause ere punishment arrive.
The law he called, comes, hears, adjudicates,
Nor does amiss i' the main,—secludes the wife
From the husband, respites the oppressed one, grants
Probation to the oppressor, could he know
The mercy of a minute's fiery purge!
The furnace-coals alike of public scorn,
Private remorse, heaped glowing on his head,

What if—the force and guile, the ore's alloy,
Eliminate, his baser soul refined—   710
The lost be saved even yet, so as by fire?
Let him, rebuked, go softly all his days
And, when no graver musings claim their due,
Meditate on a man's immense mistake
Who, fashioned to use feet and walk, deigns crawl—
Takes the unmanly means—ay, though to ends
Man scarce should make for, would but reach through wrong,—
May sin, but nowise needs shame manhood so:
Since fowlers hawk, shoot, nay and snare the game,
And yet eschew vile practice, nor find sport   720
In torch-light treachery or the luring owl.

But how hunts Guido? Why, the fraudful trap—
Late spurned to ruin by the indignant feet
Of fellows in the chase who loved fair play—
Here he picks up the fragments to the least,
Lades him and hies to the old lurking-place
Where haply he may patch again, refit
The mischief, file its blunted teeth anew,
Make sure, next time, first snap shall break the bone.
Craft, greed and violence complot revenge: 730
Craft, for its quota, schemes to bring about
And seize occasion and be safe withal:
Greed craves its act may work both far and near,
Crush the tree, branch and trunk and root beside,
Whichever twig or leaf arrests a streak
Of possible sunshine else would coin itself,
And drop down one more gold piece in the path:
Violence stipulates, "Advantage proved,
And safety sure, be pain the overplus!
Murder with jagged knife! Cut but tear too!   740
Foiled oft, starved long, glut malice for amends!"
And what, craft's scheme? scheme sorrowful and strange
As though the elements, whom mercy checked,
Had mustered hate for one eruption more,
One final deluge to surprise the Ark
Cradled and sleeping on its mountain-top:
Their outbreak-signal—what but the dove's coo,
Back with the olive in her bill for news
Sorrow was over? 'T is an infant's birth,
Guido's first-born, his son and heir, that gives   750
The occasion: other men cut free their souls
From care in such a case, fly up in thanks
To God, reach, recognize His love for once:
Guido cries, "Soul, at last the mire is thine!

Lie there in likeness of a money-bag,
My babe's birth so pins down past moving now,
That I dare cut adrift the lives I late
Scrupled to touch lest thou escape with them!
These parents and their child my wife,—touch one,
Lose all! Their rights determined on a head   760
I could but hate, not harm, since from each hair
Dangled a hope for me: now—chance and change!
No right was in their child but passes plain
To that child's child and through such child to me.
I am a father now,—come what, come will,
I represent my child; he comes between—
Cuts sudden off the sunshine of this life
From those three: why, the gold is in his curls!
Not with old Pietro's, Violante's head,
Not his gray horror, her more hideous black—   770
Go these, devoted to the knife!"
                               'T is done:
Wherefore should mind misgive, heart hesitate?
He calls to counsel, fashions certain four
Colorless natures counted clean till now,
—Rustic simplicity, uncorrupted youth,
Ignorant virtue! Here 's the gold o' the prime
When Saturn ruled, shall shock our leaden day—
The clown abash the courtier! Mark it, bards!
The courtier tries his hand on clownship here,
Speaks a word, names a crime, appoints a price,—   780
Just breathes on what, suffused with all himself,
Is red-hot henceforth past distinction now
I' the common glow of hell. And thus they break
And blaze on us at Rome, Christ's birthnight-eve!
Oh angels that sang erst "On the earth, peace!
To man, good will!"—such peace finds earth to-day!
After the seventeen hundred years, so man
Wills good to man, so Guido makes complete
His murder! what is it I said?—cuts loose
Three lives that hitherto he suffered cling,   790
Simply because each served to nail secure,
By a corner of the money-bag, his soul,—
Therefore, lives sacred till the babe's first breath
O'erweights them in the balance,—off they fly!

So is the murder managed, sin conceived
To the full: and why not crowned with triumph too?
Why must the sin, conceived thus, bring forth death?
I note how, within hair's-breadth of escape,
Impunity and the thing supposed success,

Guido is found when the check comes, the change,   800
The monitory touch o' the tether—felt
By few, not marked by many, named by none
At the moment, only recognized aright
I' the fulness of the days, for God's, lest sin
Exceed the service, leap the line: such check—
A secret which this life finds hard to keep,
And, often guessed, is never quite revealed—
Needs must trip Guido on a stumbling-block
Too vulgar, too absurdly plain i' the path!
Study this single oversight of care,   810
This hebetude that marred sagacity,
Forgetfulness of all the man best knew,—
How any stranger having need to fly,
Needs but to ask and have the means of flight.
Why, the first urchin tells you, to leave Rome,
Get horses, you must show the warrant, just
The banal scrap, clerk's scribble, a fair word buys,
Or foul one, if a ducat sweeten word,—
And straight authority will back demand,
Give you the pick o' the post-house!—how should he,   820
Then, resident at Rome for thirty years,
Guido, instruct a stranger! And himself
Forgets just this poor paper scrap, wherewith
Armed, every door he knocks at opens wide
To save him: horsed and manned, with such advance
O' the hunt behind, why, 't were the easy task
Of hours told on the fingers of one hand,
To reach the Tuscan frontier, laugh at home,
Light-hearted with his fellows of the place,—
Prepared by that strange shameful judgment, that   830
Satire upon a sentence just pronounced
By the Rota and confirmed by the Granduke,—
Ready in a circle to receive their peer,
Appreciate his good story how, when Rome,
The Pope-King and the populace of priests
Made common cause with their confederate
The other priestling who seduced his wife,
He, all unaided, wiped out the affront
With decent bloodshed and could face his friends,
Frolic it in the world's eye. Ay, such tale   840
Missed such applause, and by such oversight!
So, tired and footsore, those blood-flustered five
Went reeling on the road through dark and cold,
The few permissible miles, to sink at length,
Wallow and sleep in the first wayside straw,
As the other herd quenched, i' the wash o' the wave,

—Each swine, the devil inside him: so slept they,
And so were caught and caged—all through one trip,
One touch of fool in Guido the astute!
He curses the omission, I surmise,   850
More than the murder. Why, thou fool and blind,
It is the mercy-stroke that stops thy fate,
Hamstrings and holds thee to thy hurt,—but how?
On the edge o' the precipice! One minute more,
Thou hadst gone farther and fared worse, my son,
Fathoms down on the flint and fire beneath!
Thy comrades each and all were of one mind,
Thy murder done, to straightway murder thee
In turn, because of promised pay withheld.
So, to the last, greed found itself at odds   860
With craft in thee, and, proving conqueror,
Had sent thee, the same night that crowned thy hope,
Thither where, this same day, I see thee not,
Nor, through God's mercy, need, to-morrow, see.

Such I find Guido, midmost blotch of black
Discernible in this group of clustered crimes
Huddling together in the cave they call
Their palace, outraged day thus penetrates.
Around him ranged, now close and now remote,
Prominent or obscure to meet the needs   870
O' the mage and master, I detect each shape
Subsidiary i' the scene nor loathed the less,
All alike colored, all descried akin
By one and the same pitchy furnace stirred
At the centre: see, they lick the master's hand,—
This fox-faced horrible priest, this brother-brute
The Abate,—why, mere wolfishness looks well,
Guido stands honest in the red o' the flame,
Beside this yellow that would pass for white,
Twice Guido, all craft but no violence,   880
This copier of the mien and gait and garb
Of Peter and Paul, that he may go disguised,
Rob halt and lame, sick folk i' the temple-porch!
Armed with religion, fortified by law,
A man of peace, who trims the midnight lamp
And turns the classic page—and all for craft,
All to work harm with, yet incur no scratch!
While Guido brings the struggle to a close,
Paul steps back the due distance, clear o' the trap
He builds and baits. Guido I catch and judge;   890
Paul is past reach in this world and my time:
That is a case reserved. Pass to the next,

The boy of the brood, the young Girolamo,
Priest, Canon, and what more? nor wolf nor fox,
But hybrid, neither craft nor violence
Wholly, part violence part craft: such cross
Tempts speculation—will both blend one day,
And prove hell's better product? Or subside
And let the simple quality emerge,
Go on with Satan's service the old way?   900
Meanwhile, what promise,—what performance too!
For there 's a new distinctive touch, I see,
Lust—lacking in the two—hell's own blue tint
That gives a character and marks the man
More than a match for yellow and red. Once more,
A case reserved: why should I doubt? Then comes
The gaunt gray nightmare in the furthest smoke,
The hag that gave these three abortions birth,
Unmotherly mother and unwomanly
Woman, that near turns motherhood to shame,   910
Womanliness to loathing: no one word,
No gesture to curb cruelty a whit
More than the she-pard thwarts her playsome whelps
Trying their milk-teeth on the soft o' the throat
O' the first fawn, flung, with those beseeching eyes,
Flat in the covert! How should she but couch,
Lick the dry lips, unsheathe the blunted claw,
Catch 'twixt her placid eyewinks at what chance
Old bloody half-forgotten dream may flit,
Born when herself was novice to the taste,   920
The while she lets youth take its pleasure. Last,
These God-abandoned wretched lumps of life,
These four companions,—country-folk this time,
Not tainted by the unwholesome civic breath,
Much less the curse o' the court! Mere striplings too,
Fit to do human nature justice still!
Surely when impudence in Guido's shape
Shall propose crime and proffer money's-worth
To these stout tall rough bright-eyed black-haired boys,
The blood shall bound in answer to each cheek   930
Before the indignant outcry break from lip!
Are these i' the mood to murder, hardly loosed
From healthy autumn-finish of ploughed glebe,
Grapes in the barrel, work at happy end,
And winter near with rest and Christmas play?
How greet they Guido with his final task—
(As if he but proposed "One vineyard more
To dig, ere frost come, then relax indeed!")
"Anywhere, anyhow and anywhy,

Murder me some three people, old and young,   940
Ye never heard the names of,—and be paid
So much!" And the whole four accede at once.
Demur? Do cattle bidden march or halt?
Is it some lingering habit, old fond faith
I' the lord o' the land, instructs them,—birthright badge
Of feudal tenure claims its slaves again?
Not so at all, thou noble human heart!
All is done purely for the pay,—which, earned,
And not forthcoming at the instant, makes
Religion heresy, and the lord o' the land   950
Fit subject for a murder in his turn.
The patron with cut throat and rifled purse,
Deposited i' the roadside-ditch, his due,
Nought hinders each good fellow trudging home,
The heavier by a piece or two in poke,
And so with new zest to the common life,
Mattock and spade, plough-tail and wagon-shaft,
Till some such other piece of luck betide,
Who knows? Since this is a mere start in life,
And none of them exceeds the twentieth year.   960
Nay, more i' the background yet? Unnoticed forms
Claim to be classed, subordinately vile?
Complacent lookers-on that laugh,—perchance
Shake head as their friend's horse-play grows too rough
With the mere child he manages amiss—
But would not interfere and make bad worse
For twice the fractious tears and prayers: thou know'st
Civility better, Marzi-Medici,
Governor for thy kinsman the Granduke!
Fit representative of law, man's lamp   970
I' the magistrate's grasp full-flare, no rushlight-end
Sputtering 'twixt thumb and finger of the priest!
Whose answer to the couple's Comparini's cry for help
Is a threat,—whose remedy of Pompilia's wrong,
A shrug o' the shoulder, and facetious word
Or wink, traditional with Tuscan wits,
To Guido in the doorway. Laud to law!
The wife is pushed back to the husband, he
Who knows how these home-squabblings persecute
People who have the public good to mind,   980
And work best with a silence in the court!

Ah, but I save my word at least for thee,
Archbishop, who art under, i' the Church,
As I am under God,—thou, chosen by both
To do the shepherd's office, feed the sheep—

How of this lamb that panted at thy foot
While the wolf pressed on her within crook's reach?
Wast thou the hireling that did turn and flee?
With thee at least anon the little word!

Such denizens o' the cave now cluster round   990
And heat the furnace sevenfold: time indeed
A bolt from heaven should cleave roof and clear place,
Transfix and show the world, suspiring flame,
The main offender, scar and brand the rest
Hurrying, each miscreant to his hole: then flood
And purify the scene with outside day—
Which yet, in the absolutest drench of dark,
Ne'er wants a witness, some stray beauty-beam
To the despair of hell.

         First of the first,
Such I pronounce Pompilia, then as now   1000
Perfect in whiteness: stoop thou down, my child,
Give one good moment to the poor old Pope
Heart-sick at having all his world to blame—
Let me look at thee in the flesh as erst,
Let me enjoy the old clean linen garb,
Not the new splendid vesture! Armed and crowned,
Would Michael, yonder, be, nor crowned nor armed,
The less pre-eminent angel? Everywhere
I see in the world the intellect of man,
That sword, the energy his subtle spear,   1010
The knowledge which defends him like a shield—
Everywhere; but they make not up, I think,
The marvel of a soul like thine, earth's flower
She holds up to the softened gaze of God!
It was not given Pompilia to know much,
Speak much, to write a book, to move mankind,
Be memorized by who records my time.
Yet if in purity and patience, if
In faith held fast despite the plucking fiend,
Safe like the signet stone with the new name   1020
That saints are known by,—if in right returned
For wrong, most pardon for worst injury,
If there be any virtue, any praise,—
Then will this woman-child have proved—who knows?—
Just the one prize vouchsafed unworthy me,
Seven years a gardener of the untoward ground
I till,—this earth, my sweat and blood manure
All the long day that barrenly grows dusk:
At least one blossom makes me proud at eve
Born 'mid the briers of my enclosure! Still   1030

(Oh, here as elsewhere, nothingness of man!)
Those be the plants, imbedded yonder South
To mellow in the morning, those made fat
By the master's eye, that yield such timid leaf,
Uncertain bud, as product of his pains!
While—see how this mere chance-sown, cleft-nursed seed,
That sprang up by the wayside 'neath the foot
Of the enemy, this breaks all into blaze,
Spreads itself, one wide glory of desire
To incorporate the whole great sun it loves   1040
From the inch-height whence it looks and longs! My flower,
My rose, I gather for the breast of God,
This I praise most in thee, where all I praise,
That having been obedient to the end
According to the light allotted, law
Prescribed thy life, still tried, still standing test,—
Dutiful to the foolish parents first,
Submissive next to the bad husband,—nay,
Tolerant of those meaner miserable
That did his hests, eked out the dole of pain,—   1050
Thou, patient thus, couldst rise from law to law,
The old to the new, promoted at one cry
O' the trump of God to the new service, not
To longer bear, but henceforth fight, be found
Sublime in new impatience with the foe!
Endure man and obey God: plant firm foot
On neck of man, tread man into the hell
Meet for him, and obey God all the more!
Oh child that didst despise thy life so much
When it seemed only thine to keep or lose,   1060
How the fine ear felt fall the first low word
"Value life, and preserve life for My sake!"
Thou didst . . . how shall I say? . . . receive so long
The standing ordinance of God on earth,
What wonder if the novel claim had clashed
With old requirement, seemed to supersede
Too much the customary law? But, brave,
Thou at first prompting of what I call God,
And fools call Nature, didst hear, comprehend,
Accept the obligation laid on thee,   1070
Mother elect, to save the unborn child,
As brute and bird do, reptile and the fly,
Ay and, I nothing doubt, even tree, shrub, plant
And flower o' the field, all in a common pact
To worthily defend the trust of trusts,
Life from the Ever Living:—didst resist—
Anticipate the office that is mine—

And with his own sword stay the upraised arm,
The endeavor of the wicked, and defend
Him who—again in my default—was there   1080
For visible providence: one less true than thou
To touch, i' the past, less practised in the right,
Approved less far in all docility
To all instruction,—how had such an one
Made scruple "Is this motion a decree?"
It was authentic to the experienced ear
O' the good and faithful servant. Go past me
And get thy praise,—and be not far to seek
Presently when I follow if I may!

And surely not so very much apart   1090
Need I place thee, my warrior-priest,—in whom
What if I gain the other rose, the gold,
We grave to imitate God's miracle,
Greet monarchs with, good rose in its degree?
Irregular noble scapegrace—son the same!
Faulty—and peradventure ours the fault
Who still misteach, mislead, throw hook and line,
Thinking to land leviathan forsooth,
Tame the scaled neck, play with him as a bird,
And bind him for our maidens! Better bear   1100
The King of Pride go wantoning awhile,
Unplagued by cord in nose and thorn in jaw,
Through deep to deep, followed by all that shine,
Churning the blackness hoary: He who made
The comely terror, He shall make the sword
To match that piece of netherstone his heart,
Ay, nor miss praise thereby; who else shut fire
I' the stone, to leap from mouth at sword's first stroke,
In lamps of love and faith, the chivalry
That dares the right and disregards alike   1110
The yea and nay o' the world? Self-sacrifice,—
What if an idol took it? Ask the Church
Why she was wont to turn each Venus here,—
Poor Rome perversely lingered round, despite
Instruction, for the sake of purblind love,—
Into Madonna's shape, and waste no whit
Of aught so rare on earth as gratitude!
All this sweet savor was not ours but thine,
Nard of the rock, a natural wealth we name
Incense, and treasure up as food for saints,   1120
When flung to us—whose function was to give
Not find the costly perfume. Do I smile?
Nay, Caponsacchi, much I find amiss,

Blameworthy, punishable in this freak
Of thine, this youth prolonged, though age was ripe,
This masquerade in sober day, with change
Of motley too,—now hypocrite's disguise,
Now fool's-costume: which lie was least like truth,
Which the ungainlier, more discordant garb,
With that symmetric soul inside my son,   1130
The churchman's or the worldling's,—let him judge,
Our adversary who enjoys the task!
I rather chronicle the healthy rage,—
When the first moan broke from the martyr-maid
At that uncaging of the beasts,—made bare
My athlete on the instant, gave such good
Great undisguised leap over post and pale
Right into the mid-cirque, free fighting-place.
There may have been rash stripping—every rag
Went to the winds,—infringement manifold   1140
Of laws prescribed pudicity, I fear,
In this impulsive and prompt self-display!
Ever such tax comes of the foolish youth;
Men mulct the wiser manhood, and suspect
No veritable star swims out of cloud.
Bear thou such imputation, undergo
The penalty I nowise dare relax,—
Conventional chastisement and rebuke.
But for the outcome, the brave starry birth
Conciliating earth with all that cloud,   1150
Thank heaven as I do! Ay, such championship
Of God at first blush, such prompt cheery thud
Of glove on ground that answers ringingly
The challenge of the false knight,—watch we long,
And wait we vainly for its gallant like
From those appointed to the service, sworn
His body-guard with pay and privilege—
White-cinct, because in white walks sanctity,
Red-socked, how else proclaim fine scorn of flesh,
Unchariness of blood when blood faith begs!   1160
Where are the men-at-arms with cross on coat?
Aloof, bewraying their attire: whilst thou
In mask and motley, pledged to dance not fight,
Sprang'st forth the hero! In thought, word and deed,
How throughout all thy warfare thou wast pure,
I find it easy to believe: and if
At any fateful moment of the strange
Adventure, the strong passion of that strait,
Fear and surprise, may have revealed too much,—
As when a thundrous midnight, with black air   1170

That burns, raindrops that blister, breaks a spell,
Draws out the excessive virtue of some sheathed
Shut unsuspected flower that hoards and hides
Immensity of sweetness,—so, perchance,
Might the surprise and fear release too much
The perfect beauty of the body and soul
Thou savedst in thy passion for God's sake,
He who is Pity. Was the trial sore?
Temptation sharp? Thank God a second time!
Why comes temptation but for man to meet   1180
And master and make crouch beneath his foot,
And so be pedestalled in triumph? Pray
"Lead us into no such temptations, Lord!"
Yea, but, O Thou whose servants are the bold,
Lead such temptations by the head and hair,
Reluctant dragons, up to who dares fight,
That so he may do battle and have praise!
Do I not see the praise?—that while thy mates
Bound to deserve i' the matter, prove at need
Unprofitable through the very pains   1190
We gave to train them well and start them fair,—
Are found too stiff, with standing ranked and ranged,
For onset in good earnest, too obtuse
Of ear, through iteration of command,
For catching quick the sense of the real cry,—
Thou, whose sword-hand was used to strike the lute,
Whose sentry-station graced some wanton's gate,
Thou didst push forward and show mettle, shame
The laggards, and retrieve the day. Well done!
Be glad thou hast let light into the world,   1200
Through that irregular breach o' the boundary,—see
The same upon thy path and march assured,
Learning anew the use of soldiership,
Self-abnegation, freedom from all fear,
Loyalty to the life's end! Ruminate,
Deserve the initiatory spasm,—once more
Work, be unhappy but bear life, my son!

And troop you, somewhere 'twixt the best and worst,
Where crowd the indifferent product, all too poor
Makeshift, starved samples of humanity!   1210
Father and mother, huddle there and hide!
A gracious eye may find you! Foul and fair,
Sadly mixed natures: self-indulgent,—yet
Self-sacrificing too: how the love soars,
How the craft, avarice, vanity and spite
Sink again! So they keep the middle course,

Slide into silly crime at unaware,
Slip back upon the stupid virtue, stay
Nowhere enough for being classed, I hope
And fear. Accept the swift and rueful death,   1220
Taught, somewhat sternlier than is wont, what waits
The ambiguous creature,—how the one black tuft
Steadies the aim of the arrow just as well
As the wide faultless white on the bird's breast!
Nay, you were punished in the very part
That looked most pure of speck,—'t was honest love
Betrayed you,—did love seem most worthy pains,
Challenge such purging, since ordained survive
When all the rest of you was done with? Go!
Never again elude the choice of tints!   1230
White shall not neutralize the black, nor good
Compensate bad in man, absolve him so:
Life's business being just the terrible choice.

So do I see, pronounce on all and some
Grouped for my judgment now,—profess no doubt
While I pronounce: dark, difficult enough
The human sphere, yet eyes grow sharp by use,
I find the truth, dispart the shine from shade,
As a mere man may, with no special touch
O' the lynx-gift in each ordinary orb: 1240
Nay, if the popular notion class me right,
One of wellnigh decayed intelligence,—
What of that? Through hard labor and good will,
And habitude that gives a blind man sight
At the practised finger-ends of him, I do
Discern, and dare decree in consequence,
Whatever prove the peril of mistake.
Whence, then, this quite new quick cold thrill,—cloud-like,
This keen dread creeping from a quarter scarce
Suspected in the skies I nightly scan?   1250
What slacks the tense nerve, saps the wound-up spring
Of the act that should and shall be, sends the mount
And mass o' the whole man's-strength,—conglobed so late—
Shudderingly into dust, a moment's work?
While I stand firm, go fearless, in this world,
For this life recognize and arbitrate,
Touch and let stay, or else remove a thing,
Judge "This is right, this object out of place,"
Candle in hand that helps me and to spare,—
What if a voice deride me, "Perk and pry!   1260
Brighten each nook with thine intelligence!
Play the good householder, ply man and maid

With tasks prolonged into the midnight, test
Their work and nowise stint of the due wage
Each worthy worker: but with gyves and whip
Pay thou misprision of a single point
Plain to thy happy self who lift'st the light,
Lament'st the darkling,—bold to all beneath!
What if thyself adventure, now the place
Is purged so well? Leave pavement and mount roof,   1270
Look round thee for the light of the upper sky,
The fire which lit thy fire which finds default
In Guido Franceschini to his cost!
What if, above in the domain of light,
Thou miss the accustomed signs, remark eclipse:
Shalt thou still gaze on ground nor lift a lid,—
Steady in thy superb prerogative,
Thy inch of inkling,—nor once face the doubt
I' the sphere above thee, darkness to be felt?"

Yet my poor spark had for its source, the sun;   1280
Thither I sent the great looks which compel
Light from its fount: all that I do and am
Comes from the truth, or seen or else surmised,
Remembered or divined, as mere man may:
I know just so, nor otherwise. As I know,
I speak,—what should I know, then, and how speak
Were there a wild mistake of eye or brain
As to recorded governance above?
If my own breath, only, blew coal alight
I styled celestial and the morning-star?   1290
I, who in this world act resolvedly,
Dispose of men, their bodies and their souls,
As they acknowledge or gainsay the light
I show them,—shall I too lack courage?—leave
I, too, the post of me, like those I blame?
Refuse, with kindred inconsistency,
To grapple danger whereby souls grow strong?
I am near the end; but still not at the end;
All to the very end is trial in life:
At this stage is the trial of my soul   1300
Danger to face, or danger to refuse?
Shall I dare try the doubt now, or not dare?

O Thou,—as represented here to me
In such conception as my soul allows,—
Under Thy measureless, my atom width!—
Man's mind, what is it but a convex glass
Wherein are gathered all the scattered points
Picked out of the immensity of sky,

To reunite there, be our heaven for earth,
Our known unknown, our God revealed to man?   1310
Existent somewhere, somehow, as a whole;
Here, as a whole proportioned to our sense,—
There, (which is nowhere, speech must babble thus!)
In the absolute immensity, the whole
Appreciable solely by Thyself,—
Here, by the little mind of man, reduced
To littleness that suits his faculty,
In the degree appreciable too;
Between Thee and ourselves—nay even, again,
Below us, to the extreme of the minute,   1320
Appreciable by how many and what diverse
Modes of the life Thou madest be! (why live
Except for love,—how love unless they know?)
Each of them, only filling to the edge,
Insect or angel, his just length and breadth,
Due facet of reflection,—full, no less,
Angel or insect, as Thou framedst things.
I it is who have been appointed here
To represent Thee, in my turn, on earth,
Just as, if new philosophy know aught,   1330
This one earth, out of all the multitude
Of peopled worlds, as stars are now supposed,—
Was chosen, and no sun-star of the swarm,
For stage and scene of Thy transcendent act
Beside which even the creation fades
Into a puny exercise of power.
Choice of the world, choice of the thing I am,
Both emanate alike from Thy dread play
Of operation outside this our sphere
Where things are classed and counted small or great,—   1340
Incomprehensibly the choice is Thine!
I therefore bow my head and take Thy place.
There is, beside the works, a tale of Thee
In the world's mouth, which I find credible:
I love it with my heart: unsatisfied,
I try it with my reason, nor discept
From any point I probe and pronounce sound.
Mind is not matter nor from matter, but
Above,—leave matter then, proceed with mind!
Man's be the mind recognized at the height,—   1350
Leave the inferior minds and look at man!
Is he the strong, intelligent and good
Up to his own conceivable height? Nowise.
Enough o' the low,—soar the conceivable height,
Find cause to match the effect in evidence,

The work i' the world, not man's but God's; leave man!
Conjecture of the worker by the work:
Is there strength there?—enough: intelligence?
Ample: but goodness in a like degree?
Not to the human eye in the present state,   1360
An isosceles deficient in the base.
What lacks, then, of perfection fit for God
But just the instance which this tale supplies
Of love without a limit? So is strength,
So is intelligence; let love be so,
Unlimited in its self-sacrifice,
Then is the tale true and God shows complete.
Beyond the tale, I reach into the dark,
Feel what I cannot see, and still faith stands:
I can believe this dread machinery   1370
Of sin and sorrow, would confound me else,
Devised—all pain, at most expenditure
Of pain by Who devised pain—to evolve,
By new machinery in counterpart,
The moral qualities of man—how else?—
To make him love in turn and be beloved,
Creative and self-sacrificing too,
And thus eventually God-like, (ay,
"I have said ye are Gods,"—shall it be said for nought?)
Enable man to wring, from out all pain,   1380
All pleasure for a common heritage
To all eternity: this may be surmised,
The other is revealed,—whether a fact,
Absolute, abstract, independent truth,
Historic, not reduced to suit man's mind,—
Or only truth reverberate, changed, made pass
A spectrum into mind, the narrow eye,—
The same and not the same, else unconceived—
Though quite conceivable to the next grade
Above it in intelligence,—as truth   1390
Easy to man were blindness to the beast
By parity of procedure,—the same truth
In a new form, but changed in either case:
What matter so intelligence be filled?
To a child, the sea is angry, for it roars:
Frost bites, else why the tooth-like fret on face?
Man makes acoustics deal with the sea's wrath,
Explains the choppy cheek by chemic law,—
To man and child remains the same effect
On drum of ear and root of nose, change cause   1400
Never so thoroughly: so my heart be struck,
What care I,—by God's gloved hand or the bare?

Nor do I much perplex me with aught hard,
Dubious in the transmitting of the tale,—
No, nor with certain riddles set to solve.
This life is training and a passage; pass,—
Still, we march over some flat obstacle
We made give way before us; solid truth
In front of it, what motion for the world?
The moral sense grows but by exercise.   1410
'T is even as man grew probatively
Initiated in Godship, set to make
A fairer moral world than this he finds,
Guess now what shall be known hereafter. Deal
Thus with the present problem: as we see,
A faultless creature is destroyed, and sin
Has had its way i' the world where God should rule.
Ay, but for this irrelevant circumstance
Of inquisition after blood, we see
Pompilia lost and Guido saved: how long?   1420
For his whole life: how much is that whole life?
We are not babes, but know the minute's worth,
And feel that life is large and the world small,
So, wait till life have passed from out the world.
Neither does this astonish at the end,
That whereas I can so receive and trust,
Other men, made with hearts and souls the same,
Reject and disbelieve,—subordinate
The future to the present,—sin, nor fear.
This I refer still to the foremost fact,   1430
Life is probation and the earth no goal
But starting-point of man: compel him strive,
Which means, in man, as good as reach the goal,—
Why institute that race, his life, at all?
But this does overwhelm me with surprise,
Touch me to terror,—not that faith, the pearl,
Should be let lie by fishers wanting food,—
Nor, seen and handled by a certain few
Critical and contemptuous, straight consigned
To shore and shingle for the pebble it proves,—   1440
But that, when haply found and known and named
By the residue made rich forevermore,
These,—that these favored ones, should in a trice
Turn, and with double zest go dredge for whelks,
Mud-worms that make the savory soup! Enough
O' the disbelievers, see the faithful few!
How do the Christians here deport them, keep
Their robes of white unspotted by the world?
What is this Aretine Archbishop, this

Man under me as I am under God,   1450
This champion of the faith, I armed and decked,
Pushed forward, put upon a pinnacle,
To show the enemy his victor,—see!
What 's the best fighting when the couple close?
Pompilia cries, "Protect me from the wolf!"
He—"No, thy Guido is rough, heady, strong,
Dangerous to disquiet: let him bide!
He needs some bone to mumble, help amuse
The darkness of his den with: so, the fawn
Which limps up bleeding to my foot and lies,   1460
—Come to me, daughter!—thus I throw him back!"
Have we misjudged here, over-armed our knight,
Given gold and silk where plain hard steel serves best,
Enfeebled whom we sought to fortify,
Made an archbishop and undone a saint?
Well, then, descend these heights, this pride of life,
Sit in the ashes with a barefoot monk
Who long ago stamped out the worldly sparks,
By fasting, watching, stone cell and wire scourge,
—No such indulgence as unknits the strength—   1470
These breed the tight nerve and tough cuticle,
And the world's praise or blame runs rillet-wise
Off the broad back and brawny breast, we know!
He meets the first cold sprinkle of the world,
And shudders to the marrow. "Save this child?
Oh, my superiors, oh, the Archbishop's self!
Who was it dared lay hand upon the ark
His betters saw fall nor put finger forth?
Great ones could help yet help not: why should small?
I break my promise: let her break her heart!"   1480
These are the Christians not the worldlings, not
The sceptics, who thus battle for the faith!
If foolish virgins disobey and sleep,
What wonder? But, this time, the wise that watch,
Sell lamps and buy lutes, exchange oil for wine,
The mystic Spouse betrays the Bridegroom here.
To our last resource, then! Since all flesh is weak,
Bind weaknesses together, we get strength:
The individual weighed, found wanting, try
Some institution, honest artifice   1490
Whereby the units grow compact and firm!
Each props the other, and so stand is made
By our embodied cowards that grow brave.
The Monastery called of Convertites,
Meant to help women because these helped Christ,—
A thing existent only while it acts,

Does as designed, else a nonentity,—
For what is an idea unrealized?—
Pompilia is consigned to these for help.
They do help: they are prompt to testify   1500
To her pure life and saintly dying days.
She dies, and lo, who seemed so poor, proves rich!
What does the body that lives through helpfulness
To women for Christ's sake? The kiss turns bite,
The dove's note changes to the crow's cry: judge!
"Seeing that this our Convent claims of right
What goods belong to those we succor, be
The same proved women of dishonest life,—
And seeing that this Trial made appear
Pompilia was in such predicament,—   1510
The Convent hereupon pretends to said
Succession of Pompilia, issues writ,
And takes possession by the Fisc's advice."
Such is their attestation to the cause
Of Christ, who had one saint at least, they hoped:
But, is a title-deed to filch, a corpse
To slander, and an infant-heir to cheat?
Christ must give up his gains then! They unsay
All the fine speeches,—who was saint is whore.
Why, scripture yields no parallel for this!   1520
The soldiers only threw dice for Christ's coat;
We want another legend of the Twelve
Disputing if it was Christ's coat at all,
Claiming as prize the woof of price—for why?
The Master was a thief, purloined the same,
Or paid for it out of the common bag!
Can it be this is end and outcome, all
I take with me to show as stewardship's fruit,
The best yield of the latest time, this year
The seventeen-hundredth since God died for man?   1530
Is such effect proportionate to cause?
And still the terror keeps on the increase
When I perceive . . . how can I blink the fact?
That the fault, the obduracy to good,
Lies not with the impracticable stuff
Whence man is made, his very nature's fault,
As if it were of ice the moon may gild
Not melt, or stone 't was meant the sun should warm
Not make bear flowers,—nor ice nor stone to blame:
But it can melt, that ice, can bloom, that stone,   1540
Impassible to rule of day and night!
This terrifies me, thus compelled perceive,
Whatever love and faith we looked should spring

At advent of the authoritative star,
Which yet lie sluggish, curdled at the source,—
These have leapt forth profusely in old time,
These still respond with promptitude to-day,
At challenge of—what unacknowledged powers
O' the air, what uncommissioned meteors, warmth
By law, and light by rule should supersede?   1550
For see this priest, this Caponsacchi, stung
At the first summons,—"Help for honor's sake,
Play the man, pity the oppressed!"—no pause,
How does he lay about him in the midst,
Strike any foe, right wrong at any risk,
All blindness, bravery and obedience!—blind?
Ay, as a man would be inside the sun,
Delirious with the plenitude of light
Should interfuse him to the finger-ends—
Let him rush straight, and how shall he go wrong?   1560
Where are the Christians in their panoply?
The loins we girt about with truth, the breasts
Righteousness plated round, the shield of faith,
The helmet of salvation, and that sword
O' the Spirit, even the word of God,—where these?
Slunk into corners! Oh, I hear at once
Hubbub of protestation! "What, we monks,
We friars, of such an order, such a rule,
Have not we fought, bled, left our martyr-mark
At every point along the boundary-line   1570
'Twixt true and false, religion and the world,
Where this or the other dogma of our Church
Called for defence?" And I, despite myself,
How can I but speak loud what truth speaks low,
"Or better than the best, or nothing serves!
What boots deed, I can cap and cover straight
With such another doughtiness to match,
Done at an instinct of the natural man?"
Immolate body, sacrifice soul too,—
Do not these publicans the same? Outstrip!   1580
Or else stop race you boast runs neck and neck,
You with the wings, they with the feet,—for shame!
Oh, I remark your diligence and zeal!
Five years long, now, rounds faith into my ears,
"Help thou, or Christendom is done to death!"
Five years since, in the Province of To-kien,
Which is in China as some people know,
Maigrot, my Vicar Apostolic there,
Having a great qualm, issues a decree.
Alack, the converts use as God's name, not   1590

Tien-chu but plain *Tien* or else mere *Shang-ti,*
As Jesuits please to fancy politic,
While, say Dominicans, it calls down fire,—
For *Tien* means heaven, and *Shang-ti,* supreme prince,
While *Tien-chu* means the lord of heaven: all cry,
"There is no business urgent for dispatch
As that thou send a legate, specially
Cardinal Tournon, straight to Pekin, there
To settle and compose the difference!"
So have I seen a potentate all fume   1600
For some infringement of his realm's just right,
Some menace to a mud-built straw-thatched farm
O' the frontier; while inside the mainland lie,
Quite undisputed-for in solitude,
Whole cities plague may waste or famine sap:
What if the sun crumble, the sands encroach,
While he looks on sublimely at his ease?
How does their ruin touch the empire's bound?
And is this little all that was to be?
Where is the gloriously-decisive change,   1610
Metamorphosis the immeasurable
Of human clay to divine gold, we looked
Should, in some poor sort, justify its price?
Had an adept of the mere Rosy Cross
Spent his life to consummate the Great Work,
Would not we start to see the stuff it touched
Yield not a grain more than the vulgar got
By the old smelting-process years ago?
If this were sad to see in just the sage
Who should profess so much, perform no more,   1620
What is it when suspected in that Power
Who undertook to make and made the world,
Devised and did effect man, body and soul,
Ordained salvation for them both, and yet . . .
Well, is the thing we see, salvation?
                         I
Put no such dreadful question to myself,
Within whose circle of experience burns
The central truth, Power, Wisdom, Goodness,—God:
I must outlive a thing ere know it dead:
When I outlive the faith there is a sun,   1630
When I lie, ashes to the very soul,—
Some one, not I, must wail above the heap,
"He died in dark whence never morn arose."
While I see day succeed the deepest night—
How can I speak but as I know?—my speech
Must be, throughout the darkness, "It will end:

The light that did burn, will burn!" Clouds obscure—
But for which obscuration all were bright?
Too hastily concluded! Sun-suffused,
A cloud may soothe the eye made blind by blaze,—   1640
Better the very clarity of heaven:
The soft streaks are the beautiful and dear.
What but the weakness in a faith supplies
The incentive to humanity, no strength
Absolute, irresistible, comports?
How can man love but what he yearns to help?
And that which men think weakness within strength,
But angels know for strength and stronger yet—
What were it else but the first things made new,
But repetition of the miracle,   1650
The divine instance of self-sacrifice
That never ends and aye begins for man?
So, never I miss footing in the maze,
No,—I have light nor fear the dark at all.
But are mankind not real, who pace outside
My petty circle, world that 's measured me?
And when they stumble even as I stand,
Have I a right to stop ear when they cry,
As they were phantoms who took clouds for crags,
Tripped and fell, where man's march might safely move?   1660
Beside, the cry is other than a ghost's,
When out of the old time there pleads some bard,
Philosopher, or both, and—whispers not,
But words it boldly. "The inward work and worth
Of any mind, what other mind may judge
Save God who only knows the thing He made,
The veritable service He exacts?
It is the outward product men appraise.
Behold, an engine hoists a tower aloft:
'I looked that it should move the mountain too!'   1670
Or else 'Had just a turret toppled down,
Success enough!'—may say the Machinist
Who knows what less or more result might be:
But we, who see that done we cannot do,
'A feat beyond man's force,' we men must say.
Regard me and that shake I gave the world!
I was born, not so long before Christ's birth
As Christ's birth haply did precede thy day,—
But many a watch before the star of dawn:
Therefore I lived,—it is thy creed affirms,   1680
Pope Innocent, who art to answer me!—
Under conditions, nowise to escape,
Whereby salvation was impossible.

Each impulse to achieve the good and fair,
Each aspiration to the pure and true,
Being without a warrant or an aim,
Was just as sterile a felicity
As if the insect, born to spend his life
Soaring his circles, stopped them to describe
(Painfully motionless in the mid-air)   1690
Some word of weighty counsel for man's sake,
Some 'Know thyself' or 'Take the golden mean!'
—Forewent his happy dance and the glad ray,
Died half an hour the sooner and was dust.
I, born to perish like the brutes, or worse,
Why not live brutishly, obey brutes' law?
But I, of body as of soul complete,
A gymnast at the games, philosopher
I' the schools, who painted, and made music,—all
Glories that met upon the tragic stage   1700
When the Third Poet's tread surprised the Two,—
Whose lot fell in a land where life was great
And sense went free and beauty lay profuse,
I, untouched by one adverse circumstance,
Adopted virtue as my rule of life,
Waived all reward, loved but for loving's sake,
And, what my heart taught me, I taught the world,
And have been teaching now two thousand years.
Witness my work,—plays that should please, forsooth!
'They might please, they may displease, they shall teach,   1710
For truth's sake,' so I said, and did, and do.
Five hundred years ere Paul spoke, Felix heard,—
How much of temperance and righteousness,
Judgment to come, did I find reason for,
Corroborate with my strong style that spared
No sin, nor swerved the more from branding brow
Because the sinner was called Zeus and God?
How nearly did I guess at that Paul knew?
How closely come, in what I represent
As duty, to his doctrine yet a blank?   1720
And as that limner not untruly limns
Who draws an object round or square, which square
Or round seems to the unassisted eye,
Though Galileo's tube display the same
Oval or oblong,—so, who controverts
I rendered rightly what proves wrongly wrought
Beside Paul's picture? Mine was true for me.
I saw that there are, first and above all,
The hidden forces, blind necessities,
Named Nature, but the thing's self unconceived: 1730

Then follow—how dependent upon these,
We know not, how imposed above ourselves,
We well know—what I name the gods, a power
Various or one: for great and strong and good
Is there, and little, weak and bad there too,
Wisdom and folly: say, these make no God,—
What is it else that rules outside man's self?
A fact then,—always, to the naked eye,—
And so, the one revealment possible
Of what were unimagined else by man.   1740
Therefore, what gods do, man may criticise,
Applaud, condemn,—how should he fear the truth?—
But likewise have in awe because of power,
Venerate for the main munificence,
And give the doubtful deed its due excuse
From the acknowledged creature of a day
To the Eternal and Divine. Thus, bold
Yet self-mistrusting, should man bear himself,
Most assured on what now concerns him most—
The law of his own life, the path he prints,—   1750
Which law is virtue and not vice, I say,—
And least inquisitive where search least skills,
I' the nature we best give the clouds to keep.
What could I paint beyond a scheme like this
Out of the fragmentary truths where light
Lay fitful in a tenebrific time?
You have the sunrise now, joins truth to truth,
Shoots life and substance into death and void;
Themselves compose the whole we made before:
The forces and necessity grow God,—   1760
The beings so contrarious that seemed gods,
Prove just His operation manifold
And multiform, translated, as must be,
Into intelligible shape so far
As suits our sense and sets us free to feel.
What if I let a child think, childhood-long,
That lightning, I would have him spare his eye,
Is a real arrow shot at naked orb?
The man knows more, but shuts his lids the same:
Lightning's cause comprehends nor man nor child.   1770
Why then, my scheme, your better knowledge broke,
Presently readjusts itself, the small
Proportioned largelier, parts and whole named new:
So much, no more two thousand years have done!
Pope, dost thou dare pretend to punish me,
For not descrying sunshine at midnight,
Me who crept all-fours, found my way so far—

While thou rewardest teachers of the truth,
Who miss the plain way in the blaze of noon,—
Though just a word from that strong style of mine,   1780
Grasped honestly in hand as guiding-staff,
Had pricked them a sure path across the bog,
That mire of cowardice and slush of lies
Wherein I find them wallow in wide day!"

How should I answer this Euripides?
Paul—'t is a legend—answered Seneca,
But that was in the day-spring; noon is now,
We have got too familiar with the light.
Shall I wish back once more that thrill of dawn?
When the whole truth-touched man burned up, one fire?   1790
—Assured the trial, fiery fierce, but fleet,
Would, from his little heap of ashes, lend
Wings to that conflagration of the world
Which Christ awaits ere He makes all things new:
So should the frail become the perfect, rapt
From glory of pain to glory of joy; and so,
Even in the end,—the act renouncing earth,
Lands, houses, husbands, wives and children here,—
Begin that other act which finds all, lost,
Regained, in this time even, a hundredfold,   1800
And, in the next time, feels the finite love
Blent and embalmed with the eternal life.
So does the sun ghastlily seem to sink
In those north parts, lean all but out of life,
Desist a dread mere breathing-stop, then slow
Re-assert day, begin the endless rise.
Was this too easy for our after-stage?
Was such a lighting-up of faith, in life,
Only allowed initiate, set man's step
In the true way by help of the great glow?   1810
A way wherein it is ordained he walk,
Bearing to see the light from heaven still more
And more encroached on by the light of earth,
Tentatives earth puts forth to rival heaven,
Earthly incitements that mankind serve God
For man's sole sake, not God's and therefore man's.
Till at last, who distinguishes the sun
From a mere Druid fire on a far mount?
More praise to him who with his subtle prism
Shall decompose both beams and name the true.   1820
In such sense, who is last proves first indeed;
For how could saints and martyrs fail see truth
Streak the night's blackness? Who is faithful now,

Who untwists heaven's white from the yellow flare
O' the world's gross torch, without night's foil that helped
Produce the Christian act so possible
When in the way stood Nero's cross and stake,—
So hard now when the world smiles "Right and wise!
Faith points the politic, the thrifty way,
Will make who plods it in the end returns   1830
Beyond mere fool's-sport and improvidence.
We fools dance through the cornfield of this life,
Pluck ears to left and right and swallow raw,
—Nay, tread, at pleasure, a sheaf underfoot,
To get the better at some poppy-flower,—
Well aware we shall have so much less wheat
In the eventual harvest: you meantime
Waste not a spike,—the richlier will you reap!
What then? There will be always garnered meal
Sufficient for our comfortable loaf,   1840
While you enjoy the undiminished sack!"
Is it not this ignoble confidence,
Cowardly hardihood, that dulls and damps,
Makes the old heroism impossible?

Unless . . . what whispers me of times to come?
What if it be the mission of that age
My death will usher into life, to shake
This torpor of assurance from our creed,
Reintroduce the doubt discarded, bring
That formidable danger back, we drove   1850
Long ago to the distance and the dark?
No wild beast now prowls round the infant camp:
We have built wall and sleep in city safe:
But if some earthquake try the towers that laugh
To think they once saw lions rule outside,
And man stand out again, pale, resolute,
Prepared to die,—which means, alive at last?
As we broke up that old faith of the world,
Have we, next age, to break up this the new—
Faith, in the thing, grown faith in the report—   1860
Whence need to bravely disbelieve report
Through increased faith i' the thing reports belie?
Must we deny,—do they, these Molinists,
At peril of their body and their soul,—
Recognized truths, obedient to some truth
Unrecognized yet, but perceptible?—
Correct the portrait by the living face,
Man's God, by God's God in the mind of man?
Then, for the few that rise to the new height,

The many that must sink to the old depth,   1870
The multitude found fall away! A few,
E'en ere new law speak clear, may keep the old,
Preserve the Christian level, call good good
And evil evil, (even though razed and blank
The old titles,) helped by custom, habitude,
And all else they mistake for finer sense
O' the fact that reason warrants,—as before,
They hope perhaps, fear not impossibly.
At least some one Pompilia left the world
Will say "I know the right place by foot's feel,   1880
I took it and tread firm there; wherefore change?"
But what a multitude will surely fall
Quite through the crumbling truth, late subjacent,
Sink to the next discoverable base,
Rest upon human nature, settle there
On what is firm, the lust and pride of life!
A mass of men, whose very souls even now
Seem to need re-creating,—so they slink
Worm-like into the mud, light now lays bare,—
Whose future we dispose of with shut eyes   1890
And whisper—"They are grafted, barren twigs,
Into the living stock of Christ: may bear
One day, till when they lie death-like, not dead,"—
Those who with all the aid of Christ succumb,
How, without Christ, shall they, unaided, sink?
Whither but to this gulf before my eyes?
Do not we end, the century and I?
The impatient antimasque treads close on kibe
O' the very masque's self it will mock,—on me,
Last lingering personage, the impatient mime   1900
Pushes already,—will I block the way?
Will my slow trail of garments ne'er leave space
For pantaloon, sock, plume and castanet?
Here comes the first experimentalist
In the new order of things,—he plays a priest;
Does he take inspiration from the Church,
Directly make her rule his law of life?
Not he: his own mere impulse guides the man—
Happily sometimes, since ourselves allow
He has danced, in gayety of heart, i' the main   1910
The right step through the maze we bade him foot.
But if his heart had prompted him break loose
And mar the measure? Why, we must submit,
And thank the chance that brought him safe so far.
Will he repeat the prodigy? Perhaps.
Can he teach others how to quit themselves,

Show why this step was right while that were wrong?
How should he? "Ask your hearts as I asked mine,
And get discreetly through the morrice too;
If your hearts misdirect you,—quit the stage,   1920
And make amends,—be there amends to make!"
Such is, for the Augustin that was once,
This Canon Caponsacchi we see now.
"But my heart answers to another tune,"
Puts in the Abate, second in the suite;
"I have my taste too, and tread no such step!
You choose the glorious life, and may, for me!
I like the lowest of life's appetites,—
So you judge,—but the very truth of joy
To my own apprehension which decides.   1930
Call me knave and you get yourself called fool!
I live for greed, ambition, lust, revenge;
Attain these ends by force, guile: hypocrite,
To-day, perchance to-morrow recognized
The rational man, the type of common sense."
There 's Loyola adapted to our time!
Under such guidance Guido plays his part,
He also influencing in the due turn
These last clods where I track intelligence
By any glimmer, these four at his beck   1940
Ready to murder any, and, at their own,
As ready to murder him,—such make the world!
And, first effect of the new cause of things,
There they lie also duly,—the old pair
Of the weak head and not so wicked heart,
With the one Christian mother, wife and girl,
—Which three gifts seem to make an angel up,—
The world's first foot o' the dance is on their heads!
Still, I stand here, not off the stage though close
On the exit: and my last act, as my first,   1950
I owe the scene, and Him who armed me thus
With Paul's sword as with Peter's key. I smite
With my whole strength once more, ere end my part,
Ending, so far as man may, this offence.
And when I raise my arm, who plucks my sleeve?
Who stops me in the righteous function,—foe
Or friend? Oh, still as ever, friends are they
Who, in the interest of outraged truth
Deprecate such rough handling of a lie!
The facts being proved and incontestable,   1960
What is the last word I must listen to?
Perchance—"Spare yet a term this barren stock,

We pray thee dig about and dung and dress
Till he repent and bring forth fruit even yet!"
Perchance—"So poor and swift a punishment
Shall throw him out of life with all that sin:
Let mercy rather pile up pain on pain
Till the flesh expiate what the soul pays else!"
Nowise! Remonstrants on each side commence
Instructing, there 's a new tribunal now   1970
Higher than God's—the educated man's!
Nice sense of honor in the human breast
Supersedes here the old coarse oracle—
Confirming none the less a point or so
Wherein blind predecessors worked aright
By rule of thumb: as when Christ said,—when, where?
Enough, I find it pleaded in a place,—
"All other wrongs done, patiently I take:
But touch my honor and the case is changed!
I feel the due resentment,—*nemini*   1980
Honorem trado is my quick retort."
Right of Him, just as if pronounced to-day!
Still, should the old authority be mute
Or doubtful, or in speaking clash with new,
The younger takes permission to decide.
At last we have the instinct of the world
Ruling its household without tutelage:
And while the two laws, human and divine,
Have busied finger with this tangled case,
In pushes the brisk junior, cuts the knot,   1990
Pronounces for acquittal. How it trips
Silverly o'er the tongue! "Remit the death!
Forgive, . . . well, in the old way, if thou please,
Decency and the relics of routine
Respected,—let the Count go free as air!
Since he may plead a priest's immunity,—
The minor orders help enough for that,
With Farinacci's license,—who decides
That the mere implication of such man,
So privileged, in any cause, before   2000
Whatever Court except the Spiritual,
Straight quashes law-procedure,—quash it, then!
Remains a pretty loophole of escape
Moreover, that, beside the patent fact
O' the law's allowance, there 's involved the weal
O' the Popedom: a son's privilege at stake,
Thou wilt pretend the Church's interest,
Ignore all finer reasons to forgive!

But herein lies the crowning cogency—
(Let thy friends teach thee while thou tellest beads)—   2010
That in this case the spirit of culture speaks,
Civilization is imperative.
To her shall we remand all delicate points
Henceforth, nor take irregular advice
O' the sly, as heretofore: she used to hint
Remonstrances, when law was out of sorts
Because a saucy tongue was put to rest,
An eye that roved was cured of arrogance:
But why be forced to mumble under breath
What soon shall be acknowledged as plain fact,   2020
Outspoken, say, in thy successor's time?
Methinks we see the golden age return!
Civilization and the Emperor
Succeed to Christianity and Pope.
One Emperor then, as one Pope now: meanwhile,
Anticipate a little! We tell thee 'Take
Guido's life, sapped society shall crash,
Whereof the main prop was, is, and shall be
—Supremacy of husband over wife!'
Does the man rule i' the house, and may his mate   2030
Because of any plea dispute the same?
Oh, pleas of all sorts shall abound, be sure,
One but allowed validity,—for, harsh
And savage, for, inept and silly-sooth,
For, this and that, will the ingenious sex
Demonstrate the best master e'er graced slave:
And there 's but one short way to end the coil,—
Acknowledge right and reason steadily
I' the man and master: then the wife submits
To plain truth broadly stated. Does the time   2040
Advise we shift—a pillar? nay, a stake
Out of its place i' the social tenement?
One touch may send a shudder through the heap
And bring it toppling on our children's heads!
Moreover, if ours breed a qualm in thee,
Give thine own better feeling play for once!
Thou, whose own life winks o'er the socket-edge,
Wouldst thou it went out in such ugly snuff
As dooming sons dead, e'en though justice prompt?
Why, on a certain feast, Barabbas' self   2050
Was set free, not to cloud the general cheer:
Neither shalt thou pollute thy Sabbath close!
Mercy is safe and graceful. How one hears
The howl begin, scarce the three little taps
O' the silver mallet silent on thy brow,—

'His last act was to sacrifice a Count
And thereby screen a scandal of the Church!
Guido condemned, the Canon justified
Of course,—delinquents of his cloth go free!'
And so the Luthers chuckle, Calvins scowl,   2060
So thy hand helps Molinos to the chair
Whence he may hold forth till doom's day on just
These *petit-maître* priestlings,—in the choir
Sanctus et Benedictus, with a brush
Of soft guitar-strings that obey the thumb,
Touched by the bedside, for accompaniment!
Does this give umbrage to a husband? Death
To the fool, and to the priest impunity!
But no impunity to any friend
So simply over-loyal as these four   2070
Who made religion of their patron's cause,
Believed in him and did his bidding straight,
Asked not one question but laid down the lives
This Pope took,—all four lives together make
Just his own length of days,—so, dead they lie,
As these were times when loyalty 's a drug,
And zeal in a subordinate too cheap
And common to be saved when we spend life!
Come, 't is too much good breath we waste in words:
The pardon, Holy Father! Spare grimace,   2080
Shrugs and reluctance! Are not we the world,
Art not thou Priam? let soft culture plead
Hecuba-like, '*non tali*' (Virgil serves)
'*Auxilio*,' and the rest! Enough, it works!
The Pope relaxes, and the Prince is loth,
The father's bowels yearn, the man's will bends,
Reply is apt. Our tears on tremble, hearts
Big with a benediction, wait the word
Shall circulate through the city in a trice,
Set every window flaring, give each man   2090
O' the mob his torch to wave for gratitude.
Pronounce then, for our breath and patience fail!"

I will, Sirs: but a voice other than yours
Quickens my spirit. "*Quis pro Domino?*
Who is upon the Lord's side?" asked the Count.
I, who write—
                    "On receipt of this command,
Acquaint Count Guido and his fellows four
They die to-morrow: could it be to-night,
The better, but the work to do, takes time.
Set with all diligence a scaffold up,   2100

Not in the customary place, by Bridge
Saint Angelo, where die the common sort;
But since the man is noble, and his peers
By predilection haunt the People's Square,
There let him be beheaded in the midst,
And his companions hanged on either side:
So shall the quality see, fear, and learn.
All which work takes time: till to-morrow, then,
Let there be prayer incessant for the five!"

For the main criminal I have no hope   2110
Except in such a suddenness of fate.
I stood at Naples once, a night so dark
I could have scarce conjectured there was earth
Anywhere, sky or sea or world at all:
But the night's black was burst through by a blaze—
Thunder struck blow on blow, earth groaned and bore,
Through her whole length of mountain visible:
There lay the city thick and plain with spires,
And, like a ghost disshrouded, white the sea.
So may the truth be flashed out by one blow,   2120
And Guido see, one instant, and be saved.
Else I avert my face, nor follow him
Into that sad obscure sequestered state
Where God unmakes but to remake the soul
He else made first in vain; which must not be.
Enough, for I may die this very night:
And how should I dare die, this man let live?

Carry this forthwith to the Governor!
1868–1869

Matthew Arnold
December 24, 1822—April 15, 1888

A BIOGRAPHICAL SKETCH

Matthew Arnold was the eldest son of a man so distinguished he was a legendary prototype in the imaginations of the generation which felt the impress of his mind and personality and which succeeded him to the intellectual leadership of England. Thomas Arnold ("Arnold of Rugby" as he was somewhat majestically called) was Regius Professor of Modern History at Oxford and, from 1828 until his sudden death in 1842, the most famous headmaster in England. It was a significant period of religious renovation and intellectual expansion; and Thomas Arnold left an indelible mark on many men who, as boys, underwent the regimen of Rugby School during the period of his headmastership. (See Notes, *Rugby Chapel*, p. 687.) One of those men was Matthew Arnold. It is tempting to overinterpret the father-son interlacing in the case of the Arnolds, as much of the scholarly literature shows. But it seems clear enough that Matthew Arnold's earnest search for qualitative values, the liberality of his "imaginative reason," and the propagandist role he assumed in the second phase of his literary career (especially in cultural analysis and Biblical criticism) owed much to the genuine admiration of the son for the imposing example of the father.

Arnold's schooldays were serious and competitive. At Rugby he won a poetry prize for *Alaric at Rome* (1840), in the same year successfully competed for an open Classical Scholarship at Balliol, and in the next year won a School Exhibition. In the fall of 1841, Arnold took up residence at Balliol College, Oxford. His career there was relaxed and respectable without being meteoric. He won the Newdigate Prize for his poem *Cromwell* in 1843, but in 1844 he took a Second Class degree, having neglected to prepare with sufficient discipline for his examinations. This failure was, however, offset by his election in March 1845 as a Fellow of Oriel College, Oxford, where he took up residence for the probationary year.

Arnold had also enjoyed a number of enriching nonacademic experiences. His family had built in 1833 a retreat at Fox How in the Lake District, and they spent their summers there, maintaining friendly relationships with the Wordsworths. In 1837 he had accompanied his family on a summer tour of northern France and in the autumn of 1841 had explored southern France and the Pyrenees with his father. He was a great admirer of the works of George Sand, and in 1846 he made a pilgrimage to her home in France, combined with a visit to Switzerland. In France he became infatuated with an actress (1847) and in Switzerland (1848, 1849) with the presumed original of *Marguerite*. (See *Switzerland*, p. 573, and Notes, p. 681.)

In 1847 Arnold became private secretary to Lord Lansdowne, Lord President of the Council and chief educational officer of the government. In 1851 he was appointed by Lord Lansdowne an Inspector of Schools, a position which he held and at which he labored diligently and effectively until 1886. He was thus enabled in 1851 to marry Frances Lucy Wightman, daughter of a judge of the Court of the Queen's Bench. His marriage, though saddened by the deaths of three of his sons, was stable and rewarding.

It was not until 1853 that Arnold published a volume of poems with which he was reasonably satisfied. In 1849 he had issued *The Strayed Reveller, and Other Poems*, by "A," but almost immediately he withdrew the volume. In 1852 he issued *Empedocles on Etna, and Other Poems* but again withdrew it. He was struggling earnestly with a most distressing question—the true nature and function of the modern poet. The early poems themselves are shot through with thematic implications of the question; and his most important correspondence at this time (with his poet-friend Arthur Hugh Clough) is full of explicit and intense confrontations of it. The *Poems* of 1853 provide the first firm evidence that Arnold felt that he had at last come to terms with the question: he attached a most remarkable preface to the volume; he withdrew the major poem he had written to date, *Empedocles on Etna*; he attempted to illustrate the theory of the preface in several of the poems, most notably in *Sohrab and Rustum*; he signed his name and let the volume make its way. Arnold wrote several important poems after 1853 (e.g., *Thyrsis, Dover Beach, Rugby Chapel, Stanzas from the Grande Chartreuse, Obermann Once More*), but they are comparatively few and, except for their individual excellence, do not redefine the character of his poetic canon.

In 1857 Arnold was elected Professor of Poetry at Oxford. He held the post for two five-year terms and was required to give three lectures annually. Out of these requirements and the opportunity the post provided emerged Arnold the literary critic and cultural analyst: *On the Modern Element in Literature*, his inaugural (1857), *On Translating*

Homer (1861), *Essays in Criticism*, first series (1865), *On the Study of Celtic Literature* (1867), and *Culture and Anarchy* (1869). By 1866 he had fully earned Swinburne's accolade of the "most delicate and thoughtful of English critics . . ." and, it might be added, the most acute and provocative of English cultural analysts.

Arnold's duties as School Inspector contributed greatly to his understanding of the English society of his day—its class structure, its impediments, its chance of self-renewal. They also made him a trained expert on education itself, as seen in his discriminating and sprightly volumes, e.g., *The Popular Education of France* (1861), *A French Eton* (1864), *Schools and Universities on the Continent* (1868). In the 1870's he pursued ideas and interests, germinated from his earlier thought and from his sense of mission, through a series of reflections on religion and on the Bible's modern relevance: *St. Paul and Protestantism* (1870), *Literature and Dogma* (1873), *God and the Bible* (1875), and *Last Essays on Church and Religion* (1877), this last with a lucid and altogether satisfying preface.

It is not dismissive to see certain of Arnold's volumes as tangential to the central patterns of his canon, e.g., *Merope. A Tragedy* (1858), *England and the Italian Question* (1859), *Friendship's Garland* (1871), *Mixed Essays* (1879), *Irish Essays and Others* (1882), *Discourses in America* (1885), *Essays in Criticism, Second Series* (1888, posthumously). Everything Arnold did had a mark of distinction about it, and his works taken as a whole easily earn him the right to be called the greatest Victorian man of letters.

A BIBLIOGRAPHICAL NOTE

The standard edition of Arnold's poetry is *The Poetical Works of Matthew Arnold*, edited by C. B. Tinker and H. F. Lowry (London, New York, and Toronto: Oxford University Press, 1950), to which there is a companion handbook, *The Poetry of Matthew Arnold: A Commentary* (1940), with the same editors as authors and the same publisher. The *Complete Prose Works*, edited by R. H. Super (Ann Arbor: University of Michigan Press, 1960–) is in process. The Edition de Luxe of the *Works* (London: Macmillan, 1903–1904) has been standard since its publication. Lionel Trilling's *Matthew Arnold*, revised edition (New York: Columbia University Press, 1949), is a classic introduction to Arnold; and A. Dwight Culler's *Imaginative Reason: The Poetry of Matthew Arnold* (New Haven and London: Yale University Press, 1966) provides a challenging point of critical departure. In the absence of a genuine biography perhaps the best alternative, especially for Arnold's period of *Sturm und Drang*, is *The Letters of Matthew Arnold to Arthur Hugh Clough*, edited by

H. F. Lowry (London and New York: Oxford University Press, 1932).
The selections in this text are based on the Tinker and Lowry edition.

QUIET WORK

One lesson, Nature, let me learn of thee,
One lesson which in every wind is blown,
One lesson of two duties kept at one
Though the loud world proclaim their enmity—

Of toil unsever'd from tranquillity!
Of labour, that in lasting fruit outgrows
Far noisier schemes, accomplish'd in repose,
Too great for haste, too high for rivalry!

Yes, while on earth a thousand discords ring,
Man's fitful uproar mingling with his toil,
Still do thy sleepless ministers move on,

Their glorious tasks in silence perfecting;
Still working, blaming still our vain turmoil,
Labourers that shall not fail, when man is gone.
1849

MYCERINUS

"Not by the justice that my father spurn'd,
Not for the thousands whom my father slew,
Altars unfed and temples overturn'd,
Cold hearts and thankless tongues, where thanks are due:
Fell this dread voice from lips that cannot lie,
Stern sentence of the Powers of Destiny.

"I will unfold my sentence and my crime.
My crime—that, rapt in reverential awe,
I sate obedient, in the fiery prime
Of youth, self-govern'd, at the feet of Law;
Ennobling this dull pomp, the life of kings,
By contemplation of diviner things.

"My father loved injustice, and lived long;
Crown'd with gray hairs he died, and full of sway.

I loved the good he scorn'd, and hated wrong—
The Gods declare my recompense to-day.
I look'd for life more lasting, rule more high;
And when six years are measured, lo, I die!

"Yet surely, O my people, did I deem
Man's justice from the all-just Gods was given;   20
A light that from some upper fount did beam,
Some better archetype, whose seat was heaven;
A light that, shining from the blest abodes,
Did shadow somewhat of the life of Gods.

"Mere phantoms of man's self-tormenting heart,
Which on the sweets that woo it dares not feed!
Vain dreams, which quench our pleasures, then depart,
When the duped soul, self-master'd, claims its meed;
When, on the strenuous just man, Heaven bestows,
Crown of his struggling life, an unjust close!   30

"Seems it so light a thing, then, austere Powers,
To spurn man's common lure, life's pleasant things?
Seems there no joy in dances crown'd with flowers,
Love, free to range, and regal banquetings?
Bend ye on these, indeed, an unmoved eye,
Not Gods but ghosts, in frozen apathy?

"Or is it that some Force, too wise, too strong,
Even for yourselves to conquer or beguile,
Sweeps earth, and heaven, and men, and gods along,
Like the broad volume of the insurgent Nile?   40
And the great powers we serve, themselves may be
Slaves of a tyrannous necessity?

"Or in mid-heaven, perhaps, your golden cars,
Where earthly voice climbs never, wing their flight,
And in wild hunt, through mazy tracts of stars,
Sweep in the sounding stillness of the night?
Or in deaf ease, on thrones of dazzling sheen,
Drinking deep draughts of joy, ye dwell serene?

"Oh, wherefore cheat our youth, if thus it be,
Of one short joy, one lust, one pleasant dream?   50
Stringing vain words of powers we cannot see,
Blind divinations of a will supreme;
Lost labour! when the circumambient gloom
But hides, if Gods, Gods careless of our doom?

"The rest I give to joy. Even while I speak,
My sand runs short; and—as yon star-shot ray,

Hemm'd by two banks of cloud, peers pale and weak,
Now, as the barrier closes, dies away—
Even so do past and future intertwine,
Blotting this six years' space, which yet is mine.   60

"Six years—six little years—six drops of time!
Yet suns shall rise, and many moons shall wane,
And old men die, and young men pass their prime,
And languid pleasure fade and flower again,
And the dull Gods behold, ere these are flown,
Revels more deep, joy keener than their own.

"Into the silence of the groves and woods
I will go forth; though something would I say—
Something—yet what, I know not; for the Gods
The doom they pass revoke not, nor delay;   70
And prayers, and gifts, and tears, are fruitless all,
And the night waxes, and the shadows fall.

"Ye men of Egypt, ye have heard your king!
I go, and I return not. But the will
Of the great Gods is plain; and ye must bring
Ill deeds, ill passions, zealous to fulfil
Their pleasure, to their feet; and reap their praise,
The praise of Gods, rich boon! and length of days."

—So spake he, half in anger, half in scorn;
And one loud cry of grief and of amaze   80
Broke from his sorrowing people; so he spake,
And turning, left them there; and with brief pause,
Girt with a throng of revellers, bent his way
To the cool region of the groves he loved.
There by the river-banks he wander'd on,
From palm-grove on to palm-grove, happy trees,
Their smooth tops shining sunward, and beneath
Burying their unsunn'd stems in grass and flowers;
Where in one dream the feverish time of youth
Might fade in slumber, and the feet of joy   90
Might wander all day long and never tire.
Here came the king, holding high feast, at morn,
Rose-crown'd; and ever, when the sun went down,
A hundred lamps beam'd in the tranquil gloom,
From tree to tree all through the twinkling grove,
Revealing all the tumult of the feast—
Flush'd guests, and golden goblets foam'd with wine;
While the deep-burnish'd foliage overhead
Splinter'd the silver arrows of the moon.
    It may be that sometimes his wondering soul   100
From the loud joyful laughter of his lips

Might shrink half startled, like a guilty man
Who wrestles with his dream; as some pale shape
Gliding half hidden through the dusky stems,
Would thrust a hand before the lifted bowl,
Whispering: A *little space, and thou art mine!*
It may be on that joyless feast his eye
Dwelt with mere outward seeming; he, within,
Took measure of his soul, and knew its strength,
And by that silent knowledge, day by day,   110
Was calm'd, ennobled, comforted, sustain'd.
It may be; but not less his brow was smooth,
And his clear laugh fled ringing through the gloom,
And his mirth quail'd not at the mild reproof
Sigh'd out by winter's sad tranquillity;
Nor, pall'd with its own fulness, ebb'd and died
In the rich languor of long summer-days;
Nor wither'd when the palm-tree plumes, that roof'd
With their mild dark his grassy banquet-hall,
Bent to the cold winds of the showerless spring;   120
No, nor grew dark when autumn brought the clouds.
     So six long years he revell'd, night and day.
And when the mirth wax'd loudest, with dull sound
Sometimes from the grove's centre echoes came,
To tell his wondering people of their king;
In the still night, across the steaming flats,
Mix'd with the murmur of the moving Nile.
1849

TO A FRIEND

Who prop, thou ask'st, in these bad days, my mind?—
He much, the old man, who, clearest-soul'd of men,
Saw The Wide Prospect, and the Asian Fen,
And Tmolus hill, and Smyrna bay, though blind.

Much he, whose friendship I not long since won,
That halting slave, who in Nicopolis
Taught Arrian, when Vespasian's brutal son
Clear'd Rome of what most shamed him. But be his

My special thanks, whose even-balanced soul,
From first youth tested up to extreme old age,   10
Business could not make dull, nor passion wild;

Who saw life steadily, and saw it whole;
The mellow glory of the Attic stage,
Singer of sweet Colonus, and its child.
1849

SHAKESPEARE

Others abide our question. Thou art free.
We ask and ask—Thou smilest and art still,
Out-topping knowledge. For the loftiest hill,
Who to the stars uncrowns his majesty,

Planting his steadfast footsteps in the sea,   5
Making the heaven of heavens his dwelling-place,
Spares but the cloudy border of his base
To the foil'd searching of mortality;

And thou, who didst the stars and sunbeams know,
Self-school'd, self-scann'd, self-honor'd, self-secure,   10
Didst tread on earth unguess'd at.—Better so!

All pains the immortal spirit must endure,
All weakness which impairs, all griefs which bow,
Find their sole speech in that victorious brow.
1849

THE STRAYED REVELLER

The Portico of Circe's Palace. Evening. A Youth. Circe.

THE YOUTH. Faster, faster,
  O Circe, Goddess,
  Let the wild, thronging train,
  The bright procession
  Of eddying forms,   5
  Sweep through my soul!

  Thou standest, smiling
  Down on me! thy right arm,
  Lean'd up against the column there,
  Props thy soft cheek;   10
  Thy left holds, hanging loosely,
  The deep cup, ivy-cinctured,
  I held but now.

  Is it, then, evening
  So soon? I see, the night-dews,   15
  Cluster'd in thick beads, dim
  The agate brooch-stones

On thy white shoulder;
The cool night-wind, too,
Blows through the portico,   20
Stirs thy hair, Goddess,
Waves thy white robe!

CIRCE. Whence art thou, sleeper?

THE YOUTH. When the white dawn first
   Through the rough fir-planks   25
Of my hut, by the chestnuts,
Up at the valley-head,
Came breaking, Goddess!
I sprang up, I threw round me
My dappled fawn-skin;   30
Passing out, from the wet turf,
Where they lay, by the hut door,
I snatch'd up my vine-crown, my fir-staff,
All drench'd in dew—
Came swift down to join   35
The rout early gather'd
In the town, round the temple,
Iacchus' white fane
On yonder hill.

Quick I pass'd, following   40
The wood-cutters' cart-track
Down the dark valley;—I saw
On my left, through the beeches,
Thy palace, Goddess,
Smokeless, empty!   45
Trembling, I enter'd; beheld
The court all silent,
The lions sleeping,
On the altar this bowl.
I drank, Goddess!   50
And sank down here, sleeping,
On the steps of thy portico.

CIRCE. Foolish boy! Why tremblest thou?
   Thou lovest it, then, my wine?
Wouldst more of it? See, how glows,   55
Through the delicate, flush'd marble,
The red, creaming liquor,
Strown with dark seeds!
Drink, then! I chide thee not,
Deny thee not my bowl.   60
Come, stretch forth thy hand, then—so!
Drink—drink again!

THE YOUTH. Thanks, gracious one!
   Ah, the sweet fumes again!
   More soft, ah me,   65
   More subtle-winding
   Than Pan's flute-music!
   Faint—faint! Ah me,
   Again the sweet sleep!

CIRCE. Hist! Thou—within there!   70
   Come forth, Ulysses!
   Art tired with hunting?
   While we range the woodland,
   See what the day brings.

ULYSSES. Ever new magic!   75
   Hast thou then lured hither,
   Wonderful Goddess, by thy art,
   The young, languid-eyed Ampelus,
   Iacchus' darling—
   Or some youth beloved of Pan,   80
   Of Pan and the Nymphs?
   That he sits, bending downward
   His white, delicate neck
   To the ivy-wreathed marge
   Of thy cup; the bright, glancing vine-leaves   85
   That crown his hair,
   Falling forward, mingling
   With the dark ivy-plants—
   His fawn-skin, half untied,
   Smear'd with red wine-stains? Who is he,   90
   That he sits, overweigh'd
   By fumes of wine and sleep,
   So late, in thy portico?
   What youth, Goddess,—what guest
   Of Gods or mortals?   95

CIRCE. Hist! he wakes!
   I lured him not hither, Ulysses.
   Nay, ask him!

THE YOUTH. Who speaks? Ah, who comes forth
   To thy side, Goddess, from within?   100
   How shall I name him?
   This spare, dark-featured,
   Quick-eyed stranger?
   Ah, and I see too
   His sailor's bonnet,   105
   His short coat, travel-tarnish'd,
   With one arm bare!—

Art thou not he, whom fame
This long time rumours
The favour'd guest of Circe, brought by the waves?   110
Art thou he, stranger?
The wise Ulysses,
Laertes' son?

ULYSSES. I am Ulysses.
  And thou, too, sleeper?   115
  Thy voice is sweet. —— *i clarifies that he is a poet*
  It may be thou hast follow'd
  Through the islands some divine bard,
  By age taught many things,
  Age and the Muses;   120
  And heard him delighting
  The chiefs and people
  In the banquet, and learn'd his songs,
  Of Gods and Heroes,
  Of war and arts,   125
  And peopled cities,
  Inland, or built
  By the grey sea.—If so, then hail!
  I honour and welcome thee. —— *Description of what Gods see*

THE YOUTH. The Gods are happy.   130
  They turn on all sides
  Their shining eyes,
  And see below them
  The earth and men.

  They see Tiresias *— Greek Prophet*   135
  Sitting, staff in hand,
  On the warm, grassy
  Asopus bank,
  His robe drawn over
  His old, sightless head,   140
  Revolving inly
  The doom of Thebes.

  They see the Centaurs *— ½ man ½ horse*
  In the upper glens
  Of Pelion, in the streams,   145
  Where red-berried ashes fringe
  The clear-brown shallow pools,
  With streaming flanks, and heads
  Rear'd proudly, snuffing
  The mountain wind.   150

They see the Indian
Drifting, knife in hand,
His frail boat moor'd to
A floating isle thick-matted
With large-leaved, low-creeping melon-plants,   155
And the dark cucumber.
He reaps, and stows them,
Drifting—drifting;—round him,
Round his green harvest-plot,
Flow the cool lake-waves,   160
The mountains ring them.

They see the Scythian
On the wide stepp, unharnessing
His wheel'd house at noon.
He tethers his beast down, and makes his meal—   165
Mares' milk, and bread
Baked on the embers;—all around
The boundless, waving grass-plains stretch, thick-starr'd
With saffron and the yellow hollyhock
And flag-leaved iris-flowers.   170
Sitting in his cart
He makes his meal; before him, for long miles,
Alive with bright green lizards,
And the springing bustard-fowl,
The track, a straight black line,   175
Furrows the rich soil; here and there
Clusters of lonely mounds
Topp'd with rough-hewn,
Grey, rain-blear'd statues, overpeer
The sunny waste.   180

They see the ferry
On the broad, clay-laden
Lone Chorasmian stream;—thereon,
With snort and strain,
Two horses, strongly swimming, tow   185
The ferry-boat, with woven ropes
To either bow
Firm-harness'd by the mane; a chief,
With shout and shaken spear,
Stands at the prow, and guides them; but astern   190
The cowering merchants, in long robes,
Sit pale beside their wealth
Of silk-bales and of balsam-drops,
Of gold and ivory,
Of turquoise-earth and amethyst,   195
Jasper and chalcedony,

And milk-barr'd onyx-stones.
The loaded boat swings groaning
In the yellow eddies;
The Gods behold them.   200
They see the Heroes
Sitting in the dark ship
On the foamless, long-heaving
Violet sea,
At sunset nearing   205
The Happy Islands.

These things, Ulysses,
The wise bards also
Behold and sing.
But oh, what labour!   210
O prince, what pain!

They too can see
Tiresias;—but the Gods,
Who give them vision,
Added this law: 215
That they should bear too
His groping blindness,
His dark foreboding,
His scorn'd white hairs;
Bear Hera's anger   220
Through a life lengthen'd
To seven ages.

They see the Centaurs
On Pelion;—then they feel,
They too, the maddening wine   225
Swell their large veins to bursting; in wild pain
They feel the biting spears
Of the grim Lapithæ, and Theseus, drive,
Drive crashing through their bones; they feel,
High on a jutting rock in the red stream,   230
Alcmena's dreadful son
Ply his bow;—such a price
The Gods exact for song:
To become what we sing.

They see the Indian   235
On his mountain lake; but squalls
Make their skiff reel, and worms
In the unkind spring have gnawn
Their melon-harvest to the heart.—They see
The Scythian; but long frosts   240
Parch them in winter-time on the bare stepp,

Till they too fade like grass; they crawl
Like shadows forth in spring.

They see the merchants
On the Oxus stream;—but care   245
Must visit first them too, and make them pale.
Whether, through whirling sand,
A cloud of desert robber-horse have burst
Upon their caravan; or greedy kings,
In the wall'd cities the way passes through,   250
Crush'd them with tolls; or fever-airs,
On some great river's marge,
Mown them down, far from home.

They see the Heroes
Near harbour;—but they share   255
Their lives, and former violent toil in Thebes,
Seven-gated Thebes, or Troy;
Or where the echoing oars
Of Argo first
Startled the unknown sea.   260

The old Silenus
Came, lolling in the sunshine,
From the dewy forest-coverts,
This way, at noon.
Sitting by me, while his Fauns   265
Down at the water-side
Sprinkled and smoothed
His drooping garland,
He told me these things.

But I, Ulysses,   270
Sitting on the warm steps,
Looking over the valley,
All day long, have seen,
Without pain, without labour,
Sometimes a wild-hair'd Mænad—   275
Sometimes a Faun with torches—
And sometimes, for a moment,
Passing through the dark stems
Flowing-robed, the beloved,
The desired, the divine,   280
Beloved Iacchus.

Ah, cool night-wind, tremulous stars!
Ah, glimmering water,
Fitful earth-murmur,
Dreaming woods!   285

Ah, golden-hair'd, strangely smiling Goddess
And thou, proved, much-enduring,
Wave-toss'd Wanderer!
Who can stand still?
Ye fade, ye swim, ye waver before me— 290
The cup again!

Faster, faster,
O Circe, Goddess,
Let the wild, thronging train,
The bright procession 295
Of eddying forms,
Sweep through my soul!
1849

THE FORSAKEN MERMAN

Come, dear children, let us away;
Down and away below!
Now my brothers call from the bay,
Now the great winds shoreward blow,
Now the salt tides seaward flow; 5
Now the wild white horses play,
Champ and chafe and toss in the spray.
Children dear, let us away!
This way, this way!

Call her once before you go— 10
Call once yet!
In a voice that she will know:
'Margaret! Margaret!'
Children's voices should be dear
(Call once more) to a mother's ear; 15
Children's voices, wild with pain—
Surely she will come again!
Call her once and come away;
This way, this way!
'Mother dear, we cannot stay! 20
The wild white horses foam and fret.'
Margaret! Margaret!

Come, dear children, come away down;
Call no more!
One last look at the white-wall'd town, 25
And the little grey church on the windy shore,
Then come down!

She will not come though you call all day;
Come away, come away!

Children dear, was it yesterday   30
We heard the sweet bells over the bay?
In the caverns where we lay,
Through the surf and through the swell,
The far-off sound of a silver bell?
Sand-strewn caverns, cool and deep,   35
Where the winds are all asleep;
Where the spent lights quiver and gleam,
Where the salt weed sways in the stream,
Where the sea-beasts, ranged all round,
Feed in the ooze of their pasture-ground;   40
Where the sea-snakes coil and twine,
Dry their mail and bask in the brine;
Where great whales come sailing by,
Sail and sail, with unshut eye,
Round the world for ever and aye?   45
When did music come this way?
Children dear, was it yesterday?

Children dear, was it yesterday
(Call yet once) that she went away?
Once she sate with you and me,   50
On a red gold throne in the heart of the sea,
And the youngest sate on her knee.
She comb'd its bright hair, and she tended it well,
When down swung the sound of a far-off bell.
She sigh'd, she look'd up through the clear green sea;   55
She said: 'I must go, for my kinsfolk pray
In the little grey church on the shore to-day.
'Twill be Easter-time in the world—ah me!
And I lose my poor soul, Merman, here with thee.'
I said: 'Go up, dear heart, through the waves;   60
Say thy prayer, and come back to the kind sea-caves!'
She smiled, she went up through the surf in the bay.
Children dear, was it yesterday?

Children dear, were we long alone?
'The sea grows stormy, the little ones moan;   65
Long prayers,' I said, 'in the world they say;
Come!' I said; and we rose through the surf in the bay.
We went up the beach, by the sandy down
Where the sea-stocks bloom, to the white-wall'd town;
Through the narrow paved streets, where all was still,   70
To the little grey church on the windy hill.
From the church came a murmur of folk at their prayers,

But we stood without in the cold blowing airs.
We climb'd on the graves, on the stones worn with rains,
And we gazed up the aisle through the small leaded panes.   75
She sate by the pillar; we saw her clear;
'Margaret, hist! come quick, we are here!
Dear heart,' I said, 'we are long alone;
The sea grows stormy, the little ones moan.'
But, ah, she gave me never a look,   80
For her eyes were seal'd to the holy book!
Loud prays the priest; shut stands the door.
Come away, children, call no more!
Come away, come down, call no more!

  Down, down, down!   85
Down to the depths of the sea!
She sits at her wheel in the humming town,
Singing most joyfully.
Hark what she sings: 'O joy, O joy,
For the humming street, and the child with its toy!   90
For the priest, and the bell, and the holy well,
For the wheel where I spun,
And the blessed light of the sun!'
And so she sings her fill,
Singing most joyfully,   95
Till the spindle drops from her hand,
And the whizzing wheel stands still.
She steals to the window, and looks at the sand,
And over the sand at the sea;
And her eyes are set in a stare;   100
And anon there breaks a sigh,
And anon there drops a tear,
From a sorrow-clouded eye,
And a heart sorrow-laden,
A long, long sigh;   105
For the cold strange eyes of a little Mermaiden
And the gleam of her golden hair.

  Come away, away children;
Come children, come down!
The hoarse wind blows coldly;   110
Lights shine in the town.
She will start from her slumber
When gusts shake the door;
She will hear the winds howling,
Will hear the waves roar.   115
We shall see, while above us
The waves roar and whirl,

Description of the chamber of the mermans. Simple World.

A ceiling of amber,
A pavement of pearl.
Singing: 'Here came a mortal,   120
But faithless was she!
And alone dwell for ever
The kings of the sea.'

But, children, at midnight,
When soft the winds blow,   125
When clear falls the moonlight,
When spring-tides are low;
When sweet airs come seaward
From heaths starr'd with broom,
And high rocks throw mildly   130
On the blanch'd sands a gloom;
Up the still, glistening beaches,
Up the creeks we will hie,
Over banks of bright seaweed
The ebb-tide leaves dry.   135
We will gaze, from the sand-hills,
At the white, sleeping town;
At the church on the hill-side—
And then come back down.
Singing: 'There dwells a loved one,   140
But cruel is she!
She left lonely for ever
The kings of the sea.'
1849

Image of the mermans looking at the shore—shows tension

MEMORIAL VERSES

APRIL, 1850

Goethe in Weimar sleeps, and Greece,
Long since, saw Byron's struggle cease.
But one such death remain'd to come;
The last poetic voice is dumb—
We stand to-day by Wordsworth's tomb.   5

When Byron's eyes were shut in death,
We bow'd our head and held our breath.
He taught us little; but our soul
Had *felt* him like the thunder's roll.
With shivering heart the strife we saw   10
Of passion with eternal law;
And yet with reverential awe

We watch'd the fount of fiery life
Which served for that Titanic strife.

When Goethe's death was told, we said: 15
Sung, then, is Europe's sagest head.
Physician of the iron age,
Goethe has done his pilgrimage.
He took the suffering human race,
He read each wound, each weakness clear;   20
And struck his finger on the place,
And said: *Thou ailest here, and here!*
He look'd on Europe's dying hour
Of fitful dream and feverish power;
His eye plunged down the weltering strife,   25
The turmoil of expiring life—
He said: *The end is everywhere,*
Art still has truth, take refuge there!
And he was happy, if to know
Causes of things, and far below   30
His feet to see the lurid flow
Of terror, and insane distress,
And headlong fate, be happiness.

And Wordsworth!—Ah, pale ghosts, rejoice!
For never has such soothing voice   35
Been to your shadowy world convey'd,
Since erst, at morn, some wandering shade
Heard the clear song of Orpheus come
Through Hades, and the mournful gloom.
Wordsworth has gone from us—and ye,   40
Ah, may ye feel his voice as we!
He too upon a wintry clime
Had fallen—on this iron time
Of doubts, disputes, distractions, fears.
He found us when the age had bound   45
Our souls in its benumbing round;
He spoke, and loosed our heart in tears.
He laid us as we lay at birth
On the cool flowery lap of earth,
Smiles broke from us and we had ease;   50
The hills were round us, and the breeze
Went o'er the sun-lit fields again;
Our foreheads felt the wind and rain.
Our youth return'd; for there was shed
On spirits that had long been dead,   55
Spirits dried up and closely furl'd,
The freshness of the early world.

Ah! since dark days still bring to light
Man's prudence and man's fiery might,
Time may restore us in his course   60
Goethe's sage mind and Byron's force;
But where will Europe's latter hour
Again find Wordsworth's healing power?
Others will teach us how to dare,
And against fear our breast to steel;   65
Others will strengthen us to bear—
But who, ah! who, will make us feel?
The cloud of mortal destiny,
Others will front it fearlessly—
But who, like him, will put it by?   70

Keep fresh the grass upon his grave
O Rotha, with thy living wave!
Sing him thy best! for few or none
Hears thy voice right, now he is gone.
1850

STANZAS

IN MEMORY OF THE AUTHOR OF 'OBERMANN'

NOVEMBER, 1849

In front the awful Alpine track
Crawls up its rocky stair;
The autumn storm-winds drive the rack,
Close o'er it, in the air.

Behind are the abandon'd baths   5
Mute in their meadows lone;
The leaves are on the valley-paths,
The mists are on the Rhone—

The white mists rolling like a sea!
I hear the torrents roar.   10
—Yes, Obermann, all speaks of thee;
I feel thee near once more!

I turn thy leaves! I feel their breath
Once more upon me roll;
That air of languor, cold, and death,   15
Which brooded o'er thy soul.

Fly hence, poor wretch, whoe'er thou art,
Condemn'd to cast about,

All shipwreck in thy own weak heart,
For comfort from without!   20

A fever in these pages burns
Beneath the calm they feign;
A wounded human spirit turns,
Here, on its bed of pain.

Yes, though the virgin mountain-air   25
Fresh through these pages blows;
Though to these leaves the glaciers spare
The soul of their white snows;

Though here a mountain-murmur swells
Of many a dark-bough'd pine;   30
Though, as you read, you hear the bells
Of the high-pasturing kine—

Yet, through the hum of torrent lone,
And brooding mountain-bee,
There sobs I know not what ground-tone   35
Of human agony.

Is it for this, because the sound
Is fraught too deep with pain,
That, Obermann! the world around
So little loves thy strain?   40

Some secrets may the poet tell,
For the world loves new ways;
To tell too deep ones is not well—
It knows not what he says.

Yet, of the spirits who have reign'd   45
In this our troubled day,
I know but two, who have attain'd,
Save thee, to see their way.

By England's lakes, in grey old age,
His quiet home one keeps;   50
And one, the strong much-toiling sage,
In German Weimar sleeps.

But Wordsworth's eyes avert their ken
From half of human fate;
And Goethe's course few sons of men   55
May think to emulate.

For he pursued a lonely road,
His eyes on Nature's plan;
Neither made man too much a God,
Nor God too much a man.   60

Strong was he, with a spirit free
From mists, and sane, and clear;
Clearer, how much! than ours—yet we
Have a worse course to steer.

For though his manhood bore the blast   65
Of a tremendous time,
Yet in a tranquil world was pass'd
His tenderer youthful prime.

But we, brought forth and rear'd in hours
Of change, alarm, surprise—   70
What shelter to grow ripe is ours?
What leisure to grow wise?

Like children bathing on the shore,
Buried a wave beneath,
The second wave succeeds, before   75
We have had time to breathe.

Too fast we live, too much are tried,
Too harass'd, to attain
Wordsworth's sweet calm, or Goethe's wide
And luminous view to gain.   80

And then we turn, thou sadder sage,
To thee! we feel thy spell!
—The hopeless tangle of our age,
Thou too hast scann'd it well!

Immoveable thou sittest, still   85
As death, composed to bear!
Thy head is clear, thy feeling chill,
And icy thy despair.

Yes, as the son of Thetis said,
I hear thee saying now: 90
Greater by far than thou are dead:
Strive not! die also thou!

Ah! two desires toss about
The poet's feverish blood.
One drives him to the world without,   95
And one to solitude.

The glow, he cries, *the thrill of life,*
Where, where do these abound?—
Not in the world, not in the strife
Of men, shall they be found.   100

He who hath watch'd, not shared, the strife,
Knows how the day hath gone.
He only lives with the world's life,
Who hath renounced his own.

To thee we come, then! Clouds are roll'd   105
Where thou, O seer! art set;
Thy realm of thought is drear and cold—
The world is colder yet!

And thou hast pleasures, too, to share
With those who come to thee—   110
Balms floating on thy mountain-air,
And healing sights to see.

How often, where the slopes are green
On Jaman, hast thou sate
By some high chalet-door, and seen   115
The summer-day grow late;

And darkness steal o'er the wet grass
With the pale crocus starr'd,
And reach that glimmering sheet of glass
Beneath the piny sward,   120

Lake Leman's waters, far below!
And watch'd the rosy light
Fade from the distant peaks of snow;
And on the air of night

Heard accents of the eternal tongue   125
Through the pine branches play—
Listen'd, and felt thyself grow young!
Listen'd and wept——Away!

Away the dreams that but deceive
And thou, sad guide, adieu!   130
I go, fate drives me; but I leave
Half of my life with you.

We, in some unknown Power's employ,
Move on a rigorous line;
Can neither, when we will, enjoy,   135
Nor, when we will, resign.

I in the world must live; but thou,
Thou melancholy shade!
Wilt not, if thou canst see me now,
Condemn me, nor upbraid.   140

For thou art gone away from earth,
And place with those dost claim,
The Children of the Second Birth,
Whom the world could not tame;

And with that small, transfigured band,   145
Whom many a different way
Conducted to their common land,
Thou learn'st to think as they.

Christian and pagan, king and slave,
Soldier and anchorite,   150
Distinctions we esteem so grave,
Are nothing in their sight.

They do not ask, who pined unseen,
Who was on action hurl'd,
Whose one bond is, that all have been   155
Unspotted by the world.

There without anger thou wilt see
Him who obeys thy spell
No more, so he but rest, like thee,
Unsoil'd!—and so, farewell.   160

Farewell!—Whether thou now liest near
That much-loved inland sea,
The ripples of whose blue waves cheer
Vevey and Meillerie:

And in that gracious region bland,   165
Where with clear-rustling wave
The scented pines of Switzerland
Stand dark round thy green grave,

Between the dusty vineyard-walls
Issuing on that green place   170
The early peasant still recalls
The pensive stranger's face,

And stoops to clear thy moss-grown date
Ere he plods on again;—
Or whether, by maligner fate,   175
Among the swarms of men,

Where between granite terraces
The blue Seine rolls her wave,
The Capital of Pleasure sees
The hardly-heard-of grave;—   180

Farewell! Under the sky we part,
In this stern Alpine dell.
O unstrung will! O broken heart!
A last, a last farewell!
1852

EMPEDOCLES ON ETNA

A DRAMATIC POEM

PERSONS

EMPEDOCLES.
PAUSANIAS, *a Physician.*
CALLICLES, *a young Harp-player.*
The Scene of the Poem is on Mount Etna; at first in the forest
region, afterwards on the summit of the mountain.

ACT I. SCENE I.

Morning. A Pass in the forest region of Etna.

CALLICLES (*Alone, resting on a rock by the path*). The mules,
    I think, will not be here this hour;
They feel the cool wet turf under their feet
By the stream-side, after the dusty lanes
In which they have toil'd all night from Catana,
And scarcely will they budge a yard. O Pan,   5
How gracious is the mountain at this hour!
A thousand times have I been here alone,
Or with the revellers from the mountain-towns,
But never on so fair a morn;—the sun
Is shining on the brilliant mountain-crests,   10
And on the highest pines; but farther down,
Here in the valley, is in shade; the sward
Is dark, and on the stream the mist still hangs;
One sees one's footprints crush'd in the wet grass,
One's breath curls in the air; and on these pines   15
That climb from the stream's edge, the long grey tufts,
Which the goats love, are jewell'd thick with dew.
Here will I stay till the slow litter comes.
I have my harp too—that is well.—Apollo!
What mortal could be sick or sorry here?   20
I know not in what mind Empedocles,
Whose mules I follow'd, may be coming up,
But if, as most men say, he is half mad
With exile, and with brooding on his wrongs,
Pausanias, his sage friend, who mounts with him,   25

Could scarce have lighted on a lovelier cure.
The mules must be below, far down. I hear
Their tinkling bells, mix'd with the song of birds,
Rise faintly to me—now it stops!—Who's here?
Pausanias! and on foot? alone?

PAUSANIAS.   And thou, then?   30
I left thee supping with Peisianax,
With thy head full of wine, and thy hair crown'd,
Touching thy harp as the whim came on thee,
And praised and spoil'd by master and by guests
Almost as much as the new dancing-girl.   35
Why hast thou follow'd us?

CALLICLES.   The night was hot,
And the feast past its prime; so we slipp'd out,
Some of us, to the portico to breathe;—
Peisianax, thou know'st, drinks late;—and then,
As I was lifting my soil'd garland off,   40
I saw the mules and litter in the court,
And in the litter sate Empedocles;
Thou, too, wast with him. Straightway I sped home;
I saddled my white mule, and all night long
Through the cool lovely country follow'd you,   45
Pass'd you a little since as morning dawn'd,
And have this hour sate by the torrent here,
Till the slow mules should climb in sight again.
And now?

PAUSANIAS. And now, back to the town with speed!
Crouch in the wood first, till the mules have pass'd;   50
They do but halt, they will be here anon.
Thou must be viewless to Empedocles;
Save mine, he must not meet a human eye.
One of his moods is on him that thou know'st;
I think, thou wouldst not vex him.

CALLICLES.   No—and yet   55
I would fain stay, and help thee tend him. Once
He knew me well, and would oft notice me;
And still, I know not how, he draws me to him,
And I could watch him with his proud sad face,
His flowing locks and gold-encircled brow   60
And kingly gait, for ever; such a spell
In his severe looks, such a majesty
As drew of old the people after him,
In Agrigentum and Olympia,
When his star reign'd, before his banishment,   65
Is potent still on me in his decline.
But oh! Pausanias, he is changed of late;
There is a settled trouble in his air

Admits no momentary brightening now,
And when he comes among his friends at feasts,   70
'Tis as an orphan among prosperous boys.
Thou know'st of old he loved this harp of mine,
When first he sojourn'd with Peisianax;
He is now always moody, and I fear him;
But I would serve him, soothe him, if I could,   75
Dared one but try.
     PAUSANIAS.   Thou wast a kind child ever!
He loves thee, but he must not see thee now.
Thou hast indeed a rare touch on thy harp,
He loves that in thee, too;—there was a time
(But that is pass'd), he would have paid thy strain   80
With music to have drawn the stars from heaven.
He hath his harp and laurel with him still,
But he has laid the use of music by,
And all which might relax his settled gloom.
Yet thou may'st try thy playing, if thou wilt—   85
But thou must keep unseen; follow us on,
But at a distance! in these solitudes,
In this clear mountain-air, a voice will rise,
Though from afar, distinctly; it may soothe him.
Play when we halt, and, when the evening comes   90
And I must leave him (for his pleasure is
To be left musing these soft nights alone
In the high unfrequented mountain-spots),
Then watch him, for he ranges swift and far,
Sometimes to Etna's top, and to the cone;   95
But hide thee in the rocks a great way down,
And try thy noblest strains, my Callicles,
With the sweet night to help thy harmony!
Thou wilt earn my thanks sure, and perhaps his.
     CALLICLES. More than a day and night, Pausanias,   100
Of this fair summer-weather, on these hills,
Would I bestow to help Empedocles.
That needs no thanks; one is far better here
Than in the broiling city in these heats.
But tell me, how hast thou persuaded him   105
In this his present fierce, man-hating mood,
To bring thee out with him alone on Etna?
     PAUSANIAS. Thou hast heard all men speaking of Pantheia
The woman who at Agrigentum lay
Thirty long days in a cold trance of death,   110
And whom Empedocles call'd back to life.
Thou art too young to note it, but his power
Swells with the swelling evil of this time,
And holds men mute to see where it will rise.

He could stay swift diseases in old days, 115
Chain madmen by the music of his lyre,
Cleanse to sweet airs the breath of poisonous streams,
And in the mountain-chinks inter the winds.
This he could do of old; but now, since all
Clouds and grows daily worse in Sicily, 120
Since broils tear us in twain, since this new swarm
Of sophists has got empire in our schools
Where he was paramount, since he is banish'd
And lives a lonely man in triple gloom—
He grasps the very reins of life and death. 125
I ask'd him of Pantheia yesterday,
When we were gather'd with Peisianax,
And he made answer, I should come at night
On Etna here, and be alone with him,
And he would tell me, as his old, tried friend, 130
Who still was faithful, what might profit me;
That is, the secret of this miracle.
    CALLICLES. Bah! Thou a doctor! Thou art superstitious.
Simple Pausanias, 'twas no miracle!
Pantheia, for I know her kinsmen well, 135
Was subject to these trances from a girl.
Empedocles would say so, did he deign;
But he still lets the people, whom he scorns,
Gape and cry *wizard* at him, if they list.
But thou, thou art no company for him! 140
Thou art as cross, as sour'd as himself!
Thou hast some wrong from thine own citizens,
And then thy friend is banish'd, and on that,
Straightway thou fallest to arraign the times,
As if the sky was impious not to fall. 145
The sophists are no enemies of his;
I hear, Gorgias, their chief, speaks nobly of him,
As of his gifted master, and once friend.
He is too scornful, too high-wrought, too bitter.
'Tis not the times, 'tis not the sophists vex him; 150
There is some root of suffering in himself,
Some secret and unfollow'd vein of woe,
Which makes the time look black and sad to him.
Pester him not in this his sombre mood
With questionings about an idle tale, 155
But lead him through the lovely mountain-paths,
And keep his mind from preying on itself,
And talk to him of things at hand and common,
Not miracles! thou art a learned man,
But credulous of fables as a girl. 160
    PAUSANIAS. And thou, a boy whose tongue outruns his knowledge,

And on whose lightness blame is thrown away.
Enough of this! I see the litter wind
Up by the torrent-side, under the pines.
I must rejoin Empedocles. Do thou   165
Crouch in the brushwood till the mules have pass'd;
Then play thy kind part well. Farewell till night!

SCENE II

Noon. A Glen on the highest skirts of the woody region of Etna.

EMPEDOCLES—PAUSANIAS

PAUSANIAS. The noon is hot. When we have cross'd the stream,
We shall have left the woody tract, and come
Upon the open shoulder of the hill.
See how the giant spires of yellow bloom
Of the sun-loving gentian, in the heat,   5
Are shining on those naked slopes like flame!
Let us rest here; and now, Empedocles,
Pantheia's history! (A *harp-note below is heard.*)
    EMPEDOCLES. Hark! what sound was that
Rose from below? If it were possible,
And we were not so far from human haunt,   10
I should have said that some one touch'd a harp.
Hark! there again!
    PAUSANIAS.   'Tis the boy Callicles,
The sweetest harp-player in Catana.
He is for ever coming on these hills,
In summer, to all country-festivals,   15
With a gay revelling band; he breaks from them
Sometimes, and wanders far among the glens.
But heed him not, he will not mount to us;
I spoke with him this morning. Once more, therefore,
Instruct me of Pantheia's story, Master,   20
As I have pray'd thee.
    EMPEDOCLES.   That? and to what end?
    PAUSANIAS. It is enough that all men speak of it.
But I will also say, that when the Gods
Visit us as they do with sign and plague,
To know those spells of thine which stay their hand   25
Were to live free from terror.
    EMPEDOCLES.   Spells? Mistrust them!
Mind is the spell which governs earth and heaven.
Man has a mind with which to plan his safety;
Know that, and help thyself!
    PAUSANIAS.   But thine own words?
"The wit and counsel of man was never clear,   30
Troubles confound the little wit he has."

Mind is a light which the Gods mock us with,
To lead those false who trust it. (*The harp sounds again.*)
   EMPEDOCLES.   Hist! once more!
Listen, Pausanias!—Ay, 'tis Callicles;
I know these notes among a thousand. Hark!   35
   CALLICLES (*Sings unseen, from below*). The track winds down
      to the clear stream,
To cross the sparkling shallows; there
The cattle love to gather, on their way
To the high mountain-pastures, and to stay,
Till the rough cow-herds drive them past,   40
Knee-deep in the cool ford; for 'tis the last
Of all the woody, high, well-water'd dells
On Etna; and the beam
Of noon is broken there by chestnut-boughs
Down its steep verdant sides; the air   45
Is freshen'd by the leaping stream, which throws
Eternal showers of spray on the moss'd roots
Of trees, and veins of turf, and long dark shoots
Of ivy-plants, and fragrant hanging bells
Of hyacinths, and on late anemonies,   50
That muffle its wet banks; but glade,
And stream, and sward, and chestnut-trees,
End here; Etna beyond, in the broad glare
Of the hot noon, without a shade,
Slope behind slope, up to the peak, lies bare;   55
The peak, round which the white clouds play.

        In such a glen, on such a day,
        On Pelion, on the grassy ground,
        Chiron, the aged Centaur lay,
        The young Achilles standing by.   60
        The Centaur taught him to explore
        The mountains; where the glens are dry
        And the tired Centaurs come to rest,
        And where the soaking springs abound
        And the straight ashes grow for spears,   65
        And where the hill-goats come to feed,
        And the sea-eagles build their nest.
        He show'd him Phthia far away,
        And said: O boy, I taught this lore
        To Peleus, in long distant years!   70
        He told him of the Gods, the stars,
        The tides;—and then of mortal wars,
        And of the life which heroes lead
        Before they reach the Elysian place
        And rest in the immortal mead;   75
        And all the wisdom of his race.

  The music below ceases, and EMPEDOCLES *speaks, accompanying*
      himself in a solemn manner on his harp.

The out-spread world to span
A cord the Gods first slung,
And then the soul of man
There, like a mirror, hung,   80
And bade the winds through space impel the gusty toy.

Hither and thither spins
The wind-borne, mirroring soul,
A thousand glimpses wins,
And never sees a whole;   85
Looks once, and drives elsewhere, and leaves its last employ.

The Gods laugh in their sleeve
To watch man doubt and fear,
Who knows not what to believe
Since he sees nothing clear,   90
And dares stamp nothing false where he finds nothing sure.

Is this, Pausanias, so?
And can our souls not strive,
But with the winds must go,
And hurry where they drive?   95
Is fate indeed so strong, man's strength indeed so poor?

I will not judge. That man,
Howbeit, I judge as lost,
Whose mind allows a plan,
Which would degrade it most;   100
And he treats doubt the best who tries to see least ill.

Be not, then, fear's blind slave!
Thou art my friend; to thee,
All knowledge that I have,
All skill I wield, are free.   105
Ask not the latest news of the last miracle,

Ask not what days and nights
In trance Pantheia lay,
But ask how thou such sights
May'st see without dismay;   110
Ask what most helps when known, thou son of Anchitus!

What? hate, and awe, and shame
Fill thee to see our day;
Thou feelest thy soul's frame
Shaken and out of chime?   115
What? life and chance go hard with thee too, as with us;

Thy citizens, 'tis said,
Envy thee and oppress,

Thy goodness no men aid,
All strive to make it less; 120
Tyranny, pride, and lust, fill Sicily's abodes;

Heaven is with earth at strife,
Signs make thy soul afraid,
The dead return to life,
Rivers are dried, winds stay'd; 125
Scarce can one think in calm, so threatening are the Gods;

And we feel, day and night,
The burden of ourselves—
Well, then, the wiser wight
In his own bosom delves, 130
And asks what ails him so, and gets what cure he can.

The sophist sneers: Fool, take
Thy pleasure, right or wrong.
The pious wail: Forsake
A world these sophists throng. 135
Be neither saint nor sophist-led, but be a man!

These hundred doctors try
To preach thee to their school.
We have the truth! they cry;
And yet their oracle, 140
Trumpet it as they will, is but the same as thine.

Once read thy own breast right,
And thou hast done with fears;
Man gets no other light,
Search he a thousand years. 145
Sink in thyself! there ask what ails thee, at that shrine!

What makes thee struggle and rave?
Why are men ill at ease?—
'Tis that the lot they have
Fails their own will to please; 150
For man would make no murmuring, were his will obey'd.

And why is it, that still
Man with his lot thus fights?—
'Tis that he makes this *will*
The measure of his *rights*, 155
And believes Nature outraged if his will's gainsaid.

Couldst thou, Pausanias, learn
How deep a fault is this;
Couldst thou but once discern
Thou hast no *right* to bliss, 160
No title from the Gods to welfare and repose;

Then thou wouldst look less mazed
Whene'er of bliss debarr'd,
Nor think the Gods were crazed
When thy own lot went hard.   165
But we are all the same—the fools of our own woes!

For, from the first faint morn
Of life, the thirst for bliss
Deep in man's heart is born;
And, sceptic as he is,   170
He fails not to judge clear if this be quench'd or no.

Nor is the thirst to blame.
Man errs not that he deems
His welfare his true aim,
He errs because he dreams   175
The world does but exist that welfare to bestow.

We mortals are no kings
For each of whom to sway
A new-made world up-springs,
Meant merely for his play;   180
No, we are strangers here; the world is from of old.

In vain our pent wills fret,
And would the world subdue.
Limits we did not set
Condition all we do;   185
Born into life we are, and life must be our mould.

Born into life!—man grows
Forth from his parents' stem,
And blends their bloods, as those
Of theirs are blent in them;   190
So each new man strikes root into a far foretime.

Born into life!—we bring
A bias with us here,
And, when here, each new thing
Affects us we come near;   195
To tunes we did not call our being must keep chime.

Born into life!—in vain,
Opinions, those or these,
Unalter'd to retain
The obstinate mind decrees;   200
Experience, like a sea, soaks all-effacing in.

Born into life!—who lists
May what is false hold dear,

And for himself make mists
Through which to see less clear;   205
The world is what it is, for all our dust and din.

Born into life!—'tis we,
And not the world, are new;
Our cry for bliss, our plea,
Others have urged it too—   210
Our wants have all been felt, our errors made before.

No eye could be too sound
To observe a world so vast,
No patience too profound
To sort what's here amass'd;   215
How man may here best live no care too great to explore.

But we—as some rude guest
Would change, where'er he roam,
The manners there profess'd
To those he brings from home—   220
We mark not the world's course, but would have *it* take *ours*.

The world's course proves the terms
On which man wins content;
Reason the proof confirms—
We spurn it, and invent   225
A false course for the world, and for ourselves, false powers.

Riches we wish to get,
Yet remain spendthrifts still;
We would have health, and yet
Still use our bodies ill;   230
Bafflers of our own prayers, from youth to life's last scenes.

We would have inward peace,
Yet will not look within;
We would have misery cease,
Yet will not cease from sin;   235
We want all pleasant ends, but will use no harsh means;

We do not what we ought,
What we ought not, we do,
And lean upon the thought
That chance will bring us through;   240
But our own acts, for good or ill, are mightier powers.

Yet, even when man forsakes
All sin,—is just, is pure,
Abandons all which makes
His welfare insecure,—   245
Other existences there are, that clash with ours

Like us, the lightning-fires
Love to have scope and play;
The stream, like us, desires
An unimpeded way;   250
Like us, the Libyan wind delights to roam at large.

Streams will not curb their pride
The just man not to entomb,
Nor lightnings go aside
To give his virtues room;   255
Nor is that wind less rough which blows a good man's barge.

Nature, with equal mind,
Sees all her sons at play;
Sees man control the wind,
The wind sweep man away;   260
Allows the proudly-riding and the foundering bark.

And, lastly, though of ours
No weakness spoil our lot,
Though the non-human powers
Of Nature harm us not,   265
The ill deeds of other men make often *our* life dark.

What were the wise man's plan?—
Through this sharp, toil-set life,
To work as best he can,
And win what's won by strife.—   270
But we an easier way to cheat our pains have found.

Scratch'd by a fall, with moans
As children of weak age
Lend life to the dumb stones
Whereon to vent their rage,   275
And bend their little fists, and rate the senseless ground;

So, loath to suffer mute,
We, peopling the void air,
Make Gods to whom to impute
The ills we ought to bear;   280
With God and Fate to rail at, suffering easily.

Yet grant—as sense long miss'd
Things that are now perceived,
And much may still exist
Which is not yet believed—   285
Grant that the world were full of Gods we cannot see;

All things the world which fill
Of but one stuff are spun,

That we who rail are still,
With what we rail at, one;   290
One with the o'erlabour'd Power that through the breadth and length

Of earth, and air, and sea,
In men, and plants, and stones,
Hath toil perpetually,
And travails, pants, and moans;   295
Fain would do all things well, but sometimes fails in strength.

And patiently exact
This universal God
Alike to any act
Proceeds at any nod,   300
And quietly declaims the cursings of himself.

This is not what man hates,
Yet he can curse but this.
Harsh Gods and hostile Fates
Are dreams! this only *is*—   305
Is everywhere; sustains the wise, the foolish elf.

Nor only, in the intent
To attach blame elsewhere,
Do we at will invent
Stern Powers who make their care   310
To embitter human life, malignant Deities;

But, next, we would reverse
The scheme ourselves have spun,
And what we made to curse
We now would lean upon,   315
And feign kind Gods who perfect what man vainly tries.

Look, the world tempts our eye,
And we would know it all!
We map the starry sky,
We mine this earthen ball,   320
We measure the sea-tides, we number the sea-sands;

We scrutinise the dates
Of long-past human things,
The bounds of effaced states,
The lines of deceased kings;   325
We search out dead men's words, and works of dead men's hands;

We shut our eyes, and muse
How our own minds are made,
What springs of thought they use,
How righten'd, how betray'd—   330
And spend our wit to name what most employ unnamed.

But still, as we proceed
The mass swells more and more
Of volumes yet to read,
Of secrets yet to explore.   335
Our hair grows grey, our eyes are dimm'd, our heat is tamed;

We rest our faculties,
And thus address the Gods:
'True science if there is,
It stays in your abodes!   340
Man's measures cannot mete the immeasurable All.

"You only can take in
The world's immense design.
Our desperate search was sin,
Which henceforth we resign,   345
Sure only that your mind sees all things which befal."

Fools! that in man's brief term
He cannot all things view,
Affords no ground to affirm
That there are Gods who do;   350
Nor does being weary prove that he has where to rest.

Again.—Our youthful blood
Claims rapture as its right;
The world, a rolling flood
Of newness and delight,   355
Draws in the enamour'd gazer to its shining breast;

Pleasure, to our hot grasp,
Gives flowers after flowers;
With passionate warmth we clasp
Hand after hand in ours;   360
Now do we soon perceive how fast our youth is spent.

At once our eyes grow clear!
We see, in blank dismay,
Year posting after year,
Sense after sense decay;   365
Our shivering heart is mined by secret discontent;

Yet still, in spite of truth,
In spite of hopes entomb'd,
That longing of our youth
Burns ever unconsumed,   370
Still hungrier for delight as delights grow more rare.

We pause; we hush our heart,
And thus address the Gods:

"The world hath fail'd to impart
The joy our youth forebodes,   375
Fail'd to fill up the void which in our breasts we bear.

"Changeful till now, we still
Look'd on to something new;
Let us, with changeless will,
Henceforth look on to you,   380
To find with you the joy we in vain here require!"

Fools! That so often here
Happiness mock'd our prayer,
I think, might make us fear
A like event elsewhere;   385
Make us, not fly to dreams, but moderate desire.

And yet, for those who know
Themselves, who wisely take
Their way through life, and bow
To what they cannot break,   390
Why should I say that life need yield but *moderate* bliss?

Shall we, with temper spoil'd,
Health sapp'd by living ill,
And judgment all embroil'd
By sadness and self-will,   395
Shall *we* judge what for man is not true bliss or is?

Is it so small a thing
To have enjoy'd the sun,
To have lived light in the spring,
To have loved, to have thought, to have done;   400
To have advanced true friends, and beat down baffling foes—

That we must feign a bliss
Of doubtful future date,
And, while we dream on this,
Lose all our present state,   405
And relegate to worlds yet distant our repose?

Not much, I know, you prize
What pleasures may be had,
Who look on life with eyes
Estranged, like mine, and sad;   410
And yet the village-churl feels the truth more than you,

Who's loath to leave this life
Which to him little yields—
His hard-task'd sunburnt wife,
His often-labour'd fields,   415
The boors with whom he talk'd, the country-spots he knew.

But thou, because thou hear'st
Men scoff at Heaven and Fate,
Because the Gods thou fear'st
Fail to make blest thy state,   420
Tremblest, and wilt not dare to trust the joys there are!

I say: Fear not! Life still
Leaves human effort scope.
But, since life teems with ill,
Nurse no extravagant hope;   425
Because thou must not dream, thou need'st not then despair!

*A long pause. At the end of it the notes of a harp below are again
heard, and* CALLICLES *sings:—*

Far, far from here,
The Adriatic breaks in a warm bay
Among the green Illyrian hills; and there
The sunshine in the happy glens is fair,   430
And by the sea, and in the brakes.
The grass is cool, the sea-side air
Buoyant and fresh, the mountain flowers
More virginal and sweet than ours.
And there, they say, two bright and aged snakes,   435
Who once were Cadmus and Harmonia,
Bask in the glens or on the warm sea-shore,
In breathless quiet, after all their ills;
Nor do they see their country, nor the place
Where the Sphinx lived among the frowning hills,   440
Nor the unhappy palace of their race,
Nor Thebes, nor the Ismenus, any more.

There those two live, far in the Illyrian brakes!
They had stay'd long enough to see,
In Thebes, the billow of calamity   445
Over their own dear children roll'd,
Curse upon curse, pang upon pang,
For years, they sitting helpless in their home,
A grey old man and woman; yet of old
The Gods had to their marriage come,   450
And at the banquet all the Muses sang.

Therefore they did not end their days
In sight of blood; but were rapt, far away,
To where the west-wind plays,
And murmurs of the Adriatic come   455
To those untrodden mountain-lawns; and there
Placed safely in changed forms, the pair

Wholly forget their first sad life, and home,
And all that Theban woe, and stray
For ever through the glens, placid and dumb.   460

   EMPEDOCLES. That was my harp-player again!—where is he?
Down by the stream?
   PAUSANIAS.   Yes, Master, in the wood.
   EMPEDOCLES. He ever loved the Theban story well!
But the day wears. Go now, Pausanias,
For I must be alone. Leave me one mule;   465
Take down with thee the rest to Catana.
And for young Callicles, thank him from me;
Tell him, I never fail'd to love his lyre—
But he must follow me no more to-night.
   PAUSANIAS. Thou wilt return to-morrow to the city?   470
   EMPEDOCLES. Either to-morrow or some other day,
In the sure revolutions of the world,
Good friend, I shall revisit Catana.
I have seen many cities in my time,
Till mine eyes ache with the long spectacle,   475
And I shall doubtless see them all again;
Thou know'st me for a wanderer from of old.
Meanwhile, stay me not now. Farewell, Pausanias! (*He departs on his
      way up the mountain.*)
   PAUSANIAS (*alone*). I dare not urge him further—he must go;
But he is strangely wrought!—I will speed back   480
And bring Peisianax to him from the city;
His counsel could once soothe him. But, Apollo!
How his brow lighten'd as the music rose!
Callicles must wait here, and play to him;
I saw him through the chestnuts far below,   485
Just since, down at the stream.—Ho! Callicles! (*He descends, calling.*)

ACT II

Evening. The Summit of Etna.

   EMPEDOCLES.   Alone!—
On this charr'd, blacken'd, melancholy waste,
Crown'd by the awful peak, Etna's great mouth.
Round which the sullen vapour rolls—alone!
Pausanias is far hence, and that is well,   5
For I must henceforth speak no more with man.
He hath his lesson too, and that debt's paid;
And the good, learned, friendly, quiet man
May bravelier front his life, and in himself
Find henceforth energy and heart. But I—   10
The weary man, the banish'd citizen,

Whose banishment is not his greatest ill,
Whose weariness no energy can reach,
And for whose hurt courage is not the cure--
What should I do with life and living more?   15

   No, thou art come too late, Empedocles!
And the world hath the day, and must break thee,
Not thou the world. With men thou canst not live,
Their thoughts, their ways, their wishes, are not thine;
And being lonely thou art miserable,   20
For something has impair'd thy spirit's strength,
And dried its self-sufficing fount of joy.
Thou canst not live with men nor with thyself—
O sage! O sage!—Take then the one way left;
And turn thee to the elements, thy friends,   25
Thy well-tried friends, thy willing ministers,
And say: Ye helpers, hear Empedocles,
Who asks this final service at your hands!
Before the sophist-brood hath overlaid
The last spark of man's consciousness with words—   30
Ere quite the being of man, ere quite the world
Be disarray'd of their divinity—
Before the soul lose all her solemn joys,
And awe be dead, and hope impossible,
And the soul's deep eternal night come on—   35
Receive me, hide me, quench me, take me home!

*He advances to the edge of the crater. Smoke and fire break forth
with a loud noise, and* CALLICLES *is heard below singing:—*

The lyre's voice is lovely everywhere;
In the court of Gods, in the city of men,
And in the lonely rock-strewn mountain-glen,
In the still mountain air.   40

Only to Typho it sounds hatefully;
To Typho only, the rebel o'erthrown,
Through whose heart Etna drives her roots of stone
To imbed them in the sea.

Wherefore dost thou groan so loud?   45
Wherefore do thy nostrils flash,
Through the dark night, suddenly,
Typho, such red jets of flame?—
Is thy tortured heart still proud?
Is thy fire-scathed arm still rash?   50
Still alert thy stone-crush'd frame?
Does thy fierce soul still deplore

Thine ancient rout by the Cilician hills,
And that curst treachery on the Mount of Gore?
Do thy bloodshot eyes still weep   55
The fight which crown'd thine ills,
Thy last mischance on this Sicilian deep?
Hast thou sworn, in thy sad lair,
Where erst the strong sea-currents suck'd thee down,
Never to cease to writhe, and try to rest,   60
Letting the sea-stream wander through thy hair?
That thy groans, like thunder prest,
Begin to roll, and almost drown
The sweet notes whose lulling spell
Gods and the race of mortals love so well,   65
When through thy caves thou hearest music swell?

But an awful pleasure bland
Spreading o'er the Thunderer's face,
When the sound climbs near his seat,
The Olympian council sees;   70
As he lets his lax right hand,
Which the lightnings doth embrace,
Sink upon his mighty knees.
And the eagle, at the beck
Of the appeasing, gracious harmony,   75
Droops all his sheeny, brown, deep-feather'd neck,
Nestling nearer to Jove's feet;
While o'er his sovran eye
The curtains of the blue films slowly meet
And the white Olympus-peaks   80
Rosily brighten, and the soothed Gods smile
At one another from their golden chairs,
And no one round the charmed circle speaks.
Only the loved Hebe bears
The cup about, whose draughts beguile   85
Pain and care, with a dark store
Of fresh-pull'd violets wreathed and nodding o'er;
And her flush'd feet glow on the marbie floor.
    EMPEDOCLES. He fables, yet speaks truth!
The brave, impetuous heart yields everywhere   90
To the subtle, contriving head;
Great qualities are trodden down,
And littleness united
Is become invincible.

These rumblings are not Typho's groans, I know!   95
These angry smoke-bursts
Are not the passionate breath

Of the mountain-crush'd, tortured, intractable Titan king—
But over all the world
What suffering is there not seen   100
Of plainness oppress'd by cunning,
As the well-counsell'd Zeus oppress'd
That self-helping son of earth!
What anguish of greatness,
Rail'd and hunted from the world,   105
Because its simplicity rebukes
This envious, miserable age!

I am weary of it.
—Lie there, ye ensigns
Of my unloved preëminence   110
In an age like this!
Among a people of children,
Who throng'd me in their cities,
Who worshipp'd me in their houses,
And ask'd, not wisdom,   115
But drugs to charm with,
But spells to mutter—
All the fool's armoury of magic—Lie there,
My golden circlet,
My purple robe!   120
    CALLICLES (*from below*). As the sky-brightening south-wind clears
       the day,
And makes the mass'd clouds roll,
The music of the lyre blows away
The clouds which wrap the soul.
Oh! that Fate had let me see   125
That triumph of the sweet persuasive lyre,
That famous, final victory,
When jealous Pan with Marsyas did conspire;
When, from far Parnassus' side,
Young Apollo, all the pride   130
Of the Phrygian flutes to tame,
To the Phrygian highlands came;
Where the long green reed-beds sway
In the rippled waters grey
Of that solitary lake   135
Where Mæander's springs are born;
Whence the ridged pine-wooded roots
Of Messogis westward break,
Mounting westward, high and higher.
There was held the famous strife;   140
There the Phrygian brought his flutes,
And Apollo brought his lyre;

And, when now the westering sun
Touch'd the hills, the strife was done,
And the attentive Muses said: 145
"Marsyas, thou art vanquished!"
Then Apollo's minister
Hang'd upon a branching fir
Marsyas, that unhappy Faun,
And began to whet his knife.   150
But the Maenads, who were there,
Left their friend, and with robes flowing
In the wind, and loose dark hair
O'er their polish'd bosoms blowing,
Each her ribbon'd tambourine   155
Flinging on the mountain-sod,
With a lovely frighten'd mien
Came about the youthful God.
But he turn'd his beauteous face
Haughtily another way,   160
From the grassy sun-warm'd place
Where in proud repose he lay,
With one arm over his head,
Watching how the whetting sped.

  But aloof, on the lake-strand,   165
Did the young Olympus stand,
Weeping at his master's end;
For the Faun had been his friend.
For he taught him how to sing,
And he taught him flute-playing.   170
Many a morning had they gone
To the glimmering mountain-lakes,
And had torn up by the roots
The tall crested water-reeds
With long plumes and soft brown seeds,   175
And had carved them into flutes,
Sitting on a tabled stone
Where the shoreward ripple breaks.
And he taught him how to please
The red-snooded Phrygian girls,   180
Whom the summer evening sees
Flashing in the dance's whirls
Underneath the starlit trees
In the mountain-villages.
Therefore now Olympus stands,   185
At his master's piteous cries
Pressing fast with both his hands
His white garment to his eyes,

Not to see Apollo's scorn;—
Ah, poor Faun, poor Faun! ah, poor Faun!   190
   EMPEDOCLES. And lie thou there,
My laurel bough!
Scornful Apollo's ensign, lie thou there!
Though thou hast been my shade in the world's heat—
Though I have loved thee, lived in honouring thee—   195
Yet lie thou there,
My laurel bough!

I am weary of thee.
I am weary of the solitude
Where he who bears thee must abide—.   200
Of the rocks of Parnassus,
Of the gorge of Delphi,
Of the moonlit peaks, and the caves.
Thou guardest them, Apollo!
Over the grave of the slain Pytho,   205
Though young, intolerably severe!
Thou keepest aloof the profane,
But the solitude oppresses thy votary!
The jars of men reach him not in thy valley—
But can life reach him?   210
Thou fencest him from the multitude—
Who will fence him from himself?
He hears nothing but the cry of the torrents,
And the beating of his own heart.
The air is thin, the veins swell,   215
The temples tighten and throb there—
Air! air!

Take thy bough, set me free from my solitude;
I have been enough alone!

Where shall thy votary fly then? back to men?—   220
But they will gladly welcome him once more,
And help him to unbend his too tense thought,
And rid him of the presence of himself,
And keep their friendly chatter at his ear,
And haunt him, till the absence from himself,   225
That other torment, grow unbearable;
And he will fly to solitude again,
And he will find its air too keen for him,
And so change back; and many thousand times
Be miserably bandied to and fro   230
Like a sea-wave, betwixt the world and thee,
Thou young, implacable God! and only death

Can cut his oscillations short, and so
Bring him to poise. There is no other way.

And yet what days were those, Parmenides!   235
When we were young, when we could number friends
In all the Italian cities like ourselves,
When with elated hearts we join'd your train,
Ye Sun-born Virgins! on the road of truth.
Then we could still enjoy, then neither thought   240
Nor outward things were closed and dead to us;
But we received the shock of mighty thoughts
On simple minds with a pure natural joy;
And if the sacred load oppress'd our brain,
We had the power to feel the pressure eased,   245
The brow unbound, the thoughts flow free again,
In the delightful commerce of the world.
We had not lost our balance then, nor grown
Thought's slaves, and dead to every natural joy.
The smallest thing could give us pleasure then—   250
The sports of the country-people,
A flute-note from the woods,
Sunset over the sea;
Seed-time and harvest,
The reapers in the corn,   255
The vinedresser in his vineyard,
The village-girl at her wheel.

Fulness of life and power of feeling, ye
Are for the happy, for the souls at ease,
Who dwell on a firm basis of content!   260
But he, who has outlived his prosperous days—
But he, whose youth fell on a different world
From that on which his exiled age is thrown—
Whose mind was fed on other food, was train'd
By other rules than are in vogue to-day—   265
Whose habit of thought is fix'd, who will not change,
But, in a world he loves not, must subsist
In ceaseless opposition, be the guard
Of his own breast, fetter'd to what he guards,
That the world win no mastery over him—   270
Who has no friend, no fellow left, not one;
Who has no minute's breathing space allow'd
To nurse his dwindling faculty of joy—
Joy and the outward world must die to him,
As they are dead to me.   275

A long pause, during which EMPEDOCLES *remains motionless, plunged
in thought. The night deepens. He moves forward and gazes round
him, and proceeds:—*

And you, ye stars,
Who slowly begin to marshal,
As of old, in the fields of heaven,
Your distant, melancholy lines!
Have you, too, survived yourselves?   280
Are you, too, what I fear to become?
You, too, once lived;
You, too, moved joyfully
Among august companions,
In an older world, peopled by Gods,   285
In a mightier order,
The radiant, rejoicing, intelligent Sons of Heaven.
But now, ye kindle
Your lonely, cold-shining lights,
Unwilling lingerers   290
In the heavenly wilderness,
For a younger, ignoble world;
And renew, by necessity,
Night after night your courses,
In echoing, unnear'd silence,   295
Above a race you know not—
Uncaring and undelighted,
Without friend and without home;
Weary like us, though not
Weary with our weariness.   300

No, no, ye stars! there is no death with you,
No languor, no decay! languor and death,
They are with me, not you! ye are alive—
Ye, and the pure dark ether where ye ride
Brilliant above me! And thou, fiery world,   305
That sapp'st the vitals of this terrible mount
Upon whose charr'd and quaking crust I stand—
Thou, too, brimmest with life!—the sea of cloud,
That heaves its white and billowy vapours up
To moat this isle of ashes from the world,   310
Lives; and that other fainter sea, far down,
O'er whose lit floor a road of moonbeams leads
To Etna's Liparëan sister-fires
And the long dusky line of Italy—
That mild and luminous floor of waters lives,   315
With held-in joy swelling its heart; I only,
Whose spring of hope is dried, whose spirit has fail'd,
I, who have not, like these, in solitude
Maintain'd courage and force, and in myself
Nursed an immortal vigour—I alone   320
Am dead to life and joy, therefore I read
In all things my own deadness. (A *long silence. He continues:*)—

Oh, that I could glow like this mountain!
Oh, that my heart bounded with the swell of sea!
Oh, that my soul were full of light as the stars! 325
Oh, that it brooded over the world like the air!

But no, this heart will glow no more; thou art
A living man no more, Empedocles!
Nothing but a devouring flame of thought—
But a naked, eternally restless mind! (*After a pause:*)— 330
To the elements it came from
Everything will return—
Our bodies to earth,
Our blood to water,
Heat to fire, 335
Breath to air.
They were well born, they will be well entomb'd—
But mind? . . .

And we might gladly share the fruitful stir
Down in our mother earth's miraculous womb; 340
Well would it be
With what roll'd of us in the stormy main;
We might have joy, blent with the all-bathing air,
Or with the nimble, radiant life of fire.

But mind, but thought— 345
If these have been the master part of us—
Where will *they* find their parent element?
What will receive *them*, who will call *them* home?
But we shall still be in them, and they in us,
And we shall be the strangers of the world, 350
And they will be our lords, as they are now;
And keep us prisoners of our consciousness,
And never let us clasp and feel the All
But through their forms, and modes, and stifling veils.
And we shall be unsatisfied as now; 355
And we shall feel the agony of thirst,
The ineffable longing for the life of life
Baffled for ever; and still thought and mind
Will hurry us with them on their homeless march,
Over the unallied unopening earth, 360
Over the unrecognising sea; while air
Will blow us fiercely back to sea and earth,
And fire repel us from its living waves.
And then we shall unwillingly return
Back to this meadow of calamity, 365
This uncongenial place, this human life;

And in our individual human state
Go through the sad probation all again,
To see if we will poise our life at last,
To see if we will now at last be true   370
To our own only true, deep-buried selves,
Being one with which we are one with the whole world;
Or whether we will once more fall away
Into some bondage of the flesh or mind,
Some slough of sense, or some fantastic maze   375
Forged by the imperious lonely thinking-power.
And each succeeding age in which we are born
Will have more peril for us than the last;
Will goad our senses with a sharper spur,
Will fret our minds to an intenser play,   380
Will make ourselves harder to be discern'd.
And we shall struggle awhile, gasp and rebel—
And we shall fly for refuge to past times,
Their soul of unworn youth, their breath of greatness;
And the reality will pluck us back,   385
Knead us in its hot hand, and change our nature
And we shall feel our powers of effort flag,
And rally them for one last fight—and fail;
And we shall sink in the impossible strife,
And be astray for ever.

           Slave of sense   390
I have in no wise been;—but slave of thought? . . .
And who can say: I have been always free,
Lived ever in the light of my own soul?—
I cannot; I have lived in wrath and gloom,
Fierce, disputatious, ever at war with man,   395
Far from my own soul, far from warmth and light.
But I have not grown easy in these bonds—
But I have not denied what bonds these were.
Yea, I take myself to witness,
That I have loved no darkness,   400
Sophisticated no truth,
Nursed no delusion,
Allow'd no fear!

And therefore, O ye elements! I know—
Ye know it too—it hath been granted me   405
Not to die wholly, not to be all enslaved.
I feel it in this hour. The numbing cloud
Mounts off my soul; I feel it, I breathe free.

Is it but for a moment?
    —Ah, boil up, ye vapours!   410

Leap and roar, thou sea of fire!
My soul glows to meet you.
Ere it flag, ere the mists
Of despondency and gloom
Rush over it again,   415
Receive me, save me! (*He plunges into the crater.*)
   CALLICLES (*from below*). Through the black, rushing smoke-bursts,
Thick breaks the red flame;
All Etna heaves fiercely
Her forest-clothed frame.   420

Not here, O Apollo!
Are haunts meet for thee.
But, where Helicon breaks down
In cliff to the sea,

Where the moon-silver'd inlets   425
Send far their light voice
Up the still vale of Thisbe,
O speed, and rejoice!

On the sward at the cliff-top
Lie strewn the white flocks,   430
On the cliff-side the pigeons
Roost deep in the rocks.

In the moonlight the shepherds,
Soft lull'd by the rills,
Lie wrapt in their blankets   435
Asleep on the hills.

—What forms are these coming
So white through the gloom?
What garments out-glistening
The gold-flower'd broom?   440

What sweet-breathing presence
Out-perfumes the thyme?
What voices enrapture
The night's balmy prime?—

'Tis Apollo comes leading   445
His choir, the Nine.
—The leader is fairest,
But all are divine.

They are lost in the hollows!
They stream up again!   450
What seeks on this mountain
The glorified train?—

They bathe on this mountain,
In the spring by their road;
Then on to Olympus, 455
Their endless abode.

—Whose praise do they mention?
Of what is it told?—
What will be for ever; 460
What was from of old.

First hymn they the Father
Of all things; and then,
The rest of immortals,
The action of men.

465
The day in his hotness,
The strife with the palm;
The night in her silence,
The stars in their calm.
1852

from SWITZERLAND

4. ISOLATION. TO MARGUERITE

We were apart; yet, day by day,
I bade my heart more constant be.
I bade it keep the world away,
And grow a home for only thee;
Nor fear'd but thy love likewise grew, 5
Like mine, each day, more tried, more true.

The fault was grave! I might have known,
What far too soon, alas! I learn'd—
The heart can bind itself alone,
And faith may oft be unreturn'd. 10
Self-sway'd our feelings ebb and swell—
Thou lov'st no more;—Farewell! Farewell!

Farewell!—and thou, thou lonely heart,
Which never yet without remorse
Even for a moment didst depart 15
From thy remote and spheréd course

To haunt the place where passions reign—
Back to thy solitude again!

Back! with the conscious thrill of shame
Which Luna felt, that summer-night,   20
Flash through her pure immortal frame,
When she forsook the starry height
To hang over Endymion's sleep
Upon the pine-grown Latmian steep.

Yet she, chaste queen, had never proved   25
How vain a thing is mortal love,
Wandering in Heaven, far removed.
But thou hast long had place to prove
This truth—to prove, and make thine own:
'Thou hast been, shalt be, art, alone.'   30

Or, if not quite alone, yet they
Which touch thee are unmating things—
Ocean and clouds and night and day;
Lorn autumns and triumphant springs;
And life, and others' joy and pain,   35
And love, if love, of happier men.

Of happier men—for they, at least,
Have *dream'd* two human hearts might blend
In one, and were through faith released
From isolation without end   40
Prolong'd; nor knew, although not less
Alone than thou, their loneliness.
1852

5. TO MARGUERITE—CONTINUED

Yes! in the sea of life enisled,
With echoing straits between us thrown,
Dotting the shoreless watery wild,
We mortal millions live *alone*.
The islands feel the enclasping flow,   5
And then their endless bounds they know.

But when the moon their hollows lights,
And they are swept by balms of spring,
And in their glens, on starry nights,
The nightingales divinely sing;   10
And lovely notes, from shore to shore,
Across the sounds and channels pour—

Oh! then a longing like despair
Is to their farthest caverns sent;
For surely once, they feel, we were   15
Parts of a single continent!
Now round us spreads the watery plain—
Oh might our marges meet again!

Who order'd, that their longing's fire
Should be, as soon as kindled, cool'd?   20
Who renders vain their deep desire?—
A God, a God their severance ruled!
And bade betwixt their shores to be
The unplumb'd, salt, estranging sea.
1852

THE BURIED LIFE

Light flows our war of mocking words, and yet,
Behold, with tears mine eyes are wet!
I feel a nameless sadness o'er me roll.
Yes, yes, we know that we can jest,
We know, we know that we can smile!   5
But there's a something in this breast,
To which thy light words bring no rest,
And thy gay smiles no anodyne.
Give me thy hand, and hush awhile,
And turn those limpid eyes on mine,   10
And let me read there, love! thy inmost soul.

Alas! is even love too weak
To unlock the heart, and let it speak?
Are even lovers powerless to reveal
To one another what indeed they feel?   15
I knew the mass of men conceal'd
Their thoughts, for fear that if reveal'd
They would by other men be met
With blank indifference, or with blame reproved;
I knew they lived and moved   20
Trick'd in disguises, alien to the rest
Of men, and alien to themselves—and yet
The same heart beats in every human breast!

But we, my love!—doth a like spell benumb
Our hearts, our voices?—must we too be dumb?   25

Ah, well for us, if even we,
Even for a moment, can get free

Our heart, and have our lips unchain'd;
For that which seals them hath been deep-ordain'd!

Fate, which foresaw   30
How frivolous a baby man would be—
By what distractions he would be possess'd,
How he would pour himself in every strife,
And well-nigh change his own identity—
That it might keep from his capricious play   35
His genuine self, and force him to obey
Even in his own despite his being's law,
Bade through the deep recesses of our breast
The unregarded river of our life
Pursue with indiscernible flow its way;   40
And that we should not see
The buried stream, and seem to be
Eddying at large in blind uncertainty,
Though driving on with it eternally.

But often, in the world's most crowded streets,   45
But often, in the din of strife,
There rises an unspeakable desire
After the knowledge of our buried life;
A thirst to spend our fire and restless force
In tracking out our true, original course;   50
A longing to inquire
Into the mystery of this heart which beats
So wild, so deep in us—to know
Whence our lives come and where they go.
And many a man in his own breast then delves,   55
But deep enough, alas! none ever mines.
And we have been on many thousand lines,
And we have shown, on each, spirit and power;
But hardly have we, for one little hour,
Been on our own line, have we been ourselves—   60
Hardly had skill to utter one of all
The nameless feelings that course through our breast,
But they course on for ever unexpress'd.
And long we try in vain to speak and act
Our hidden self, and what we say and do   65
Is eloquent, is well—but 'tis not true!
And then we will no more be rack'd
With inward striving, and demand
Of all the thousand nothings of the hour
Their stupefying power;   70
Ah yes, and they benumb us at our call!
Yet still, from time to time, vague and forlorn,
From the soul's subterranean depth upborne

As from an infinitely distant land,
Come airs, and floating echoes, and convey   75
A melancholy into all our day.

Only—but this is rare—
When a belovéd hand is laid in ours,
When, jaded with the rush and glare
Of the interminable hours,   80
Our eyes can in another's eyes read clear,
When our world-deafen'd ear
Is by the tones of a loved voice caress'd—
A bolt is shot back somewhere in our breast,
And a lost pulse of feeling stirs again.   85
The eye sinks inward, and the heart lies plain,
And what we mean, we say, and what we would, we know.
A man becomes aware of his life's flow,
And hears its winding murmur; and he sees
The meadows where it glides, the sun, the breeze.   90

And there arrives a lull in the hot race
Wherein he doth for ever chase
That flying and elusive shadow, rest.
An air of coolness plays upon his face,
And an unwonted calm pervades his breast.   95
And then he thinks he knows
The hills where his life rose,
And the sea where it goes.
1852

SELF-DEPENDENCE

Weary of myself, and sick of asking
What I am, and what I ought to be,
At this vessel's prow I stand, which bears me
Forwards, forwards, o'er the starlit sea.

And a look of passionate desire   5
O'er the sea and to the stars I send:
'Ye who from my childhood up have calm'd me,
Calm me, ah, compose me to the end!

'Ah, once more,' I cried, 'ye stars, ye waters,
On my heart your mighty charm renew;   10
Still, still let me, as I gaze upon you,
Feel my soul becoming vast like you!'

From the intense, clear, star-sown vault of heaven,
Over the lit sea's unquiet way,
In the rustling night-air came the answer: 15
'Wouldst thou *be* as these are? *Live* as they.

'Unaffrighted by the silence round them.
Undistracted by the sights they see,
These demand not that the things without them
Yield them love, amusement, sympathy.   20

'And with joy the stars perform their shining,
And the sea its long moon-silver'd roll;
For self-poised they live, nor pine with noting
All the fever of some differing soul.

'Bounded by themselves, and unregardful   25
In what state God's other works may be,
In their own tasks all their powers pouring,
These attain the mighty life you see.'

O air-born voice! long since, severely clear,
A cry like thine in mine own heart I hear: 30
'Resolve to be thyself; and know that he,
Who finds himself, loses his misery!'
1852

MORALITY

We cannot kindle when we will
The fire which in the heart resides;
The spirit bloweth and is still,
In mystery our soul abides.
   But tasks in hours of insight will'd   5
   Can be through hours of gloom fulfill'd

With aching hands and bleeding feet
We dig and heap, lay stone on stone;
We bear the burden and the heat
Of the long day, and wish 'twere done.   10
   Nor till the hours of light return,
   All we have built do we discern.

Then, when the clouds are off the soul,
When thou dost bask in Nature's eye,
Ask, how *she* view'd thy self-control,   15
Thy struggling, task'd morality—
   Nature, whose free, light, cheerful air,
   Oft made thee, in thy gloom, despair.

And she, whose censure thou dost dread,
Whose eyes thou wast afraid to seek, 20
See, on her face a glow is spread,
A strong emotion on her cheek!
    'Ah, child,' she cries, 'that strife divine,
    Whence was it, for it is not mine?

'There is no effort on *my* brow— 25
I do not strive, I do not weep;
I rush with the swift spheres and glow
In joy, and when I will, I sleep.
    Yet that severe, that earnest air,
    I saw, I felt it once—but where? 30

'I knew not yet the gauge of time,
Nor wore the manacles of space;
I felt it in some other clime,
I saw it in some other place.
    'Twas when the heavenly house I trod, 35
    And lay upon the breast of God.'
1852

LINES

WRITTEN IN KENSINGTON GARDENS

In this lone, open glade I lie,
Screen'd by deep boughs on either hand;
And at its end, to stay the eye,
Those black-crown'd, red-boled pine-trees stand!

Birds here make song, each bird has his, 5
Across the girdling city's hum.
How green under the boughs it is!
How thick the tremulous sheep-cries come!

Sometimes a child will cross the glade
To take his nurse his broken toy; 10
Sometimes a thrush flit overhead
Deep in her unknown day's employ.

Here at my feet what wonders pass,
What endless, active life is here!
What blowing daisies, fragrant grass! 15
An air-stirr'd forest, fresh and clear.

Scarce fresher is the mountain-sod
Where the tired angler lies, stretch'd out,

And, eased of basket and of rod,
Counts his day's spoil, the spotted trout.   20

In the huge world, which roars hard by,
Be others happy if they can!
But in my helpless cradle I
Was breathed on by the rural Pan.

I, on men's impious uproar hurl'd,   25
Think often, as I hear them rave,
That peace has left the upper world
And now keeps only in the grave.

Yet here is peace for ever new!
When I who watch them am away,   30
Still all things in this glade go through
The changes of their quiet day.

Then to their happy rest they pass!
The flowers upclose, the birds are fed,
The night comes down upon the grass,   35
The child sleeps warmly in his bed.

Calm soul of all things! make it mine
To feel, amid the city's jar,
That there abides a peace of thine,
Man did not make, and cannot mar.   40

The will to neither strive nor cry,
The power to feel with others give!
Calm, calm me more! nor let me die
Before I have begun to live.
1852

THE SCHOLAR-GIPSY

Go, for they call you, shepherd, from the hill;
    Go, shepherd, and untie the wattled cotes!
        No longer leave thy wistful flock unfed,
    Nor let thy bawling fellows rack their throats,
        Nor the cropp'd herbage shoot another head.   5
            But when the fields are still,
    And the tired men and dogs all gone to rest,
        And only the white sheep are sometimes seen
        Cross and recross the strips of moon-blanch'd green,
    Come, shepherd, and again begin the quest!   10

Here, where the reaper was at work of late—
　In this high field's dark corner, where he leaves
　　His coat, his basket, and his earthen cruse,
　And in the sun all morning binds the sheaves,
　　Then here, at noon, comes back his stores to use—　15
　　　Here will I sit and wait,
　While to my ear from uplands far away
　　The bleating of the folded flocks is borne,
　　With distant cries of reapers in the corn—
　All the live murmur of a summer's day.　20

Screen'd in this nook o'er the high, half-reap'd field,
　And here till sun-down, shepherd! will I be.
　　Through the thick corn the scarlet poppies peep,
　And round green roots and yellowing stalks I see
　　Pale pink convolvulus in tendrils creep;　25
　　　And air-swept lindens yield
　Their scent, and rustle down their perfumed showers
　　Of bloom on the bent grass where I am laid,
　　And bower me from the August sun with shade;
　And the eye travels down to Oxford's towers.　30

And near me on the grass lies Glanvil's book—
　Come, let me read the oft-read tale again!
　　The story of the Oxford scholar poor,
　Of pregnant parts and quick inventive brain,
　　Who, tired of knocking at preferment's door,　35
　　　One summer-morn forsook
　His friends, and went to learn the gipsy-lore,
　　And roam'd the world with that wild brotherhood,
　　And came, as most men deem'd, to little good,
　But came to Oxford and his friends no more.　40

But once, years after, in the country-lanes,
　Two scholars, whom at college erst he knew,
　　Met him, and of his way of life enquired;
　Whereat he answer'd, that the gipsy-crew,
　　His mates, had arts to rule as they desired　45
　　　The workings of men's brains,
　And they can bind them to what thoughts they will.
　　'And I,' he said, 'the secret of their art,
　　When fully learn'd, will to the world impart;
　But it needs heaven-sent moments for this skill.'　50

This said, he left them, and return'd no more.—
　But rumours hung about the country-side,
　　That the lost Scholar long was seen to stray,
　Seen by rare glimpses, pensive and tongue-tied,
　　In hat of antique shape, and cloak of grey,　55

The same the gipsies wore.
Shepherds had met him on the Hurst in spring;
    At some lone alehouse in the Berkshire moors,
    On the warm ingle-bench, the smock-frock'd boors
Had found him seated at their entering,   60

But, 'mid their drink and clatter, he would fly.
And I myself seem half to know thy looks,
    And put the shepherds, wanderer! on thy trace;
And boys who in lone wheatfields scare the rooks
    I ask if thou hast pass'd their quiet place;   65
        Or in my boat I lie
Moor'd to the cool bank in the summer-heats,
    'Mid wide grass meadows which the sunshine fills,
    And watch the warm, green-muffled Cumner hills,
And wonder if thou haunt'st their shy retreats.   70

For most, I know, thou lov'st retired ground!
    Thee at the ferry Oxford riders blithe,
    Returning home on summer-nights, have met
Crossing the stripling Thames at Bab-lock-hithe,
    Trailing in the cool stream thy fingers wet,   75
        As the punt's rope chops round;
And leaning backward in a pensive dream,
    And fostering in thy lap a heap of flowers
    Pluck'd in shy fields and distant Wychwood bowers,
And thine eyes resting on the moonlit stream.   80

And then they land, and thou art seen no more!—
    Maidens, who from the distant hamlets come
    To dance around the Fyfield elm in May,
Oft through the darkening fields have seen thee roam,
    Or cross a stile into the public way.   85
        Oft thou hast given them store
Of flowers—the frail-leaf'd, white anemony,
    Dark bluebells drench'd with dews of summer eves,
    And purple orchises with spotted leaves—
But none hath words she can report of thee.   90

And, above Godstow Bridge, when hay-time's here
    In June, and many a scythe in sunshine flames,
    Men who through those wide fields of breezy grass
Where black-wing'd swallows haunt the glittering Thames,
    To bathe in the abandon'd lasher pass,   95
        Have often pass'd thee near
Sitting upon the river bank o'ergrown;
    Mark'd thine outlandish garb, thy figure spare,
    Thy dark vague eyes, and soft abstracted air—
But, when they came from bathing, thou wast gone!   100

At some lone homestead in the Cumner hills,
  Where at her open door the housewife darns,
    Thou hast been seen, or hanging on a gate
  To watch the threshers in the mossy barns.
      Children, who early range these slopes and late   105
        For cresses from the rills,
  Have known thee eying, all an April-day,
    The springing pastures and the feeding kine;
    And mark'd thee, when the stars come out and shine,
  Through the long dewy grass move slow away.   110

In autumn, on the skirts of Bagley Wood—
  Where most the gipsies by the turf-edged way
    Pitch their smoked tents, and every bush you see
  With scarlet patches tagg'd and shreds of grey,
      Above the forest-ground called Thessaly—   115
        The blackbird, picking food,
  Sees thee, nor stops his meal, nor fears at all;
    So often has he known thee past him stray,
    Rapt, twirling in thy hand a wither'd spray,
  And waiting for the spark from heaven to fall.   120

And once, in winter, on the causeway chill
  Where home through flooded fields foot-travellers go,
    Have I not pass'd thee on the wooden bridge,
  Wrapt in thy cloak and battling with the snow,
      Thy face tow'rd Hinksey and its wintry ridge?   125
        And thou hast climb'd the hill,
  And gain'd the white brow of the Cumner range;
    Turn'd once to watch, while thick the snowflakes fall,
    The line of festal light in Christ-Church hall—
  Then sought thy straw in some sequester'd grange.   130

But what—I dream! Two hundred years are flown
  Since first thy story ran through Oxford halls,
    And the grave Glanvil did the tale inscribe
  That thou wert wander'd from the studious walls
      To learn strange arts, and join a gipsy-tribe;   135
        And thou from earth art gone
  Long since, and in some quiet churchyard laid—
    Some country-nook, where o'er thy unknown grave
    Tall grasses and white flowering nettles wave,
  Under a dark, red-fruited yew-tree's shade.   140

—No, no, thou hast not felt the lapse of hours!
  For what wears out the life of mortal men?
    'Tis that from change to change their being rolls;
    'Tis that repeated shocks, again, again,
      Exhaust the energy of strongest souls   145

And numb the elastic powers.
Till having used our nerves with bliss and teen,
And tired upon a thousand schemes our wit,
To the just-pausing Genius we remit
Our worn-out life, and are—what we have been.   150

Thou hast not lived, why should'st thou perish, so?
Thou hadst *one* aim, *one* business, *one* desire;
Else wert thou long since number'd with the dead!
Else hadst thou spent, like other men, thy fire!
The generations of thy peers are fled,   155
And we ourselves shall go;
But thou possessest an immortal lot,
And we imagine thee exempt from age
And living as thou liv'st on Glanvil's page,
Because thou hadst—what we, alas! have not.   160

For early didst thou leave the world, with powers
Fresh, undiverted to the world without,
Firm to their mark, not spent on other things;
Free from the sick fatigue, the languid doubt,
Which much to have tried, in much been baffled, brings.   165
O life unlike to ours!
Who fluctuate idly without term or scope,
Of whom each strives, nor knows for what he strives,
And each half lives a hundred different lives;
Who wait like thee, but not, like thee, in hope.   170

Thou waitest for the spark from heaven! and we,
Light half-believers of our casual creeds,
Who never deeply felt, nor clearly will'd,
Whose insight never has borne fruit in deeds,
Whose vague resolves never have been fulfill'd;   175
For whom each year we see
Breeds new beginnings, disappointments new;
Who hesitate and falter life away,
And lose to-morrow the ground won to-day—
Ah! do not we, wanderer! await it too?   180

Yes, we await it!—but it still delays,
And then we suffer! and amongst us one,
Who most has suffer'd, takes dejectedly
His seat upon the intellectual throne;
And all his store of sad experience he   185
Lays bare of wretched days;
Tells us his misery's birth and growth and signs,
And how the dying spark of hope was fed,
And how the breast was soothed, and how the head,
And all his hourly varied anodynes.   190

This for our wisest! and we others pine,
  And wish the long unhappy dream would end,
    And waive all claim to bliss, and try to bear;
  With close-lipp'd patience for our only friend,
    Sad patience, too near neighbour to despair—   195
      But none has hope like thine!
  Thou through the fields and through the woods dost stray,
    Roaming the country-side, a truant boy,
    Nursing thy project in unclouded joy,
  And every doubt long blown by time away.   200

O born in days when wits were fresh and clear,
  And life ran gaily as the sparkling Thames;
    Before this strange disease of modern life,
  With its sick hurry, its divided aims,
    Its heads o'ertax'd its palsied hearts, was rife—   205
      Fly hence, our contact fear!
  Still fly, plunge deeper in the bowering wood!
    Averse, as Dido did with gesture stern
    From her false friend's approach in Hades turn,
  Wave us away, and keep thy solitude!   210

Still nursing the unconquerable hope,
  Still clutching the inviolable shade,
    With a free, onward impulse brushing through,
  By night, the silver'd branches of the glade—
    Far on the forest-skirts, where none pursue,   215
      On some mild pastoral slope
  Emerge, and resting on the moonlit pales
    Freshen thy flowers as in former years
    With dew, or listen with enchanted ears,
  From the dark dingles, to the nightingales!   220

But fly our paths, our feverish contact fly!
  For strong the infection of our mental strife,
    Which, though it gives no bliss, yet spoils for rest;
  And we should win thee from thy own fair life,
    Like us distracted, and like us unblest.   225
      Soon, soon thy cheer would die,
  Thy hopes grow timorous, and unfix'd thy powers,
    And thy clear aims be cross and shifting made;
    And then thy glad perennial youth would fade,
  Fade, and grow old at last, and die like ours.   230

Then fly our greetings, fly our speech and smiles!
  —As some grave Tyrian trader, from the sea,
    Descried at sunrise an emerging prow
  Lifting the cool-hair'd creepers stealthily,

The fringes of a southward-facing brow   235
    Among the Ægæan isles;
And saw the merry Grecian coaster come,
    Freighted with amber grapes, and Chian wine,
    Green, bursting figs, and tunnies steeped in brine—
And knew the intruders on his ancient home,   240

The young light-hearted masters of the waves—
    And snatch'd his rudder, and shook out more sail;
    And day and night held on indignantly
O'er the blue Midland waters with the gale,
    Betwixt the Syrtes and soft Sicily,   245
      To where the Atlantic raves
Outside the western straits; and unbent sails
    There, where down cloudy cliffs, through sheets of foam,
    Shy traffickers, the dark Iberians come;
And on the beach undid his corded bales.   250
1853

SOHRAB AND RUSTUM

AN EPISODE

And the first grey of morning fill'd the east,
And the fog rose out of the Oxus stream.
But all the Tartar camp along the stream
Was hush'd, and still the men were plunged in sleep;
Sohrab alone, he slept not; all night long   5
He had lain wakeful, tossing on his bed;
But when the grey dawn stole into his tent,
He rose, and clad himself, and girt his sword,
And took his horseman's cloak, and left his tent,
And went abroad into the cold wet fog,   10
Through the dim camp to Peran-Wisa's tent.
    Through the black Tartar tents he pass'd, which stood
Clustering like bee-hives on the low flat strand
Of Oxus, where the summer-floods o'erflow
When the sun melts the snows in high Pamere;   15
Through the black tents he pass'd, o'er that low strand,
And to a hillock came, a little back
From the stream's brink—the spot where first a boat,
Crossing the stream in summer, scrapes the land.
The men of former times had crown'd the top   20
With a clay fort; but that was fall'n, and now
The Tartars built there Peran-Wisa's tent,
A dome of laths, and o'er it felts were spread.

And Sohrab came there, and went in, and stood
Upon the thick piled carpets in the tent,   25
And found the old man sleeping on his bed
Of rugs and felts, and near him lay his arms.
And Peran-Wisa heard him, though the step
Was dull'd; for he slept light, an old man's sleep;
And he rose quickly on one arm, and said:—   30
   'Who art thou? for it is not yet clear dawn.
Speak! is there news, or any night alarm?'
   But Sohrab came to the bedside, and said:—
'Thou know'st me, Peran-Wisa! it is I.
The sun is not yet risen, and the foe   35
Sleep; but I sleep not; all night long I lie
Tossing and wakeful, and I come to thee.
For so did King Afrasiab bid me seek
Thy counsel, and to heed thee as thy son,
In Samarcand, before the army march'd;   40
And I will tell thee what my heart desires
Thou know'st if, since from Ader-baijan first
I came among the Tartars and bore arms,
I have still served Afrasiab well, and shown,
At my boy's years, the courage of a man.   45
This too thou know'st, that while I still bear on
The conquering Tartar ensigns through the world,
And beat the Persians back on every field,
I seek one man, one man, and one alone—
Rustum, my father; who I hoped should greet,   50
Should one day greet, upon some well-fought field,
His not unworthy, not inglorious son.
So I long hoped, but him I never find.
Come then, hear now, and grant me what I ask.
Let the two armies rest to-day; but I   55
Will challenge forth the bravest Persian lords
To meet me, man to man; if I prevail,
Rustum will surely hear it; if I fall—
Old man, the dead need no one, claim no kin.
Dim is the rumour of a common fight,   60
Where host meets host, and many names are sunk;
But of a single combat fame speaks clear.'
   He spoke; and Peran-Wisa took the hand
Of the young man in his, and sigh'd, and said:—
   'O Sohrab, an unquiet heart is thine!   65
Canst thou not rest among the Tartar chiefs,
And share the battle's common chance with us
Who love thee, but must press for ever first,
In single fight incurring single risk,
To find a father thou hast never seen?   70

That were far best, my son, to stay with us
Unmurmuring; in our tents, while it is war,
And when 'tis truce, then in Afrasiab's towns.
But, if this one desire indeed rules all,
To seek out Rustum—seek him not through fight!　　75
Seek him in peace, and carry to his arms,
O Sohrab, carry an unwounded son!
But far hence seek him, for he is not here.
For now it is not as when I was young,
When Rustum was in front of every fray;　　80
But now he keeps apart, and sits at home,
In Seistan, with Zal, his father old.
Whether that his own mighty strength at last
Feels the abhorr'd approaches of old age,
Or in some quarrel with the Persian King.　　85
There go!—Thou wilt not? Yet my heart forebodes
Danger or death awaits thee on this field.
Fain would I know thee safe and well, though lost
To us; fain therefore send thee hence, in peace
To seek thy father, not seek single fights　　90
In vain;—but who can keep the lion's cub
From ravening, and who govern Rustum's son?
Go, I will grant thee what thy heart desires.'
　　So said he, and dropp'd Sohrab's hand, and left
His bed, and the warm rugs whereon he lay;　　95
And o'er his chilly limbs his woollen coat
He pass'd, and tied his sandals on his feet,
And threw a white cloak round him, and he took
In his right hand a ruler's staff, no sword;
And on his head he set his sheep-skin cap,　　100
Black, glossy, curl'd, the fleece of Kara-Kul;
And raised the curtain of his tent, and call'd
His herald to his side, and went abroad.
　　The sun by this had risen, and clear'd the fog
From the broad Oxus and the glittering sands.　　105
And from their tents the Tartar horsemen filed
Into the open plain; so Haman bade—
Haman, who next to Peran-Wisa ruled
The host, and still was in his lusty prime.
From their black tents, long files of horse, they stream'd;　　110
As when some grey November morn the files,
In marching order spread, of long-necked cranes
Stream over Casbin and the southern slopes
Of Elburz, from the Aralian estuaries,
Or some frore Caspian reed-bed, southward bound　　115
For the warm Persian sea-board—so they stream'd.
The Tartars of the Oxus, the King's guard,

First, with black sheep-skin caps and with long spears;
Large men, large steeds; who from Bokhara come
And Khiva, and ferment the milk of mares.   120
Next, the more temperate Toorkmuns of the south,
The Tukas, and the lances of Salore,
And those from Attruck and the Caspian sands;
Light men and on light steeds, who only drink
The acrid milk of camels, and their wells.   125
And then a swarm of wandering horse, who came
From afar, and a more doubtful service own'd;
The Tartars of Ferghana, from the banks
Of the Jaxartes, men with scanty beards
And close-set skull-caps; and those wilder hordes   130
Who roam o'er Kipchak and the northern waste,
Kalmucks and unkempt Kuzzaks, tribes who stray
Nearest the Pole, and wandering Kirghizzes,
Who come on shaggy ponies from Pamere;
These all filed out from camp into the plain.   135
And on the other side the Persians form'd;—
First a light cloud of horse, Tartars they seem'd,
The Ilyats of Khorassan; and behind,
The royal troops of Persia, horse and foot,
Marshall'd battalions bright in burnish'd steel.   140
But Peran-Wisa with his herald came,
Threading the Tartar squadrons to the front,
And with his staff kept back the foremost ranks.
And when Ferood, who led the Persians, saw
That Peran-Wisa kept the Tartars back,   145
He took his spear, and to the front he came,
And check'd his ranks, and fix'd them where they stood.
And the old Tartar came upon the sand
Betwixt the silent hosts, and spake, and said:—
    'Ferood, and ye, Persians and Tartars, hear!   150
Let there be truce between the hosts to-day.
But choose a champion from the Persian lords
To fight our champion Sohrab, man to man.'
    As, in the country, on a morn in June,
When the dew glistens on the pearled ears,   155
A shiver runs through the deep corn for joy—
So, when they heard what Peran-Wisa said,
A thrill through all the Tartar squadrons ran
Of pride and hope for Sohrab, whom they loved.
    But as a troop of pedlars, from Cabool,   160
Cross underneath the Indian Caucasus,
That vast sky-neighbouring mountain of milk snow;
Crossing so high, that, as they mount, they pass
Long flocks of travelling birds dead on the snow,

Choked by the air, and scarce can they themselves   165
Slake their parch'd throats with sugar'd mulberries—
In single file they move, and stop their breath,
For fear they should dislodge the o'er-hanging snows—
So the pale Persians held their breath with fear.
　　And to Ferood his brother chiefs came up   170
To counsel; Gudurz and Zoarrah came,
And Feraburz, who ruled the Persian host
Second, and was the uncle of the King;
These came and counsell'd, and then Gudurz said:—
　　'Ferood, shame bids us take their challenge up,   175
Yet champion have we none to match this youth.
He has the wild stag's foot, the lion's heart.
But Rustum came last night; aloof he sits
And sullen, and has pitch'd his tents apart.
Him will I seek, and carry to his ear   180
The Tartar challenge, and this young man's name.
Haply he will forget his wrath, and fight.
Stand forth the while, and take their challenge up.'
　　So spake he; and Ferood stood forth and cried:—
'Old man, be it agreed as thou hast said!   185
Let Sohrab arm, and we will find a man.'
　　He spake: and Peran-Wisa turn'd, and strode
Back through the opening squadrons to his tent.
But through the anxious Persians Gudurz ran,
And cross'd the camp which lay behind, and reach'd,   190
Out on the sands beyond it, Rustum's tents.
Of scarlet cloth they were, and glittering gay,
Just pitch'd: the high pavilion in the midst
Was Rustum's, and his men lay camp'd around.
And Gudurz enter'd Rustum's tent, and found   195
Rustum; his morning meal was done, but still
The table stood before him, charged with food—
A side of roasted sheep, and cakes of bread,
And dark green melons; and there Rustum sate
Listless, and held a falcon on his wrist,   200
And play'd with it; but Gudurz came and stood
Before him; and he look'd, and saw him stand,
And with a cry sprang up and dropp'd the bird,
And greeted Gudurz with both hands, and said:—
　　'Welcome! these eyes could see no better sight.   205
What news? but sit down first, and eat and drink.'
　　But Gudurz stood in the tent-door, and said:—
'Not now! a time will come to eat and drink,
But not to-day; to-day has other needs.
The armies are drawn out, and stand at gaze;   210
For from the Tartars is a challenge brought

To pick a champion from the Persian lords
To fight their champion—and thou know'st his name—
Sohrab men call him, but his birth is hid.
O Rustum, like thy might is this young man's!   215
He has the wild stag's foot, the lion's heart;
And he is young, and Iran's chiefs are old,
Or else too weak; and all eyes turn to thee.
Come down and help us, Rustum, or we lose!'
    He spoke; but Rustum answer'd with a smile:—   220
'Go to! if Iran's chiefs are old, then I
Am older; if the young are weak, the King
Errs strangely; for the King, for Kai-Khosroo,
Himself is young, and honours younger men,
And lets the aged moulder to their graves.   225
Rustum he loves no more, but loves the young—
The young may rise at Sohrab's vaunts, not I.
For what care I, though all speak Sohrab's fame?
For would that I myself had such a son,
And not that one slight helpless girl I have—   230
A son so famed, so brave, to send to war,
And I to tarry with the snow-hair'd Zal,
My father, whom the robber Afghans vex,
And clip his borders short, and drive his herds,
And he has none to guard his weak old age.   235
There would I go, and hang my armour up,
And with my great name fence that weak old man,
And spend the goodly treasures I have got,
And rest my age, and hear of Sohrab's fame,
And leave to death the hosts of thankless kings,   240
And with these slaughterous hands draw sword no more.'
    He spoke, and smiled; and Gudurz made reply:—
'What then, O Rustum, will men say to this,
When Sohrab dares our bravest forth, and seeks
Thee most of all, and thou, whom most he seeks,   245
Hidest thy face? Take heed, lest men should say:
Like some old miser, Rustum hoards his fame,
And shuns to peril it with younger men.'
    And, greatly moved, then Rustum made reply:—
"O Gudurz, wherefore dost thou say such words?   250
Thou knowest better words than this to say.
What is one more, one less, obscure or famed,
Valiant or craven, young or old, to me?
Are not they mortal, am not I myself?
But who for men of nought would do great deeds?   255
Come, thou shall see how Rustum hoards his fame!
But I will fight unknown, and in plain arms;
Let not men say of Rustum, he was match'd

In single fight with any mortal man.'
   He spoke, and frown'd; and Gudurz turn'd, and ran   260
Back quickly through the camp in fear and joy—
Fear at his wrath, but joy that Rustum came.
But Rustum strode to his tent, and call'd
His followers in, and bade them bring his arms,
And clad himself in steel; the arms he chose   265
Were plain, and on his shield was no device,
Only his helm was rich, inlaid with gold,
And, from the fluted spine atop, a plume
Of horsehair waved, a scarlet horsehair plume.
So arm'd, he issued forth; and Ruksh, his horse,   270
Follow'd him like a faithful hound at heel—
Ruksh, whose renown was noised through all the earth,
The horse, whom Rustum on a foray once
Did in Bokhara by the river find
A colt beneath its dam, and drove him home,   275
And rear'd him; a bright bay, with lofty crest,
Dight with a saddle-cloth of broider'd green
Crusted with gold, and on the ground were work'd
All beasts of chase, all beasts which hunters know.
So follow'd, Rustum left his tents, and cross'd   280
The camp, and to the Persian host appear'd.
And all the Persians knew him, and with shouts
Hail'd; but the Tartars knew not who he was.
And dear as the wet diver to the eyes
Of his pale wife who waits and weeps on shore,   285
By sandy Bahrein, in the Persian Gulf,
Plunging all day in the blue waves, at night,
Having made up his tale of precious pearls,
Rejoins her in their hut upon the sands—
So dear to the pale Persians Rustum came.   290
   And Rustum to the Persian front advanced,
And Sohrab arm'd in Haman's tent, and came.
And as afield the reapers cut a swath
Down through the middle of a rich man's corn,
And on each side are squares of standing corn,   295
And in the midst a stubble, short and bare—
So on each side were squares of men, with spears
Bristling, and in the midst, the open sand.
And Rustum came upon the sand, and cast
His eyes toward the Tartar tents, and saw   300
Sohrab come forth, and eyed him as he came.
   As some rich woman, on a winter's morn,
Eyes through her silken curtains the poor drudge
Who with numb blacken'd fingers makes her fire—
At cock-crow, on a starlit winter's morn,   305

When the frost flowers the whiten'd window-panes—
And wonders how she lives, and what the thoughts
Of that poor drudge may be; so Rustum eyed
The unknown adventurous youth, who from afar
Came seeking Rustum, and defying forth   310
All the most valiant chiefs; long he perused
His spirited air, and wonder'd who he was.
For very young he seem'd, tenderly rear'd;
Like some young cypress, tall, and dark, and straight,
Which in a queen's secluded garden throws   315
Its slight dark shadow on the moonlit turf,
By midnight, to a bubbling fountain's sound—
So slender Sohrab seem'd, so softly rear'd.
And a deep pity enter'd Rustum's soul
As he beheld him coming; and he stood,   320
And beckon'd to him with his hand, and said:—
  'O thou young man, the air of Heaven is soft,
And warm, and pleasant; but the grave is cold!
Heaven's air is better than the cold dead grave.
Behold me! I am vast, and clad in iron,   325
And tried; and I have stood on many a field
Of blood, and I have fought with many a foe—
Never was that field lost, or that foe saved.
O Sohrab, wherefore wilt thou rush on death?
Be govern'd! quit the Tartar host, and come   330
To Iran, and be as my son to me,
And fight beneath my banner till I die!
There are no youths in Iran brave as thou.'
  So he spake, mildly; Sohrab heard his voice,
The mighty voice of Rustum, and he saw   335
His giant figure planted on the sand,
Sole, like some single tower, which a chief
Hath builded on the waste in former years
Against the robbers; and he saw that head,
Streaked with its first grey hairs;—hope filled his soul,   340
And he ran forward and embraced his knees,
And clasp'd his hand within his own, and said:—
  'O, by thy father's head! by thine own soul!
Art thou not Rustum? speak! art thou not he?'
  But Rustum eyed askance the kneeling youth,   345
And turn'd away, and spake to his own soul:—
  'Ah me, I muse what this young fox may mean!
False, wily, boastful, are these Tartar boys.
For if I now confess this thing he asks,
And hide it not, but say: *Rustum is here!*   350
He will not yield indeed, nor quit our foes,
But he will find some pretext not to fight,

And praise my fame, and proffer courteous gifts,
A belt or sword perhaps, and go his way.
And on a feast-tide, in Afrasiab's hall,   355
In Samarcand, he will arise and cry:
"I challenged once, when the two armies camp'd
Beside the Oxus, all the Persian lords
To cope with me in single fight; but they
Shrank, only Rustum dared; then he and I   360
Changed gifts, and went on equal terms away."
So will he speak, perhaps, while men applaud;
Then were the chiefs of Iran shamed through me.'
    And then he turn'd, and sternly spake aloud:—
'Rise! wherefore dost thou vainly question thus   365
Of Rustum? I am here, whom thou hast call'd
By challenge forth; make good thy vaunt, or yield!
Is it with Rustum only thou wouldst fight?
Rash boy, men look on Rustum's face and flee!
For well I know, that did great Rustum stand   370
Before thy face this day, and were reveal'd,
There would be then no talk of fighting more.
But being what I am, I tell thee this—
Do thou record it in thine inmost soul:
Either thou shalt renounce thy vaunt and yield,   375
Or else thy bones shall strew this sand, till winds
Bleach them, or Oxus with his summer-floods,
Oxus in summer wash them all away.'
    He spoke; and Sohrab answer'd, on his feet:—
'Art thou so fierce? Thou wilt not fright me so!   380
I am no girl, to be made pale by words.
Yet this thou has said well, did Rustum stand
Here on this field, there were no fighting then.
But Rustum is far hence, and we stand here.
Begin! thou art more vast, more dread than I,   385
And thou art proved, I know, and I am young—
But yet success sways with the breath of Heaven.
And though thou thinkest that thou knowest sure
Thy victory, yet thou canst not surely know.
For we are all, like swimmers in the sea,   390
Poised on the top of a huge wave of fate,
Which hangs uncertain to which side to fall.
And whether it will heave us up to land,
Or whether it will roll us out to sea,
Back out to sea, to the deep waves of death,   395
We know not, and no search will make us know;
Only the event will teach us in its hour.'
    He spoke, and Rustum answer'd not, but hurl'd
His spear; down from the shoulder, down it came,

As on some partridge in the corn a hawk,   400
That long has tower'd in the airy clouds,
Drops like a plummet; Sohrab saw it come,
And sprang aside, quick as a flash; the spear
Hiss'd, and went quivering down into the sand,
Which it sent flying wide;—then Sohrab threw   405
In turn, and full struck Rustum's shield; sharp rang,
The iron plates rang sharp, but turn'd the spear.
And Rustum seized his club, which none but he
Could wield; an unlopp'd trunk it was, and huge,
Still rough—like those which men in treeless plains   410
To build them boats fish from the flooded rivers,
Hyphasis or Hydaspes, when, high up
By their dark springs, the wind in winter-time
Hath made in Himalayan forests wrack,
And strewn the channels with torn boughs—so huge   415
The club which Rustum lifted now, and struck
One stroke; but again Sohrab sprang aside,
Lithe as the glancing snake, and the club came
Thundering to earth, and leapt from Rustum's hand.
And Rustum follow'd his own blow, and fell   420
To his knees, and with his fingers clutch'd the sand;
And now might Sohrab have unsheathed his sword,
And pierced the mighty Rustum while he lay
Dizzy, and on his knees, and choked with sand;
But he look'd on, and smiled, nor bared his sword,   425
But courteously drew back, and spoke, and said:—
   'Thou strik'st too hard! that club of thine will float
Upon the summer-floods, and not my bones.
But rise, and be not wroth! not wroth am I;
No, when I see thee, wrath forsakes my soul.   430
Thou say'st, thou art not Rustum; be it so!
Who art thou then, that canst so touch my soul?
Boy as I am, I have seen battles too—
Have waded foremost in their bloody waves,
And heard their hollow roar of dying men;   435
But never was my heart thus touch'd before.
Are they from Heaven, these softenings of the heart?
O thou old warrior, let us yield to Heaven!
Come, plant we here in earth our angry spears,
And make a truce, and sit upon this sand,   440
And pledge each other in red wine, like friends,
And thou shalt talk to me of Rustum's deeds.
There are enough foes in the Persian host,
Whom I may meet, and strike, and feel no pang;
Champions enough Afrasiab has, whom thou   445
Mayst fight; fight *them*, when they confront thy spear!

But oh, let there be peace 'twixt thee and me!'
  He ceased, but while he spake, Rustum had risen,
And stood erect, trembling with rage; his club
He left to lie, but had regain'd his spear, 450
Whose fiery point now in his mail'd right-hand
Blazed bright and baleful, like that autumn-star,
The baleful sign of fevers; dust had soil'd
His stately crest, and dimm'd his glittering arms.
His breast heaved, his lips foam'd, and twice his voice 455
Was choked with rage; at last these words broke way:—
  'Girl! nimble with thy feet, not with thy hands!
Curl'd minion, dancer, coiner of sweet words!
Fight, let me hear thy hateful voice no more!
Thou art not in Afrasiab's gardens now 460
With Tartar girls, with whom thou art wont to dance;
But on the Oxus-sands, and in the dance
Of battle, and with me, who make no play
Of war; I fight it out, and hand to hand.
Speak not to me of truce, and pledge, and wine! 465
Remember all thy valour; try thy feints
And cunning! all the pity I had is gone;
Because thou hast shamed me before both the hosts
With thy light skipping tricks, and thy girl's wiles.'
  He spoke, and Sohrab kindled at his taunts, 470
And he too drew his sword; at once they rush'd
Together, as two eagles on one prey
Come rushing down together from the clouds,
One from the east, one from the west; their shields
Dash'd with a clang together, and a din 475
Rose, such as that the sinewy woodcutters
Make often in the forest's heart at morn,
Of hewing axes, crashing trees—such blows
Rustum and Sohrab on each other hail'd.
And you would say that sun and stars took part 480
In that unnatural conflict; for a cloud
Grew suddenly in Heaven, and dark'd the sun
Over the fighters' heads; and a wind rose
Under their feet, and moaning swept the plain,
And in a sandy whirlwind wrapp'd the pair. 485
In gloom they twain were wrapp'd, and they alone;
For both the on-looking hosts on either hand
Stood in broad daylight, and the sky was pure,
And the sun sparkled on the Oxus stream.
But in the gloom they fought, with bloodshot eyes 490
And labouring breath; first Rustum struck the shield
Which Sohrab held stiff out; the steel-spiked spear
Rent the tough plates, but fail'd to reach the skin,

And Rustum pluck'd it back with angry groan.
Then Sohrab with his sword smote Rustum's helm,   495
Nor clove its steel quite through; but all the crest
He shore away, and that proud horsehair plume,
Never till now defiled, sank to the dust;
And Rustum bow'd his head; but then the gloom
Grew blacker, thunder rumbled in the air,   500
And lightnings rent the cloud; and Ruksh, the horse,
Who stood at hand, utter'd a dreadful cry;—
No horse's cry was that, most like the roar
Of some pain'd desert lion, who all day
Hath trail'd the hunter's javelin in his side,   505
And comes at night to die upon the sand.
The two hosts heard that cry, and quaked for fear,
And Oxus curdled as it cross'd his stream.
But Sohrab heard, and quail'd not, but rush'd on,
And struck again; and again Rustum bow'd   510
His head; but this time all the blade, like glass,
Sprang in a thousand shivers on the helm,
And in his hand the hilt remain'd alone.
Then Rustum raised his head; his dreadful eyes
Glared, and he shook on high his menacing spear,   515
And shouted: *Rustum!*—Sohrab heard that shout,
And shrank amazed; back he recoil'd one step,
And scann'd with blinking eyes the advancing form;
And then he stood bewilder'd; and he dropp'd
His covering shield, and the spear pierced his side.   520
He reel'd, and staggering back, sank to the ground;
And then the gloom dispersed, and the wind fell,
And the bright sun broke forth, and melted all
The cloud; and the two armies saw the pair—
Saw Rustum standing, safe upon his feet,   525
And Sohrab, wounded, on the bloody sand.
    Then with a bitter smile, Rustum began:—
'Sohrab, thou thoughtest in thy mind to kill
A Persian lord this day, and strip his corpse,
And bear thy trophies to Afrasiab's tent.   530
Or else that the great Rustum would come down
Himself to fight, and that thy wiles would move
His heart to take a gift, and let thee go.
And then that all the Tartar host would praise
Thy courage or thy craft, and spread thy fame,   535
To glad thy father in his weak old age.
Fool, thou art slain, and by an unknown man!
Dearer to the red jackals shalt thou be
Than to thy friends, and to thy father old.'
    And, with a fearless mien, Sohrab replied:—   540

'Unknown thou art; yet thy fierce vaunt is vain.
Thou dost not slay me, proud and boastful man!
No! Rustum slays me, and this filial heart.
For were I match'd with ten such men as thee,
And I were that which till to-day I was,   545
They should be lying here, I standing there.
But that belovèd name unnerved my arm—
That name, and something, I confess, in thee,
Which troubles all my heart, and made my shield
Fall; and thy spear transfix'd an unarm'd foe.   550
And now thou boastest, and insult'st my fate.
But hear thou this, fierce man, tremble to hear:
The mighty Rustum shall avenge my death!
My father, whom I seek through all the world,
He shall avenge my death, and punish thee!'   555
    As when some hunter in the spring hath found
A breeding eagle sitting on her nest,
Upon the craggy isle of a hill-lake,
And pierced her with an arrow as she rose,
And follow'd her to find her where she fell   560
Far off;—anon her mate comes winging back
From hunting, and a great way off descries
His huddling young left sole; at that, he checks
His pinion, and with short uneasy sweeps
Circles above his eyry, with loud screams   565
Chiding his mate back to her nest; but she
Lies dying, with the arrow in her side,
In some far stony gorge out of his ken,
A heap of fluttering feathers—never more
Shall the lake glass her, flying over it;   570
Never the black and dripping precipices
Echo her stormy scream as she sails by—
As that poor bird flies home, nor knows his loss,
So Rustum knew not his own loss, but stood
Over his dying son, and knew him not.   575
    But, with a cold incredulous voice, he said:—
'What prate is this of fathers and revenge?
The mighty Rustum never had a son.'
    And, with a failing voice, Sohrab replied:—
'Ah yes, he had! and that lost son am I.   580
Surely the news will one day reach his ear,
Reach Rustum, where he sits, and tarries long,
Somewhere, I know not where, but far from here;
And pierce him like a stab, and make him leap
To arms, and cry for vengeance upon thee.   585
Fierce man, bethink thee, for an only son!
What will that grief, what will that vengeance be?

Oh, could I live, till I that grief had seen!
Yet him I pity not so much, but her,
My mother, who in Ader-baijan dwells   590
With that old king, her father, who grows grey
With age, and rules over the valiant Koords.
Her most I pity, who no more will see
Sohrab returning from the Tartar camp,
With spoils and honour, when the war is done.   595
But a dark rumour will be bruited up,
From tribe to tribe, until it reach her ear;
And then will that defenceless woman learn
That Sohrab will rejoice her sight no more,
But that in battle with a nameless foe,   600
By the far-distant Oxus, he is slain.'
    He spoke; and as he ceased, he wept aloud,
Thinking of her he left, and his own death.
He spoke; but Rustum listen'd, plunged in thought.
Nor did he yet believe it was his son   605
Who spoke, although he call'd back names he knew;
For he had had sure tidings that the babe,
Which was in Ader-baijan born to him,
Had been a puny girl, no boy at all—
So that sad mother sent him word, for fear   610
Rustum should seek the boy, to train in arms.
And so he deem'd that either Sohrab took,
By a false boast, the style of Rustum's son;
Or that men gave it him, to swell his fame.
So deem'd he; yet he listen'd, plunged in thought   615
And his soul set to grief, as the vast tide
Of the bright rocking Ocean sets to shore
At the full moon; tears gather'd in his eyes;
For he remember'd his own early youth,
And all its bounding rapture; as, at dawn,   620
The shepherd from his mountain-lodge descries
A far, bright city, smitten by the sun,
Through many rolling clouds—so Rustum saw
His youth; saw Sohrab's mother, in her bloom;
And that old king, her father, who loved well   625
His wandering guest, and gave him his fair child
With joy; and all the pleasant life they led,
They three, in that long-distant summertime—
The castle, and the dewy woods, and hunt
And hound, and morn on those delightful hills   630
In Ader-baijan. And he saw that youth,
Of age and looks to be his own dear son,
Piteous and lovely, lying on the sand,
Like some rich hyacinth which by the scythe

Of an unskillful gardener has been cut, 635
Mowing the garden grass-plots near its bed,
And lies, a fragrant tower of purple bloom,
On the mown, dying grass—so Sohrab lay,
Lovely in death, upon the common sand.
And Rustum gazed on him with grief, and said:— 640
    'O Sohrab, thou indeed art such a son
Whom Rustum, wert thou his, might well have loved.
Yet here thou errest, Sohrab, or else men
Have told thee false—thou art not Rustum's son.
For Rustum had no son; one child he had— 645
But one—a girl; who with her mother now
Plies some light female task, nor dreams of us—
Of us she dreams not, nor of wounds, nor war.'
    But Sohrab answer'd him in wrath; for now
The anguish of the deep-fix'd spear grew fierce, 650
And he desired to draw forth the steel,
And let the blood flow free, and so to die—
But first he would convince his stubborn foe;
And, rising sternly on one arm, he said:—
    'Man, who art thou who dost deny my words? 655
Truth sits upon the lips of dying men,
And falsehood, while I lived, was far from mine.
I tell thee, prick'd upon this arm I bear
That seal which Rustum to my mother gave,
That she might prick it on the babe she bore.' 660
    He spoke; and all the blood left Rustum's cheeks,
And his knees totter'd, and he smote his hand
Against his breast, his heavy mailed hand,
That the hard iron corslet clank'd aloud;
And to his heart he press'd the other hand, 665
And in a hollow voice he spake, and said:—
    'Sohrab, that were a proof which could not lie!
If thou show this, then art thou Rustum's son.'
    Then, with weak hasty fingers, Sohrab loosed
His belt, and near the shoulder bared his arm, 670
And show'd a sign in faint vermilion points
Prick'd; as a cunning workman, in Pekin,
Pricks with vermilion some clear porcelain vase,
An emperor's gift—at early morn he paints,
And all day long, and, when night comes, the lamp 675
Lights up his studious forehead and thin hands—
So delicately prick'd the sign appear'd
On Sohrab's arm, the sign of Rustum's seal.
It was that griffin, which of old rear'd Zal,
Rustum's great father, whom they left to die, 680
A helpless babe, among the mountain-rocks;

Him that kind creature found, and rear'd, and loved—
Then Rustum took it for his glorious sign.
And Sohrab bared that image on his arm,
And himself scann'd it long with mournful eyes, 685
And then he touch'd it with his hand and said:—
    'How say'st thou? Is that sign the proper sign
Of Rustum's son, or of some other man's?'
    He spoke; but Rustum gazed, and gazed, and stood
Speechless; and then he utter'd one sharp cry: 690
"O boy—*thy father!*"—and his voice choked there.
And then a dark cloud pass'd before his eyes,
And his head swam, and he sank down to earth.
But Sohrab crawl'd to where he lay, and cast
His arms about his neck, and kiss'd his lips, 695
And with fond faltering fingers stroked his cheeks,
Trying to call him back to life; and life
Came back to Rustum, and he oped his eyes,
And they stood wide with horror; and he seized
In both his hands the dust which lay around, 700
And threw it on his head, and smirch'd his hair,—
His hair, and face, and beard, and glittering arms;
And strong convulsive groanings shook his breast,
And his sobs choked him; and he clutch'd his sword,
To draw it, and for ever let life out. 705
But Sohrab saw his thought, and held his hands,
And with a soothing voice he spake, and said:—
    'Father, forbear! for I but meet to-day
The doom which at my birth was written down
In Heaven, and thou art Heaven's unconscious hand. 710
Surely my heart cried out that it was thou,
When first I saw thee; and thy heart spoke too,
I know it! but fate trod those promptings down
Under its iron heel; fate, fate engaged
The strife, and hurl'd me on my father's spear. 715
But let us speak no more of this! I find
My father; let me feel that I have found!
Come, sit beside me on this sand, and take
My head betwixt thy hands, and kiss my cheeks,
And wash them with thy tears, and say: *My son!* 720
Quick! quick! for number'd are my sands of life,
And swift; for like the lightning to this field
I came, and like the wind I go away—
Sudden, and swift, and like a passing wind.
But it was writ in Heaven that this should be.' 725
    So said he, and his voice released the heart
Of Rustum, and his tears broke forth; he cast
His arms round his son's neck, and wept aloud,

And kiss'd him. And awe fell on both the hosts,
When they saw Rustum's grief; and Ruksh, the horse,   730
With his head bowing to the ground and mane
Sweeping the dust, came near, and in mute woe
First to the one, then to the other moved
His head, as if inquiring what their grief
Might mean; and from his dark, compassionate eyes,   735
The big warm tears roll'd down, and caked the sand.
But Rustum chid him with stern voice, and said:—
    'Ruksh, now thou grievest; but, O Ruksh, thy feet
Should first have rotted on their nimble joints,
Or ere they brought thy master to this field!'   740
    But Sohrab look'd upon the horse and said;—
'Is this, then, Ruksh? How often, in past days,
My mother told me of thee, thou brave steed,
My terrible father's terrible horse! and said,
That I should one day find thy lord and thee.   745
Come, let me lay my hand upon thy mane!
O Ruksh, thou art more fortunate than I;
For thou hast gone where I shall never go,
And snuff'd the breezes of my father's home.
And thou hast trod the sands of Seistan,   750
And seen the River of Helmund, and the Lake
Of Zirrah; and the aged Zal himself
Has often stroked thy neck, and given thee food,
Corn in a golden platter soak'd with wine,
And said: *O Ruksh! bear Rustum well!*—but I   755
Have never known my grandsire's furrow'd face,
Nor seen his lofty house in Seistan,
Nor slaked my thirst at the clear Helmund stream;
But lodged among my father's foes, and seen
Afrasiab's cities only, Samarcand,   760
Bokhara, and lone Khiva in the waste,
And the black Toorkmun tents; and only drunk
The desert rivers, Moorghab and Tejend,
Kohik, and where the Kalmuks feed their sheep,
The northern Sir; and this great Oxus stream,   765
The yellow Oxus, by whose brink I die.'
    Then, with a heavy groan, Rustum bewail'd:—
'Oh, that its waves were flowing over me!
Oh, that I saw its grains of yellow silt
Roll tumbling in the current o'er my head!'   770
    But, with a grave mild voice, Sohrab replied:—
'Desire not that, my father! thou must live.
For some are born to do great deeds, and live,
As some are born to be obscured, and die.
Do thou the deeds I die too young to do,   775

And reap a second glory in thine age;
Thou art my father, and thy gain is mine.
But come! thou seest this great host of men
Which follow me; I pray thee, slay not these!
Let me entreat for them; what have they done?   780
They follow'd me, my hope, my fame, my star.
Let them all cross the Oxus back in peace.
But me thou must bear hence, not send with them,
But carry me with thee to Seistan,
And place me on a bed, and mourn for me,   785
Thou, and the snow-hair'd Zal, and all thy friends.
And thou must lay me in that lovely earth,
And heap a stately mound above my bones,
And plant a far-seen pillar over all.
That so the passing horseman on the waste   790
May see my tomb a great way off, and cry:
Sohrab, the mighty Rustum's son, lies there,
Whom his great father did in ignorance kill!
And I be not forgotten in my grave.'
        And with a mournful voice, Rustum replied:—   795
'Fear not! as thou hast said, Sohrab, my son,
So shall it be; for I will burn my tents,
And quit the host, and bear thee hence with me,
And carry thee away to Seistan,
And place thee on a bed, and mourn for thee,   800
With the snow-headed Zal, and all my friends.
And I will lay thee in that lovely earth,
And heap a stately mound above thy bones,
And plant a far-seen pillar over all,
And men shall not forget thee in thy grave.   805
And I will spare thy host; yea, let them go!
Let them all cross the Oxus back in peace!
What should I do with slaying any more?
For would that all whom I have ever slain
Might be once more alive; my bitterest foes,   810
And they who were call'd champions in their time,
And through whose death I won that fame I have—
And I were nothing but a common man,
A poor, mean soldier, and without renown,
So thou mightest live too, my son, my son!   815
Or rather would that I, even I myself,
Might now be lying on this bloody sand,
Near death, and by an ignorant stroke of thine,
Not thou of mine! and I might die, not thou;
And I, not thou, be borne to Seistan;   820
And Zal might weep above my grave, not thine;
And say: *O son, I weep thee not too sore,*

For willingly, I know, thou met'st thine end!
But now in blood and battles was my youth,
And full of blood and battles is my age,   825
And I shall never end this life of blood.'
    Then, at the point of death, Sohrab replied:—
'A life of blood indeed, thou dreadful man!
But thou shalt yet have peace; only not now,
Not yet! but thou shalt have it on that day,   830
When thou shalt sail in a high-masted ship,
Thou and the other peers of Kai Khosroo,
Returning home over the salt blue sea,
From laying thy dear master in his grave.'
    And Rustum gazed in Sohrab's face, and said:—   835
'Soon be that day, my son, and deep that sea!
Till then, if fate so wills, let me endure.'
    He spoke; and Sohrab smiled on him, and took
The spear, and drew it from his side, and eased
His wound's imperious anguish; but the blood   840
Came welling from the open gash, and life
Flow'd with the stream;—all down his cold white side
The crimson torrent ran, dim now and soil'd
Like the soil'd tissue of white violets
Left, freshly gather'd, on their native bank,   845
By children whom their nurses call with haste
Indoors from the sun's eye; his head droop'd low,
His limbs grew slack; motionless, white, he lay—
White, with eyes closed; only when heavy gasps,
Deep heavy gasps quivering through all his frame,   850
Convulsed him back to life, he open'd them,
And fix'd them feebly on his father's face;
Till now all strength was ebb'd, and from his limbs
Unwillingly the spirit fled away,
Regretting the warm mansion which it left,   855
And youth, and bloom, and this delightful world.
    So, on the bloody sand, Sohrab lay dead;
And the great Rustum drew his horseman's cloak
Down o'er his face, and sate by his dead son.
As those black granite pillars, once high-rear'd   860
By Jemshid in Persepolis, to bear
His house, now 'mid their broken flights of steps
Lie prone, enormous, down the mountain side—
So in the sand lay Rustum by his son.
    And night came down over the solemn waste,   865
And the two gazing hosts, and that sole pair,
And darken'd all; and a cold fog, with night,
Crept from the Oxus. Soon a hum arose,
As of a great assembly loosed, and fires

870
Began to twinkle through the fog; for now
Both armies moved to camp, and took their meal;
The Persians took it on the open sands
Southward, the Tartars by the river marge;
And Rustum and his son were left alone.
   But the majestic river floated on,   875
Out of the mist and hum of that low land,
Into the frosty starlight, and there moved,
Rejoicing, through the hush'd Chorasmian waste,
Under the solitary moon;—he flow'd
Right for the polar star, past Orgunjè,   880
Brimming, and bright, and large; then sands begin
To hem his watery march, and dam his streams,
And split his currents; that for many a league
The shorn and parcell'd Oxus strains along
Through beds of sand and matted rushy isles—   885
Oxus, forgetting the bright speed he had
In his high mountain-cradle in Pamere,
A foil'd circuitous wanderer—till at last
The long'd-for dash of waves is heard, and wide
His luminous home of waters opens, bright   890
And tranquil, from whose floor the new-bathed stars
Emerge, and shine upon the Aral Sea.
1853

PHILOMELA

Hark! ah, the nightingale—
The tawny-throated!
Hark, from that moonlit cedar what a burst!
What triumph! hark!—what pain!   5
O wanderer from a Grecian shore,
Still, after many years, in distant lands,
Still nourishing in thy bewilder'd brain
That wild, unquench'd, deep-sunken, old-world pain—
Say, will it never heal?   10
And can this fragrant lawn
With its cool trees, and night,
And the sweet, tranquil Thames,
And moonshine, and the dew,
To thy rack'd heart and brain   15
Afford no balm?

Dost thou to-night behold,
Here, through the moonlight on this English grass,

The unfriendly palace in the Thracian wild?
Dost thou again peruse
With hot cheeks and sear'd eyes   20
The too clear web, and thy dumb sister's shame?
Dost thou once more assay
Thy flight, and feel come over thee,
Poor fugitive, the feathery change
Once more, and once more seem to make resound   25
With love and hate, triumph and agony,
Lone Daulis, and the high Cephissian vale?
Listen, Eugenia—
How thick the bursts come crowding through the leaves!
Again—thou hearest?   30
Eternal passion!
Eternal pain!
1853

REQUIESCAT

Strew on her roses, roses,
    And never a spray of yew!
In quiet she reposes;
    Ah, would that I did too!

Her mirth the world required;   5
    She bathed it in smiles of glee.
But her heart was tired, tired,
    And now they let her be.

Her life was turning, turning,
    In mazes of heat and sound.   10
But for peace her soul was yearning,
    And now peace laps her round.

Her cabin'd, ample spirit,
    It flutter'd and fail'd for breath.
To-night it doth inherit   15
    The vasty hall of death.
1853

STANZAS FROM THE GRANDE CHARTREUSE

Through Alpine meadows soft-suffused
With rain, where thick the crocus blows,
Past the dark forges long disused,

The mule-track from Saint Laurent goes.
The bridge is cross'd, and slow we ride,   5
Through forest, up the mountain-side.

The autumnal evening darkens round,
The wind is up, and drives the rain;
While, hark! far down, with strangled sound
Doth the Dead Guier's stream complain,   10
Where that wet smoke, among the woods,
Over his boiling cauldron broods.

Swift rush the spectral vapours white
Past limestone scars with ragged pines,
Showing—then blotting from our sight!—   15
Halt—through the cloud-drift something shines!
High in the valley, wet and drear,
The huts of Courrerie appear.

Strike leftward! cries our guide; and higher
Mounts up the stony forest-way.   20
At last the encircling trees retire;
Look! through the showery twilight grey
What pointed roofs are these advance?—
A palace of the Kings of France?

Approach, for what we seek is here!   25
Alight, and sparely sup, and wait
For rest in this outbuilding near;
Then cross the sward and reach that gate
Knock; pass the wicket! Thou art come
To the Carthusians' world-famed home.   30

The silent courts, where night and day
Into their stone-carved basins cold
The splashing icy fountains play—
The humid corridors behold!
Where, ghostlike in the deepening night,   35
Cowl'd forms brush by in gleaming white.

The chapel, where no organ's peal
Invests the stern and naked prayer—
With penitential cries they kneel
And wrestle; rising then, with bare   40
And white uplifted faces stand,
Passing the Host from hand to hand;

Each takes, and then his visage wan
Is buried in his cowl once more.

The cells!—the suffering Son of Man   45
Upon the wall—the knee-worn floor—
And where they sleep, that wooden bed,
Which shall their coffin be, when dead!

The library, where tract and tome
Not to feed priestly pride are there,   50
To hymn the conquering march of Rome,
Nor yet to amuse, as ours are!
They paint of souls the inner strife,
Their drops of blood, their death in life.

The garden, overgrown—yet mild,   55
See, fragrant herbs are flowering there!
Strong children of the Alpine wild
Whose culture is the brethren's care;
Of human tasks their only one,
And cheerful works beneath the sun.   60

Those halls, too, destined to contain
Each its own pilgrim-host of old,
From England, Germany, or Spain—
All are before me! I behold
The House, the Brotherhood austere!   65
—And what am I, that I am here?

For rigorous teachers seized my youth,
And purged its faith, and trimm'd its fire,
Show'd me the high, white star of Truth,
There bade me gaze, and there aspire.   70
Even now their whispers pierce the gloom:
What dost thou in this living tomb?

Forgive me, masters of the mind!
At whose behest I long ago
So much unlearnt, so much resign'd—   75
I come not here to be your foe!
I seek these anchorites, not in ruth,
To curse and to deny your truth;

Not as their friend, or child, I speak!
But as, on some far northern strand,   80
Thinking of his own Gods, a Greek
In pity and mournful awe might stand
Before some fallen Runic stone—
For both were faiths, and both are gone.

Wandering between two worlds, one dead,   85
The other powerless to be born,
With nowhere yet to rest my head,

Like these, on earth I wait forlorn.
Their faith, my tears, the world deride—
I come to shed them at their side. 90

Oh, hide me in your gloom profound,
Ye solemn seats of holy pain!
Take me, cowl'd forms, and fence me round,
Till I possess my soul again; 95
Till free my thoughts before me roll,
Not chafed by hourly false control!

For the world cries your faith is now
But a dead time's exploded dream;
My melancholy, sciolists say,
Is a pass'd mode, an outworn theme— 100
As if the world had ever had
A faith, or sciolists been sad!

Ah, if it *be* pass'd, take away,
At least, the restlessness, the pain;
Be man henceforth no more a prey 105
To these out-dated stings again!
The nobleness of grief is gone—
Ah, leave us not the fret alone!

But—if you cannot give us ease—
Last of the race of them who grieve 110
Here leave us to die out with these
Last of the people who believe!
Silent, while years engrave the brow;
Silent—the best are silent now.

Achilles ponders in his tent, 115
The kings of modern thought are dumb;
Silent they are, though not content,
And wait to see the future come.
They have the grief men had of yore,
But they contend and cry no more. 120

Our fathers water'd with their tears
This sea of time whereon we sail,
Their voices were in all men's ears
Who pass'd within their puissant hail.
Still the same ocean round us raves, 125
But we stand mute, and watch the waves.

For what avail'd it, all the noise
And outcry of the former men?—
Say, have their sons achieved more joys,

Say, is life lighter now than then?   130
The sufferers died, they left their pain—
The pangs which tortured them remain.

What helps it now, that Byron bore,
With haughty scorn which mock'd the smart,
Through Europe to the Ætolian shore   135
The pageant of his bleeding heart?
That thousands counted every groan,
And Europe made his woe her own?

What boots it, Shelley! that the breeze
Carried thy lovely wail away,   140
Musical through Italian trees
Which fringe thy soft blue Spezzian bay?
Inheritors of thy distress
Have restless hearts one throb the less?

Or are we easier, to have read,   145
O Obermann! the sad, stern page,
Which tells us how thou hidd'st thy head
From the fierce tempest of thine age
In the lone brakes of Fontainebleau,
Or chalets near the Alpine snow?   150

Ye slumber in your silent grave!—
The world, which for an idle day
Grace to your mood of sadness gave,
Long since hath flung her weeds away.
The eternal trifler breaks your spell;   155
But we—we learnt your lore too well!

Years hence, perhaps, may dawn an age,
More fortunate, alas! than we,
Which without hardness will be sage,
And gay without frivolity.   160
Sons of the world, oh, speed those years;
But, while we wait, allow our tears!

Allow them! We admire with awe
The exulting thunder of your race;
You give the universe your law,   165
You triumph over time and space!
Your pride of life, your tireless powers,
We laud them, but they are not ours.

We are like children rear'd in shade
Beneath some old-world abbey wall,   170

Forgotten in a forest-glade,
And secret from the eyes of all.
Deep, deep the greenwood round them waves,
Their abbey, and its close of graves!

But, where the road runs near the stream,   175
Oft through the trees they catch a glance
Of passing troops in the sun's beam—
Pennon, and plume, and flashing lance!
Forth to the world those soldiers fare,
To life, to cities, and to war!   180

And through the wood, another way,
Faint bugle-notes from far are borne,
Where hunters gather, staghounds bay,
Round some fair forest-lodge at morn.
Gay dames are there, in sylvan green;   185
Laughter and cries—those notes between!

The banners flashing through the trees
Make their blood dance and chain their eyes;
That bugle-music on the breeze
Arrests them with a charm'd surprise.   190
Banner by turns and bugle woo:
Ye shy recluses, follow too!

O children, what do ye reply?—
'Action and pleasure, will ye roam
Through these secluded dells to cry   195
And call us?—but too late ye come!
Too late for us your call ye blow,
Whose bent was taken long ago.

'Long since we pace this shadow'd nave;
We watch those yellow tapers shine,   200
Emblems of hope over the grave,
In the high altar's depth divine;
The organ carries to our ear
Its accents of another sphere.

'Fenced early in this cloistral round   205
Of reverie, of shade, of prayer,
How should we grow in other ground?
How can we flower in foreign air?
—Pass, banners, pass, and bugles, cease;
And leave our desert to its peace!'   210
1855

THYRSIS

A MONODY, TO COMMEMORATE THE AUTHOR'S FRIEND,
ARTHUR HUGH CLOUGH, WHO DIED AT FLORENCE, 1861

How changed is here each spot man makes or fills!
  In the two Hinkseys nothing keeps the same;
    The village street its haunted mansion lacks,
  And from the sign is gone Sibylla's name,
    And from the roofs the twisted chimney-stacks—   5
      Are ye too changed, ye hills?
  See, 'tis no foot of unfamiliar men
    To-night from Oxford up your pathway strays!
    Here came I often, often, in old days—
  Thyrsis and I; we still had Thyrsis then.   10

Runs it not here, the track by Childsworth Farm,
  Past the high wood, to where the elm-tree crowns
    The hill behind whose ridge the sunset flames?
  The signal-elm, that looks on Ilsley Downs,
    The Vale, the three lone weirs, the youthful Thames?—   15
      This winter-eve is warm,
  Humid the air! leafless, yet soft as spring,
    The tender purple spray on copse and briers!
    And that sweet city with her dreaming spires,
  She needs not June for beauty's heightening,   20

Lovely all times she lies, lovely to-night!—
  Only, methinks, some loss of habit's power
    Befalls me wandering through this upland dim.
  Once pass'd I blindfold here, at any hour;
    Now seldom come I, since I came with him.   25
      That single elm-tree bright
  Against the west—I miss it! is it gone?
    We prized it dearly; while it stood, we said,
    Our friend, the Gipsy-Scholar, was not dead;
  While the tree lived, he in these fields lived on.   30

Too rare, too rare, grow now my visits here,
  But once I knew each field, each flower, each stick;
    And with the country-folk acquaintance made
  By barn in threshing-time, by new-built rick.
    Here, too, our shepherd-pipes we first assay'd.   35
      Ah me! this many a year

My pipe is lost, my shepherd's holiday!
　Needs must I lose them, needs with heavy heart
　　Into the world and wave of men depart;
But Thyrsis of his own will went away.   40

It irk'd him to be here, he could not rest.
　He loved each simple joy the country yields,
　　He loved his mates; but yet he could not keep,
For that a shadow lour'd on the fields,
　　Here with the shepherds and the silly sheep.   45
　　　Some life of men unblest
He knew, which made him droop, and fill'd his head.
　He went; his piping took a troubled sound
　Of storms that rage outside our happy ground;
He could not wait their passing, he is dead.   50

So, some tempestuous morn in early June,
　When the year's primal burst of bloom is o'er,
　　Before the roses and the longest day—
When garden-walks and all the grassy floor
　　With blossoms red and white of fallen May   55
　　　And chestnut-flowers are strewn—
So have I heard the cuckoo's parting cry,
　From the wet field, through the vext garden-trees,
　Come with the volleying rain and tossing breeze:
The bloom is gone, and with the bloom go I!   60

Too quick despairer, wherefore wilt thou go?
　Soon will the high Midsummer pomps come on,
　　Soon will the musk carnations break and swell,
Soon shall we have gold-dusted snapdragon,
　　Sweet-William with his homely cottage-smell,   65
　　　And stocks in fragrant blow;
Roses that down the alleys shine afar,
　And open, jasmine-muffled lattices,
　And groups under the dreaming garden-trees,
And the full moon, and the white evening-star.   70

He harkens not! light comer, he is flown!
　What matters it? next year he will return,
　　And we shall have him in the sweet spring-days,
With whitening hedges, and uncrumpling fern,
　　And blue-bells trembling by the forest-ways,   75
　　　And scent of hay new-mown.
But Thyrsis never more we swains shall see;
　See him come back, and cut a smoother reed,
　And blow a strain the world at last shall heed—
For Time, not Corydon, hath conquer'd thee!   80

Alack, for Corydon no rival now!—
  But when Sicilian shepherds lost a mate,
    Some good survivor with his flute would go,
  Piping a ditty sad for Bion's fate;
    And cross the unpermitted ferry's flow,   85
      And relax Pluto's brow,
  And make leap up with joy the beauteous head
    Of Proserpine, among whose crowned hair
    Are flowers first open'd on Sicilian air,
  And flute his friend, like Orpheus, from the dead.   90

O easy access to the hearer's grace
  When Dorian shepherds sang to Proserpine!
    For she herself had trod Sicilian fields,
  She knew the Dorian water's gush divine,
    She knew each lily white which Enna yields,   95
      Each rose with blushing face;
  She loved the Dorian pipe, the Dorian strain.
    But ah, of our poor Thames she never heard!
    Her foot the Cumner cowslips never stirr'd;
  And we should tease her with our plaint in vain!   100

Well! wind-dispersed and vain the words will be,
  Yet, Thyrsis, let me give my grief its hour
    In the old haunt, and find our tree-topp'd hill!
  Who, if not I, for questing here hath power?
    I know the wood which hides the daffodil,   105
      I know the Fyfield tree,
  I know what white, what purple fritillaries
    The grassy harvest of the river-fields,
    Above by Ensham, down by Sanford, yields,
  And what sedged brooks are Thames's tributaries;   110

I know these slopes; who knows them if not I?—
  But many a dingle on the loved hill-side,
    With thorns once studded, old, white-blossom'd trees,
  Where thick the cowslips grew, and far descried
    High tower'd the spikes of purple orchises,   115
      Hath since our day put by
  The coronals of that forgotten time;
    Down each green bank hath gone the ploughboy's team,
    And only in the hidden brookside gleam
  Primroses, orphans of the flowery prime.   120

Where is the girl, who by the boatman's door,
  Above the locks, above the boating throng,
    Unmoor'd our skiff when through the Wytham flats,
  Red loosestrife and blond meadow-sweet among

And darting swallows and light water-gnats,   125
  We track'd the shy Thames shore?
    Where are the mowers, who, as the tiny swell
    Of our boat passing heaved the river-grass,
      Stood with suspended scythe to see us pass?—
They all are gone, and thou art gone as well!   130

Yes, thou art gone! and round me too the night
  In ever-nearing circle weaves her shade.
    I see her veil draw soft across the day,
  I feel her slowly chilling breath invade
    The cheek grown thin, the brown hair sprent with grey;   135
      I feel her finger light
  Laid pausefully upon life's headlong train;—
    The foot less prompt to meet the morning dew,
    The heart less bounding at emotion new,
  And hope, once crush'd, less quick to spring again.   140

And long the way appears, which seem'd so short
  To the less practised eye of sanguine youth;
    And high the mountain-tops, in cloudy air,
  The mountain-tops where is the throne of Truth,
    Tops in life's morning-sun so bright and bare!   145
      Unbreachable the fort
  Of the long-batter'd world uplifts its wall;
    And strange and vain the earthly turmoil grows,
    And near and real the charm of thy repose,
  And night as welcome as a friend would fall.   150

But hush! the upland hath a sudden loss
  Of quiet!—Look, adown the dusk hill-side,
    A troop of Oxford hunters going home,
  As in old days, jovial and talking, ride!
    From hunting with the Berkshire hounds they come,   155
      Quick! let me fly, and cross
  Into yon farther field!—'Tis done; and see,
    Back'd by the sunset, which doth glorify
    The orange and pale violet evening-sky,
  Bare on its lonely ridge, the Tree! the Tree!   160

I take the omen! Eve lets down her veil,
  The white fog creeps from bush to bush about,
    The west unflushes, the high stars grow bright,
  And in the scatter'd farms the lights come out.
    I cannot reach the signal-tree to-night,   165
      Yet, happy omen, hail!
  Hear it from thy broad lucent Arno-vale
    (For there thine earth-forgetting eyelids keep

The morningless and unawakening sleep
Under the flowery oleanders pale),   170

Hear it, O Thyrsis, still our tree is there!—
    Ah, vain! These English fields, this upland dim,
        These brambles pale with mist engarlanded,
    That lone, sky-pointing tree, are not for him;
        To a boon southern country he is fled,   175
            And now in happier air,
    Wandering with the great Mother's train divine
        (And purer or more subtle soul than thee,
        I trow, the mighty Mother doth not see)
    Within a folding of the Apennine,   180

Thou hearest the immortal chants of old!—
    Putting his sickle to the perilous grain
        In the hot cornfield of the Phrygian king,
    For thee the Lityerses-song again
        Young Daphnis with his silver voice doth sing;   185
            Sings his Sicilian fold,
    His sheep, his hapless love, his blinded eyes—
        And how a call celestial round him rang,
        And heavenward from the fountain-brink he sprang,
    And all the marvel of the golden skies.   190

There thou art gone, and me thou leavest here
    Sole in these fields! yet will I not despair.
        Despair I will not, while I yet descry
    'Neath the mild canopy of English air
        That lonely tree against the western sky.   195
            Still, still these slopes, 'tis clear,
    Our Gipsy-Scholar haunts, outliving thee!
        Fields where soft sheep from cages pull the hay,
        Woods with anemonies in flower till May,
    Know him a wanderer still; then why not me?   200

A fugitive and gracious light he seeks,
    Shy to illumine; and I seek it too.
        This does not come with houses or with gold,
    With place, with honour, and a flattering crew;
        'Tis not in the world's market bought and sold—   205
            But the smooth-slipping weeks
    Drop by, and leave its seeker still untired;
        Out of the heed of mortals he is gone,
        He wends unfollow'd, he must house alone;
    Yet on he fares by his own heart inspired.   210

Thou too, O Thyrsis, on like quest wast bound;
    Thou wanderedst with me for a little hour!

Men gave thee nothing; but this happy quest,
If men esteem'd thee feeble, gave thee power,
  If men procured thee trouble, gave thee rest.   215
    And this rude Cumner ground,
Its fir-topped Hurst, its farms, its quiet fields,
  Here cam'st thou in thy jocund youthful time,
  Here was thine height of strength, thy golden prime!
And still the haunt beloved a virtue yields.   220

What though the music of thy rustic flute
  Kept not for long its happy, country tone;
    Lost it too soon, and learnt a stormy note
Of men contention-tost, of men who groan,
  Which task'd thy pipe too sore, and tired thy throat—   225
    It fail'd, and thou wast mute!
Yet hadst thou alway visions of our light,
  And long with men of care thou couldst not stay,
  And soon thy foot resumed its wandering way,
Left human haunt, and on alone till night.   230

Too rare, too rare, grow now my visits here!
  'Mid city-noise, not, as with thee of yore,
    Thyrsis! in reach of sheep-bells is my home.
  —Then through the great town's harsh, heart-wearying roar,
  Let in thy voice a whisper often come,   235
    To chase fatigue and fear:
Why faintest thou? I wander'd till I died.
  Roam on! The light we sought is shining still.
  Dost thou ask proof? Our tree yet crowns the hill,
Our Scholar travels yet the loved hill-side.   240
1866

DOVER BEACH

The sea is calm to-night.
The tide is full, the moon lies fair
Upon the straits;—on the French coast the light
Gleams and is gone; the cliffs of England stand,
Glimmering and vast, out in the tranquil bay.   5
Come to the window, sweet is the night-air!
Only, from the long line of spray
Where the sea meets the moon-blanch'd land,
Listen! you hear the grating roar
Of pebbles which the waves draw back, and fling,   10
At their return, up the high strand,
Begin, and cease, and then again begin,

With tremulous cadence slow, and bring
The eternal note of sadness in.

Sophocles long ago   15
Heard it on the Ægæan, and it brought
Into his mind the turbid ebb and flow
Of human misery; we
Find also in the sound a thought,
Hearing it by this distant northern sea.   20

The Sea of Faith
Was once, too, at the full, and round earth's shore
Lay like the folds of a bright girdle furl'd.
But now I only hear
Its melancholy, long, withdrawing roar,   25
Retreating, to the breath
Of the night-wind, down the vast edges drear
And naked shingles of the world.

Ah, love, let us be true
To one another! for the world, which seems   30
To lie before us like a land of dreams,
So various, so beautiful, so new,
Hath really neither joy, nor love, nor light,
Nor certitude, nor peace, nor help for pain;
And we are here as on a darkling plain   35
Swept with confused alarms of struggle and flight,
Where ignorant armies clash by night.
1867

RUGBY CHAPEL

NOVEMBER 1857

Coldly, sadly descends
The autumn-evening. The field
Strewn with its dank yellow drifts
Of wither'd leaves, and the elms,
Fade into dimness apace,   5
Silent;—hardly a shout
From a few boys late at their play!
The lights come out in the street,
In the school-room windows;—but cold,
Solemn, unlighted, austere,   10
Through the gathering darkness, arise
The chapel-walls, in whose bound
Thou, my father! art laid.

There thou dost lie, in the gloom
Of the autumn evening. But ah!   15
That word, *gloom*, to my mind
Brings thee back, in the light
Of thy radiant vigour, again;
In the gloom of November we pass'd
Days not dark at thy side;   20
Seasons impair'd not the ray
Of thy buoyant cheerfulness clear.
Such thou wast! and I stand
In the autumn evening, and think
Of bygone autumns with thee.   25

Fifteen years have gone round
Since thou arosest to tread,
In the summer-morning, the road
Of death, at a call unforeseen,
Sudden. For fifteen years,   30
We who till then in thy shade
Rested as under the boughs
Of a mighty oak, have endured
Sunshine and rain as we might,
Bare, unshaded, alone,   35
Lacking the shelter of thee.

O strong soul, by what shore
Tarriest thou now? For that force,
Surely, has not been left vain!
Somewhere, surely, afar,   40
In the sounding labour-house vast
Of being, is practised that strength,
Zealous, beneficent, firm!

Yes, in some far-shining sphere,
Conscious or not of the past,   45
Still thou performest the word
Of the Spirit in whom thou dost live—
Prompt, unwearied, as here!
Still thou upraisest with zeal
The humble good from the ground,   50
Sternly repressest the bad!
Still, like a trumpet, dost rouse
Those who with half-open eyes
Tread the border-land dim
'Twixt vice and virtue; reviv'st,   55
Succourest!—this was thy work,
This was thy life upon earth.

What is the course of the life
Of mortal men on the earth?—
Most men eddy about   60
Here and there—eat and drink,
Chatter and love and hate,
Gather and squander, are raised
Aloft, are hurl'd in the dust,
Striving blindly, achieving   65
Nothing; and then they die—
Perish;—and no one asks
Who or what they have been,
More than he asks what waves,
In the moonlit solitudes mild   70
Of the midmost Ocean, have swell'd,
Foam'd for a moment, and gone.

And there are some, whom a thirst
Ardent, unquenchable, fires,
Not with the crowd to be spent,   75
Not without aim to go round
In an eddy of purposeless dust,
Effort unmeaning and vain.
Ah yes! some of us strive
Not without action to die   80
Fruitless, but something to snatch
From dull oblivion, nor all
Glut the devouring grave!
We, we have chosen our path—
Path to a clear-purposed goal,   85
Path of advance!—but it leads
A long, steep journey, through sunk
Gorges, o'er mountains in snow.
Cheerful, with friends, we set forth—
Then, on the height, comes the storm.   90
Thunder crashes from rock
To rock, the cataracts reply,
Lightnings dazzle our eyes.
Roaring torrents have breach'd
The track, the stream-bed descends   95
In the place where the wayfarer once
Planted his footsteps—the spray
Boils o'er its borders! aloft
The unseen snow-beds dislodge
Their hanging ruin; alas,   100
Havoc is made in our train!
Friends, who set forth at our side,
Falter, are lost in the storm.

We, we only are left!
With frowning foreheads, with lips   105
Sternly compress'd, we strain on,
On—and at nightfall at last
Come to the end of our way,
To the lonely inn 'mid the rocks;
Where the gaunt and taciturn host   110
Stands on the threshold, the wind
Shaking his thin white hairs—
Holds his lantern to scan
Our storm-beat figures, and asks:
Whom in our party we bring?   115
Whom we have left in the snow?

Sadly we answer: We bring
Only ourselves! we lost
Sight of the rest in the storm.
Hardly ourselves we fought through,   120
Stripp'd, without friends, as we are.
Friends, companions, and train,
The avalanche swept from our side.

But thou would'st not *alone*
Be saved, my father! *alone*   125
Conquer and come to thy goal,
Leaving the rest in the wild.
We were weary, and we
Fearful, and we in our march
Fain to drop down and to die.   130
Still thou turnedst, and still
Beckonedst the trembler, and still
Gavest the weary thy hand.

If, in the paths of the world,
Stones might have wounded thy feet,   135
Toil or dejection have tried
Thy spirit, of that we saw
Nothing—to us thou wast still
Cheerful, and helpful, and firm!
Therefore to thee it was given   140
Many to save with thyself;
And, at the end of thy day,
O faithful shepherd! to come,
Bringing thy sheep in thy hand.

And through thee I believe   145
In the noble and great who are gone;
Pure souls honour'd and blest

By former ages, who else—
Such, so soulless, so poor,
Is the race of men whom I see—   150
Seem'd but a dream of the heart,
Seem'd but a cry of desire.
Yes! I believe that there lived
Others like thee in the past,
Not like the men of the crowd   155
Who all round me to-day
Bluster or cringe, and make life
Hideous, and arid, and vile;
But souls temper'd with fire,
Fervent, heroic, and good,   160
Helpers and friends of mankind.

Servants of God!—or sons
Shall I not call you? because
Not as servants ye knew
Your Father's innermost mind,   165
His, who unwillingly sees
One of his little ones lost—
Yours is the praise, if mankind
Hath not as yet in its march
Fainted, and fallen, and died!   170

See! In the rocks of the world
Marches the host of mankind,
A feeble, wavering line.
Where are they tending?—A God
Marshall'd them, gave them their goal.   175
Ah, but the way is so long!
Years they have been in the wild!
Sore thirst plagues them, the rocks,
Rising all round, overawe;
Factions divide them, their host   180
Threatens to break, to dissolve.
—Ah, keep, keep them combined!
Else, of the myriads who fill
That army, not one shall arrive;
Sole they shall stray; in the rocks   185
Stagger for ever in vain,
Die one by one in the waste.

Then, in such hour of need
Of your fainting, dispirited race,
Ye, like angels, appear,   190
Radiant with ardour divine!
Beacons of hope, ye appear!

Languor is not in your heart,
Weakness is not in your word,
Weariness not on your brow. 195
Ye alight in our van! at your voice,
Panic, despair, flee away.
Ye move through the ranks, recall
The stragglers, refresh the outworn,
Praise, re-inspire the brave! 200
Order, courage, return.
Eyes rekindling, and prayers,
Follow your steps as ye go.
Ye fill up the gaps in our files,
Strengthen the wavering line, 205
Stablish, continue our march,
On, to the bound of the waste,
On, to the City of God.
1867

OBERMANN ONCE MORE

Savez-vous quelque bien qui console du regret d'un monde?—Obermann

Glion?——Ah, twenty years, it cuts
All meaning from a name!
White houses prank where once were huts.
Glion, but not the same!

And yet I know not! All unchanged
The turf, the pines, the sky!
The hills in their old order ranged;
The lake, with Chillon by!

And, 'neath those chestnut-trees, where stiff
And stony mounts the way, 10
The crackling husk-heaps burn, as if
I left them yesterday!

Across the valley, on that slope,
The huts of Avant shine!
Its pines, under their branches, ope
Ways for the pasturing kine.

Full-foaming milk-pails, Alpine fare,
Sweet heaps of fresh-cut grass,
Invite to rest the traveller there
Before he climb the pass— 20

The gentian-flower'd pass, its crown
With yellow spires aflame;
Whence drops the path to Allière down,
And walls where Byron came,

By their green river, who doth change
His birth-name just below;
Orchard, and croft, and full-stored grange
Nursed by his pastoral flow.

But stop!—to fetch back thoughts that stray
Beyond this gracious bound,   30
The cone of Jaman, pale and grey,
See, in the blue profound!

Ah, Jaman! delicately tall
Above his sun-warm'd firs—
What thoughts to me his rocks recall,
What memories he stirs!

And who but thou must be, in truth,
Obermann! with me here?
Thou master of my wandering youth,
But left this many a year!   40

Yes, I forget the world's work wrought,
Its warfare waged with pain;
An eremite with thee, in thought
Once more I slip my chain,

And to thy mountain-chalet come,
And lie beside its door,
And hear the wild bee's Alpine hum,
And thy sad, tranquil lore!

Again I feel the words inspire
Their mournful calm; serene,   50
Yet tinged with infinite desire
For all that *might* have been—

The harmony from which man swerved
Made his life's rule once more!
The universal order served,
Earth happier than before!

—While thus I mused, night gently ran
Down over hill and wood.
Then, still and sudden, Obermann
On the grass near me stood.   60

Those pensive features well I knew,
On my mind, years before,
Imaged so oft! imaged so true!
—A shepherd's garb he wore,

A mountain-flower was in his hand,
A book was in his breast.
Bent on my face, with gaze which scann'd
My soul, his eyes did rest.

"And is it thou," he cried, "so long
Held by the world which we   70
Loved not, who turnest from the throng
Back to thy youth and me?

"And from thy world, with heart opprest,
Choosest thou *now* to turn?—
Ah me! we anchorites read things best,
Clearest their course discern!

"Thou fledst me when the ungenial earth,
Man's work-place, lay in gloom.
Return'st thou in her hour of birth,
Of hopes and hearts in bloom?   80

"Perceiv'st thou not the change of day?
Ah! Carry back thy ken,
What, some two thousand years! Survey
The world as it was then!

"Like ours it look'd in outward air.
Its head was clear and true,
Sumptuous its clothing, rich its fare,
No pause its action knew;

"Stout was its arm, each thew and bone
Seem'd puissant and alive—   90
But, ah! its heart, its heart was stone,
And so it could not thrive!

"On that hard Pagan world disgust
And secret loathing fell.
Deep weariness and sated lust
Made human life a hell.

"In his cool hall, with haggard eyes,
The Roman noble lay;
He drove abroad, in furious guise,
Along the Appian way.   100

"He made a feast, drank fierce and fast,
And crown'd his hair with flowers—
No easier nor no quicker pass'd
The impracticable hours.

"The brooding East with awe beheld
Her impious younger world.
The Roman tempest swell'd and swell'd,
And on her head was hurl'd.

"The East bow'd low before the blast
In patient, deep disdain;   110
She let the legions thunder past,
And plunged in thought again.

"So well she mused, a morning broke
Across her spirit grey;
A conquering, new-born joy awoke,
And fill'd her life with day.

" 'Poor world,' she cried, 'so deep accurst,
That runn'st from pole to pole
To seek a draught to slake thy thirst—
Go, seek it in thy soul!'   120

"She heard it, the victorious West,
In crown and sword array'd!
She felt the void which mined her breast,
She shiver'd and obey'd.

"She veil'd her eagles, snapp'd her sword,
And laid her sceptre down;
Her stately purple she abhorr'd,
And her imperial crown.

"She broke her flutes, she stopp'd her sports,
Her artists could not please;   130
She tore her books, she shut her courts,
She fled her palaces;

"Lust of the eye and pride of life
She left it all behind,
And hurried, torn with inward strife,
The wilderness to find.

"Tears wash'd the trouble from her face!
She changed into a child!
'Mid weeds and wrecks she stood—a place
Of ruin—but she smiled!   140

"Oh, had I lived in that great day,
How had its glory new
Fill'd earth and heaven, and caught away
My ravish'd spirit too!

"No thoughts that to the world belong
Had stood against the wave
Of love which set so deep and strong
From Christ's then open grave.

"No cloister-floor of humid stone
Had been too cold for me.
For me no Eastern desert lone
Had been too far to flee.

"No lonely life had pass'd too slow,
When I could hourly scan
Upon his Cross, with head sunk low,
That nail'd thorn-crowned Man!

"Could see the Mother with her Child
Whose tender winning arts
Have to his little arms beguiled
So many wounded hearts!

"And centuries came and ran their course,
And unspent all that time
Still, still went forth that Child's dear force,
And still was at its prime.

"Ay, ages long endured his span
Of life—'tis true received—
That gracious Child, that thorn-crown'd Man!
—He lived while we believed.

"While we believed, on earth we went,
And open stood his grave.
Men call'd from chamber, church, and tent;
And Christ was by to save.

"Now he is dead! Far hence he lies
In the lorn Syrian town;
And on his grave, with shining eyes,
The Syrian stars look down.

"In vain men still, with hoping new,
Regard his death-place dumb,
And say the stone is not yet to,
And wait for words to come.

150

160

170

180

"Ah, o'er that silent sacred land,
Of sun, and arid stone,
And crumbling wall, and sultry sand,
Sounds now one word alone!

"*Unduped of fancy, henceforth man*
Must labour!—must resign
His all too human creeds, and scan
Simply the way divine!

"But slow that tide of common thought,
Which bathed our life, retired;   190
Slow, slow the old world wore to naught,
And pulse by pulse expired.

"Its frame yet stood without a breach
When blood and warmth were fled;
And still it spake its wonted speech—
But every word was dead.

"And oh, we cried, that on this corse
Might fall a freshening storm!
Rive its dry bones, and with new force
A new-sprung world inform!   200

"—Down came the storm! O'er France it pass'd
In sheets of scathing fire;
All Europe felt that fiery blast,
And shook as it rush'd by her.

"Down came the storm! In ruins fell
The worn-out world we knew.
It pass'd, that elemental swell!
Again appear'd the blue;

"The sun shone in the new-wash'd sky,
And what from heaven saw he?   210
Blocks of the past, like icebergs high,
Float on a rolling sea!

"Upon them plies the race of man
All it before endeavour'd;
'Ye live,' I cried, 'ye work and plan,
And know not ye are sever'd!

" 'Poor fragments of a broken world
Whereon men pitch their tent!
Why were ye too to death not hurl'd
When your world's day was spent?   220

" 'That glow of central fire is done
Which with its fusing flame

Knit all your parts, and kept you one—
But ye, ye are the same!

" 'The past, its mask of union on,
Had ceased to live and thrive.
The past, its mask of union gone,
Say, is it more alive?

" 'Your creeds are dead, your rites are dead,
Your social order too!
Where tarries he, the Power who said:
See, I make all things new?

" 'The millions suffer still, and grieve,
And what can helpers heal
With old-world cures men half believe
For woes they wholly feel?

" 'And yet men have such need of joy!
But joy whose grounds are true;
And joy that should all hearts employ
As when the past was new.

" 'Ah, not the emotion of that past,
Its common hope, were vain!
Some new such hope must dawn at last,
Or man must toss in pain.

" 'But now the old is out of date,
The new is not yet born,
And who can be *alone* elate,
While the world lies forlorn?'

"Then to the wilderness I fled.—
There among Alpine snows
And pastoral huts I hid my head,
And sought and found repose.

"It was not yet the appointed hour.
Sad, patient, and resign'd,
I watch'd the crocus fade and flower,
I felt the sun and wind.

"The day I lived in was not mine,
Man gets no second day.
In dreams I saw the future shine—
But ah! I could not stay!

"Action I had not, followers, fame;
I pass'd obscure, alone.
The after-world forgets my name,
Nor do I wish it known.

230

240

250

260

"Composed to bear, I lived and died,
And knew my life was vain,
With fate I murmur not, nor chide,
At Sèvres by the Seine

"(If Paris that brief flight allow)
My humble tomb explore!   270
It bears: *Eternity, be thou
My refuge!* and no more.

"But thou, whom fellowship of mood
Did make from haunts of strife
Come to my mountain-solitude,
And learn my frustrate life;

"O thou, who, ere thy flying span
Was past of cheerful youth,
Didst find the solitary man
And love his cheerless truth—   280

"Despair not thou as I despair'd,
Nor be cold gloom thy prison!
Forward the gracious hours have fared,
And see! the sun is risen!

"He breaks the winter of the past;
A green, new earth appears.
Millions, whose life in ice lay fast,
Have thoughts, and smiles, and tears.

"What though there still need effort, strife?
Though much be still unwon?   290
Yet warm it mounts, the hour of life!
Death's frozen hour is done!

"The world's great order dawns in sheen,
After long darkness rude,
Divinelier imaged, clearer seen,
With happier zeal pursued.

"With hope extinct and brow composed
I mark'd the present die;
Its term of life was nearly closed,
Yet it had more than I.   300

"But thou, though to the world's new hour
Thou come with aspect marr'd,
Shorn of the joy, the bloom, the power
Which best befits its bard—

"Though more than half thy years be past,
And spent thy youthful prime;

Though, round thy firmer manhood cast,
Hang weeds of our sad time

"Whereof thy youth felt all the spell,
And traversed all the shade— 310
Though late, though dimm'd, though weak, yet tell
Hope to a world new-made!

"Help it to fill that deep desire,
The want which rack'd our brain,
Consumed our heart with thirst like fire,
Immedicable pain;

"Which to the wilderness drove out
Our life, to Alpine snow,
And palsied all our word with doubt,
And all our work with woe— 320

"What still of strength is left, employ
That end to help attain:
One common wave of thought and joy
Lifting mankind again!"

—The vision ended. I awoke
As out of sleep, and no
Voice moved;—only the torrent broke
The silence, far below.

Soft darkness on the turf did lie.
Solemn, o'er hut and wood, 330
In the yet star-sown nightly sky,
The peak of Jaman stood.

Still in my soul the voice I heard
Of Obermann!——away
I turned; by some vague impulse stirr'd,
Along the rocks of Naye

Past Sonchaud's piny flanks I gaze
And the blanch'd summit bare
Of Malatrait, to where in haze
The Valais opens fair, 340

And the domed Velan, with his snows,
Behind the upcrowding hills,
Doth all the heavenly opening close
Which the Rhone's murmur fills;—

And glorious there, without a sound,
Across the glimmering lake,
High in the Valais-depth profound,
I saw the morning break.
1867

Notes

TENNYSON

ODE TO MEMORY (p. 5). Although "Written very Early in Life" as the subtitle in 1830 suggested, and clearly the work of an apprentice, this ode is highly significant thematically. Like Wordsworth, the speaker posits "Recollections of Early Childhood" as the major agency of psychological, moral, and imaginative well-being; like Carlyle, he pairs Memory with Hope, and assigns to both mystical qualities by which one can retain his identity in the uncongenial present and face the future ("Tho' deep not fathomless . . .").

RECOLLECTIONS OF THE ARABIAN NIGHTS (p. 8). This poem reads like an illustrative confirmation of the "Ode to Memory." Based on recollections of early childhood, the "dewy dawn of memory," the poem creates, through the fiction of a dream-voyage, an artifact of the poetic imagination. It reaches back toward Coleridge's *Kubla Khan* and forward toward Yeats's *Sailing to Byzantium*. But it is unique, both in this tradition and in the canon of Tennyson's poetry, because no counter-tension is established to its youthful exuberance and unadulterated joy. Yet its intention is complex, reversing time, uniting fragments of experience into quintessence, inserting night within night and dream within dream. It is the poem of Tennyson's in which the "lost paradise" is recovered without psychological anxiety or moral misgiving.

MARIANA (p. 11). Often cited for its pre-Symbolist qualities, *Mariana* shares with *Recollections of the Arabian Nights* several significant characteristics: the experience in each poem is presented without thematic gloss— that is, the experience presented is its own commentary; each is an adaptation of the ballad form, though freely and differently executed; each is a "lyrical" ballad, in which contrasting experiences of zest and fulfilment on the one hand, exhaustion and desolation on the other, are rendered through common devices—situation, details of setting, line measure, and a masterly control of the music of vowels.

THE LADY OF SHALOTT (p. 13). Although he uses an Italian source for this poem (*Donna di Scalotta*), the Lady and Elaine of the *Idylls* ("the lily maid of Astolat") are the same person, and in the two poems they represent variations on a single theme. Critics agree that (1) the poem is an extraordinary example of verbal music and (2) the narrative is either symbolic or parabolic or allegorical, depending on the individual critic's persuasion of the symbols' consistency and complexity. Relevant to an allegorical reading are the unexplained curse under which she labors, the "ivory" tower in which she lives and works, the nature of her labor (weaving a history of her "knowledge of life" into a tapestry), and the conditioned source of that knowledge, as reflected in a mirror. Tennyson himself has given authority to the interpretation that her sudden vision of Lancelot and "the new-born love" she feels for him make her defy the curse and accept death as preferable to a life of shadows. The reader, however, has at least two justifications not to settle for this reading of the Lady's motivation: (1) Tennyson elsewhere insists that with allegorical poetry one cannot say "*this* means *that*"; (2) in l. 105 of the poem, she sees Lancelot in a very special way, "From the bank and from the river"—that is, she sees him from her habitual angle of vision, but also sees him as a reflection of a reflection, which is a way of seeing her own plight in a devastating new perspective.

Two additional points are worth making. If *Mariana* is a pre-Symbolist poem, so is *The Lady of Shalott*: it is its own commentary. Secondly, those critics who shy away from the art-life allegory of the poem because of the "startling statement" thus posited are perhaps doing the poet a disservice by assuming that a theme rendered in the poem is also a personal statement of the poet. It is more in keeping with Tennyson's maturing work to recognize that he was exploring, quite impersonatively, many credible as well as startling alternatives.

ŒNONE (p. 17). The first of a cluster of poems which refurbish classical myths, *Œnone* is also a dramatic confirmation of Tennyson's succession to Milton, Wordsworth, and Keats as a master of blank verse. The central "event" of the poem is, of course, "The Judgment of Paris," and the fact that Tennyson entered the lists of poets and painters who had treated the subject suggests a degree of confidence or, at least, boldness. Critics continue occasionally to chide Tennyson for the "Victorian" rather than the "Greek" sentiments expressed by Here (Juno), queen of heaven; Pallas (Minerva), goddess of wisdom; and Aphrodite (Venus), goddess of love. None of these critics has clearly demarcated Greek from Victorian thought in this context; and the point, even when made, is probably irrelevant anyway. The "modernization of myth" does not demand a hands-off application of historically pure ideas to contemporary dilemmas. Rather, myth is a public, or semi-public, configuration of situation and typical choice through which an artist can add freshness to the known and put the present into perspective. Paris chooses among three precisely defined ways of viewing "the fairest"; and he is "everyman" in the sense that he chooses her who offers him "The fairest and most loving wife in Greece." But his choice also assumes his character as developed in the poem: he chooses not what he might be, but what he is.

The uniqueness of Tennyson's treatment, however, derives from his development of Œnone's sensibility. Her confession/lamentation takes place long after the central event, when the Trojan War is already in progress and her love-hate response to Paris is near fulfillment. She will refuse him succor and die on his funeral pyre. Thus the "fiery thoughts" of Œnone (l. 242), the "fire" that dances before Cassandra (l. 260), the "burning brand" of Hecuba's dream, the fiery "fruit of pure Hesperian gold" (l. 65), and the conflagration of Troy all meet in a passionate image of dissolution.

Several lesser motifs are clear, if unpressed, in the poem: like the speaker in *In Memoriam*, Oenone justifies relating her history so that her "heart may wander from its deepest woe"; like Camelot, Troy "Rose slowly to a music slowly breathed" (l. 40); like Camelot again, Troy was destroyed by a complex of unreasoning passions.

TO ——, WITH THE FOLLOWING POEM (p. 23) and THE PALACE OF ART (p. 24). The dedicatory lines, it is always assumed, are addressed to R. C. Trench, also a member of the Cambridge Apostles, who had said to the poet, "Tennyson, we cannot live in art." Of the "following poem" Tennyson remarked "'The Palace of Art' is the embodiment of my own belief that the God like life is with man and for man."

The progress of the poem from the first phrase ("I built," l. 1) to the last ("my guilt," l. 296) is managed by a curious device: the "I" of the narrator and the "Soul" who inhabits the palace are divided aspects of the same Self. Further, the "I" not only monitors the narrative and glosses it (see esp. ll. 221–224), but is also architect and artist, building the extravagantly ornate palace and selecting the subjects (the legends, the wise men, the chronicle of human bondage, liberation, and change) he portrays there. The "Soul," on the other hand, is entirely sterile in her self-indulgence: she holds no creeds; even her songs are drawn from her as from a statue and are savored as mere echoes. In short, the poem progresses, by a kind of creative exorcism, into "The abysmal deeps of personality" (l. 223) in order to purge the diseased Soul of its Faust-like arrogance. The equivocal ending of the poem is entirely suited not to a firm declaration of the unity of art and life, as some critics wish, but to the enfeebled state of the personality that has just emerged from its identity crisis. The Soul, then, represents a particular phase in the earlier history of the "I's" development. (Cf. *Great Expectations* and *The Way of All Flesh*.)

Two aspects of the poem, one technical, the other thematic, are particularly noteworthy. (1) Like many poets, Tennyson worked much in the "picturesque" tradition, that is, painted verbal pictures. The landscapes of ll. 61 ff. and the portraits of ll. 132 ff. clearly illustrate this. (2) In ll. 233–236, "memory" is cited as the source of the "strong foundation-stones" of the Soul's sense of identity.

Saint Cecily, line 99: patron saint of music. *Houris*, 102: maidens in the Islamic paradise. *Uther's son*, 105–108: Arthur and his earthly paradise. *Ausonian*, 111: legendary Italian king counseled by the nymph Egeria. *Indian Cama*, 115: Hindu god of love. *Europa*, 117: Phoenician princess abducted by Zeus in the form of a white bull. *Ganymede*, 121: Trojan boy carried to Olympus by an eagle (Zeus) to become cupbearer of the gods. *Ionian father*, 137: Homer. *beast of burden, tiger, athlete, sick man*, 149 ff.: sometimes translated, respectively, as slavery, rebellion, democracy, anarchy. *Verulam*, 163: Lord Bacon. *Memnon*, 171: statue in Thebes reputed to sing when struck by the sun's first rays. *anadems*, 186: garlands. *devil*, 203: allusion to the Gadarene swine, possessed and drowned by the devils cast out of a man. *Herod*, 219: Herod was smitten because "he gave not God the glory." *Mene*, 227: the writing on the wall at Belshazzar's feast interpreted by Daniel as "God hath numbered thy kingdom and finished it."

THE HESPERIDES (p. 31). Suppressed from the Tennyson canon and long ignored by critics, this poem has enjoyed, in recent years, a greater resurgence than any other of Tennyson's poems. Borrowing from Milton's *Comus* for the epigraph and following Hesiod's account of the myth, Tennyson produced a sort of fragment of a masque. The narrative frame, provided by the account of Zidonian (that is, Carthaginian) Hanno, places the geography on the West African coast, but it also supplies the poem's motivation: Hanno the navigator is becalmed in strange waters rife with mysterious legends; the daughters of the evening star who guard the golden apple are

anxious "Lest one from the East come and take it away" (1. 42)—Hanno
now, Hercules later. The poem demands association with *The Lotos-Eaters*
(see 1. 7), but it operates on an entirely different principle. Here the choric
song is sung by the Hesperides themselves, in *The Lotos-Eaters* it is sung
by Odysseus's men. Thus in the latter poem a contention between two
value-systems holds the poem together and explicates it. *The Hesperides* is
not at all explicable in the same sense. The incantation of its verse, the
free association by which its sentiments progress, the vagueness of its nu-
merology, the indistinctness of its symbolism, all suggest that, however in-
geniously one may draw the poem into the group of "art" poems Tennyson
wrote at about this time, "an awful mystery" or fabulous riddle is the
poem's ultimate and intentional effect.

THE LOTOS-EATERS (p. 34). Based on an episode in the *Odyssey* (Bk. IX),
with a soupçon of Lucretius added later (see ll. 156–161), this poem renders
a variation on a recurrent theme in Tennyson's poetry—namely, the gods
being so careless, the struggle availing so little, the ultimate outcome being
so uncertain, why not drop out? He chooses a myth that offers the most
compelling case for giving up: after fighting the Trojan War and battling
strange hostile elements for years, Ulysses' men try to return to Ithaca, half-
convinced that, even if they arrive, all will be cold, broken, and overthrown.
    The poem is introduced with five lush Spenserian stanzas, in which
Odysseus's call for "Courage!" is contrasted with the appearance of the
"mild-eyed melancholy Lotos-eaters," symbols of a narcotic death-in-life.
This contrast supplies one implicit corrective to the lotos-temptation. The
"Choric Song" itself, with its varied but carefully measured prosody, ultimately climaxes in a revival of vigor and an oblique indication that the
mariners, despite all their arguments to the contrary, recognize a predominant
responsibility. Ll. 150 ff. (stanza VIII) confirm the former; the too urgent
insistence of "Surely, surely" (1. 171) confirms the latter. They *will* "wander
more."

ULYSSES (p. 38). This poem has persistently received critical kudos even from
readers generally unsympathetic to Tennyson. *Ulysses* rose out of the same
seed-time as *In Memoriam* (Autumn, 1833), and Tennyson said that it expressed perhaps more simply than anything in *In Memoriam* his feelings
about the need for going forward, for braving the struggle of life. But here
again one should guard against taking a truth for the whole truth.
    Tennyson's most immediate source for the poem was Dante's *Inferno*,
Canto XXVI, in which the fabulous voyager is condemned as an Evil
Counselor, or spiritual thief. Some of Tennyson's warmest admirers, while
recognizing the source, have ignored its relevance and have read the poem
as an exaltation of "the eternally restless aspiration." It seems more likely
that the poem rests on a double recognition, of the genuinely heroic spirit
and of the overreacher doomed to a tragic catastrophe. Note the peevish,
impatient, ego-oriented tone of the opening lines; compare the poem with
its companion piece, *Tithonus* (p. 40); and contrast its sentiments with
those expressed by Arthur at the end of *The Holy Grail* (p. 188).

TITHONUS (p. 40). See the note to *Ulysses*. Tithonus, a mortal, was the
beloved of Eos (or Aurora), goddess of the Dawn. She interceded with Zeus
to get Tithonus immortality, but she failed to gain for him eternal youth
also. Thus his ever-ageing life became an intolerable burden to him, and

he prayed for death. The gods cannot cancel their gifts, although they can add to them. He was ultimately changed into a grasshopper. (Cf. Swift's Struldbrugs in *Gulliver's Travels*.)

"BREAK, BREAK, BREAK" (p. 42). This poem belongs to the poems stimulated by the sudden death of Arthur Hallam. Although "made in a Lincolnshire lane at five o'clock in the morning between blossoming hedges," it seems to take its setting from the seashore and thus to become an imaginary seascape.

THE EPIC (p. 42) and MORTE D'ARTHUR (p. 43). *Morte d'Arthur*, with its curiously domestic and somewhat banteringly defensive frame, is Tennyson's earliest and most lasting extended treatment of Arthurian materials. It became ll. 170–440 of *The Passing of Arthur* (1869). Moreover, it constituted for him an "older," consciously epic style which, even in the late 1860's, served as a compelling model. (See the note to *Idylls of the King*.)

The frame itself ("The Epic") is teasing for several reasons: (1) the poet of the piece, Hall, is carefully distinguished from its "I," so that while the former can give "a mint of reasons" against old subject matter and classical style, the latter can be totally caught up in this mythic world where "dreams / Begin to feel the truth and stir of day, . . ."; (2) the portrait of the parson, Holmes, though lightly sketched, is highly significant, for the imaginative re-creation of the noble King gives a real significance to the Christ-myth untouched by the "harping," "hawking," "grunting" parson; (3) the "modern touches" of lines 329–330 are, in context and at one level, positively sarcastic, because not only had Tennyson been personally abused by the critics for a lack of modern relevance in his two previous volumes, but from the early 1830's to the late 1860's there was immense critical pressure on all poets to address their talents explicitly to contemporary ("modern") problems.

Tennyson began *Morte d'Arthur* in the months immediately following Arthur Hallam's death, and it therefore has relevance both to *Ulysses* and to *In Memoriam*.

church-commissioners, line 15: Ecclesiastical Commission established in 1835–1836, which included among its duties administering the revenues of the Church of England; *geology and schism*, 16: Charles Lyell's *Principles of Geology* (1831–1833) unsettled the religious beliefs of many early Victorians, including Tennyson.

LOCKSLEY HALL (p. 50). This is a pivotal poem in the Tennyson canon since it makes a number of demands upon the reader which may be considered characteristic: the speaker, the setting, and the fiction are entirely imaginary; the verse is normative, which means it is successful to the degree that it is a dimension of character revelation; however many details typical of the early Victorian period one may find in the poem, its ultimate validity depends upon the reader's estimate of the representative psychological truth it embodies.

In the first place, the speaker is a young man of twenty with a "good side," "deficiencies," and "yearnings" (the words are Tennyson's). He is an incorrigible idealist, an orphan, a complete secularist (his only deity is "Mother-Age"), an activist, and he has recently discovered that the one relative he loved intensely and spiritually is fickle. One "early morn" he separates himself from his hunting companions and tries to put himself together again.

His efforts to establish a viable identity are deeply affected by his acute self-awareness ("bluster," "mad," "angry," "passionate," "wild") and his out-ranging fancy. In a manner strongly suggestive of one of the basic psychological perceptions which George Eliot emphasized twenty years later (e.g., in *Silas Marner*), the speaker rediscovers his identity and cures a temporarily diseased imagination by building his future on memories of "a youth sublime" (l. 11). Thus three comparable passages represent his progress from health to health through periods interspersed with generalized rage and sick fantasy: (1) 7–16; (2) 109–130; (3) 181–188. It is significant that the middle passage is induced by an act of will (l. 107) and that the understandable yearning for escape to a primitive paradise (ll. 157–171) is immediately recognized as a foolish dream.

The "poet" (l. 75) is Dante.

songs from THE PRINCESS (p. 56). Throughout his long career as a poet, Tennyson relished his unparalleled gift as a lyric songwriter, surpassing— by a combination of number and quality—his great Elizabethan and Jacobean predecessors. "Sweet and Low," for example, is a familiar lullaby throughout the English-speaking world. Two of the more famous among critics are "Tears, Idle Tears" and "Come Down, O Maid," both notably in blank verse. Of the former, Tennyson said: "The passion of the past, the abiding in the transient, was expressed in *Tears, Idle Tears*, which was written in the yellowing autumntide at Tintern Abbey, full for me of its by-gone memories." It is a superbly clear, modest, haunting, and penetrating creation of the mystery of life and death, having compelling associations with Wordsworthian memory and Keats's "unheard" melodies.

IN MEMORIAM (p. 59). A comparison of *In Memoriam* with other elegies in English (e.g., Milton's *Lycidas*, Shelley's *Adonais*, Arnold's *Thyrsis*) goes a long way to define Tennyson's distinctive stature as a poet: thoroughly idiosyncratic (he "invented" the quatrain for *In Memoriam*); deeply immersed in the elegiac tradition; determined to carry his difficult subject to its genuine center—which rendered his elegy broader in its implications and deeper in its perceptions than any of its predecessors; thoroughly committed to the public responsibility of making his work representative of and accessible to the broadly literate man.

Tennyson's own statements about the poem are useful. (1) It is "a kind of *Divina Commedia*, ending in happiness." (2) In it, the poet tried to portray "different moods of sorrow as in a drama." (3) The poem expresses the poet's conviction that "anxieties of heart" rising out of fear, doubt, and suffering will find relief "only through Faith in a God of Love." (4) The poem is divided according to the Christmas sections: XXVII, LXXVIII, CIV. (5) The poem falls into "nine natural groupings" marking the stages of his grief and his thought: (a) I–VIII, (b) IX–XIX, (c) XX–XXVII, (d) XXVIII–XLIX, (e) L–LVIII, (f) LIX–LXXI, (g) LXXII–XCVIII, (h) XCIX–CIII, (i) CIV–CXXXI. (6) "*In Memoriam* is a poem, *not* an actual biography. . . . 'I' is not always the author speaking of himself, but the voice of the human race speaking through him."

This last point is perhaps the most important caution the poet has given us. Admittedly the word *always* is a bit confusing. It is likely that Tennyson inserted the word for two reasons: (1) however generalized the "I" may be, it is still the product of the heart and brain of Alfred Tennyson; (2) he did not want to weaken his dedication to the memory of Arthur Henry Hallam, although it is clear, within the poem, that the dead man undergoes a transformation very much in the direction of Arthur the King (CXI, p. 120). But Tennyson still intends the poem to be read as a formal modern elegy with the elegist inside, *not outside*, the poem. Some readers have been distracted from this intention by the number of biographical or autobiographical points of reference in the poem: e.g., "Dark house," l. 165; "Fair ship," l. 201; "The Danube to the Severn gave," Section XIX; "those five years," l. 916; "thro' summer France," l. 1324; "cypress of her orange flower," l. 1559; "reverend walls," l. 1729; "On that last night before we went," Section CIII. Further, there are sections addressed to his brother Charles and to his friend Edmund Lushington, whose marriage to Tennyson's sister Cecilia is celebrated in the epithalamium, especially ll. 2777–2824. But it should be noted that the speaker, despite the many classical and scientific allusions and despite the unobtrusive introduction of the conventions of the pastoral elegy, never loses his identity as a modern man passing through "the night of fear" in which "faith and form" are sundered (CXXVII), facing and laying "the spectres of the mind" (XCVI).

In Memoriam is the most Wordsworthian of Tennyson's poems in language, in simplicity of stanza form, in theme, in assimilation of scientific knowledge or theory, and most of all in its recognition of the function of memory in human psychology. This last point is signaled by the allusion to Goethe in the first quatrain of the first section:

> I held it truth, with him who sings
> To one clear harp in divers tones,
> That men may rise on stepping-stones
> Of their dead selves to higher things.

It is this belief which has received an elemental shock, as stanza two shows:

> But who shall so forecast the years
> And find in loss a gain to match?
> Or reach a hand thro' time to catch
> The far-off interest of tears?

Thus the spiritual quest pursued in the poem is given a primary rooting in personality: not the mind alone, but the total sense of self has been all but shattered; the past has ceased to be a trustworthy emblem of the future, and until this belief can be reconfirmed, the poet-speaker must endure a necessarily prolonged period dominated at intervals by "fears, and fancies, . . . Dim sadness—and blind thoughts. . . ." (Wordsworth, *Resolution and Independence*). It should be noted, too, that like Wordsworth the speaker in *In Memoriam* posits several principles essential to the poem's credibility: (1) although he says that death has

> stunn'd me from my power to think
> And all my knowledge of myself. (XVI)

even at the nadir of his grief he still faintly trusts; (2) the past with which his memory feeds him back to health is joyful and open-ended; (3) it is fruitless to try to resolve his dilemma by crushing sorrow

> like a vice of blood,
> Upon the threshold of the mind? (III)

because the mind is only one element—and a secondary element—in his total personality and his total grief; (4) the "will" to live, to emerge triumphant from the Slough of Despond, "not [to] be the fool of loss" (IV), is a fundamental dimension of the speaker from the beginning.

Variations on the word *memory* and illustrations of its function (including the fantasies and dreams which it engenders) constitute the dominant motivational assumption of the poet-speaker. One illustration will perhaps suffice. There are two climaxes, one mystical (XCV), the other consciously allegorical (CIII), which move the poem to its full and final affirmation. The first of these (XCV) is carefully prepared for (LXXXVII–XCIV)—although no less mystical for all that—by a sequence of "emblematic narratives" in the manner of Wordsworth's *Prelude*. Within these a combination of memory, affirmation, and yearning induces the mystical experience. (In at least two passages—XLIV–XLV, and the epilogue—thoughts about pre-existence and post-existence closely analogous to those expressed, in Wordsworth's *Intimations* are tentatively explored.)

Although the poet-speaker welcomes to his consciousness "random influences" "From art, from nature, from the schools," he denies any formal philosophical intent (XLVIII); it is an important aspect of the poem's distinctiveness that it neither rejects nor adopts a formal religion, though it does "glance" against aspects or various "schools"—e.g., atheism, materialism, scientism, transcendentalism. The theme of spiritual and psychological recovery emerges at the experiential rather than the argumentative level. But the "I" of the poem, not Tennyson, is equally not any ordinary man. He is a poet; and poetry is integral to a search for the kind of truth *In Memoriam* achieves or aspires to.

In single lines and whole sections, sometimes explicitly, sometimes allegorically, the reader is persistently reminded of the speaker's identity as a poet and is given perspectives on the poem: the poet's motivation, the relationship between his emotional moods and his poetic practice, the functions and limitations of his verse-writing, his austerely circumscribed intentions. (See especially Sections V, VIII, XIX, XXI, XXIII, XXXVI, XXXVII, XXXVIII, XLVIII–XLIX, LII, LXV, LXXV, LXXVI–LXXVII, and LXXXV.) The climax of progression, on both the personal and the symbolic levels, is reached in CIII, a dream-vision which leaves his "after-morn content." The allegory has been variously interpreted, but the following seems fair. The poet-speaker has been isolated in his grief, with only the muses to sustain him. At the centre is a statue of Hallam behind a veil, though the poet is secure in his knowledge and love of the object hidden. The poet himself is summoned by death and, in company with the muses travels from life to life, passing beyond the veil of death, undergoing a lordly magnification and being at last re-united with the man who died. The muses, too, are admitted so that, according to Tennyson, "everything that made Life beautiful here, we may hope may pass on with us beyond the grave." The allegory seems to suggest, also, that without the muses—without the "strong imagination," "Fancy," "symbols," "memory," "dreams"—the recovery of spirit could not have been achieved, nor the fundamental perception of "the Reality of the Unseen," common to both *In Memoriam* and *The Holy Grail*, arrived at. Thus poetic imagination becomes a mode of spiritual insight and the modern poet a modern seer. This, in turn, suggests that Tennyson had as a fundamental concern throughout *In Memoriam*

Goethe's position on the relationship of poetry and truth (*Dichtung und Wahrheit*).

him, line 45: Goethe; *Dark house*, 165: 67 Wimpole Street, London residence of Arthur Hallam; *Fair ship*, 201: the funeral ship, bearing Hallam's body to England; *hushes half the babbling Wye*, 407: the part that is tidal, when the tide is full; *Pan*, 496: god of all nature; *Argive*, 506: Greek; *Arcady*, 508: poetical for Arcadia, idyllic region of Greece; *Lazarus*, 637: dead man raised to life by Christ according to St. John (*that Evangelist*, 652); *Olivet*, 648: the Mount of Olives in the life of Christ; *bathes the Saviour's feet*, 663: by Mary, sister of Lazarus; *Aeonian*, 711: timeless; *the Word*, 733: St. John, "In the beginning was the Word"; *Urania*, 741: Muse of Astronomy or heavenly poetry; *Melpomene*, 749: Muse of elegy or earthly poetry; *Lethean*, 882: of Lethe, river of forgetfulness; *the sinless years*, 1011: the life of Christ; *broad water of the west*, 1255: the Severn River; *thro' summer France*, 1324: reference to travels by Tennyson and Hallam in 1830; *mimic picture*, 1455: charades; *thee*, 1466: Tennyson's brother Charles; *cypress of her orange flower*, 1559: Emily Tennyson's symbol of marriage was changed to a symbol of mourning by the death of her fiancé; LXXXV: addressed to Edmund Lushington, engaged to marry Tennyson's sister Cecilia; *reverend walls*, 1729: Trinity College, Cambridge; *over . . . Angelo*, 1767–8: Hallam once said, "Alfred, look over my eyes; surely I have the bar of Michael Angelo"; *this flat lawn*, 1782: at Somersby, where Hallam visited the Tennyson family; *purlieus of the law*, 1792: after Cambridge, Hallam studied law at the Inner Temple; *Tuscan poets*, 1804: Dante and Petrarch; *star*, 1827: Venus, in the context of the nebular hypothesis by which the sun is the nebulous source of all the planets; *sea-blue bird*, 1860: the kingfisher; *You*, 2045: Charles Tennyson, planning a wedding trip to Vienna; *the Lesser Wain*, 2127: the Little Dipper; *maidens*, 2170: "the muses, arts"; *Anakim*, 2195: giant sons of Onak; *Her pillars*, 2440: pillars of Hercules; *Pallas*, 2448: goddess of wisdom (Roman Minerva); *Hesper-Phosphor*, 2565, 2573, 2581–2: Evening-morning stars, used by analogy with Omega-Alpha; *fool-fury . . . dead*, 2675–6: one of the several blood-lettings in revolutionary France.

THE EAGLE (p. 133). This has always been one of Tennyson's most admired short poems. *falls*, l. 6: dives for his prey.

THE CHARGE OF THE LIGHT BRIGADE (p. 134). This "occasional piece"—the "occasion" being the battle of Balaklava in the ambiguous Crimean War—was generated by the pervasive war fever at home and a phrase in *The Times*, "someone had blundered" (l. 12). Obviously calculated to catch the popular ear, the poem celebrates the nobility of both the living and the dead in the vigorous performance of duty despite the overwhelming odds against them and their awareness that the order was a blunder. The Russian forces held the valley, with cavalry and infantry and gun implacements, on both sides and at one end; of the 670 men in the "Light Brigade," fewer than thirty per cent survived the charge.

MAUD (p. 135). Tennyson's first major poetic effort after the publication of *In Memoriam* was devoted to *Maud*, "a little Hamlet, history of a morbid poetic soul, under the blighting influence of a recklessly speculative age." Perhaps prompted by widespread critical dissent from the poem, Tennyson goes on to tell us more about his speaker in the poem than about any other of his creations: "He is the heir of madness, an egoist with the makings of a cynic, raised to sanity by a pure and holy' love which elevates his whole nature, passing from the height of triumph to the lowest depth of misery, driven into madness by the loss of her whom he has loved, and, when he has at length passed through the fiery furnace, and has recovered his reason, giving himself up to work for the good of mankind through the unselfishness born of his great passion." About the form, as distinct from the speaker, Tennyson comments: "The peculiarity of this poem is that different phases of passion in one person take the place of different characters." The seed-lyric for the poem ("O that 'twere possible," Part II, section IV) was composed during the years when Tennyson was still very actively at work on *In Memoriam*.

Those who give their efforts, however far-fetched, to find a self-portrait in each of Tennyson's speakers have not ignored *Maud*, even though the fiction of the drama, including the personality of the protagonist, has a precise and clear definition entirely independent of the author, and even though Tennyson was manifestly attempting one of the boldest literary experiments since the Elizabethans. He recognized, as Arnold recognized in the Preface to *Poems* (1853), that "the dialogue of the mind with itself has commenced; modern problems have presented themselves; we hear already the doubts, we witness the discouragement, of Hamlet and of Faust." Although Tennyson called the poem "a little *Hamlet*," the speaker's kinship with Faust is also unmistakable. Tennyson, like Browning, recognized that a psychological anatomization of the recesses of personality was one of the chief obligations of the new literature and that, by the authority of Shakespeare himself, this could be most economically and credibly accomplished by the soliloquy or monologue, a device in which motivation and inhibition could be controlled entirely from within the personality of the speaker. He perceived, further, that his choice of protagonist ("a morbid poetic soul") provided, within the frame of character conception, a full range of poetic variety. Finally, the poem seems to be a fully developed example of what a major poet, in response to critical pressure and his own felt need, might do to give mature poetic attention to contemporary problems, without easy, sentimental moralism and without jingoistic pandering to popular emotions.

Maud; A Monodrama appears to be a far more ambitious, complex, and poetically subtle development of the same conception which underlies *Locksley Hall*. This speaker is some five years older than the other. His prevailing memory is not of "a youth sublime," but of "a horror of shatter'd limbs and a wretched swindler's lie" (l. 56). His love for Maud, unlike the other speaker's love for Amy, is not the central shattering experience from which he must recover; in fact, it becomes the "one thing bright" (Part III, l. 17) to which, through dream, his memory can lighten his despair. Its development and climax in Part I, ll. 162–923, makes credible his return, in Part III, from his mythological journey to the Underworld in Part II, ll. 239–342. Finally, the speaker in *Maud* is more explicitly poetic; and the effort to accommodate a wide variety of verse forms to a wide variety of moods is a bold central concern of the author.

Tennyson has been persistently criticized, as some students read the poem, for his advocacy of war in general and of the Crimean War in particular. This again insists upon an unjustifiable identification between author and *persona*. The speaker is, after all, a man of the 1850's and the poem is clearly concerned with contemporary relevance. It was quite possible for even an alienated man of the 1850's to see the British forces in the Baltic as pursuing a just and God-appointed course.

In a significant sense, the issue is incidental. *Maud* is not a poem about war, but a poem about the search of a morbidly self-conscious man for an alternative to burying himself in himself, the dominant ethical/psychological problem of the century. He rejects the civil war of commerce, the "well-practised" eye but "bounded" spirit of science, the "folly and vice" of the "passionate poet." His defensive retreat into the "passionless peace" of philosophical stoicism is annuled by his "pure and holy" love affair with Maud, which, despite its tragic outcome, magnifies his spirit enough to make ultimate retreat into the dungeon of himself impossible. His final resolution, normed down to his clearly fallible personality, is essentially Arthurian: to "embrace the purpose of God, and the doom assign'd" by joining a crusade of modern knights righting human wrong.

Part I: *centre-bits*, line 41: the brace and bit used by thieves; *Mammonite*, 45: worshiper of Mammon, god of wealth—probably an allusion to Carlyle's *Past and Present*; *Timour*, 46: Tamurlane, Mongol conqueror of the 14th century; *Isis*, 144: Egyptian goddess of fertility; *Poland . . . Hungary*, 147: Poland fell to Russia under Nicholas I, and Hungary led an unsuccessful revolt against Austrian rule in 1849; *Assyrian bull*, 233: gross, with curled hair; *cap and bells*, 251: traditional accoutrements of court fools; *broad-brimm'd hawker*, 370: a Quaker, or pacifist; *King Charley*, 441: a spaniel; *Gorgonised*, 464: turned into stone; *truest breath*, 651: according to Tennyson, "This is the central idea, the holy power of Love."

Part II: *section II*: according to Tennyson, "The shell undestroyed amid the storm perhaps symbolizes to him his own first and highest nature preserved amid the storms of passion"; *Lamech*, line 96: in Genesis 4:23 Lamech "said unto his wives . . . , 'hearken unto my speech: for I have slain a man to my wounding, and a young man to my hurt'"; *prophecy*, 280: in Luke 12:2–3, "there is nothing covered, that shall not be revealed; . . . that which ye have spoken in the ear in closets shall be proclaimed upon the housetops."

Part III: *Charioteer*, line 6, *Gemini*, 7, *Orion*, 8, *the Lion*, 14: constellations as they are positioned in late Spring, with Leo (the Lion) symbol of Britain.

LUCRETIUS (p. 170). It was quite common for the Victorian poets to select a crucial moment in the life of a real or imaginary (but in either case representative) pagan spokesman and to explore dramatically the value-system he embodied. *Lucretius* is such a poem, as are Browning's *Cleon*, Arnold's *Empedocles on Etna*, and Swinburne's *Hymn to Proserpine*. Lucretius was a Roman poet, philosopher, and scientist (c. 96–55 B.C.). The long poem in hexameters (l. 11), which fused all three of his distinguished talents, is *De Rerum Natura* ("Of the Nature of Things"), one of the final great philosophical statements of the pagan world. Lucretius posited an atomistic theory of the universe that included man, and, like his master Epicurus (l. 13), proffered as a model for man "the sober majesties / Of settled, sweet, Epicurean life" described in lines 217–218. The tradition that Lucretius killed himself because a love-potion administered by his "petulant" wife had destroyed his "Tranquillity" and made his life an intolerable nightmare is the frame of this turbulent monologue.

Critics credit Tennyson with a fair distillation of Lucretian thought in the monologue. Hence we may assume that any thematic gloss suggested by the poem probably resides in a combination of this thought and its situational context. For example: (1) Lucilia, though not above blame for her jealousy and deviousness, is in fact a dutiful wife unable to understand or support the austere withdrawal from both pleasure and pain to which her husband aspires, under the dual influence of Epicurus and his own ambition to write an "immortal" poem; (2) Lucretius's final remark (ll. 279–280)—clearly meant to suggest an analogy with Pilate's "What is truth?"—shows him cynically unresponsive to human needs and to values undreamed of in his philosophy; (3) Lucretius kills himself out of loathing for the "brute brain," an animalism revitalized by the potion and one aspect of the complex pluralism of man he ignored in his philosophy and in his later life with Lucilia (cf. *Dr. Jekyll and Mr. Hyde*); (4) his state is induced by three dreams (ll. 36–43, 47–59, 60–66) which occur in quick succession on the threshold of awakening, suggesting that, in the "abysmal deeps of [his unconscious] personality," there is a revolt raging against his superimposed, systematic rationality and his orderly materialism; (5) at one point (ll. 205–207) Lucretius's conscious mind is divided between the desire to enjoy and the desire to destroy; (6) although throughout the poem Lucretius is presented as both philosopher-scientist and poet, it seems clear that poetry becomes his primary consideration (ll. 92–104, 222–225, 258–264), and thus it may not be fanciful to wonder if, in the over-all parabolic suggestiveness of the poem, the poet does not undermine the philosopher-scientist in Lucretius.

Teacher, line 13: Epicurus, Greek philosopher (342–270 B.C.); *Sylla*, 47: Sulla, cruel and dissolute Roman dictator (138–78 B.C.); *Cadmean teeth*, 50: Cadmus, founder of Thebes, sowed dragon teeth, from which warriors sprang up, as contrasted with the sexy dancing girls (*Hetairai*, 52) of Lucretius's dream; *Dictator's*, 54: Sulla's; *Helen*, 61: Helen of Troy; *procemion*, 70: invocation to Venus with which *De Rerum Natura* begins; *Mavors*, 82: Mars; 85–92: the Venus addressed was not the popular mythological goddess of Love in the fables of Anchises, Adonis, or Paris, but (96–98) the Venus Genetrix, universal mother of "Great Nature" (245); *Sicilian*, 93: Empedocles; *Calliope*, 94: muse of epic poetry; *Kypris*, 95: Cyprus, sacred to Venus; *his*, 118: Epicurus's; *Memmius*, 119: son-in-law of Sulla to whom *De Rerum Natura* is dedicated; *where he says*, 147: Phaedo; *Picus and Faunus*, 182: rural deities whom Egeria instructed the Roman Numa to snare and to learn from them the laws of nature; *her*, 235: Lucretia, raped by the son of King Tarquin, killed herself, thus precipitating a rebellion and the establishment of the Commonwealth; *Ixionian wheel*, 260: symbol of eternal punishment (or hell), the existence of which Lucretius denied.

from IDYLLS OF THE KING (p. 177). No major poem of Tennyson's has been received with more critical mystification than *Idylls of the King*. It ranges from Carlyle ("the inward perfection of vacancy") through Meredith ("fluting of creatures that have not a breath of humanity in them") to Jerome H. Buckley: "Yet the *Idylls* taken singly repay close analysis, and as a sequence they represent the most sustained effort of any Victorian poet to deal with the moral problems of a society in crisis." Thus right up to our time, even thoroughly appreciative Tennysonians hedge on the *Idylls*.

It is not surprising that Tennyson's contemporaries had difficulty gaining a critical-interpretive overview of the poem. It was worked on, in a fragmentary way, from 1830 ("Sir Launcelot and Queen Guinevere") until 1885 ("Balin and Balan") and was not given its final arrangement until 1888:

Dedication (to Prince Albert)	1862
The Coming of Arthur	1869
Gareth and Lynette	1872
The Marriage of Geraint	1859
Geraint and Enid	1859
Balin and Balan	1885
Merlin and Vivien	1859
Lancelot and Elaine	1859
The Holy Grail	1869
Pelleas and Ettarre	1869
The Last Tournament	1871
Guinevere	1859
The Passing of Arthur	1869
To the Queen (Victoria)	1872

Thus, though the *Idylls* derive from the predominant creative effort of Tennyson's whole life, none of his contemporaries ever had a chance to read it through "at one sitting" as they could, to its advantage, *Paradise Lost*. It must be recognized, too, that when Tennyson's first installment of *Idylls* appeared in 1859 it followed upon two major poems (*In Memoriam* and *Maud*) of the profoundest and most explicit contemporary relevance. Even the careful reader of that volume in 1859 had an excuse for missing the central spiritual theme which would emerge in the volume of 1869 and be reenforced by *The Last Tournament* (1871) and *To the Queen* (1872).

That the *Idylls*, lacking a corpus of firm critical assent, should have lapsed into the category of schoolboy literature for about a half century was perhaps the likeliest result of a concurrence of forces: the nature of the poem itself—muted allegory, epic-non-epic form, apparent predominance of romantic narrative for its own sake (which all who ran could read); the "new" poetry struggling toward an idiom quite different from the "sweet and lovely language" of the Spenser-Tennyson tradition; the cultural rebellion which sought to dump all things "Victorian"; and the emergence of schools of literary criticism which looked elsewhere for examples to illustrate their sense of the excellent in poetry. Although the Tennyson revival began modestly in the 1920's and is now in full flood, it is only within the last decade that the perception of the *Idylls* as a lightly veiled but profound examination of the cyclic, universal human condition has begun to be accepted.

THE COMING OF ARTHUR (p. 177). When he published his second set of idylls in 1869, Tennyson had arrived at the central spiritual perception of the poem and wished to establish the over-all structure which the *Idylls*, when completed, would have. Thus *The Coming of Arthur*, *The Holy Grail*, and *The Passing of Arthur* (see *Morte d'Arthur*, p. 43) correspond to the Aristotelian requirements of beginning, middle, and end. The central issue in the first idyll is Arthur's authenticity or credibility, and in the tradition of medieval debate-literature, Leodogran sifts the evidence and tries to resolve an inward dilemma. Significantly it is impossible to establish Arthur's right on scientific or rational bases. So Leodogran arrives at his confirmation of Arthur through a dream-vision, at a level of personality deeper than levels accessible by knowledge and reason. Essentially he makes an act of faith in the compelling reality of the unknowable. Merlin's riddles, so exasperating to Bellicent in her eager search for "truth," "half reveal / And half conceal the Soul within," like "nature" in *In Memoriam*. Clearly, too, the knights like Lancelot (ll. 127–129), who "know" Arthur for their King, do so because of the mysterious magnification they see in him—"the fire of God" (l. 127), "a secret . . ." (ll. 488, 500). The primary questions raised by the *Idylls*, therefore, concern ways of knowing and the relation of personality to "knowledge," or, put another way, they suggest the interaction of a dual quest, for identity and for authority.

Cuckoo, line 166: cuckoos lay their eggs in the nests of other birds; *three fair queens*, 275: Faith, Hope, and Charity, or, more generally, "three of the noblest of women"; *Lady of the Lake*, 282: the Christian Religion or Church; *hind*, 431: farmer, plowman.

THE HOLY GRAIL (p. 188). Tennyson considered this idyll one of the most imaginative of his pieces and described its theme as follows: "I have expressed there my strong feeling of the Reality of the Unseen. The end, when the king speaks of his work and of his visions, is intended to be the summing up of all in the highest note by the highest of human men. These three lines in Arthur's speech are the (spiritually) central lines in the *Idylls*:

> In moments when he feels he cannot die,
> And knows himself no vision to himself,
> Nor the High God a vision."

The allegory is many faceted, and the network of symbols is not easy to read exhaustively (for example, ll. 489–539, Galahad's crossing of the river of death and his entry into the spiritual city). The major motifs, however, seem to be these. (1) There are two distinct ways of seeking holiness, which is complete immersion in and devotion to the Reality of the Unseen: (a) withdrawal from the world and singular spiritual discipline in the eradication of self-regard—the way, in differing degrees, of the "holy nun," Galahad, and Percivale; (b) a dedication "With strength and will to right the wrong'd, or power / To lay the sudden heads of violence flat," (ll. 309–310)—the way of Arthur and, heretofore, of the Round Table. (2) The ascetic way is yielded full legitimacy, though only for the "happy few." For the vast majority it is one of the subtlest and most dangerous temptations, likely to end in futility and, ironically, to destroy the fellowship of social responsibility and service which was sacrificed for it. Thus (3) the good is in mysterious conflict with the good.

Five of the knights are particularized in their quest. Percivale, who has promulgated the Grail story as related by his sister and who first swears the vow, pursues the most elaborate *rite de passage*. Setting out in a state of acute and acutely deceptive self-consciousness, he vacillates between extremes of buoyancy and depression, of expectation and guilt. On the one hand, he creates phantoms or mirages of bodily comfort and satisfaction (ll. 379–390), of comforting human fellowship and domesticity (ll. 391–400), of magnificence (ll. 401–420), and of worldly acclaim (ll. 421–439). On the other hand, so great is his spiritual dryness that his phantoms fall into dust "in a land of sand and thorns." Percivale's self-delusions progress in an ascending order and presumably the last is self-corrective or cathartic for he seeks out a "holy hermit" in a "lowly vale" and is instructed in "true humility"—lose oneself in order to save oneself. Thus instructed, he is succored by Galahad and sees the Holy Grail at a great distance. Galahad represents unadulterated and inexplicable holiness; once taught to see the Grail, he never loses sight of it. On the strength of it, he wages for a time a crusade against "evil customs everywhere." But his service is short-termed and he goes to be crowned "king / Far in the spiritual city" (ll. 482–483).

Sir Bors is perhaps the most Arthurian and at the same time the most barometrically human of the Grail knights. He pursues the quest without self-regard. Even his sight of the "Holy Cup of healing" he would gladly give, if he could, to his tortured cousin Lancelot. With "grief and love" he knows that dissolution is at hand. Lancelot is handled here, as elsewhere in the *Idylls*, with great delicacy: in him we have "Sense at war with Soul" fully focused and unresolved.

We doubt neither Lancelot's nobility nor his adultery, and the mad heat with which he pursues his quest is spent, not on losing himself, but on trying to free himself from an agonizing duality. He fails, of course, but in view of Arthur's commentary (ll. 877–883), and of the fact that Lancelot sees the "veil'd" Grail the reader is persuaded that, on humbler terms, Lancelot will finally achieve purification. Gawain, the sensualist, not only abandons before anyone else the quest for which he had sworn the loudest vow, but also attempts to discredit the ascetic way to holiness.

Arthur sums up the Appearance-Reality theme (*seems* vs. *is*) at the end.

The narrative method of this idyll deserves a word of comment. After a brief introduction, the idyll proceeds in the form of a colloquy between two monks who, despite their vastly different personalities and life-experiences, love each other well, a love which is all the more secure because each speaker has a firm and hard-won knowledge of himself. Ambrosius, the "old badger in his earth," is a humble, parochial man who understands that he has given up "the warmth of double life" because he is "plagued with dreams of something sweet / Beyond all sweetness in a life so rich." Although sympathetic, he is inclined at first to view the Grail as a phantom. Thus Percivale's recollections, punctuated with perceptive questions from Ambrosius, are calculated to demonstrate the reality of the Holy Grail to a credulous but inquisitive audience. Percivale, in turn, demonstrates his humility (recognition of his own limitations) in the final line: "So spake the King; I knew not all he meant." Thus Percivale's stature is specifically normed, though it is difficult to agree with those critics who see him as "the man of average sensibility."

smoke, line 15: pollen; *Aromat*, 48: Arimathea, near Jerusalem; Joseph of Arimathea is said to have brought the cup (variously that of the Last Supper or that with which Christ's blood was caught at the Crucifixion) to Glastonbury; *Arviragus*, 61: an early king of Britain; *Siege*, 172: seat, characterized by Tennyson as the "spiritual imagination"; *golden dragon*, 263: symbol of Arthur and of British sovereignty; *Taliessin*, 300: most famous early Welsh bard (the analogy, along with the characterization of "Siege Perilous" as "spiritual imagination," plus the analogy between Lancelot's madness and "the sacred madness of the bard," all together suggest that the art-escape vs. art-responsibility theme is in the back of the poet's mind here); *wyvern . . . swan*, 350: heraldic devices; *she*, 449: humility; *Paynim*, 661: pagan (in this case, Druids); *him of Cana*, 759: allusion to Christ's changing of water into wine at the marriage feast, thus the better wine being served after the inferior; *Carbonek*, 810: legendary castle built to house the Holy Grail; *deafer . . . cat*, 862: a whimsical correlation cited in Darwin's *Origin of Species*.

THE LAST TOURNAMENT (p. 209). The *Idylls* now are moving rapidly toward their tragic close. In the preceding idyll (*Pelleas and Ettarre*), Gawain has been unequivocally exposed as traitor, liar, and adulterer; in the following (*Guinevere*), the Queen will fully recognize both her culpability and Arthur's true magnitude:

> Ah great and gentle lord,
> Who wast, as is the conscience of a saint
> Among his warring senses, to thy knights—
> To whom my false voluptuous pride, that took
> Full easily all impressions from below,
> Would not look up, or half-despised the height
> To which I would not or I could not climb—
> I thought I could not breathe in that fine air,
> That pure severity of perfect light—
> I yearn'd for warmth and color which I found
> In Lancelot—now I see thee what thou art,
> Thou art the highest and most human too,
> Not Lancelot, nor another.

In *The Last Tournament*, Tennyson reworked, in a highly original way, a legend fascinating to nineteenth-century poets and artists, that of Tristram and the two Isolts. Tristram of the Woods is a late-comer to the Round Table. Although he has sworn the vows, he has never experienced the act of faith in Arthur's Christ-like kingship which gave the Order its original unity and strength. Rather, coming late from "rough Lyonesse," he has simply been awed by the king's presence and by the "mystic babble" surrounding him. Hence he has no genuine understanding of the underlying concept of fidelity to vow, king, or lady. He lacks the fullness of both courtesy and valor and represents, instead, an amoral animalism with the motto "We love but while we may."

The idyll is full of pain, mockery, wrath, and wretchedness. At its center is the sad interpretive figure of "Dagonet, the fool." He opens and closes the idyll, and his dialogue with Tristram (ll. 240–359) constitutes one of the key glosses on the entire poem. In the first place, Dagonet identifies himself and Arthur with "poor Innocence" and thus defines his role as fool: "Innocence the King's" Innocent. Secondly, he identifies the worm in the apple: "too much wit / Makes the world rotten." Thus the cause assigned to the dissolution of the Round Table is the same as that assigned in *Paradise Lost* to the loss of the Garden of Eden:

> 'Ay, and when the land
> Was freed, and the Queen false, ye set yourself
> To babble about him, all to show your wit—
> And whether he were king by courtesy,
> Or king by right—and so went harping down
> The black king's highway, got so far and grew
> So witty that ye play'd at ducks and drakes
> With Arthur's vows on the great lake of fire.'
> (ll. 338–345)

Finally, the contrast between the harmony of the spheres ("It makes a silent music up in heaven," l. 349) and the "broken music" of these later days clarifies the meaning of the riddle in *Gareth and Lynette*, "city built to music." At the beginning, the mind and soul had made a single, harmonious act of faith—the vows had been a total experimental affirmation; but now knowledge and faith have suffered dislocation, and the former creates discord with the latter. It is a theme expressed earlier in the invocation (or Prologue) to *In Memoriam*:

> Let knowledge grow from more to more,
>   But more of reverence in us dwell;
>   That mind and soul, according well,
> May make one music as before,
>
> But vaster.

(ll. 25–29)

THE PASSING OF ARTHUR. See MORTE D'ARTHUR (p. 43).

THE VOYAGE OF MAELDUNE (p. 227). This is another quest-allegory similar, in some respects, to several of Tennyson's early poems, but with these significant differences: the poet draws upon medieval Irish legend; the most conspicuous polarity in the poem is between pagan revenge and Christian forgiveness; the protagonists undergo a clear conversion from one value-system to another. It seems clear that the odyssey through which the men experience, allegorically, various ways of facing life is a necessary preparation for their acceptance, anew and vicariously, of the Christian message. The emblematic episodes through which they pass may suggest different nuances to different readers, but it is clear that the twelve parts into which the poem is divided suggest, in miniature, analogy with the classical epic. The following suggestions are very tentative: III, the Silent Isle: Life-in-Death, before the Word; IV, the Isle of Shouting: after the Word, babble, or Babel; V, the Isle of Flowers: the narcotic world of aesthetic escape, of beauty without truth; VI, the Isle of Fruits: the swine-like world of sensuous self-indulgence; VII, the contrasting worlds of flagrant passion (the Isle of Fire) and return to the womb of the lost Paradise (that undersea isle); VIII, the Bounteous Isle: the world of plenty, in which there is no challenge and in which courage must be mimicked; IX, the Isle of Witches: lascivious sexuality; X, the Isle of the Double Towers: religious partisanship, controversy, and wars.

Finn, line 48: great legendary Irish chieftain; Saint Brendan, 115: sailor-saint of sixth-century Ireland.

RIZPAH (p. 231). This poem is a compelling example of Tennyson's perception of recurring patterns in human suffering: on the one hand, he was thinking of the Biblical Rizpah who guarded the bones of her sons hanged by the Gibeonites (II Samuel 21:8 ff.); on the other, he had in mind the story from a penny magazine of an old woman of Brighton in the eighteenth century who gathered the bones of her son, hanged for robbing the mail coach, and having finally got them all, buried them "in the hallowed enclosure of old Shoreham Churchyard."

Rizpah is probably Tennyson's finest achievement in the dramatic monologue. The old woman, lying on her deathbed in company with some evangelical sister of mercy, reviews, through rapidly varying moods of sorrow, madness, suspicion, anger, remorse, and blasphemy, the catastrophe of her son and the life she has spent bearing him a second time in defiance of social law. She puts him together again, bone by bone, so that he " 'ill rise up whole when the trumpet of judgment 'ill sound. . . ."

DEMETER AND PERSEPHONE (p. 234). Although a monologue, this poem is not a "dramatic monologue" in the technical sense; it is more like a soliloquy with a listener. (Contrast, for example, the dramatic tension of *Rizpah*).

Demeter, the Earth Goddess, controlled the seasons and the regeneration of nature. With the permission of Zeus ("The Bright one," l. 93), Aidoneus, king of the underworld ("the Dark one," l. 94), carried off Demeter's daughter Persephone to become queen of Hades. Demeter wanders through the world in search of her lost daughter and is finally informed of what has happened by "the God of dreams." In anger Demeter curses the gods and neglects the seasons upon which man, bird, beast, and even the gods (in sacrifices) depend. Zeus finally compromises, allowing Persephone to spend nine months (cycle of regeneration) on earth and three months (hibernation and dormancy) in Hades. Although reconciled to this dispensation of the gods, Demeter's faith in their nobility has been shaken, and she predicts their overthrow and their replacement by "younger, kindlier Gods" grown from the "souls of men," with a gospel of Love. Thus, according to Tennyson's intention the "antique" myth is given a "modern frame of reference."

(*In Enna*): the Vale of Enna, near Athens; *God of ghosts*, line 5: Hermes, messenger of Zeus; *Eleusis*, 6: town sacred to Demeter; *Phlegethon*, 28: fiery river of Hades; *three gray heads*, 82: the Fates (cf. ll. 127–130); *God of dreams*, 90: Hermes again.

CROSSING THE BAR (p. 241). At Tennyson's request, this poem is placed "at the end of all editions" of his poems.

BROWNING

MY LAST DUCHESS (p. 244). This poem is generally grouped with a relatively small number of "perfect" dramatic monologues in the Browning canon. It does accomplish, with the sharpest economy, the three classical elements of the dramatic monologue: (1) a single speaker, (2) an audience, and (3) intense dramatic tension between (1) and (2). The poem is so subtly balanced that interpretive criticism of even its major nuances is quite disparate. The arrogant, cultivated vanity of the speaker seems certain enough, as does the innocent simplicity of the duchess. The painting, as well as the duke's unsatisfactory explanation of how she offended him, work ironically against him. She does seem alive, and he progressively unmasks not her but himself. But both the imaginary artist, Fra Pandolf, and the unnamed legate raise some teasing questions. Pandolf is a friar, and he has given the duchess a second immortality on canvas. Did she inspire him on purely aesthetic or spiritual (Madonna-like) or courtly grounds, as rumor may have had it? The poem contains hints (ll. 5, 12–13, 34–35, 43–44, 47, 53–54) that the legate is deeply moved by the portrait, that he is thoroughly and transparently incredulous of the duke's explanations, and even that he pushes his way out of the gallery in disgust. Thus the duchess is magnified, the duke diminished. Some critics even see here a hint that the legate perceives his mission as tragic, as agency of the catastrophic bondage of the *next* duchess.

Browning's use of heroic couplets for this poem is a mark of the subtle balance already mentioned; the formality is functional, and yet it does not intrude artificially upon the duke's exposition.

I gave commands; (l. 45): according to Browning, "the commands were that she should be put to death, or he might have had her shut up in a convent."

Neptune . . . Claus of Innsbruck (ll. 54–56): the artist is imaginary, but the statue of Neptune may be seen (a) as a symbol of the duke's domination or (b) as a symbol of the entirely unreal, mythical concept he has of himself.

COUNT GISMOND (p. 246). This is a companion poem to *My Last Duchess* in that chivalric France is contrasted with Renaissance Italy. It, too, is a dramatic monologue, but of a sharply differentiated kind. It is more conspicuously lyrical; its drama resides more in the recollected narrative than in any tension between speaker and audience; and it breathes the atmosphere of southern France and the spirit of the troubadours: simple unequivocal religious faith and wholesome sexual love.

there, 'twill last, line 46: a momentary fainting spell brought on by vivid memory; *second death,* 100: eternal damnation; *tercel,* 124: hunting falcon.

SOLILOQUY OF THE SPANISH CLOISTER (p. 249). This self-revelation of a dog-in-the-manger monk is an illuminating example of Browning's many and varied uses of "the grotesque." The grotesque is a literary mode which combines the tragic with the comic; the "serious grotesque" reaches toward the tragic, the "comic grotesque" toward the comic. In either case, humor, however wry, is an indispensable ingredient. *Soliloquy* is a clear paradigm of the comic grotesque. From its opening "Gr-r-r" to its concluding "you swine!" it operates on a broad acrobatic level of incident and rhyme, of pettiness and far-fetched deviousness. This makes humor the predominant effect. The fact that the monk is antipodal to the ideal of his tribe (Brother Lawrence, perhaps) introduces an undertone of tragic possibility, but the tone of the speaker rebuts a morally intense reading of the poem. Even the "great text in Galatians" is probably more significant on the level of rhythm and rhyme than on the level of a subtle meaning for the "Twenty-nine distinct damnations."

Salve tibi, line 10: "Hail to thee"—the manner, ironically, of Gabriel's address to the Virgin Mary; *Barbary corsair,* 31: pirate on the Barbary coast; *Arian,* 39: heretics who denied the Trinity; *Manichee,* 56: heretics dividing the world equally and eternally between good (God) and evil (Devil); *Hy, Zy, Hine,* 70: perhaps an imitation of the sounds of the Vesper bells; *Plena,* 71–72: "Hail, Virgin, full of grace."

JOHANNES AGRICOLA IN MEDITATION (p. 251). Browning used a quotation from Daniel Defoe's *Dictionary of All Religions* (1704) as a preface to this poem: "Antinomians, so denominated for rejecting the Law as a thing of no use under the Gospel dispensation: they say, that good works do not further, nor evil works hinder salvation; that the child of God cannot sin, that God never chastiseth him, that murder, drunkenness, etc. are sins in the wicked but not in him, that the child of grace being once assured of salvation, afterwards never doubteth . . . that God did not love any man for his holiness, that sanctification is no evidence of justification, etc. Potanus, in his Catalogue of Heresies, says John Agricola was the author of this sect, A.D. 1535."

The Antinomians rose out of the cradle of the Reformation, but their doctrines still had currency in various fundamentalist sects early in the nineteenth century, and the handbooks of Protestantism kept the controversy of faith vs. good works very much alive. (Witness, for example, Burns's *Holy Willie* and James Hogg's *Justified Sinner*.)

Johannes Agricola was grouped with *Prophyria's Lover* (p. 253) under the caption *Madhouse Cells*, thus glossing the poet's intention to expose a basic aberration from the norm. On the other hand, although Johannes is dominated by a thoroughly horrifying self-regard, he is not a mean personality like Holy Willie. He is poetic, mystical, sympathetic, and does not pretend to understand. He only "knows."

PORPHYRIA'S LOVER (p. 253). See the note to Johannes Agricola. The characters are, of course, imaginary.

PICTOR IGNOTUS (p. 254). This is one of Browning's early "artist-poems" in which he obliquely explores the personal qualities of an individual as he stands before a watershed period in Italian art. This "Unknown Painter" is a contemporary of Raphael and Michelangelo, but he has chosen (l. 57) a "monotonous" career within the well-established tradition, even though he knows this work has no continuing vitality; "So, die my pictures! surely, gently die!" (l. 69). The poem explores *why*, the same question which lies behind *Fra Lippo Lippi* and *Andrea del Sarto*, Browning's more famous artist-poems.

In the first place, from the beginning the speaker is fully, painfully aware of the choice he has made—"ah, thought which saddens while it soothes!" (l. 3). (The degree of self-awareness is always a crucial ingredient in Browning's dramatic monologues.) Such awareness of choice and acceptance of consequences seem to contradict a reading of the speaker as timid, envious, and self-deceiving. Moreover, the suggestion that dwarfs prudence as his monitor forces him to choose a safe mediocrity oversimplifies his choice.

The text seems fully to justify interpreting the "voice" (l. 41) as conscience, not prudence. The conflict which it introduces is essentially that between a Christian set of values and a resurgent pagan secularism—"like the revels through a door / Of some strange house of idols at its rites!" (ll. 42–43). After all, the net result of his exaltation in ll. 2–40 has been the "wildly dear" desire for a purely earthly fame. Hence he chooses to be a good Christian rather than a great painter in the Renaissance tradition, in which "Mixed with my loving trusting ones, there trooped . . . [satyrs, pagan gods, pre-Christian myths?]" (l. 45). In this interpretation, it is to the speaker's credit that, having made so fundamental a decision, he accepts with a sad lucidity the monotony of his professional career, the recurrent doubts ("at whiles / My heart sinks"), and the inevitable fading of his slight mark upon the world.

THE ENGLISHMAN IN ITALY (p. 256). In some respects, this is an "inventory" poem. The speaker catalogues, with vivid detail, the colors and rituals, the minutiae and topographical grandeur of Southern Italy, from the plain of Sorrento ("Piano di Sorrento") to the top of Mt. Calvano (l. 171). The fictional situation, however, is an Englishman attempting to allay a young Italian girl's fear of the tempestuous Scirocco, a hot dry wind from North Africa that brings about seasonal change and, at the same time, some inevitable violence and destruction. It is also a "sensibility" poem, in which the speaker attempts to ground in reality his recognition that a hot wind of righteous revolution is sweeping across both Italy and his native England (see, esp., ll. 286–292).

frails, line 47: rush baskets; *love-apple*, 87: tomato; *sorbs*, 138: species of apple tree; *isles of the siren*, 199: as recounted in the Odyssey; *Bellini . . . Auber*, 265; popular Italian and French composers, respectively; *Corn-laws*, 289: protective tariffs, the economic effects of which caused much political and social unrest and violence until their repeal in 1846.

HOME-THOUGHTS, FROM ABROAD (p. 262). The opening lines are some of the best known of Browning. The contrast between "brighter" England and "gaudy" Italy is explained by the fondness of absence.

THE BISHOP ORDERS HIS TOMB . . . (p. 263). It was Browning's persistent habit to bring a moment of history and a moment in the history of a soul into significant relationship. John Ruskin, the period's most distinguished aesthetician, noted the former quality of *The Bishop:* "I know no other piece of modern English, prose or poetry, in which there is so much told, as in these lines, of the Renaissance spirit,—its worldliness, inconsistency, pride, hypocrisy, ignorance of itself, love of art, of luxury, and of good Latin."

Whether or not "ignorance of itself" is truly a characteristic of the Renaissance spirit (Raphael? Michelangelo?), it is certainly a predominant trait of the Bishop: "ah, God, I know not!" (l. 3); "Ah, God, I know not, I!" (l. 39). Ruskin's sweeping indictment of the Renaissance spirit needs qualification; it is clear that he is expressing a private, though educated, judgment as much as a commentary on this poem.

There are many ironic twists in the poem: The worldly bishop orders his tomb in the church of a holy virgin who distributed her wealth among the poor. The Church Latin which he condemns was the true idiom of medieval Catholicism. The bishop maintains a "fleshly" frame of reference ("Blue as a vein o'er the Madonna's breast," l. 44; "Pan / Ready to twitch the nymph's last garment off," ll. 60–61); the proffered prayer to Saint Praxed for "mistresses with great smooth marbly limbs" (l. 75) is joined with the moment of his fleshly dissolution; and, finally, the bishop generally mingles naturalistic (pagan) and supernatural (Christian) sets of values.

The poem still succeeds in eliciting for the bishop a significant portion of reader-sympathy. His incompetence both as a churchman and as a human being emerges out of a pathetically dwarfed rather than a malicious character: his vague sense of self, his growing sense of failure, and the final recoil to Gandolf's envy as his only means of self-definition.

Vanity, line 1: Ecclesiastes, 2; *Nephews*, 3: a conventional euphemism for illegitimate sons, here ambiguously used; *epistle-side*, 21: to the congregation, the right-hand side; *tabernacle*, 26: canopy; *onion-stone*, 31: inferior peeling marble; *conflagration*, 34: did he burn his own church or did he merely purloin the undetected *lapis lazuli*, a magnificent blue stone?; *shuttle*, 51: Job 7:6; *antique-black*, 54: the bishop's enthusiasm (or ambition) is running higher than the basalt of 25; *tripod, thyrsus*, 58: the tripod of Apollo, the thyrsus of Dionysus; *glory*, 60: halo; *travertine*, 66: limestone; *tomb-top*, 67: effigy; *Tully's*, 77: Cicero's; *Ulpian*, 79: Roman jurist in the "decadent" third century; *God made and eaten*, 82: transubstantiation and communion, phrased in a particularly sensuous way; *mortcloth*, 89: funeral pall or death-sheet; *sermon on the mount*, 95: like Everyman, the bishop is losing his wits; *Elucescebat*, 99: "He was illustrious" in a decadent form; *vizor, term*, 108: mask, pedestal; *Gritstone*, 116: porous sandstone.

FRA LIPPO LIPPI (p. 266). Fra Lippo Lippi is one of Browning's most exuberant characters and one who gets from the reader resounding applause. Drawing upon details from Giorgio Vasari's *Lives of the Painters*, Browning has here mixed fact with fancy to give both individuality and emblematic relevance to this early Renaissance painter (1406–1469).

Two main lines of observation constitute the critical commentary on the poem: (1) its excellence as an example of the poet's achievement with dramatic monologue and (2) the skill with which the poet obliquely posits his own artistic creed. Concerning the first point, the major considerations are (a) the dramatic situation out of which Lippi's "deposition" proceeds, (b) the interpenetration of speaker and listener, and (c) the personal elan and colloquial vigor with which the speaker has his say. It is as though for the first time Lippi has found the right moment to unburden himself and the right audience. The main tenets of Lippi's artistic creed, with widely varying significance, are these: (a) the early culture of the artist has little to do with the standard fare of schools, rather it is dependent upon experience that teaches the significance behind a look or gesture; (b) the greatest impediment to the artist and to an appreciation of his works is the conventional, a priori notion that art can be defined independently of the artist and that the purpose of art is to inculcate principles and platitudes rather than portray beauty; (c) even if natural beauty could be separated from such spiritual realities as "hope, fear, / Sorrow or joy" (which it cannot), it would still be the surest token of a transcendent reality; (d) nature imitates art in the sense that reality for the most part goes unnoticed until it has been "formed" or "framed" by the artist.

As thematically important as Lippi's artistic creed is, it seems a secondary rather than the primary concern of the poem. He is a painter, true; but even more significantly, he is an unpretentious but profoundly impressive personality who unequivocably knows *who he is:* "I am poor brother Lippo, by your leave!" (l. 1). That he is neither celibate nor ascetic is perfectly clear. Equally clear is the fact that he is a profoundly religious man whose very celebration of "The beauty and the wonder and the power" (l. 283) of the world is an act of adoration. Although he is the least haughty of men (generous, forgiving, confidential, permissive, and without guile—the *reader* is more suspicious of the relationship between the Prior and his "niece" than Lippi is), he insists upon being himself and upon extending to others the same courtesy. "Death for us all, and his own life for each!"

Zooks, line 3: Gadzooks, an inoffensive oath; *Cosimo . . . Medici*, 17: banker, art patron, and lion of Florence; *pilchards*, 23: fish; *the Eight*, 121: the magistrates; *antiphonary*, 130: book of responses for chanting the office; *Preaching Friars*, 140: Dominicans; *safe*, 150: claiming sanctuary; *Giotto*, 189: a painter and architect who had flourished a century before Lippi and whom Browning greatly admired but whom Lippi refuses to accept as having defined the limits of realism; *Herodias*, 196: the Prior significantly confuses the mother with the daughter, Salome; *Angelico . . . Lorenzo*, 235–236: Fra Angelico and Lorenzo Monaco, painters whose conventions were antipodal to those espoused by Lippi; *Hulking Tom*, 277: Tomasco Guidi, or Masaccio, variously cited as master and disciple of Lippi; *cullion*, 307: rascal; *Laurence*, 323: a martyr who was broiled to death; *Saint Ambrogio*, 346: church of the convent of St. Ambrose for which Lippi painted "The Coronation of the

Virgin," described in 347–387; *camel-hair*, 375: St. John's clothing; *Iste . . .* , 377: "This man accomplished the work."

A TOCCATA OF GALUPPI'S (p. 274). As Browning analogized the poet with the painter, so he did the poet with the composer. His music analogies ranged from improvisation as in this poem and ABT VOGLER (p. 337) to Beethoven's Fifth Symphony in *The Ring and the Book*.

Baldassare Galuppi (1706–1785) was a popular Venetian composer in his day. The *toccata*, or "touch piece," was one of his favorite forms, and its light, capricious, seemingly unpredictable mode of evolving seems to simulate the frivolous gaiety of Venice at the time, as well as to norm it down. This poem both imitates and analyzes the toccata.

The central spiritual movement of the poem takes place in the speaker himself, a sensitive, reflective man of the nineteenth century, possibly a professional scientist, probably an avid amateur. At first he responds to Galuppi's light touch with a supercilious condescension toward its apparent triviality in manner and substance. Afterwards, however, he begins to experience the ironic critique, of Venice and of himself, contained in the "cold music," l. 33. In stanza XIII its ironic significance is emphasized.

Doges, line 6: rulers of Venice; *rings:* annual ceremony of wedding the Adriatic with Venice, the dominant party; *Shylock's bridge*, 8: the Rialto.

AN EPISTLE . . . OF KARSHISH . . . (p. 276) and CLEON (p. 326). It is customary (and not unprofitable) to study these two poems together and to find significance for each in the points of comparison and contrast they provide. For example, while they are both verse epistles, each "writer" has taken quite a different measure of himself and assumes a distinctly different attitude toward his "audience." Both characters cross, obliquely, the path of the historical Christ and respond, in diametrically opposed ways, to the incipient propagation of Christianity. One is an Arab scientist doggedly pursuing, in the face of much danger and discomfort in an alien land, the "crumbs" of useful knowledge. The other is a Greek philosopher, poet, and jack-of-all-arts, an aging naturalist who has written "the fiction out" of religion and who faces death with a thinly disguised despair.

But it has also been customary (somewhat less profitably) to emphasize Karshish and Cleon as typical Oriental and typical hellenistic Greek. This imposes upon Browning a naïve ethnological assumption which becomes quickly reductive. To see these characters ethnologically as one of the suggestive outreaches of the poems is fair enough; to see this as the poet's principal purpose contradicts both his poetic theory and the practice of the poems themselves. In theory, Browning concentrated on "a moment in the history of the development of *a* soul"; in practice, he concentrated his greatest efforts on the individualized identity of the principal in each of his poems. In *Karshish* and *Cleon*, for example, each speaker tells us immediately who he is: Karshish is

> the picker-up of learning's crumbs,
> The not-incurious in God's handiwork . . .

while Cleon is

> the poet (from the sprinkled isles,
> Lily on lily, that o'erlace the sea,
> And laugh their pride when the light wave lisps "Greece")—. . . .

Karshish is warm and deferential, freely expressing his debt to and affection for his teacher, near-contemporary, and friend. Cleon is elegant and formalistic, intent upon confirming the justness of the Tyrant's praises and wholly insensitive to the urgent human need beneath the compliments, gifts, and queries of Protus. Karshish, despite his genuine devotion to exact knowledge, cannot subdue in himself the pressure of intuition and the haunting reality of experience for which science offers no adequate explanation. Cleon has packaged life with the strapping of his own ego; he is a sophist who attempts to veil with a flimsy stoicism the discrepancy between his self-praise and his confession of failure. Karshish has come in search of what the Jews have to offer; Cleon dismisses the Jews superciliously and out of hand even though they offer the one thing necessary. Karshish is inductive throughout, embarrassed by his discovery but determined to present this strange case history and its possible implications. Cleon is deductive, semantical, and contemptuous of the possible relevance of anything outside his ken; he has been so light-handed gathering his "facts" from bystanders that he isn't even sure that Christ and Paul are not one and the same person.

What, in fact, may be truer to Browning's purpose than presenting Cleon as a typical hellenistic Greek is presenting him as a typical chauvinistic provincial without enough genuine curiosity either to welcome or to understand new experience. After all, the poem's epigraph comes from Acts (17:28–34), which tells of Paul's remarks from the Areopagus at Athens, where he spoke at the invitation of very curious Stoic and Epicurean philosophers.

snakestone, line 17: "old wives" cure for snakebite; V*espasian*, 28: the Romans invaded Jerusalem in 66 A.D. and in 70; *tertians*, 43: recurrent fevers; *falling-sickness*, 44: either epilepsy or dropsy; *porphyry*, 57: the bowl in which the *gum-tragacanth* (55) is prepared; *earthquake*, 252: the upheaval that accompanied the Crucifixion; *borage*, 281: a medicinal plant. (For annotation of details in *Cleon*, see page 659.)

"CHILDE ROLAND TO THE DARK TOWER CAME" (p. 283). First, we have Browning's own comment on this poem: "Childe Roland came upon me as a kind of dream. I had to write it, then and there, and I finished it the same day, I believe. But it was simply that I had to do it. I did not know then what I meant beyond that, and I'm sure I don't know now. But I am very fond of it." He reiterated that he "was conscious of no allegorical intention in writing it. . . ." Further, modern scholarship has teasingly demonstrated that the chief source of the poem's unusual imagery was a chapter from Browning's favorite childhood book, Gerard de Lairesse's *The Art of Painting in All Its Branches*, Chapter XVII: "Of Things Deformed and Broken, Falsely Called Painter-like." A combination of these suggestions leads to the conclusion that *Childe Roland* is a recollection of an indelible imaginative experience in early youth. It follows the formulary of mythic quest but substitutes a surrealistic landscape for a romantic one and a psychological expectation of the minimum of endurance for an expectation of high spiritual conquest. Browning had no predecessor in such a rigorous use of the wasteland motif for the terrifying, nightmarish quality of Roland's *rite de passage*. Even the relief of memory (stanzas 15–17) is denied him since he can recall only the lecherous Cuthbert and the traitorous Giles.

Critics generally pinpoint lines 41–43 as the thematic keynote of the poem

Childe, title: an unproved aspirant after knighthood; *Edgar's Song*, epigraph:

> Child Rowland to the dark tower came,
> His word was still—Fie, foh, and fum,
> I smell the blood of a British man.

estray, line 48: lost wanderer; *bents*, 68: coarse grass; *colloped*, 80: folded; *Tophet*, 143: Hell; *Apollyon*, 160: the Devil; *penned*, 161: pinioned; *slughorn*, 203: trumpet.

BISHOP BLOUGRAM'S APOLOGY (p. 289). Several characteristics justify this monologue's reputation for subtlety and superb literary finesse: (1) The imaginative situation is entirely fresh and apposite. A sixty-year-old Bishop and a thirty-year-old journalist who has evidenced some slight journalistic skill sit across the table —of gracious living, of generations, of temperaments, of value-systems, of religious convictions—and have an eyeball-to-eyeball conversation. (What the journalist has said is implicit in what the Bishop says.) (2) The "moment" is crucial in several senses. Three hundred years ago in the "age of faith," it would have lacked tension, as it would have seventy years ago in the "age of disbelief," an age in which the full impact of Voltaire and empirical rationalism was felt. But at this moment something new has happened. On the Protestant side, Evangelicalism and Tractarianism have given new vitality, social respectability, and credibility to faith. On the Catholic side, English Catholics have been emancipated (1829), Newman and a host of his Oxford sympathizers have "gone over" to Rome, and the Catholic hierarchy has been re-established with the new Bishop of Westminster primate of England. Also, the Catholic Church under Pius IX is confronting or preparing to confront the wave of liberalism (defined by Newman as the position that there is no *necessary* truth in religion) with dogmatic declarations, for example, the Immaculate Conception (1854) and Infallibility (1870). (3) The Bishop assumes, in the intimacy of the situation, the role of a latter-day casuist, attempting "in equilibrium [to] keep / The giddy line midway . . ." (ll. 399–400) between "one who studies and resolves cases of conscience or conduct," and "an oversubtle or disingenuous reasoner" of conscience or conduct.

That young Gigadibs is "worsted" or "bested" seems clear enough. He gives up the unequal struggle, buys settlers' implements, and goes to Australia. Just what our ultimate evaluation of the Bishop should be criticism in no way makes clear. Some students of Browning read the poem as unfriendly to the Catholic Church, even suggesting that Browning compensated for it with his sympathetic delineation of Innocent XII in *The Ring and the Book*. Others see the Bishop as brilliant, wholly attuned to the necessities of his office in the modern world, and as sympathetic as a religious realist can be.

It does seem clear, however, that one must adjudge the Bishop ultimately not by the cogency of his arguments but by the identity which emerges during the course of his exposition. His arguments are very telling. Honest doubt is as much subject to doubt as faith is. You either have faith or you don't have it; and if you profess faith in the fundamental attributes of a Christian God (omnipotence, omniscience, benevolence) such dogmatic or miraculous details as the Immaculate Conception, the Virgin's winks, and the Naples liquefactions need not be boggled at. A fundamental distinction must be made between Luther in the sixteenth century and Strauss in the nineteenth:

although Luther broke from Rome, it was his surplus of fire that impelled him; while Strauss lacks all faith, foresees no future, and is a cold analyst who may, if only on "that plaguy hundredth chance," be wrong (ll. 576–591). Bishops are bishops and should satisfy the expectations of laymen, wear bishops' robes and live in bishops' palaces. That bishops should "believe . . . statedly . . . and fixedly / And absolutely and exclusively" (ll. 150–152) represents a simplistic and doctrinaire view of the nature of the assenting mind. Belief or unbelief is no trivial matter but "Bears upon life, determines its whole course, / Begins at its beginning" (ll. 229–230). Even the "natural man" provides an analogue to the man credulous of the supernatural in that he disciplines his life beyond natural license "Through certain instincts, blind, unreasoned-out, / You dare not set aside, you can't tell why, / But there they are, and so you let them rule" (ll. 838–840).

But Blougram's real motor force is his high degree of self-awareness, his keen sense of who he is. This is more significant, he feels, than "historic knowledge, logic sound, / And metaphysical acumen. . . ." (ll. 624–625). I am what I am, he says, and "My business is not to remake myself, / But make the absolute best of what God made" (ll. 354–355). Two passages pinpoint this explicitly: ll. 322–340, 845–852. Whether one "likes" him or not is a personal matter, and it would be hard to deny that the poem's ultimate effect is ambiguous. One can, with Kingsley on Newman, say that he is either a fool or a knave, but one must admit that Browning, to a very impressive degree and a decade earlier than Newman's *Apologia*, has Blougram answer what was to be Newman's central question: " 'What does Dr. Newman mean?' It pointed in the very same direction into which my musings had turned me already. He asks what I *mean*; not about my words, not about my arguments, not about my actions, as his ultimate point, but about that living intelligence, by which I write and argue, and act. He asks about my Mind and its Beliefs and its sentiments. . . ." (Preface, *Apologia*)

To have made Blougram an obvious knave or an equally obvious saint would have immobilized Browning's purpose in the poem. But, along with his gamesmanship with Gigadibs, Browning allows oblique suggestions of the genuine depth and quality of Blougram's personality: e.g., ll. 599–623, 647–675, 693–712.

Abbey, line 3: Westminster Abbey; *Pugin's*, 6: A. W. N. Pugin, late convert and architect; *Count D'Orsay*, 54: Victorian dandy; *tire-room*, 70: dressing room; *Jerome*, 113: Correggio's painting of St. Jerome; *Hildebrand's*, 316: Pope Gregory VII; *Schelling's*, 411: German idealistic philosopher in the Kantian tradition; *Romano . . . Dowland*, 516: Renaissance painter and Elizabethan musician/composer, respectively; *Pandulph*, 519: in Shakespeare's King John; *Re-opens a shut book*, 572: lays new stress upon the Bible and its accessibility through the vernacular; *Strauss*, 577: David Friedrich Strauss, historical critic of the Bible and author of the most important *Life of Jesus* in the nineteenth century; *Newman*, 703: John Henry Newman (1801–1890), convert and "defender of the faith"; *King Bomba's lazzaroni*, 715: beggars in Ferdinand II's Sicily; *Antonelli*, 716: cardinal secretary to Pius IX; *Naples' liquefaction*, 728: a popular belief that the blood of Januarius, patron of Naples, liquefied on his Feast Day; *Fichte*, 744: Johann Gottlieb Fichte (1762–1814), German philosopher who held that God existed only in the mind of man; *in partibus,* 972: before becoming Archbishop of Westminster, Bishop Wiseman, the "original" of Bishop Blougram, had been titular bishop of Melipotamus, "in the territories of infidels"; *St. John,* 1014: the subject of Browning's "A Death in the Desert."

ANDREA DEL SARTO (p. 311). Commentators on this poem generally agree on three points: (1) that it is one of Browning's finest poetic achievements; (2) that Browning's judgment, which was based upon Vasari's *Lives of the Painters* and his own prolonged study of Andrea's self-portrait with wife in the Pitti Palace, of del Sarto's relative failure as a painter with extraordinary gifts is just; and (3) that it contains the quintessential statement of Browning's so-called "philosophy of the imperfect," especially in two passages:

> Well, less is more, Lucrezia: I am judged.   (l. 78)

> Ah, but a man's reach should exceed his grasp,
> Or what's a heaven for?   (ll. 97–98)

Despite the genuine relevance of points 2 and 3, it is the first point that magnetizes critical attention.

Essentially, the poem must be judged as a profoundly subtle self-revelation. Browning had clearly adopted Vasari's reading of the painter's talents and character:

> In Andre del Sarto nature and art combined to show all that may be done in painting, when design, coloring and invention unite in one and the same person: Had this master possessed a somewhat bolder and more elevated mind; had he been as much distinguished for higher qualifications as he was for genius and depth of judgment in the art he practiced, he would, beyond all doubt, have been without an equal. But there was a certain timidity of mind, a sort of diffidence and want of force in his nature. . . .

Browning set himself to write a surrogate poem, a poetic substitute for the portrait of Andrea and his wife hanging in the Pitti Palace, intending to assimilate into the monologue "the design, coloring and invention" of the painting. In short, he chose to present Andrea as judged, not by Vasari, but by himself. Thus he imagines the scene as a twilight moment between the garish turbulence of quarrel and the darkness of inescapable acceptance, a moment of truth in which the two dominant dimensions of del Sarto's identity (his undeniable talent as an artist, his fully confessed weakness for an unworthy woman) are fully delineated:

> days decrease,
> And autumn grows, autumn in everything.
> Eh? the whole seems to fall into a shape
> As if I saw alike my work and self
> And all that I was born to be and do
> A twilight-piece.

The muted tone of the poem is corroborated throughout. Andrea emerges as pathetic rather than tragic. Although fully aware of the essential flaws in Lucrezia and in himself, he acquiesces in his failure. Although cognizant of the contempt men have for him because he betrayed King Francis and callously neglected his parents, he hides behind a fragile *que sera sera* fatalism which enables him to escape a just burden of guilt. Even the dramatic interplay between speaker and audience unravels in a minor key.

Fiesole, line 15: a suburb of Florence; *Someone,* 76: Michelangelo; *Morello,* 93: a mountain peak north of Florence; *The Urbinate,* 105: Raphael; *Agnolo,* 130: Michelangelo; *Francis,* 149: Francis I of France was Andrea's patron for a fruitful period at Fontainebleau, from which Andrea departed with a sum of money he appropriated for his own uses; *Roman,* 178: Raphael; *New Jerusalem,* 261: Heaven; *Leonard,* 263: Leonardo da Vinci.

SAUL (p. 317). *Saul* is perhaps the most appropriate of all of Browning's poems for a concentrated study of how the poet fused his peculiar religious outlook with his theory of poetry, its sanction, its highest possibilities, its function. From the Bible (I Samuel 16:14–23), Browning took the simple fact that David played before Saul and cured him of his evil spirit.

The poem progresses through several well-defined stages. First, David sings a series of simple folk songs—a shepherd's song, a reaper's song, a wine song, a dirge, a marriage hymn, an altar chorus. Having aroused Saul from the depths of spiritual lethargy, David next sings (lines 68–96) of the joy and richness of life, climaxing in a paean to Saul himself. Saul's deepest agony has been relieved (his "slow heavings subsided"), but he still has not found hope. David then sings (lines 147–190) an exultant song of the soul, celebrating Saul's enduring fame for posterity, a secular kind of immortality. Finally, the singer becomes the seer, and poet becomes prophet (lines 238–312); the immortality of the soul replaces lasting fame among men, and the God of law becomes also the God of love—prophecy of the coming of Christ.

The ultimate sanction of poetry, then, is a religious sanction. At its highest, it abandons tradition and formal convention ("Then the truth came upon me. No harp more—no song more!") and relies on divine inspiration. Then the poet-seer, as Browning himself said, will be "impelled to embody the thing he perceives not so much with reference to the many below, as to the one above him, the supreme Intelligence which apprehends all things in their absolute truth." The function of poetry is to move its audience to action. Thus the mounting ecstasy of David's songs leads Saul out of the dark night (lines 23–76) of the soul.

David is the speaker in the poem. His narrative uses both the past tense and the present tense, the latter portions being direct quotations of what was said and sung.

Abner, line 1: commander of Saul's army and David's uncle; *king-serpent,* 31: the boa-constrictor, "caught in his pangs" of shedding his old skin; *jerboa,* 45: a "flying" mouse; *paper-reeds,* 188: papyrus plant; *Hebron,* 203: a mountain; *Kidron,* 204: a brook; *error,* 213: his disobedience to the commands of Jehovah; *Sabaoth,* 291: biblical armies or hosts.

CLEON (p. 326). (For general comments on *Cleon,* see *An Epistle,* p. 654.)
As certain also . . . , epigraph: Acts 17:28, "For in him we live and move and have our being; as certain also of your poets have said, For we are also his offspring"; *sprinkled isles,* line 1: islands off the Greek coast; *his Tyranny,* 4: his kingship; *phare,* 51: lighthouse; *Poecile,* 53: the portico at Athens; *moods,* 60: scales or modes; *rhomb, lozenge, trapezoid,* 83–84: distinct variations on four-sided geometrical figures; *drupe,* 132: wild, uncultivated plum; *Terpander,* 140: most famous of early Greek musicians; *Phidias,* 141: most famous Greek sculptor; *Naiad,* 252: water nymph.

A GRAMMARIAN'S FUNERAL (p. 334) and RABBI BEN EZRA (p. 340). It has been customary to read these two poems as exhilarating manifestoes of several of Browning's deeply held beliefs, buoyant expressions of an indomitable optimism. Recently a rift has appeared in that critical lute.

Read as a poem that "conveys the adventurous spirit, the hunger for knowledge," A Grammarian's Funeral may serve as a reassuring testament to the aging scholar or professor, but very few younger readers can be comfortable with the severely circumscribed life-style adopted by the Grammarian or the timid—at best—motives with which he avoids tasting life. Three or four aspects of the poem suggest that its intention is deeply ironic and that the author is concerned with the death-in-life of the unadventurous spirit. (1) The first reference to the Grammarian is to "this corpse" (l. 1). (2) The singers' attitude toward ordinary mankind, like their mentor's, is arrogantly contemptuous (ll. 3, 13, 29, 83). (3) The comparison between the Grammarian and "Lyric Apollo" (l. 34) is grotesquely extravagant. (4) The Grammarian is allowed to characterize himself in verse that is devastatingly comic (esp. ll. 57–64). (5) The students' summary of his highest achievement (ll. 123–132) is, in both language and substance, clearly more grub than butterfly.

Rabbi Ben Ezra, while not mock-serious in the comic manner of A Grammarian's Funeral, presents a philosophy of life which few thoughtful people could easily adopt. Iba Ezra and Omar Khayyam were contemporaries (the former died in 1167, the latter around 1123) and Browning may have been, to a degree at least, prompted to write his poem by the publication of Fitzgerald's Rubaiyat in 1859. It does not necessarily follow that Browning therefore intended Rabbi Ben Ezra "to serve as a reply to Omar's carpe diem hedonism." It might be argued instead that Browning, with his characteristic sense of the dramatic, presented an alternative, twelfth-century, non-Christian world view, vigorous, declamatory, and optimistic rather than languid, reflective, and world-weary. And his purpose in the poem was to make the speaker (who seems to have no particular audience) vivid and interesting rather than right.

Calculus, line 86: gallstones; Tussis, 88: a persistent cough, perhaps tubercular; hydroptic, 95: thirsty; the rattle, 127: the death rattle; Hoti . . . Oun . . . De, 129–131: Greek particles meaning, respectively, that, therefore, and toward. (For annotation of details in Rabbi Ben Ezra, see p. 661.)

ABT VOGLER (p. 337). Another of Browning's "musical analogues," Abt Vogler posits and explores certain "intimations of immortality." The good Abbe (1749–1814) was both a devoted religious and a composer. He is presented here as a virtuoso in both worlds of religion and intuitive composition, pushing to the limit the possibilities of the orchestrion, which he had invented. The importance of extemporization to the poem's form and theme is that it stresses process rather than the less dynamic result of process. The gifted musician creates his "palace built to music," his reality of the unseen, more purely than does either painter or poet. Even though the infinite moment which he thus momentarily perceives dissolves and is gone, it will repeat itself temporally and, by analogy, eternally. The groundtone—"The C Major of this life"—is the basic human condition, but God occasionally "whispers in the ear" of musicians and then they "know." Thus Abt Vogler, like David in Saul, represents the ex tempore prophetic seer, to whom the painter, the lover, and the bard are all analogues.

Solomon willed, line 3: King Solomon was said to have the powers described by virtue of a seal bearing the "ineffable name" of God; *Protoplast*, 34: first created thing; *a star*, 52: that is, a metaphor of celestial beauty; *houses not made with hands*, 66: St. Paul speaks of "a building of God, an house not made with hands, eternal in the heavens" (cf. Camelot in Tennyson's *Idylls*); *common chord*, etc., 91–96: musical metaphors by which Vogler descends, by degrees, to the natural scale, pausing for a moment on a "ninth," or unresolved chord, to review the "heights" where he had been; *sleep*, 96: though some critics read this as a metaphor for death, it may also suggest a concept very much like Wordsworth's "Our birth is but a sleep and a forgetting. . . ."

RABBI BEN EZRA (p. 340). (For general comments on *Rabbi Ben Ezra*, see the note A *Grammarian's Funeral* p. 660.)

Ay, note that Potter's wheel, / That metaphor!, ll. 151–152: a rather extended use of the same metaphor in *The Rubaiyat* is one of the strongest arguments for connecting the two poems. *Potter and clay endure*, l. 162: it is possible, of course, to resolve the difficulty in these metaphors by arguing that by "clay" Ben Ezra means the soul rather than the body; but it is also possible to argue that here, as elsewhere (ll. 40–43, e.g.), the Rabbi, despite his spiritual bravado, is both perplexing and perplexed.

THE RING AND THE BOOK (p. 346). *The Ring and the Book* (1868–1869) was Browning's most ambitious effort in poetry and is certainly one of the greatest poetic achievements of the Victorian period. Based on evidence—some printed, some manuscript—that he had first found bound in parchment, *The Old Yellow Book*, on a bookstall in Florence in 1860, the poem provides the ultimate test of Browning's chief poetic formula, the dramatic monologue. In its more than 20,000 lines, Browning explores—while he demonstrates—the relationship between Poetry (the Ring) and Truth (the Book). The poem is structured as follows:

I. *The Ring and the Book* (the poet-narrator speaks)
II. *Half-Rome* (pro-Guido)
III. *The Other Half-Rome* (pro-Pompilia)
IV. *Tertium Quid* (the "educated" analyst, above gross choice)
V. *Count Guido Franceschini* (principal)
VI. *Giuseppe Caponsacchi* (principal)
VII. *Pompilia* (principal)
VIII. *Dominus Hyacinthus De Archangelis* (pro-Guido)
IX. *Juris Doctor Johannes-Baptista Bottinus* (pro-Pompilia)
X. *The Pope* (final earthly adjudicator)
XI. *Guido* (the convict unmasked)
XII. *The Book and the Ring* (the poet-narrator again)

Books I and XII function, outside the art-ring metaphor, as General Prologue and General Epilogue. Books II, III, and IV form a movement of popular judgment, balanced by Books VIII, IX, and X, the official representatives of justice. Further, each of the earlier books balances each of the later, e.g., Book IV and Book X project fundamental contrasts. At the center of the poem are the self-revelations of the principals (Books V, VI, and VII), whose monologues in turn floodlight the characters and qualities of the other speakers. In each instance the speaker sees the case with varying relativism, his apprehension of Truth dependent upon his degree of genuine self-awareness and his capacity for self-immolation.

The simple stock of the story is this. Count Guido Franceschini—a Florentine nobleman getting on in years, down at fortune's heel, and having failed to obtain ecclesiastical preferment—decides, with the connivance of his brother, a priest, to repair his fortunes through marriage. Pompilia Comparini, supposed daughter and heir of Pietro and Violante Comparini, an apparently well-propertied couple, is chosen, and Guido and Pompilia are married at Rome in 1693. The Comparinis go to live with the Franceschinis at Guido's home in Arezzo. Almost immediately tensions and hostilities pervade the Franceschini home. Pietro and Violante return to Rome, where they let out the true story of Pompilia's parentage—she is the accidental daughter of a prostitute whom Violante, past child-bearing, has bought. Pietro then sues for a return of Pompilia's dowry. At first the suit is decided in Guido's favor, but an appeal is entered, and the matter remains unsettled.

Pompilia continues at Arezzo in an increasingly wretched situation. Her desperate appeals—to the Archbishop, to the Governor—for relief from at least her connubial obligations prove futile. Finally she discovers that she is pregnant and makes a fresh plea to a young Canon of the town, Giuseppe Caponsacchi. After some days' hesitation, Caponsacchi makes the necessary arrangements and starts with Pompilia for Rome. At Castelnuovo, a village some fifteen miles outside Rome, the exhausted pair rest. The next morning they are taken into custody on the complaint of Guido, who has overtaken them. After trial before the Tribunal of the Governor, the following decision is handed down: Pompilia is sent to a convent, and Caponsacchi is suspended for three years and exiled in the seaport town of Civita Vecchia.

As Pompilia comes closer to term, she is transferred to the home of her foster parents, and there, on December 18, 1697, she gives birth to a son, Gaetano. Guido's hatred continues to fester, and on the night of January 2, 1698, he and four hired confederates gain entrance, through a ruse, to the Comparini home, violently kill Pietro and Violante, and leave Pompilia for dead. (Gaetano had been prudently sequestered.) Guido and his accomplices, having failed to obtain a routine permit, cannot hire horses and have to travel on foot. They are captured before they can reach the safety of their own border.

V. COUNT GUIDO FRANCESCHINI (p. 346) and XI. GUIDO. The villain of the piece, Count Guido, is given two monologues: the first before the criminal court of secular law; the second, from midnight to dawn, before the Abate and Cardinal who have come to shrive his soul and prepare him, penitent, for death.

Browning is sometimes criticized for having offended his own "technique of indirection," of having, as it were, unmasked Guido in Book XI and thus placed a "mediate word" between the reader and the poem in contradiction to his declared method. And the masked/unmasked argument has some force: "Count Guido Franceschini" with the eight-hundred-years-old name and the presumption of privilege and impunity in Book V is, at the level of external trappings at least, in marked contrast to the naked wolf, who has called a truce to nonsense and sheep's clothing, in Book XI—even though the central core of character is obviously common to both.

Ultimately, the more compelling critical judgment is not made on method and architectonics, but on thematic depth and perspective: does Book XI contribute significantly (and therefore indispensably) to the poem's "exploration of truth"?

In Book V, Count Guido Franceschini stands self-indicted (though, with a fine irony, he is entirely insensible of the fact) on three counts that in turn reflect three dimensions of personality or character. (1) The tone of voice which he assumes—purring, oily, obsequious, martyr-saturate—implies a cynical, condescending attitude toward both his judges and the whole machinery of justice. It indicates his assumption that, with an eye to rhetoric and some adroit play-acting, he can use his head to save his neck, independently of the issues of moral depravity and guilt. In other words, he sees moral justice as subordinate to wily casuistry. (2) He gives startling evidence of his megalomania by comparing himself to Christ (ll. 4–6). (3) He asserts a thesis— "Law is law" (l. 11)—upon which his defense turns and collapses. These three motifs, with inventive variations, dominate his monologue and, thus, the identity which he projects.

Throughout Count Guido makes a series of concessions. He did kill Pompilia and her foster parents (ll. 109–112). He did come to Rome to gamble at the casino of patronage and lost (the gambling analogy—ll. 369–396—is shot through with worldly cynicism). He did, he brutally avows, barter his Franceschinihood for the Comparini wealth, even "gilding fact by fraud" (ll. 434–497). He did demand from his child-wife a passionate sexuality that she could not give (ll. 602–604, 610–611, 694–703—the "dirty old man" theme), and the more unmalleable she became, the more he applied the "short chain and sharp scourge" (l. 739). He did forge the letter in which Pompilia disavowed her parents (ll. 841–845). He did breathe "threatenings, rage and slaughter" (l. 931). He did, when Pompilia and Caponsacchi were apprehended at Castelnuovo, play the coward (ll. 1089–1099). He did accept, without appeal, law's earlier dispositions in the case—the light sentences dealt Pompilia and Caponsacchi (ll. 1250f.), the rejection of his suit for divorce, and the release of Pompilia to the care of the Comparini (ll. 1303f.). Although he asserts that, on receipt of word of Pompilia's child, he "rose up like fire, and fire-like roared" (l. 1476), he did take four hired assassins with him (ll. 1548f.) and he did hesitate for at least ten days before committing the act (ll. 1574f.). He did use deception to gain entrance to the Comparini house (ll. 1621–1627).

Recurrent, too, is his arrogant self-magnification. Having begun with a comparison of himself with Christ, he ends with a comparison with God the Father (l. 2037), with implied comparisons, en route, with St. Francis (ll. 140–156), the Church (ll. 740–741), the agent of miracles (ll. 1518, 2016–2017), of biblical innocence (ll. 1660f.), and of social and moral renovation (ll. 2024–2036).

"I began life," says Count Guido in a deeply ironic assertion towards the end of his monologue, "I began life by hanging to the law, / To the law it is I hang till life shall end" (ll. 1739–1740). The fact is, of course, that he has bruised or broken every code of conduct by which man is measured estimable: the code of religious service he converted into a drawn-out, angry, unsuccessful quest for patronage; the code of marriage he turned into fraudulent barter; his sexual demands upon his child-wife were absolutely lacking in the slightest touch of chivalry; he took full advantage of the rigid timidity of the Archbishop and the Governor in refusing, in name of the law, Pompilia's pleas for sanctuary; he violated the admissible law of justified righteous wrath by playing "prodigy / Of patience which the world [rightly] calls cowardice . . ." (ll. 1869–1870); finally, he set out in the Christmastide to set aside the law of the church, state, and nature ("a voice beyond the law / Enters my heart, *Quis est pro Domino?*"—ll. 1541–1542).

Count Guido, then, is patently guilty. He is a bitter, distorted man who has never asked himself, "Who am I? What do I believe?" His life has simply been an assertion, "I am Count Guido Franceschini, and in this world of topsy-turvy social leveling—in which the grandsons of tripe-sellers are adding towers to their palaces and lacqueys' sons are choosing coats-of-arms to go with their new estates—I mean to have my share."

Book XI is full of a defiant, though deeply fallible, bravado. Guido sees himself as the personification of "Rank, privilege, indulgence" (ll. 1771–1773) and, as such, the scapegoat of a "sneaking burgess-spirit" that is winning the day. He throws aside the sheep's skin and bares the wolf's fangs; he condemns the Pope—his "murderer"—to hell, denies the validity of Christianity (the fables of children, the make-believe of magicians, the ravings of madmen), takes pleasure in defying his would-be confessors, and rejects the crucifix throughout. To a degree he is the arch-deceiver still: his very show of impenitence is a ruse to put off his execution (ll. 2222–2224). At the end he breaks down completely and prays his litany of terror (ll. 2407–2417).

But two quite disparate new dimensions of Guido as a character emerge in Book XI. He assumes a culture-function, becomes an embodiment of the materialism and naturalism which are sweeping the Christian world; and he comes very close to the truth when he perceives that the warfare between him and Pompilia has been a struggle between inviolate good and inexplicable evil—between what in more primitive religious vocabularies would be called God and the Devil.

Three passages clearly demonstrate the cultural-ideological movement for which Guido serves as spokesman.

XI, 512–542: Hobbesian utilitarianism—hedonistic, epicurean
XI, 1967–1995: Neopaganism, in the manner of Swinburne's *Poems and Ballads*, First Series, "Thou has conquered, O Pale Galilean . . ."
XI, 2295–2310: Determinism, survival of the fittest, natural selection, struggle for existence, in which *crime* is not a meaningful word, only *blunder*

These three corroborative, cultural-ideological movements compose colossal threats to the fundamental tenets (mystery and miracle, the existence of the nonsensual world, free will, a hierarchy of moral values, the individual functioning with a nonegocentric style) upon which nondogmatic, fallible, credible religion has traditionally been erected.

Guido does recognize in Pompilia a haunting antipodal force he associates with God, although he cannot "like" her for it:

This self-possession to the uttermost,
How does it differ in aught, save degree,
From the terrible patience of God?
(XI, 1372–1374)

just one ghost-thing half on earth,
Half out of it,—as if she held God's hand
While she leant back and looked her last at me,

Forgiving me (here monks begin to weep)
Oh, from her very soul, commending mine
To heavenly mercies which are infinite— . . .
(XI, 1720–1724)

She had committed the offense of seeing at once into the blackness of his soul (ll. 971–985); his ineradicable haunting thought of her is of those accusing eyes (ll. 2067–2077).

One could make the argument that this confessed recognition and grudging concession of Pompilia's inviolate virtue justifies Guido's deathbed confession. It seems more consonant with Browning's purpose to let Guido's paroxysm of fear account for that, while the sources of his evil, however clear their manifestations, remain ultimately unexplained.

and not vinegar and gall, line 5: an implicit comparison of himself with Christ on the cross; *a rhetorician's trick,* 78: Guido sees himself as a suave and cultured man like his peers on the bench; *very like our Lord,* 156: again, by analogy, he means himself; *Molinos,* 203: Miguel de Molinos (1627–1696) was a Spanish mystic condemned for heresy in 1687, four years before the Papacy of Innocent XII, who ironically shared to a degree Molinos's emphasis on the individual's spiritual state and nature rather than the "laws" of Church and State which Guido attempts to make so much of; *Utrique sic paratus,* 284: prepared for either event; *the last Pope his certain obstinate sore,* 300; *My father's chaplain's nephew, Chamberlain,* 308: in both cases, Guido insinuates vague, coarse accusations; *New Prisons from Tordinona,* 324: where the accused were held; *seventh climacteric,* 344: change of life or menopause; *a sors,* 401: a lot, that is, opening Virgil at random for guidance in a moment of crisis; *Pietro of Cortona . . . Ciro Ferri,* 486–487: a late painter of frescoes and his pupil, respectively; *Ser Franco,* 558: author of ribald tales; *troll,* 592: a pun on trull, meaning slut; *cockatrice,* 655: a serpent—hatched from a cock's egg—whose very glance is fatal; *Thyrsis to Neaera,* 670: swain and sweetheart in Virgil's *Eclogues; Church's mode,* 741: another of Guido's arrogant self-analogies; *turtle,* 751: turtle-dove; *Locusta's wile,* 809: poisoner and henchwoman of Nero; *Bilboa,* 848: Spanish cutlass; *Stans pede in uno,* 920: standing on one foot; *Malchus,* 965: St. Peter cut off the ear of Malchus; *calash,* 1024: hooded carriage; *poltroon,* 1091: craven coward; *passim,* 1141f. that the letters are counterfeit is suggested by the artificial, conventionally mythological style in which they are written; *doctus,* 1205: learned; *pudency,* 1230: modesty, which Guido's lascivious vulgarity belies, suggesting sex organs; *Ultima Thule . . . Proxima Civitas,* 1277–1278: a joke, "farthest north" vs. "nearest town"; *Ovid's art . . . his "Summa,"* 1351–1352: that is, knew Ovid's *Art of Love* better than St. Thomas Aquinas's *Summa Theologica; Corinna,* 1353: poetical for Ovid's mistress; *merum sal,* 1359: pure salt, or wit; *leviathan,* 1498: fabulous whale or other sea-monster; *Quis est pro Domino,* 1542: Who is on the Lord's side? —another arrogant self-analogy; *florid prose / As smooth as mine is rough,* 1684–1685: this inverted contrast of their styles is an important key to Guido's disingenuousness; *Ad judices meos,* 1749: Leave him to his judges; *Justinian's Pandects,* 1770: digests of Roman Law prepared under the Emperor Justinian; *Shimei,* 2009: II Samuel 16, 5–14, cast stones at David; *Belial,* 2034: a fallen angel, or even Satan himself; *then will I set my son at my right-hand,* 2037: a final arrogant self-analogy, this time with God the Father Himself.

VI. GIUSEPPE [MARIA] CAPONSACCHI (p. 390). Guido, it seems, represents a terrifying, not entirely explicable, evil force in the world of the poem; Pompilia is a mysterious miracle of goodness and compels the reader's cathartic sympathy.

Caponsacchi is the poem's dynamic center. It is he who can credibly "bow . . . blessed / By the revelation of Pompilia" (ll. 1837–1838). It is he who, temperamentally, craves a mission that will catalyze his entire personality, his whole ME—"my eyes and ears and brain and heart" (l. 190). It is he who, through the baptism of elemental experience, learns some of the wisdom of Innocent himself: that the attributes of the God that he had once dilettantishly served are indeed "great, just, good" (l. 2076); that ministers of the gospel and the law, since they have not studied "passion," can be of little shepherd-value to mankind "in passionate extremes" (ll. 2051–2052); that the world of man is in fact a grotesque marriage of good and evil (ll. 1446–1478); and that the price of moral wisdom is an eternal note of sadness (ll. 2072–2075).

Caponsacchi and Guido show significant points of contrast. They vie for the oldest and second-oldest names in Arezzo; but while Guido "remembers" his family's roots through the grandsire who "drew rein, slipped saddle, and stabbed knave / For daring gibe" (XI, 104–105), Caponsacchi remembers his through his "father's father's brother" who "spent to the last doit / His bishop's-revenue among the poor, / And used to tend the needy and the sick, / Barefoot, because of his humility" ((ll. 241–244). Both enter the service of the Church. Although Guido prudently keeps his tonsured head in both worlds, Caponsacchi is plagued with scruples of unworthiness, grows restive under the sportive, half-secular regimen of the modern Church, and longs to be a genuine Primitive Christian. Both make their second depositions before the same criminal court—Guido in a voice and posture of obsequious sychophancy, Caponsacchi in a mood of moral outrage, undisguised hostility, grieving bitterness, and careless contempt for judicial, moral, and religious blindness. (Besides the opening foray, see such passages as ll. 1754–1764.) Finally, both Guido and Caponsacchi, with diametrically opposite results, have the experience of Pompilia.

There are four critical moments in the moral and religious baptism through which Caponsacchi passes. One has already been cited—his perception of the grotesque marriage of good and evil (ll. 1446–1478) and the total, though momentary, paralysis which is the result of this terrifying perception. A second moment is his immediate and unequivocal recognition of the pure affinity between himself and Pompilia, also the operation of what is called "elective affinity," and the sense of rebirth and ecstasy Caponsacchi experiences as a result of it (ll. 916–921, 929–958). The third is a rather extensive "interior monologue" (ll. 980–1047), in which Caponsacchi is caught between two appearances of duty—obedience to custom, prudence, self-abnegation and obedience to the electric perception that his true vocation has come. Finally, there is that sublime passage (*sublime* in the strict aesthetic sense of the word) in which Caponsacchi pronounces the sentence which his own experience and personality dictate for Guido (ll. 1879–1925).

Browning uses Caponsacchi to ground the potentiality for spiritual growth in humanity. Both Guido and Pompilia, however opposite they may be in the poem's spiritual framework, are polar, are too far from the center. But against Caponsacchi one can at least measure his conscience and his capacity for singular action.

an old book, line 49: the Bible, which recounts how the soldiers cast lots for Christ's "coat"; *The glory of life . . .* , 118–119: a light suggestion of the Litany of the Virgin; *my eyes and ears and brain and heart*, 190: that is, my whole identity or being; *Old Mercato*, 230: that is, Mercato Vecchio, in Florence; *Ferdinand*, 245: Ferdinand II, "Granduke" of Tuscany (1621–1670); *Diocletian*, 290: Roman Emperor and persecutor of the Christians; *Onesimus*, 314: In Philemon 11–18, Paul asks forgiveness of his son Onesimus and offers to pay anything Onesimus may owe Philemon; *Agrippa*, 316: King Agrippa, by whom St. Paul was sympathetically received; *Fénelon*, 319: French prelate and writer (1651–1715); *Marinesque Adoniad*, 329: that is, write an epic about Adonis like Giovanni Battista Marino's (1569–1625); *Pieve*, 342: the church where he served as Canon; *tarocs*, 345: a card game; *body o' Bacchus*, 382: an elegant "classical" oath; *Catullus*, 384: Catullus's elegiacs are marked by a subtle and original control of the caesura; *Priscian's head*, 385: that is, give the great grammarian a migraine by reciting degenerate Church Latin; *You've Ovid*, 387: afterwards, you can read Ovid to recover; *facchini*, 398: porters; *In ex-cel-sis . . .* , 434–447: in a sacrilegious comic passage, Conti's gossiping is interspersed with over-loud snatches of the vesper service; *passim*, 454–457: an important blending of Caponsacchi's aesthetic and religious sensibilities; *canzonet*, 462: a little love lyric; *Summa*, 479: the *Summa Theologica*, which throughout serves as an inadequate guide to Caponsacchi's noblest impulses; *Thyrsis . . . Myrtilla*, 551: conventional figures in pastoral love poetry, wholly out of keeping with Pompilia's character; *Philomel*, 574: Philomela was raped by her brother-in-law and her tongue cut out so she could not tell, being transformed, according to Ovid, into a nightingale; *Our Lady of all the Sorrows*, 695: one of many comparisons of Pompilia with the Virgin; *Cephisian*, 946: of the Athenian river Cephisus; *corona*, 973: heavenly crown; *fabled garden*, 987: garden of the Hesperides (see Tennyson's poem); *passim*, 995–1047: in this passage, Caponsacchi is caught in the central dilemma of conflicting appearances of duty or obedience; *Our Lady's girdle*, 1086: at the Assumption, the Virgin was said to drop her girdle to Doubting Thomas as proof of the miracle; *God's sea, glassed in gold . . .* , 1143: allusion to the Heavenly City of Revelation; *Parian— coprolite*, 1151: that is, confuse high quality Parian marble with petrified dung; *Vulcan pursuing Mars*, 1434: Venus, wife of Vulcan, was having an affair with Mars; *Cyclops*, 1436: vassals of Vulcan's forge; *Moliere's self*, 1462: in his satire generally, but especially in *Don Juan*; *paten*, 1594: the plate held under the chin of the communicant to catch any particles of the host which may fall; *Pasquin*, 1633: a statue on which scurrilous burlesques were posted; *Bembo*, 1640: a distinguished Italian writer and churchman; *Sub imputatione meretricis / Laborat*, 1665–1666: labors under the charge of being a whore; *Joseph . . . Potiphar*, 1702–1705: Giuseppe, like the biblical Joseph, is innocent of wrong-doing with Potiphar's wife, but is made the occasion for some light banter; *De Raptu Helenae*, 1720–1726: rather poor literary wit based on a rather poor poetic account of the flight of Paris and Helen; *Scazons*, 1724: hexameters with a spondee variation in the sixth foot; *passim*, 1879–1925: this is one of the aesthetically sublime passages in the poem, in which with fearful justice a myth of perversion is the punishment for both Guido and Judas, Guido's prototype; *cockatrice . . . basilisk*, 1921: fabulous serpents, archetypal reptiles, deadly even with a glance; *Probationis ob defectum*, 1984: because of a lack of proof; *Augustinian*, 2031: Pompilia's deathbed confessor.

VII. POMPILIA (p. 436). The challenge that Browning faced in Pompilia's monologue was surely the subtlest in the whole poem. She speaks sixth (after the Prologue) in the accretion of judgments. Although the justness and credibility of her conduct have been more confirmed than undermined, this probability imposes upon the poet's presentation of her even larger demands of tact. If he overscores her inviolate sanctity—makes her a sort of fairy figure above the world's filth—then he has abdicated his avowed purpose of inducing truth out of a genuine complex of conflicting evidence and testimony. If he implicitly assigns to her false motives, then he has broken her will and, with it, her spiritual, moral, and psychological credibility. Several of the chief characteristics of her monologue seem to be the result of the poet's care to avoid these patent pitfalls.

In the first place, she speaks the shortest of the principal monologues; she is "on stage" less expansively. Secondly, she does not protest her own innocence, does not even perceive it as an issue. She knows that some of her closest sympathizers see her and Caponsacchi's relationship as romantic love, but she cannot even bring the idea into focal relationship with knowledge of her own identity or her perception of Caponsacchi's:

> To make me and my friend unself ourselves,
> Be other man and woman than we were!
> (VII, 701–702)

Thirdly, Pompilia lifts her story above the danger of mere pity not only by her persistent resistance to the painful recollections but principally by her irresistible recognition that, although she has lost the lamb-life of her premarital childhood, she has gained infinitely as a result of her ordeal in self-knowledge and the understanding of life:

> I see how needful now,
> Of understanding somewhat of my past,—
> Know life a little, I should leave so soon.
> (VII, 1648–1650)

Further, Pompilia's ordeal of violated innocence is brutally sexual even in her muted account of it. The Archbishop's sophistry first converts her deposit of integrity into heresy (ll. 749–765), then into gross psychological and sexual perversion (ll. 810–840). There is an unmistakable suggestion that the Canon's effrontery has been grossly depraved. Thus she loses, through the forces against her, all sense of the sacredness of her body as a temple of the soul and is driven back upon the soul itself. This fact and the prolonged, humiliating, horrifying sexual abuses to which she must submit (for years, in Percivale's phrase, she is forced to couple with a wolf) is fundamental to an understanding of several of her statements and descriptions of experience: her statement that, after all is said and done, "God plants us where we grow" (l. 298); her epiphanic response to realizing she is pregnant (ll. 1212–1248); the nadir of her spiritual crisis, when she confesses that she is on the brink of the sin of sins—"The frightfulness of my despair in God" (l. 1274); her "elective affinity" for Caponsacchi, that is, her recognition that he is an angelic messenger sent to save her (ll. 1370–1433); the sincerity with which she can even thank Guido (l. 1722) for murdering her—"He burned that garment spotted by the flesh" (l. 1718).

Finally, Pompilia is not aggressively judgmental in her account of her life-adversaries. Violante, who lacked intuition (ll. 323–326), did not realize the nature of genuine truth (ll. 303–309) and made evil out of good intentions.

The Archbishop proved that he "was just man, / And hardly that, and certainly no more" (ll. 842–843). Even Guido, whose "hate was thus the truth of him" (l. 1710), is not without his moral mystery: "So he was made; he nowise made himself . . ." (l. 1714).

Thus Pompilia, although she perceives the opposites of good and evil and their subtler gray gradations, does not try to explain them. She moves rather on an experiential than a rationalistic plane:

> It seems absurd, impossible to-day;
> So seems so much else not explained but known.
> (VII, 1749–1750)

In this she differs significantly from the Pope, who falters in his efforts to "explain" Guido's evil. She posits ultimately only an act of faith in which both innocence and experience unite in a simple but unequivocal affirmation:

> God stooping shows sufficient of His light
> For us i' the dark to rise by. And I rise.
> (VII, 1827–1828)

It is highly significant in appraising Browning's handling of this monologue that it requires little or no annotation. Perhaps only the tapestry of lines 183ff. and 382ff. requires a word of explanation. In the first passage, she and Tisbe identify themselves with the chaste Diana and Daphne, the nymph who escaped the advances of Apollo by having herself changed into a laurel tree; in the second, Perseus is rescuing Andromeda from a sea monster, a leviathan. Browning was perhaps most strongly confirmed in his conception of Pompilia by the testimony, among his sources, of Pompilia's confessor, Don Celestine (l. 31):

I, the undersigned, barefooted Augustinian priest, pledge my faith that inasmuch as I was present, helping Signora Francesca Comparini from the first instant of her pitiable case, even to the very end of her life, I say and attest on my priestly oath, in the presence of the God who must judge me, that to my own confusion I have discovered and marvelled at an innocent and saintly conscience in that ever-blessed child. During the four days she survived, when exhorted by me to pardon her husband, she replied with tears in her eyes and with a placid and compassionate voice: "May Jesus pardon him, as I have already done with all my heart." But what is more to be wondered at is that, although she suffered great pain, I never heard her speak an offensive or impatient word, nor show the slightest outward vexation either toward God or those near by.

You should therefore say that this girl was all goodness and modesty, since with all ease and gladness she performed virtuous and modest deeds even at the very end of her life. Moreover she has died with strong love for God, with great composure, with all the sacred sacraments of the Church, and with the admiration of all bystanders, who blessed her as a saint. I do not say more lest I be taxed with partiality. I know very well that God alone is the searcher of hearts, but I also know that from the abundance of the heart the mouth speaks; and that my great St. Augustine says: "As the life, so its end."

Therefore, having noted in that ever blessed child saintly words, virtuous deeds, most modest acts, and the death of a soul in great fear of God, for the relief of my conscience I am compelled to say, and cannot do otherwise, that necessarily she has ever been a good, modest, and honourable girl, etc.

X. THE POPE (p. 476). It is common in the literature on *The Ring and the Book* to see the Pope as a spokesman for Browning. For example: "The views which he expresses . . . are the views of Robert Browning, and the section of the poem which presents them affords what is often regarded as Browning's finest expression of his philosophical and religious ideas. In an important sense, *The Pope* is more intimately Browning's own monologue than either the first or the last book of the poem, where he speaks in his own person."

Without denying for a moment that the Pope emerges from his monologue as a deeply sympathetic human being or that, like the speakers in other poems (Fra Lippo Lippi, for example, and Andrea del Sarto and Bishop Blougram), he expresses certain ideas and attitudes that are consonant with what we know of Browning's world view, one can still cite several significant bases against viewing the Pope's monologue as "Browning's own." In the first place, such a view stands in flat contradiction to the whole artistic creed upon which the poem rests:

> . . . Art may tell a truth
> Obliquely, do the thing shall breed the thought,
> Nor wrong the thought, missing the mediate word.
> (XII, 851–853)

If the Pope stands between the facts (truth) and the meaning of the facts (Truth) and thus figures as a poet-planted interpreter of the poem, he becomes "the mediate word" and destroys the experiential or "sensational" premise by which, according to Browning, "Art remains the one way possible / Of speaking truth. . . ." (XII, 835–836). Secondly, such a view ultimately diminishes or at least equivocates Browning's achievement in this, one of his most superb dramatic delineations. Setting aside the questionable delicacy of having one who speaks for God the spokesman for oneself ("I it is who have been appointed here / To represent Thee, in my turn, on earth" —X, 1328–1329), a reader who has come to expect from Browning's most inspired efforts a fully projected, distinctive, and credible personality in a critical moment of its development, accustomed to characters subtly integrated on coordinates of emotion, belief, training, memory, historical time, aspiration or the lack of it, the counterplay of public opinion, the necessity of making choices and/or living with the consequences, such a reader has some right to be impatient with the implication that the Pope is not a character of this kind but a half-real, half-imaginary personality got up to enunciate the "philosophical and religious ideas" of a middle-aged Victorian poet. It is surely more just to see the Pope's monologue as a fascinating example in Browning of what Mark Shorer calls "technique as discovery"—that is, an imaginative situation so dynamic and compelling that it becomes a vehicle not for positing ideas but for discovering them. Finally, in his monologue the Pope not only eschews infallibility, he demonstrates his own fallibility in the unsatisfactory manner in which he tries to explicate evil (ll. 398–435). That he functions as a casuist, studying and judging cases of conscience and conduct, is inevitable. He is, after all, the final court of appeal. Nor does one object to his thus talking to himself—Innocent XII to Antonio Pignatelli, "thou / My ancient self" (ll. 382–397). But as a public explanation of the origin of evil, the Pope's exposition does not satisfy; by denying Guido even an average conscience, he has begged not the fact but the question.

[Guido] pines
After the good things just outside the gate,
With less monition, fainter conscience-twitch,
Rarer instinctive qualm at the first feel
Of the unseemly greed and grasp undue,
Than nature furnishes the main mankind,— . . .
(X, 417–422)

Significantly, the Pope does not try to explain Pompilia's goodness, although he extols it above all of his life-experiences and accepts it as a miraculous manifestation of God. Significantly, too, his proffered explanation of Guido's reprobation contradicts his central conception of man's severe circumscription (X, 1303–1367), especially ll. 1337–1341:

Choice of the world, choice of the thing I am,
Both emanate alike from the dread play
Of operation outside this our sphere
Where things are classed and counted small or great,—
Incomprehensibly the choice is Thine!

And it is fair to assume that this wholly human limitation of the Pope was a part of Browning's conscious and careful attention.

The Pope's monologue, like Andrea del Sarto's, is a twilight piece: the twilight of a winter day, of his life and reign, perhaps even of the Christian era. He looks around his post-Renaissance world and through the case before him analyzes the present and prophesies the future. He is conscious of two "luminously self-evident beings," himself and his Creator:

We men, in our degree, may know
There, simply, instantaneously, as here
After long time and amid many lies,
Whatever we dare think we know indeed
—That I am I, as He is He,—what else?
(X, 376–380)

But the self, the identity, he relies on is not that of a Pope with a presumption of infallibility but that of Antonio Pignatelli, "the mere old man of the world, / Supposed inquisitive and dispassionate . . ." (X, 392–393). It is on the basis of his faith in God and his knowledge of himself that he pronounces with complete resolution the degrees of guilt and innocence among the *dramatis personae*. In each case, he sees motive and personality intertwined and inseparable. Thus Guido's motive is gold, his method craft and masked cruelty, with violence unleashed only when safety seemed assured.* Pompilia's motives are the birth of her son and the eradication of evil ("lay low/ The neutraliser of all good and truth," VII, 1579–1580), and her methods are flight and healthy rage:

Thou, patient thus, couldst rise from law to law,
The old to the new, promoted at one cry
O' the trump of God to the new service, not
To longer bear, but henceforth fight, be found
Sublime in new impatience with the foe!
(X, 1050–1055)

* Guido, in his combination of religious fraud, greed, and sexual depravity, reminds one of Chaucer's Pardoner. Certainly he is an exemplum of *Cupiditas est omnium malorum radix.*

Caponsacchi's motive is Pompilia's salvation on both the temporal and the eternal levels, and he springs "Right into the mid-cirque, free fighting-place" (X, 1142), athlete and warrior. Also in the case of each of the principals, the Pope sees an element of the unpredictable and marvelous: Pompilia, the "mere chance-sown, cleft-nursed seed" (X, 1035), flowers into a rose "for the breast of God" (X, 1041); Caponsacchi "In mask and motley, pledged to dance not fight, / Sprang'st forth the hero" (X, 1162–1163); Guido "the astute" perishes because of the simplest, most foolish of oversights, forgetting the warrant or pass (X, 818–852).

The Pope's monologue broadens out to a panoramic overview at l. 1303. Beginning with an extended metaphor of man's mind,

> a convex glass
> Wherein are gathered all the scattered points
> Picked out of the immensity of sky,
> To reunite there, be our heaven on earth,
> Our known unknown, our God revealed to man?
>   (X, 1306–1310)

he proceeds to prophesy the question that Voltaire would articulate in the next century and to answer it:

> Is there strength there?—enough: intelligence?
> Ample: but goodness in a like degree?
> Not to the human eye in the present state,
> This isosceles deficient in the base.
> What lacks, then, of perfection fit for God
> But just the instance which this tale supplies
> Of love without a limit? So is strength,
> So is intelligence; then love is so,
> Unlimited in its self-sacrifice:
> Then is the tale true and God shows complete.
>   (X, 1358–1369)

And his answer to those who see an insuperable difficulty between God's omniscience and benevolence, on the one hand, and the colossus of human suffering, on the other, is the same as that which Hopkins would later make the central theme of *The Wreck of the Deutschland*: "so our heart be struck, / What care I,—by God's gloved hand or the bare?" (X, 1401–1402).

Having reconfirmed "The central truth, Power, Wisdom, Goodness,—God" (X, 1628), he looks, without personal doubt, at the terrifying prospect of individuals and institutions that make up this latter-day Christianity. What he sees is a homocentric world, rife with theories of the noble savage, social amelioration, "the spirit of culture," "Civilization and the Emperor," the "new tribunal" of "the educated man's" (X, 1970–1971), but in which "love and faith" "lie sluggish, curdled at the source . . ." (X, 1543–1545). By contrast, how much worthier of admiration was the tentative search for truth as pursued by Euripides in his pagan ambiance than the "torpor of assurance" with which Christians dull their daily lives seventeen hundred years after the Incarnation? In a passage highly suggestive of Yeats's "The Second Coming," the Pope sees portents of "some revelation":

> No wild beast now prowls round the infant camp;
> We have built wall and sleep in city safe:
> But if the earthquake try the towers, that laugh
> To think they once saw lions rule outside,

Till man stand out again, pale, resolute,
Prepared to die,—that is, alive at last?
As we broke up that old faith of the world,
Have we, next age, to break up this the new— . . .
(X, 1852–1859)

At least for Guido, the quintessence of a world without faith or love (only their counterfeits), this seems the single hope:

So may the truth be flashed out by one blow,
And Guido see, one instant, and be saved.
(X, 2120–2121)

Ahasuerus, line 1: the king in Esther 6:1 who could not sleep and had the chronicles read to him; *Peter . . . Alexander,* 11: that is, St. Peter and Alexander VIII, the preceding Pope; *funeral cyst,* 23: coffin; *passim,* 24–161: the "Formosus question" is a dramatic illustration that, despite the general assumption of infallibility (it was not formally declared a doctrine until 1870), the example of his predecessors is not re-assuring to Innocent XII; IXΘΥΣ, 89: the Greek word for *fish,* each letter being, also, the first letter of the Greek words for *Jesus Christ, God's Son, Saviour,* a symbol of the early Christians and of the Pope; *Fisherman,* 91: Christ made Peter, the first Pope, "a fisher of men"; *Luitprand,* 121: a chronicler of the papacy in its most turbulent days; *Eude,* 133: Odo, king of the West Franks (888–898); *Auxilius,* 136: another medieval chronicler of the papacy; *man's assize to mine,* 169: as a holder of minor orders (beneath those requiring celibacy), Guido could claim the jurisdiction of the Church; *clear rede,* 227: a straight story, no riddle; *Swede,* 292: unidentified; *dip in Virgil,* 296: the *sortes Virgilian,* opening Virgil at random for guidance; *posset,* 327: a drink; *passim,* 382–397: the Pope examines the case, not from the vantage point of papal prerogatives, but that of an experienced man, Antonio Pignatelli, student, priest, bishop, diplomat; *cirque,* 416: arena; *sunscreen, paravent and ombrifuge,* 465: screens from the elements, sun, wind, and rain; *with fifties,* 474: at the miracle of the loaves and fishes, the "companies" "sat down in ranks, by hundreds, and by fifties," Mark 6: 39–40; *soldier-crab,* 509: hermit crab, which inhabits the abandoned shells of others; *gor-crow,* 578: carrion-crow; *Aretine,* 652: Peter Aretine (1492–1557), also a citizen of Arezzo, ribald poet and playwright; *Pieve,* 695: Caponsacchi's church; *the dove's coo,* 747: in Genesis 8, the dove's return to the ark with an olive leaf signals that the flood has subsided; *When Saturn ruled,* 777: that is, the golden age before Zeus, used here to satirize the "noble savage" theme gaining currency; *hebetude,* 811: dull obtuseness; *passim,* 814–828: the Pope sees the hand of God in the absurdity of wily Guido's forgetting the requisite pass; *Rota,* 832: the supreme tribunal in Tuscany; *Abate,* 877: Abbot; *Paul is past reach,* 891: that is, has fled Rome and disappeared, as has Girolamo, 903–905; *new splendid vesture,* 1006: the heavenly garment she will soon wear; *Michael, yonder,* 1007: a statue on top of the Castel S. Angelo; *signet stone,* 1020: "the seal of the living God," Revelation 7: 2–4; *novel claim,* 1065: her pregnancy, which revolutionizes her view of duty; *Him,* 1080: Caponsacchi; *the other rose, the gold,* 1092: the golden rose which the Pope blesses every Lent and presents to a monarch; *leviathan,* 1098: whale or other sea-monster; *lynx-gift,* 1240: sharp-eyed; *misprison,* 1266: a wrong impression; *new philosophy,* 1330: new science, especially astronomy; *transcendent act,* 1334: the Incarnation; *discept / From,* 1346–1347: disagree with; *Convertites,*

1494: a convent of nuns whose work was the rehabilitation of fallen women; *the Fisc*, 1513: Bottinius, prosecutor of Guido, defender of Pompilia, and speaker of Book IX of *The Ring and the Book*; *To-kien*, 1586: Fokien or Fukien; *Maigrot*, 1588: the Pope's Vicar Apostolic in China, who condemned "creeping Confucianism" in the Jesuit teaching of Christian doctrine to the Chinese; *Tournon*, 1598: then Papal Legate to India; *Rosy Cross*, 1614: a Rosicrucian, that is, a member of a sect claiming to be able to change base metal into pure gold; *passim*, 1664–1784: spoken by an imaginary Euripides, Browning's favorite Greek dramatist; *"Know thyself,"* 1692: the motto on the temple at Delphi; *"Take the golden mean!"* 1692: the Aristotelian moral maxim, belonging to the Greeks generally; *the Two*, 1701: Sophocles and Aeschylus; *Paul . . . Felix*, 1711: St. Paul taught Christian principles to Felix, Roman governor of Jerusalem; *Galileo's tube*, 1724: the telescope; *Paul . . . Seneca*, 1786: the "legend" that St. Paul and Seneca corresponded with each other; *Nero's cross*, 1827: on which the early Christians were martyred; *Molinists*, 1863: see note to l. 203, "Count Guido Franceschini"; *antimasque . . . kibe*, 1898: a comic interlude on the "heel" of the masque itself; *first experimentalist*, 1904: Caponsacchi; *morrice*, 1919: a dance as complicated as a maze; *Loyola*, 1936: Ignatius Loyola (1491–1556), founder of the Jesuits; *nemini / Honorem trado*, 1980–1981: I trust my fame to no one's keeping; *Farinacci*, 1998: a late authority on canon law; *Barabbas*, 2050: Pilate offered the people the freedom of Christ or of Barabbas, and they claimed Barabbas; *three little taps*, 2054: the taps on the forehead with a silver mallet before the Chamberlain announces the Pope's death; *petit-maitre priestlings*, 2063: little puffed-up worldly priests; *Sanctus et Benedictus*, 2064: Holy and Blessed; *non tali . . . / Auxilio*, 2083–2084: the words of Hecuba to Priam (Aeneid, II, 521–522) meaning the times do not call for such help as Innocent is prepared to give.

ARNOLD

QUIET WORK (p. 526). Arnold considered this Petrarchan sonnet, from his first verses to the final arrangement of his poetry, as a kind of motto not only for his poetic labors but for his life.

MYCERINUS (p. 526). In a note Arnold tells part of the story of Herodotus which provided the seed of the poem's fiction.

After Cephren, Mycerinus, son of Cheops, reigned over Egypt. He abhorred his father's courses, and judged his subjects more justly than any of their kings had done. —To him there came an oracle from the city of Buto, to the effect that he was to live but six years longer, and to die in the seventh year from that time. [*Here Arnold's note ends.*] The king deemed this unjust, and sent back to the oracle a message of reproach, blaming the god: why must he die so soon who was pious, whereas his father and his uncle had lived long, who shut up the temples, and regarded not the gods, and destroyed men? But a second utterance from the place of divination declared to him that his good deeds were the very cause of shortening his life; for he had done what was contrary to fate; Egypt should have been afflicted for an hundred and fifty years, whereof the two kings before him had been aware, but not Mycerinus. Hearing this, he knew that his doom was fixed. Therefore he caused many lamps to be made, and would light these at nightfall and drink and make merry; by day or night he never ceased from reveling, roaming to the marsh country and the groves and wherever he heard of the likeliest places of pleasure. Thus he planned, that by turning night into day he might make his six years into twelve and so prove the oracle false.

From this account of fate's irony and of man's ingenious but self-defeating efforts to outwit the gods, and from the domestic proverb that "the good die young," Arnold created one of his most accomplished early poems, presenting a new mytho-historical archetype of the disillusioned idealist and the cluster of intellectual and moral questions he must face. The first part of the poem (ll. 1–78) is dramatically conceived; there is a carefully muted tension between the speaker's resolve and the questions with which he is haunted. This has its counterpart in the blank verse narrative of the poem's second part (ll. 79–127), signaled by the series of alternative readings that are introduced with "It may be. . . ."

TO A FRIEND (p. 529).
thou, line 1: unidentified for certain, but perhaps Arthur Hugh Clough; *these bad days*, 1: perhaps the "bad days" of "French Revolutions, Chartism, Manchester Insurrections" of which Carlyle had written in *Past and Present*; *old man*, 2: Homer; *he*, 5: Epictetus, Stoic philosopher of the first century A.D., banished from Rome by the Emperor Domitian; *Arrian*, 7: pupil of Epictetus and Greek historian; *his*, 8: Sophocles.

SHAKESPEARE (p. 530). Shakespeare is here viewed as an exemplification of the "Olympian" poet described in lines 130–206 of *The Strayed Reveller*.

THE STRAYED REVELLER (p. 530). In this brief dramatic interlude, with its admirable experimental use of free verse, Arnold presents his first allegory of the poetic life and the options available to the poet. (It was the title poem in his first volume.) The youth is obviously a poet-aspirant who has seen the "wild-hair'd Maenad," the "Faun with torches," "The desired, the divine, / Beloved Iacchus," and been instructed by Silenus, satyr and tutor of Dionysus (Bacchus), that the Gods extract from bards the "labour" and "pain" of becoming what they sing. The youth has neither the experience nor the fortitude to assume this last Romantic role of the poet (ll. 207–260); the "Olympian" role of classical, detached objectivity (ll. 130–206) is not available to him; hence he "strays" into the portico of Circe's Palace in search of an alternative, a narcotic magnification of "the wild, thronging train, / The bright procession / Of eddying forms . . ." (ll. 3–5, 294–296) with which he has had some experience already (ll. 270–281). Again it should be noted that he is a *strayed* reveller.

Iacchus, line 38: Bacchus or Dionysus; *Ampelus*, 78: son of a satyr and a nymph and beloved of Bacchus; *Tiresias*, 135: called upon by Zeus and Hera to judge which sex derives more pleasure from love-making, Tiresias sided with Zeus that women do, and he was struck blind by the angry Hera and, by the grateful Zeus, given the powers of a seer and life for seven generations; *Centaurs*, 143: wild, lusty, uncivilized "people," half man, half horse; *Scythian*, 162: nomadic tribe north of the Black Sea; *Chorasmian stream*, 183: the Oxus river south of the Aral Sea; *Lapithae . . . Alcmena's dreadful son*, 228–231: at the marriage feast of the king of the Lapiths, a Centaur got drunk and tried to carry off the bride, bringing down the ire and the arms of the Lapiths (aided by Theseus, king of Athens) upon the Centaurs, an incident repeated by a Centaur against Hercules' wife, for which he was killed; *Argo*, 259: ship of Jason and the Argonauts in search of the Golden Fleece; *Silenus*, 261: satyr and tutor of Bacchus.

THE FORSAKEN MERMAN (p. 537). Arnold has adroitly reinterpreted the Danish ballad and has created a uniquely lyrical dramatic monologue. The tone of the poem has a quality of "eternal sadness" like *Dover Beach*; the theme, with only a slight change in perspective, is very much like that of *To Marguerite—Continued*:

> A God, a God their severance ruled!
> And bade betwixt their shores to be
> The unplumb'd, salt, estranging sea.

It is significant that, although the merman's personality or character is fully and sympathetically elaborated, the loneliness and nostalgic longing of Margaret as she fulfills the demands of her humanity relieve her of any personal charge of betrayal. This separation of the primitive and the societal happened long, long ago and was nobody's fault. Finally, the poet imitates with remarkable success in his verse the sounds/voices of the sea which induce mermaid legends.

MEMORIAL VERSES (p. 540). Wordsworth died on April 23, 1850; the fair copy manuscript of the poem is dated "April 27th 1850."

STANZAS IN MEMORY OF THE AUTHOR OF 'OBERMANN' (p. 542). Like so many of Arnold's poems, these elegiac stanzas attempt to pinpoint the cultural significance of a creative historical figure who is both individual and, to a degree, representative. Thus in his note to the poem Arnold stressed the mirror function of Senancour, author of the letters entitled *Obermann*: "The stir of all the main forces, by which modern life is and has been impelled, lives in the letters of *Obermann*; the dissolving agencies of the eighteenth century, the fiery storm of the French Revolution, the first faint promise and dawn of the new world which our own time is but now more fully bringing to light,—all these are to be felt, almost to be touched, there." Again, in his essay on Senancour (*Essays in Criticism*, Third Series), Arnold made important distinctions between this author's responses to these forces and the responses of other representative contemporaries:

> His constant inwardness, his unremitting occupation with that question which haunted St. Bernard—*Bernarde, ad quid veniste?*—distinguished him from Goethe and Wordsworth, whose study of this question [*why were you born?*] is relieved by the thousand distractions of a poetic interest in nature and in man. His severe sincerity distinguished him from Rousseau, Chateaubriand, or Byron, who in their dealing with this question are so often attitudinising and thinking of the effect of what they say on the public. His exquisite feeling for nature, though always dominated by his inward self-converse and by

his melancholy, yet distinguished him from the men simply absorbed in philosophical or religious concerns, and places him in the rank of men of poetry and imagination.

That Arnold felt an acute sympathy for the response to "The hopeless tangle of [his] age" symbolized by Obermann seems clear enough (he underscores it as a genuine alternative in *Empedocles on Etna,* in *Stanzas from the Grande Chartreuse,* and elsewhere); but it is also clear that he was acutely critical, with himself and others, of this response.

Obermann, title: Etienne Pivert de Senancour "was born in 1770. He was educated for the priesthood, and passed some time in the seminary of St. Sulpice; broke away from the seminary and from France itself, and passed some years in Switzerland, where he married; returned to France in middle life, and followed thenceforward the career of a man of letters, but with hardly any fame or success. He died an old man in 1846, desiring that on his grave might be placed these words only: *Eternite, deviens mon asile!"* (Arnold's note); *baths,* line 5: "The Baths of Leuk. This poem was conceived, and partly composed in the valley going down from the foot of the Gemmi Pass towards the Rhone." (Arnold's note); *tranquil world,* 67: that is, the third quarter of the eighteenth century, before revolutionary forces reached their zenith; *son of Thetis,* 89: Achilles, lamenting the death of Patroclus; *Jaman,* 114: a peak in the Alps; *Lake Leman,* 121: the Lake of Geneva; *Children of the Second Birth,* 143: "Marvel not that I say unto you, ye must be born again" (Arnold to Clough); *anchorite,* 150: monk or hermit; V*evey and Meillerie,* 164: towns along the Lake of Geneva; *grave,* 180: Senancour was buried at Sevres, near Paris.

EMPEDOCLES ON ETNA (p. 547). It is now generally held that *Empedocles on Etna* is Arnold's chief single poem. Like *In Memoriam* but for a sharply delimited audience, it is one of the most significant poetic productions of the period. Further, it represents a unique phase in Arnold's evolving poetic theory and poetic practice: he worked on it from 1849 to 1852; it was the title piece of his second volume, *Empedocles on Etna, and Other Poems* (1852); it was dropped from his canon in 1853 and "censured" in the crucial preface of that year; it was reprinted in 1867, according to Arnold, "at the request of a man of genius, whom it had the honor and the good fortune to interest,—Mr. Robert Browning." Arnold's basic reason for excluding the poem was given in the 1853 preface:

> What, then, are the situations, from the representation of which, though accurate, no poetical enjoyment can be derived? They are those in which the suffering finds no vent in action; in which a continuous state of mental distress is prolonged, unrelieved by incident, hope, or resistance; in which there is everything to be endured, nothing to be done. In such situations there is inevitably something morbid, in the description of them something monotonous. When they occur in actual life, they are painful, not tragic; the representation of them in poetry is painful also.

In this preface, Arnold was trying to accomplish several things. He was trying to correct a prevalent theory of poetry—the theory that "A true allegory of the state of one's own mind in a representative history is perhaps the highest thing that one can attempt in the way of poetry." He was trying to reassert, in his own terms, some of the forgotten sanity of Wordsworth's preface of 1800. He was trying, especially for himself and hence nonprescriptively, to identify the modern relevance of classical models: ". . . in the sincere endeavour to learn and practise, amid the bewildering confusion of our times, what is true and sound in poetic art, I seemed to myself to find the only sure guidance, the only solid footing, among the ancients." *Empedocles on Etna*, he seemed to feel, for all its classical sources and subject matter and accuracy, had been contaminated by the spirit of his own bewildered age. In a letter to Clough, dated September 23, 1849, Arnold had written: "these are damned times—everything is against one—the height to which knowledge is come, the spread of luxury, our physical enervation, the absence of great *natures*, the unavoidable contact with millions of small ones, newspapers, cities, light profligate friends, moral desperadoes like Carlyle, —our own selves, and the sickening consciousness of our difficulties."

It is not surprising, then, that *Empedocles on Etna* has a high degree of relevance to Arnold's own spiritual and cultural climate. That was what the modern poet—the critic of life—was all about. In fact, as the letters to Clough, the preface, and the inaugural lecture as professor of poetry at Oxford (1857) all show, Arnold's prevailing concern during the 1850's was the question of poetry's relevance. Nothing long held his attention unless it contained a high and fundamental degree of relevance; he even defined the "modern element in literature" as, not that which is newest or most contemporaneous, but that which is most relevant. Looking back on his then all-but-complete poetic career, Arnold wrote in 1869: "My poems represent, on the whole, the main movement of mind of the last quarter of a century, and thus they will probably have their day as people become conscious to themselves of what that movement of mind is, and interested in the literary productions which reflect it. It might be fairly urged that I have less poetical sentiment than Tennyson, and less intellectual vigor and abundance than Browning; yet, because I have perhaps more of a fusion of the two than either of them, and have more regularly applied that fusion to the main line of modern development, I am likely enough to have my turn as they have had theirs."

However, emphasis on the modern applicability in *Empedocles on Etna* has sometimes led to two critical distortions in commentary on the poem: that the poem has *more* to do with *Arnold's age* than with that of Empedocles; that the poem has *more* to do with *Arnold himself* than with Empedocles.

To the first distortion, one can reply simply, *not proved*. None of the commentators who have made the assertion has demonstrated a knowledge of the subject more expert than Arnold's own; and while Arnold censured the poem for its inadequacy as a tragic representation, he maintained that it was an "accurate" and "interesting" representation. The second distortion is at once more crucial and more slippery: more crucial because it ultimately represents a challenge to the poet's integrity; more slippery because it is too attractive a premise to a large readership ever to be successfully contradicted. Arnold himself denied, rather assertively, that the poem was philosophically autobiographical:

> Empedocles was composed fifteen years ago, when I had been much studying the remains of the early Greek religious philosophers, as they are called; he greatly impressed me, and I desired to gather up and

draw out as a whole the hints which his remains offered. Traces of an impatience with the language and assumptions of the popular theology of the day may very likely be visible in my work, and I have now, and no doubt had still more then, a sympathy with the figure Empedocles presents to the imagination; but neither then nor now would my creed, if I wished or were able to draw it out in black and white, be by any means identical with that contained in the preachment of Empedocles.

"Tut, Tut, Matthew," say the commentators, "we have found you out. Why, it's probably even true that you suppressed the poem, not for the reasons you assert, but for the reasons we have discovered—namely, you had inadvertently exposed the real you." Their argument runs something like this: in the poem there are parallels ("influences") to Senancour, Carlyle, Byron, Shakespeare, Goethe, and so forth; therefore, *Empedocles* is indeed Arnold's *Werther*, etc. Why not reason instead that Arnold, through his own sensibility and his sympathetic reading of significant Elizabethan and post-Elizabethan authors, had perceived the world of the modern intellectual to be one from which "the calm, the cheerfulness, the disinterested objectivity have disappeared." He discerned: "The dialogue of the mind with itself has commenced; modern problems have presented themselves; we hear . . . the doubts, we witness the discouragement, of Hamlet and of Faust." Then he discovered Empedocles and was struck by profound parallels between the ancient Sicilian and the modern European, between the philosopher-poet in exile in the fifth century B.C. and a philosopher-poet alien in his own world of the seventeenth, eighteenth, and nineteenth centuries. Placed in that cultural frame, Empedocles is no more Arnold than Manfred is—or than Hamlet, Faust, Mycerinus, Antigone, and Sohrab are. Arnold's prose outline of the poem confirms the objective nature of his treatment:

He is a philosopher.

He has not the religious consolation of other men, facile because adapted to their weaknesses, or because shared by all around and charging the atmosphere they breathe.

He sees things as they are—the world as it is—God as he is: in their stern simplicity.

The sight is a severe and mind-tasking one: to know the mysteries which are communicated to others by fragments, in parables.

But he started towards it in hope: his first glimpses of it filled him with joy: he had friends who shared his hope and joy and communicated to him theirs: even now he does not deny that the sight is capable of affording rapture and the purest peace.

But his friends are dead: the world is all against him, and incredulous of the truth: his mind is overtasked by the effort to hold fast so great and severe a truth in solitude: the atmosphere he breathes not being modified by the presence of human life, is too rare for him. He perceives still the truth of the truth, but cannot be transported and rapturously agitated by its grandeur: his spring and elasticity of mind are gone: he is clouded, oppressed, dispirited, without hope and energy.

Before he becomes the victim of depression and overtension of mind, to the utter deadness of joy, grandeur, spirit, and animated life, he desires to die; to be reunited with the universe, before by exaggerating his human side he has become utterly estranged from it.

In the preface Arnold speaks of his "sympathy with the figure Empedocles presents to the imagination. . . ." The center of his interest in Empedocles was dramatic, not argumentative, more psychological than philosophical. He was fascinated with how this ancient prototype of modernism faced his problem and how he answered the question which *Hamlet* phrased for all later generations:

> To be, or not to be—that is the question.
> Whether 'tis nobler in the mind to suffer
> The slings and arrows of outrageous fortune,
> Or to take arms against a sea of troubles
> And by opposing end them. (III, i)

The fundamental reason for Empedocles' suicide, elaborated in Act II, ll. 218–234, demonstrates that the poem is *primarily* psychological, *secondarily* philosophical. It is not despair of faith that drives Empedocles to the crater, but *ennui* or *Weltschmerz*—the imperious, unsatisfying wandering between the marketplace with its idols and the Ivory Tower with its austerity and loneliness. Hence the last emblem which he puts aside is the "laurel bough" and his address to Apollo is "Thou young, implacable God!"

The three characters in the poem (all of whom are treated sympathetically) represent three stages in the pilgrimage of man. Callicles is the young poet, filled with the freshness of the early world. He is joyful and credulous, seeing without misgiving Apollo and the Muses marching round him, and in love with all the mythology he sings about. Like Empedocles, however, he has begun although unconsciously to develop the inevitable pattern. His life oscillates between the fun-loving crowd and an escape into the hills with his harp. He, too, will be a wanderer between two worlds, and one day like Empedocles he will face the ultimate dilemma. Pausanias stands between them. He is practical and sympathetic, yet like the generality of men relies not on wisdom but on "drugs to charm with / . . . spells to mutter— / All the fool's armoury of magic!" (Act II, ll. 116–118). The long ode Empedocles chants (I, ii, 77–426) is his way of repaying Pausanias for his devotion, and of giving him a wisdom superior to "spells."

In this ode Empedocles preaches stoical moderation (ll. 422–436). Then why does he commit suicide? On the psychological level, he doesn't: he acts out of faith, not despair; he seeks salvation, not (like Dr. Faustus) annihilation. In his last speech his mood is exultant (ll. 404–416).

I, i: *Catana,* line 4: village at the foot of Mt. Etna; *Agrigentum, and Olympia,* 64: cities in Sicily and Greece, respectively; *Peisianax,* 73: a wealthy patron in Syracuse.

I, ii: *passim,* lines 57–76: both Achilles and his father Peleus were instructed by Chiron in the rudiments of the heroic life; Empedocles in turn will instruct Pausanias (77ff.) to face fundamentally changed conditions with stoical moderation; *Cadmus and Harmonia,* 436: Cadmus, the founder of Thebes, married Harmonia, daughter of Ares and Aphrodite, and was favored by the gods until he killed a snake, sacred to Mars; after much calamity, both he and Harmonia were turned into snakes at their request; *Ismenus,* 442: a river near Thebes.

II: *Typho,* line 41: "Mount Haemus, so called, said the legend, from Typho's blood spilt on it in his last battle with Zeus, when the giant's strength failed, owing to the Destinies having a short time before given treacherously to him, for his refreshment, perishable fruits" (Arnold's note); *Marsyas,* 128: a faun who, because of the urging of Pan, challenged Apollo to a musical contest and when he lost was flayed alive; *Pytho*, 205: a serpent slain by Apollo. *Parmenides*, 235: a philosopher and contemporary of Empedocles; *Sun-born Virgins*, 239: daughters of Helios, patron of Sicily; *Helicon*, 423: Mount of the Muses ("the Nine").

ISOLATION. TO MARGUERITE (p. 573) and TO MARGUERITE—CONTINUED (p. 574) are two from the cluster of love poems having the umbrella-title *Switzerland* and centering around a girl called Marguerite, apparently pronounced MAR·GRET, as in *The Forsaken Merman*. The evidence that she was a real girl with whom Arnold had a crucial affair of the heart is tenuous, although the poems, especially as Arnold viewed them in retrospect (he altered titles and arrangement until 1869), do seem to reflect a decisive moment in his life. The poems' *literary* analogues (in Wordsworth, Keats, Goethe, Ugo Foscolo, and the canon of Arnold's poems generally) suggest that their "fiction" is imaginary.

Luna, line 20: Diana, goddess of the moon, the hunt, and chastity, fell in love with Endymion when she saw the young shepherd sleeping on Mt. Latmos.

THE BURIED LIFE (p. 575). This is another of the "Know then thyself" poems recurrent, not only in the Arnold canon (cf. "Self-Dependence" and "Dover Beach") but also in classical (Sophocles), neoclassical (Pope), and romantic (Wordsworth) literature. Like "Dover Beach" it is cast in the form of a dramatic monologue. Like "To Marguerite—Continued," it concerns the piercing sense of estrangement—even from his "love," even from himself—which haunts the sensitive, reflective man. Like "Dover Beach" the poem progresses dramatically from one sense of reality to another, but by a different route and to a different resolution. In "Dover Beach" the movement is from "calm" to "clash"; in "The Buried Life" from "a war of mocking words" to a deep psychological and spiritual awareness of self.

SELF-DEPENDENCE (p. 577). On February 12, 1853, Arnold had written to Clough as follows: "You ask me in what I think or have thought you going wrong: in this: that you would never take your assiette as something determined final and unchangeable for you and proceed to work away on the basis of that: but were always poking and patching and cobbling at the assiette itself—could never finally, as it seemed—'resolve to be thyself'—. . . ."

LINES WRITTEN IN KENSINGTON GARDENS (p. 579) and MORALITY (p. 578). These two poems are frequently cited by critics documenting recurrent Wordsworthian motifs in Arnold's poetry. The former is seen as reminiscent of *Composed upon Westminster Bridge*, the latter of *Intimations of Immortality*. This is fair as far as it goes, but it should be noted that in both of Arnold's poems a would-be consoling perception is counterpointed by a persistent anxiety and longing.

THE SCHOLAR-GIPSY (p. 580) and THYRSIS (p. 612). These two poems, which some critics have classed as Arnold's finest, are companion pieces. They employ the same stanza form, the same "artless" diction, and the same reliance upon the pastoral tradition—"the old beautiful use of the language of shepherds, of flocks and pipes" (Swinburne). Both celebrate a particular topography inextricably joined with a recollected spiritual phase of the speaker's life. Arthur Hugh Clough and the Scholar-Gipsy (*his* quest, *their* quest for him) figure predominantly in both poems., *Thyrsis* is, of course, specifically an elegy for a dead poet-friend; but Arnold chose to use the pastoral tradition as a controlling distance, something he had established a decade earlier in *The Scholar-Gipsy.* Thus Arnold admitted that "if one reads the poem as a memorial poem, . . . not enough is said about Clough in it; I feel this so much that I do not send the poem to Mrs. Clough. Still Clough *had* this idyllic [as opposed to a prophetic] side, too; to deal with this suited my desire to deal with that Cumner country: anyway, only so could I treat the matter this time." Thus he disciplined his elegiac stanzas to the model of poets like Theocritus and Milton rather than to the dark night of *In Memoriam.*

As Arnold himself acknowledged, a passage in Joseph Glanvil's *The Vanity of Dogmatizing* (1661) was "the oft-real tale" which supplied the legend for *The Scholar-Gipsy*:

There was very lately a Lad in the *University of Oxford,* who being of very pregnant and ready parts, and yet wanting the encouragement of preferment; was by his poverty forc'd to leave his studies there, and to cast himself upon the wide world for a livelyhood. Now, his necessities growing dayly on him, and wanting the help of friends to relieve him; he was at last forced to joyn himself to a company of *Vagabond Gypsies,* whom occasionally he met with, and to follow their Trade for a maintenance. Among these extravagant people, by the insinuating subtilty of his carriage, he quickly got so much of their love, and esteem; as that they discover'd to him their *Mystery:* in the practice of which, by the pregnancy of his wit and parts he soon grew so good a proficient, as to be able to out-do his Instructours. After he had been a pretty while well exercis'd in the Trade; there chanc'd to ride by a couple of *Scholars* who had formerly bin of his acquaintance. The *Scholars* had quickly spyed out their old friend, among the *Gypsies*; and their amazement to see him among such society, had well-nigh discover'd him: but by a sign he prevented their owning him before that Crew: and taking one of them aside privately, desired him with his friend to go to an *Inn,* not far distant thence, promising there to come to them. They accordingly went thither, and he follows: after their first salutations, his friends enquire how he came to lead so odd a life as that was, and to joyn himself to such a *cheating beggerly* company. The Scholar-Gipsy having given them an account of the necessity, which drove him to that kind of life; told them, that the people he went with were not such *Impostours* as they were taken for, but that they had a *traditional* kind of *learning* among them, and could do wonders by the power of Imagination, and that himself had learnt much of their Art, and improved it further then themselves could. And to evince the truth of what he told them, he said, he'd remove into another room, leaving them to discourse together and upon his return tell them the sum of what they had talked of: which accordingly he perform'd, giving them a full account of what had pass'd between them in his absence. The Scholars being amaz'd at so unexpected a discovery, earnestly desir'd him to unriddle the *mystery.* In which he gave them satisfaction, by telling them, that what he did was by the power of *Imagination,* his Phancy *binding* theirs; and that himself had dictated to them the discourse, they held together, while he was from them: That there were warrantable wayes of heightening the *Imagination* to that pitch, as to bind anothers; and that when he had compass'd the whole *secret,* some parts of which he said he was yet ignorant of, he intended to leave their company, and give the world an account of what he had learned.

Arthur Hugh Clough (1819–1861) preceded Matthew Arnold both to Rugby and to Oxford, but they "launched" their poetic careers in the same year (1849). One of the most gifted and honest intellectuals of his generation, Clough carried forward a supportive friendship and substantive dialogue with Arnold especially during the late '40's and early '50's, when the latter was trying to get perspective on both life and art. (Arnold's letters to Clough, edited by H. F. Lowry, Oxford, 1932, are indispensable for a study of Arnold's inner life during this period.) For example, on November 30, 1853, Arnold wrote to Clough about *The Scholar-Gipsy*:

> I am glad you like the Gipsy Scholar—but what does it *do* for you? Homer *animates*—Shakespeare *animates*—in its poor way I think Sohrab and Rustum *animates*—the Gipsy Scholar at best awakens a pleasing melancholy. But this is not what we want.
>
> > The complaining millions of men
> > Darken in labour and pain—
>
> what they want is something to *animate* and *ennoble* them—not merely to add zest to their melancholy or grace to their dreams. —I believe a feeling of this kind is the basis of my nature—and of my poetics.

(For annotation of details in *Thyrsis*, see p. 686.)

wattled cotes, line 2: sheepfolds made of woven twigs; *the quest,* 10: for the Scholar-Gipsy; *Hurst,* 57: Cumner Hurst, a hill near Oxford; *Berkshire,* 58: the county separated from Oxfordshire by the Thames; *ingle-bench,* 59: that is, in the chimney corner; *punt's rope,* 76: ferry-boat's rope, vibrating in the wind; *Christ-Church hall,* 129: dining hall at Christ Church College; *teen,* 147: sorrow; *just-passing Genius,* 149: perhaps the Spirit of Life *and* Death, to whom our existence is a mere matter of seconds; *one,* 182, and *wisest,* 191: Carlyle, Goethe, and Tennyson have all been suggested, the last on the basis of *In Memoriam; anodynes,* 190: drugs to assuage pain; *Dido,* 208: Dido scorned Aeneas, whose desertion had brought about her death, when they met in Hades; *Tyrian,* 232: a Phoenician from Tyre; *Midland waters,* 244: the Mediterranean; *Syrtes,* 245: gulfs of Sidra and Cabes on the northern coast of Africa; *western straits,* 247: Straits of Gibraltar; *Iberians,* 249: primitive inhabitants of the Iberian (Spanish-Portuguese) peninsula; *passim,* 232–250: this is an example of the "codas" with which Arnold sometimes ended his poems, providing in miniature a metaphoric analogue with which to gloss the preceding stanzas.

SOHRAB AND RUSTUM (p. 586). *Sohrab and Rustum* was the lead-off poem in Arnold's *Poems* of 1853, taking the place which (the now-suppressed) *Empedocles on Etna* held in the volume of 1852. It seems altogether likely, then, that Arnold meant *Sohrab and Rustum* to illustrate in a positive way the poetic principles he laid down in the preface of 1853: namely, to create a great and noble action through which to trace "the great primary human affections"; to present that action so that "the feeling . . . developed gives importance to the action and situation, and not the action and situation to the feeling"; to provide a high degree of poetical enjoyment by telling a genuine tragic action in language that does not detract from that action by attracting attention to itself

Sohrab and Rustum is called "An Episode," and this fact suggests that Arnold intended the poem as a self-contained "mirror portion" of what one could imagine to be a larger epic. Arnold was not posturing as an epic poet.

He did borrow from the epic tradition in obvious ways: he begins *in medias res*; he gives his narrative a heroic setting and variations on the heroic type; he uses the nearest English equivalent of heroic narrative verse, namely blank verse; he employs epic roll-calls and epic similes. But he was not writing a miniature epic; he was testing and illustrating a corrective theory of narrative/dramatic poetry.

That Arnold succeeded in giving "poetical enjoyment" is undeniable. *Sohrab and Rustum* has been a favorite of more than four generations of poetry-readers. That the unfamiliar myth had a high degree of modern relevance even unsuspecting critics have confirmed. They have read the conflict of Thomas Arnold and Matthew Arnold into the poem. They have called it, by analogy with T. S. Eliot, another *Waste Land*. They have seen in it the lonely alienation of modern life: Sohrab is unknown even to his own father; he is a soldier in an alien army; he is, in a sense, searching for his own identity. Rustum, himself far from home and out of harmony with man and nature, appears upon the field of combat *in disguise*. The grand "modern" irony of the situation is that Sohrab unwittingly battles his father in order to find his father, and Rustum battles his unknown son with a fury half-inspired by belief that he has no son. That the poet succeeded in subordinating language to action can be shown with three climactic lines (857–859):

> So, on the bloody sand, Sohrab lay dead;
> And the great Rustum drew his horseman's cloak
> Down o'er his face, and sate by his dead son.

The image is everything; the language serves only to make the image possible. All critics do not agree that the action of the episode is genuinely tragic. Certainly the effect of the poem hardly rises above the pathetic if Sohrab is seen as the protagonist. But Arnold insists upon a character flaw in Rustum which brings about the tragedy: he is peevish over neglect, rebellious against the fate that has given him a daughter, stung into action by pride, jealous of his fame, merciless toward Sohrab in the contest before onlooking armies. Moreover, Rustum does gain self-knowledge, and his heart pent up with pride does, through suffering, will its own punishment.

In Arnold's own note for this poem, he gives his source of the story as Sir John Malcolm's *History of Persia* and then quotes it directly:

> The young Sohrab was the fruit of one of Rustum's early amours. He has left his mother, and sought fame under the banners of Afrasiab, whose armies he commanded and soon obtained a renown beyond that of all contemporary heroes but his father. He had carried death and dismay into the ranks of the Persians, and had terrified the boldest warriors of that country, before Rustum encountered him, which at last that hero resolved to do, under a feigned name. They met three times. The first time they parted by mutual consent, though Sohrab had the advantage; the second, the youth obtained a victory, but granted life to his unknown father; the third was fatal to Sohrab, who, when writhing in the pangs of death, warned his conqueror to shun the vengeance that is inspired by parental woes, and bade him dread the rage of the mighty Rustum, who must soon learn that he had slain his son Sohrab. These words, we are told, were as death to the aged hero; and when he recovered from a trance, he called in despair for proofs of what Sohrab had said. The afflicted and dying youth tore open his mail, and showed his father a seal which his mother had placed on his arm when she discovered to him the secret of his birth,

and bade him seek his father. The sight of his own signet rendered Rustum quite frantic; he cursed himself, attempting to put an end to his existence, and was only prevented by the efforts of his expiring son. After Sohrab's death, he burnt his tents and all his goods, and carried the corpse to Seistan, where it was interred; the army of Turan was, agreeably to the last request of Sohrab, permitted to cross the Oxus unmolested. To reconcile us to the improbability of this tale, we are informed that Rustum could have no idea his son was in existence. The mother of Sohrab had written to him her child was a daughter, fearing to lose her darling infant if she revealed the truth; and Rustum, as before stated, fought under a feigned name, an usage not uncommon in the chivalrous combats of those days.

Oxus, line 2: river in central Asia; *Peran-Wisa*, 11: leader of the Tartars; *Pamere*, 15: plateau in the Caucasus mountains; *thick piled*, 25: heavy-napped; *Afrasiab*, 38: king of the Tartars; *Samarcand*, 40: luxurious commercial city in Turkestan; *Ader-baijan*, 42: Persian home of Sohrab's mother; *Seistan*, 82: region east of the Persian Gulf; *Persian King*, 85: Kai Khosroo; *Kara-Kul*, 101: Bakhara, province famous for its sheep; *Casbin*, 113: city in northern Persia; *Elburz*, 114: mountain in northern Persia; *Aralian*, 114: of the Aral Sea; *frore*, 115: frozen; *Khiva*, 120: region south of the Aral Sea; *ferment*, 120: Kumiss, a drink made of mare's milk; *Toorkmuns*, 121: a Turkish tribe; *Tukas*, 122: a tribe from northwest Persia; *Salore*, 122: a tribe from east of the Caspian Sea; *Attruck*, 123: river in northern Persia; *Ferghans*, 128: region in Turkestan; *Jaxartes*, river in Turkestan; *Kipchak*, 131: region east of the Aral Sea; *Kuz-zaks*, 132: Cossacks; *Kirghizzes*, 133: nomadic tribes from northern Turkestan; *Ilyats of Khorassan*, 138: tribes from northeastern Persia; *Cabool*, 160: Kabul, in Afghanistan; *Indian Caucasus*, 161: mountains between Turkestan and Afghanistan; *snow-hair'd Zal*, 232: Rustum's father, born with the disgrace of snow-white hair, was left in the mountains to die but was rescued by a griffin; *plain arms*, 257: his disguise; *Bahrein*, 286: islands famous for their pearl beds; *tale*, 288: number; *Hyphasis or Hydaspes*, 412: rivers in northern India; *autumn star*, 452: the Dog Star, symbol of the "dog days"; *Koords*, 592: tribes in northwestern Persia; *Sir*, 765: another name for the Jaxartes River; *Jemshid in Persepolis*, 861: Jemshid, Persian king and legendary founder of Persepolis, was said to have ruled for 700 years; *Chorasmian waste*, 878: desert south of the Aral Sea; *Orgunje*, 880: town on the Oxus.

PHILOMELA (p. 605). There are several versions of the legend this poem is based on, including some which switch the roles of Philomela as a nightingale and Procne as a swallow. (Some modern poets, for example Keats, make the nightingale a metaphor for the poet and some, for example Tennyson, make the swallow that metaphor.) Arnold's version, it seems, was this: Tereus, king of Daulis, married Philomela, daughter of the king of Attica and sister of Procne. Tired of Philomela and lustful for her sister, he raped Procne and cut out her tongue so she could not tell. Procne wove the story into a tapestry and informed her sister. Philomela, horrified, took revenge by killing Itylus, Tereus's son and hers, and serving him to the king for dinner. Tereus discovered the crime and pursued the sisters to slay them. The gods interceded by turning Philomela into a nightingale and Procne into a swallow. (In some versions, Tereus was turned into a hoopoe.)

To appreciate the tone and rhetorical manner of the poem, it is essential to keep in mind that this is a dramatic monologue.

STANZAS FROM THE GRANDE CHARTREUSE (p. 606). This poem provides a useful illustration of the disservice done to Arnold's poetry by aggressively equating the "I" of his poems with Arnold himself. One commentator sees the poem as a reflection of "Arnold's attitude towards the so-called Oxford or Tractarian Movement (1833–45)." Another glosses ll. 67–70 as follows: "The men of the Enlightenment and their nineteenth-century heirs who insisted he aspire to truth by following fact and reason, to the resulting exclusion not only of Catholic Christianity, Roman and Anglican, but even of his father's Liberal Protestantism (cf. lines 73–75)." Such assumed autobiographical associations are critical impediments to the poem's vision of a representative and recurrent alienation from alternative value-systems for a certain classless minority and also to the poem's recognition that, however disciplined a mind may be, depths of personal need are not satisfied in that way. Monasticism has persistently fascinated the passionate pilgrim: the "Greek" of ll. 80–83, the "forlorn" speaker of the poem. The fact that such a way of life has become "impossible" to an incredulous generation ("a dead time's exploded dream") does not necessarily make, for certain temperaments at least, an emotionally credible alternative out of either hard-fisted action ("To life, to cities, and to war!") or frivolous pleasure (the metaphor of the hunt). For these there are no vicarious substitutes: they must wander "between two worlds, one dead, / The other powerless to be born. . . ."

   Grande Chartreuse, title: the chief monastery of the Carthusians (an austere religious order) in the mountains near Grenoble, France, and which Arnold visited on his honeymoon in 1851; Saint Laurent, line 4: a nearby village; Dead Guier's stream, 10: a nearby river, the Guiers Mort River; Courrerie, 18: another village; Host, 42: the consecrated Eucharist; since it is not usually passed from hand to hand, either Arnold made a mistake or the monks had an extraordinary dispensation; not in ruth, 77: that is, not in remorse over my training; Runic stone, 83: a lettered stone used by the Germanic peoples from about the third century; sciolists, 99: people superficially and pretentiously learned; Achilles, 115: at the siege of Troy, Achilles refusing to fight withdrew to his tent because of a dispute with Agamemnon over a captive maid; the contemporary allusion may be to Carlyle; Ætolian shore, 135: the Greek shore where Byron died; Spezzian bay, 142: Shelley was drowned in the Bay of Spezzia; Obermann, 146: see the notes to Stanzas in Memory of the Author of "Obermann," p. 676; weeds, 154: mourning garments.

THYRSIS (p. 612). (For general comments on Thyrsis, see the note on The Scholar-Gipsy, p. 681.)
   Thyrsis, title: Thyrsis appears as the shepherd-poet in Theocritus and in Virgil, both of whom deeply influenced Arnold's handling of the pastoral elegy; two Hinkseys, line 2: North and South Hinksey, between Oxford and Cumner; haunted mansion, 3: a house in North Hinksey associated in the popular mind with witchcraft; Sibylla, 4: Sibylla Kerr, proprietress of a pub in South Hinksey; Childsworth Farm, etc., 11 passim: all of the place names are from the Oxford area, in Oxfordshire or in Berkshire; weirs, 15: dammed areas of a river; youthful Thames, 15: near its source; went away, 40: Clough resigned his Oriel Fellowship in 1848 because he could not subscribe to the Thirty-nine Articles; silly, 45: innocent; Corydon, 80: a conventional name in pastoral poetry and specifically in Virgil's seventh Eclogue, the victor in a musical contest with Thyrsis; Bion's fate, 84: a reference to the Lament for Bion by

Moschus, the lament of one Sicilian pastoral poet for the passing of another; *unpermitted ferry*, 85: that is, across the River Styx, permitted only to the dead; *Pluto's brow*, 86: Pluto, god of the underworld, had stolen Proserpine from the vale of Enna in Sicily and made her his queen; *Orpheus*, 90: the son of Apollo and Calliope who so pleased Pluto with his music that he won conditional release from Hades for his wife Euridyce; *Dorian*, 92: simple strain of the Sicilian pastoral poets; *Fyfield tree*, 106: the symbolic elm; *fritillaries*, 107: flowers resembling lilies; *Arno-vale*, 167: Clough was buried in Florence, in the valley of the Arno River; *great Mother*, 177: Cybele, goddess of nature; *Apennine*, 180: mountain range near Florence; *passim*, 181–190: Arnold's note to this stanza is taken from Servius's commentary on Virgil's *Eclogues*: "Daphnis, the ideal Sicilian shepherd of Greek pastoral poetry, was said to have followed into Phrygia his mistress Piplea, who had been carried off by robbers, and to have found her in the power of the king of Phrygia, Lityerses. Lityerses used to make strangers try a contest with him in reaping corn, and to put them to death if he overcame them. Hercules arrived in time to save Daphnis, took upon himself the reaping-contest with Lityerses, overcame him, and slew him. The Lityerses-song connected with this tradition was, like the Linus-song, one of the early plaintive strains of Greek popular poetry, and used to be sung by corn-reapers. Other traditions represented Daphnis as beloved by a nymph who exacted from him an oath to love no one else. He fell in love with a princess, and was struck blind by the jealous nymph. Mercury, who was his father, raised him to Heaven, and made a fountain spring up in the place from which he ascended. At this fountain the Sicilians offered yearly sacrifices.—"

DOVER BEACH (p. 617). This is Arnold's most popular poem. It contains some of Arnold's deftest felicities: the realization of a *tremulo* in ll. 10–13, the impressive opening up of *a*'s and *o*'s to reveal the sound that provokes the thought in ll. 24–25, and the memorable figures of speech in ll. 26–28 and 35–37. But the more remarkable aspect of the poem is its progress, in thirty-seven short lines, from the peace and quiet joy of the opening stanza to the desperate anguish with which the poem ends. Yet, in its dramatic framework (it is a dramatic monologue) the movement, although achieved in so short a space, is wholly credible. The basic contrast is between the *appearance* of the first stanza and the *reality* of the last. The sound of the ebb and flow is one stimulus; the memory of the tragic vision of Sophocles is another; the speaker's sudden, analogical perception of the death of the Christian era—a temporary compensation for the tragic awareness of Sophocles—is the third. The speaker is thus thrown back upon his own resources, of which human love is at once the most fragile and intelligible.

RUGBY CHAPEL (p. 618). Matthew Arnold's father, "Arnold of Rugby," was a headmaster whose reputation assumed legendary proportions, and, like other legends, was subjected to various interpretations. By some, he was credited with having sensitized the consciences of a generation. Samuel Butler, in *The Way of All Flesh*, saw him as the source of a new unhealthy wave of moral earnestness. In January, 1858, in a review of *Tom Brown's School Days*, Fitzjames Stephen presented him as "a narrow bustling fanatic" utterly lacking in humor. It was this last commentary that, as Arnold tells us, "moved [him] first to the poem."

OBERMANN ONCE MORE (p. 623). This poem was obviously conceived, thematically and psychologically, as a companion piece to *Stanzas in Memory of the Author of "Obermann"* (see p. 542 and Notes, p. 676). "Twenty years" have passed, and certain superficial changes have taken place: "White houses prank where once were huts." Behind this facade of change, there is an elemental constancy—in the hills, the sky, the lakes, the mountains. What has changed most dramatically is the world view of the speaker. He has found a new harmony, a new vitality, and joy in an adequate degree. Arnold recognizes that the contrast in the speakers of the two poems, though real, is not odious. The Obermann of twenty years ago did function for the speaker as the *Stanzas* had portrayed him; and the change, although philosophical in expression, has psychological roots. Hence the technique of a dream-vision, in which Obermann puts the anguish he symbolized for the speaker into historical perspective, is both a cathartic for the spiritual state which "palsied all our word with doubt, / And all our work with woe" and also a credible validation of the speaker's growth in maturity and resolution.

Savez-vous . . . , motto: "Do you know anything that heals sorrow for a lost world?"; *Glion*, line 1: "Probably all who know the Vevey end of the Lake of Geneva, will recollect Glion, the mountain-village above the castle of Chillon. Glion now has hotels, *pensions*, and villas; but twenty years ago it was hardly more than the huts of Avant opposite to it,—huts through which goes that beautiful path over the Col de Jaman, followed by so many foot-travelers on their way from Vevey to the Simmenthal and Thun." (Arnold's note); *Byron*, 24: Byron visited Montbovon, in the district of Alliere; *birth-name*, 26: the River Saane becomes the Sarine below Montbovon; *Appian way*, 100: greatest of the ancient Roman roads; *Syrian town*, 174: Jerusalem; *the storm*, 201: the French Revolution; *See, I* . . . , 232: Revelation 21:5, "Behold, I make all things new"; *Sèvres*, 268: Senancour's burial place near Paris; *rocks of Naye*, 336: the Rockers de Naye at the eastern end of Lake Geneva; *Sonchaud*, 337, *Malatrait*, 339: mountains; *Valais*, 340: a district high above Lake Geneva; *Velan*, 341: a high mountain peak in the Alps.